SURVEY OF BRITISH COMMONWEALTH AFFAIRS

VOLUME I

PROBLEMS OF NATIONALITY 1918—1936

BY

W. K. HANCOCK

Professor of History in the University of Birmingham; Former Fellow of All Souls College, Oxford

WITH A SUPPLEMENTARY LEGAL CHAPTER BY

R. T. E. LATHAM

of Lincoln's Inn, Barrister-at-Law; Fellow of All Souls College, Oxford; Assistant Lecturer in Laws in King's College, University of London

OXFORD UNIVERSITY PRESS
LONDON NEW YORK TORONTO
1937

OXFORD UNIVERSITY PRESS
AMEN HOUSE, E.C. 4
LONDON EDINBURGH GLASGOW NEW YORK
TORONTO MELBOURNE CAPETOWN BOMBAY
CALCUTTA MADRAS
HUMPHREY MILFORD
PUBLISHER TO THE UNIVERSITY

PRINTED IN GREAT BRITAIN

SURVEY OF
BRITISH COMMONWEALTH
AFFAIRS

The Royal Institute of International Affairs is an unofficial and non-political body, founded in 1920 to encourage and facilitate the scientific study of international questions.

The Institute, as such, is precluded by its rules from expressing an opinion on any aspect of international affairs; opinions expressed in this book are, therefore, purely individual.

TO MY

FATHER AND MOTHER

PREFACE

THE present volume does not deal at length with problems of defence; but its contents may best be indicated by reference to a memorandum dealing with the relations between defence and policy, written by a great public servant in the year 1907. The memorandum emphasizes the dependence of an island kingdom, and an oceanic empire, upon naval power.

> 'Sea power [it continues] is more potent than land power, because it is as pervading as the element in which it moves and has its being. Its formidable character makes itself felt the more directly that a maritime State is, in the literal sense of the word, the neighbour of every country accessible by sea. It would, therefore, be but natural that the power of a State supreme at sea should inspire universal jealousy and fear, and be ever exposed to the danger of being overwhelmed by a combination of the world. Against such a combination no single nation could in the long run stand, least of all a small island kingdom not possessed of the military strength of a people trained to arms, and dependent for its food supply on oversea commerce. This danger can in practice only be averted—and history shows that it has been so averted—on condition that the national policy of the insular and naval State is so directed as to harmonize with the general desires and ideals common to all mankind, and more particularly that it is closely identified with the primary and vital interests of a majority, or as many as possible, of the other nations.'

The memorandum argued that the British Empire had in two important particulars harmonized its policy with the interests of the majority of nations. In the first place, it had steadily championed the principle of national independence against the aggressions of preponderant power. In the second place, it had aimed at promoting 'the largest measure of general freedom of commerce'.

> 'This is an aspect of the free trade question which is apt to be overlooked. It has been well said that every country, if it had the option, would, of course, prefer itself to hold the power of supremacy at sea, but that, this choice being excluded, it would rather see England hold that power than any other State.'

The writer of the memorandum did not inquire to what extent the foreign commercial policy of Great Britain was dependent upon a possibly ephemeral balance of domestic interests. But he argued that Great Britain's policy of encouraging national independence had a permanent basis. It was, he said, the natural extension of principles which, 'by a sound instinct', had been steadily pursued within the British Empire.

'No other State has ever gone so far and so steadily as the British Empire in the direction of giving free scope to the play of national forces in the internal organization of the divers peoples gathered under the King's sceptre. It is perhaps England's good fortune, as much as her merit, that taking this view of the manner in which the solution of the higher problems of national life must be sought, she has had but to apply the same principle to the field of external policy in order to arrive at the theory and practice governing her action as one of the international community of States.'[1]

It is not necessary to inquire whether or not this statement of British policy corresponded to the facts of 1907. The statement may be accepted as a useful mapping of the ground which has to be covered in a Survey of British Commonwealth Affairs between 1918 and 1936. There are two outstanding topics to be investigated—the national question and the economic question. The first question is the subject of the present volume. It is hoped to tackle the second question in a later volume. But it must be understood that the separation of the two questions is only partial and provisional. It has been necessary to inject here and there into the present volume —for example, into the second Irish chapter—some economic analysis. It will not be possible or desirable to ignore, in the second volume, the effect of nationalism, or of simpler forms of social consciousness, upon economic life and policy. In both volumes the concern of the writer will be with politics in the widest sense of the word.

The title of the book may need explanation. A Survey of British Commonwealth Affairs excludes both international affairs at large and the domestic affairs of the various members of the British Commonwealth. But on neither side does there exist a rigid separation, and in following his theme the writer has at times been led, sometimes into the one field, and sometimes into the other. He hopes, nevertheless, that he will not be considered a trespasser upon ground outside his own province. If, for example, he has written about Palestine, he has done so because Palestine, although not within the area of the British Empire, is within the area of British responsibility and because events in Palestine are pertinent to the communal problem, which has been exercising British statesmanship in a number of territories under the sovereignty of the British Crown.

[1] Memorandum by Mr. (later Sir) Eyre Crowe, 1st January 1907. See *British Documents on the Origins of the War*, edited by G. P. Gooch and Harold Temperley (H.M. Stationery Office), vol. iii, pp. 402–3, 406.

The method of the book is microcosmic rather than encyclopaedic. The writer has preferred to deal exactly with selected topics rather than to cover inexactly all the countries and all the problems of the Empire. The unity of the book therefore depends on the significance or insignificance of the problems selected. In Chapter VIII the writer reviews his argument from this point of view. In the same chapter he drags into the light of day the theories which are implied in his interpretations of events. The reader, therefore, will have no ground for complaining that he has been coaxed to swallow the writer's political philosophy, together with his history.

In documentation, the writer has chosen to err on the side of pedantry. He thought it desirable, in handling history which lies so close to the dangers and opportunities of the present, to give precise authority for statements of fact. He also thought it desirable to give guidance to readers who might desire to explore the background of any particular topic. This guidance is in the footnotes; there is no general bibliography. A discriminating bibliography of British Commonwealth affairs at large would be a book in itself. Moreover, every student of the contemporary world learns as much from men as he learns from books. The author of this book remembers with deep gratitude all the friends and helpers who have given him information or criticism or the stimulus of lively discussion. He would like to thank them by name, but the list would be long and perhaps some of them would prefer not to appear upon it. The form of his acknowledgement must be general, but it is addressed to every individual helper.

One acknowledgement the author feels that he can make in specific form. It has been a very great pleasure to him to work under the oversight of the Publications Committee of Chatham House. His freedom has been completely unfettered. To the Director of Studies at Chatham House, Professor A. J. Toynbee, he owes a great deal in friendship, encouragement, and that suggestive word which so frequently starts a train of profitable thought. To Miss Margaret Cleeve and Miss H. G. Liddell he is indebted for many aids which have helped to relieve the pressure of work and time under which he has been compelled to write. Finally, he wishes to express his great pleasure at having secured a contribution on the legal problems of the British Commonwealth from Mr. R. T. E. Latham, with whom he is joined by close ties of association both in Australia and in England.

CONTENTS

MAPS

CHAPTER I

PERSPECTIVE VIEW

I

A New Theory of Empire

In the constitutional history of the British Empire the years of emergence from the Great War were a period of unusual self-consciousness. Leading statesmen of Great Britain and the Dominions, assembled in conference, looked at their Empire with a fresh awareness and wonder—as if it were an Ethiopian who had changed his skin, or, more surprisingly, a skin which had changed its Ethiopian. In its outward aspect, in its proportion and form and ceremonial decoration, the Empire retained its traditional appearance: it was the inner life which seemed different. The outward forms were forms of command and subordination; the inner reality was equality and co-operation. A chorus of orators exulted in this transformation. 'We are still unconscious', declared Mr. A. J. Balfour, 'of the extraordinary novelty, the extraordinary greatness, and the extraordinary success of this unique experiment in human co-operation.' 'The British Empire', said General Smuts, 'is the only successful experiment in international government that has ever been made. . . . It is a congeries of nations . . . not merely a state but a system of states.' Australians, Canadians, and New Zealanders added their joyful testimony. 'We are a League of Free Nations', cried Mr. Hughes. 'We are an Imperial Commonwealth of United Nations', declared Sir Robert Borden. 'We are coming together', Mr. Massey said, 'not . . . as the United Kingdom and its dependencies. . . . We are coming together as the United Nations of the Empire, and on equal terms . . .'[1]

Was it a sudden transformation? More than ten years later, statesmen showed themselves still preoccupied with its processes. On 16th July 1931 the Minister of External Affairs in the Irish Free State announced the final demolition of 'the system which it took centuries to build'. 'The former legal unitary state', asserted the Minister, 'has gone the way of the former political unitary state and the former diplomatic unitary state.' He spoke as if this impressive work of demolition had been achieved within the past few years. Mr. Winston Churchill spoke in a similar strain in the British House of Commons:

[1] Imperial War Conferences of 1917 and 1918, Cd. 8566, pp. 41, 45, 46, 47; Cd. 9177, pp. 19, 146.

B

'We accepted in this Motherland the view of those who wish to state the imperial obligation and imperial ties at their minimum; we abandoned the whole apparatus of sovereignty and constitutional law to which our ancestors, and even the later Victorians, had attached the greatest importance.'[1] The changes which most preoccupied Mr. Churchill were changes which had occurred since the war. It seems clear, therefore, that the orators of 1918 were over-confident in hailing so soon the complete achievement of an imperial transformation. Yet it is equally clear that the orators of 1931 laid too much stress upon the latter stages of this transformation. Even the men of 1918 were inclined to shorten their perspective unduly. For they were not the first to perceive that a new association was growing within the framework of the old Empire. 'We are now a family of nations',[2] declared the Australian Prime Minister in 1911. Six years previously Mr. Joseph Chamberlain had asserted that the British Empire was not really an empire; nor were the colonies really colonies. 'What are we all? We are sister states.'[3] As far back as 1864 a great Canadian statesman had observed this same process of transformation. 'The colonies are now in a transition state. Gradually a different colonial system is being developed—and it will become, year by year, less a case of dependence on our part, and of over-ruling protection on the part of the Mother Country, and more a case of healthy and cordial alliance.'[4]

The spirit of these pronouncements, assembled with little trouble from the pronouncements of half a century, shows no essential change. They testify to the working out of a single principle, rather than to the entry, at any point—in 1917 or 1926 or 1931—of a new principle. Is there any difference in emphasis between the earlier and the later pronouncements? Before the war the emphasis fell first upon liberty, which was understood in the sense of national self-government. 'Decentralization and liberty', said General Botha in 1911, 'have done wonders.' 'It is the policy of decentralization', he repeated, 'which has made the British Empire.'[5] In the minds of these men liberty and empire were not opposed: liberty was the cement of empire. 'The policy which was supposed to weaken the Empire', asserted Sir Robert Borden, 'has really strengthened it.'[6] From

[1] A. Berriedale Keith, *Speeches and Documents on the British Dominions* (Oxford University Press, 1932), pp. 231, 236, 275 (Debates on the Statute of Westminster).

[2] Cd. 5745 of 1911, p. 98 (Mr. Andrew Fisher).

[3] Speech of 27th June 1905.

[4] W. P. M. Kennedy, *Statutes, Treaties, and Documents of the Canadian Constitution, 1713–1929*, 2nd ed. (Milford, 1930), p. 617 (Sir John A. Macdonald).

[5] Cd. 4745 of 1911, pp. 40, 42.

[6] Cd. 8566 of 1917, p. 41.

liberty the emphasis passed quite naturally to unity. Mr. Asquith summed up the matter in his opening address to the Imperial Conference of 1911:

> 'Whether in this United Kingdom, or in any one of the great communities which you represent, we each of us are, and we each of us intend to remain, masters in our own house. This is . . . the life-blood of our polity. It is the *articulus stantis aut cadentis imperii*. . . . It is none the less true that we are, and intend to remain, units indeed, but units in a greater unity.'[1]

Let us compare Mr. Asquith's statement with the famous italicized sentence of the report of the Inter-Imperial Relations Committee of 1926. We shall see that there is added in the latter a third object of emphasis which was not present in the former. The report thus describes the group of self-governing communities composed of Great Britain and the Dominions:

> 'They are autonomous communities within the British Empire, equal in status, in no way subordinate one to another in any aspect of their domestic or external affairs, though united by a common allegiance to the Crown, and freely associated as members of the British Commonwealth of Nations.'[2]

The new object of emphasis is equality of status. But equality of status did not make its first appearance in the pronouncement of 1926. It was explicitly and repeatedly affirmed during the Imperial War Conferences of 1917 and 1918. Sometimes it was affirmed as a principle already realized: as 'what has been achieved now': sometimes it was appealed to as a principle in process of realization, still imperfectly recognized and applied.[3] Throughout this period there was a frequent confusion in the minds of statesmen between ideal and fact, between fact and form. But the important thing to notice is that from 1917 onwards there was continuity in the explicit enunciation of the principle of equality as a necessary condition of an enduring imperial partnership. Implicitly, this principle made its appearance even before the war. It was, for example, implied in Sir John Macdonald's vision of an empire transformed into a 'permanent alliance'. In truth, among nations as among individuals, the acceptance of liberty as a principle leads inevitably to the acceptance of equality as a principle.[4] The new emphasis laid, at the conclusion

[1] Cd. 4745, p. 23. [2] Cd. 2768 of 1905, p. 14.

[3] One South African, Mr. Burton, refers to equality as 'what has been achieved now' (Cd. 9177, p. 160); another, General Smuts, appeals to it as a principle which 'will have to be recognized to a very large extent' (Cd. 8566, p. 47). See Cd. 8566, pp. 41, 45, 52, 55, 59; Cd. 9177, pp. 155 ff., 201, 203.

[4] Not necessarily, as the 1926 report made clear, as an abstract dogma, but as a

of the war, upon the equality of the self-governing communities of the British Empire, was in part an assertion, within the constitutional pattern of the Empire, of that emphatic national feeling which the war everywhere produced. But it was also a reiteration, in the new circumstances of the war and the peace, of the old emphasis upon liberty. Equality supplied the logical bridge between Mr. Asquith's terminal points, Liberty: Unity. The revised articles of faith—frankly enunciated in 1917, emphatically reasserted in 1926, and thereafter pursued with great persistence through complicated technicalities to the statutory enactment of 1931—were, Liberty: Equality: Unity.[1]

Did it ever occur to the statesmen of Great Britain and the Dominions, as they stated and restated these principles, that they were but affirming, sometimes in economical and felicitous English, sometimes with vague and puffy periphrasis, the famous French triad, Liberty: Equality: Fraternity? The suggestion would have been unwelcome. Their prevailing mood (challenged but scarcely shaken by Irish scepticism) was that of God's Englishmen to whom a precious and peculiar revelation has been vouchsafed. Their Empire, they said, defied classification and bore no real resemblance to any other political organization which existed or had ever been attempted. They viewed it as 'a unique experiment in human co-operation'; they admired its 'extraordinary novelty'.[2] It was unique because of its modernity. It was unique because of some peculiar British quality belonging to it.

The statesmen who affirmed these convictions in 1917 and 1926 may have been uniquely British, but they were not uniquely modern. This same assurance of a peculiar way of life embodied in a peculiar constitution is already apparent in the first treatise on government to be written in the English tongue. The writer of this treatise, a fifteenth-century chief justice, coins a new phrase to describe the English constitutional system, although he gives his readers to understand —in this, too, he is perhaps very English—that he has found the phrase already coined in the classic medieval authorities. And he paints in lurid colours the contrast, so dear to Englishmen for so many cen-

form of development in varying historical circumstances. See Edwin De Witt Dickinson, *Equality of States in International Law* (Harvard University Press, 1920). Or see the 1789 principle of 'equality before the law'.

[1] Might not the urge to equality drive out unity? The writer is discussing now the ideals which were professed, and is content that his whole narrative should gradually reveal underlying forces and the problems raised by their action.

[2] Novelty of content, not of form, e.g. General Smuts in 1917: 'The British Monarchy is the key of the constitutional arch' (Cd. 8566, p. 47). See the minutes of proceedings of all imperial conferences, *passim*.

turies, between the lusty vigour of England's law-abiding freedom and the oppressions with which England's continental neighbours are afflicted.[1] An afterglow of this vivid antithesis lingers as late as Professor Dicey's treatise on the English constitution. The antithesis is perhaps most eloquently and persuasively expressed in a famous pamphlet of the latter part of the seventeenth century, Halifax's *Character of a Trimmer*. Englishmen, Halifax says, have found happy escape from the dilemma posed by advocates of monarchy (i.e. absolute monarchy) and of commonwealth (i.e. a republic).

> 'We in England, by a happy use of this controversy, conclude them both in the wrong, and reject them both from being our pattern, taking the words in the utmost extent, which is—Monarchy, a thing that alloweth men no liberty, and a Commonwealth, such as alloweth no quiet. . . . We take from one the too great power of doing hurt, and yet leave enough to govern and protect us; we take from the other the animosities and the licence, and yet reserve a due care of such a liberty as may consist with men's allegiance.'

The student of the British Commonwealth of Nations may find in these classic writers a clue which will help him in his modern inquiries. He will notice in Halifax, and in Fortescue, the search for a middle term between accepted political concepts; he will perceive in both an incorrigible disposition to escape from a logical dilemma. He will be moved, as he reads the *Character of a Trimmer*, by the writer's passion for liberty—'the only seasoning that giveth a virtue to life'—by his devotion to the laws, those jewels 'which are nowhere better set than in the constitution of our English government', by his exaltation of 'the principle of love', without which 'there can be no true allegiance'. He will observe that in every essential the faith held by Halifax re-expresses itself in the eloquence—not quite so eloquent as his—of the conferences of 1911, 1917, and 1926. But there comes a sentence in which the persuasive Halifax attempts too much: 'Our government', he says, 'is like our climate.' At this point a writer who is not an Englishman feels his enthusiasm begin to freeze. He is reminded of the vice generally ascribed to Englishmen of idealizing everything with which they happen to be concerned. Possibly this disease has been carried by Englishmen throughout the Empire? The historian remembers that he must be suspicious of oratory. He must be careful to disentangle ideal and fact.

[1] The treatise called the *Governance of England*, by Sir John Fortescue. The term which he coins is *dominium politicum et regale*, standing midway between *dominium politicum* and *dominium regale*. It does not mean constitutional monarchy in the modern sense. For Whiggish misinterpretations see *Transactions of the Royal Historical Society*, 4th series, vol. xvii, pp. 117 ff.

II

The Old Empire: The Logic of the Schools

Less than a century after Halifax wrote *The Character of a Trimmer* British statesmen obstinately insisted on facing a dilemma, and thereby broke the first British Empire. Since an equally obstinate avoidance of the same dilemma has brought into existence the British Commonwealth of Nations, it is necessary to examine what the dilemma was, and how it came to be there. Machiavelli stated it in a general way when he remarked, 'Of all servitudes, the most insupportable is the one which makes you subject to a free people.'[1] This was a fair generalization from the history of the Athenian Empire, or from the history of Machiavelli's own Florence in its relations with Pisa. And it has been argued in support of the generalization that the progress of self-government in Great Britain was paid for by the loss of America—and perhaps the loss of Ireland.

The argument is a daring one, and needs qualification, but let us see how it develops. It starts from a general view of English constitutional history. The technique by which Englishmen have achieved what they call constitutional freedom is, if we look at it in its broadest aspects, a simple one. They regularized and limited the power of the monarchy by 'tying the instruments it was to act by'.[2] The royal power, by a judicious process of specialization which dispersed the original concentration in the royal council, flowed gently through separate customary channels, a protection to the subject against violent and incalculable irruptions. The King was the fountain of justice; but, as Coke explained to James I, his irrigating flood could flow only through the courts. The King issued commands; but they were authentic commands only if they were conveyed in customary form and marked with the seals for which particular officers were responsible. The King could make statutes, but he must make them with the co-operation of the Lords and Commons.

Thus arose the limited monarchy which Sir John Fortescue praised. It was not yet the constitutional monarchy with which we are familiar. What powers the King had, he had absolutely. There was not yet injected into the constitution a rival power strong enough and ambitious to share with the King, or to take from him, his function of

[1] 'Di tutte le servitù, quella è durissima che ti sottomette ad una repubblica.' See Burke, 'They found that the tyranny of a free people could of all tyrannies the least be endured' (*Speech on Conciliation*).

[2] Sir Roger Twysden, *Certayne Considerations upon the Government of England* (Camden Society), p. 11.

sovereign rule. That struggle for power occurred in the seventeenth century. Its first result was to establish what lawyers call the sovereignty of parliament. Its second result, which took some time to work out, was a parliamentary executive, or cabinet government. These two achievements, underlined by the later progress of democracy, are the core of British self-government. Public acts are still acts of the King, but public power, both in the making of laws and in executive government, is ultimately in the constituencies.

In the eighteenth century aristocratic and mercantile interests were supreme in the constituencies. It was these interests, therefore, which in effect exercised the King's authority over the King's subjects overseas. It was they who determined the legislation of the imperial parliament binding upon the colonies. It was, indirectly, they who sent to the colonies the governors who ruled there—very ineffectively—in the King's name. The augmentation of self-government at home had obviously created a new subordination abroad. It was that kind of subordination which Machiavelli declared to be the most insupportable. A gifted American writer has taken Machiavelli's generalization as the thesis of his study of the American Revolution. 'Parliamentary government is probably the most developed form of representative institutions now known', he says, '. . . but it has the defects of its merits, that it makes "the government of dependencies" illogical and almost impossible.'[1] The British parliament faced the King's subjects overseas with that formidable engine of sovereignty which it had forged in the seventeenth century. 'In all forms of government', Blackstone wrote, 'there must be a supreme, irresistible, absolute and uncontrolled power, in which the *jura summi imperii*, or rights of sovereignty, reside.' A parliament representing only the aristocratic society of Great Britain claimed this supreme, irresistible, absolute, and uncontrolled power over the whole British Empire. What rights were left to the King's subjects overseas? 'In sovereignty', declared Dr. Johnson, 'there are no gradations.' Lord Mansfield affirmed that the American colonies were 'all on the same footing as our great corporations of London'. Governor Hutchinson declared that he knew of 'no line that can be drawn between the supreme authority of Parliament and the total independence of the colonies'.[2] Englishmen thought of the colonies in words first used in 1649 by the Long Parliament in the statute which constituted the Commonwealth—as dominions 'belonging' to the people of England. English

[1] C. H. McIlwain, *The American Revolution* (Macmillan, 1923), p. 159.

[2] The quotations are taken from R. G. Adams, *Political Ideas of the American Revolution* (Trinity College Press, Durham, N.C., 1922), pp. 24, 75.

constitutional theory stated the problem of *imperium et libertas* as an inescapable dilemma.

What was the reply of the King's subjects overseas to this theory? It depended upon circumstances. It also depended in part upon the character of the King's subjects overseas. There were different kinds of them. Swift, in *Gulliver's Travels*, has given a most unpleasing picture of empire-building.

> 'A crew of pirates', he says, 'are driven by a storm, they know not whither; at length a boy discovers land from the topmast; they go on shore to rob and plunder; they see a harmless people, are entertained with kindness; they give the country a new name; they take formal possession of it for their king; they set up a rotten plank or stone for a memorial; they murder two or three dozen of the natives, bring away a couple more by force for a sample, return home, and get their pardon. Here commences a new dominion, acquired with a title by divine right. Ships are sent with the first opportunity; the natives driven out or destroyed; their princes tortured to discover their gold; a free licence given to all acts of inhumanity and lust; the earth reeking with the blood of its inhabitants; and this execrable crew of butchers employed in so pious an expedition is a modern colony sent out to convert and civilise an idolatrous and barbarous people.'

This seems rather rough on the Pilgrim Fathers. Yet Swift does not so very much exaggerate the treatment which the natives of America suffered even at the hands of godly Puritans. John Winthrop, the governor of the Massachusetts Bay Company, calmly reflected that God in His Providence had cleared by plague the regions which He had appointed as a refuge for His faithful Englishmen. English jurisprudence, in contrast with Spanish jurisprudence, was fundamentally inhumane in its attitude to the heathen; it allowed them no place at all in the 'natural society' of peoples; it ascribed to them no rights, not even the right of being conquered.[1] Twelve of the thirteen mainland colonies of America were therefore,

[1] Spanish opinion was not unanimous; cf. the controversy between Las Casas and Sepúlveda. The point is that the Spanish government itself took an interest in the controversy, i.e. it admitted a problem of right. The controversy was summed up by the Spanish jurist, Franciscus de Victoria, who asserted that there is a *societas naturalis*, bound by the *ius gentium*, of which all peoples, even heathen, are members. English thought, on the other hand (e.g. Wyclif), held that heathen tribes had no true *dominium*, a theory which is apparent in the early colonization charters which gave authority to individuals or companies to colonize and settle 'land not occupied by any Christian prince'. See Arnold J. Toynbee, *A Study of History* (Oxford University Press, 1934), vol. i, pp. 464–5 for 'The Historical Antecedents and the Vein of Ruthlessness in the Modern English Method of Overseas Settlement.' On the Spaniards see Franciscus de Victoria, *De Indis et de Jure Belli Relectiones* (Carnegie Institute, 1917) and F. Scott Brown, *The Spanish Origins of International Law* (Carnegie Institute, 1934).

in the verbiage of English law, 'settled colonies'. The thirteenth colony, New York, had, like Canada, been peopled by other European colonists before the English took it. There the King acquired 'new subjects' who were not of British stock. The legal position in these 'conquered' colonies was that they remained under their old law until the King was pleased to change it.[1] There was in fact a strong tendency to assimilate their position to that of the settled colonies, if only with the intention of inducing Englishmen to settle in them. The problem of *imperium et libertas*, therefore, presented itself in the first place most forcibly as a problem of the relationship between Englishmen abroad and Englishmen at home. Even in Ireland it will be useful for the present to consider the problem in this simple form; for in the eighteenth century it was 'the garrison', 'the Protestant Ascendancy' of Scots and English, which first challenged the theories of Blackstone and Mansfield and Dr. Johnson.

It may be said in general that the English theory was not energetically challenged except when concrete applications of it impinged drastically upon the lives of Englishmen overseas, endangering their interests or their self-respect or their idea, whatever it happened to be—it was not always admirable—of what was for them the good life. The colony of Barbadoes challenged the theory in 1649, when the Long Parliament first enunciated it; for Barbadoes was royalist. 'Shall we be bound', demanded the assembly, 'to the Government and Lordship of a Parliament in which we have no Representatives or persons chosen by us?' 'In truth', it answered, 'this would be a slavery far exceeding all that the British nation hath yet suffered.' The colony of Jamaica challenged the theory in the nineteenth century, when the British parliament abolished slavery throughout the British Empire. The assembly of Jamaica professed itself in 1833 willing to admit 'the supremacy of a common sovereign over the whole empire'; but it refused to admit the supremacy of 'one portion of His Majesty's subjects residing in the parent state over another portion of their fellow subjects residing in Jamaica'.[2] The most persistent protests against the British theory of parliamentary sovereignty came from Ireland. They began in 1649, and continued in an unbroken tradition through Molyneux and Swift, Grattan and Flood, down to Arthur Griffith and Sinn Fein. The historical argumentation of the Irish case—that parliamentary legislation for Ireland was a revolutionary usurpation arising from the Great Rebellion and a violation of

[1] The classic case is *Campbell* v. *Hall*, 20 State Trials, 239.

[2] R. L. Schuyler, *Parliament and the British Empire* (Columbia University Press, 1929), p. 178.

established constitutional right—is weak.[1] But the Irish are not the only people who have supported a strong case with bad history. In the eighteenth century the urge to resist the sovereignty of parliament by 'any and every means' was irresistible; for that sovereignty was pressing remorselessly upon Ireland and beating down her strength.

The thirteen colonies of America were sheltered by distance. New England, in the late seventeenth century, appeared to orthodox mercantilists to be 'the most prejudicial Plantation to this Kingdom'; but distance and the circumstances of New England's immature growth saved it from the heavy blows of sovereignty which Ireland had to bear; against the worst consequences of this sovereignty, as against a federative reformation of it, *opposuit natura*.[2] Even so, the New England economy, as it grew, developed a structure fundamentally irreconcilable with the theories of mercantilist imperialism; New England's very solvency was hardly compatible with observance of the laws of trade ordained by the sovereign parliament.[3] Fortunately, it was easy to evade and defy these laws: there was therefore no occasion to question obstinately parliament's right to make them. The occasion arose after the Seven Years' War, when plans of imperial reconstruction, of which there was urgent need, pointed to a time soon to come when the laws of trade would be more strictly enforced, and at the same time, by seeking 'a regular Plantation Parliamentary revenue', outraged a love of liberty which, like that of Englishmen, had 'fixed and attached on this specific point of taxing'.[4] The Americans, like the Irish, were now driven to think fundamentally about their status.

The history of the American controversy can be viewed from two standpoints. Attention can be focused on the revolutionary minority which forced the controversy from one resting-point to another until the colonists found themselves at last facing the dilemma, British sovereignty or American independence—and chose the latter. But it

[1] Historically Parliament is the King-in-Council, and the jurisdiction of the King-in-Council was not limited to any one part of his Dominions.

[2] Burke, *Speech on Conciliation*. 'In large bodies', he says, 'the circulation of power must be less vigorous at the extremities. Nature has said it.'

[3] There was, for example, the problem of paying for British manufactures, since New England could not produce goods which Great Britain would admit. The attempt to find a solution through the stimulation of naval stores could not be completely successful; New England naturally began to meet the problem by a trade of mutual advantage with the French sugar islands—lumber and provisions for sugar and molasses (to be turned into rum).

[4] Burke, op. cit. He also calls self-taxation 'the characteristic mark and seal of British freedom'.

is probably truer to admit the sincerity and the very great significance of the efforts which most of the leading Americans made, at one point or another, to reconcile empire and liberty. Men like Benjamin Franklin, John Adams, and Stephen Hopkins did persistently and honestly seek for a theory which would, in Maitland's phrase, 'have mediated between absolute dependence and absolute independence'.[1] Beginning with a denial of the power of parliament to levy internal taxation in America, they were led by logical necessity to deny its power to tax at all, and finally to deny its legislative supremacy. But this denial of parliamentary sovereignty did not, until the final decision was forced upon them, carry with it a repudiation of their allegiance. 'I am a subject of the Crown of Great Britain', said Franklin; but he added—'America is no part of the dominions of Great Britain, but of the King's Dominions.' 'All the members of the British Empire', declared Thomas Wilson, 'are distinct states, independent of each other, but connected together under the same sovereign, in right of the same crown.' And Stephen Hopkins envisaged 'an imperial state', consisting of 'many separate governments, in which no single part, though greater than any other part, is by that superiority entitled to make laws for, or tax, such other part'.[2] This conception was unintelligible to British lawyers and statesmen of the eighteenth century. But something very like it became the official British theory during the first decade after the War of 1914–18. In its spirit, and even in its language, the vision of Stephen Hopkins anticipates the declaration of 1926.[3]

It must not be imagined that any serious attempt has been made, in the preceding paragraphs, to summarize the history of the American Revolution. It is not suggested that men deliberately made theories, and then found them incompatible, and therefore decided to fight about them. Nevertheless men did attempt at every stage of the conflict to state in terms of political principle the issues involved, with the result that the manifold oppositions of interest and sentiment and policy were generalized and simplified as an issue of status. Attention was focused upon the British theory of parliamentary supremacy, which the Americans rejected because it made all their liberties precarious. Logically, it left them no more liberty than

[1] O. von Gierke, *Political Theories of the Middle Ages,* (trans. F. W. Maitland, Cambridge 1900), p. x.

[2] Adams, *Political Ideas of the American Revolution*, pp. 45, 53–4.

[3] e.g. *The Washington Post* (quoted *Canadian Annual Review*, 1926–7, p. 132): 'If the Government of George III had possessed the wisdom of the Government of George V, there would have been no Declaration of Independence, and the United States would now be part of the British Commonwealth.'

James I's theory of divine right, which also possessed historical justifications, had left to his English subjects. The Americans, like their English forefathers, honestly attempted to save both their 'birthright' and their allegiance. By their theory of a multi-cellular commonwealth of free communities under a common crown they attempted to reconcile liberty and imperial unity. They were able to achieve this conception because their thought derived from the early seventeenth century, when the idea of law was still in large measure consciously attached to the ideas of reason and justice, rather than to those of will and power.[1] From the eighteenth-century point of view, the American colonists were absurdly old-fashioned. They clung to their charters, which assured to them 'all liberties, franchises, and immunities of Englishmen'. When English lawyers pointed out that they were exactly on the same footing as the great corporations of London, and, like these corporations, subject to parliamentary omnipotence, they appealed to a fundamental law which guarded their liberties, a law which parliament could not alter. They appealed, in fact, from the new conception of law to the old. 'Magna Carta is such a fellow he will have no sovereign.' They could quote Coke for that. And they could quote Cromwell. 'In every government there must be somewhat fundamental, somewhat like a Magna Carta, that should be standing and immutable.'[2]

Among English statesmen there was only one who really understood their theory. Burke, for all his generosity and imagination, did not understand it. Burke's plan of declaring sovereignty, and using moderation in the exercise of it, was inadequate to meet a situation which, through mishandling, had grown into a dispute about status. But Camden understood the earlier conception of law to which the Americans still clung. The Declaratory Act, he affirmed, was 'absolutely illegal, contrary to the fundamental laws of the constitution'.

> 'My Lords,' he exclaimed, 'he who disputes the authority of any supreme legislature, treads on very tender ground. In my opinion, the

[1] See C. H. McIlwain, *The Growth of Political Thought in the West* (Macmillan, 1932), p. 387: 'The English civil wars of the seventeenth century roughly threw English thought out of its true orbit and substituted a theory of might for a theory of law; and the English theory of sovereignty, as well as the American theory derived from it, has been eccentric ever since in its adherence to the ideas of Hobbes and Austin —a costly aberration, which lost for England one great empire and would soon have lost another if practice had not fortunately departed from theory just before it was too late . . .' The writer is aware that Austin has been frequently misinterpreted and that the theory of sovereignty has been so restated (e.g. by Professor Dickinson) as to free it from many crudities historically associated with it. He believes, however, that his historical argument may stand, just because the crudities expounded in the text were in fact associated with it.

[2] T. Carlyle, *Letters and Speeches of Oliver Cromwell* (ed. Lomas, 1904), vol. ii, p. 382.

legislature has no right to make this law. The sovereign authority, the omnipotence of the legislature, is a favourite doctrine, but there are some things which you cannot do.'[1]

This doctrine was quite unintelligible to an eighteenth-century House of Lords. It is even now difficult doctrine for a generation which has taken its ideas of the constitution from Delolme and Dicey. But it is a doctrine which has now returned, although not in the exact form in which Camden stated it, to a central place in English constitutional theory. The unity of the British Commonwealth of Nations now rests upon a theory which cuts the claws of sovereignty. An illustration may be taken from a parliamentary document of the year 1935. It is the report of the joint committee of both houses which considered whether the petition of the state of Western Australia, asking for the introduction and passage of a bill enabling Western Australia to withdraw from the Commonwealth of Australia, was proper to be received.

> 'It is true', reported the joint committee, 'that, as things stand, the Parliament of the United Kingdom alone can pass an Act which would have that result. It is true also that this Parliament has in law full competence to do so, even against the wish and without the consent of the Commonwealth. To do so would not be outside its competence in the strict legal sense. But it would be outside its competence, if the established constitutional conventions of the Empire are to be observed, as observed they must be. . . . Hence what the Petition prays for is, in that sense, something which is beyond the jurisdiction claimed by the Parliament of the United Kingdom.'[2]

Thus, by way of a new distinction between what is legal and what is constitutional, the mother of parliaments has repudiated Dr. Johnson's theory that in sovereignty there are no gradations, and has asserted Lord Camden's theory, a theory which is now more modern as it is more ancient—that there are things which parliament cannot do.

III

The Logic of Experience: Dominion Self-government

There occurred, after the American Revolution, no repudiation or mitigation of the juristic theory which asserted that there was nothing which parliament could not do. On the contrary, the notions of law as a command, and of parliament as the omnipotent commanding

[1] *Parliamentary History*, vol. xvi, pp. 161 ff., 177 ff.; Adams, *Political Ideas of the American Revolution*, pp. 127, 139.

[2] *The Times*, 25th May 1935.

authority, entrenched themselves almost impregnably in English minds through crude popularizations of Jeremy Bentham and John Austin. It followed inevitably from these notions—assuming them to be true and immutable—that new disruptions of Empire must some day succeed the American disruption. For the unlimited supremacy of a parliament chosen by British constituencies condemned to perpetual inequality and insecurity the British communities overseas, unless they should take the extreme step of separation. And this step, surely, they would one day take. For experience had shown that emigrant Englishmen possessed a craving for liberty no less obstinate than that of the Englishmen who had stayed at home.

All those people, therefore, whose view of the imperial problem was determined by the accepted theory, were convinced that there was no solution of the problem short of imperial disruption. 'There cannot be two imperial legislatures in one Empire.' 'A self-governing dependency is a contradiction in terms.' 'Emancipation is as natural an event in the history of the colonies as death to an individual.' 'Does anybody believe that a population of twenty millions in Australia would remain subject to a population of forty millions in the British Isles?' These are typical pronouncements from the lips of nineteenth-century statesmen, public servants, and publicists.[1] The mood in which one doctrinaire or another pronounced judgement depended upon his individual temperament and standard of values. If he had thought of the Empire as profit, he could cheerfully contemplate its dissolution, because new and revered teachers were making it quite obvious that 'economics of sovereignty' were fallacious and expensive economics. It became fashionable among Englishmen to wish themselves good riddance of the colonies because there was nothing to be made out of them. 'The monopoly', Adam Smith had said, 'is the chief badge of their dependency, and it is the sole fruit which has hitherto been gathered from that dependency.' During the nineteenth century the majority of Englishmen came to the conclusion that the fruit was not worth the cost of collection. There were better ways of growing rich. Why struggle, why protest, against the inevitable disruption? . . . But the Empire might have military and strategic advantages. There were other Englishmen who thought of it in terms of power politics. From this point of view the

[1] Sir William Molesworth in 1850; Sir G. Cornewall Lewis in 1841 (*Government of Dependencies*, p. 289); Mr. Warburton in 1837 (*Hansard*, vol. xl, p. 108); A. Trollope in 1872 (*Australia and New Zealand*, vol. i, p. 356). For a survey of this phase of thought see C. A. Bodelsen, *Studies in Mid-Victorian Imperialism* (Copenhagen, 1924), and R. L. Schuyler, 'The Climax of Anti-Imperialism in England', in *Political Science Quarterly*, vol. xxxvi, no. 4.

Indian and tropical dependencies certainly seemed to be worth while. They supported military establishments, they were 'a nursery of our statesman and warriors', their vast populations were obedient to the word of command. The colonies of British settlers were another matter. Emigrant Englishmen were intractable. 'What is the use of these colonial deadweights which we cannot govern?'[1] They might even get us into expensive trouble. To Disraeli, India was a great British interest and a great British pride: Canada was a liability. There were many who agreed with him. 'Our relations with North America are of a very delicate character,' wrote Lord Granville. 'The best solution of them would probably be that in the course of time and in the most friendly spirit the Dominion should find itself strong enough to proclaim her independence.'[2] Obviously, the 'inevitable day' of a second imperial disruption, when it dawned, would dawn not unwelcome to a considerable section of influential Englishmen.

There was, however, another section of thoughtful Englishmen who contemplated this same inevitable day with different feelings. Theirs was an attitude towards the colonies which expressed itself not in 'good riddance' but in 'good luck'. Accepting regretfully the proposition that a self-governing dependency was a contradiction in terms, they resigned themselves to colonial independence because they believed in colonial self-government. Taking it on trust from established theory that empire and liberty were irreconcilable, they declared themselves for liberty. Liberty without disruption, full liberty as the foundation of empire, would have been their choice, had it occurred to them as a possible one. But the orthodoxies of the theory of sovereignty made it impossible for them to conceive of bonds of empire which were not in some degree a bondage of subjection. Their dream, of which they were but half conscious, was a refashioning of the Empire upon the principle of equal liberty of the parts and free association of the whole; but such a refashioning could not happen by quiet growth, and the gradual diffusion of the living principle of liberty throughout the old structure, and its ultimate transformation. The necessities of imperial command and colonial subjection could not be evaded in this way. There must, therefore, be a moment of disruption. It was the only possible way of achieving unfettered freedom. But it might be followed by a moment of

[1] G. E. Buckle, *Life of Disraeli* (Murray, 1916), vol. iv, p. 476. Also his famous exclamation, 'These wretched colonies . . . are a millstone around our necks', recorded by Lord Malmsbury, *Memoirs of an Ex-Minister* (1884), vol. i, p. 334. Disraeli's later profession of faith (1822) was not without reservations.

[2] Lord Fitzmaurice, *Life of Lord Granville*, 1905, vol. ii, p. 22.

re-integration. Within the space of three years three notable books advocated this neat but rather perilous manœuvre. The colonies were to assume full freedom by assuming sovereignty. Thereafter they were to accept a treaty with Great Britain; as free communities they would join a free association. This was the proposal of Lord Thring in 1865, of Viscount Bury in 1866, of Sir Charles Dilke in 1867.[1] It is in all essentials the proposal on which Mr. De Valera took his stand in 1921. The Articles of Agreement for a Treaty between Great Britain and Ireland are a half-way house between these ingenious mid-nineteenth-century suggestions and the actual experience of the Dominions, which, between 1867 and 1921, was solving the problem of liberty and unity, by the method of pushing to one side its impressive theoretical impossibilities.

Until the end of the nineteenth century there were still in the overseas Empire many thoughtful individuals who, like their English contemporaries, judged more by theory than by their unfolding experience. And their judgement tended to coincide with that of the English doctrinaires. In so far as they remained emigrant British, they were not content with an inferior measure of British liberty. In so far as they were becoming aware of their own environment and their peculiar destiny as members of individual communities, their impatience with legal frustrations of their freedom was sharpened. The new nationalisms which were becoming self-conscious in Australia and Canada could not submit to an empire which meant dependence. If freedom meant separation, they must demand separation. If self-government and empire were contradictories, they must repudiate empire. But there was an underlying reluctance to accept the dilemma. And so, from Australia as from Great Britain, there came voices which preached 'Separation and Nationalism with a subsequent Anglo-Saxon alliance'. An independent federated Australia, they argued, would, under wise councils, be only preliminary to a Union with England. To men of this stamp separation was desirable because it was the only road to mature freedom. Freedom, they hoped, would mean free association. By 1900 the majority of them had realized that free association could be achieved without the moment of disintegration. In the first year of the Australian Commonwealth, one of their leaders confessed that experience had disproved preconceived theory. His speech was valedictory to those

[1] Henry (afterwards Lord) Thring, *Suggestions for Colonial Reform*, 1865; Viscount Bury, *Exodus of the Western Nations*, 1866; Sir Charles Dilke, *Problems of Greater Britain*, 1867. Dilke envisaged some kind of partnership for the whole 'Saxon' race, in whose vigour and virtue (the only race capable of freedom) he was a great believer. His 'Greater Britain' included the United States of America.

idealists, 'of whom I was one', who had believed that Australia could realize her national destiny 'only by establishing an independent entity as the preliminary to a closer alliance with Great Britain'.[1]

Looking back upon these fumblings with the problem of *imperium et libertas,* we now see clearly that their awkwardness was due to the existence of a theoretical obstacle which interfered with the natural disposition of Englishmen and colonists to trust their own experience. Experience was demonstrating with increasing emphasis that liberty was the cement of empire, that each extension of it mitigated irritations, removed frustrations, and liberated an active will for partnership in a common way of life. Experience was progressively refuting the maxim that in sovereignty there are no gradations. This demonstration and this refutation did not, it is true, possess any inherent and eternal doctrinal validity; but they were valid under the existing conditions of time and circumstance. It was the error of the established juristic doctrine, or at least of the current political translations of it, to rule out dogmatically any mitigating possibilities of circumstance. Theory continued to demonstrate that some time, at some point, sovereignty must inevitably operate as a check upon liberty, expressing intolerably in outward relationships its inner nature of command and obedience, superiority and inferiority. It was intellectual subservience to this theory, together with an emotional repudiation of it, which stimulated the doctrinaires to their Humpty-Dumpty performances of pulling down the Empire, which meant sovereignty, as a preliminary to putting it up again in the form of a perpetual alliance. The doctrinaires, had they been consistent, would have been forced to confess that all the King's horses and all the King's men could do nothing with the Empire's broken pieces. For, if law inevitably meant merely the command of a superior—and it was this assumption which necessitated the imperial disruption—the refashioning upon a basis of equality could not be binding: unless, indeed, the disrupted Empire reformed itself as a vast state with a single sovereignty. Failing this heroic solution, which was not contemplated by the advocates of an 'alliance', the separated units of a disrupted constitutional structure must henceforth face each other in a state of nature. The moment of independence could not possibly introduce a moment of reunion. The separation must be perpetual.[2]

[1] See Henry L. Hall, *Australia and England* (Longmans, 1934), ch. iv.

[2] Nineteenth-century Austinians, such as Dicey, held that, while the sovereign could give away no part of its power, it could abdicate wholly in favour of a new sovereign: and that this had in fact happened at the union of England and Scotland.

There was only one sensible attitude for statesmen to take towards a political distortion of legal theory which so muddled their heads and thwarted their intentions. The intelligent thing to do with this doctrine was to forget about it, following the lessons of experience until there should emerge a new theory which would help rather than hinder the interpretation of experience.[1] For such an attitude there was good precedent. Burke had advised it. Leave theories to the schools, he had said; 'for there only they may be discussed with safety'. Burke's own theory of sovereignty was no more helpful than that of his contemporaries; it was enshrined in the Declaratory Act; it raised a formal barrier to the principle of equality which we have now accepted as a necessary complement to the principle of liberty. But Burke was not greatly interested in this theory: his thought had a different starting-point. 'I am not determining a point of law; I am restoring tranquillity; and the general character and situation of a people must determine what sort of government is fitted for them.' What sort of government was fitted for colonists of British stock? Surely a free government, a government in accord with 'the antient policy of this Kingdom'.

> 'When this child of ours wishes to assimilate to its parent, and to reflect with a true filial resemblance the beauteous countenance of British liberty; are we to turn to them the shameful parts of our Constitution? are we to give them our weakness for their strength? our opprobrium for their glory? and the slough of slavery, which we are not able to work off, to serve them for their freedom?'

The British Commonwealth of to-day, it has been said, is a remarkable product of the political philosophy of Burke.[2] If we are content to ignore Burke's legalistic theory and emphasize, as he emphasized, the unimportance of theory in comparison with experience, we may accept this statement as true. It is indeed tempting to imagine a kind of apostolic succession of magnanimous Whig statesmen who hand on from one to another the virtue which has recreated the Empire upon the principle of broadening freedom. Burke uses the

[1] There was one mid-nineteenth-century publicist who attempted, not without some incoherence and inconsistency in the use of words, to modify the theory of sovereignty to fit the trend of experience. See Herman Merivale, *Colonization and Colonies*, 1841, vol. ii, p. 293: 'It does not follow that the attainment of domestic freedom is inconsistent with continued dependence upon Imperial sovereignty. . . . Union might be preserved long after the sense of necessary dependence has gone. . . . And the Crown may remain at last, in solitary supremacy the only common authority, recognized by many different legislatures, by many different nations, politically and socially distinct.'

[2] Nicholas Mansergh, *The Irish Free State: its Government and Politics* (Allen & Unwin, 1934), p. 270.

blessed word, 'assimilation'. 'This child of ours', he says, 'wishes to assimilate to its parent, and to reflect with a true filial resemblance the beauteous countenance of British liberty.' Fox re-echoes Burke's phrase. 'The principle laid down', he says in 1774, '. . . has been this, that the government of the colony ought to be assimilated, as much as possible, with that of the mother country.' And in 1791 he repeats the word and gives it the widest possible interpretation. Canada is capable of enjoying liberty in its fullest extent, and—'Canada must be preserved to Great Britain by the choice of its inhabitants'. In Fox's view, empire and liberty are not contradictories: empire is achieved through liberty. Nearly half a century later, Lord Durham, holding the same faith, convinces his doubting countrymen that the Canadians must have a constitution assimilated in the essential matter of executive government to the English model. . . From one liberal Englishman to another the torch of colonial freedom is handed on. Reactionary Tories dash in to snatch at it and hurl it to the ground. There is, for example, Thurlow, the formidable antagonist of Fox, both in 1774 and in 1791. Assimilation, he grumbles, cannot be applied to the constitution of a colony. 'It is a grossness—it is making two allied kingdoms, totally out of our power . . .' 'If political liberty, the governing principle of our constitution, be established in a colony, the sovereignty will be established there—and consequently independence.' Liberty by this argument is proper for Englishmen, not for colonists.[1]

Nevertheless, it is quite false to think of the refashioning of the Empire on the principle of liberty as the methodical working-out by English Whigs of a kind of hundred years' plan of liberal imperialism. The historical reality is far more complicated. Pitt, a Tory, is responsible for the instalment of 'assimilation' which is contained in the Act of 1791. Russell, a Whig, resists the further instalment proposed by Lord Durham in 1839. Thurlow's statement of theory is almost universally accepted by Whig and Tory alike, though varying deductions are made from it. The doctrine of assimilation is given a reactionary twist by English governors on Canadian soil, who interpret it in the sense of establishing there the conservative elements of English social and political life as a counterpoise to the equalitarian spirit of American democracy.[2] Its more liberal

[1] Useful extracts from the debates on the Quebec Act, 1774, and the Constitution Act of 1791 are in Kennedy, *Statutes, Treaties and Documents of the Canadian Constitution 1713–1929* (2nd edition, Milford, 1930), Nos. XXIX and LIV.

[2] Ibid., No. LXI (Governor Milnes), No. LIX (Governor Simcoe—in Upper Canada). Mr. John W. Dafoe in *Canada, An American Nation* (Columbia University Press, 1935) stresses justly, though perhaps a little too emphatically, the English and

interpretation is rejected by the loyalist emigrants from the revolted colonies to Canada, although it had in 1791 been asserted primarily for their benefit. These loyalists, like Ulster Protestants, ground their own ascendancy in the community upon its political subordination, which is challenged by the majority of their countrymen. They persuade themselves that this subordination constitutes the essential part of the imperial connexion; they make its acceptance the test of 'loyalty'. Assimilation to British practice by the institution of parliamentary executives would in one Canadian province give the power of government to a majority composed largely of dissenters and democrats of American origin: in the other province it would put it in the hands of French Catholics.

The stubborn fact of French-Canadian nationality cuts right across the constitutional problem and makes it impossible to study the doctrine of assimilation merely as a proposition of governmental theory. The doctrine may be shown, in its origins, to have had emphatic racial connotations. 'Do you propose to take away liberty from the Englishman', cried Burke, 'because you will not give it to the French? I would give it to the Englishman, although ten thousand Frenchmen should take it against their will.'[1] To Fox, a constitutional assimilation of Canada to Great Britain was bound up with a racial assimilation of French Canadians to the dominant British. He wished them to 'unite and coalesce, as it were, into one body'. The early governors of Canada—from motives which, it is true, were mixed—had resisted claims to British freedom which would have given power to a tiny British minority to legislate against French nationality. These military reactionaries had a vision of freedom as national tolerance; they formulated on behalf of the French-Canadians a doctrine of trusteeship. But the governors after 1800 joined with English Whigs and Canadian loyalists in a campaign of racial imperialism. The French element must be swamped by a British immigration. 'The Province must be converted into an English Colony, or it will ultimately be lost to England.' The Canadian population must be 'overwhelmed' with English Protestants.[2] Lord Durham himself failed to disentangle the constitutional and racial implications of assimilation. He had no tolerance

aristocratic aspects of assimilation which opposed the American and democratic content of Canadian life. His reflections suggest a counter movement of assimilation —the penetration of the Empire by American-democratic ideas—which would be a fruitful theme to develop.

[1] Kennedy, *Statutes, Treaties and Documents of the Canadian Constitution*, p. 135.

[2] Kennedy, op. cit., dispatches of Milnes and Craig; cf. the views of Black, Ryland, and C. J. Sewell.

for 'the miserable spirit of nationality', for 'the idle and petty notion of a visionary nationality'. He wished Canada to be free in the English way; but he thought it indispensable to put a majority of British race in control of this freedom. Would it then be freedom for the French ? Perhaps it would, when they had been taught not to be French. . . . British constitutional principle was still interwoven with British racial prejudice. The most liberal Englishmen had not yet learnt that the liberty which they valued might be a wholesome diet for people of another nationality.

It is therefore utterly surprising to find French-Canadians asserting, less than forty years after the Durham Report, that they desire the federated Canada which they are helping to make, to remain 'a British colony'. The French want to remain 'British' in order that they may remain French.[1] This means that somehow, between 1839 and 1865, the doctrine of assimilation has shed its racial implications. It has been discovered that Frenchmen need not cease to be Frenchmen in order to share with Englishmen the difficult privileges of self-government. The discovery is perhaps hardly less significant, achieved as it was in an age of bitter national antagonisms, than the principle of 'liberty for tender consciences' towards which men of goodwill struggled in the age of religious wars. Both in seventeenth-century England and in nineteenth-century Canada, the new principle to which society ultimately rallied was discovered and applied in despite of preconceived theory and prejudice.[2] It was wrested out of conflict; it was seized upon and proclaimed by creative leaders whose imaginations were quicker and more generous than those of the majority of men; but it was also in the end achieved by the plain common sense of ordinary individuals honestly learning the lessons of experience. It was a synthesis hammered out by the contrasted ideals, interests, and wills of English Whigs and Tories, of Canadian-British and Canadian-French, of Canadian rebels and Canadian reactionaries, of conflicting creeds and classes and localities. The bitterness of conflict was moderated by old traditions of British constitutional method, of local autonomy, of respect for individual conscience and a rooted dislike of force. Amidst the disorder of interests and beliefs there was one unifying principle, the principle of liberty. At the beginning it had been assumed that the constitutional liberty

[1] Kennedy, op. cit., pp. 622 ff.

[2] In the seventeenth century the preconceived theory, hardly to be questioned, was identity of 'Church and Commonwealth'. The necessity for common religious belief in the state is nowhere more firmly insisted on than in the reasonable and enlightened pages of Richard Hooker. In the nineteenth century the preconceived theory was that of the uni-national state.

which the English valued, and the national liberty which the French valued, were contradictories. Searching their experience, British and French came to understand that they could achieve neither, except in a free federated community where both values were ultimately shared.

Lord Durham and his disciples set out to solve a problem of constitutional freedom, and, in solving it, achieved a triumph greater than the one which they had at first imagined. They appeased warring nations. Moreover, they raised a standard which in other countries and other circumstances would encourage those who came after them to face courageously the inescapable and intractable issues of race and nationality which constitute the supreme challenge to the British Commonwealth. Race and nationality will be recurring themes in this book. For the present, however, it will be profitable to keep to the central problem raised in this chapter, the formal problem of *imperium et libertas*, of reconciling the equal freedom of the parts of an association with the unity of the whole.

British statesmanship chose to leave difficult theories to the schools, and to follow the path of liberty, walking rather by faith than by sight. But there were moments when the theoretical reason of statesmen uttered emphatic protests. Such a moment occurred during the thirties and forties of the last century. Here was the turning-point of imperial constitutional history. Lord Durham had carried the principle of assimilation into the sphere of executive government; Canada, like Great Britain, was to be ruled by ministers responsible to parliament. This raised in a new and even more acute form the dilemma which had wrecked the first British Empire. Imagination which had boggled at the vision of co-ordinate parliaments in the same empire must boggle still more at the vision of co-ordinate parliamentary executives in the same empire. Responsible government, said Lord John Russell, was 'a condition which can exist only in one place, namely the seat of empire'. Logically, the existence of separate parliamentary executives involved the acceptance by the Crown of separate advice. The advice might be conflicting. The unity of the Crown, and of the Empire, would then be at an end. Durham and the Canadian reformers thought that they could evade the dilemma by drawing a line between matters which were local and matters which were imperial. In the former, the governor would act on the advice of his Canadian ministers: in the latter, he would follow the instructions of Her Majesty's government. The legislative competence of the Canadian parliament would also be limited to this local field. Russell denied that a line of demarcation could be drawn. Obviously the Canadian constitution could not be assimilated to the British in the sphere of external relations, for nobody would recommend separate executive decision in 'the questions of foreign war and international relations, whether of trade or diplomacy'. According to Russell, assimilation was equally impossible in internal government. 'There are some cases of internal government', he said, 'in which the honour of the Crown, or the faith of Parliament, or the safety of the state, are so seriously involved, that it would not be possible for Her Majesty to delegate her authority to a ministry in a colony'. The reformers of the North American provinces nevertheless argued that a line could be drawn. Doctrinaires in England and in Australia, later on, desired the line to be rigidly defined. But on this matter Russell was right. Experience proved that self-government, to be effective, must be free to expand indefinitely with the expansion of interests and strength in the new communities. The spheres of land policy, constitutions, tariffs, which Durham would have reserved to imperial authority, were soon occupied. More slowly, but definitely, self-government began to expand into the sphere of foreign relations, where, so Russell had said—and there was nobody who ventured to contradict him—unity of control was indispensable.[1]

Lord John Russell was extremely far-sighted, but it may sometimes happen that the wisest statesmanship is content not to see too far. The immediate and pressing problem at the time was to extend liberty; the extensions of liberty would create new problems which must be solved in their turn. Astute reasonings might be framed, declared the Canadian reformer Baldwin, and fine distinctions might be drawn; 'but the plain common sense and practical view' of Canadians resented a system which, in the name of imperial unity, subjected the colonial majority to rule by a colonial minority. The remedy, the only remedy, was assimilation of Canadian to British practice. 'Your Lordship', wrote Baldwin to Durham, 'must adapt the Government to the genius of the people upon whom it is to act.

[1] Among those who favoured a rigid limitation of the colonial sphere were Sir William Molesworth and Gladstone in England and G. Higinbotham in Victoria. Russell's admirably clear arguments are well illustrated by various excerpts in Kennedy, *Statutes, Treaties and Documents of the Canadian Constitution*. K. C. Wheare explains in *The Statute of Westminster* (Oxford University Press, 1933), pp. 31–2, that 'What Gladstone and the framers of the New South Wales and Victorian Bills had in mind was not a division of the legislative field into mutually exclusive spheres, imperial and colonial. They merely desired that one part of the field—and that the greater part—should be free from the intervention of the Imperial Government by veto while a smaller part should be liable to veto on imperial grounds.' Imperial intervention did, in fact, follow these lines.

It is the genius of the English race in both hemispheres to be concerned in the government of themselves.' The Nova Scotian reformer, Joseph Howe, demanded nothing which was not 'extremely simple and eminently British'.

> 'It seems strange', he wrote to Russell, 'that those who live within the British Empire should be governed by other principles than those of the British Constitution; and yet it is true, notwithstanding.... Why should we run counter to the whole stream of British experience; and seek, for no object worthy of the sacrifice, to govern on one side of the Atlantic by principles the very reverse of those found to work so admirably on the other?'[1]

In dealing with the thirteen colonies, the British, so Burke had complained, practised 'too much logick and too little sense': in dealing with the Canadians they were persuaded to follow 'the plain common sense and practical view' of the matter. Lord John Russell himself, as Colonial Secretary, played a notable part in evading his own dilemma.[2] Honest rigid men were appalled at the experiment in which they found themselves called upon to take part. The Empire was being wrecked, Canada was being surrendered to republicans and disloyalists; and the governor was expected to assist at the surrender.[3] But there were other statesmen, British and Canadian, who followed their experience with an expanding enthusiasm. In their speeches and dispatches we feel a stir of excitement. They feel that their faith is visibly working miracles. Liberty, instead of disrupting the Empire, is re-creating it. Lord Elgin, Durham's son-in-law, beholds an empire 'growing, expanding, strengthening itself from age to age, striking its roots deep in fresh earth and drawing new supplies of vitality from its virgin soils'. He writes to Earl Grey—'I have been possessed with the idea that it is possible to maintain on this soil of North America and in the face of Republican America, British connexion and British institutions, if you give the latter freely and trustingly.'[4]

In Canada, New Zealand, Australia, and South Africa, colonies and provinces joined with each other in federations or unions under the British Crown. They assumed the new style of 'self-governing Dominions';[5] they emphasized their awareness of deepening national

[1] Kennedy, *Statutes, Treaties and Documents of the Canadian Constitution*, Nos. CVI–CIX.

[2] Ibid., No. CXIII, the tenure of offices dispatch.

[3] Kennedy, op. cit., No. CLXI, and other dispatches of Sir Charles Metcalfe.

[4] Chester Martin, *Empire and Commonwealth* (Oxford University Press, 1929), p. 341.

[5] The new style dates from the Colonial Conference of 1907, Cd. 3523, pp. 31, 72–83.

individuality; their expanding interests and vitality pushed them forwards in the direction of unfettered and complete national self-government. There remained, it is true, imposing limitations on their power. In their capital cities there was a governor-general, appointed by the Sovereign on the advice of his British ministers, and performing in the Dominions not only the tasks of constitutional headship which the Sovereign himself performed in the United Kingdom, but also special duties enjoined upon him as an imperial officer. The governor-general was the channel through which His Majesty's government sent such communications as it saw fit to make to dominion governments on matters of foreign policy, which, except in the more local and less formal matters, remained outside dominion competence. Over the legislative power of dominion parliaments there lay a 'triple veto'. The governor-general might refuse his assent to a Bill passed by both houses of parliament; or he might reserve the Bill for the Sovereign's pleasure; or—even if the governor-general did neither of these things—the Sovereign, advised by his ministers in the United Kingdom, might himself within one year of the final passing of the act in the dominion disallow it and thereby annul it as law. There was in addition the overriding legislative power of the imperial parliament elected by the constituencies of the United Kingdom. The Colonial Laws Validity Act of 1865, although it removed doubts as to the powers of colonial legislatures within their own sphere, emphasized the fact of their subordination. In legal theory, there were still no gradations in sovereignty. The dominion constitutions were themselves derived from acts of the imperial parliament, and the power which conferred right could also revoke it. The imperial parliament could, if it chose, annihilate the whole constitutional structure of dominion freedom.

This imposing legal system has been described in many books.[1] The point which it is necessary to make now is that theory had very little relation to practice. In practice, none of the formidable restrictions which have been mentioned interfered with dominion freedom in the spheres marked out by dominion constitutions. They operated only in the field where co-ordination of legislation and policy were deemed essential in the interests of imperial unity. In matters of merchant shipping and the extradition of criminals, for example, there were effective legal barriers to dominion action. Yet even

[1] Notably those of Professor Berriedale Keith. On the conventions of the system students are awaiting a book by Mr. K. C. Wheare. The same author's *Statute of Westminster* contains in its early chapters the best short outline account of the system as a whole.

within the field deemed to be imperial, many of the weapons of imperial restriction were rusting through disuse. The 'triple veto' is a phrase with repressive implications which, one can imagine, might provoke the most extreme revolutionary fury: a single veto, in the early stages of the French Revolution, was a godsend to demagogic agitators playing upon the emotions of the mob. But in Australia and Canada, where self-assertive nationalism certainly did not lack its uncompromising champions, nobody thought of making play with the phrase. The triple veto was in fact attenuated by the obsolescence of the governor-general's power to reject bills and the Sovereign's power to disallow acts. Even the power of reservation tended to become a device for securing consultation upon matters of common imperial interest; in Canada the practice was to find a substitute for it in suspending clauses inserted in acts of the dominion parliament, providing that they should not come into effect unless by proclamation. This gave to the imperial government opportunity to consider their bearing upon imperial interests. Similarly, the British parliament, which once had been accustomed to legislate in its imperial capacity without paying particular attention to colonial susceptibilities, gradually fell into the practice of choosing 'a form of legislation enacted to secure the co-operation of Dominion legislation for the common end'.[1]

Facts and forms did not correspond with each other. The facts were facts of a liberty which was growing towards equality and seeking a new form of unity through voluntary co-operation. The forms were forms of subordination. They still, in a narrowing field, performed a useful function; but in 1917 General Smuts in effect gave notice that some other way would have to be found of performing that function. 'Too much, if I may say so, of the old ideas still clings to the new organism which is growing. I think that although in practice there is great freedom, yet in actual theory the status of the Dominions is of a subject character.'[2] General Smuts demanded that the forms of the constitution should be brought into correspondence with its facts—a demand which was repeated at later imperial conferences and which produced radical changes in the legal structure.

[1] A. Berriedale Keith, *Responsible Government in the Dominions* (Oxford, Clarendon Press, 1928 edition), vol. ii, p. 761. 'This indeed', adds Keith, 'constitutes the whole history of the control exercised by the Imperial Government and Parliament over the Dominions . . . It has gradually been transformed into co-operation on a footing which steadily approaches more closely to the ideal of a Commonwealth of equal nations.' Much has been done since this sentence was written.

[2] Cd. 8566 of 1917, p. 47.

Sir Robert Borden in 1917 replied to General Smuts by enunciating a principle which did not deny, but which effectively mitigated, the rigours of juristic theory. The principle was a restatement, in a slightly novel way, of constitutional experience. It had long been the fashion to distinguish between the strict law of the constitution and its conventions or customs. In the former were included obsolete procedures such as the Royal Veto and the Act of Attainder; from the latter had grown the cabinet system. In the actual working of the constitution, each had an essential part to play. Sir Robert Borden had in mind this distinction between the law and the custom of the constitution; but his statement enunciated a further distinction between things which—whether legal or customary—were constitutional, and could be done; and other things which—though legal—were unconstitutional, and therefore could not be done.

> 'It is to be observed [he said] . . . that constitutional writers draw a distinction between legal power and constitutional right. The British parliament has technically the legal power to repeal the British North America Act—taking our Dominion as an illustration. But there is no constitutional right to do so without our assent, and therefore, while there is the theory of predominance, there is not the constitutional right of predominance in practice, even at present.'[1]

This is precisely the doctrine which, according to the joint committee of the House of Lords and the House of Commons quoted at the conclusion of the previous section, is enshrined in the Statute of Westminster. It is a sufficiently effective amendment to the doctrine of the sovereignty of the British parliament. A sovereignty which carries with it no inherent constitutional right need have no terrors for those who live under constitutions assimilated to the constitution of Great Britain. Sir Robert Borden's principle—which in 1917 was a convention of the constitution and is now constitutional law[2]—illustrates the persistence of a peculiar technique which dominion statesmen inherited from seven or eight centuries of English practice. Just as Englishmen had safeguarded themselves against the power of the Crown, not by denying it, but by 'tying the instruments it was to act by'; so now the Canadians set out, not to destroy, but—a subtler task—to harness the sovereign parliament. They led their captivity captive. They so bound imperial sovereignty—a dangerous monster once, but now an amiable, complaisant creature—that it could move, in their business, only at their bidding.

[1] Cd. 8566, p. 59.

[2] The Statute of Westminster, 1931 (22 Geo. V, c. 4), section 4. It is the request and consent of a dominion which confers on the imperial parliament the constitutional right to legislate for it.

In the period covered by this volume, the Australians and New Zealanders were inclined to deprecate what they regarded as the excessive zeal with which the Canadians addressed themselves to this task. The Irish and the South Africans, on the other hand, gradually showed themselves resolved to end, and not merely to amend, this theoretical subordination to the imperial parliament. They were resolved to assert their own self-derived statehood. Thus there arose, as will be seen later, differences between the theories held in London and Dublin, Canberra and Pretoria. In practice, these differences of theory were no obstacle to co-operation, which tended always towards the same end. That end is sometimes declared to be the disintegration of a great society. More commonly it is affirmed to be the transformation of it. The historian who writes to-day cannot look back upon a completed journey. He cannot define an end which has not yet been reached. He must be content to contribute such understanding as may be won from a study of the beginnings of the journey, and of its gradually opening prospects.

IV

The Logic of Experience: The Imperial Conference

At the end of the nineteenth century and early in the twentieth there still survived a nicely patterned network of relations based upon superiority and subordination. But the network was fraying, and experience suggested that the Dominions would free themselves from those parts of it, at least, which impeded their activity or offended their pride. What, then, would happen to the unity of the Empire?—for legally and historically its unity seemed inseparably interwoven with the forms of predominance. Experience, not always as yet rightly interpreted, was provisionally answering this question also. Beneath the old formal pattern, a new 'network of contacts'[4] was being woven by the voluntary action of free partners.

One example of this tentative experiment in a new design may be taken from a correspondence between the British and Canadian governments in 1879. The Canadian government at the time was pressing for the removal of anomalies which survived from days when the governor did not as yet act through the agency of ministers; and its concern with these matters suggested the question whether the governor, whose functions were, normally, those of a formal head of a state, was an adequate channel of communication between Great Britain and Canada. Canada's expanding interests necessitated

[4] The phrase is Mr. Baldwin's: Imperial Conference, 1926 (Cmd. 2769, p. 8).

direct contact between those who were in fact responsible for her government, and the responsible ministers of Great Britain. In matters of trade she was feeling the need of establishing from time to time direct contact with foreign governments also. A dispatch of August 1879 laid stress upon both these matters, and proposed new means 'of constant and confidential communication between Her Majesty's government and her local advisors in Canada, in extension of the more formal relations subsisting through the correspondence of the Secretary of State for the Colonies with the Governor-General'. The precise suggestion was that the British government should receive an official representative of Canada who would be 'specially entrusted with the general supervision of all the political, material, and financial interests of Canada in England', and who would also be specially accredited by the Sovereign to negotiate, in association with a British diplomatist, any trade treaty which Canada desired to conclude with a foreign government. The Canadian government desired 'to surround the proposed appointment with all the importance which should attach to an official charged with such high duties'; it suggested that he should be designated Resident Minister, and that he should be given 'a quasi-diplomatic position at the Court of St. James's'. The wording of this last proposal disturbed Her Majesty's government. Diplomatic status, it replied, was hardly appropriate to the position of Canada as an integral part of the Empire. For this reason it preferred rather to confer on the official the title of '"Dominion" or "Canadian Commissioner" than . . . any title implying a diplomatic status or position'. The time was to come when the Canadian phraseology would cease to sound shocking, and even in 1879 the Canadian rejoinder expounded with persuasive firmness the realities of the situation.

> 'In considering many questions of the highest importance . . . the imperial government and parliament have so far transferred to Canada an independent control that their discussion and settlement have become matters for mutual assent and concert, and therefore have, it is thought, assumed a quasi-diplomatic character as between Her Majesty's government representing the United Kingdom *per se* and the Dominion, without in any manner derogating from their general control and authority as rulers of the entire Empire.'

The Canadian government was, however, content to leave in the hands of the British government the question of status, and it now suggested for its representative the title of 'High Commissioner'. The suggestion was accepted, and a precedent was set which the other Dominions later followed. Nearly two generations were to pass before there was serious thought of reciprocal appointments by the government of the United Kingdom; but the correspondence of 1879 clearly enunciates a principle of growth whose elaboration, to which there need be no other limit than that of convenience, can only emphasize the inherent quality of 'mutual assent and concert'.[1]

The second example of experiment in the new design—an example which must be considered with some care—is the imperial conference. The first thing which is apparent about the origin of this institution is that it does not arise from any conscious plan of substituting a new system of relationships, similar to that which now exists, for the old system. In 1887 the British government took advantage of the fervour associated with the Queen's jubilee, the anxiety arising from recent international complications, and the strong tide of reaction against mid-Victorian disillusionment with the Empire, to assemble in London a spectacular gathering of colonial personalities. This first colonial conference was a motley assembly of 121 delegates, representing the United Kingdom, the self-governing colonies, the Crown colonies, and the protectorates. It had no resemblance in principle to the modern conference of governments claiming to represent nations which are equal in status.

In summoning the conference, the Colonial Secretary referred to a growing desire to draw closer the bonds of the Empire; he deprecated, however, discussion of 'subjects falling within the range of what is known as Political Federation'.[2] This statement is significant, not only for the gathering of 1887, but for many of those which followed it. There did exist a plan for an imperial reconstruction; but it never became practical politics. The plan which commended itself to most theoretical students of imperial affairs differed widely from that system of relationships which has in fact been achieved. For forty years imperial federation continued to be urged as the only satisfactory solution of the imperial problem; and all this time the current of actual change was running strongly in a contrary direction. In one sense the project of federation dominated the colonial and imperial conferences;[3] for it was continually present to the minds of statesmen as the only scheme of complete political logic which had been propounded. In another sense it was irrelevant to their discussions, which tended persistently to concentrate upon their con-

[1] The documents quoted are in Kennedy, *Statutes, Treaties and Documents of the Canadian Constitution*, Nos. CLXXXV, CLXXXVI.

[2] Letter of Rt. Hon. E. Stanhope to the governors of colonies under responsible government, 25th November 1886. C. 5091, p. vii.

[3] The Colonial Conference of 1907 decided on the change of name. In this chapter it will be convenient to use the later name even for the earlier conferences.

crete interests and to solve experimentally each specific problem which presented itself.

As a political ideal, imperial federation had to be taken very seriously. It had behind it a rising flood of imperial fervour, and from the early seventies onwards it enlisted the support of persistent and enthusiastic champions. The Imperial Federation League, founded in 1884, produced during its decade of life well over a hundred pamphlets. The ideal survived the league.[1] Chamberlain was a convert to it. 'I am told on every hand', he declared, 'that imperial federation is a vain and empty dream. . . . Dreams of that kind which have so powerful an influence upon the imagination of men, have somehow or other an unaccountable way of being realized in their own time.'[2] It was not only among Englishmen that the ideal won converts. Its original apostles in Great Britain had been predominantly Australians—absentee Australians, it is true. It won converts in every dominion, especially among persons of university education. In Sir Joseph Ward, the Premier of New Zealand, it had a most enthusiastic advocate, who in 1911 expounded his plan in what was perhaps the longest speech which has ever been made at an imperial conference. At this time too the *Round Table*, with its groups of well-informed and respected associates planted in every dominion, devoted itself to the cause. The original crudities and uncertainties of the early days of the movement had now long since disappeared. The proposals put forward by Mr. Lionel Curtis, for example, were precise in detail and extremely cogent in their logic. Ultimately, they rested on the postulate of sovereignty which, if accepted—and the sport of sovereignty-baiting had not yet become fashionable—could be reconciled with formal equality in no other way than that of federation.[3] Whatever may have been the desires, conscious or unconscious, of some of the earlier protagonists of the federation movement, its later champions had no wish to arrest the growth of freedom in the Dominions. On the contrary, they stressed the fact that the growth remained incomplete. It had stopped short of the supreme essential power, foreign policy. It was inconceivable that the Dominions would remain content with this arrested growth. It was certain that they would not for ever allow others to decide for them the issues of peace and war which touched them so nearly. But

[1] See Bodelsen, *Studies in Mid-Victorian Imperialism*, on the origins of the movement.

[2] J. L. Garvin, *Life of Chamberlain* (Macmillan 1934), vol. iii, p. 56.

[3] Maitland's legal and political theories had not yet become currency for publicists. The *Federalist* supplied most of the ammunition used by imperial idealists; Alexander Hamilton's arguments reached a wide public through F. S. Oliver's biography of him.

it was equally certain that they would not acquiesce in political separation, as an unfortunate but inevitable incident of their maturity. Yet only a deliberate effort of reason and will could avert this consequence. The dilemma which Lord John Russell had propounded in 1839 could no longer be evaded or postponed. The day was now rapidly approaching when the Sovereign would be offered separate advice by separate governments in the supreme issues of peace and war. That day would bring the dissolution of the Empire and a crushing blow to the forces of freedom. But the day need never come. Courage and intelligence might bring instead a day of achievement. The United Kingdom and the Dominions, like Rousseau's natural men, might surrender their natural freedom in exchange for the fuller freedom of a common citizenship. A new social compact might establish a new sovereignty to which all would be equally subject and in which all would be equal sharers.

The criticism of this argument dealt chiefly with points such as What would be the position of India ?, What would be in fact the voting strength of the Dominions ?, which need not be discussed here. The points were, from the practical point of view, well made; but their chief significance lies in their cumulative effect in revealing intense national attachments which refused to make the surrender required by a vast super-nationalism claiming for itself the coercive equipment of a sovereign state.[1] On the whole, the response to the federationist argument was emotional rather than logical; whereas the argument itself was both. 'We are one,' affirmed the federationists; 'we must will the means necessary to our unity.' 'We are many,' replied their opponents, 'we cannot surrender our individuality. The means you urge are irrelevant, for your ends are not ours. All the same, we hope that the disasters which you prophesy will not occur.'

According to the logic of sovereignty, the disasters needs must occur. If we look at the problem for a moment from another angle, we shall see how it was bound to vex the minds of thoughtful men and torment their loyalties. As early as the sixties of last century, Australian democracy was rebelling against tutelage to British foreign policy. The tone of Australian political thought was given by English, Irish, and Scottish democrats—then in process of finding common ground in Australian nationalism—at a time when the tone of British thought was still predominantly aristocratic and upper-

[1] The demand is thus made by L. Curtis, *The Commonwealth of Nations* (London, 1916), p. 678: 'Allegiance can no more be rendered by one citizen to two Commonwealths than homage can be paid by one subject to two Kings. The people of Britain and those of the Dominions have yet to decide whether it is to this mighty Commonwealth as a whole or merely to the territory in which they live that their final allegiance is due.'

middle class. Australia naturally adopted the 'two hemispheres' view of international relations which the Canadians breathed from their North American air; the old continents were given up to aristocracy, aggression, and wrong; the new continents belonged to the people, to peace, and to justice. Isolationism was the natural result of this simple diagnosis; for the just do not consort with sinners. Taught by President Monroe, American citizens strove earnestly not to consort with sinners. But what could virtuous Australians do? When the King, advised by British ministers, was at war, his Australian subjects were also at war. They discussed their difficult position in the press and even in their parliaments. Some of them found it intolerable. 'In any just and necessary war', they would cheerfully join; but it was hateful to be dragged by Englishmen who were probably aristocrats into conflicts which were probably unjust. If it could have been contrived that all the wars of the Empire were, as a matter of course, just wars, they would have been spared their searchings of conscience.[1] But, since such a contriving was improbable, they must take steps on their own account to preserve their virtue unblemished. Some of them advocated independence. An Englishman who hated war, John Bright, made this suggestion to a kindred spirit in Victoria, Charles Gavan Duffy. But Duffy wrote in his memoirs—'I did not sympathize with Mr. Bright's policy.' Surely there was available some less catastrophic procedure? Duffy suggested neutrality. 'When the contest was one for defence, I say we should be bound to take our share in it. Where the contest was one for ambition . . . we might properly stand aside.' The colonies, then, would constitute themselves judges of the justice of imperial foreign policy. By their own decision they would free themselves from its taint when it was sinful; on their own responsibility they would—with terrific moral effect—defend it when it was righteous.

This solution of the problem caused by the extension of self-government towards the sphere of foreign affairs, was actually propounded by a Victorian Royal Commission on Australian Federation which reported in 1870. The same solution was urged repeatedly, over a long period of years, by the more radical and influential of Melbourne's two great daily papers. It found persistent support in other radical quarters. But the arguments in its favour were not always so highly moral. The Queen's colonial subjects did not forget

[1] The Covenant of the League of Nations has importance from this point of view as an attempt to anchor foreign policy to justice. There is a great deal to be said for the view that this lightened the strain upon imperial unity at a time when the problem of co-ordination in foreign policy had not yet been solved.

the dangers and the expenses of war. War on the responsibility of others, they frequently argued, endangered their interests no less than their honour. Why should Victorians suffer in their trade and prosperity, perhaps even in their security and life, because England had ambitions in Africa or the Middle East? But they had still another grievance against Downing Street. Policies of expansion, which seemed sinful in other continents and oceans, wore a different appearance in the seas adjacent to Australia. They bitterly complained that Great Britain had allowed other Europeans to enter their seas—seas which Providence had set aside for the British race. The effete English were betraying the vital interests of a more virile British stock. Not only must Australia keep herself 'clear and free, unhampered, uncompromised, safely separate from the war perils of the old world', she must also be free to fulfil her manifest destiny in the ocean which washed her eastern shores.[1]

All these protests, taken together, had behind them a strong emotional force but little practical reason. In the controversy were muddled inconsistent grievances and imperfectly defined and separated remedies. Critics had at the time little difficulty in disposing of the various points separately, and less difficulty in refuting the argument as a whole. France, Germany, and Japan had established themselves or were establishing themselves in the Pacific Ocean. Could Australia face them, or one of them, with her own power? This was enough to rule out independence. And, as for neutrality, would these Powers respect it? They would do so only if it served their interests. Was it even true that by neutrality Australians might protect their virtue? There was another point of view. 'This colony would be British only so long as Britain served her turn, but neutral, or un-British, the very moment that help was required or that there was danger to be encountered.' And, in the last analysis, if the existing realities of international relations were honestly faced, neutrality was indistinguishable from independence.

The colonial neutrality argument, in fact, was then the expression

[1] The quotations contained in the previous paragraphs are taken chiefly from Hall, *Australia and England*, esp. chapters iv and v. See also W. K. Hancock, *Australia* (Benn, 1930), chap. iv. A similar picture of the moods and mental processes of immature nationalism would fit Canadian radicals of a rather later period, e.g. W. S. Ewart, *Kingdom Papers* (Ottawa, 1912), *passim* and *Canada and British Wars* (Ottawa, 1923); or Mr. Bourassa, *Que devons-nous à l'Angleterre?* (Montreal, 1915). J. W. Dafoe in *Canada, An American Nation*, has recently stressed again an historical interpretation depending on a contrast between English aristocracy and Canadian democracy. At the present time it is the European 'financiers' or 'imperialists' who taint the Empire with sin. For a criticism of the whole argument see A. G. Dewey, *The Dominions and Diplomacy* (Longmans, 1929), *passim*.

of an immature nationalism. But that was the very problem which statesmanship had to face. Immature nationalism, in this tentative effort to forecast the line of its future inevitable growth, was attracted by expedients which logically ended in imperial disintegration. This strengthened the logical case of the imperial federationists. They argued that their solution both satisfied the demands which immature nationalism was attempting to formulate, and at the same time preserved unity. Their way was the one true way of bringing the Dominions to maturity. Assuming the existence of an imperial nationalism stronger than dominion nationalism, and assuming the postulate of sovereignty, they were right. The Dominions, announced Sir Joseph Ward in 1911, would no longer accept the old relation of 'mother and infants'. And his argument, although confused in statement, was logical in its general conclusion. 'If the people of New Zealand are to take their responsibilities . . . in connection with the general defence of the Empire . . . they are entitled to some representation on some body that has got the power of saying when New Zealand should go into war.'[1]

Imperial federationist argument, therefore, was a constant background to the imperial conference; sometimes, as in 1911, it boldly stepped into the foreground; more often it tentatively insinuated itself into the discussions.[2] But, whenever questions of policy and organization were under discussion, the question was never far from the minds of statesmen. Is this leading towards imperial federation? Or is it leading in the other direction? The results of this preoccupation were not always fortunate. Important matters which deserved to be considered on their own merits were confused with the federation issue. Nationalist stalwarts—both in Great Britain and the Dominions—tended to suspect federationist manœuvres which did not always exist. For, stronger than the influence of a persuasive theory, was the natural disposition of British and dominion statesmen, even statesmen of marked imperial conviction, to fight shy of ambitious constitutional constructions. 'There is nothing,' said Lord Salisbury in 1902, 'there is no danger that appears more serious for

[1] Cd. 5745, p. 61. Sir R. Borden had put forward the same argument in Canada (*House of Commons Debates*, Session 1909–10, col. 4137 ff.).

[2] Chamberlain in 1902 proposed an advisory imperial council as a 'preliminary step' to a 'Council with executive functions, and perhaps also legislative functions'. Cd. 1299, p. 4. Similarly Dr. Jameson, in supporting Deakin's secretariat proposal in 1907—a proposal which had no necessary connexion with federation—let slip: 'We want no new departure . . . but you must put the seed in first that it may begin to grow.' This was sufficient to frighten Laurier and Botha (Cd. 3523, pp. 35–40). Cf. the position ten years earlier, when Seddon and Braddon alone express discontent with existing arrangements (C. 8596, p. 15).

the time that lies before us than an attempt to force various parts of the Empire into a mutual subordination and arrangement for which they are not ready.'[1] The majority of the statesmen who met at the imperial conference were content to solve immediate problems. The immediate problem which most preoccupied the United Kingdom was the problem of defence. The immediate problem which most preoccupied the Dominions was the problem of trade.

A Bismarckian centralization of the scattered British Empire, said Lord Salisbury in his opening speech at the Colonial Conference of 1887, was impossible. A tariff union on the German model was also impossible, for the reason that Great Britain forty years earlier had rejected the policy of tariffs. But a defence union like Germany's—a *Kriegsverein*—was possible and should be pursued. And yet, after twenty years of pursuit, British statesmen were forced to give up the quest as hopeless. They had on the whole the better of the argument. Their diagnosis of international relationships was more realistic than the colonial diagnosis which we have examined: it was truer to say that armaments were necessary 'for the maintenance of imperial trade and of imperial interests all over the world'—though an 'imperial' interest might easily be confused with a British interest—than to argue that the colonies, themselves no liability to the Empire, were embroiled by imperial diplomacy.[2] Their diagnosis of the strategy of defence was hardly disputable. Repeatedly they emphasized the influence of sea-power upon history, and the historical character of the Empire as a sea-commonwealth. 'The sea is the link that joins us together. It was the reason of your up-rising. It is our first defence. It is the origin of our great commerce. . . . There is one sea, there is one Empire, and there is one Navy. . . .'[3] Surely it was madness to deny the necessity of a single navy under a single control? The situation in the Pacific, said Mr. Churchill as late as March 1914, would be determined absolutely by the situation in European waters. Two or three Australian and New Zealand battleships in the North Sea might decide the issue and make victory certain; the same ships in Pacific waters would be useless after the defeat of the British navy in the danger centre. 'Their existence would only serve to pro-

[1] H. E. Egerton, *Short History of British Colonial Policy* (Methuen's Colonial Library, 1897), p. 433.

[2] At almost every conference the British representatives insisted on this view of international realities, e.g. Lord Salisbury in 1887: 'Supposing that the Colonies were independent . . . do you think they would be safe?' C. 5091, p. 5. Chamberlain in 1897: '. . . every war . . . has had at bottom a colonial interest . . .' (C. 8596, p. 7.) See also Cd. 1299 of 1902, p. 9.

[3] Cd. 3523, p. 129 Lord Tweedmouth at the Colonial Conference, 1907.

long the agony without altering the course of events.' New Zealand, with minor reservations, accepted this argument. As late as 1902, an Australian Minister of Defence urged it no less forcibly than the British strategic experts. 'There is only one sea to be supreme over, and we want one fleet to be mistress over that sea.'[1] But Australian nationalism wanted a fleet of its own in Australian waters. Even in 1887, when the Australian colonies were doing nothing more than contribute to a British squadron, they compelled the Admiralty to agree that the squadron should be withdrawn from Australian waters 'only with the consent of the Colonial governments'.[2] After 1902, opinion in the Commonwealth vehemently attacked the principle of Australian contributions in money and men to an imperial fleet under British control. It was unworthy of a rising nation with its own challenging policies and its own responsibilities. By 1907 Australia had decided to possess her own separate navy. National sentiment triumphed over imperial sentiment, supported though it was by a most cogent strategic argument. It triumphed even in the area of greatest isolation and insecurity.

The Dominions, as Lord Selborne feared, were becoming 'continentally minded'. In military preparation this 'continental mindedness' was certain to be still more marked than it was in naval defence. According to the strategists, some kind of imperial military force was a necessary supplement to the imperial navy; the navy would keep open the seas for transports which might carry troops to any part of the Empire which found itself in trouble. In 1902, Mr. Seddon, the Prime Minister of New Zealand, moved for the establishment of 'an Imperial Reserve Force in each of His Majesty's Dominions over the seas for service in case of emergency outside the Dominion or Colony in which such reserve is formed'. The Canadian and Australian representatives replied that this proposal was 'objectionable in principle as derogating from the powers of self-government enjoyed by them'.[3] This meant that the Canadian militia and the Australian citizen-forces, to be instituted a few years later, must be solely under the control of their respective governments. Australia and Canada, therefore, might refuse to send away their troops in an imperial emergency. The claim of national self-government, if it meant anything, meant this. Sir Wilfrid Laurier, in particular, took care that there should be no ambiguity. 'I claim for Canada this,' he said in 1900, 'that in future Canada shall be at liberty to act or not act, to interfere or not interfere, to do just as she pleases, and that she shall

[1] Cd. 1299, p. 13. [2] C. 5091, p. 44.
[3] Cd. 1299, p. 32. See Appendix VI, ibid., at p. 73.

reserve to herself the right to judge whether or not there is cause for her to act.' From 1900 to 1914 Laurier reiterated this doctrine that Canadian defence was the business of the Canadian government; that Canada was not bound to take part in British wars.[1]

Suppose that the contrary proposition had been accepted? Laurier argued that common military liability would imply common political control. 'Under that condition of things, which does not exist, we should have the right to say to Great Britain: If you want us to help you, call us to your councils . . .' Chamberlain replied that Great Britain did want the help of her daughter-nations: she would call them to her councils. Like every other imperialist, he stressed the necessary connexion between defence and foreign policy. The argument led through unity of sacrifice towards unity of control. Its logical conclusion was, therefore, federation. This was the reason why Laurier had taken pains to make his argument hypothetical. Certainly, common military liability would imply a common control of foreign policy. But common military liability did not exist. The reverse was the position. Did not then the reverse consequence follow? Did not separate control of defence lead inevitably to separate control of separate foreign policies? Laurier was content not to see too far. He accepted the present fact that Canada did not possess a personality in international law. He accepted the shelter of subordinate status, which protected Canada from the impact of a dangerous world and the difficult decisions which it forced upon those who lived in it.[2] This hesitation was bound to increase the uneasiness of the imperialists and stimulate their activities. Canadian nationalism, they knew, would not always mark time. Canada would not always be content with subordination. They interpreted correctly the trend of events by which Canada was steadily moving towards the day when she would have a foreign policy of her own.

From defence, discussion sometimes turned also to the large subject of commercial policy. There was a natural approach through finance.

[1] Speech of 6th February 1900, quoted in Dewey, *The Dominions and Diplomacy*, vol. i, p. 235. There is ambiguity in the phrase about taking part in British wars. Laurier did not deny that Canada was legally involved: 'taking part' meant to him sending troops. He was in fact asserting a doctrine of 'passive belligerency'. Dewey contends justly that his standpoint was relevant only in an era of small local wars, when Canada's hand could not be forced by the active operations of states with whom she was legally at war.

[2] e.g. at the Conference of 1911: '. . . It must be recognised that in that family of nations by far the greater burden has to be carried on the shoulders of the Government of the United Kingdom. The diplomatic part of the Government of the Empire has of necessity to be carried on by the Government of the United Kingdom' (Cd. 5745, p. 116).

A common organization for defence suggests a common fund to pay for it: in 1887 Hofmeyr had proposed 'an Imperial Customs tariff, the revenue derived from such tariff to be devoted to the general defence of the Empire'. He believed that his imperial tariff—its average rate need not be more than 2 per cent.—could be levied on the foreigner without interfering with the existing tariffs which the colonies levied on all comers, including the British. Chamberlain went a good deal farther than this. His pronouncements illuminate the beginnings of that strange retreat of the newly risen political class of industrial England—its retreat, in free-trade fervour, along protectionist paths. The imperial system which Chamberlain desired was in substance the old mercantilist system: Great Britain would be the workshop for her economic dependencies; these in turn would supply her with raw materials; and the combination, surrounded by an unbroken tariff wall built against the foreigner, would as an economic unit pursue prosperity and power. As against the outer world this design of empire was exclusive and menacing; but its essential quality was cloaked from Chamberlain's followers by the accident of the Empire's vast size. An area extending over one-quarter of the world seemed, in a peroration, the world itself. The design, declared Chamberlain to the congress of chambers of commerce, might 'commend itself to an orthodox free trader'. It would be 'the greatest victory for free trade since Cobden's day'. His free-trade enthusiasm kindled at the prospect of demolishing irrational customs barriers built by the colonies. He told the Canadian Club in 1896 that 'protection must disappear' within the Empire. But a new imperial protection would take its place! This, he conceded, might appear 'a derogation from the high principles of free trade'. But it was a matter of subordinate importance. It need not prevent a 'satisfactory arrangement', if only the colonies would consider his proposition. The pieties and precisions of free-trade doctrine were swept away at last in a magnificent visionary enthusiasm. 'To organise an empire—one may almost say to create an empire—greater and more potent for peace and the civilisation of the world than any that history has ever known—that is a dream if you like, but a dream of which no man need be ashamed.'[1]

To the self-governing communities assembled in the Conference of 1897 this dream appeared a nightmare. Chamberlain was in effect proposing the abolition of colonial nationalism. He was unconsciously imitating Disraeli in hankering after a great scheme of imperial consolidation which involved the annihilation of colonial

[1] Garvin, *Life of Chamberlain*, vol. iii, pp. 180, 182. See also Cd. 1299, p. 6.

self-government in the economic sphere. The initiative in economic policy had, in fact, already passed to the free communities of the outer empire. They, too, had their imperial visions; but these were more in accord with the existing realities. They assumed their own established structure as distinct economic units. They then demanded that these units should link themselves in a combination of mutual advantage against the outside world. Sincerely they repeated Chamberlain's phrases of glowing imperial patriotism with a fervour equal to his own. But, whereas he called for an *imperial 'zollverein'*, they called for *imperial preference*. His proposal meant that they should assimilate their economic policies to the policy of the United Kingdom. Their demand meant that the United Kingdom should reverse her economic policy in order to conform with theirs. His proposal was in some degree a rationalization of the desires of the exporting industrial interests of Great Britain. Their proposal was in some degree a rationalization of the desires of their own industrial interests for predominance in a protected local market. Their proposal had the more promising future. The farmers and graziers of the outer empire, resentful at the burden of local industrial costs, might tend at first to support the idea of a *zollverein*; but, failing this, they would see in preference the means to a sheltered market in Great Britain which would compensate them for the costs laid upon them. British industrialists, threatened or annoyed at home and in the Empire by foreign competitors, might see visions of a happier day to be reached along the path of protection and preference. Even British farmers might possibly dream of a far-distant day when New Zealand exporters would be kept at bay in the name of the Empire. These were the interests which were operating in the controversy; but it is impossible to measure either their relative or their total strength. All that need be concluded at present is that the alignment of interests quickly proved the notion of a *zollverein* to be Utopian. In the early days of the Conference of 1902 it passed definitely out of practical, though not out of journalistic, politics.[1] For the next thirty years imperial preference held the stage as the only possible scheme of imperial fiscal reconstruction. Chamberlain himself was a

[1] Garvin, *Life of Chamberlain*, vol. iii, p. 191, quotes from the unpublished report of the discussions: 'Permit me to say that very definite suggestions have been before the Conference, and one of them has, to a certain extent, been approved, and another has been undoubtedly rejected by the general opinion of the Conference. The one which was rejected was the proposal for a *zollverein* with free trade in the British Empire . . .' The proposal was never again seriously entertained by any responsible minister anywhere in the British Empire, but in 1930 Lord Beaverbrook was 'crusading' for 'Empire Free Trade' in the newspapers which he controlled.

convert to it. Dominion statesmen, disregarding 'little Englander' protests, preached with apostolic fervour to the unconverted English. 'This', said Deakin in 1907, 'is a political gospel.'[1]

It would be out of place to open in this chapter an inquiry into the economics of the 'gospel'. But it will be useful to state shortly what it meant in sentiment, loyalties, and political aspiration. It was interwoven with a patriotism which those Englishmen who envisaged the Empire as 'forever broadening England', 'a vast English nation', 'the all-Saxon home',[2] could not understand. It was difficult for Englishmen who held these quite natural preconceptions to understand that the self-governing communities overseas did not admit an overriding loyalty to an 'organic' empire, a whole which was prior to those parts of which they were members. The first English publicist who thoroughly understood dominion loyalties was Mr. Richard Jebb, who published in 1905 his *Studies in Colonial Nationalism.* Mr. Jebb explained to readers in Great Britain—and to readers in the outer empire also, for there, also, enlightenment was often needed—that Canada, Australia, New Zealand, and South Africa were all travelling the same road to national status and mature national consciousness, although they were at different stages on that road. But the independence at which they aimed was not a denial of interdependence in foreign policy, or in commercial policy, or in law. Nationalism would accept the limitations of membership in a common society. National loyalties, so far from being disruptive of the Empire, were the stuff out of which it must be re-created.

Mr. Jebb's counsel was to begin the work of re-creation on an economic basis—protection and preference all round. A generation passed before the United Kingdom was willing to try this experiment. In the meantime, therefore, nationalism in tariffs operated without any attempt at systematic imperial co-ordination. It brought the Dominions into direct touch with the outer world at large, without defining those 'workable limits' for which Mr. Jebb had pleaded. It is interesting to observe, in the records of the imperial conference and elsewhere, the manner in which the genuine imperial sentiment of the Dominions served the purposes which their more immediate and ever-deepening national sentiment was pursuing. With sincere

[1] Cd. 3523, p. 239. But there was no gospel note in the speech of another Australian representative, Sir William Lyne (pp. 324 ff.). Lloyd George and Churchill, supported by Laurier, claimed for Great Britain the same right of self-government in economic affairs as the Dominions enjoyed. Churchill argued that 'the system of imperial preference inevitably brings colonial affairs into the parliamentary and party area'.

[2] The phrases come from Tennyson, Seeley, and Carlyle respectively. 'Organic' was a favourite word of the *Round Table.*

imperial enthusiasm they pursued their essentially national aims. Thus, at the Ottawa Conference of 1894—a conference called on Canadian initiative and one in which Great Britain did not actively participate—they fervently advocated preference as a policy of imperial patriotism. Canada shortly afterwards granted preferences to Great Britain: the other daughter-nations were ready to do the same. But, in order to be effectively patriotic, they needed new powers. The Australasian representatives at Ottawa demanded that their countries, like Canada, should be freed of constitutional obstacles which prevented them from instituting differential duties outside the Australasian area. All the representatives demanded that they should be freed from existing treaty obstacles to the preferential policy which they wished to pursue. They repeated the demand in 1897, and in the following year Great Britain denounced the offending treaties which had been made in 1865 and 1867 with Belgium and the German *Zollverein*. In the name of the Empire, the Dominions were liberating themselves from the last vestiges of imperial constraint on their economic freedom. They established the two principles of optional withdrawal from imperial commercial treaties and optional inclusion in them; thus they retained the commercial advantages of membership in a great empire and at the same time escaped the disadvantages. Their acquisition of new powers had also its more positive side in relation to the outer world. It was natural, when demanding specific powers in the name of an imperial ideal, to forget that other powers of a similar nature served no obvious imperial purpose. These powers they claimed for their own sake. Thus, even at the Conference of 1887, New Zealand had claimed the limited rights already enjoyed by Canada of negotiating, in association with British diplomatists, her own separate commercial treaties with foreign states. A South Australian delegate then pointed out that this policy would create a 'mutuality of interest' with foreigners which was in direct contradiction with the imperial purposes which the delegates had been professing. But not even New Zealand, the most 'home-loving' of all the daughter-nations of Great Britain, was willing to forgo a power essential to economic and political maturity. New Zealand pilots might hoist imperial ensigns, and the crew might cheer, but it was a nationalist wind which was filling the sails of the ship of state. The irresistible current of national self-government was sweeping all the Dominions—it mattered not whether they were nonchalant, or exultant, or uneasy—out into the open sea of international relationships. By 1907 all familiar landmarks had disappeared, save one. They did their own business in the direct negotiation of commercial treaties with foreign Powers; but they still acted in formal association with a British representative and under formal powers granted to them by the King on the advice of British ministers. A Canadian minister negotiating with the French government was in form a British plenipotentiary. In fact he was politically responsible to the government at Ottawa.

> 'Thus on the political side the relations of the parts of the Empire to one another were tending steadily to become those of independent nations, and the efforts of one of them to delimit the scope or direct the operation of another's activities would present the same difficulties as arise in the case of similar efforts among independent nations.'[1]

In the sphere of general international relations the same tendency was operating at a slower pace. In 1871 there was one Canadian commissioner among a body of five representatives appointed by the British government to conduct the negotiations, on a miscellaneous programme which jostled together Fenian raids, *Alabama* controversies, and Canadian fisheries, which led eventually to the Treaty of Washington. In 1897 the reverse position obtained: on the joint high commission appointed in that year to settle outstanding questions between the United States and Canada there were four members of the Canadian government and one representative of Great Britain. In the Alaskan boundary arbitration of 1903 the proportion was one to three. The vote of this single British representative—he was the Lord Chief Justice of the United Kingdom—decided the arbitration in favour of the United States, and stirred up the old bitter complaint that Canadian interests were perpetually sacrificed to British diplomacy. 'The difficulty as I conceive it to be', said Sir Wilfrid Laurier, 'is that so long as Canada remains a dependency of the British Crown, the present powers that we have are not sufficient for the maintenance of our rights.' A Canadian writer has asserted that in this moment 'a definite turning was taken'—'the Canadian people passed at a single stride from the plane of willing dependency to one of conscious aspiration for the powers of nationhood'.[2] In the permanent International Joint Commission instituted in 1909 by treaty between Great Britain and the United States, the Canadian people

[1] Dewey, *The Dominions and Diplomacy*, vol. i, p. 186. It should be noticed that Lord Ripon's dispatch of 28th June 1895, which satisfied the practical needs of the Dominions while explicitly withholding from them the treaty power, also laid down fundamental principles as to substance: (1) that there should be no infringement of the treaty right to most-favoured-nation treatment enjoyed by any foreign nation; (2) that no foreign nation should be granted privileges superior to those which the members of the Empire possessed.

[2] Dafoe, *Canada, An American Nation*, p. 71.

in effect exercised the powers of nationhood: three Canadian members met on equal terms with three American members. Two years previously the Canadian government had taken a distinct step forward in Canadian participation in Pacific politics; responding directly to Japanese initiative, and with only a perfunctory communication with the British government, it sent emissaries to Tokio to discuss the extremely dangerous topic of the wrongs suffered by Japanese subjects on Canadian soil. In the very different sphere of international technical conferences there was advance of a more formal kind. In 1912 and 1914 Canadian representatives, although their powers derived from action of the imperial government, met the representatives of other nations, with a separate and equal status 'on behalf of Canada'.

From whatever angle we view the trend of dominion development, we see that it was leading towards effective national independence. According to the logic of sovereignty and the teaching of the imperial federationists, this meant—failing the one appropriate remedy—imperial disintegration. But, in practice, common sense seemed to be finding a middle way between dependence and disruption. The best example of what was in fact happening can be found in that sphere which to imperialists was the sphere of primary importance, the sphere of defence. The Dominions were resolute in vindicating the principle of national organization and control both of their armies and navies. Logically this principle led to chaos and inefficiency—weapons of different pattern, different notions of tactics and strategy, impossibility of a common plan. In practice, the Dominions proved themselves willing so to manage their own separate organizations that they might fit together, if the need should arise, as voluntary units operating in a greater organization. Australia, for example, established an Australian navy; but this navy was also one of three British Empire fleet-units in the Pacific Ocean. The navy served Australian purposes and was subject to Australian control;[1] but, 'subject to approval of the Commonwealth government on declaration of war', it would play its part according to the plan of the Admiralty for the common defence of the British Empire.[2] The same

[1] As a necessary legal preliminary to the establishment of dominion navies an explicit extension of legislative power beyond the local territorial sphere was secured by imperial Act (The Naval Discipline (Dominion Naval Forces) Act, 1911).

[2] The fleet-unit principle was adopted at the Defence sub-Conference of 1909 (Cd. 4948). New Zealand preferred to contribute to the China fleet-unit. In 1911 an agreement between the governments of the United Kingdom, Canada, and Australia defined the relation of the Australian and Canadian fleets to the royal navy. Canada, with two coasts, was not willing to establish a Canadian navy as a fourth Pacific fleet-unit. In 1914 the Canadian navy was negligible. The liberal government

principle operated with regard to dominion land forces. Every student of the Conferences of 1907, 1909, and 1911 must be profoundly impressed with the penetration, ability, and tact of Haldane, who was in charge of the British War Office. He understood perfectly the determination of the Dominions to control their own forces, and he also understood that this determination was not a denial, but rather the condition, of mutual support backed by mutual loyalty. Haldane swept aside all notions of command or of centralization working from above. This cleared the ground for the idea of co-operation, of co-ordination pursued as a matter of free choice and common sense. It freed the self-governing communities of the British Empire from inhibitions which might have frustrated their natural disposition to stand together. The Conference of 1907 agreed to use the newly established general staff as a 'common school' at the disposal of the various national organizations within the Empire. 'It is', said Haldane, 'a purely advisory organization of which command is not a function.' And he concluded a paper which in masterly fashion exposed the principles of imperial defence with the words:

'We know that this thing must be founded simply upon the attaining of a common purpose, the fulfilment of a common end. It cannot be by the imposing of restrictions or by rigid plans which might not suit the idiosyncracies of particular countries.'

The initiative, then, lay with the Dominions. It was for them to decide their own needs and policies, bearing only in mind that, as members of a family, they might need help and might wish to give it. Controlw as separate; but—again it was Haldane's phrase—the same 'expert' was 'called in'.[1]

It would have been absurd to do anything else. For, if they had failed to co-ordinate their military technique, they would have made mutual support impossible, or, at the least, costly and inefficient. In the sub-conference of 1909 Haldane raised the practical issues in a series of blunt questions:

'1. Is each part of the Empire willing to make its preparations on such lines as will enable it, should it so desire, to take its share in the general defence of the Empire?

'2. Shall the war establishments of dominion forces be assimilated as far as possible to the approved war establishments of units of the regular forces?

'3. Will the Dominions endeavour to organize their existing forces so

of Sir Wilfrid Laurier had done little to create the fleet for which an act of 1910 had made legal provision. Sir Robert Borden's government proposed instead a direct grant of $35,000,000 to the British government, but this proposal was blocked by the liberal majority in the Senate.

[1] Cd. 3523, pp. 94 ff.

as to be capable of mobilizing in accordance with the above establishments for a common imperial object?

'4. Will the Dominions adopt, as far as practicable, the field service regulations and training manuals issued to the Home Regular Army as the basis of their organization, administration, and training of their troops?

'5. Are the Dominions prepared to adopt, as far as possible, imperial patterns of arms, equipment, and stores?'

To all these questions the Dominions answered 'Yes'. No other answer was consistent with common sense. The general principle asserted was simply that 'each part of the Empire is willing to make its preparations on such lines as will enable it, should it so desire, to take its share in the general defence of the Empire'.[1] The basic idea was decision by each self-governing community. This in turn became the starting-point for voluntary reintegration.

The advocates of imperial federation, well drilled in the lessons of American constitution-making, were fond of quoting a saying of Washington's, 'Influence is not government'. Nor is it. But, as a method of achieving desired results in certain circumstances, it is not necessarily inferior to government. More influence and less government in Ireland during the War of 1914–18 would have made a less tragic history. The overseas Dominions before the War had in successive conferences flatly rejected British plans of defence based on the idea of control from a centre. In 1907 British statesmen, and even their attendant experts, accepted the dominion verdict as irrevocable. Influence—not merely the influence of persuasive personalities, but rather the compelling influence of facts operating directly upon the minds of statesmen—took the place of government. The results proved satisfactory.

This new method of achieving a common end was no isolated procedure. The mutual arrangements for defence accepted by the different communities represented at the imperial conference accurately reflected the political relations which they were establishing with each other. In 1887 the self-governing colonies had been jumbled together with Crown colonies and protectorates. In 1894, on their own initiative, they met at Ottawa in a society of their own. From 1897 onwards there was no questioning of the principle that self-government was an indispensable condition of representation at the conference.[2] The words 'inner empire' and 'outer empire', hitherto understood geographically, might now have been used with a new

[1] Cd. 4948, pp. 29, 38. Even so, the Canadians adopted a separate pattern of rifle (the Ross rifle) with some resulting inconvenience when war came.

[2] e.g. Sir William Lyne's words in 1907, objecting to a speech of the Secretary of

significance: the conference communities were in a real sense constituting themselves as an inner circle of the privileged—of those privileged to govern themselves, and to discuss on terms of equality the common concerns of all. It was a symptom of growing equality that both Great Britain and Canada should in 1905 propose the substitution of the word 'imperial' for the word 'colonial'— a substitution which was effected at the Conference of 1907.[1] This same conference discarded the noun 'colony' with the adjective 'colonial', and from now on the conference circle was constituted by the United Kingdom and the 'self-governing Dominions beyond the seas'. At the same time there was a clear definition of the relation in which these communities stood to each other at the conference. It was a conference of governments; one government, one vote. In practice, resolutions were never carried by majority decision. 'Nothing will be done', said Dr. Jameson, 'unless we are unanimous.'[2] He might have added that, strictly speaking, nothing could in any circumstances be 'done' by the imperial conference. It had neither executive nor legislative powers. Its resolutions were merely recommendations for action to be undertaken by the governments and parliaments of the separate Dominions. Complaints were made from time to time that conference resolutions were not systematically followed up. But in matters of chief importance the action agreed to be desirable almost invariably followed. The technique of persuasion and agreement, which was taking the place of command, was adequate for the conditions of that time because there was no dispute about basic principles. Agreement about essentials existed in advance; the need, therefore, was to elicit it and state it, rather than create it and impose it. Mr. Asquith showed true insight in 1911 when he defined the Empire in terms of the values which it professed to serve—liberty, the rule of law, loyalty to a common head. Defined in this way the Empire appeared living and strong. Defined institutionally it would have appeared a ramshackle structure, for its compulsive machinery was rusting into obsolescence and its co-operative

State for India: 'India is not a self-governing colony in the sense in which we are' —and, in general, her conditions are not those of a member of the conference (Cd. 3523, p. 325).

[1] The proposal for the new name occurred in correspondence on the Lyttelton proposals of 1905 (Cd. 2785; see also Cd. 3523, pp. 78 ff.).

[2] Cd. 3523, p. 33. General Smuts later protested against departure from the convention in the matter of Indian emigration (Cmd. 1988 of 1923, p. 115): 'That is why I think the resolution passed in 1921 was a mistake. . . . We got on the wrong road there. For the first time we passed a motion through this conference by a majority. It has never been done before and I do hope it will never occur again.' In the early conferences the unanimity convention was not established, e.g. 1897 (Cd. 8596, p. 15).

machinery was a scanty, untidy heap of improvised parts. Institutionally, the British Empire seemed to be reaching the extreme limit of decentralization. Students of British history might, however, have taken comfort from the reflection that Great Britain, judged by standards of continental centralization and state-worship, had been traditionally an undergoverned, chaotic country, whose spontaneous unity seemed a recurring miracle.

There were, however, answers which might properly have been offered to this reflection. Had not Great Britain paid a heavy price for her contempt of organization, and had she not been forced in the nineteenth century to repair the defect? Apart from this, was not the lack of organization exaggerated? There was still the Colonial Office. Important parts of the old organization still functioned; it was the new principle, the developing principle of free co-operation, which lacked necessary instruments. Deakin, in 1907, attacked the dead hand of the past, and pleaded for a deliberately organized future. If the procedure of the imperial conference truly reflected the real relationship of the free communities within the Empire—a direct relationship between government and government—why did the Colonial Office survive as the organizing centre? The Colonial Office was merely a department of the British government, a department, too, with associations reminiscent of colonial subordination, and manners offensive to dominion pride and zeal—'a certain impenetrability, a certain remoteness—a certain weariness of people much pressed with affairs, and greatly overburdened, whose natural desire is to say, "Kindly postpone this; do not press that, do not trouble us; what does it matter? we have enough to do already . . ."' Let the Colonial Office continue to organize the affairs of those territories which were still in a colonial relation to Great Britain. For the communities of the conference circle Deakin demanded a secretariat which would 'represent all these governments', 'a new department which would be in a sense a joint department, though under the ministerial direction of the Prime Minister of England', a truly imperial institution based on the idea of 'joint cost and responsibility'. Undoubtedly this would have been a more logical embodiment in administration of the principle of co-operation by equals, which the imperial conference embodied. But opponents of the proposal—and indeed, to some extent, its champions—saw in it a tactical move of the imperial federationists. British liberal statesmen and Canadian liberal statesmen united in opposing it. Would not these imperial bureaucrats trench on the powers of responsible governments? They might become, argued Lord Elgin, 'a danger to the autonomy of us all'. 'Whom are they going to advise?' inquired Sir Wilfrid Laurier. 'Whose suggestions are they to receive? On what authority are they to act? What work shall they do? What advice shall they give? Shall they give independent advice?' Underlying these doubts was the fear that an imperial secretariat implied, if it were to be effective—and otherwise it was mischievous—an imperial executive control. This was not a necessary implication, as the experience of the League of Nations secretariat has since demonstrated. But it was sufficient to defeat Deakin's plan of co-operative organization.[1] And, since organization of some kind was necessary, it remained in the hands of the Colonial Office. A separate department of that office was named the Dominions Department and put under the charge of a senior-assistant secretary charged to act as permanent secretary to the imperial conference. 'All that appears to have been accomplished', complained the Australian government, 'is that a sub-department has been renamed.'[2]

The whole discussion is extremely illuminating. It is a reminder that imperial development was still hesitating at a provisional and ambiguous stage. Dominion equality, copiously watered by aspiration and oratory, was growing into a healthy plant and had already yielded some fruit. But the young plant was growing in the protecting shade of a 'British ascendancy'[3] which was real and not merely formal. Great Britain was still performing on behalf of the whole Empire functions which its self-governing members were not yet ready to share or assume. The secretariat of the conference of equal governments remained inside a British department of state. The Committee of Imperial Defence was a committee constituted by the British Prime Minister and whomsoever he chose to summon. Dominion representatives might receive a summons if they wished; but the committee remained essentially the creation of one government extending its action over the whole imperial field.[4] It was the same with foreign

[1] Cd. 3523, pp. 37–73. See also Cd. 5745, pp. 75 ff. and 173 ff.; and Cd. 5746–1, pp. 212–14, for 1911 proposals. The institution which most completely embodies to-day the principle of 'joint cost and responsibility' is the Imperial War Graves Commission. An Australian Prime Minister, Mr. S. M. Bruce, several times made the suggestion that an imperial secretariat should be instituted on this model. See Gerald Palmer, *Consultation and Co-operation in the British Commonwealth* (Oxford University Press, 1934), pp. 210–11, 217–18.

[2] Cd. 3795; Cd. 5273.

[3] The phrase is R. Jebb's, see *The Britannic Question* (Longmans, 1917), pp. 42 ff.

[4] Cf. Dewey, *The Dominions and Diplomacy*, vol. i, pp. 294 ff. After the change of government in 1914, Canadian ministers made considerable use of the committee. There is perhaps some analogy with the Judicial Committee of the Privy Council, an imperial institution of the old model which, however, since 1895 might be on occasion 'afforced' by the presence of Privy Councillors who have held high judicial office in the Dominions.

policy. Dominion governments were beginning to do direct business with their foreign neighbours; but high policy—foreign policy in supreme issues affecting all the members of the Empire—remained exclusively in the control of the British cabinet. 'That authority', said Mr. Asquith in 1911, 'cannot be shared.' The Canadian liberal government wanted no share: it even deprecated the idea that dominion governments should be informed and consulted. These large questions, said Sir Wilfrid Laurier, were 'eminently in the domain of the United Kingdom'. By this he meant that they *ought* to remain within the domain of the United Kingdom, for he hoped that by escaping consultation Canada would escape liability. The hope was an illusion, as Canada was to learn three years later. The more realistic Labour Prime Minister of Australia requested in 1911 that the Dominions should be consulted before the negotiation of international agreements affecting them; but he qualified his request with the words, 'as far as possible'. The conference took special pains to underline the reservation:

> 'General Botha: "I want it clear. I do not want to handicap the British Government. I want them to undertake the full responsibility."
>
> 'The President: "The British Government do not want to shovel it off on the Dominions."
>
> 'Mr. Fisher: "I do not want to handicap you either. We want to be associated as far as possible."'[1]

The champions of imperial federation might therefore have argued that their thesis had not yet been refuted. The Empire remained provisionally a unity because the Dominions remained provisionally content to linger in the shelter of inferior status and powers. On the other hand, it might have been answered that the goodwill and fertility of expedient which in the past had reconciled unity and freedom would continue to do so even when freedom swept the Dominions into the difficult seas of high policy. The controversy lasted into the War. Even yet there is no definite conclusive answer which would satisfy both parties to it. The historian of to-day, contemplating the Empire's development in the generation preceding the War and the testing which it underwent during the War itself, may be content to record that the Empire at that time was moving between two worlds and enjoying the benefits of each. There was the old world of United Kingdom ascendancy. This still survived sufficiently to ensure effective leadership in policy and organization.

[1] Cd. 5745, pp. 97–131. The original Australian motion referred to the Declaration of London, and the assurance given by Sir Edward Grey referred particularly to international conferences. Fisher did not grasp the fact that all high policy ultimately affected the Dominions, a fact of which Sir Robert Borden was fully conscious.

There was the new world of dominion equality. This was sufficiently mature to call forth comradeship. The Dominions went to war on the volunteer principle.

The new strength of this principle cut channels of its own, but it also poured vigorously through the traditional channels of the British state. The most notable institutional expression of this moment in imperial development was the improvisation known as the Imperial War Cabinet. In 1917 the British Prime Minister invited the Prime Ministers of the Dominions to sit in common council with the five members of the British War Cabinet. Sir Robert Borden described this improvisation as 'a cabinet of governments'. He shared the prevailing opinion that it represented an important step forward in the permanent constitutional organization of the Empire. In reality it represented not only 'the almost unlimited flexibility' of the British monarchy, but also the exceptional response to the challenge of an emergency. Both in Great Britain and the Dominions the normal conditions of parliamentary responsibility were, with the consent of parliaments and electorates, in abeyance. This fact enabled the British Prime Minister to create a policy-making directive committee whose members, whether drawn from the inner or the outer empire, had the status of privy councillors. What was legally possible then could not have become a normal constitutional practice. The essential characteristics of a true cabinet are common responsibility to a single legislature and decision by a majority vote. The Imperial War Cabinet possessed neither of these characteristics; it was therefore misnamed. It was in reality simply the British Cabinet 'afforced' with dominion representatives. And yet it had historical importance as the expression—none the less striking because it ignored rather than embodied normal constitutional categories—of the new principle of empire, the principle of liberty growing into equality and proving itself willing, under trial, to accept so much unity as was necessary to defend its basic values. Sir Robert Borden appropriately recalled the not very distant past of doctrinaire resignation and disillusionment.

> 'Less than half a century had passed since the most commanding figures in the statesmanship of Britain anticipated and even hoped for the disruption of the Empire. . . . Now a million fighting men from free self-governing nations were in the Empire's battle line, and dominion statesmen took their equal parts at the Empire's council table in the supreme test of its destiny.'[1]

[1] Sir Robert Laird Borden, *Canadian Constitutional Studies* (University of Toronto Press, 1921), pp. 109–10. See Keith, *Speeches and Documents on the British Dominions,*

V

A New Name for the British Empire

According to Aristotle, friendship is an essential element in the life of a true community, and friendship presupposes a real equality of some kind. The statesmen of Great Britain and the Dominions claimed these blessings. They testified to the 'warm vein of friendship' which ran throughout the Empire, to 'the refreshment of spirit' which came to them in their conferences with each other.[1] To equality they paid unceasing homage. 'The only possibility of a continuance of the British Empire', declared Lord Milner in 1919, 'is on a basis of absolute out-and-out equal partnership between the United Kingdom and the Dominions. I say this without any kind of reservation whatsoever.' There was not a statesman in the Dominions who would have confessed himself unwilling to repeat the assertion without any kind of reservation whatsoever. And yet, as Lord Milner went on to say, to translate equality into forms and institutions without destroying the Empire's unity 'was one of the most complicated tasks which statesmanship has ever had to face'.[2] Both in Great Britain and the Dominions statesmen differed from each other in the degree of their enthusiasm for this task. For more than a decade after the War conservatism struggled with impatience, appeasement with discontent, timidity with daring. Legal theory, said General Smuts in 1917, must be adapted to political fact. Constitutional custom, answered Sir Robert Borden, was more important than legal theory. We want no constitution-making, said Mr. Hughes in 1921. 'What is there that we cannot do now? What could the Dominions do as independent nations that they cannot do now?' This was the perpetual Australian refrain. We want no written constitution, said Mr. Bruce in 1926. We want no formal document, declared Mr. Scullin in 1930. Our relations, said an Australian opponent of Mr. Scullin, are like the relations of a family; and he added: 'I do not want the relations of myself and my children to be determined by rules written in a book, to which each of us must refer to discover who is right and who is wrong.' To this attitude the New Zealanders subscribed even more emphatically. But the South Africans, the Irish, and frequently the Canadians, took the contrary point of view. Failure to define the principle of equality, they maintained, was

pp. 3–8, and (for criticism of the term 'imperial cabinet') *Imperial Unity and the Dominions* (Oxford University Press, 1917), p. 545, and *Letters on Imperial Relations* (Oxford University Press, 1935), No. 15.

[1] Cmd. 2769 of 1926, p. 410.

[2] *The Times*, 10th July 1919.

equivalent to an abandonment of the principle. Perpetuation of the forms of subordination implied the recognition of a subordination existing in fact. Acquiescence in surviving inequalities would destroy friendship. South Africa, declared General Hertzog in 1926, could not give loyalty to an empire which failed to realize its own aspirations.

> 'I think, Sir, it will be generally agreed that the corner-stone of the Empire is the will, the goodwill, of those who compose it. . . . If, therefore, the Empire is to be maintained . . . we must see that the will to live in the Empire, as a Commonwealth of free nations, will in future, as it is to-day, be present and active with every one of its constituent elements.'

Did the conditions for ensuring the permanency of that goodwill exist? General Hertzog told the Conference of 1926 that they did not. But, a few months later, he told the people of South Africa that the conference had created them.[1]

'The Empire as a Commonwealth of free nations.' General Hertzog was repeating a phrase which during the War had begun to take hold of public imagination, which from 1917 onwards began to appear with increasing frequency in the records of imperial conferences, and which in 1921 established itself as a new official designation of the Empire. What did the new name signify? The men who popularized it intended it to signify the transformation of the Empire by the principle of liberty. They intended it to signify their faith that liberty, even when it had grown into equality, would bring not disintegration but a deeper unity. The name, therefore, embodied an interpretation of past history and a prophecy of the future. It was not a scientific description. Its associations were poetic, rhetorical, legendary. A short investigation of them will not be out of place: it will shed some light on emotions and ideals which were in part a reaction to change and in part a cause of it.[2] 'The names of such things as affect us

[1] The quotations are taken from the proceedings of the Conferences of 1917, 1921, 1926 and 1930: Cd. 8566, pp. 46, 59; Cmd. 1474, p. 22; Cmd. 2769, pp. 19, 24; Cmd. 3718, p. 13. For Mr. Latham's speech see Keith, *Speeches and Documents on the British Commonwealth*, p. 264. For General Hertzog's speech on his return to South Africa see *The Times*, 14th December, 1926. 'He said emphatically that he no longer feared the Empire.... There was no question any longer of domination or superiority over the Dominions. . . .'

[2] The name is foreshadowed in the famous resolution IX of the Imperial War Conference of 1917, recommending that as soon as possible after the War a special conference should be held for the readjustment of the constitutional relations of the various parts of the Empire, 'based upon a full recognition of the Dominions as autonomous nations of an Imperial Commonwealth, and of India as an important part of the same' (Cd. 8566, p. 5). Sir Robert Borden at this conference used the phrase: 'Imperial Commonwealth of United Nations.' In the following year (Cmd.

[Thomas Hobbes has said] . . . are in the common discourses of men of "inconstant" signification. For seeing that all names are imposed to signify our conceptions, and all our affections are but

9177, p. 18) General Smuts used the form 'British Commonwealth of Nations'. But orators continued to vary the phrase at their fancy, e.g. the forms 'Britannic Commonwealth of Nations', 'Commonwealth of British Nations' were used indifferently. Even the Articles of Agreement for a treaty between Great Britain and Ireland, which establish the term as official, refer both to 'the Community of Nations known as the British Empire' (Art. 1) and 'the group of nations forming the British Commonwealth of Nations' (Art. 4). In 1926 General Hertzog in a single sentence employs the terms 'Commonwealth of Nations', 'Empire', and 'British Community of Nations', without any distinction in their meaning. This matter has some importance, as is shown on p. 60.

The origin of the phrase has some interest. Lord Rosebery used it in a prophetic speech delivered at Adelaide in 1884 (Lord Crewe, *Lord Rosebery* (Murray 1931), vol. i, p. 186). But Lord Rosebery seems to have forgotten his phrase and nobody else remembered it. It was Mr. Lionel Curtis who coined the name to express what he considered to be the true principle of development in the British Empire. He has kindly given to the writer the following account:

'What happened was this: we had all been nourished in the true milk of the Kiplingian word when we set out to inquire what the British Empire meant and stood for. After some years' work I came to think that it stood for something very different from "dominion over palm and pine', that its function in the world was to promote the government of men by themselves. I caused grave searchings of heart by beginning to argue that that principle must be applied to India as well as the Dominions. I developed the argument to show that the Empire could not become self-governing in the real sense of the term until people all over it had the same responsibility in respect of the issues of peace and war and external affairs as a British citizen had who happens to live in England. The upshot was that I came to regard the word "Empire" as a misnomer. Hunting about for a good Saxon word to express the kind of state for which it stood I naturally lit on the word "Commonwealth." I developed the theme that while the Greeks had achieved the city-commonwealth, England had made an immense advance in achieving a national commonwealth; but this was by no means the end of the process of development. The next step in the history of mankind must be the creation of an international commonwealth. The so-called British Empire was not such a commonwealth because responsibility in respect of the things which affected us as a whole was confined to the people of Great Britain.

'My book in its first form was printed for private circulation among the *Round Table* groups under the title "The Project of a Commonwealth." This title was based on the phrase used by Adam Smith when he described the British Empire not as an Empire but as the project of an Empire. But I was not satisfied with this title and I can now remember the exact place on a lonely country walk when the title "A Commonwealth of Nations" occurred to me as the phrase for which I was looking. The book was ultimately published under this title; but long before it had been published Philip Kerr began to use it in his articles in the *Round Table*. It corresponded to what was in the minds of a growing number of people, who were not satisfied with the old Kiplingian conception, and caught on. During the War when we were busy contrasting our ideals with those of the empires of Central Europe, with which we were fighting, the statesmen began to use the phrase in their speeches. After the War it began to creep into official documents. . . .'

It should be remembered that the statesmen who adopted the name which Mr. Curtis had made did not adopt his proposals for the constitutional organization of the Commonwealth of Nations.

conceptions, when we conceive the same things differently we can hardly avoid the different naming of them.'[1] For this reason a political society or institution may suffer in public esteem because its name remains associated with situations or transactions which awaken in the public mind feelings of resentment, repugnance, disapproval, or mere weariness. If this disfavour derives chiefly from transient misfortunes or mistakes of the society, and not from its essential nature, a change of name will help to revive the society's prestige. The change may even assist in making the members of the society aware of true purposes already pursued but not yet stated. If, on the contrary, the old name has won disfavour because of vices inherent in the society, the new name, however nobly-sounding, will soon fall into a similar contempt.

In the first two decades of the twentieth century the word empire was rapidly losing its prestige. During the Middle Ages the word had enjoyed the prestige of universalist ideals and pretensions; thereafter the national states which challenged these ideals and destroyed these pretensions appropriated to themselves the imperial title. *Rex est imperator in regno suo*, declared Philip the Fair of France; this declaration, inspired by the Roman lawyers, challenged the basic assumptions of medieval unity. Two centuries later Henry VIII effectively repeated the challenge in England. The Act of Appeals declared England to be an empire independent of all outward jurisdiction and authority. In Henry VIII's day empire signified national sovereignty. But already in the next reign its signification was expanding to include the conception of a composite state formed through the union of two separate states. The Protector Somerset, whose ideal was a union of Scots and English 'with the sea for a wall and mutual love for a garrison', proposed, in deference to Scottish sensibilities, that the united kingdoms, surrendering their separate designations, should style themselves the Empire, and their sovereign the Emperor, of Great Britain. After the union of crowns in 1603, the phrase, which James I found pleasing, won considerable popular acceptance. Gradually the 'Brittanick Empire' came to include the

[1] *Leviathan*, Bk. I, ch. iv. Hobbes continues '. . . And therefore in reasoning a man must take heed of words, which, besides the signification of what we imagine their nature, have a signification also of the nature, disposition, and interest of the speaker; such as are the names of virtues and vices; for one man calleth "wisdom" what another calleth "fear", and one "cruelty" what another "justice". . . . And therefore such names can never be true grounds of any ratiocination. No more can metaphors and tropes of speech; but these are less dangerous, because they profess their inconstancy, which the other do not.' On the necessary and proper use of metaphors or 'fictions' in historical narrative, see Toynbee, *A Study of History*, vol. i, pp. 441–64.

'daughter nations' also.[1] In the eighteenth century British Empire meant as a matter of course all the territories united to the Crown. But the word inherited from this century had associations of overbearing power which were repugnant to the new nationalisms of the twentieth century, and inconsistent with the ideal of equality. Radical nationalists in Canada and other Dominions vehemently repudiated 'the idea of ascendancy and domination' associated with the word.[2] The propaganda of the nationalists at first penetrated slowly. For it met the great wave of imperial enthusiasm which followed the long trough of mid-Victorian disillusionment. That enthusiasm, however, suffered from its own indiscriminate fervour. It began as an idealistic protest against the severing of ties between kindred free communities. It soon became compromised by association with missions of civilization, the white man's burden, and jingo patriotism exulting in a map painted red. The association was, strictly speaking, accidental, and both among the fervent and their critics it was due largely to the use of one word to cover two distinct movements. Idealists who were afire with the idea of re-creating the unity of the Empire on the principles of freedom and equality innocently adopted the new word imperialism.[3] At the same time socialist criticism was exposing the jingo creed as the ideological expression of economic exploitation at home and abroad; and was using the word imperialism to describe both.[4] Add to this the natural reaction in taste and ethics after Mr. Kipling's prodigious literary success. The word imperialism came badly torn out of all these trials, and the word empire shared its discredit. To cap all, there was the War. Imperialism became a handy term of abuse for the policy of enemy empires. British statesmen were anxious to prove that their empire was not like other people's empires. It was therefore tempting, it was fitting, to give it a different name.

The name commonwealth had a history which for many centuries had run parallel with that of empire; but this history, except for one brief period, had a content which was far deeper intellectually, and far richer in emotional colour. Commonwealth is a distinctive English word current from the fifteenth century onwards. But the word became the vehicle for ideas and aspirations whose history stretches

[1] See C. H. Firth in *Scottish Historical Review*, vol. xv, no. 59, pp. 185 ff., and J. T. Adams in *American Historical Review*, vol. xxvii, pp. 487 ff.

[2] e.g. W. S. Ewart, *The Kingdom of Canada* (Toronto, 1908), pp. 56 ff. *Kingdom Papers* (Ottawa 1912), vol. i, no. 1; vol. ii, no. 21, *passim*.

[3] Lord Carnarvon wrote in 1878: 'I have heard of imperial policy and imperial interests, but imperialism, as such, is new to me.'

[4] See, for example, J. A. Hobson's powerful book, *Imperialism* (London, 1902).

far back into classical antiquity. Commonwealth meant *res publica*, the true society grounded upon the rule of law and the common good.[1] Empire, on the other hand, derived from *imperium*, the function of command (and especially military command) in this society. During the Middle Ages the empire was merely one aspect of the *res publica generis humani*. When the national state appropriated to itself imperial sovereignty, it filched also that magnificent creation of human aspiration and intellect embodied in the writings of St. Thomas Aquinas and Dante. Instead of a single Christian commonwealth, men spoke now of 'divers Christian commonwealths', and surrendered themselves wholly to their own. Their passion for a social order which would reflect the harmony and justice of Divine Reason narrowed and deepened into patriotism; became devotion to 'the comyn wele here in our own nacyon'. The word commonwealth is the watchword of England's greatest creative age; the visions which the word summons are medieval visions lingering in the English air. There is the vision of harmony achieved through the just distribution of function, 'where as all the parts, as members of one body, be knit together in perfect love and unity; every one doing his office and duty'. There is the vision of justice and truth, in which 'the public weal is a body living . . . governed by the rule and moderation of reason. . . .' There is, above all, the vision of brotherhood, no longer the brotherhood of all Christians, but the brotherhood of all Englishmen. 'God hath so placed us Englishmen here in one commonwealth, also in one church, as in one ship together; let us not mangle or divide the ship, which being divided perisheth. . . .' Englishmen of the Tudor age were sailing in stormy seas. 'A very and true commonweal' was the vision which guided, governed, restrained, inspired their passionate, quarrelsome, romantic, victorious adventure. But the vision faded. Stuart England fell into faction, and commonwealth became the symbol of a faction. It became the name with which a 'rump' flattered its unlawful sovereignty. It was imprisoned within the narrow framework of Puritan and republican association. Yet the imprisonment was short-lived, and lax even while it lasted. This irrepressible word persisted in breaking bounds. Political scientists like Locke continued using

[1] 'Est igitur, inquit Africanus, res publica res populi, populus autem non omnis hominum coetus quoquo modo congregatus, sed coetus multitudinis iuris consensu et utilitatis communione sociatus' (Cicero, *De Re publica*, i. 25). In the sixteenth century the stilted form *public weal* competed with *common weal*: it was thought to be nearer to the Latin *res publica*. Sir Thomas More, among others, usually prefers to write of 'weal publique'. The *O.E.D.* gives the first reference to the words 'common weal' in 1479. Even to-day the noun and adjective making the compound word frequently split apart.

it as the Romans used *res publica*, and as we to-day write of the state. Literary men such as Swift employed the word metaphorically and sometimes ironically to describe any form of association—'the spacious commonwealth of writers', 'the commonwealth of wit and learning', 'the commonwealth of dogs'. Gradually the word shed its seditious connotations. It became again respectable in monarchical England. And at last, in the nineteenth century, the warmth and glow of courageous idealism began to flow into the word again. Both to William Morris, the romantic socialist, and to those Australian idealists who embodied in a constitution their vision of 'a nation for a continent and a continent for a nation', the name commonwealth signified a new adventure in brotherly living. The political scientists had long since realized the futility of hoping to appropriate to their purposes of cool analysis a compound which at any moment was liable to split into its component parts and transform itself into a passionate manifesto. But it was a manifesto which the Australians wanted. And similarly, it was as a manifesto, as a declaration of faith in a way of life, rather than as an accurate description in terms known to political science, that this word commonwealth was chosen by the free association of self-governing nations under the British Crown. The name commonwealth is a programme in itself.[1]

But the name empire has proved itself tough. It has retained the favour of the plain blunt men—and these are probably the majority, not only in Great Britain, but in the Dominions as well—who are not troubled with scruples about words and their histories, and who feel uncomfortable in an atmosphere of political evangelism pitching its professions and aspirations very high. Even some of the champions of the name and ideal of commonwealth may find—have indeed found—their championship embarrassing to them. For the word is full of contradictory echoes from contradictory epochs of history. A British Commonwealth of Tudor pattern would be an 'organic' state with coercive machinery. This was desired by Mr. Curtis who coined the new name for empire, but not by General Smuts who adopted it. General Smuts's ideal was, in its constitutional expressions, closer to the medieval ideal of a Christian commonwealth, joined by law but not bound beneath a sovereignty. Such a commonwealth might by its example and by its co-operation with internationalist idealism lead the world back towards the unity shattered

[1] Innumerable quotations similar to those in the text will be found in publications of the Early English Text Society (Crowley, Lever, Forrest, and others) in Holinshed, and indeed in practically all Tudor writers, including Shakespeare. The author has adapted some paragraphs from an article of his in *The Australian Rhodes Review*, no. 1.

by the modern sovereign state. 'The tents have been struck and the great caravan of Humanity is once more on the march.' General Smuts did not doubt in 1918 that the British Commonwealth would be in the van of that march. He insisted repeatedly upon the quality of the British Commonwealth as a league of nations. His imagination foreshadowed some kind of interlocking between the British league —which nevertheless would not lose its distinct identity—and the Genevan league. He reiterated this conviction in 1923.[1] And yet the conception led naturally to interpretations which were dangerous to the Prime Minister of South Africa. For behind the ideal of a Christian commonwealth was the Christian-Stoic assumption of the equality of all men. In 1921 and 1923 the representatives of India at the Imperial Conference vehemently demanded equality of Indians with European South Africans under the franchise laws of South Africa. This, rejoined General Smuts, was an 'impossibility'; 'no government could for a moment either tamper with this position or do anything to meet the Indian point of view'. General Smuts advanced reasons of constitutional law and political philosophy, as well as reasons of economic and political necessity, to prove that the inferiority of Indian subjects of the King on South African soil was no contradiction of the commonwealth ideal.[2] The offended pride of Indians brushed these reasons aside as mere sophistry. To them the commonwealth ideal of equality meant equality of the kind which they valued and desired. The denial of their interpretation stirred them to angry and rebellious brooding. There always is this inevitable danger in raising a standard, in launching a manifesto. The name commonwealth, in the twentieth century as in the sixteenth, was a standard and a manifesto. In both centuries it produced the fervour of rebellion as well as the fervour of loyalty. For manifestoes arouse expectations, and breed impatience. Behind standards warring interests group themselves. Standard-bearers grow satisfied and smug; the dissatisfied and the ardent press forward to snatch the standard from them.

In the years which followed the Irish Treaty a conservative interpretation of the name commonwealth began to gain currency. This interpretation emphasized heavily the difference between the fully

[1] Cmd. 1988, p. 61: 'I am sure the League is adding a new bond to the Empire. I am sure the time is coming when the young nations of the British Empire will be prepared to support any line of action, not merely to support Great Britain, but because the League is being flouted, because the League is being attacked, and they stand by the League. These young nations will have an added reason for coming forward and supporting the international action of Great Britain.' See the note on p. 33 on the importance of anchoring British foreign policy to principles of justice.

[2] See Chapter IV below.

free and all the others. There were citizens, and there were subjects. There were, so to speak, those who were justified, and those who were under the law. There was an inner circle of the privileged. This was the commonwealth. Outside was the empire. For the British Commonwealth was not coextensive with the British Empire: the British Commonwealth was a group of communities within it. . . . There were some arguments in favour of such an interpretation. There was the administrative separation in the United Kingdom of dominion and colonial affairs, initiated after the Conference of 1907, and completed after the Conference of 1926. There was dominion status, progressively defined by resolutions of the imperial conference, by the Statute of Westminster, and by decisions of the Privy Council. There was the imperial conference, which some people preferred to call the commonwealth conference. There was, in short, 'the Commonwealth', the fact, and not merely the ideal, of liberty, fully grown into equality: whereas in 'the Empire' subordination and inequality still survived. It was not necessary for those who held this interpretation to repudiate the ideal of equality as ultimately valid for all the peoples, tongues, kindreds, and languages, under the British Crown.[1] To many of them the existing 'commonwealth within the empire' was the model to which 'the empire' must eventually conform. Yet insistence on the existing antithesis between commonwealth and empire did tend to strengthen the hands of conservatives, who supported their resistance to every step in transformation with the argument that conditions in the 'empire', especially conditions arising from racial difference, rendered it incapable of 'commonwealth' privileges. Interpreted in this way, the new name—a name for the exclusive few—might signify the repudiation of aspirations which its adoption had helped to stimulate, and the extinction of an idealism which it had helped to kindle.

There was, however, insufficient ground for adopting this antithesis between empire and commonwealth.[2] Life within the Empire was

[1] e.g. Wheare, *The Statute of Westminster*, p. 8; A. J. Toynbee, *The Conduct of British Empire Foreign Relations since the Peace Settlement* (Oxford University Press, 1928), esp. pp. 16, 27, 40; R. C. Coupland, *The Empire in These Days* (Macmillan, 1935), pp. 50–56; and J. Coatman, *Magna Britannia* (Cape, 1935), pp. 60 ff. See also these works passim.

[2] Professor A. B. Keith rightly refuses to accept the word Commonwealth as the description of one part, and the word Empire as the description of another part, of the King's Dominions. See Keith, *Speeches and Documents on the British Dominions*, p. xlvii. This distinction has never been consistently adopted in any public document—not even in the 1926 Report on Inter-Imperial Relations. The most extreme expression of it by a public man was probably that of the Solicitor General on the 24th November 1931. The British Empire, he said, meant in practice the Empire *minus* the Dominions; the British Commonwealth meant the Dominions (ibid., p. 231).

flowing too vigorously to let itself be congealed in two separate seas. There was, for example, the position which since 1917 India had held at the imperial conference. By admitting India, the conference circle had irrevocably committed itself against any general theory of European racial exclusiveness. From 1917 onwards India was accepted in the conference circle as 'the juniormost traveller on the highroad of self-government'[1]—the same road which the Dominions had already travelled. There were indeed anomalies in India's presence at the conference which were bluntly pointed out.[2] But it was assumed that these anomalies were in process of disappearing. From the point of view of domestic self-government, India's position was inferior to that of every other conference member, including Newfoundland. From the point of view of international status, she ranked, in virtue of her League membership, with the other Dominions above Newfoundland. Newfoundland was, indeed, destined to lose, at least temporarily, both her domestic self-government and her conference membership. She passed out of the inner circle. Southern Rhodesia, on the other hand, was approaching that circle. Ceylon, with no representation at the conference, moved quicker than India along the road of self-government. Malta witnessed the novel experiment of 'a constitution for a battleship'—an experiment which was suspended. Under widely different conditions and in diverse forms, hopefully or with hesitation, tentatively or with a confident touch, the British Empire was experimenting in the art of 'the government of men by themselves'. It is best to regard the British Commonwealth, not as part of the British Empire, but as the whole British Empire, viewed in the light of this experiment. In this view, the British Commonwealth is nothing else than the 'nature' of the British Empire defined, in Aristotelian fashion, by its end. This is the best way of making sense out of official documents and the speeches of statesmen. It depends upon a speaker's mood and temperament and train of thought, upon conditions of time and place, upon the character of his audience, whether or not he speaks of the British Empire or the British Commonwealth. The two names jostle each other in a competition which is perhaps symbolical of the struggle between liberty and necessity, ideal and fact, aspiration and limiting condition —a struggle which is fought continuously in every creative society.

It is fitting that this chapter should conclude, as it opened, with its emphasis chiefly upon the liberty, the ideal, the aspiration—upon

[1] Cmd. 2769 of 1926, p. 31.

[2] e.g. by the Irish Free State representative in 1923. Cmd. 1988, p. 118. On India as a conference member see Chapter IV.

the *mythus* of the Commonwealth of Nations. Critics who think they have cause already to condemn the writer's facile enthusiasm may be fairly invited to suspend judgement until they have read farther. The enthusiasm is not something which the writer has injected into his narrative; it permeates the records which he has been handling. Written history is a narrative not only of the enterprises which men undertake, but of the spirit and mood in which they undertake them. Ideals, even when they are in large measure illusions, may have some influence upon events, at least upon immediate events. When they are grounded upon a true appreciation of some powerful tendency in the past and present they may contribute powerfully to moulding the future. But even then they are always simplifications, and therefore to some extent distortions, of history; with the result that future events themselves will criticize them, and, in the process, lead to a change or modification of mood.

The criticism of events soon revealed divergences and complexities which the statesmen of the British Commonwealth had shown few signs of perceiving during the years of struggle and victory. And with the arrival of these complexities there crept into the oratory of confident evangelism a new note of doubt. The following chapter will seek to recapture a more sober mood which was arising—a mood of uncertainty and hesitation.

CHAPTER II

THE END OF THE WAR

I

'PEACEMAKING 1919'

BEFORE the war dominion self-government had decentralized everything except high policy. The Dominions were already masters of their destinies in everything except the issues of peace and war. Here the British government still exercised a 'trusteeship' on their behalf. That authority, declared Mr. Asquith, it could not share. But it was ready to gratify a natural thirst for knowledge. Solicitously, like a virtuous and rather self-conscious parent who believes that the time has come for his children to be told the "facts of life," the British government in 1911 led the dominion prime ministers into the Committee of Imperial Defence, there to behold the *arcana imperii*.

A few years later the Dominions were learning at first hand through their own direct experience what high policy meant. A million of their men were learning on parade grounds, in the trenches, in sickness and wounds and death, as much as the common soldier ever knows. So far from thinking themselves pupils of the British soldier, these men imagined that they could teach him a thing or two. They were hardly 'patriotic', perhaps not quite 'loyal', according to some popular understandings of these words. There was little to suggest that they cared for the Empire, or reverenced England, or loved Englishmen. Their homesickness was for their own countries, their comradeship for their own countrymen, their pride for their own armies.[1] Before the end of the war, Canadians and Australians were fighting under their own commanders. They had in London their own head-quarters administrations. The Canadian administration was controlled by a minister resident in London, with ultimate responsibility to the government and parliament of Canada. At the same time this autonomous national effort took its place without strain or friction in the effort of the whole Empire which was organized by the British high command.[2] The same dovetailing occurred

[1] For a vivid picture of the spirit of the Australian Imperial Force (with plenty of emphasis on its anti-English aspects) see the novel by Leonard Mann, *Flesh in Armour* (Sydney, 1932). One might indeed cite prose and verse of a different tendency, and a full study of Australian or Canadian loyalties would reveal a very frequent double patriotism.

[2] See Borden, *Canadian Constitutional Studies* pp. 99–100.

in the sphere of political control. In 1915 the Canadian Prime Minister was summoned to a meeting of the British Cabinet: commentators duly noted that this was 'totally without precedent'.[1] In December 1916 the five dominion prime ministers were invited to attend an 'Imperial War Cabinet'. From March to May 1917, and again from June to August 1918, they sat with the five members of the British War Cabinet, sharing its deliberations on the vital issues of the war. Were these sessions the sessions of a conference, or of a cabinet? 'Each minister or group of ministers', Sir Robert Borden has written, 'represented a government, and the conference might fairly be termed a cabinet of governments.' This argument has been criticized. It is said, with justice, that the word cabinet can only be properly applied to an executive body corporately responsible to a single legislature. But the constitutional significance of the Imperial War Cabinet is of secondary importance. It is the political fact which counts. At the 'Imperial War Cabinet' the heads of dominion governments made direct contact with the realities of high policy. Their initiation, like that of the soldiers, was sudden, violent, and complete.

They were, in fact, too much engaged by the impact of political facts to spare time for constitutional problems. Even the 1917 and 1918 sessions of the Imperial War Conference, which might have permitted them to enjoy some relief from the short perspective of day-to-day executive decision, focused their attention predominantly upon matters of immediate concern. The 1917 Conference definitely recorded its opinion that constitutional readjustment was too intricate and important a matter to be handled during the stress of the war. It should be handled by a special conference to be called as soon as possible after the end of the war. But there were certain facts which had already been established, certain principles which must be asserted now. The prime ministers felt it their duty to state that the Dominions would never again be content to leave the issues of high policy to the British government. For the 'autonomous nations of an Imperial Commonwealth' they claimed 'an adequate voice in foreign policy'. In order to make this voice continuously effective, it would be necessary later on to devise 'effective arrangements for continuous consultation in all important matters of common imperial concern, and for such necessary concerted action, founded on consultation, as the several governments may determine'.[2]

[1] Keith, *Imperial Unity and the Dominions*, p. 545.

[2] Cd. 8566, p. 5, Resolution IX. It was drafted by Borden and Smuts. On the motion of Sir Satyendra Sinha, an additional reference to India as 'an important part' of the imperial commonwealth was added.

Public opinion, both in the United Kingdom and in the Dominions was by now well prepared for this claim of right. From the early days of the war, professors, journalists, and politicians had kept repeating that things could never again be as they had been: the Dominions had passed from the status of the protected colony to that of the participating nation. 'The protected colony was rightly voiceless; the participating nation cannot remain so.'[1] There was urgency in this declaration. The Dominions demanded a voice here and now. They were concerned, not merely with the issues of peace and war in general (this was the constitutional question which they were not yet ready to face), but with the issues of the present war and of the coming peace. South Africa, Australia, and New Zealand had gathered booty, and intended to have a say in the disposal of it. Canada had no special territorial interests, but her interest in the larger issues, quickened by the belligerency and idealism of the United States, surpassed that of all the other dominion governments except the South African. The dominion governments intended to take a hand in shaping the peace. As early as March 1915 Viscount Milner had laid stress on the need for meeting their demand. 'Remember that on a previous and most disastrous occasion it was not war—not the strain of war—which disrupted the Empire, but the aftermath of war. This is a risk which we ought not to run. . . .' British statesmen had no intention of running it. In April 1915 the Colonial Secretary told the House of Commons that the government intended to consult the Dominions with regard to the terms of peace, and had informed them of this intention. In 1917 and 1918 this engagement was many times reaffirmed. Officials and students who remembered the dispatches of Lord John Russell and had absorbed the arguments of the *Round Table* hoped for some preliminary scheme of imperial co-ordination which would blend the dominion voices at the Peace Conference in one harmonious imperial choir.[2] But, when the War was over, the Dominions turned up at the Peace Conference in the same individualistic, haphazard, unorthodox manner in which they had turned up on the battlefields.

The story of their advent, which has often been told at length,[3]

[1] Hon. C. J. Doherty (Canada) quoted in *Round Table*, vol. v, p. 428. There is a very full account of these war declarations in Dewey, *The Dominions and Diplomacy*, vol. ii, pp. 2–17.

[2] e.g. *Round Table*, vol. v, pp. 325–44, vol. vii, pp. 1–13.

[3] e.g. in the books cited, by Borden and Dewey. The most useful printed collection of documents is *Correspondence and Documents relative to the representation of Canada at the Peace Conference and to the ratification of the Treaty of Peace with Germany* (10 Geo. V, Sessional Paper, No. 41 J.A., Ottawa, 1919).

can best be summarized from the Canadian angle. On 27th October 1918 Mr. Lloyd George telegraphed to Sir Robert Borden, urging him to come immediately to London. In his reply two days later, Sir Robert stated that the Canadian people took it for granted that Canada would be represented at the conference. He requested Mr. Lloyd George to bear in mind the fact that 'a very unfortunate impression would be created and possibly a dangerous feeling might be aroused if the difficulties are not overcome by some solution which will meet the national spirit of the Canadians'. After Sir Robert Borden had arrived in London, his cabinet kept sending him telegrams to the same effect. They were concerned with Canadian prestige in the eyes of Canada's powerful neighbour. 'Canada has had as many casualties as the United States and probably more actual deaths. Canadian people would not appreciate five American delegates throughout the whole conference and probably no Canadian to sit throughout the conference, nor would they appreciate several representatives from Great Britain and Canada none.' The other dominion governments accepted the Canadian point of view; the Australian Prime Minister had already protested against Great Britain's acceptance of conditions for an armistice which contained also the agreed principles of peace. But the Dominions had no serious cause of complaint against the British attitude; Mr. Lloyd George made their cause his own. The Imperial War Cabinet accepted Sir Robert Borden's proposals, which projected into the international sphere the disorderly unity of the war-time Empire. The Imperial War Cabinet transferred itself to Paris, taking the new title of British Empire Delegation. Here the participating nations of the Empire took their full share of responsibility for the affairs of the Empire as a whole and of the world at large. They sat on committees; they took their turn, by means of a panel system, in acting as plenipotentiary delegates at sessions of the Peace Conference; they met continually, often with Sir Robert Borden in the chair in place of Mr. Lloyd George, to review from the Empire angle the progress of negotiations. As member nations of the Empire the Dominions ascended to the high places of high politics. But this was not all. In their own right, as 'belligerent nations with special interests', they enjoyed a distinctive representation. They appeared at the Peace Conference in their multiplicity as well as in their unity. In this way, as Sir Robert Borden very mildly said, they 'secured a peculiarly effective position'. They had their cake and they ate it. If foreign nations admitted their privileged position only after a tussle, this was not due merely to that alleged defect in all foreigners which prevents them from rising superior to logic, as the gifted British do so easily. There was also in foreign breasts a natural jealousy of the unique British skill in making the best of both worlds. 'Are you one or are you many?', foreigners asked; and the British answered innocently—or were they so very innocent?—'We are one, and we are many.'[1]

In the signature of the peace treaties, no less than in their negotiation, the British Empire presented itself to international society as the one and the many. On 12th March 1919 Sir Robert Borden circulated to the other dominion prime ministers a memorandum which urged, first, that the dominion plenipotentiaries should personally sign the treaties, and secondly, that the dominion legislatures should have the right of approving them.

> 'The procedure [argued Sir Robert] is in consonance with the principles of constitutional government that obtain throughout the Empire. The Crown is the supreme Executive in the United Kingdom and in all the Dominions, but it acts on the advice of different constitutional units; and under resolution of the Imperial War Conference, 1917, the organisation of the Empire is to be based upon equality of nationhood.'

Sir Robert, having established this principle, took pains to ensure that the fact of separate and direct dominion advice to the Crown should formally appear on the records.[2] With regard to the form of the treaties, he considered that his proposals necessitated but little alteration; both in the preambles to and in the signature of the treaties the general heading British Empire would be further explained by the sub-headings United Kingdom, Dominion of Canada, Commonwealth of Australia, &c. The plenipotentiaries of the participating units of the Empire would sign under the appropriate headings. The British Empire Delegation accepted this suggestion with one alteration: whereas the dominion plenipotentiaries affixed their signatures on behalf of their respective governments, the British plenipotentiaries affixed their signatures, not merely on behalf of the

[1] Canada, Australia, South Africa, India were under the rules of the Peace Conference each represented by two delegates: New Zealand by one. It is interesting to note that the 'inner circle' of the Empire, when projected into the international sphere, was undergoing some change. India, with a recent and anomalous status at the imperial conference, had equal international representation; whereas Newfoundland, an original conference member, was represented only through the British Empire delegation.

[2] It was accordingly as the result of a Canadian Order-in-Council that the King issued full powers to the Canadian plenipotentiaries. The instrument of issue was Letters Patent which bear the King's signature without the counter signature of a British minister. But was the British government eliminated? See Keith, *Responsible Government in the Dominions*, pp. 881–2.

United Kingdom, which was not mentioned at all, but on behalf of the whole British Empire.

In the Covenant of the League of Nations there was a similar assertion of multiplicity and unity, with considerably more stress on the multiplicity. The earlier drafts of the Covenant were modified with the express purpose of securing for the Dominions original and independent membership of the League. In the Assembly they would vote as separate nations. In the Council, however, it was the British Empire, not the United Kingdom and its non-self-governing dependencies, which was granted permanent representation.[1] Yet Sir Robert Borden secured from Clemenceau, Wilson, and Lloyd George an authoritative interpretation of Article 4 of the Covenant which asserted the right of dominion representatives to sit as non-permanent members of the Council. There was thus a possibility—although imperialists were relucant to admit it[2]—of the British Empire and the Dominion of Canada taking their separate seats on the central organ of the League and giving their separate decisions—perhaps conflicting decisions—on the issues of peace and war.

II

The Parliaments of the Empire and their Questionings

There was one more stage in the succession of acts by which the Dominions, at the time of the peace settlement, emphasized their distinct personality. As the result of direct dominion advice, the King had issued to their plenipotentiaries the full powers necessary for their attendance and action at the Paris Conference. The plenipotentiaries had taken an active part in the business of that conference. On behalf of their several countries, they had formally signed the treaty which they had helped to make. It was now the turn of their parliaments. Sir Robert Borden had insisted that the Canadian parliament must approve the treaties with Germany and with the other Powers before the King ratified them on behalf of Canada. But this involved delay. In July 1919 the British government telegraphed that it hoped for immediate ratification of the German treaty. Sir Robert Borden, in reply, insisted that he must fulfil his pledge to the

[1] This arrangement came under criticism. See, for Canada, *J.P.E.*, vol. ii, p. 335. The Minister of Justice, answering a criticism, said: 'It was urged at the time that the United Kingdom with the Crown colonies and dependencies should have been one member, and we should have been the others, all together going to make up the British Empire. We were not able to put it that way. . . .' The anomaly was corrected in 1926, so far as treaty-making procedure was concerned.

[2] e.g. *Round Table*, vol. ix, p. 491.

Canadian parliament. Lord Milner thereupon reminded Sir Robert that under the British constitution ratification belonged to the King, and not to parliament. The Canadian Prime Minister answered with an appeal from the law of the constitution to constitutional practice. He appealed also to political expediency. 'I cannot emphasize too strongly', he cabled, 'the unfortunate results which would certainly ensue from ratification before the Canadian parliament has had an opportunity of considering the treaty.' The British government gave way. In September the Canadian parliament passed in both houses resolutions assenting to the peace treaty with Germany. Thereafter the Canadian government issued orders in council requesting the final act of ratification by the King.[1] The Canadian parliament followed the same procedure with regard to the Austrian and Bulgarian treaties, although Canadian representatives had not taken any real part in their negotiation. The other dominion parliaments acted generally in a similar fashion. This did not conclude their activities with regard to the peace settlement. It was also necessary for them to legislate in order to carry into effect those parts of the treaties—for example, the mandates provisions—which directly affected them.

All this meant that the dominion prime ministers had to explain and justify to their parliaments and peoples the action which they had taken at London and Paris. This, surely, would be an easy task. The prime ministers and their colleagues returned home glowing with pride in the achievement of their countries and with faith in the future. The Dominions had achieved new weight and honour in the councils of the Empire and of the world. And what they had achieved they had achieved in comradeship. Never had they been more truly themselves, never had they been in truer unity with each other and with Great Britain. The Dominions were now the equals of Great Britain. The Dominions were now individual nations. They counted for something. But they counted as members of one another. This was in general the message of the prime ministers, although in each case the emphasis tended to be different. Sir Robert Borden traced carefully, step by step, the process by which Canada had achieved her new status in the British Commonwealth, at the Peace Conference, and in the League of Nations. Canada had won her title-deeds of nationhood in the War.

> 'The same indomitable spirit which made Canada capable of that effort and sacrifice made her equally incapable of accepting, at the

[1] See *Correspondence and Documents relative to the representation of Canada*, &c., pp. 10 ff. The parliaments of Australia, South Africa, and New Zealand passed similar resolutions in September 1919.

Peace Conference, in the League of Nations, or elsewhere, a status inferior to that accorded to nations less advanced in their development, less amply endowed in their wealth, resources, and population, no more complete in their sovereignty, and far less conspicuous in their sacrifice.'

The new status certainly necessitated a remodelling of imperial relationships. That would be the task of the coming constitutional conference. But the principles of the new imperial order were already clear. They were equality and partnership.

'Each nation must preserve its own autonomy, but it must likewise have its voice as to those external relations which involve the issues of peace and war. So that the British Commonwealth is itself a community or league of nations which may serve as an exemplar to that world-wide League of Nations which was founded in Paris on the 28th of last June.'[1]

General Botha was not present to speak in the South African parliament. He had died on 28th August 1919. Between him and Sir Robert Borden there had been a complete unity of purpose.

'I fought against the British [he had said to Borden] but I am a firm upholder of the Commonwealth. In South Africa we enjoy all the liberty that we could have as an independent nation, and far greater security against external aggression; we have complete powers of self-government; we control the development of our country; and in the affairs of the world we take a place far higher and render a service more notable and useful than we could attain or give as a separate nation.'[2]

This was the spirit in which General Smuts, Botha's friend and successor, addressed the parliament of the Union a month after Botha's death. Like Borden, he depicted the British Commonwealth as 'a league of free, equal states, working together for the great ideals of human government'. Like Borden, he emphasized the new status of equality which belonged to the dominions in the Commonwealth and in the League. His emphasis was doubly stressed because he had to face the lament and suspicion of men who remembered their old freedom which the British had taken from them. He told them that the old freedom, for which he too had fought, was gone for ever; even if the forms of it could be recovered, it would not be freedom. The new freedom was a deeper and wider one.

'Let us not mope over the past. To-day we have every opportunity to build our nation; and I am standing here to make the strongest, the most urgent appeal to this House and the country to live in the present and the future. Let us get off our ant-heap of grief over the past and let us concentrate on the great things which the future holds for us.'[3]

[1] *J.P.E.*, vol. i, pp. 87 ff.
[2] Sir Robert Borden, *Canada in the Commonwealth* (Clarendon Press, 1929), p. 105.
[3] *J.P.E.*, vol. i, pp. 193 ff.

The Australian Prime Minister had no similar challenge to meet. He faced a parliament which was content to take for granted the national status, and which showed little interest in constitutional theory. What interested parliament, and what interested the Prime Minister, was one of the concrete results of the new status—that Australia had become a mandatory Power in the Pacific Ocean. The debate became almost entirely a debate on Australia's national security. One or two speakers feared that Australia was moving into an exposed and lonely position among the struggling nations, but Mr. Hughes believed that there was no security without Australian control of the ramparts covering the Australian coast. He would have preferred outright annexation of New Guinea, but a C mandate was the next best thing.

In New Zealand, the debates covered a wider range. Here the Prime Minister and his colleagues had to face, not the suspicions of nationalists, but the distrust of imperialists. This separate signature and approval of treaties, this separate membership of the League, this mandate in Samoa—might not they imply a weakening of the bonds which bound New Zealand to the mother country? Perplexing legal issues were touched upon. But Mr. Massey had little interest in legal forms. He did not understand that to others, to South Africans and to Canadians, these forms might have a different meaning; that these others might force their interpretation of words and acts upon New Zealand and drag her along a path she did not wish to travel. What was real to him was the comradeship of the battlefields, of the Imperial War Cabinet, and of the British Empire Delegation. The new freedom meant simply a deeper partnership. The dominion signatures upon the peace treaty were no act of national self-assertion; but rather an act of imperial duty and devotion. 'We signed it, not as independent nations in the ordinary sense of the term. We signed it as the representatives of the self-governing nations within the Empire; we signed it as partners in the Empire—partners, with everything the names implies.'[1]

Things which had seemed simple in London and in Paris, nevertheless, began to appear difficult and dubious in the atmosphere of the scattered parliaments of the Empire. The War had given to the dominion prime ministers an overriding authority; they spoke for their countries without fear of challenge; perhaps they tended to forget that at home there were oppositions, and that some day these oppositions might become governments.[2] They were men of similar intentions and ideals, they understood each other, and if they

[1] *J.P.E.*, vol. i, pp. 124 ff., 133 ff., 156 ff., 172.

[2] It is worth remembering that the circumstances of war had led to party splits

sometimes differed from each other in what they emphasized, it was easy for them to find reassurance by reaffirming the fundamental articles of belief which they held in common. Back in their own countries, differences of emphasis took on a greater importance. They had to some extent lost touch with their parliaments and constituencies—one of them, Mr. Hughes, had been absent in Europe for sixteen continuous months. Their first task was to get close again to their own peoples. In doing this, they lost something of their intimate contact with each other. Each of them enjoyed for the time a secure position in parliament. There was no question of the parliaments refusing to pass the resolutions and legislation which they desired. Their view of the significance of recent happenings could command imposing majorities. But the great questions under discussion were not of the kind to be settled permanently by majority decisions.

The mere fact that these questions became the object of party controversy was of itself significant. Of equal importance was the lack of intellectual clarity in the party duel. The Canadian parliament became hopelessly muddled. Liberal orators, in opposition to the Prime Minister's vindication of Canada's new status, took first of all the line that nothing had happened. This so-called new status was 'a colossal humbug, designed to impose on a credulous parliament and a too innocent people'. Had the British North America Act been amended? And if not, did not things remain as they were? 'Gentlemen who contended that they had achieved an advanced status ought to be able to show them the public act by which that status had been secured.' Nobody would assert that Canada was a sovereign state. And only sovereign states had anything to do with the framing of treaties. It was therefore mere window-dressing to introduce into the Canadian parliament a motion to give assent to the treaty. Canada would be bound by British ratification, whether the Canadian parliament assented or not. Legally, this was true. And it pleased some of the Canadian politicians to state a legal proposition, and then to deduce from it the most extreme consequences—for example, it belonged to sovereign states to accredit diplomatic representatives: Canada was not a sovereign state, therefore Canada could not send even a consul to Washington.[1] Ministers mocked at a pedantry which

or shiftings and to governmental coalitions—more or less complete and formal—in Great Britain, Canada, Australia, and New Zealand. In South Africa, the old opposition (South Africa party) supported the Botha government. In all the Dominions, except New Zealand, the formation of these 'win-the-war' majorities was paid for in varying degrees by intensifying bitterness between the majorities and the truncated minorities. The arrival of the latter to power was delayed, but was liable to cause some breach of continuity when it occurred.

[1] *J.P.E.*, vol. i, p. 315.

rejected all facts that could not be fitted into the paragraphs of text-books. The text-books were out of date; the facts were new. Their critics were clinging to a colonialism which had passed away. In truth, the argument of legal subordination merged insensibly into an argument of political expediency. In one breath the critics maintained that nothing had happened; in the next they argued that something very unfortunate had happened. Canada had lost her old freedom. The old status was good enough. Canada was safer when she had no voice in foreign policy. 'Let well enough alone; let us not be involved in the domestic affairs of the United Kingdom or its foreign policy.' To one section of critics the much-vaunted new status was part of an imperialist plot; 'a fever of imperialism' was sweeping Canada into the vortex of British world policy. The Imperial War Cabinet and the British Empire Delegation were the first step, the much advertised constitutional conference would be the second, along a road which would mortgage Canada's men and money and annihilate her right to abstain from fighting in British wars. But another section of critics made a diametrically opposite complaint. Canada was mortgaging her freedom, not to Great Britain, but to powers outside the Empire. As a separate and individual nation she had undertaken obligations which might conceivably commit her to war against the British government itself. It was safer to leave high policy in the hands of those who had managed it in the past. The Hon. W. S. Fielding 'was firmly persuaded that the assertion of a separate interest on the part of Canada and the other Dominions was the beginning of the evolution of separation'.[1] Both these contrasted forebodings were advanced by members of the same party: both could not be true. Canada could not be simultaneously surrendering to imperialism and deserting the Empire. Yet both complaints revealed an attitude to the outside world which was at bottom identical. It was the traditional attitude of Sir Wilfrid Laurier and the liberal party. Sir Wilfrid had always assumed that the British Empire effectively screened Canada from the hurly-burly of world politics; the outer world could force no decisions upon her; Canada herself was free to make decisions—to fight or not to fight—which concerned nobody outside the British Empire. Now the screen was broken through. Canada was in the hurly-burly. There could be Canadian wars. Whether the new status

[1] *J.P.E.*, vol. i, p. 327; cf. p. 484. Mr. Lemieux: 'Do not let us meddle in the affairs of the Mother Country, and the Mother Country will let us govern ourselves. We have governed ourselves during the last twenty years according to British traditions. Do not accustom the people to think that the ministers of a Canadian government view with a light heart the loosening of the moorings which bind us to the Mother Country.'

meant partnership in imperial obligations or whether it meant individual liability, it brought Canada into direct contact with the dangerous world of international rivalry. The opposition blamed the government's rashness for this calamity. Yet it was not the theorizing of Sir Robert Borden, it was the challenge of the World War and Canada's response to it, which had closed an epoch in Canadian history and transformed the relationship of Canada both to the British Empire and to the world at large.

The Borden government continued to tread the path which it believed to be marked out for Canada. Perhaps it took some pleasure in confounding those critics who saw the society of nations under text-books headings. The British Commonwealth which was coming into being, meant, in despite of text-books, equality; on the motion of the government, parliament moved that a humble address be presented to His Majesty to submit to the parliament of the United Kingdom an amendment of the British North America Act which would establish the extra-territorial operation of Canadian legislation 'in the like manner and to the same extent as if enacted by the parliament of the United Kingdom'.[1] The Covenant of the League of Nations and the convention establishing the Permanent Court of International Justice defined certain rights and privileges enjoyed by nationals of the members of the League; the Canadian government therefore introduced legislation to define a Canadian national. 'As far as I am concerned,' groaned a member of the opposition, 'to be a Canadian citizen and a British subject is enough for me'; but the government spokesmen had no difficulty in showing that a Canadian law defining a certain kind of British subject, who, in addition to his rights and obligations as a British subject, possessed also particular rights in virtue of his Canadian nationality, did not falsify, but recognized, the facts of the world in which Canada moved.[2] Critics who had cast doubts on Canada's status in the League of Nations were faced with the fact that the Canadian representatives at the first Assembly had taken an independent line of their own; the Empire's multiplicity was asserting itself in policy at Geneva—yet not, the government asserted, to the danger of its essential unity.[3] Finally,

[1] *J.P.E.*, vol. i, p. 646. The power was not established till the Statute of Westminster, 1931.

[2] *J.P.E.*, vol. ii, pp. 327 ff. The status of 'Canadian citizen' had already been created by the Canadian Immigration Act of 1910 (Revised Statutes of Canada, 1927, c. 93).

[3] *J.P.E.*, vol. ii, pp. 310 ff. Mr. Rowell cites the South African proposal, seconded by Canada, for the admission of Albania to the League—a proposal opposed by Great Britain and France.

it had pleased those learned in text-book knowledge to assert as 'the ABC of international law' that a legal dependency, such as Canada, could not make direct diplomatic contact with foreign Powers. The Borden government disposed of this assertion by assuming for Canada —with the approval of the British government—the right of legation. On 10th May 1920 the announcement was made both in the British and the Canadian parliaments that His Majesty, on the advice of his Canadian ministers, would appoint a minister plenipotentiary at Washington who would have charge of Canadian affairs and be the ordinary channel of communication with the United States government in matters of purely Canadian concern. At the same time, the Canadian minister would, in the absence of the British ambassador, take charge of the whole Embassy and of the representation of imperial as well as Canadian interests. Here again the multiplicity and unity of the Empire which had been the note of the Paris Conference was projected into the field of international relations, this time at a foreign capital. The diplomatic individuality of Canada was asserted; the diplomatic unity of the Empire was in definite terms protested. But then followed a long delay. Year after year the necessary supply was voted by parliament; but the actual appointment was not made until February 1927—three years after the Irish Free State had actually exercised the same right. There was therefore ample leisure for debating the venture. Earlier criticisms made a good deal of play with text-books smartness. Why this delay in making the appointment? Because—despite all the posturing—Canada, as a non-sovereign state, did not possess the power. Because—did not the secrecy of the affair make it certain?—the Foreign Office was objecting. And was there not reason in the objection? Was not the present position good enough? Why should Canada dive 'into the very vortex which had created the whole situation in Europe?' Would not a keen trade commissioner be sufficient for her needs? But all these objections were offered with diminishing frequency and with diminishing conviction. From the very beginning the main point of criticism had been the dual status and the dual responsibility of the minister plenipotentiary. Would the people of Canada be responsible for his actions while he was representing the British government? Would the people of Britain be content for their vice-ambassador to be appointed by the Canadian government? Which government would have the right to recall him when he was acting in this anomalous position? Mr. Mackenzie King, in the first debate upon the new venture, accepted its nationalist but not its imperialist implications.

> 'What seemed the more reasonable course was the middle one, that in matters between Canada and other countries Canada should manage her own affairs, and that in matters between Great Britain and other countries Great Britain should manage her own affairs, always when necessary with co-operation and consultation between the two.'[1]

It was along these lines that Canada's political attitude gradually defined itself, not only with regard to the Washington Embassy, but with regard to the whole question of status, both within the Empire and—for the two aspects could not be separated—in the international world. When old-fashioned imperialists like Sir George Parkin opposed the new status because it implied imperial disintegration, liberals like Mr. Lemieux, who had used exactly the same words, realized that they were moving in strange company. The Canadian liberal party was in process of recovering from the shock dealt to it by the conscription issue—it was recovering, not only in numbers, but in coherence of outlook. The Laurier attitude, which had been good enough to work with in a period of sheltered isolation, had proved inadequate in the day when Canada, challenged by the outer world, had revealed herself to the world as in fact a nation. There were, however, elements in the Laurier tradition which could be carried over into the new situation, once it was accepted. Laurier himself had once been the proponent of direct diplomatic contact between Canada and the United States. He had also, while insisting upon the legal unity of the Empire, resisted every move towards political integration. He was first and foremost an autonomist. When it recovered from its bewilderment, the Canadian liberal party found itself ready to agree with Sir Robert Borden that autonomy nowadays meant a distinct international status. At the same time it sought by every means to curtail the obligations arising out of that status. Since the most pressing of these obligations were likely to come through partnership in the Empire, it showed itself particularly shy of co-operationist proposals. The question might have been raised whether this political aloofness was ultimately reconcilable with common legal liability; but parliamentary politics seldom concern themselves with ultimate questions. The Canadian people were cautiously feeling their way along the new path which they were compelled to tread, and they were finding themselves on the whole to be more of one mind than the performances of their party chieftains had suggested. The new liberalism—in particular the liberalism of the prairie

[1] For the announcement of 10th May 1920, see Keith, *Speeches and Documents on the British Dominions*, p. 38. For the first full-dress debate see *J.P.E.*, vol. i, pp. 476 ff.

from the British Empire. Having thus fairly faced his catechizers, the Prime Minister proceeded to take the offensive. He would ask General Hertzog a question: Supposing the nationalists got a majority at the next election and decided to secede from the Empire, would they use force against the minority? General Hertzog parried the question by saying that he would be bound by the decision of his party. General Smuts thereupon appealed to parliament and the country to recognize three fundamental principles—first, the British connexion, 'the British League of Nations', in which they would find full national freedom; secondly, a powerful sentiment of distinct South African nationhood, as the bond holding the white races together; and thirdly, to admit that the great task ahead of them was the economic development of their country.[1]

In the congress of the nationalist party which met next day General Hertzog similarly laid down three principles, which the party agreed to—first, acceptance of the Union as fundamental; secondly, assertion of the right of secession, as the party's ideal for the Union; thirdly, that the party should decide, according to circumstances, whether or not to press the issue of secession as a matter of practical politics. In this programme there may be seen a distinction between secession and the right to secede; it might be held that full freedom was satisfied by the possession of the latter, without its exercise. A speech in the House of Commons by Mr. Bonar Law, the leader of the conservative party and of the House, suggested that the Dominions already enjoyed the right to secede. 'If the self-governing Dominions', he declared in March 1920, '. . . chose tomorrow to say, "We will no longer make a part of the British Empire", we would not try to force them. Dominion Home Rule means the right to decide their own destinies.'[2] In answer to the nationalists who joyfully quoted this utterance, General Smuts denied that it admitted a constitutional right. It was merely a declaration that Great Britain would not apply 'sanctions' against a seceding dominion. The real sanctions supporting the South African constitution, he said, were South African sanctions.

> 'For secession means not only secession from the British Empire, it means also secession of Dutch-speaking from English-speaking South Africans, who made together a solemn pact at the Union. It means secession of one province of the Union from another and the break-up of the Union, which is the noblest legacy of our great statesmen, the

[1] *J.P.E.*, vol. i, pp. 193 ff., esp. pp. 209, 212, 213, 214; *Round Table*, vol. ix, pp. 194 ff.; vol. x, pp. 186 ff.; vol. xi, pp. 193 ff.

[2] Bonar Law was speaking on the Government of Ireland Bill.

consecration of all the sacrifices of the past. It means the secession of the natives, whose devotion to the British connexion is historical. It means the complete isolation of Dutch-speaking Africa, and in that isolation its stranglement and decay. It means the blasting of all the great hopes which have sustained our people in the past. It means that a civilized South Africa becomes a dream, and that the white people of this country has decided to commit political suicide.'[1]

Party struggle exaggerated the differences between General Smuts and General Hertzog. The controversy between them was in a large measure an academic one. General Hertzog's programme did not advocate the act of secession. It professed the ideal of secession, and it claimed the right. It claimed the right, not merely as something to be won, but as something which existed. If dominion status really meant the right of the Dominions 'to decide their own destinies', was it not cheating to exclude separation, if this should prove to be the destiny which a dominion chose? General Smuts, on his side, was willing to admit that there was 'no limit to the future political development of the country'. He demanded, however, that there should be no majority coercion; that change in the future, as in the fruitful past which had made the Union, should be the work of all sections of the white population acting together.[2] This was a limiting condition which in practice General Hertzog was certain to observe. Closely examined, the differences between the programmes of the two leaders narrowed down to a hair-splitting debate about the theoretical implications of South African status. Did it or did it not include a certain right, the conditions for whose exercise were non-existent? It was not, however, programmes, it was symbols and the memories and loyalties attaching to symbols, which divided the two parties. General Smuts demanded of his old comrades that they should lower the republican flag. To him this was no surrender. The smaller still lived in the greater, the freedom of the republics in the wider freedom of the Union. The contradictions of history could be resolved in the achievement of 'South Africa a nation'; the impossible dream of 'South Africa a republic' would perpetuate them to the ruin of both freedoms, the greater and the less. This teaching was too hard for many who had ridden in the commandos. Their old

[1] Speech at Pretoria, 3rd December 1920; see *Round Table*, vol. xi, p. 435.

[2] Ibid., p. 198. This was the first point of form which Smuts laid down as the basis for negotiation with the nationalists in October 1920. The other points were that there should be no agitation for constitutional change but that this should be left 'to the natural course of events'; that no obligations to other parts of the Empire which were contrary to South African interests or which detracted from her status should be admitted; that no distinction between British and Afrikaner should be permitted to influence policy.

loyalties were deep. In practice, they might come to terms with circumstances. But they could not deny the republican idea.

General Smuts joined battle with them. In the elections of March 1920, the South African party and the unionist party (which, without sharing office, had during the War and after supported the governments of Botha and Smuts) both lost heavily. The nationalists increased their numbers in the lower house from 27 to 45; the labour party rose from 6 to 21. General Smuts survived a session, because these two parties, divided on the constitutional issue, could not join to outvote the supporters of his government. But the situation was too precarious to continue. The four parties must be reduced to three. Attempts to bring the South African party and the nationalists together split on the rock of secession. The nationalists would not agree to let that issue sleep. Thereupon General Smuts called upon 'all right-minded South Africans' to unite in a single party which would stand at the same time for the British Commonwealth, the equality of the self-governing nations of that Commonwealth, and the unity of the South African nation. On this platform the unionist party consented to merge itself in the South African party. On this platform General Smuts dissolved and fought an election in January and February 1921. Secession was not strictly an issue at the election, for the nationalist party pledged itself to consult the people in a referendum before taking any steps to separate the Union from the British Commonwealth. But the party also asserted that the right of secession was 'an ever-existing and lasting right'. Thus the election was fought, not on policies, but on political ideals and theories. The South African party triumphed, chiefly at the expense of the labour party. The nationalists maintained their position exactly.

How did these controversies impress the other Dominions in the South Seas? New Zealanders might draw some comfort from the success of General Smuts. But, if they followed carefully South African events, they would soon see that his triumph was precarious; on the Rand trouble was brewing, and events were preparing an understanding between the nationalist and labour parties which in a few years would bring the terrible General Hertzog to power. They could not, from their distance, perceive the operation of circumstances which was making the nationalist party more nationalist, and less republican. They could not understand that the gap between General Smuts and General Hertzog was narrowing. Besides, the new conception of the British Commonwealth which made possible the narrowing of that gap was strange and disturbing to them.

General Smuts himself was sufficiently alarming. Like Sir Robert Borden, he seemed willing that South Africa should plunge separately into the world of nations. He boasted that he had scotched imperial federation in 1917. He said that he would accept no obligations to other parts of the Empire which were contrary to South Africa's interests (and how would these interests be judged?) or in derogation of her status. In order to demonstrate the reality of that status and its international recognition, he harped on all that had happened at Paris and afterwards. He accepted a mandate which came direct from foreign Powers, without providing (as the dutiful New Zealanders provided[1]) for the recognition of imperial authority. He approved—and even the Australians incomprehensibly approved[2]—of the sending of dominion ministers to foreign capitals. There was, he had said, no single power which could speak for the whole Commonwealth, 'but six free, equal members of this great League'.[3] Did not this mean that the British Empire had dwindled into a personal union, like the former association of Great Britain and Hanover? Before the governments of the British Commonwealth (and the government of New Zealand with the rest of them) allowed themselves to rush into peace conferences and international leagues, they should have carried through 'an organic change in the constitution of the British Empire'. Where was sovereignty now? It was going a-begging. Perhaps New Zealand herself had become an independent sovereignty which some day might find itself standing alone in the face of foreign aggression. . . . In successive sessions members of parliament reiterated their fears. The government, with diminishing assurance, reiterated its consolations. The constitutional conference, provided for in 1917, would soon come. The conference would clear up all the muddle. An imperial executive would be established under the leadership of the British Prime Minister—but the doubters refused to be comforted. 'Have we been,' one of them asked, 'without our desire and without our knowledge, unloosed from the silken bond?'[4]

There was a small sprinkling of labour members who spoke in a different tone. The comfort which the Prime Minister offered to troubled imperial loyalty was an irritant to their ideals. They were content to be joined to Great Britain by 'the strong natural ties of blood'; but they were opposed to schemes of constitutional adjustment which would 'bind the Dominion to the imperial chariot'. In this

[1] In taking over the Samoan mandate New Zealand resorted to the Foreign Jurisdiction Act and imperial orders in council issued under it.

[2] *J.P.E.*, vol. i, p. 695. [3] Ibid., p. 546. [4] Ibid., vol. ii, p. 645.

they echoed, rather faintly, the vigorous assertions of the Australian labour movement. The Australian Workers' Union, the strongest body of organized labour within the Commonwealth, had in 1917 answered the propaganda of imperial federation by placing on record 'its stoutest opposition to this Dominion of the Empire being governed by the plutocrats of England, which the proposed scheme would involve'. The labour movement was full of vigorous incompatibilities—American syndicalist theories, echoes of Leninism, echoes of Wilsonism, odds and ends of Marx, British pacificism, and robust Australian nationalism. It was easy enough to reconcile all these conflicting elements in a vendetta against Mr. Hughes, who had been driven from the party in 1916 on the conscription issue, and since then had made his political fortune—this is what labour men said—with capitalists and imperialists in Australia and London. The labour party was staunch in its anti-imperialism, but this did not signify much more than a strenuous democratic nationalism and a dislike of capitalists. The cry of 'loyalty', unfairly used in successive elections, helped to keep labour out of power in the Australian Commonwealth for more than a decade after the War; but in fact, as regards relations with Great Britain, Australian labour was likely to be more conservative than the Canadian liberals or even the Canadian conservatives. It was only faintly interested in dominion status; the idea of secession simply did not occur to it. But it was not going to allow Mr. Hughes to tie Australia up in any scheme of organization produced in high capitalistic, academic, and political society on the other side of the world. This was the last thing which Mr. Hughes was likely to do. He was a strong Australian nationalist and at the same time (if the phrase may be allowed for want of a better) a British racialist. He was acutely conscious of 'white' Australia's exposed position facing an awakening Asia. Australia must be ready to look after herself as best she could, and at the same time must do all she could to support British power at sea. He did not think that constitution-making would help. He trusted to the natural solidarity of British peoples united by the Crown, by their common sympathies and interests, by their freedom. He told the Australian parliament that a haphazard adaptable constitution suited the British Empire best; logical rearrangement would be certain to make trouble by interfering with national liberties.[1] However much the labour men might dislike Mr. Hughes, he said pretty much what they thought. He said what almost all Australians thought—let well alone: the Empire would hang together. A minority of thoughtful people

[1] Ibid., pp. 354 ff.

refused to be reassured so easily; they complained that there had been insufficient debate of serious problems. What exactly was Australia's new international status? Lawyers assured them that it did not impair the legal and diplomatic unity of the British Empire; for what the Dominions had done, and what they might do, *vis-à-vis* foreign nations, was done and would be done, in the name of the common Crown. Moreover, the instruments and channels through which dominion governments received their powers of international action were in the last resort controlled by a British minister: there was a supremacy in His Majesty's government in Great Britain which had not been annihilated.[1] But were not these legal and formal checks flimsy in comparison with the political realities? Might not the theory of a common Crown become a fiction masking disintegration? Were not the political realities of to-day the legal forms of to-morrow? These or similar reflections suggested to one or two public men—especially to Mr. Watt, a former lieutenant of the Prime Minister who had fallen out with him—the desirability of a withdrawal to a less exposed position in the international world. Such a proposal came from England in the form of a *Round Table* article urging a limited membership of the League which would have the effect of substituting for the separate dominion voices at Geneva some kind of British Empire delegation.[2] None of these suggestions interested Mr. Hughes. While he believed in the British navy more than he believed in the League of Nations, he saw no reason for surrendering a status which Australia had fairly won. At the same time, his policy was not merely negative. He chid the intellectuals for their constitution-making; but he was alive to the need of finding political machinery and constitutional conventions which would bridge 'that apparently impassable chasm which divides complete autonomy of the several parts of the Empire from united action upon matters affecting us all'.[3]

Throughout 1918 and 1919 it had been a regular habit in the parliaments of the British Commonwealth to look forward—whenever debate revealed the disorder and uncertainty of the new imperial dispensation—to the special constitutional conference which had been agreed upon by the Imperial War Conference of 1917. The constitutional conference, declared Mr. Massey, would remove all fears for the unity of the Empire. The constitutional conference,

[1] Keith, *Responsible Government in the Dominions*, vol. ii, pp. 840 ff. P. E. Corbett and H. A. Smith, *Canada and World Politics* (Faber & Gwyer, 1928), pp. 148–52.

[2] *Round Table*, vol. x, pp. 895 ff.; vol. xi, pp. 1 ff., 321 ff., and 676; cf. *J.P.E.*, vol. ii, p. 613 (Mr. Watt).

[3] Cmd. 1474 of 1921, p. 18.

said General Smuts, would remove all doubts about South Africa's national status. Gradually it penetrated into the minds of the interested public in the different dominions that different spokesmen were saying different things about the coming conference. English peers who came to Canada to lecture, confer, and feast announced that the constitutional conference would furnish the British Empire with an imperial cabinet.[1] At once the Canadian nationalists suspected a conspiracy of centralization. The government made reassuring statements; but the opposition continued to nag. In June 1920 Lord Milner made a statement in the House of Lords. The conference, he said, would be in the nature of a constituent assembly. He hoped that it would not separate without having provided the British Empire with some organ of government based upon the recognition of the complete equality and independence of its several parts, which would, nevertheless, enable them to act promptly and efficiently together, and to exercise in peace a measure of the beneficent co-operation which was so brilliantly illustrated in the War. But the conference, he added, could not meet this year because all the governments of the Commonwealth were necessarily intent upon their internal affairs; he hoped that it would meet in the following year. This statement was intended to reassure both parties to the controversy which was being waged with greater or less vigour throughout the British Commonwealth—both those who were fearful of a drift into disintegration, and those who were afraid of a centralizing plot. However, some careless sentences in the statement gave occasion for renewed nationalist suspicions in South Africa, and reiterated assurances from General Smuts. In the end nothing came of the whole proposal except endless reassertions of the principles asserted in 1917. Early in 1921, it was announced in the parliaments of the Empire that the special constitutional conference would not be held that year. In its stead there would be held a conference of prime ministers to consider specific matters of urgency. What would this assembly be called? It was not an ordinary imperial conference. It was not the much-advertised constitutional conference. It was not the Imperial War Cabinet, for the Empire was at peace. Mr. Churchill spoke of it as an Imperial Peace Cabinet, and drew protests from irritated lawyers and alarmed nationalists. The printed report of the proceedings, avoiding controversy at the price of clumsiness, described the gathering as a 'Conference of the Prime Ministers and Representatives of the United Kingdom, the Dominions, and India, held in June, July, and August 1921'. Among the con-

[1] *Round Table*, vol. xi, p. 153; *J.P.E.*, vol. ii, pp. 312–14.

clusions reached by the prime ministers and representatives was the following:

> '. . . Having regard to the constitutional developments since 1917, no advantage is to be gained by holding a constitutional conference.'[1]

III

'A Dying Illumination'

It was the Australian Prime Minister, Mr. W. M. Hughes, who most strongly attacked the project of a constitutional conference.

> 'It may be that I am very dense [he declared], but I am totally at a loss to understand what it is that this constitutional conference proposes to do. Is it that the Dominions are seeking new powers, or are desirous of using powers they already have, or is the conference to draw up a declaration of rights, to set down in black and white the relations between Britain and the Dominions? What is this conference to do? What is the reason for calling it together? I know, of course, the resolution of the 1917 Conference. But much water has run under the bridge since then. Surely this conference is not intended to limit the rights we now have. Yet what new right, what extension of power, can it give us? What is there that we cannot do now? . . .'

Addressing himself to General Smuts, the Australian Prime Minister urged him to let well alone. The presence of the dominion prime ministers at the council table of the British Empire was evidence enough of Britannic equality. There was practical work to be done. 'We, the representatives of the Dominions, are met together to formulate a foreign policy for the Empire. What greater advance is conceivable? What remains to us? We are like so many Alexanders. What other worlds have we to conquer?'[2]

The Conference of Prime Ministers which met in 1921 did in fact formulate a foreign policy for the Empire. The published record of its deliberations is meagre; but it reveals beyond doubt an active partnership in imperial policy reminiscent of the days of the War. The affairs of Upper Silesia, Egypt, the Ruhr, the League, the Japanese Alliance, Pacific policy in general came under review. Decisions of great importance were taken, decisive political events were prepared. It was natural that this should be so. It was an old and tried team which assembled in the summer of 1921. Mr. Lloyd George, Mr. Hughes, Mr. Massey, General Smuts, had stood together in 1917, 1918, and 1919. Sir Robert Borden was no longer with them; but in his place was Mr. Meighen, Sir Robert's successor in the same

[1] Cmd. 1474, p. 9. [2] Ibid., pp. 22–3.

party and the same parliament. Between the prime ministers there was a complete personal understanding, a complete unity of essential purpose which seemed to make irrelevant the divergent attitudes which they perforce had taken in their own parliaments. Yet one of them, at least, realized that their unity might prove itself a transitory makeshift. Prime ministers could not always be travelling twelve thousand miles to meet each other, and leaving their parliaments for six months at a time. And prime ministers would not always be old friends and comrades. Somehow or other, insisted Mr. Hughes, a sure and practical way must be found of bridging time and distance. Somehow or other the second part of the 1917 resolution—that part which promised 'effective arrangements for continuous consultation in all important matters of common imperial concern'—must be carried into effect, as the affirmation of dominion equality had been. This was not a matter for constitution-making; it was a matter of practical arrangement. And it was urgent. 'That we must do something is essential if this conference is not to be a last magnificent flare of a dying illumination.'[1]

This time Mr. Hughes did not get his way. If he helped in obstructing, or at least in postponing, a declaration of dominion rights, he failed to achieve an ordered system of imperial co-operation. Possibly, as the conference became involved in things which needed doing at once, he forgot his resolve to insist upon the construction of means to future common action. Immediate things were a pressing challenge. The challenge was triumphantly met. The last flare of war-time unity and power was indeed magnificent. It carried the British Commonwealth of Nations into a creative work for the organization of peace. The conference of the statesmen of the Commonwealth was an indispensable preliminary to the international conference held at Washington. This was perhaps the most constructive effort in international agreement which occurred during the decade which followed the War. Its history does not come within the scope of this book. But it is necessary to refer briefly to the influence of the Washington Conference on the relations of the nations of the British Commonwealth with each other. Their practical unity had been effective in creating conditions necessary for its success. But the sequel of their effective unity was a renewed emphasis on their multiplicity. Even the most unlikely springs were swelling the stream of nationalistic separateness.[2]

[1] Cmd. 1474, p. 18.

[2] A full treatment of the Washington Conference from this angle is in Dewey, *The Dominions and Diplomacy*, vol. ii, pp. 80–93, and A. J. Toynbee, *The Conduct of British Empire Foreign Relations since the Peace Settlement* (Milford 1928), pp. 83 ff.

The United States government did not invite the Dominions to be represented at the Washington Conference. Possibly this was a deliberate reminder that the greatest of world Powers had not yet recognized the new status which the Dominions believed they had won at the Paris Conference and in the League of Nations.[1] The British government at once attempted to soften the blow. It took steps to associate dominion delegates—from Canada, Australia, and India—with the three delegates of the United Kingdom. There would therefore be six British Empire delegates. But this was not enough for General Smuts. General Hertzog was watching him. The snub which had come from the outside world was a serious matter for him. He demanded that the precedents of Paris should be followed now and at every subsequent conference.

> 'I want the British Empire [he said] to be represented through its constituent equal states. There is no other way to give it representation. The United Kingdom is not the British Empire, and a United Kingdom delegation does not become an Empire delegation merely by slipping some dominion statesmen through a back door.'[2]

Mr. Lloyd George expressed complete agreement with General Smuts's views, and so far as the British government was able, he met them. Dominion representatives were given full powers to sign individually on behalf of their countries. The effect of this would be, said Mr. Lloyd George, that they would hold the same status which they had held at the Peace Conference. In addition to the signatures of the British delegation, the signature of each dominion would be necessary to commit the British Empire as a whole to anything decided at the conference.[3] General Smuts professed himself content. The American government raised no objection. But the incident revealed the precariousness of the new international status of the Dominions. American tolerance had for the moment accepted the 1919 compromise. But foreign Powers might not always be so tolerant. If the Dominions were to maintain the ground which they had won, they might have to advance further.[4]

The most important official sources are Sir Robert Borden's report (*Canadian Sessional Papers*, 1922, No. 47) and Sir John Salmond's report (New Zealand, *Parliamentary Papers*, 1922, A. 5).

[1] This was the opinion of Professor Keith, see Dewey, op. cit., p. 83.

[2] *J.P.E.*, vol. iv, p. 678.

[3] Ibid., p. 590.

[4] Dewey points out that General Smuts had already gone further than Sir Robert Borden had gone at Paris. The latter had then argued that the internal constitution of the British Empire—its multiplicity in unity—was no concern of foreign Powers. The former was now demanding international recognition of the multiplicity. The Montreal *Star* commented: 'It is not the business of any foreign Power to assume that the British Empire is not a unit in its foreign relations . . .'

The ambiguity of the position already achieved was well illustrated by two highly contrasted reports on the significance of the Dominions' part in the Washington settlement. The report of Canada's representative, Sir Robert Borden, was in the spirit of his deliverances upon the Paris Conference; for it laid stress both on the personality of each separate unit and upon the partnership of them all. All derived their powers from one source, the Crown; all were members of one delegation and communicated with foreign Powers through its head; all were emissaries of the Empire equally. Yet each was in constant communication with its government at home; each was able to secure proper weight for its separate views, and each could refuse agreement. From the point of view of dominion status, this last right—the right to stand alone—was surely the essential thing. Sir Robert asserted it as 'a recognized convention based upon a definite principle'.

> 'In order to commit the British Empire delegation as a whole [he continued] to any agreement reached at the Conference, the signature of each dominion delegate was necessary in addition to that of others, and any dominion delegate could, if convinced or instructed that its duty lay that way, reserve assent on behalf of his government.'

From this it would follow that if the Canadian representative refused to sign, or if the Canadian parliament refused to approve his signature, Canada would not be 'committed' by the signature of the British plenipotentiaries, nor (presumably) by the King's ratification. This argument was flatly controverted by the New Zealand representative, Sir John Salmond.

> 'The true significance of the presence of representatives of the Dominions [he said in his report] is not that the Dominions have acquired for either international or constitutional purposes any form of independent status, but that they have now been given a voice in the management of the international relations of the British Empire as a single, undivided unity—relations which were formerly in the exclusive control of the government of Great Britain.'

He referred to the form of the invitation which the United States had issued, and to the form of the British Empire appointments, which was determined within the Empire itself. He rejected the argument that the new status was a derivation of dominion self-government: if this were so, how account for India's representation? The procedure of the conference, from whatever point of view it was regarded, showed that the Dominions were not represented as quasi-independent states. The British delegation did not consist of seven co-ordinate plenipotentiaries, but of 'three such plenipotentiaries, with whom were associated the four dominion representatives each of whom had authority in respect of his Dominion only'. And that authority was not a power to stand apart from the British Empire. If dominion representatives had refused their signature, His Majesty's general plenipotentiaries would no doubt have sought (if it were at all possible) for a compromise enabling all to sign. But they would if necessary have signed alone, and their action would have bound the whole Empire.

> 'The fact that the delegate of one of the British Dominions had failed to sign the treaty on behalf of the Dominion would have had no effect on the international operation and obligation of the treaty. Any difficulty so unfortunately resulting would have been matter for negotiation and settlement within the borders of the Empire itself, but would have in no way affected the external relations between the Empire and the other contracting Powers.'[1]

For New Zealanders, this report was a comforting document. In the last analysis the British Empire was still one, and New Zealand was still a dependency. But what would the South Africans think about it? And the Canadians? Sir Robert Borden had denied this argument of dependent status. Which was right, the New Zealand representative or the Canadian? ... They were talking about different things. Sir John Salmond was talking about the present relation in law of the British Empire to the outside world. Sir Robert Borden was talking of constitutional and political relations within the British Commonwealth of Nations. Both, inevitably, trespassed a little on each other's ground, for in the last analysis the two matters were not separable. There must be some levelling up or levelling down between legal and political facts, between international and intra-Commonwealth status. Which direction would the adjustment take? . . . Within a few months the Italian government issued separate invitations to the Dominions to attend an economic conference at Genoa. This indicated how things would go. The lawyer's analysis had been true at the time, but the tendency was for it to become rapidly out of date. In the immediate future, at least, it was the political facts which would count most. Their pressure would force a whole series of adjustments in legal rules and theories. The New Zealanders soon learnt that their lawyer's comfort was cold comfort. They watched from their lonely and mistrustful remoteness the fall of General Smuts and Mr. Meighen. They watched the welcome of Sinn Féin to the inner circle of the British Commonwealth.

[1] References in note 2 on pp. 87–8.

From their point of view the years which followed were wretched years in the Empire's history. From the Imperial Conferences of 1907, 1911, 1917, 1918, and 1921, they had each time hoped for some creative act which would constitute the British Empire as an organic whole. From the Conferences of 1923, 1926, and 1930, they each time would fear the worst. The best which might happen would be something to stop the rot which had been spreading now from Canada, now from South Africa, now from the Irish Free State. . . . Gradually the New Zealanders might accustom themselves to the changing order of things. They might even at last come to agree that the transformation which the British Commonwealth was undergoing was the best guarantee of its permanence. But for some time to come they would look back wistfully on 1921 as the last of the good years. When would the Commonwealth of Nations recover the comradeship, the confidence of those years? When would its leaders speak again as Lloyd George had spoken in 1921 to the Conference of Prime Ministers?

Three years after the War, Mr. Lloyd George could still kindle the faith and fire of the victory years.

> 'The British Empire [he declared] is a saving fact in a distracted world. It is the most hopeful experiment in human organization which the world has yet seen. It is not so much that it combines men of many races, tongues, traditions and creeds in one system of government. Other empires have done that; but the British Empire differs from all in one essential respect. It is based not on force but on goodwill and a common understanding. . . . Think of what we stand for in this room to-day. . . .'

And the long recital of the Empire's diversities, liberties, wealth, power, and loyalty, ended with an affirmation of faith in the willingness of all its members to maintain their strength both moral and material, to keep themselves 'a united power for justice, liberty, and peace'.[1]

The illumination of those years flared brilliantly even as it was dying.

[1] Cmd. 1474, pp. 15, 16.

CHAPTER III

SAORSTÁT ÉIREANN

I

FROM HOME RULE TO INDEPENDENCE

THROUGHOUT the nineteenth century the 'Irish Question' was in form a domestic problem of the United Kingdom. In fact it was an Empire matter also, for Irish brains and brawn were playing more than their proportionate part in building the new British communities beyond the seas. In more than one of these communities men of Irish name predominated in the opinion-making professions of the publican, the policeman, the poet, and the politician. Ireland's influence upon the Empire was considerable, although it was indirect. In 1923 it became direct influence. In that year the Irish Free State took her place at the Imperial Conference. She was an equal but junior member, coming in order of precedence before India, but after Canada, Australia, New Zealand, and South Africa. Her influence at once brought reinforcement to the decentralizing forces within the Conference; it may even appear to observers who will see these years in more distant perspective that its tendency was decisively disintegrating. There is something obviously anomalous in the entry of Ireland into the family circle of British Dominions. For what in fact was a dominion? All the Dominions hitherto existing were New World countries peopled by emigrants from the Old World. These communities had but recently emerged, or were still emerging, from colonial tutelage into national self-consciousness. But Ireland was a European country, a 'mother country', a giver of emigrants. The Irish, so they claimed, were 'an ancient nation', 'the children of a foregathered race which has acted highly, which distinguished itself in Europe . . . long centuries before any of the new states now being set up were ever heard of'.[1] This claim was, if anything, too modest. Between the sixth and eleventh centuries Ireland had been the home of something more distinctive than race or nation; she had been the home of a civilization.[2] Surely it is

[1] 'Message to the Free Nations of the World', 21st January 1919. In *Dáil Éireann, Tuairisg Oifiguil* (Official Report), 21st January 1919–18th June 1922 (Stationery Office, Dublin), p. 17. The volume will be cited as *First Dáil.*

[2] Toynbee, *A Study of History,* vol. ii, pp. 322–40 and 427–33, on 'The Abortive Far-Western Civilisation'.

paradoxical to see her appear, in 1923, as a new-comer among the daughter-nations of the British Crown?

This paradoxical transformation was effected by the 'Articles of Agreement for a Treaty between Great Britain and Ireland'[1] signed on the 6th December 1921. We shall not be able to understand this most important document without giving some attention to events during the previous decade. In August 1914 Sir Edward Grey had declared that Ireland was 'the one bright spot'. In December 1918 Mr. Lloyd George might have been tempted to confess that Ireland was the one dark spot. Elsewhere, what brightness! The British peoples in the Old World and the New were once again exulting in their victory and their liberty. Once again: for a hundred years back there was Napoleon; another hundred years, and there was Louis; another century behind Louis passed Philip of Spain. For the fourth time within three centuries God's Englishmen had put despots to flight. England was safe. The Empire and the world were safe. They claimed now, as they had claimed in the past, that the war had been no selfish struggle. This time they had fought for the 'little nations'.[2] . . . Amidst their clamour of joy and self-righteousness a little nation recited its ancient wrongs. Ireland accused 'the pretensions of England founded in fraud and sustained only by an overwhelming military occupation'. 'Ireland', declaimed Dáil Éireann, 'dêmands to be confronted publicly with England at the Congress of the Nations, in order that the civilised world, having judged between English wrong and Irish right, may guarantee to Ireland its permanent support for the maintenance of her national independence.'[3]

During the two and a half years which followed, Irish history is the record of an uncompromising struggle to make this challenge effective. Gradually, the British people began to realize that a great majority of the Irish seriously meant what their elected representatives said and did. At the beginning, British public opinion was totally unprepared for the bitterness and desperation of the challenge which the Irish were prepared to offer. Now, as so often before, British heads were full of preoccupations with Europe, and the continents of the New World, and all the oceans. Their awareness of Ireland—despite the intimate irritations of the past century—remained curiously reluctant and superficial. This traditional compla-

[1] Cmd. 1560 of 1921.

[2] *Dáil Éireann, Tuairisg Oifigiuil,* 16th August 1921–8th June 1922 (to be cited as *Second Dáil*), p. 10. President De Valera quotes Mr. Lloyd George: 'The world is a world for the weak as well as the strong; if not, why did God make little nations?'

[2] *First Dáil,* p. 17 (Message to the Free Nations of the World).

cency, not easily ruffled, had frequently in the past provoked scornful and impotent protest from foreign rulers, who had perforce to submit to sermons on their short-comings from the righteous British.[1] It had goaded the Irish—even the Irish of the Protestant Ascendancy—to recurrent spasms of exquisite irritation. 'They look upon us', raged Swift, 'as a sort of Savage Irish, whom our Ancestors conquered several hundred years ago, and if I should describe the *Britains* to you as they were in *Caesar's* Time, when they *Painted their Bodies, or cloathed themselves with the Skins of Beasts*, I would act full as reasonably as they do. . . .'[2] In the history of England and Ireland, St. George's Channel has been like an ocean, so widely has it separated English and Irish minds. During the middle and later years of the war that ocean broadened until Ireland lay in a remoteness which even diligent and resolute goodwill could never penetrate, which only an inspired imagination might enter. In 1919 it was utterly beyond possibility that England and Ireland should understand each other. It must have been hard enough for the Irish to understand themselves—to realize the extent of that self-transformation, or self-discovery, which they had experienced within a few years. How came it that within four years they had crossed the chasm which separates the Home Rule Act of 1914 from the Declaration of Independence of 1919? The historian of the British Commonwealth cannot escape the duty of making some attempt—forlorn though it may be—to cross the chasm with them.

The act which Redmond was willing to accept from Parliament as 'a final settlement'—Sinn Féin would never allow Redmond to forget that disastrous phrase—was nothing more than a scheme of provincial autonomy. It was a scheme of provincial autonomy so circumscribed that an Australian colony, even sixty or seventy years earlier, would have rejected it with indignation. It contained 'limitations' excluding from the competence of the Irish parliament trade regulation in all its forms, navigation, postal services, and trademarks. In addition it specified certain 'reserved' matters—not counting truly imperial matters such as foreign policy and defence—which might pass to Irish control only at a later date. Among these 'reserved' matters were police, savings banks, friendly societies, and public loans raised before the passing of the act. Ireland, to all intents and purposes, remained within the British financial system:

[1] 'We never impose our advice on him [Palmerston] in relation to Ireland; let him spare himself the trouble of advising us on the subject of Lombardy.' Circular dispatch of Prince Schwarzenburg, 4th December 1848. Quoted by A. J. P. Taylor in *The Italian Problem in European Diplomacy, 1847–9* (Manchester, 1934), p. 191.

[2] Swift, *The Drapier's Fourth Letter* p. 496.

at the head of six limitations on her fiscal autonomy customs and excise were listed. Ireland, in the future as in the past, would send representatives to Westminster. The act left intact the framework of the United Kingdom. If this was what home rule meant, home rule—although its excited partisans and opponents could not see it—was in fact another form of unionism.[1]

In method and theory also the Irish leaders who were willing to accept this act worked within the framework of the United Kingdom. Their strategy and tactics assumed the validity of the Act of Union. 'Nationalist Ireland', says Professor Henry, 'had been officially committed to a peaceful and constitutional policy since the inception of the Home Rule movement in 1870.'[2] The Irish had accepted English rules—those rules of respect for law, of persuasion and majority decision as the means of changing the law, which the English boasted were an essential quality of their civilized living. The Irish accepted the constitutional principle of the sovereignty of parliament. They staked everything upon this principle. They lost their stake.

It was not the content of the Home Rule Act—which, from the later standpoint of Ireland's 'separate and distinct nationhood', was absurdly inadequate—that ruined Redmond and his followers. Slogans may mean more than clauses, and in 1913, in 1914, and still later, home rule was still an 'emotional flag'[3] to wave in the air. But gradually the enemies of the nationalist party and of the British government convinced Ireland that there was truth in their gibe: 'The Act on the Statute Book is a mere invoice, and there is no intention of delivering the goods.'[4] In truth, the goods were never delivered. The 'loyalty' of Ulstermen in 1913 and 1914 made it certain that they would not be delivered. The notion of loyalty is one which demands careful analysis; we must be content here to suggest, by citing one illuminating historical parallel, one of the issues which were hidden in the cloak of that word. In the eighteen-thirties and forties the United Empire Loyalists of Canada, like the Ulster unionists, propounded a theory of loyalty which made it the exclusive possession of a specially privileged, specially dutiful, minority. The English—except the reforming English—were loyal: the Catholic French were not. In opposition to this theory Lord Elgin

[1] Government of Ireland Act, 1914, 4 & 5 Geo. V, Ch. 90. See especially sections 2, 5, 15. The executive would have been a difficult form of diarchy.

[2] R. M. Henry, *The Evolution of Sinn Féin* (Dublin, Talbot Press, 1920), p. 129.

[3] Royal Commission on the 1916 rebellion. Quoted *Sinn Féin Rebellion Handbook* (Dublin, 1916), p. 151.

[4] Sir Horace Plunkett in public letter of June 1916.

maintained the historic English interpretation, according to which loyalty is due equally from all subjects to the King—a constitutional monarch who acts according to the law and custom of the realm. The United Empire Loyalists separated King and constitution: Lord Elgin refused to do so. Consistently with their theory, the loyalists assaulted the King's representative as he was driving away from Parliament where he had done his constitutional duty. Lord Elgin stuck to his guns and the British government backed up Lord Elgin. . . . But in 1914 the British government 'lowered its eyes' (to adopt Mr. Colvin's phrase[1]) before the challenge of loyal Ulster, backed by the leaders of the unionist party.

The optimistic constitutionalists of the nineteenth century had been prone to imagine that the principle of majority decision, once it had been established in a community, would work with the unfailing regularity of a natural law. This volume will have to deal repeatedly with facts which prove the relativity of the majority principle. It depends upon 'an inarticulate major premiss'. The use of majority decision to register agreement in all particulars is possible only in those communities which already possess agreement upon essentials. The events of 1913 and 1914 proved that this condition did not exist in the United Kingdom. Against the constitution, Ulster and her supporters asserted with effect the 'right to resist'. From this there followed logically and necessarily, though not immediately, the ruin of the nationalist party and the collapse of constitutional government. To the majority of Irishmen it came to seem as if the English were saying: 'You have been imagining for fifty years that you were playing this game according to our English rules. And so you were. But now that you have won the game by our rules, it is time for us to change them.' Into Irish minds there flashed the memory of old treacheries. 'We must never trust the English. They'll *rat* on us as they did at Limerick.'[2] A tiny revolutionary minority had persistently preached that English rules were a snare and a sham. This minority at once became aggressive and hopeful. It hailed the Ulstermen as brothers who were breaking the long spell of cringing subservience to the Union and its parliament, who were recalling Irishmen to their own rules of national life, the true rules of defiance and armed resistance to an alien law.[3] In November 1913, a year after the signing of the

[1] Ian Colvin, *Life of Sir Edward Carson* (Gollancz, 1934), vol. ii.

[2] The writer is quoting the interpretation and the words of an Irishman of the old 'Ascendancy', one of the many Irishmen with whom he has discussed these changes.

[3] Cf. an article of P. H. Pearse in *Irish Freedom* (quoted Henry, *Evolution of Sinn Féin*, p. 126): 'One great source of misunderstanding has now disappeared: it has

Covenant, Dublin imitated Belfast and began to drill. The Irish Volunteers set themselves up, with a distinguished Gaelic scholar, Professor Eoin MacNeill, as their first president.

To those who are familiar with the history of revolutionary nationalism in continental Europe the part played by scholars and poets in the Irish revolution will be easy to understand. The language of eighteenth-century revolution is the cosmopolitan language of natural right. Nationalist revolutionaries of the nineteenth and twentieth centuries do not discard natural right. But they inject into it an historical content. They claim this right for the living individual peoples which they believe that they have discovered in history. Eighteenth-century rationalism asserts the rights of man: nineteenth-century romanticism proclaims that man is a national animal; and historical research joins in to remind the rediscovered nations of their past glories and their wrongs. In Ireland the union of these forces was long delayed. The Gaelic League was not founded until 1893. Its founders were scholars, and its aim was scholarship. But its effects were ultimately political, because it challenged the denationalizing and provincializing tendencies which one hundred years of the Union had brought almost to completion. The scholars and poets were rediscovering the ancient Irish civilization; at the same time they were re-creating modern Irish idealism. They found in Ireland's past, beauty, romance, and, above all, heroism. They did not create the Irish ideal of the hero-martyr—that ideal was already the inspiration of innumerable popular plaintive ditties—but they accepted that ideal and made fine poetry of it. For example, it is a central theme in the early work of W. B. Yeats. The Countess Cathleen, Yeats's first heroine, barters not only her life, but her soul, to save the people. Michael, in *Cathleen ni Houlihan* (1902), renounces his bride and offers his life to the old woman who is type and parable of Ireland, who lives for one hope—'the hope of getting my four beautiful fields back again; the hope of putting the strangers out of my house'. He goes with the old woman just because she demands complete sacrifice. 'If any one would give me help he must give me himself, he must give me all. . . .' To those who give all she offers immortality in legend—

> They shall be remembered for ever,
> They shall be alive for ever,
> They shall be speaking for ever,
> The people shall hear them for ever.

become clear . . . that the Orangeman is now no more loyal to England than we are . . .' '. . . The Orangeman with a rifle is a much less ridiculous figure than the Nationalist without a rifle. . . .'

Cathleen ni Houlihan is a drama of the rising of 1798; it is also a dream of the yet unacted 1916 rebellion. The theme of heroic martyrdom passes from politics into literature; it then passes from literature into politics again. The Easter Rebellion is, literally, a tragedy, first rehearsed, then performed in life and death. Padraic Pearse, president of the provisional government, acts in the flesh the part of martyr-saviour which he has conceived in his play, *The Singer*. One man gives his blood to redeem the people. What if the British had not taken blood? What if they had failed to play the part which Pearse had plotted for them? . . . As the defeated rebels were marched by their captors through the streets of Dublin, there came to their ears, every now and then, a subdued jeering and hissing. Suddenly broke in a girl's voice, shrill and lonely, crying, 'Long live the Republic'. For the most part the watching crowds were silent and hostile.[1] The carefully plotted tragedy was not yet complete. Perhaps for a moment Pearse dreaded that it might collapse into anticlimax and farce. General Maxwell's firing parties saved the play.[2]

The ordinary Englishman regarded the Easter Rebellion as a wanton blow aimed at England and the cause of freedom. But in Ireland it had a different meaning.

> 'From that moment the old and deep but hitherto submerged emotions resumed full sway of the national imagination, and jostled out the novel and superficial emotions induced by the war and Ireland's earlier participation in it.'[3]

This, or something like it, is all that the historian can say; and it is utterly inadequate. Historical narrative cannot express the reality of the spiritual revolution which completed the physical defiance of Easter 1916; only Irish imaginations, working in an Irish mental idiom, may symbolize it in drama and dialogue. Poets and story-tellers and dramatists have expressed fragments of it. Within a few

[1] This is the picture which remains in the mind of an acquaintance of the writer, one of the men who was marched through the streets—a friend of Arthur Griffith, a sober and truthful man. Cf. P. S. O'Hegarty, *The Victory of Sinn Féin* (Dublin, Talbot Press, 1924), p. 3: 'The insurrection was . . . universally and explosively unpopular.'

[2] Fifteen men were shot, in executions drawn out from 3rd May to 12th May. Five men were sentenced to life imprisonment. Hundreds were exiled and imprisoned. 3,149 men and 77 women passed through Richmond barracks. The question whether this suppression was vindictive or not (compared, say, with Austrian practice) is not here discussed. The only point made is that the British acted the part Pearse cast for them: for him one execution would have sufficed.

[3] W. B. Wells and N. Marlowe, *The Irish Convention and Sinn Féin* (Dublin, Maunsel & Co., 1918), p. 9.

days of the rebellion, a sensitive Irish writer living in London half divined and half explained the changing mood of Ireland.

> 'She was not with the Rebellion, but she will be, and her heart, which was withering, will be warmed by the knowledge that men thought her worth dying for. . . . If freedom is to come to Ireland, as I believe it is, then the Easter Revolution is the only thing which would have happened. . . . We might have crept into liberty like some domesticated man, whereas now we may be allowed to march into liberty with the honours of war.'[1]

Yet even this interpretation, brilliant as it was, did not lay bare the bitter resolution of the new mood and the new men. A few months before he died in the rôle which he had conceived for himself, Pearse had systematically and deliberately set himself the task of defining that 'redemption' which his martyrdom was to achieve:

> 'I make the contention that the national demand of Ireland is fixed and determined; that that demand has been made by every generation; that we of this generation receive it as a trust from our fathers; that we are bound by it; that we have not the right to alter it or to abate it by one jot or tittle; and that any undertaking to accept in full satisfaction anything less than the generations of Ireland have stood for is null and void, binding on Ireland neither by the law of God nor by the law of nations. . . . Ireland's historic claim is for separation. Ireland has authorised no man to abate that claim. The man who, in the name of Ireland, accepts as a "final settlement" anything less by one portion of an iota than separation from England will be repudiated by the new generation as surely as O'Connell was repudiated by the generation that came after him, . . . is guilty of so immense an infidelity, so immense a crime against the Irish nation, that one can only say of him that it were better for that man . . . that he had not been born.'[2]

These words, this implacable spirit, must often have haunted the minds of Irish leaders who in later days found themselves negotiating with English statesmen. These leaders carried a heavy burden of responsibility towards the living; but upon their shoulders lay also a dreadful tyranny of the dead.

Until the elections of December 1918 the old leaders of the nationalist party were still the nominal spokesmen for the majority of Ireland; and these leaders were ready to continue negotiations on the old basis. Successful negotiation was the one chance of saving the nationalist party, the Home Rule Act, the unity of Ireland, and

[1] James Stephens, quoted ibid.

[2] Pádraic H. Pearse, *Collected Works, Political Writings and Speeches* (Dublin, Talbot Press, 1917), p. 230. From pamphlet *Ghosts*. With this there needs to be read also *The Separatist Idea, The Sovereign People, The Spiritual Nation.*

at the same time the unity of the United Kingdom. On the 7th March 1917 Redmond warned the House of Commons and the government: 'If the constitutional movement in Ireland disappears, the Prime Minister will find himself face to face with the Revolutionary Movement, and he will have to govern Ireland by the naked sword.' The British government understood the danger. Mr. Asquith had announced to the House of Commons on 25th May 1916 that the machinery of government had broken down. He believed that there was 'a unique opportunity for a settlement of outstanding problems by general consent', and he persuaded Mr. Lloyd George to preside over its negotiation. The negotiation petered out in ambiguities, recriminations, self-justifications, and intensified suspicions of bad faith. 'Some tragic fatality', cried Redmond, 'seems to dog the footsteps of this government in all their dealings with Ireland.'[1] But it was not fate or accident that ruined the negotiation; the position remained exactly as it was in 1913 and 1914, when the British repudiated their own constitutional rule of political life. Improvisation could put nothing in its place. Lloyd George, again aided by the nationalist party and by idealists like Sir Horace Plunkett, made another effort to cover or to conceal (for at this time the United States was hesitating before its entry into the war) the crack which was splitting the United Kingdom. An Irish Convention deliberated from July 1917 to April 1918.[2] It began bravely with a communiqué accepting 'the dominion principle of self-government'. But its report, when it was at last published, was peppered with minority protests repudiating the recommendations (themselves far short of the dominion principle) on which the majority agreed. The task of manipulating warring groups—which now had clearly emerged as sequel to the abandonment of normal constitutional method—was so impossible that the British government did not further attempt it. Instead, it attempted to force conscription on Ireland, and by so doing drove even the nationalist party on to the Sinn Féin platform of Ireland's 'separate and distinct nationhood'.

It is an interesting indication of the remoteness from England into

[1] Hansard, *House of Commons Debates*, vol. lxxxiv, 24th July 1916, col. 1338. Cf. *Headings of a Settlement as to the Government of Ireland*, Cd. 8310 of 1916. For a defence of Redmond against the Sinn Féin accusation that he accepted partition, see letter by John D. Nugent in *Irish News* (Belfast), 12th Aug. 1933.

[2] *Report of the Proceedings of the Irish Convention*, Cd. 9019 of 1918. Perhaps the most important result of the Convention was the definite separation between the unionists of north-east Ulster and those of the rest of Ireland. The latter from now on are ready for a move—though not a sudden one—towards Dominionism.

which nationalist Ireland had now passed, that a review like the *Round Table*, pledged to the principle of self-government as the bond of Empire, should denounce the extremists *within* the Convention.[1] Yet only one member of the Convention had been in prison—and he by an error of the police. Sinn Féin had refused to enter the Convention. Men who had been in prison—De Valera, Cosgrave, Griffith—were winning by-elections while the Convention was sitting. Sinn Féin was already certain of the overwhelming triumph which it won in December 1918. While England was voting 'khaki', Ireland chose the rebels. The unionists won only 26 seats. The nationalists won 6; and 4 of these they owed to bargains (in some doubtful Ulster constituencies) with Sinn Féin. Even in Ulster the unionists had a majority in four counties only out of nine. Even in Ulster Sinn Féin won 10 seats.[2] In Connaught Sinn Féin won every seat. Both in Leinster and in Munster it captured every seat but one. Its gains throughout all Ireland were 73, out of a possible 105. It is necessary to insist on the fact that Sinn Féin achieved this triumph before the British government had begun to lose physical mastery of Ireland. One after another, the Sinn Féin directors of elections had followed each other to prison. Forty of the elected candidates were in prison on the day when their constituents elected them. Only twenty-six of them were able to celebrate their victories in their constituencies.

Here, in this election, is a rough external measure of the emotional revolution which separated Redmond's Ireland from De Valera's. Was the revolution entirely emotional? Or had the party which De Valera led a theory and a method to put in the place of the constitutional theory and method for which the ruined nationalist party had stood?

In the ferment of revolution no theory was clearly stated. But there were in the background two contrasted theories, each of which had an historic ancestry. The first of them may be called the Sister Kingdom theory. It is explicitly enunciated as early as 1649, in answer to the assertion—then the revolutionary assertion of a revolutionary parliament—that Ireland (together with the other territories 'belonging' to the 'People of England') is to be governed by 'the Supreme Authority of this Nation, the Representatives of the People in Parliament'. Irishmen then answered that they owed 'superiority, allegiance, and subjection only to the King's sacred Majesty'. This argument is repeated by a long line of eminent

[1] *Round Table*, vol. viii, p. 519.

[2] In Belfast and the four adjoining counties the 'garrison' was unshaken.

Irishmen—Molyneux, Swift, Grattan, Griffith. 'I declare, next under God,' cries Swift, 'I depend only on the King my Sovereign, and on the laws of my own country.'[1] Grattan forced from Great Britain admission of the Sister Kingdom theory in the Renunciatory Act of 1783, which enacted that

> 'the said right claimed by the people of Ireland to be bound only by laws enacted by his Majesty and the Parliament of that Kingdom, . . . shall be, and is hereafter declared to be, established and ascertained forever, and shall, at no time hereafter, be questioned or questionable.'

On this statute Griffith, the founder of the Sinn Féin movement, took his stand. His argument had no legal validity: probably it never had possessed legal validity.[2] Yet Griffith intended it as a claim of constitutional right, not as an appeal to revolutionary force. The method he advocated was that the elected representatives of Ireland, instead of attending at Westminster, should resume their former constitutional right of assembling in Dublin as an Irish Assembly, and should there initiate a national economic and social programme which would rebuild the fortunes of their country. No doubt he was at fault in imagining that this programme could be carried through without revolution. He was influenced by the Hungarian example in politics. He was also influenced by German economic doctrine. But both his politics and his economics had a distinguished Protestant Irish ancestry; his politics may be found in Swift, and his economics in Berkeley.[3]

The second theory cannot claim such an extended pedigree. The father of this theory is Wolfe Tone, who popularized in Ireland French revolutionary ideas of natural right and the republic. Wolfe Tone reached his theory by gradual stages of disillusionment with Grattan's half-achieved, and therefore wholly ruined, Sister King-

[1] Swift, *The Drapier's Fourth Letter*, p. 494.

[2] Professor McIlwain, in his stimulating book, *The American Revolution*, links these Irish protests with the protests of the American colonists before they reached their final stage of natural right and rebellion against the King. He argues that the protests were valid from the legal point of view. Professor A. Berriedale Keith will not accept the argument as having any force.

[3] See Arthur Griffith, *The Resurrection of Hungary* (Dublin, 1903), and George Berkeley, *The Querist* (Dublin, 1725), Query 129: 'Whether one may not be allowed to conceive and suppose a Society or Nation of Human Creatures, clad in Woollen Cloaths and Stuffs, eating good Bread, Beef, Mutton, Poultry, and Fish in great Plenty, drinking Ale, Mead, and Cyder, inhabiting decent Houses built of Brick and Marble, taking their Pleasure in fair Parks and Gardens, depending on no foreign Imports either of Food or Raiment; and whether such People ought much to be pitied?' Query 130: 'Whether Ireland be not as well qualified for such a State as any Nation under the Sun?' Cf. Queries 115, 165, 168. With equal vigour but less subtlety Swift himself advocates the same economic programme, cf. *A Proposal for the Universal Use of Irish Manufactures*.

dom. Disillusionment grew into desperation. 'He did not think of separation', his widow once testified, 'until every other hope had failed.'[1] And he did not think of a republic until he had convinced himself that it was the only possible symbol for an independent and united Ireland. Separation 'under any form of government'[2] was what he wanted. But in 1795 he assured the French—whose support was necessary to him—that a republic was the only form of government to which the Irish would rally. It was for the republic that he died. There is therefore a direct link between him and Pearse, who places him first in that faithful band—from which Grattan and O'Connell are excluded—of 'those who have thought most authentically for Ireland'.[3] From Wolfe Tone to Pearse the republican tradition was, in appearance at least, continuous. Its professed guardians during the previous half-century had been the members of a secret society, the Irish Republican Brotherhood, founded in 1858. But the Irish Republican Brotherhood was neglected and forgotten by the Irish people. 'Ireland', one of its members has testified, '. . . knew nothing of the I.R.B.'[4] Probably it would be true to add—although the history of a secret society is inevitably controversial—that the I.R.B., despite its name, was not particularly interested in republican theory nor particularly committed to it.[5] It existed for revolutionary action. The witness who has been quoted above goes on to assert that the I.R.B., implacable and efficient, hiding itself even from the apparent leaders of militant nationalism, plotted and controlled every revolutionary event from the formation of the Volunteers until the Easter rising. Of the seven members of the provisional government who proclaimed the Easter rising, all but one—James Connolly, commander of the labour Citizen Army, who was with the I.R.B. in spirit—were members of that secret band.

The proclamation of Easter 1916 asserted the independence of the Irish nation under the republican form.[6] In the circumstances,

[1] *Letters of Theobald Wolfe Tone*, ed. Bulmer Hobson (Dublin, Lester, 1921), p. 163. This letter was written in old age—1842.

[2] *The Life of Wolfe Tone written by himself*, ed. Bulmer Hobson (Dublin, Lester, 1920), p. 73.

[3] In the pamphlet *Ghosts*. See his *Political Writings and Speeches*, p. 249.

[4] O'Hegarty, *The Victory of Sinn Féin*, p. 3.

[5] The writer is acquainted with a former member of the I.R.B. whose political theory at the time of his membership was Catholic monarchism.

[6] The undated poster by which the Irish Republic was declared on 24th April 1916 bears the heading: 'Poblacht Na H Éireann. The Provisional Government of the Irish Republic to the Irish People.' Some of the pamphlet literature is worth referring to, e.g. *Twenty Plain Facts for Irishmen*. 'It is the natural right of the people of every nation to have the free control of their own national affairs and any body of the people is entitled to assert that right in the name of the people.'

this was inevitable. The revolutionaries were bound to proclaim a separate Irish government which could claim *immediate* authority; and the *immediate* form and symbolism of national separation could be none other than republican. But this form and symbolism, like the government itself, might be provisional. National revolt, should it succeed, would be free to clothe the established national state in whatever form and symbolism it might deem expedient.[1] If, on the other hand, the revolt should fail, and fail heroically, the republican symbolism would be hallowed by martyrdom. This happened. The Easter rising gave a halo to the abstract theory of republicanism. The theory now occupied 'that misty sphere of the mind where feelings are just emerging into ideas with the help of catchwords'.[2] Yet in the Sinn Féin party, which was Griffith's foundation, the old idea of a Dual Monarchy remained deeply rooted. This represented not so much a constitutional dogma as a working method of achieving national freedom; it was the product of a practical temper aware of the limitations inherent in changing circumstance and unwilling to fix any abstract label on the national struggle and turn that label into a test for patriots. When, therefore, Sinn Féin became in 1917 the party of the great majority of nationalists, it had to find room for two strongly contrasted political tendencies. On the one side was the dogma of the undying republic, won by the blood of the martyrs, living in its own right, needing no ratification by popular vote, but needing only resolution and arms. For this living republic Sinn Féin was trustee, claiming full loyalty and obedience. Here in germ was the party-state. But on the other side was nationalistic democracy, equally resolute for Irish independence, but admitting the right of the Irish people to choose the symbolism and forms of government in which that independence would express itself. This theory subjected Sinn Féin itself to the suffrage of the people. In the early months of 1922 these conflicting theories and methods came into conflict, split Sinn Féin, split the Dáil, and plunged Ireland into civil war. But from 1918 to 1921 all theories and all temperaments were united in pursuing the immediate object of separation from England—'under any form of government'. The party congress of 25th–26th October 1917, which defined the programme to be put before the people, found room for both points of view. The Sinn Féin manifesto recited 'the supreme courage and glorious sacrifices' which had 'united the

[1] From the source mentioned in note 5, p. 103, the writer had been informed that even in the inner circle there was in 1916 some talk—how serious he cannot say—of choosing a German prince as king.

[2] G. M. Young, *Charles I and Cromwell* (Peter Davies, 1936), p. 74.

Irish people under the flag of the Irish Republic'. It appealed to the republican proclamation of Easter 1916 as if that proclamation still had validity. But it then went on to speak of the republic as something which would come into existence in the future, by way of international recognition. It also promised the people that 'having achieved that status' they might 'by referendum choose their own form of government'. The immediate programme to which the party pledged itself was—with modifications arising out of the existing international situation—Griffith's programme. The Irish representatives were to withdraw from the British parliament. They were to constitute themselves as a national constituent assembly in Dublin. They were to appeal to the Peace Conference for recognition of Irish independence. That independence, however—here the other theory reasserted itself—was to be republican in form. The essential all-reconciling pledge, proposed by Eamonn De Valera, the new president of Sinn Féin—who called on the congress to salute the flag of the republic with the words, *Esto perpetua*, and yet proclaimed himself 'no doctrinaire republican'—was a pledge 'to make use of any and every means available to render impotent the power of England to hold Ireland in subjection by military force or otherwise'. For the present that objective united Sinn Féin and united the people.[1]

It may therefore be disputed whether the Irish people in December 1918 voted for a republic. It is beyond dispute that they voted for secession from the United Kingdom. And, as in 1916, secession demanded in practice a republican form. Whatever might be the form of a future national state, the immediate need was an act repudiating the existing monarchy. On 21st January 1919 twenty-seven Sinn Féin deputies (for the majority of Sinn Féin representatives could not attend: the unionists and nationalists would not) met in the Mansion House in Dublin as Dáil Éireann, adopted a short, business-like constitution, and then, in a declaration faithfully echoing the phrases of Europe's revolutionary tradition—the phrases of 1776 and 1789 and 1848—reaffirmed the act of Easter 1916:

> 'Now therefore we, the elected representatives of the ancient Irish people in National Parliament assembled, do, in the name of the Irish nation, ratify the establishment of the Irish Republic and pledge ourselves and our people to make this declaration effective by every means at our command.'[2]

[1] Sinn Féin Constitution (in Irish, with English translation), Dublin, 1917. Cf. the election manifesto of December 1918.

[2] *First Dáil*, pp. 14 ff. Cf. Mr. De Valera, 16th August 1921 (*Second Dáil*, p. 9), referring to the answer of the Irish people given in this election. 'I do not say that

II

The Struggle, 1919–1921

Even the declaration of a republic did not end all ambiguity. It could not prevent men feeling and thinking after their several fashions. To some men the declaration was a solemn act of creation and consecration; from now and for ever, surely, all doubts were silenced; the republic really existed; denial of it 'by one portion of an iota' was the blackest treachery. Other men persisted in thinking that it was the Irish people, and not a declaration on a constitution or a symbol, who made Ireland. To these men the republic was no more than a banner beneath which the Irish people marched forward. Deep in their hearts was the feeling that it was the forward march, not the banner, which mattered most. And yet they knew that the banner itself did matter. With reservations of which they were perhaps themselves unconscious, they fell into step behind it.

There was another element of ambiguity. The declaration of independence, like all the formal proceedings of Dáil Éireann, was in the Irish speech. Here lay possibilities of confusion which, failing a saving moderation, might ruin the whole plan of national unity and independence. Pearse had dramatized Ireland's national struggle as a revolt of the 'Gael' against the 'Gall'.[1] This racial conception of nationality, if one can imagine it being pressed to its logical end, implies 'undoing the conquest' by the expulsion or the subjugation of all the foreign elements which have entered Ireland since Strongbow's day—to go no farther back. It means a *jacquerie*, it means civil war. And suppose that the 'Gall', entrenched in the six counties around Belfast, is strong enough to stave off subjugation ? The theory then means a perpetual partition of Ireland. Apart from this, it means—and this perhaps is sufficient to prove that it can never be pushed to its extreme conclusion—repudiation by Ireland of Ireland's most famous rebels, including Tone himself. An alternative view of Irish nationality therefore offers itself, a view which escapes these awkward consequences. This view professes a resolute historical realism; it accepts and welcomes 'every element of strength, Gaelic

that answer was for a form of government so much, because we are not Republican doctrinaires, but it was for Irish freedom and Irish independence, and it was obvious to every one who considered the question that Irish independence could not be realised at the present time in any way so suitably as through a Republic. Hence it was that the Irish Republic as such was sanctioned by the representatives of the people . . .'

[1] Cf. *The Singer*.

or Norman or British, Catholic or Protestant, Democratic or Conservative, which constitutes the actual Irish nation, such as History has bequeathed it to us'.[1] At first sight this theory appears more reasonable and more intelligent than the former one; yet it, too, may be pushed to extremes—it may even be pushed to the extreme of denying Irish nationality altogether, for what history bequeathed after a century of the Union was an all-but triumphant anglicization. If there is to be any accommodation between the two theories, the 'Gael' must repudiate the extreme racialist implications of his theory, and the 'Gall' must accept Gaelic culture as a precious inheritance which lives, and which has creative work to do, in a living Irish nation.

It is almost impossible to state these issues without over-simplifying them. To begin with, 'Gael' and 'Gall' are poetic images; they are not distinct individuals or definite racial groups. They do not even appear in coherent theoretical systems held by rival schools. They appear most frequently as theories which are merely implied in affirmations and denials which are primarily emotional. These affirmations and denials follow and contradict each other within a single individual and within a single party. Both views of nationality struggled together within Sinn Féin and Dáil Éireann; in moments of sentiment and on ritual occasions the first tended to prevail; in moments of reflection and argument, the second.[2] It might have been expected that the more extreme conception of nationality would be allied with the more uncompromising theory of politics. But, by a curious though natural chance, the Gaelic aspirations which determined the language of the original declaration of independence, played the republicans false. For the ancient Irish civilization had no theoretical conception of a republic. The original thought of the declaration of independence is republican, and the word republic appears in the English and French versions of it. But the original version in Irish uses the words *Saorstát Éireann*. These words passed, nearly three years later, into the Irish Treaty, where they were retranslated with literal accuracy, as Irish Free State.[3]

[1] William O'Brien, *The Irish Revolution and How it came about* (Dublin, Talbot Press, 1923), p. 411.

[2] Cf. repudiation of 'two nations theory' in pamphlets on Ulster by E. MacNeill and P. S. O'Hegarty.

[3] F. Pakenham, *Peace by Ordeal* (Cape, 1935), p. 244, gives 'a fragment of dialogue of 24th November 1921:

'Griffith: "You may prefer to translate 'Saorstát Éireann' by 'Free State' (instead of Republic). We shall not quarrel with your translation."

'Lord Birkenhead: "The title, Free State, can go into the Treaty."'

For this reason the Irish Republican Army, refusing to recognize the Free State, has

Despite the hesitations, confusions, and ambiguities to which reference has been made, three things are perfectly plain: that Dáil Éireann claimed to be the sovereign authority in an Irish republic existing *de jure*: that the Dáil and the ministry which it appointed struggled to establish the republic *de facto*: and that the Dáil won the backing of a great majority of the Irish people. In a revolution, one cannot measure the movement of opinion by figures. There is indeed some evidence in the figures of the local government elections of 1920, which were held under a system of proportional representation introduced with the direct purpose of weakening Sinn Féin.[1] At the elections to the second Dáil in the following year, when the Irish turned to their own purposes the occasion provided by the Government of Ireland Act 1920,[2] a single party held a control which no minority dared challenge. The narrative will reveal how this party was able to win the popular backing which was the indispensable condition of its monopoly.

The narrative must of necessity be incomplete. The records of the Dáil are fragmentary, and only the records of its public sessions have been printed. The records of the revolutionary government and its departments are not available for consultation; it would besides be absurd to expect to find in them the system and completeness proper to an established state. On the other hand, there is a very extensive newspaper and pamphlet literature, and the testimony of actors in these events who are still living, if checked with caution, provides the contemporary writer with material which future historians, who in other respects will be more fortunate, will have to do without.

yet been unable to appeal to the original phrase of the declaration of independence. It has, however, been able to quote the proclamation of 1916 for its own word *Poblacht*. But Pakenham, *Peace by Ordeal*, p. 82, utters a justified protest against making too much of these linguistic trifles.

[1] 9 & 10 Geo. V, c. 19. In the whole of Ireland there were 62 townships with republican majorities, 25 with mixed republican and nationalist majorities, and 24 with unionist majorities.

[2] 10 & 11 Geo. V, c. 67. The 3rd May 1921 was fixed as the day for the establishment of the separate parliaments of Southern and Northern Ireland. On 11th March 1921 Mr. De Valera moved in the Dáil '1. That the Parliamentary elections which are to take place during the present month be regarded as elections to Dáil Éireann. 2. That all deputies duly returned at these elections be regarded as members of Dáil Éireann and allowed to take their seats on subscribing to the Oath of Allegiance. That the present Dáil dissolve automatically as soon as the new body has been summoned by the President and called to order' (*First Dáil*, p. 291). One hundred and twenty-four members who pledged themselves to the republic were returned without opposition. Four representatives (from Trinity College) out of 128 recognized the Government of Ireland Act and English authority by attending the opening of the 'parliament of Southern Ireland' on 28th June 1921. Fifteen senators, out of 64, attended. The second Dáil met on 16th August for its first public session.

Certainly there is now material enough for reconstructing the main outline of the revolution and—what is equally important—recapturing its mood.

In January 1919 a truncated Dáil assembled. On the second day of its first session (22nd January) twenty-four members answered the roll. The deputies were for the time content with declarations and gestures. At their first meeting they adopted a short constitution, proclaimed the national republic, issued a message to the free nations of the world, and voted a 'democratic programme'.[1] On the following day they elected a ministry with Cathal Brugha president *pro tem.* Then followed a long pause. In March large numbers of Sinn Féin prisoners were released from English prisons. On the 1st April fifty-two deputies answered the roll at a private session of the Dáil. They made some amendments to the constitution and elected De Valera as their president. On the following day the president nominated his ministry. The revolution was beginning to move. It still moved in a cloud of rhetoric[2]; but the rhetoric had its importance; it testified at least to an energetic process of auto-suggestion and a quickening conviction of republican right. That conviction was not shaken when the Peace Conference refused to receive the Irish emissaries. They published their letters to M. Clemenceau and to the other plenipotentiaries in a booklet[3] which made good propaganda: its theme was the heroic pronouncement of Cardinal Mercier: 'The authority of that power is no lawful authority. Therefore in soul and conscience you owe it neither respect nor attachment nor obedience.' The activities of Saorstát Éireann's ministry of foreign affairs and of its agents abroad only pretended to be diplomatic; in fact they were propagandist, addressing themselves, not to governments, but to the opponents of governments, and especially to the opponents of President Wilson in America.[4] On 11th April an Irish-American delegation listened while the sovereign Dáil demonstrated with profuse rhetoric that Irish independence would solve the problem of the freedom of the seas; on 17th June the Dáil listened to a letter from its president,

[1] Its rhetoric traces back through Pearse to Lalor; its proposals rather resemble those of Australian labour about the year 1900—but they do not have the same ring of clear-cut practicability.

[2] e.g. 'The Message to the Irish abroad', *First Dáil*, p. 55.

[3] *The Irish Republic and the Peace Conference.*

[4] See *Second Dáil*, pp. 16 ff., for summary of 'the foreign establishments of the Republic'. On 29th January 1920, the Dáil had passed a vote authorizing Mr. De Valera to spend a sum not exceeding 500,000 dollars in connexion with the presidential election in America, and a sum not exceeding 1,000,000 dollars to secure American recognition for the Republic (*First Dáil*, p. 71).

informing it that he himself had gone to America and that he nominated Arthur Griffith as acting president. These activities among the Irish abroad, within the British Empire and outside it, had considerable importance; but they were stamped with the character of a 'movement', with which the 'Irish race', and its enemies, were already familiar.[1]

Within Ireland, republicanism was ceasing to be a 'movement'; it was becoming a government, not only in its claims, but in fact. It is interesting, in view of the later attitude of Arthur Griffith, that it was he who guided this transformation. On 19th August he announced in the Dáil that all justices of inferior and supreme courts would be required to pledge their allegiance to the republic.[2] On 30th August he supported a motion of Cathal Brugha, Minister of Defence, setting out a form of oath and ordering its imposition upon deputies, volunteers, officers, and clerks of the Dáil, and every other individual who in the opinion of the Dáil should take it. 'They should realise', said Griffith, 'that they were the government of the country. This oath would regularise the situation.' 'If they were not a regular government,' he declared, 'then they were shams and imposters.'[3]

Enough has now been said to illustrate the resolution and persistence with which Dáil Éireann asserted the existence *de jure* of the Irish republic. Those members of the Dáil who were not 'wedded and glued to forms of government', who cared more for the substance than the forms of national freedom, had nevertheless pledged themselves to go forward now under the republican banner. Recollection of this oath, little more than two years hence, was to mean a searing of many men's consciences and a bitter division between loyal comrades. In 1920 there was little sign of this tragic division. The oath to the republic was more than a gesture; it was, perhaps, in the desperate situation which the Dáil was now facing, a necessity. If Dáil Éireann and its officers made no claim to represent a rightful

[1] Even Mr. De Valera, as late as August 1921, spoke of the Dáil's work as a 'movement'. *Second Dáil*, p. 25.

[2] *First Dáil*, p. 141.

[3] *First Dáil*, pp. 151, 152. The form of the oath was: 'I, A.B., do solemnly swear (or affirm) that I do not and shall not yield a voluntary support to any pretended government, authority, or power within Ireland hostile and inimical thereto, and I do further swear (or affirm) that to the best of my knowledge and ability I will support and defend the Irish Republic and the Government of the Irish Republic which is Dáil Éireann, against all enemies, foreign and domestic, and I will bear true faith and allegiance to the same, and that I take this obligation freely without any mental reservation or purpose of evasion, so help me God.' The voting was 30 to 3 in favour of this form of oath.

power, they must be what their enemies called them—a murder gang. For they were killing and ordering to kill.

The British government assumed that it had been in lawful possession of Ireland for centuries, and never doubted its legal right to kill. Irish logic—to British minds unimaginably wrong-headed and topsy-turvy—insisted that the British were invaders who wantonly and without provocation were harassing the peaceful activities of the legitimate Irish government, Dáil Éireann. Dáil Éireann empowered the Minister of Defence to take all necessary measures to repel British aggression.

Logically, according to this view of things, the peaceful work of the Dáil comes first, and it is necessary to examine this before considering the military operations. The question of right could not, in truth, be separated from the question of fact; gangsters can give themselves high-sounding titles, and not even its election mandate would justify the high claims of the Dáil and its desperation in defence of them, unless it should succeed, or give some substantial promise of succeeding, in the peaceful tasks of a government which pursues the common weal and is supported by the common will.[1] The Dáil in fact set out to 'form a polity within a polity'. An Irishman who hated the savagery which grew out of revolution and repression has written of the peaceful work of the Dáil:

> 'It brought about a situation wherein we in Ireland had two governments; one, our own, which was effective, but outlawed; and the other which had all the outward machinery of government, but nobody to govern. It drove home to everybody in Ireland the fact that the British government in Ireland was an alien and an unconstitutional government. In effect it ousted it.'[2]

These assertions may be to some extent exaggerated; but it is nevertheless possible to trace the main lines of the process by which a native Irish state began to form itself within the shell of an alien coercive authority.[3]

[1] It is only fair to quote the comment on this paragraph of an Irish critic: 'Our revolutionary fighters felt no need for the sanction of a government.' But Mr. De Valera thought differently: e.g. 'The first duty, therefore, of the Ministry was to set about making the *de jure* Republic a *de facto* Republic.' *Second Dáil*, p. 9.

Jurists of the Italian Renaissance, compelled by circumstances to face the problem of 'illegitimacy' in government, propound two tests of it—defective title, and failure to use power rightly. Cf. Bartolus, *De Tyrannia*.

[2] O'Hegarty, *The Victory of Sinn Féin*, p. 36. The 'outlawing' touched more than the government. A proclamation of 25th November 1919 suppressed Sinn Féin, the Sinn Féin Clubs, the Volunteers, the Gaelic League, Cummann na M'Ban. 'The English government in Ireland', commented Griffith, 'has now proclaimed the whole Irish Nation.' *Irish Bulletin*, 27th November 1919.

[3] Revolutionaries elsewhere took lessons from the Irish. The writer has been

According to Irish theory, sovereign authority over the whole of Ireland was vested in Dáil Éireann; but the Dáil entrusted executive power to the ministry which it had elected. In fact, the Dáil was little more than a machine for registering the decisions of the ministry.[1] The ministry assumed the form of a British cabinet; it was an executive committee whose members were heads of departments of state. In this there was an element of fiction. Conditions did not make possible the regular and orderly performance of public business. The Dáil itself, in the times of crisis which intermittently arose, bore the outward appearance of a handful of conspirators secretly assembling[2]; and departmental heads were frequently 'on the run' from hiding-place to hiding-place. Many of the so-called departments were shadow departments which never assumed substance. In the reports presented to the second Dáil there is a large element of play-acting and pretence. The ministry of foreign affairs, as has been seen, never pursued 'diplomatic practice' as it is understood in the comity of nations. The ministry of education secured from the bishops promises of support for the revival of the Irish language, instituted inter-family competitions in Irish, and tried to improve its status in the universities. The activities of this ministry were rather those of a 'movement' than of an administrative department. The ministry of fisheries attempted to stimulate the formation of co-operative societies, expressed opinions on the marketing of fish at home and abroad, assisted the people of Gorumma to purchase a motor-boat called the *Little Flower*, and itself purchased a steam trawler for the transport of fish to the Welsh coast. The trawler was lost at sea—'but the insurance was recovered'.[3] Was this a triumph for the sovereign government of Saorstát Éireann? The departments of trade and industry, which were very closely associated, achieved little more. The social regeneration of Ireland by way of economic nationalism had been in the forefront of Griffith's programme at the time when he first founded Sinn Féin.[2] But Griffith had not then clearly realized that the achievement of this programme could only

informed that Indian terrorists were very interested in Dan Breen, the Irish gunman. Congress at one period appears to have attempted to copy the tactics of the Dáil.

[1] *First Dáil*, p. 214, 17th September 1920. J. MacEntee deplores lack of discussion and the dictatorship of the ministry. Collins in reply says that 'the real difficulty was to get practical assistance from members. . . . The Dáil had absolute power to remove any minister'.

[2] For example, at No. 3, Mountjoy Square, where there were ingenious devices for concealing arms, documents, &c.

[3] *Second Dáil*, p. 51.

[4] Cf. his pamphlet of 1919, *To Rebuild the Irish Nation*. It is still in the spirit of *The Querist*.

follow, that it could not precede or accompany, the establishment of an Irish government with unchallenged coercive authority. In the early days of the first Dáil too much was hoped from a commission of inquiry into industries, trade, and commerce, with Mr. Darrel Figgis as secretary. The activities of the commission could mean little more than a gesture. The realities of the situation were admitted in a decree passed by the Dáil in September 1920.

> 'It is impossible', the decree stated, 'at the present juncture to establish a customs tariff and impose regular duties upon foreign goods on their entry into Ireland, and in consequence the protection of Irish industries must take the form chiefly of discrimination by individual citizens in favour of Irish products.'

The decree instructed the ministry of trade and commerce to compile a schedule which would aid the Irish people to exercise this discrimination.[1] But the procedure stamps the activities of this department also as those of a 'movement', not those of a government.

It is thus apparent that all the government 'departments' hitherto considered should be written in inverted commas; they did not govern, they did not administer, they did not substitute themselves for the British departments. It is also apparent that success in the more strictly political departments must be a prior condition to success in the public service departments.[2] The new polity began to take form within the old when it vindicated its authority in the spheres of local government and justice. The considerable measure of success which it won in these spheres was entangled (both as cause and effect) with the considerable measure of success achieved by the defence department. This in turn was interwoven in the same manner with the activities of the department of finance. The last mentioned did not indeed have to go very far in substituting itself for the British financial authority. What happened was that the British government lost a large amount of Irish revenue, and that the government of Saorstát Éireann was able to raise a sum sufficient to pay its employees and to wage its war.[3]

[1] *First Dáil*, p. 229.

[2] An important exception is the department of agriculture—the reason being that, in the conditions of Irish peasant society, it was able to exercise judicial functions. Its activities in land disputes will be considered shortly under the head of justice.

[3] On 21st August 1919 came the first public announcement of a loan, £250,000 to be subscribed in Ireland, £250,000 in America. Mr. De Valera was later allowed to increase the American issue. The Irish issue was closed in July 1920, having been oversubscribed by £179,000. Naturally, the raising of the loan was attended with great difficulties, as all activities in connexion with it were treated as illegal by the British government. For a discussion of taxation proposals, see *First Dáil*, pp. 180 ff. The finance of the Irish Revolution would repay study.

A writer in the *Irish Year Book* of 1921 described the local government bodies established by the Act of 1898 as 'the only English institution that has become a living and popular organism'.[1] In the elections of 1920 the republicans gained almost complete control of this living organism. Town councils and county councils throughout the greater part of Ireland mirrored the loyalties of Dáil Éireann. They took the oath to the republic prescribed by the Dáil. But they did not immediately break their connexion with the British central authority, the Local Government Board, from which they received grants. On 29th June 1920, the Minister of Finance, Michael Collins, argued that 'to send minutes to the English Local Government Board would be a recognition of their authority'.[2] He favoured a complete break with the Board, and the Dáil appointed a commission to consider the matter. The commission reported on 17th September recommending the break. This would involve the loss of the grants in aid, which amounted to one-eighth of the income of local authorities. To make good this loss the commission recommended the withholding of principal and interest on British debts, and in addition the drastic curtailment of expenditure on hospitals, child welfare, and health services for tuberculosis and venereal disease. This would save £370,000, but would still leave a deficit of £270,000, which, the commission suggested, might be met by diverting land annuities and income-tax to the Dáil's use. The Dáil did not accept all these drastic recommendations, but it accepted the principle of the 'clean cut' and proceeded to carry it through.[3] From October 1920 practically all the local government bodies performed their functions under the supervision of the local government department of Saorstát Éireann, which had its staff of medical, engineering, and accountancy officials operating throughout the country. The transfer of allegiance and effective jurisdiction was not effected without struggle; a detailed study of it would be closely interwoven with a study of military operations. The British authorities announced that local rates would be held liable for war damages; the Irish authorities proclaimed that the government would resist and punish any attempt to secure payment in this way. The Irish Republican Army destroyed the Customs House, and thereby 'eliminated the British Local Government Board as a serious factor in the situation'.[4] The British authorities warned the ratepayers that payments were invalid unless they were made to a 'duly authorised collector', and from time to time took unauthorized

[1] Kevin O'Shiel in *Leabhar Na h Éireann* (Dublin, 1921), p. 7.
[2] *First Dáil*, p. 184.
[3] op. cit., p. 212.
[4] *Second Dáil*, p. 35.

collectors into custody. In the struggle for control the efficiency of local government suffered; but services were in some fashion or other maintained, and maintained, for the most part, in the name of Saorstát Éireann. The department of local government, administered by Mr. Cosgrave, need not be placed between inverted commas.

Of equal importance was the success—although it was later interrupted—of the republican courts. 'It was a necessary, logical step of the Republic to withdraw litigation from British courts and put it in national courts.'[1] But the step was, at first, tentative and uncertain. 'Criminal courts'—the inverted commas are necessary—of a very rough and ready kind came into existence spontaneously; but civil courts owed their origin to a decree of the Dáil in June 1919. This decree aimed to establish national arbitration courts, whose proceedings would depend upon the consent of both parties; but it contained no plan for their institution. The next move was with local initiative. Within a fortnight West Clare had established an arbitration court consisting of the elected member, the president of the Sinn Féin club, and 'three other justices'. Galway quickly followed this example, which became the model of the general scheme adopted by the Dáil in March 1920 for the whole country. So far there was no direct defiance of British jurisdiction; for British law permits voluntary arbitration proceedings. Moreover, the Irish arbitration courts had not begun to compete seriously with the British machinery of justice. 'At first their operations were small and they received little publicity or attention, except in their immediate neighbourhood, till the great wave of land hunger which swept over the west in the Spring of 1920 gave them and the Republic at once the greatest test and the greatest opportunity.'[2]

It was the agrarian crisis of 1920 which brought republican justice 'out of the cellars'. That crisis had been chronic throughout the previous century, especially in the west. The British land-purchase acts had grappled with one aspect of it; they had achieved considerable success in fixing upon the land the occupiers of it. But they had done little to meet the problem of land-hunger among the landless, or among the equally large number of people existing on hopelessly uneconomic holdings. The cessation of emigration overseas during the War made this problem acute; it shut the customary safety-valve. Moreover, Sinn Féin propaganda and the rhetoric of militant

[1] *The Constructive Work of Dáil Éireann. The National Police and Courts of Justice* (Dublin, Talbot Press, 1923), p. 2.

[2] *Second Dáil*, p. 58. 'A Brief Survey of the Work done by the Department of Agriculture', presented by Mr. Art O'Connor.

nationalism had stirred up a revolutionary passion hungrier and more primitive than that which inflamed the imaginations of orators in the Dáil. In the congested districts of the west, national struggle meant a peasant's revolt. The reconquest of Ireland meant to thousands of starved and crowded families the conquest of their neighbour's farms. The war of independence meant a land war. Nationalist leaders of the past had frequently allied themselves with agrarian misery. The Easter rising had behind it not only a nationalistic but a social revolutionary force. But among the leaders of 1920 there was no partnership like that of Connolly and Pearse. The Sinn Féin movement revealed itself in this crisis as bourgeois nationalism of the nineteenth-century brand. It snatched at the opportunity of saving the threatened social order. In June 1920 an apprehensive Dáil considered it necessary to proclaim: 'All our energies must be directed, not towards clearing out the occupier of this or that piece of land—but the foreign invader of our country.'

'Big ranch and little farm were invaded indiscriminately—the small farms with so much frequency as to indicate the adoption of a policy of least resistance, till no holder felt his title or possession safe.'[1] British power was too shaken to grapple with this upheaval. Even individuals of British sympathies turned for protection to republican authority. 'Society'—that is to say everybody who had land to lose—'turned to the Arbitration Courts to save it from anarchy.'[2] But the Arbitration Courts were composed of local notabilities deeply implicated in local contentions, and they had not as yet asserted authority to compel individuals to enter them and to accept their decisions. The Dáil found itself face to face with a challenge and an opportunity. In May 1920 it sent Mr. Art O'Connor to the west with wide authority to act. On the 17th May Mr. O'Connor held at Ballinrobe the 'first public sitting of any court directly under the Dáil'. Two individuals, Hyland and Murphy, held jointly a farm of about 100 acres. On to this farm there had swarmed a crowd of peasant families. Hyland and Murphy, both of whom had large families to support, brought their grievance before the court by filling in a printed submission-form set out under the heading 'Dáil Éireann Arbitration Courts'. The court decided in their favour; but the aggrieved claimants refused to surrender what they had seized, and

> 'went throughout the fairs boasting of their contumacy and waxing eloquent on the futility of the Dáil's authority. But the Republic had a longer arm than they had given her credit for, and one night about a

[1] *Second Dáil*, p. 57. [2] op. cit., pp. 56, 60.

fortnight after the issue of the judgment the captain of the local company of the I.R.A. descended upon them with a squad of his men—sons of very small farmers like themselves—arrested four of them, and brought them off to that very effective Republican prison—an unknown destination'.[1]

From this time onwards republican justice took the offensive. 'In a few days public Courts were being held all over the country, and the Republic was making its first great constructive advance, and the outposts of the enemy were being correspondingly driven in.' The republican advance took two forms. In the first place, there were measures specially devised to meet the land crisis. Land courts established through the agency of the ministry of agriculture handled a multitude of claims to land. The number and recklessness of these claims became so embarrassing that on 29th June 1920 a decree of the republican government enacted that a licence must be obtained from the ministry of home affairs before a claim could be made in court.[2] At the same time the department of agriculture launched a land-acquisition scheme in an attempt to remove the causes of the agitation. In September 1920 the Dáil established a National Land Commission[3] to carry on both the judicial and economic-administrative sides of the land policy.

In addition to these special measures designed to meet the challenge of the land crisis, Dáil Éireann, taking heart from the decisive success which it was winning, made an ambitious attempt to substitute generally its own courts for the British courts. The decree of 29th June, referred to above, also established courts of justice and equity, and empowered the ministry of home affairs, if it deemed fit, to set up courts with criminal jurisdiction. The ministry quickly made use of its powers. By September 1920 the following organization was in existence:

(1) Parish Courts, composed of three members, meeting once a week and dealing with small civil and criminal cases.

(2) District Courts, composed of five members, meeting once a month, and dealing with more important civil and criminal

[1] op. cit., p. 60. [2] *First Dáil*, p. 196.

[3] op. cit., p. 231. The establishment of the Land Commission illustrates very well the ambiguities of this curious revolution. It was established by a decree of the Dáil. But it was constituted according to English law, 'a body corporate with a common seal'. Its functions were to 'hear and determine all matters whether of law or fact relating to land other than matters properly referable to the Common Law Court and Chancery Division', for which purpose it could compel the attendance of witnesses; and to receive applications for recommendation to the national co-operative bank or to a joint-stock bank for the acquisition of untenanted land for leasing or purchase.

cases, or cases which came by appeal from the parish courts. In addition, at three sessions during the year a circuit judge presided over the district court, which then became a 'circuit court' with unlimited civil and criminal jurisdiction. There were four circuit judges and four circuit districts.

(3) A Supreme Court at Dublin, composed of not less than three members appointed for three years, functioning both as a court of first instance and of appeal.

The legal code which the republican courts upheld was the law as it stood on 2nd January 1919, save as amended by the Dáil[1]—that is to say, it was English law.

In Munster and Connaught and in parts of Leinster the British machinery of justice almost entirely collapsed, and the republican machinery in greater or less degree supplied the needs of society. Even in Dublin republican courts contrived from time to time to sit, to give judgement, and to ensure that judgement was obeyed. The legal profession adjusted itself to the new order of things. Some individual members of the profession, even in the west, refused to appear before the republican courts, and for the time being gave up practice altogether. Others competed strenuously for their share in a diminishing volume of business. The Incorporated Law Society considered a resolution which aimed at preventing solicitors from appearing before parish and district courts; but the resolution was dropped. The Council of the Bar of Ireland passed a resolution declaring it unprofessional for counsel to appear before the republican courts; but a general meeting of the Bar decided to take no action against counsel who ignored the resolution. In the tribunals set up by Dáil Éireann the new polity was taking definite shape within the shell of the old one.

British power was now faced with the alternative of admitting its own futility or of crushing the republican courts by the systematic use of force. In choosing the latter alternative it had to face a tactical embarrassment, for the Irish courts still professed to be courts of arbitration. The British government claimed the right to use force, not on the ground that litigation and arbitration outside British courts were illegal, but on the ground that 'the courts functioned under the authority of Dáil Éireann and that this treasonable name appeared on paper in court or in the possession of individual judges,

[1] The Minister of Home Affairs was given power by the Dáil to declare inoperative any act of parliament, and the local government board was given power to amend the existing code, which otherwise was adopted. But there were few amendments to English law.

registrars, solicitors, or litigants, rendering the tribunals seditious and those appearing in them criminals'.[1] In addition, the British government attacked the revolutionary usurpation of police functions. On 6th July 1920 the Inspector-General of the Royal Irish Constabulary issued an order forbidding unauthorized persons to arrogate to themselves the duties of the police.

This is the logical point at which a study of the peaceful activities of Dáil Éireann might merge into a study of its military activities. For it marks the clash between two forces, each claiming the exercise of police functions, and each deriving its authority from a rival source. Logical analysis, however, distorts the disorderly succession of events by forcing it into a neat and tidy frame. The reality was far from tidy. Fighting did not wait upon the enunciation of logical propositions and the recognition of their conclusions. Yet, provided that the essential disorder of the struggle is not forgotten, it is profitable to consider now the theories by which the actors in the struggle explained it. Logical relations are not time-sequences or relations of cause and effect; but they are a help towards the understanding of those others.

The British and Irish notions of police activity may, therefore, serve to introduce the topic of the military struggle. The British policemen were half soldiers; the Irish soldiers were half policemen. The Royal Irish Constabulary had never been police in the English sense—people's police, village constables sharing in the village jokes. They lived in barracks, they carried arms, they were associated with memories of eviction and 'coercion'; they were not necessarily hated by the village, but they were outside its intimate life; they were at the orders of the district inspector and the resident magistrate who might be liked as individuals, but who nevertheless were members of an alien society. One did not call in the police when one had a difference with one's neighbour. Moreover, except when it was in the grip of a land crisis, the Irish village was over-policed in relation to its crime-producing capacity. The Church looked after faith and morals. And village opinion, though it showed patriotic tolerance of crime in the abstract (that is to say of crime at a distance), was zealous for good order in its own immediate affairs; it was quick to seize the difference between 'a gallows story and a dirty deed'.[2] It is this class of fact which explains the quick displacement of British police authority in the country, and the comparative tranquillity of

[1] *The Constructive Work of Dáil Éireann*, No. 1, p. 27, quoting statement by Mr. Lloyd George in the House of Commons at Westminster on 24th July 1920.

[2] Cf. Synge's *Playboy of the Western World*.

a largely self-policed society during the struggle which followed. The successes of Dáil Éireann in local government and the administration of justice could not have been won if the R.I.C. had kept control of the country-side. It was necessary to break what nationalist theory described as 'the intelligence branch of the British army in Ireland'. This was rougher work than theorizing in Dáil Éireann. Dáil Éireann indeed decreed that no Irishman might without treachery to his nation join the alien police.[1] It thus gave impetus to a movement which, by stopping recruiting in Ireland and by starting a rush of resignations, did in fact transform the R.I.C. into a force chiefly alien and, therefore, ineffective. Dáil Éireann also propounded the theories necessary for the legitimization of violence and its absorption into the life of a national state struggling to emerge. But the task of expelling the R.I.C. from their blockhouses was undertaken, not by formal order and decision of the Dáil, but by action of resolute bodies of the Irish Volunteers. By the spring of 1920 the British police had been driven out of the majority of villages in the west and south. British authority was confined to the towns. But what was the fate of village society, now that the customary defenders of law and order had been expelled? Seed-time and harvest, birth, death, and marriage, continued as of yore. The Church remained as the upholder of faith and morals. In matters of urgency, if any should occur, the local squad of the Irish Republican Army—energetic farmers' sons not unwilling to supervise their neighbour's affairs—were ready to do rough justice. They were the new 'police'. But the village was not conscious that a new state, called Saorstát Éireann, had taken form; for the time being village society, with its own resources, was keeping itself in rudimentary but sufficient motion. Then, in the late summer and autumn of 1920, British power tried to reassert itself in the country-side with the aid of new levies and mechanical transport. Lorries full of 'Black and Tans' roared along the roads at night with search-lights blazing. The 'Black and Tans' were ready to shoot. The villagers kept off the roads. The theory of the Dáil now became a reality to them. They felt that the foreigner was invading their country. They looked on the I.R.A. as their defenders.

In the theory of the Dáil the I.R.A. was only secondarily, almost as an afterthought, 'the republican police'; primarily it was the defence-force of Saorstát Éireann. Yet, as a matter of history, it had existed before Saorstát Éireann was dreamt of. The Irish Volunteers had been founded in November 1913; they were an autonomous

[1] Decree of 20th April 1919.

body, keeping themselves free from the control of politicians and aiming to be 'broadly national'.[1] They were governed by an executive elected annually at their own convention.[2] John Redmond succeeded, in 1914, in nominating twenty-five 'representative members' to the executive; but in the early stages of the Great War the original body, greatly reduced, regained its freedom by splitting from Redmond's national volunteers. From behind the scenes the Irish Republican Brotherhood controlled the Irish Volunteers; the price paid for this secret plotting was the indecision and ineffectiveness of the titular leaders and the main body at the time of the Easter Rebellion. After 1916 the organization was for a time driven underground. It began to emerge again with the rise of the Sinn Féin party. In August 1918 appeared the first number of its new official paper, *An t-Óglách*, which took up again the tradition of Professor MacNeill's paper, the *Irish Volunteer*—a paper which had not appeared since Easter 1916. The first number of *An t-Óglách* told the Volunteers that they were 'the Army of the Irish Republic, the agents of the National Will'. It told them that their function was defensive, but added that 'volunteers with weapons in their hands must *never surrender without a fight*'. It reminded them that they were not politicians; their duty was to obey the leaders whom they had chosen in convention.[3] It was the business of these leaders to conform the policy of the Volunteers to the national will, by co-operating with those bodies and institutions which 'in other departments of the national life are striving to make an Irish Republic a tangible reality'. The constitution of Dáil Éireann in January 1919 altered the situation. The leaders of the Irish Volunteers maintained that the republic had become in fact a tangible reality. Instead of co-operation their duty was obedience. The Volunteers must surrender their autonomy and accept the authority of the Minister of Defence responsible to the Dáil. As the army of a lawfully constituted government, they possessed a legal and moral right to kill.

> 'If they are called on to shed their blood in defence of the new-born Republic', declared *An t-Óglách*,[4] 'they will not shrink from the sacrifice. For the authority of the nation is behind them, embodied in a lawfully constituted authority, whose moral sanction every theologian will

[1] See The O'Rahilly, *The Secret History of the Irish Volunteers* (Dublin, Wheelan & Sons). The O'Rahilly was treasurer of the organization.

[2] A convention was held on 27th October 1918, and thereafter none was held till 1922, after the treaty split. The 1918 Convention elected De Valera president and Cathal Brugha chief of staff.

[3] *An t-Óglách*, vol. i, no. 1, 15th August 1918.

[4] Ibid., vol. i, no. 10, 31st January 1919.

recognise, an authority claiming the same right to inflict death on the enemies of the Saorstát Éireann, as every national government claims in such a case. . . . Dáil Éireann, in its message to the Free Nations of the World, declares a "state of war" to exist between Ireland and England. . . . The "state of war" which is thus declared to exist, renders the National Army the most important national service of the moment. It justifies the Irish Volunteers in treating the armed forces of the enemy—whether soldiers or policemen—exactly as a National Army would treat the members of an invading army.'

There is some support for the claim of an adventurous gunman that the 'war' began with his private enterprise;[1] but the leaders of the Volunteers made strenuous efforts to legalize all irregularities. Cathal Brugha had been the elected chief of staff; but he was now Minister of Defence. The basis of his authority was thus entirely altered. He accepted definite responsibility to the Dáil and submitted a report at every meeting; the Dáil passed votes of money to the army, and gave it a free hand in its operations.[2] After 30th August 1919 every volunteer took the oath to the republic. Gradually the old title of 'Irish Volunteers' went out of fashion. The Volunteers began to call themselves the army of Ireland, the army of the republic, the 'Irish Republican Army'. It was the last phrase, usually abbreviated to I.R.A., which stuck. The symbol of the republic began to take hold of the imaginations of the volunteers, who were taught in every number of *An t-Óglách* that they were the *real* army of a *real* republic. After the treaty the leaders of the majority found themselves embarrassed by the results of their too-successful indoctrination. *An t-Óglách* now attempted to state a strictly democratic, rather than a strictly republican, view of the military power. 'The Army is of the people, for the people, an instrument of the will of the people constitutionally expressed.' It was set up 'to safeguard the common rights and liberties of all the people of Ireland'.[3] But in

[1] Cf. Dan Breen, *My Fight for Irish Freedom* (Dublin, Talbot Press, 1924).

[2] e.g. on 29th June 1920 it voted 1,000,000 dollars to defence out of the American loan. *First Dáil*, pp. 172 ff. The work actually was not done by Cathal Brugha (who had continued in his candle-making business and would receive no salary) but by Richard Mulcahy, assistant Minister of Defence and chief of staff, with Michael Collins playing an increasing part. This is one of the origins of the feud of Brugha against Collins.

[3] *An t-Óglách*, vol. ii, no. 42 (13th January 1922); cf. vol. iii, nos. 43 and 49, where the sectional convention of 26th March 1922 is denounced as an 'act of military despotism' by men who want to be 'the masters and not the servants of the Irish nation'. At this convention Cathal Brugha and his followers repudiated both the majority of G.H.Q. and the Dáil—on the ground that these had repudiated the Republic and were no longer a rightful authority. Cathal Brugha's claims for the 'army' as a lawful power were similar to those made by Cromwell in 1648—but 'providences' were not so kind to him.

the following months a section of the higher command, with Cathal Brugha at its head, took up the position that the army was set up as trustee for the republic, to which the majority had been false. These leaders and their followers appropriated the title I.R.A. In effect they were assuming the autonomy which they had possessed prior to the constitution of the Dáil, and were denying the authority of the civil power.

Between January 1919 and November 1921, however, there was almost complete unanimity within the army and the Dáil in upholding the view that the army was waging a lawful war under the authority of a duly constituted civil power.[1] The irregularities of ambushing and shooting soldiers and policemen by gunmen in civilian clothes were officially designated 'guerrilla warfare'. The English designated these activities 'serious political crime'[2] or, more bluntly, 'murder'.[3] The Irish had an answer to the reproach of not fighting in uniform; in 1916 they had fought in uniform, but had not been granted the privileges of war; their uniformed leaders had been taken and shot. In 1916, and still more in 1919–21, common men on each side had conflicting ideas of fairness.[4]

The conflicting theories of the fighting which were held on the opposing sides, and the conflicting grievances and passions which accompanied the theories, ensured that the fighting would produce the maximum of squalor and savagery. General Macready, who commanded the British forces in Ireland, repeatedly urged that the government 'should recognise that the country was in a state of war'. If that had been done, the soldier's job would, he argued, have been easy. The enemy would have been forced into uniform, for every armed man taken in civilian clothes would have been shot out of hand. The country would have been under martial law; the military would have had undivided responsibility for its pacification, and un-

[1] *First Dáil*, p. 243, 25th January 1921. Mr. Sweetman, member for Wexford North, is attacked for accepting the British theory of the fighting. 'Mr. Sweetman seemed to agree with the British government that it was simply war when they did any killing but when it was done on the other side it was murder.'

[2] Sir A. S. Queckett, *The Constitution of Northern Ireland* (Belfast, H.M.S.O., 1928), vol. i, p. 15.

[3] Sir Neville Macready, *Annals of an Active Life* (Hutchinson, 1924), vol. ii, p. 437.

[4] e.g. Sean O'Casey's rendering of it in *The Plough and the Stars*:

'Sergeant Tinley . . Gang hof Hassassins potting at hus from behind roofs. That's not ploying the goime; why down't they come hinto the howpen hand foight fair!

'Fluther (*unable to stand the slight*). Fight fair! A few hundhred scrawls o' chaps with a couple o' guns an' Rosary beads, again' a hundhred thousand thrained men with horse, fut an' artillery . . . an' he wants us to fight fair! (*To* Sergeant) D'ye want us to come out in our skins an' throw stones?'

divided power.[1] Beyond question this course of action would have been more humane and far more effective than the course actually followed. But it would have meant acceptance of the Irish theory, and the recognition of Dáil Éireann as a belligerent authority. The British government would not admit a state of war, it would not even admit a state of insurrection; all it would admit was the activity of a 'murder gang' whose criminal operations were so persistent and widespread that the military must continue to act 'in support of the civil power'. The military authorities considered the action of the 'civil power' uncivilized, and hardly less embarrassing than the activities of the Irish. General Macready desired recognition of a state of war, partly to subdue the rebels, partly to 'enforce discipline among the police'. In January 1920 a recruiting office for the Royal Irish Constabulary had been opened in London, to fill the gap caused by the cessation of recruiting in Ireland and the stream of resignations. The new drafts wore the black belts and caps of the R.I.C., but owing to a shortage of equipment they were clothed in khaki uniforms. The Irish christened them the 'Black and Tans'.[2] In July 1920 an auxiliary force of cadets—nicknamed the 'Auxis'—was constituted to support the R.I.C. This force was well paid and contained a large proportion of ex-officers of the British army. General Macready would have preferred soldiers under military discipline. He thought them 'a tough lot'. 'As policemen they were useless.' There were good men among them, but under bad officers the 'Black and Tans' and the 'Auxis' 'became a danger to their friends and a disgrace to the uniform'. 'The only excuse that can be made', General Macready concluded, 'is that their methods did not surpass those of the rebels from whom they took their cue.'[3] A courageous judge, presiding over a court of the King in the west of Ireland, risked the vengeance of both sides when he denounced their activities impartially as 'a competition in crime'.[4]

Any attempt to describe the details of the fighting would be outside the scope of this book.[5] Broadly speaking, the struggle may be

[1] Macready, *Annals of an Active Life*, vol. ii, pp. 444, 470, 473, 474, 504, 534.

[2] The name of a well-known hunting pack of County Galway. A man named Sullivan—so the story goes—looked out of his window, saw a body of the new recruits in their novel rig, and exclaimed, 'There go the Black and Tans'.

[3] Macready, op. cit., vol. ii, pp. 481, 504, 521. Macready states—what Sir Hamar Greenwood denied at the time in the House of Commons—that a body of 'Auxis' was responsible for the burning of Cork on 11th December 1920.

[4] Mr. McDonnell Bodkin, K.C., County Court Judge for Co. Clare. At Ennis Quarter Sessions, 7th February 1921.

[5] From the Irish point of view the fullest account is in P. Beaslai's *Michael Collins and the Making of the New Ireland* (Dublin, 1926).

divided into three phases. In the first phase, which lasted to the summer of 1920, the Irish, despite their theory of lawful possession wantonly challenged by foreign invasion, were in fact taking the offensive. In Dublin, 'executions' planned by Michael Collins were breaking the intelligence system of Dublin Castle; in the country, a series of ambushes and attacks on police barracks, usually carried through by Collins's 'Squad', was driving the R.I.C. into the towns. Without these operations the Republican courts could hardly have substituted themselves for the British courts. But the British decided to regain their jurisdiction. A counter-offensive was forecast in March 1920 by the appointment of Sir Hamar Greenwood as Chief Secretary and of Sir Neville Macready as Commander-in-Chief. The spear-head of the counter-offensive was the new recruitment of 'Black and Tans' and 'Auxis', equipped with adequate mechanical transport. The new forces began to operate systematically in the summer of 1920, and they succeeded in driving republican jurisdiction 'into the cellars' again. This was the second phase of the conflict. The third phase is less clear-cut, for it is a period in which the British government began to oscillate uncertainly between the alternatives of a more ruthless coercion and of negotiation. It is the phase leading up to the truce of July 1921. Possibly it may be said to open as early as October 1920, when *The Times* published suggestions for a truce and negotiations between plenipotentiaries of both sides, under a procedure 'analogous to that of an international conference'.[1] In December, through the medium of an Australian Roman Catholic archbishop, unofficial discussions actually began. But the British Prime Minister shrank from open and equal negotiation with men like Michael Collins, and allowed himself to be persuaded that the 'extremists' were weakening.[2] On 23rd December the Government of Ireland Act 1920—called by the Irish the Partition Act—received the royal assent. In the succeeding months the fighting grew more violent. General Macready adopted a policy of systematic 'reprisals', not merely to intimidate the Irish, but in order to prevent or mitigate the far more shocking unofficial reprisals which would have taken place if the troops, like the police, had got

[1] *The Times*, 6th October 1920. Letter of Brigadier-General Cockerell, C.B., M.P.

[2] See *First Dáil*, pp. 241 ff. Collins believed that Father O'Flanagan and some members of Galway Council had given the impression that Sinn Féin was showing the 'white feather' and that this encouraged Lloyd George to smash through. He resisted a suggestion from De Valera that, while maintaining their front, they should lighten the burden on the Irish people. England, he said, was in a hurry to end the war, but Ireland was not. For the later moves leading up to Lloyd George's *volte-face* in June see Pakenham, *Peace by Ordeal*, Part III, ch. i.

out of hand. The Irish retorted with house burnings, 'executions', and attacks on military lorries. Both sides held hostages. The war was becoming more terrible. The British people began to realize that they were facing Machiavelli's terrible dilemma; things had come to such a pass that they must either exterminate the Irish or satisfy them. Sir Henry Wilson had put this dilemma in a curt phrase: 'Go all out or get out.'[1] The British government could not command sufficient nerve and ruthlessness to 'go all out'. It oscillated back towards negotiation. On 24th June Mr. Lloyd George addressed Mr. De Valera as 'the chosen leader of the great majority in Southern Ireland', and invited him to a conference in London at which the Premier of Northern Ireland would also be present. The form of the invitation was unacceptable to the Irish leaders; but on 8th July Mr. De Valera consented at least to discuss the bases on which a conference of reconciliation might profitably meet. A truce was subsequently declared, to date from noon on 11th July. The truce of arms was preface to a war of words.

III

The Treaty

Why did the British government reverse its course, eat its words, and offer negotiation to the Irish leaders? The military men lamented afterwards that the truce came when they had the rebels almost beaten. In the early summer of 1921, however, their reports were far less confident.[2] Moreover, the Irish struggle, formidable in itself, was encouraging revolutionary nationalism in India and Egypt, and was becoming a scandal and a danger within the British Commonwealth, and a stumbling-block to Anglo-American friendship. The direct and indirect costs of repression alarmed coolly thinking realists. But more important even than the calculations of British prudence was the revolt of the British conscience. The soldiers were forced to confess that their drastic plans were useless because England was not with them.[3] In scores of pamphlets and newspaper articles, appeals to British decency appeared over signatures which carried weight in England and Ireland and the whole civilized world. Sir John Simon asserted that Britain's conduct in

[1] Quoted Macready, *Annals of an Active Life*, vol. ii, p. 565.

[2] Winston Churchill, *The Aftermath* (Thornton Butterworth, 1929), p. 293.

[3] *Diary of Sir Henry Wilson* (Cassell, 1927), vol. ii, p. 295. Wilson was against martial law 'unless England was on our side'. Macready, too, was forced to adopt this opinion. See his *Annals of an Active Life*, vol. ii, p. 564.

Ireland was 'turning Mr. Lloyd George's heroics about the rights of small nations into nauseating cant'. Mr. G. K. Chesterton declared that Great Britain had 'crossed a line'—the same line which she had accused the Germans of crossing in Belgium, the line which divides civilized living from frightfulness. Mr. A. Clutton Brock compared the atrocities of the British government with the brutalities of Russian despotism. 'Not by calling in the aid of the devil', cried the Archbishop of Canterbury in the House of Lords, 'will you cast out devils.' The revolt of conscience expressed itself in newspapers so various as the *Manchester Guardian*, *The Times*, and the *Daily Mail*. In parliament it extended from the labour and liberal parties to conservative supporters of the coalition. Men whose names were inseparably linked with the high political traditions of their country, men like Lord Robert Cecil and Lord Henry Cavendish-Bentinck, separated themselves on this issue from the governing majority. The revolt of conscience spread into the cabinet itself. There it met and drew support from King George's deep desire, declared to the world in words spoken at Belfast on 24th June 1921, for 'a new era of peace, contentment, and goodwill'.[1]

The *Round Table* had denounced England's methods in Ireland as a policy in conflict with her own institutions. 'If the British Commonwealth can only be preserved by such means', it declared, 'it would become a negation of the principle for which it has stood.'[2] But in what form might the principle of the Commonwealth be rediscovered and expressed in the relations of Great Britain and Ireland? What could the British government offer? Hitherto it had obstinately kept its feet on the path along which it had shuffled and been pushed in 1913 and 1914. By following that path it had translated Irish dissension into a legalized territorial partition. In June of 1914 the project of home rule with exclusion for Ulster first took precise shape.[3] In September of that year the government gained time in United Kingdom politics, and lost ground in Ireland, by securing a Suspensory Act to accompany the Home Rule Act. In the discussions of 1916 and 1918 the area which would certainly demand exclusion from a home-rule Ireland clearly defined itself as six out of

[1] Typical material in: *Report of the Labour Commission to Ireland: An Analysis of Government Admissions*, by Sir John Simon; *Peace or ——?* by A. Clutton Brock; *What are Reprisals?* by G. K. Chesterton. Cf. many pamphlets by J. L. Hammond, 'A.E.', Brig.-Gen. Sir Henry Lawson (two very fair reports of fact), Captain Henry Harrison, and others. For the not unfavourable Sinn Féin reception of the King's speech, see *Irish Bulletin*, 30th June 1921.

[2] *Round Table*, vol. xi, p. 466.

[3] In the bill introduced by the Marquis of Crewe, 23rd June 1914.

Ulster's nine counties.[1] In 1920 the government had to face the expiry of the Suspensory Act which had postponed the 1914 measure of home rule. Either it must permit that measure to come into operation, or it must introduce new legislation. It chose the latter course. The Government of Ireland Act 1920 received the royal assent on 23rd December. This act was an exercise of legal sovereignty which paid no regard to the wishes either of the 'rebellious' or the 'loyal' Irish. The former wanted complete independence for a united Ireland. The latter abhorred the slightest tampering with the perfections of the United Kingdom. But, since some tampering was inevitable, they accepted provincial self-government merely as a means of separating themselves from the nationalistic south. The Act of 1920 partitioned Ireland into two entities with strictly limited powers of self-government, and with an attenuated link, the 'Council of Ireland', to mitigate the evils of present disunity and to keep alive hopes of re-created unity in the future.[2]

Even when it passed this Act, parliament was aware that it would not be accepted outside the six counties. The Act contained a provision for crown-colony government in 'Southern Ireland', which would come into force if a majority of elected members failed to take the oath of allegiance to the King. Only the four members for Trinity College took the oath. The one hundred and twenty-four Sinn Féin deputies were resolved to constitute themselves as the second Dáil, the sovereign authority of the Irish nation. . . . That was how things stood in June 1921. If the British government was now seriously seeking peace, it must produce proposals based upon an entirely new principle. In the old path there was no hope of peace. Nothing in the previous resounding controversies of union and home rule was relevant to Saorstát Éireann. Nothing in the domestic experience of the United Kingdom had any relevance to this new intractable will of nationalistic Ireland. But perhaps there was something relevant in the recent transformations within the 'outer Empire'? In Canada and South Africa bitter racial conflicts had been assuaged, ardent nationalist aspirations had been realized, within the framework of constitutional monarchy. Might not Ireland find contentment by taking her equal place among the 'autonomous nations of an Imperial Commonwealth'? Throughout 1919, 1920, and 1921 a small band of Irish idealists pleaded

[1] *Headings of a Settlement as to the Government of Ireland*, Cd. 8310 of 1916, and *Report of the Proceedings of the Irish Convention*, Cd. 9019 of 1918.

[2] 10 & 11 Geo. V, c. 67. Among powers withheld were income-tax, customs, and excise. The parliament of Northern Ireland still functions under this Act.

patiently, obstinately, against the violence and legalism of the British and against the loyalist or republican ruthlessness of their own countrymen, for the unity of Ireland as a self-governing nation within the British Commonwealth. On 9th May 1921 these idealists addressed to Mr. Lloyd George a memorial containing a concrete plan.

> 'It proposes that the Ulster Unionists should be asked, without abandoning the powers and privileges assured to them by the Government of Ireland Act 1920, to join with their fellow countrymen in an all-Ireland Conference with the aim of keeping Ireland contentedly in the British Commonwealth, and that those entitled to speak for the majority of the Irish people should be asked to abandon separation for the sake of unity.'

Supposing that the Ulster unionists refused to make this sacrifice for Irish and imperial unity? The document repudiated any design of compelling them, and pleaded that the British government, despite their intransigence, should take the initiative in offering to the twenty-six counties the status of a dominion, with such safeguards as might be necessary in the spheres of defence and foreign affairs.[1] Similar suggestions, hitherto obstinately rejected, had been made repeatedly by Mr. Asquith and other English leaders. They were now strongly urged by the dominion leaders gathered for the 1921 Conference, and particularly by General Smuts.[2] They did not altogether fit Irish circumstance. There seems something wooden and unimaginative in an attempt to shape an 'ancient nation' according to the dominion model. But the dominion model was something proved and definite, the product of experience which had justified itself elsewhere. It was a remedy lying to hand. It offered to Great Britain the chance of a last-minute escape from 'a policy in conflict with her own institutions'.

Why should the nationalist leaders consent to negotiate? There is no accepted record of their crucial discussions in the midsummer

[1] *Memorial of Certain Irishmen.* This was one of the publications of the Irish Dominion League of which Sir Horace Plunkett was president and Captain Henry Harrison, M.C., secretary. The League was founded in June 1919 and dissolved in November 1921. It published seven pamphlets written by Sir Horace Plunkett and numerous ones by others. The first prominent English statesman to advocate dominion home rule was Mr. Asquith, on 4th October 1920. Cf. his *Memories and Reflections, 1857–1927* (Cassell, 1928), vol. ii, pp. 187 ff.

[2] King George is said to have consulted General Smuts before his Belfast speech (Pakenham, *Peace by Ordeal*, p. 77). In a letter of 4th August Smuts strongly urged De Valera to accept Lloyd George's dominion proposals. The letter was published in *The Times* on 15th August to the indignation of the Irish (*Irish Bulletin*, vol. v, no. 53, 13th August 1921).

of 1921; only a great deal of controversy about them. It is nevertheless abundantly plain, from what both sides to the controversy have admitted, that there was a general readiness for some degree of compromise.[1] But what degree? That probably was not clear. It is likely that Cathal Brugha hoped merely for a truce which would make possible rearmament and reorganization, and that almost any conceivable treaty would have been repugnant to him. It is also likely that the rest of his colleagues were agreed in distrusting both his political and military judgement. They did not yet know the limits of British concession in negotiation; and they were beginning to realize the limits of their success in fighting. The republican courts were now hardly working.[2] The military reports were far from reassuring. There seemed no prospect of driving the British army out of Ireland. 'We have not been able', the chief of staff declared later, 'to drive the enemy from anything but from a fairly good-sized police barracks.'[3] Fighting had not yet established the republic. Dáil Éireann professed to have set itself the task of translating a republic *de jure* into a republic *de facto*, with what measure of success we have already seen. Some departments of government were chiefly make-believe, others were functioning with a fair degree

[1] This is proved by the scanty references in public session of the Dáil to the presumably fuller discussions about the oath which took place in private session. The Second Dáil took the same oath to the republic as the First Dáil had taken (for its terms see footnote on p. 110). On 26th August the ministry resigned 'on an issue of peace and war' and was re-elected. It took the oath again. But in his speech of 16th August Mr. De Valera had kept the door open for interpretations which qualify by conditions of circumstance the republican allegiance. Referring to the election of the First Dáil, he said: 'I do not say that that answer was for a form of government so much, because we are not Republican doctrinaires, but it was for Irish freedom and Irish independence, and it was obvious to every one that Irish independence could not be realised at the present time in any other way so suitably as through a Republic.' He then went on to recall the sanctioning of the republic, and the solemn declaration of the representatives of the people that they would give their lives in the endeavour to make the republic effective and secure recognition for it. On the occasion of his election as President in private session of Dáil Éireann, Mr. De Valera gave an interpretation of the republican oath which would seem to allow a still greater latitude of interpretation. In the treaty debate on 19th December 1921, Griffith thus referred to it: 'We took an oath to the Irish Republic, but, as President De Valera himself said, he understood that oath to bind him to do the best he could for Ireland.' De Valera referred to the occasion in these words: 'Before I was elected President at the private session, I said "Remember I do not take, as far as I am concerned, oaths as regards forms of government. I regard myself here to maintain the independence of Ireland and to do the best for the Irish people".' *Treaty Debate*, pp. 23, 25. The author prefers not to refer to other alleged pronouncements of the President whose authenticity is a matter of dispute.

[2] But some time previously Mr. De Valera had expressed a hope of getting them started again. *First Dáil*, p. 244.

[3] General Mulcahy. See *Official Report, Debate on Treaty between Great Britain and Ireland* (Dublin, Talbot Press), p. 143 (22nd December 1921).

of efficiency. A living Irish polity was beginning to form itself within the shell of the British polity; but it had not yet come into existence. At best, a republic *de facto* half existed. And had not Dáil Éireann begged the question of a republic *de jure*? No member of the Society of Nations had recognized the lawful existence of Saorstát Éireann. The only right on which Dáil Éireann could take its stand was natural right; the only recognition which Mr. De Valera could claim was 'self-recognition'.[1] By entering upon negotiations with the British, the Irish leaders hoped to gain from them that essential recognition which no single member of the international community had been willing to grant.[2] They had in addition a tactical motive. The relative success which they had so far won was due, not merely to physical force, but to the moral force behind it. Great Britain's weakness was due to her lack of moral support, within Ireland, throughout the world, throughout the Empire, within her own borders. But if the advances of a repentant Britain were flatly rejected by an implacable Ireland, the positions of the two countries might be reversed.

Tactics merged with principle in determining both on the English and the Irish side the methods of approach. You are the chosen leader of Southern Ireland, Mr. Lloyd George adroitly conceded to Mr. De Valera. His letter went on to assume that there was also a chosen leader of Northern Ireland enjoying equal authority. For the Irish to let this pass would have meant the acceptance of the Government of Ireland Act and the whole system of British law as the basis from which negotiation would take its departure. Mr. De Valera was equally adroit. I am spokesman for the Irish nation, he replied, and the man whom you call the premier of Northern Ireland is merely one representative of the political minority with whom I have to discuss Irish affairs in Ireland. Sir James Craig promptly repudiated this interpretation of his status, by accepting the invitation which Mr. Lloyd George had sent to him as premier, and by refusing to meet Mr. De Valera. There was therefore no basis upon which the three men could come together. De Valera, nevertheless, consented to meet Lloyd George in conference—in order to seek a basis for conference. This was the slender foundation for the truce

[1] The phrase occurs in De Valera's telegraphed communication to Lloyd George, 17th September 1921. 'Surely you must understand', adds Mr. De Valera, 'that we can only recognise ourselves for what we are.' Cmd. 1539 of 1921, No. XII.

[2] Cf. Michael Collins on 19th December 1921 (*Treaty Debate*, p. 35): 'I say that this Treaty gives us, not recognition of the Irish Republic, but it gives us more recognition on the part of Great Britain and the associated States than we have got from any other nation.'

of 11th July and for the four meetings between De Valera and Lloyd George during the same month.[1]

At these meetings each of the two men spoke in the language of his own theory, and each was unable, or professed himself unable, to understand the language of the other. But Sir James Craig, after a separate interview with the British Prime Minister, permitted himself an exercise in the phrases of natural right. Since self-determination was put forward as a principle, he would accept it on behalf of the people of Northern Ireland, who in the recent election had already by an overwhelming majority 'determined' their own parliament.[2] . . . The tests of nationality are in the last resort subjective: it is under different objective conditions that diverse communities in the same spirit declare themselves 'We Englishmen', 'We Swiss', 'We Germans', 'We South Africans'. Both in Dublin and in Belfast the people declared themselves Irish; but they qualified their declaration with adjectives—'We loyal Irish', 'We true Irish'—whose power to separate was, for the time being at any rate, stronger than the uniting force of the name they both claimed. To be 'true Irish' signified a will to separate from Britain, to be 'loyal Irish' signified a determination to remain in communion with Great Britain. But tests of such an extreme emotional subjectivity may be employed in an almost endless series of refinements. If the majority in the six counties were able to claim self-determination against the majority of Ireland, the majority of Fermanagh and Tyrone might in their turn claim self-determination against the majority in the six counties. The fragmentation and anarchy implicit in the principle might in theory produce an infinite variety of possible results; but in practice its action would be qualified by the effective will of a majority within a specific area. The area in which the 'loyal Irish' were able to make their will effective was the six-county area defined by parliament; and it was upon parliamentary enactment that Sir James Craig, despite his little excursion into Dublin dialectics, really took his stand. In this he showed tactical wisdom. Statesmen may try to assume a posture of lonely grandeur upon the 'rock of justice', but it is a slippery, overcrowded rock, and the jostling politicians and peoples perpetually push each other off it like children playing the old game

[1] The correspondence is in Dáil Éireann, *Official Correspondence relating to the Peace Negotiations*, June–September 1921, Part 1 (24th June–9th July). Lord Midleton, for the Southern unionists, accepted De Valera's invitation to confer in Dublin.

[2] Statement by Sir James Craig in *The Times*, 19th July 1921. Mr. De Valera, seemingly, admitted this argument in the Dáil on 17th August 'In the same way that the people of the North can recognise themselves if they want to, we recognise ourselves.' *Second Dáil*, p. 14.

'King of the Castle'. Even in Saorstát Éireann, the leaders would some day be forced to seek a securer foothold.

Mr. Lloyd George had in the recent past used all the phrases of self-determination and natural justice, but in his dealings with Sinn Féin he spoke from first to last in the language of constitutional monarchy. In this language were couched the 'Proposals of the British Government for an Irish Settlement', dated 20th July.[1] Only in one particular did the proposals seem to meet the Irish claim that the relations between Great Britain and Ireland were international relations. They suggested that the settlement between the two countries should be 'embodied in the form of a Treaty'. But the substance of the proposed treaty was dominion self-government, with safeguards for British security and for the fiscal unity of the old United Kingdom area. These safeguards were alleged to be necessary on the ground of geographical and economic fact. As for Northern Ireland, its status must not be altered by compulsion: the unity which was so desirable must be allowed to grow, as it had grown in Canada and South Africa. To the experience of those countries, the British document eloquently appealed. Ireland's road to freedom was the road which they had followed. Freedom would not be won by a repudiation of the Crown, but rather by that familiar transformation of it which filled the channels of monarchical authority with the strong current of popular will.

The British government offered Ireland freedom as a reality which could be secured and enlarged by means of the conventions and symbols of the British monarchy. To this the Irish replied that the offer was hypocritical, and that it would be unacceptable even if it were sincere. It was hypocritical in two respects. Nothing was offered to *Ireland*; something was offered only to one fragment of that Ireland which the British had broken into two pieces. And the something which was offered to this fragment fell far short of dominion status. The Dominions owed their freedom, not to the law and custom of the British monarchy, but to geography. If the Dominions felt themselves free, that was because the Crown was too far distant to interfere in their community life. But the Crown entrenched in the constitution of Ireland would be an interfering Crown. Moreover, the Crown had no right in the constitution of Ireland. From the arguments of expediency, the Irish now turned to the argument of natural justice. 'Ireland's right to choose for herself the path she shall take to realise her own destiny must be accepted as indefeasible.' This was De Valera's reply to Lloyd

[1] Cmd. 1470 of 1921, no. 1.

George.[1] To Dáil Eireann he declared that Ireland could deal with England on no other basis. 'It is as a separate nation that we are talking.'[2]

The exchanges, so far, had given small cause of hope for a fruitful negotiation. And yet they continued. Mr. De Valera's task was particularly difficult. He must avoid any concession which would enable the English to start whittling down the Irish demands. He must at the same time avoid any affirmation so uncompromising as to make the English despair completely of negotiation. Mr. Lloyd George showed himself ready to continue the discussion so long as the word republic was not mentioned. Both sides had reasons, which have already been examined, for seeking by negotiation objectives which fighting had failed to gain. De Valera added another reason. Ireland, he told Lloyd George, was willing to compromise on that 'absolute but amicable separation' which was her desire, in order to win for the nation 'the allegiance of the present dissenting minority'. How far would the compromise extend? Neither party to the negotiations knew as yet the limits beyond which the other party would refuse to go. Might not Lloyd George be moved at last to surrender the forms of monarchy for the facts of Irish reconciliation and a permanent association? Might not De Valera be moved at last to surrender the forms of republicanism for the facts of Irish freedom?

The two statesmen continued in correspondence with each other, and continued also at cross-purposes. Great Britain would never admit a right of secession, declared Mr. Lloyd George. Ireland could not secede, rejoined Mr. De Valera, from a partnership which she had not accepted. The reservations to the offer of dominion status, declared Mr. Lloyd George, were imposed by the force of geographical and historical facts. These very facts, retorted Mr. De Valera, compelled Ireland to secure additional guarantees against British domination. Both Mr. Lloyd George and Mr. De Valera appealed to the principle of government by consent of the governed, and each of them ridiculed the other's interpretation of that principle. Mr. Lloyd George cited the racial reconciliation in Canada as testi-

[1] Cmd. 1470, no. 11 (10th August).

[2] *Second Dáil*, pp. 10, 14. Mr. De Valera goes on to develop his idea of 'self-recognition'; cf. p. 82. 'We cannot change our position, because it is fundamentally sound and just. And the moment we get off that fundamental rock of right and justice, we have no case whatever. No fight can be made except on that rock, and on that rock we shall stand.' Cf. *Irish Bulletin*, vol. v, no. 28 (9th July 1926), quoting interview of De Valera to *New York World*: 'The world must support Ireland's natural right to be free.'

mony to the healing properties of a system of government by consent actually embodied in institutions of British origin. We do not consent, retorted Mr. De Valera, to that particular embodiment of the principle. The Ulster men followed the controversy and commented on it. If the British will consent to 'stand aside', argued Mr. De Valera, the Irishmen of North and South will settle their differences on the principle of government by consent. But we do not consent, interjected the northerners, to the British consenting to 'stand aside'. It is by our consent that the King is in our Parliament. . . . Who was the victor in these disputations? There could be no victor, since there was no common ground on which to fight. It was like the great debate between Cromwell and the English Levellers. Cromwell's wisdom of history and experience could not refute the logic of natural right, although it might win and persuade some of the logicians. And Cromwell, vexed with the fundamental problems of peace and unity, exclaimed at last to an unbending antagonist, 'I am as much for government by consent as any man, but where are we to find that consent?'

Neither Lloyd George nor De Valera won a doctrinal triumph.[1] But Lloyd George won a definite tactical advantage. It is true that the actual formula which finally made serious negotiation possible involved no surrender of the Irish position; for the conference was to meet 'with a view to ascertaining how the association of Ireland with the community of nations known as the British Empire may best be reconciled with the Irish national aspirations'. Reconciliation might conceivably come through an independent Irish republic choosing freely to associate itself with the British community of nations. And De Valera had suggested, if he had not stated, that, in 'self-recognition', Ireland was an independent republic. Not once, however, had he put forward a demand for British recognition. Not

[1] The correspondence is in Cmd. 1470 and Cmd. 1539 of 1921. The author cannot quite agree with Mr. Pakenham, *Peace by Ordeal*, p. 89, that Mr. De Valera won a dialectical triumph. It is true that Mr. Lloyd George gives an impression of humbugging, when one remembers his war-time pronouncements on self-determination. He would have accepted the De Valera argument of government by consent if it had been applied to an insurgent nationality within the 'ramshackle Empire' of Austria-Hungary; but he would not have it applied to an insurgent nationality within the British Empire! All the same, the writer thinks that Mr. Lloyd George had shifted to a view of government by consent which is truer to fact; although the manner of his shifting, in response to a British interest, may justly provoke cynical comment. Consent to government, either by an individual or a nation, may be looked on *a priori* as something 'original'. Or it may be conceived to be something which must be built up by experience in the process of history. The first view was implied in Mr. De Valera's letters, the second in Mr. Lloyd George's. The two views are well discussed in A. D. Lindsay, *The Essentials of Democracy* (Oxford University Press, 1929).

once had he insisted that a British refusal to grant this recognition would mean the end of negotiations and the resumption of hostilities. In general, De Valera and the members of Dáil Éireann took a higher line in debate among themselves than they did in discussion with the English—although, as we have seen, even in the Dáil they left themselves free not to insist upon a strict republican interpretation of the oath. On the British side there was no trace of ambiguity. When it agreed to negotiate with Sinn Féin, the British government was in advance of a large section of its supporters. It had to make it clear to these supporters, and indeed to the whole nation, that it would not compromise on the issue of allegiance to the Crown. On six separate occasions Lloyd George insisted in writing that Great Britain would under no circumstances agree to any abandonment, however informal, of the principle of allegiance to the King, upon which the whole fabric of the Empire and every constitution within it was based. Despite this reiterated warning, the Irish agreed to enter into formal conference. The presumption was that they were prepared, in the last resort, to yield on the issue of crown and empire. It is difficult not to agree with Michael Collins's defence of himself: 'It was the acceptance of the invitation that formed the compromise.'[1]

It is not necessary to follow closely the discussions of the Anglo-Irish conference, for its unfolding drama has already been revealed by the Honourable Frank Pakenham in his vivid book, *Peace by Ordeal*. This narrative need attempt no more than to review once again those principles and loyalties whose struggle has been its constant theme, clashing now in a moment of supreme decision.

The conference continued from 11th October until 6th December. It sat, not in a time of peace, but during a truce. The different theories of the British and the Irish had this common implication, that a failure to agree would involve the resumption of fighting.[2] During the last hours Lloyd George revealed this consequence—which, more or less veiled, was from the beginning of the conference until

[1] Dáil Éireann, *Treaty Debate*, January 1922, vol. i, p. 32. Cf. Griffith, at p. 21: 'In the letters that preceded the negotiations not once was a demand made for the recognition of the Irish Republic.' See also the interview of De Valera given to the *New York Herald* on 7th July, and quoted in the *Irish Bulletin*, vol. v, no. 28. 'Is there', the American journalist asked, 'anything in the constitution of the Irish Republic which makes it impossible to present to the Irish people any proposition coming from the British Government with respect to some new political relationship between the peoples of the two islands?' 'No', was the clear reply.

[2] The Irish leaders saw this clearly and kept it before the public. Cf. *Irish Bulletin*, vol. v, no. 33 (15th July 1921), vol. v, no. 40 (26th July 1921), vol. v, no. 81 (22nd September 1921), vol. v, no. 94 (11th October 1921), vol. vi, no. 8 (31st October 1921).

its end constantly in the minds of the two delegations—as an 'immediate and terrible' one.

On the issue which they considered vital, the British took pains to reiterate those clear and precise declarations which had been a feature of their written communications. If they had to fight on fundamentals, they insisted, 'there was no help for it'. Allegiance was fundamental. 'Any British government that attempted to propose to the British people the abrogation of the Crown would be smashed to atoms.' 'On the Crown they had no alternative, they must fight.' Repeatedly the British forced this issue to the front of the discussions. Here there was no concealment, no ambiguity, no imprecision.[1]

On the Irish side, the great weakness was imprecision. The Irish failed to make clear early and unmistakably to the British the limit where they were resolved to surrender their hopes of a treaty and allow the truce to lapse. They never stated clearly and challengingly Ireland's 'fundamentals'. Their failure was due not merely to the individual weaknesses of the delegates, or of the cabinet, or of the deputies of Dáil Éireann. It had a deeper cause. They did not know what their 'fundamentals' were. To Cathal Brugha, the republic was doubtless fundamental, and he was willing to take extreme measures to forestall and thwart any agreement which failed to secure recognition for it. To others, the fundamental thing was to 'do their best for Ireland', to get the most that could be got in extension of the British proposals.[2] The Irish leaders had not as yet worked out their counter-proposals. They had not in their own minds an agreed breaking-point. Their own success, the retreat of the British government to ground where it might stand with the support of the British people and a large measure of approval from the outside world, had removed the pressure which had closed Irish ranks in 1917. The Sinn Féin conference of 1917 had pledged itself 'to make use of any and every means available to render impotent the power of England to hold Ireland in subjection by military force or otherwise'. This pledge had united the champions of two historic theories, the sister kingdom theory and the republican theory. It had united the champions of two conflicting methods, the party-state method, which looked upon Sinn Féin as trustee of the undying republic, and the ordinary democratic method, which would submit

[1] Pakenham, *Peace by Ordeal*, pp. 181, 249.

[2] To what extent were these opposing views made explicit at the time? And where did Mr. De Valera then stand? Treaty supporters would say that he *later* shifted to Brugha's side, thereby making its strength. Treaty opponents would deny this.

both the party and its republican symbols to the vote of the Irish people.[1] So long as the British fought for the military subjection of Ireland, Dáil Éireann kept a united front as a coalition of patriots. Both parties to the coalition followed the republican banner, for beneath it was the rallying-point of defiance to an implacable foe. Every patriot would fight under this banner for the substance and the symbols of national freedom. But supposing that their fight had won the substance, would they still fight for the symbols alone? They valued and interpreted the symbols in accordance with their different habits of thought and feeling. When the foe was no longer implacable, when it confessed itself by its actions to be half beaten and half repentant, when it lost the will to military domination—then the different political theories and methods and the different temperaments which existed among Irishmen began to find themselves once again in opposition with each other. In October 1921 this opposition was still hidden, but an unconscious fear of awakening it warned the Irish leaders against probing too deeply into fundamentals. This at any rate appears a likely interpretation.

Irish champions of the treaty go farther; they maintain that the cabinet was at this time definitely ready to accept something less than the republic. If that were so, the division which was to split them came by a later reaction. Yet, even on this interpretation, the way was prepared—was it consciously prepared, and at the instance of Cathal Brugha?—for the reaction. There were sown now the seeds of the later controversy about the status of the negotiators. The cabinet chose five men to conduct the negotiation, and the Dáil unanimously ratified their appointment. The President issued credentials to them as 'Envoys plenipotentiaries from the elected Government of the Republic of Ireland', with power to 'negotiate and conclude' a treaty on behalf of Ireland. These credentials were sealed with the official seal of Dáil Éireann. But thereafter the President also gave to the duly appointed plenipotentiaries a second document—instructions which enjoined them to notify the cabinet of the final decisions which they intended to make, and to await a reply before they made these decisions. Did the second document destroy the force of the first one?[2] Was the first document intended primarily to trick the British into recognition of the republic? If so, it failed to achieve that aim. There was no formal presenting and accepting of credentials. So far as the formalities of negotiation were concerned, the

[1] See above, pp. 104–5.

[2] The credentials and instructions were quoted in the *Treaty Debate*, pp. 8 and 11, and led to endless controversy.

republican status of the Irish delegation never passed the bounds of 'self-recognition'.[1]

Mr. De Valera, by his own casting vote given in cabinet, excluded himself from the delegation. Griffith was chosen as leader. Collins reluctantly accepted nomination, and went to London leaving enemies behind him in the cabinet. As the negotiations proceeded, Collins found himself working in close harmony with Griffith, and these two were supported by a third member, Duggan; but Barton and Gavan Duffy, the remaining two members, found themselves criticizing their leader and inclining to the stiff republicanism of the secretary, Erskine Childers. At what time did this division begin to appear openly? Probably there was not much sign of it prior to Mr. De Valera's telegram to the Pope in the third week of October. At the beginning, cabinet and delegation were both unanimous about the course which they thought good to follow. There was to be no challenging demand for recognition of the republic. The republic was, if possible, to be smuggled into the treaty. Its existence was not to be acknowledged, but implied. These tactics necessitated a persistence in ambiguities. Only one document had been put forward as a basis of discussion. That was the British document which cabinet and Dáil had rejected. But the British had nevertheless made it plain that they would open discussion on a dominion basis. The Irish had no counter-suggestions ready. The Irish delegation brought with them to London an uncompleted document called Draft Treaty A, which contained in it the germ of 'external association'. But 'external association' was as yet only a vague idea; it was not a plan worked out in detail. Moreover, the 'Ulster clause' was not ready. Throughout, it was British pressure which forced the Irish towards precision.[2]

Inevitably, therefore, the initiative was taken by the British, and the discussion opened on the dominion plan, the Irish representatives challenging the reservations with which the offer of dominion status had been qualified. Draft Treaty A was not put on the table until the seventh and last plenary session of the conference, on 24th October. At the previous session Lloyd George, stung to action by the uncompromising stand on natural right taken by De Valera in

[1] Collins said in the *Treaty Debate* (p. 13) that the credentials were presented but not accepted. Griffith (p. 14) corrected this: 'I believe Mr. Lloyd George saw the document. They were neither presented nor accepted.'

[2] Pakenham, *Peace by Ordeal*, p. 172, describes the Irish proposals as 'discreet' both in their content and their omissions. On the delay in completing Draft Treaty A, ibid., pp. 145 and 152–3. On the vagueness of the Ulster clause even when it arrived, ibid., p. 159. On cabinet approval for these temporizing tactics, ibid., p. 145.

his telegram to the Pope,[1] had forced the Irish delegates from their reserve by demanding from them a plain yea or nay on the question of allegiance. But Draft Treaty A contained no plain answer. Lloyd George probed for one. What did the Irish mean when they said that they were ready for association with the British Commonwealth for all purposes of agreed common concern? What was the difference between adhering to the Empire and coming into it? 'By "adhere" you don't accept the link of the Crown?' 'We will accept the Crown', replied Griffith, 'as head of the association.' 'As allies?' inquired Lloyd George. 'Something more,' answered Griffith, 'permanent allies, not temporary.' . . . Long ago in 1867 Sir John Macdonald had described the substance of Canada's evolving relation with Great Britain as 'permanent alliance'. But Lloyd George was fighting for more than a relationship of substance. And De Valera was already insisting that more must not be conceded. 'There can be no question', he wrote to Griffith, 'of our asking the Irish people to enter into an arrangement which would make them subject to the Crown, or demand from them allegiance to the King.' But the delegation wrote back insisting on its freedom to negotiate, and pointing out that every association must have a head.[2] From this time onward the idea of external association began to take clearer form. Ireland could without inconsistency 'for the purpose of the association recognise the Crown as symbol and accepted head of the combination of signatory states'.[3] Such an offer would not admit the Crown into the inner life of Saorstát Éireann. 'For external affairs', explained Griffith later, 'such as peace and war and defence, Ireland will recognise the British Crown in the way we have explained, while for internal affairs she will retain the Republic.'[4] Out of the give and take of debate there had emerged a plan which was not impracticable, and which was capable of quieting tender consciences and saving the unity of the Irish nationalists. During the concluding days of the conference, the Irish delegation, after consultation with the President and cabinet in Dublin, and with their backing, offered a contribution to the King's civil list and even an oath—'I do solemnly swear true faith and allegiance to the Constitution of the Irish Free State, to the Treaty of Association, and to recognise the King of Great Britain as Head of the Associa-

[1] *Irish Bulletin*, vol. vi, no. 2 (21st October 1921); Pakenham, *Peace by Ordeal*, pp. 165 ff.

[2] Ibid., pp. 178, 182. On the same occasion Griffith put forward the idea of 'reciprocal citizenship' which is logically bound up with the external-association conception. See below, Chapter VI, p. 379.

[3] Pakenham, *Peace by Ordeal*, p. 193.

[4] Ibid., p. 244.

tion.'[1] But the British continued to demand an unqualified allegiance. And the British might argue that these slowly elaborated plans of external association, even with the oath added, fell short of what the Irish had already offered. On 4th December Gavan Duffy explained that the Irish difficulty was 'coming into the Empire'. Yet more than a month previously Griffith, in order to provide a basis from which Lloyd George could open fire upon Craig, had offered on behalf of Ireland 'free partnership with the other States associated within the British Commonwealth'.[2] The President was notified of this offer, and did not question it. But was it not natural to interpret these words as meaning that Saorstát Éireann, like Australia or Canada, should be 'within' the Commonwealth.[3] Lloyd George acted upon this interpretation, and in his letter to Sir James Craig of 10th November defined the first principle of a settlement in these words: 'Ireland would give her allegiance to the Throne and would take her place in the partnership of Free States comprised in the British Empire.'[4]

Sir James Craig had been on the wings of the conference; he had not been a party to it. He could not be a party to it because of the fundamental disagreement about his status. Sinn Féin would not admit his separate status as political head of a distinct community established by British statute, and Craig could not confess himself to be nothing more than the leader of a local minority within the sovereign national state called Saorstát Éireann. But, although the Ulster leader was not a party to the congress, he realized that its results might have important implications for the community whom he represented. His aim was to prevent the established separate and equal status of Ulster being bartered away by the British in order to achieve a settlement with the nationalist Irish leaders. While protesting that Ulster would not block the way of an agreement between Great Britain and Southern Ireland, he asserted that she had already, 'in agreeing to self-government', made sacrifices in the cause of peace, and he demanded that the British should keep faith with her by respecting 'the just equality exhibited throughout the Government of Ireland Act'.[5]

[1] Ibid., p. 261. The Crown as head of the association came to be known as the 'Chartres Crown'. There is uncertainty about a small point: whether 'associated states' or 'association' occurred in the form of oath accepted by the cabinet.

[2] Ibid., p. 199.

[3] An Irish critic rejects this interpretation, and the writer is not inclined to press it unduly: it is enough to state that it was a possible interpretation which Lloyd George adopted.

[4] Letter of 10th November 1921 in Cmd. 1561, p. 2.

[5] Sir James Craig to Mr. Lloyd George, 29th July 1921. Published in *The Times*, 15th August 1921.

The British delegates at the conference, no less than the Irish, had strong motives for attempting to move Craig from this position. They believed that if only they could persuade Ulster they would win a settlement by general consent. They believed that the emotional satisfaction of most Irishmen with the double achievement of unity and self-government would be infinitely stronger than the regrets of some Irishmen for the lost republican symbols. They wanted the unity of Ireland for the sake of the unity of the Empire. Sinn Féin wanted the unity of Ireland for its own sake, and was willing to pay a considerable price for it. But Ulster wanted unity with Great Britain. For this she was ready to sacrifice the unity of Ireland.

Supposing that the conference broke down on the issue of Irish unity? This would be a tactical advantage for Sinn Féin, for in the eyes of the outside world it would seem more reasonable to reject partition than to reject the real freedom which satisfied Canada and South Africa. It would be easy to say that Ulster prejudice was to blame for the renewal of fighting. The British then might find it impossible to command the moral support necessary for resolute fighting. Tactics, no less than principle, made it inevitable that Ulster would play a considerable part in the conference. But the weapons of tactics were double-edged. Just because the Irish delegates hoped to win Ulster, or hoped, if they failed to win her, to prove her unreasonable, they were compelled first of all to demonstrate their own reasonableness. It was in order to demonstrate this that they had offered 'free partnership with the other States associated within the British Commonwealth', and had thereby given the occasion for Lloyd George's approach to Craig on the basis of Irish allegiance to the Throne and Irish partnership in the Commonwealth.

Lloyd George, it must be admitted, had already made concessions at the expense of Ulster. He had raised the question of her territorial definition. What was Ulster? Was she the historic province of nine counties? Or was she the six-county area defined in the Act of 1920? Or was she an area of self-determination liable to be clipped and cut by a more exact application of the principle of self-determination? Lloyd George had allowed this last interpretation to come under discussion with the Irish delegation, and he attempted to make it a basis of discussion with Sir James Craig. In brief, his letter of 10th November proposed to Craig that Northern Ireland, while retaining her existing legislative powers, should surrender some of her existing territory, and should exchange her immediate legislative subordination to the parliament of the United Kingdom for an immediate legislative subordination to the proposed all-Ireland parliament.[1] Craig refused to confer on this basis. He insisted that the boundaries contained in the Act of 1920 were 'no less essential a part of the Act than the powers conferred upon the Northern parliament'.[2] And he rejected the idea of an all-Ireland parliament. Never would Ulster allow herself to 'be placed under Sinn Féin'.[3] If the British were bent on thrusting Ulster out of the United Kingdom, he argued with obstinate devotion, let them thrust her into the position of a dominion. Equality between the two areas of north and south was the principle of the 1920 Act. Equality now would create beside the Sinn Féin dominion another Irish dominion fervently loyal to the Throne. If separation were decided on, let Ulster be granted the power to separate herself from the separatists, and to march step by step with her British comrades.

> 'To sum up,' Sir James Craig argued, 'if you force Ulster to leave the United Kingdom against the wishes of her people, she desires to be left in a position to make her own fiscal and international policy conform as nearly as possible with the policy of the Mother Country, and to retain British traditions, British currency, British ideals, and the British language, and in this way render the disadvantages entailed by her separation from Great Britain as slight as possible.'[4]

Against this impressive devotion to the United Kingdom, the vision and subtlety of the new imperial statesmanship achieved nothing. Ulster had ruined the chances of an Anglo-Irish reconciliation grounded without ambiguity on the reconciliation of a united Irish people. The British delegation kept this door to peace formally open, and it also kept the plan of frontier rectification as a threat which might after all push Ulster through the door. But it turned again to the task of winning Sinn Féin from republicanism, without being able to promise the grand compensation of Irish unity. The Irish delegates, however, had already compromised their republican-

[1] In the letter of 10th November the plan of rectifying the frontier of Northern Ireland was thus expressed: '(5) The question of the area within the special jurisdiction of the Northern Parliament we have reserved for discussion with you. The creation of an all-Ireland Parliament would clearly further an amicable settlement of this problem.'

[2] Cmd. 1561, p. 5 (11th November 1921).

[3] Ibid., p. 10.

[4] This suggests a doubt of recent suggestions (by an Irish writer in the *Round Table*, vol. xxv, p. 40) that Irish unity might be reached if the British should confer dominion status willy-nilly on Ulster. The theory is that if Great Britain would 'stand aside' in this way, Ulster would move towards unity with the south. But might not Ulster use her dominion powers, as Craig suggested in 1921, to keep herself distant from Dublin and close to London?

ism in the hope either of Irish unity or a break on the issue of Irish unity. Moreover, a slip on Griffith's part made it difficult for them to exploit even the tactical advantage of Ulster's intransigence.[1] During the last days of the conference, therefore, the issue of peace and war narrowed itself down to the issue of external association versus allegiance.

The Irish objections to the Crown were of two kinds, emotional and practical. They had sworn an oath to the republic, and how could they swear allegiance to the King? To accept allegiance would inevitably create the most profound disturbances of sentiment and of conscience. Practically, they argued that by letting the King into their constitution they would drive out national freedom. The legal powers of the Crown, which meant nothing in distant Ottawa, would mean everything in Dublin. 'The Crown far away would never menace the Dominions with its powers. The Crown close at hand would prove a constant menace of this kind.'[2] Their insistence on this point had an important effect on the shaping of the treaty. Consistently with the method which they had adopted of veiling their republican aspirations, they emphasized, not their emotional, but their practical objections to the Crown. The British cut the ground from under their feet by offering them 'any phrase they liked which would ensure that the position of the Crown in Ireland should be no more in practice than it was in Canada or in any other Dominion'. They could write into their constitution, not only the law, but the custom, of dominion self-government.

This was the position on 2nd December, when the Irish delegation left London to confer with the cabinet in Dublin. The conference occurred next day, and laid bare divisions of opinion which were deep, but imprecisely marked. All members of the delegation and of the cabinet were agreed that the British proposals as they still stood were unacceptable, but there was no definition of the modifications which would make the proposals acceptable. Griffith made it clear that he would not break with the British on the Crown, and he insisted that no settlement was possible without an oath. But others would not accept the oath as it stood in the final draft. What oath, then? A possible alternative form was roughly drafted. Imprecision was now rooted in a deepening disunity.[3] The members of the delega-

[1] Pakenham gives a full account, *Peace by Ordeal*, part iii, chapters xii–xv; part iv, chapter ii.

[2] Erskine Childers in particular had developed this line of argument. See his Memorandum quoted in Pakenham, op. cit., pp. 247–8.

[3] Even Stack gives striking evidence of this imprecision. Quotation in Pakenham, op. cit., p. 331.

tion returned to London with contradictory impressions about the substance of the programme which had been decided upon in Dublin. Before long they were maintaining contradictory arguments about their own powers and responsibilities. Thus it happened that the signature of the treaty in the small hours of the morning of 6th December, although the prospect of 'immediate and terrible war'[1] made it the signature of all of the delegates, became matter for bitter personal recrimination. Individual hatreds envenomed the conflict of principle which from now onwards split the patriotic front.

But this narrative need say nothing about these personal recriminations and hatreds. The time will come when Ireland herself will approach without the bitterness of partisanship this period of her history, and will deal calmly and generously both with Cathal Brugha and Michael Collins, as Englishmen to-day can appraise and appreciate both Hampden and Falkland. Let us be content to say, as Mr. Pakenham has said, that 'Ireland had moved too rapidly to freedom to be certain where its essence lay'.[2] And let us for the moment consider only this aspect of the treaty, that instead of the 'external' Crown which a united Dáil would have accepted,[3] it retained in nationalist Ireland the symbolism of Britannic monarchy. It was on this that the nationalists divided. Some men believed themselves sworn to fight the treaty. It is 'a subversion of the Irish Republic', declared Cathal Brugha.[4] 'The meaning of it is that you are British subjects,' said Austin Stack.[5] 'The King will be part of the legislature of this island,' said Erskine Childers.[6] Other men believed that they might now with honour set themselves to constructive work in a free Ireland. 'I don't want a lecture from anybody as to what my principles are to be now,' cried Michael Collins. 'I am just a representative of plain Irish stock whose principles have been burnt into them.'[7] Griffith believed that he had done the best for Ireland according to his conscience and the true spirit of his oath. 'The difference in this Cabinet and in this House', he said, 'is between half-recognising the British King and the British Empire and in marching in . . . with our heads up.'[8] In the minds of De Valera and

[1] Mr. Pakenham says that Lloyd George's ultimatum was a brutal use of violence, and also that it was a bluff which the Irish, if they had kept cool, could easily have called. Is there not some contradiction between the two judgements?

[2] Pakenham, op. cit., p. 320.

[3] De Valera again put external association before the Dáil—academically—in Document No. 2, submitted in private session. It is printed in *Leahbar Na h Éireann* (The Irish Year Book), 1922, pp. 253 et seq.

[4] *Treaty Debate*, p. 403.

[5] Ibid., p. 28.

[6] Ibid., p. 39.

[7] Ibid., p. 35.

[8] Ibid., p. 20.

Brugha and Childers there was a bitter consciousness of what they had failed to win by fighting and conference—the republic: in the minds of Griffith and Collins and Cosgrave there was pride in what they had won—military evacuation by the British, an independence which was real and strong now and would be stronger in the future, the power to refashion a living Irish nation.

IV

The Dominion

The first sentence of the Articles of Agreement for a Treaty between Great Britain and Ireland laid it down that Ireland should have 'the same constitutional status in the Community of Nations known as the British Empire as the Dominion of Canada, the Commonwealth of Australia, the Dominion of New Zealand, and the Union of South Africa . . .'. This meant that Saorstát Éireann, if it ratified the signature of its representatives, accepted the status of a dominion. But Saorstát Éireann would be a most unusual dominion. Ireland's peculiar history compelled peculiar modifications and adaptations of the dominion model. The British reading of historical and geographical fact expressed itself in limitations, which might in part be temporary limitations, upon that right of individual self-defence which the other Dominions possessed. In addition, Ireland's withdrawal from the constitutional unit of the United Kingdom necessitated adjustments of financial and administrative questions. The treaty made provision for these matters.[1] But the treaty also gave repeated recognition to the Irish interpretation of Ireland's history. It stretched the framework of dominion status in the attempt to make room within it for 'the national and self-derived statehood' which Ireland claimed.

It was a truism that the Dominions enjoyed by custom and constitutional practice a status of equality which was not theirs in law. The treaty gave to Ireland a legal guarantee of this actual status. It thereby marked an important step in the process by which the customary content of dominion nationhood was transformed into positive law. In one or two particulars—the appointment of the Governor-General and the relations of executive and legislature were the two most notable examples[2]—the treaty itself made specific

[1] Articles 7 and 8 and the Annex dealt with defence. Article 7, as was pointed out both in the Dáil and in the House of Commons, negatived in fact the claim to neutrality which the Irish had put forward.

[2] Article 1 laid it down that the executive should be responsible to a 'Parliament having powers to make laws for the peace, order and good government of Ireland'.

reference to this content. In general, however, the treaty reflected the view then prevalent that a detailed definition of rights which were still expanding would have a restrictive effect.[1] The result was to bring Irish reinforcements to those nationalistic forces at the imperial conference, whose aim was to state in legal terms the transformation which the British Commonwealth had undergone in practice.

Another sign of the peculiar individuality of the new Dominion was the form of parliamentary oath for which the treaty made provision. The monarchical symbolism of the oath proved itself to be the most obvious stumbling-block to that appeasement which the treaty aimed to achieve. Yet there was a marked deviation from the form of oath which was the rule in Great Britain and the Dominions. The Irish representative was not called upon to swear direct allegiance to the King. He must swear true faith and allegiance to the constitution of the Irish Free State as by law established. Thereafter, he must swear that he would be *faithful* to His Majesty the King and his successors 'in virtue of the common citizenship of Ireland with Great Britain and her adherence to and membership of the group of nations forming the British Commonwealth of Nations'. The primary obligation solemnly recognized in the oath was to the Irish constitution. The obligation to the King was secondary and—so it was argued both in the Dáil and the House of Commons—conditional. 'Paradoxical as it might seem,' writes Dr. Kohn, 'it was the expression of the Free State's adherence to the British Commonwealth in the feudal rite of an oath of fidelity to a sovereign liege which symbolised the full measure of its freedom in the new bond of association.'[2]

There was another recognition, still more striking, of the Irish interpretation of Ireland's history. This recognition was contained in the very form and title of the signed document. The document was an agreement for a treaty between 'Great Britain and Ireland'. Here was the British acceptance of the claim put forward by Dáil Éireann to speak for a united Ireland. This acceptance was empha-

Article 2 provided that Canadian practice should govern the relationship between the representative of the Crown and the Free State. Article 3 provided for the Canadian method of appointment. Mr. Lloyd George put on record in a letter to Mr. Griffith what the method was.

[1] Cf. Mr. Churchill, Hansard, *House of Commons Debates*, vol. cli, 2nd March 1922, col. 686: 'What the British Empire exhibits more than anything else is the result of freedom of growth.' The champions of the treaty in the Dáil agreed with its opponents that it could not represent a 'final settlement', but they disagreed with them (*a*) in insisting that the practical equality of dominion status nullified theoretical subjection, and (*b*) that the treaty, so far from being an inflexible limitation of Irish growth, would make possible peaceful growth in the future.

[2] Leo Kohn, *The Constitution of the Irish Free State* (Allen & Unwin, 1932), p. 56. Loc. cit. for excellent discussion of oath and references.

sized in articles 11 to 15 of the document, and was implied even in the annex to it. In the duel of principle and tactics which had been opened in June between Mr. De Valera and Sir James Craig, the latter was now marked definitely as the loser. In theory Ulster had been 'placed under Sinn Féin'. In theory the formal recognition of the unity of Ireland within the political form of Saorstát Éireann nullified the partition of 1920. In practice, however, careful provision was made for maintaining the actual status of Northern Ireland, by permitting her to perform a definite act of withdrawal from Saorstát Éireann. She might perform this act by means of an address, from both Houses of the Parliament of Northern Ireland, presented to His Majesty within one month from the passing of the British act ratifying the articles of agreement.[1] In the meantime, the powers of the Irish Free State would not extend to Northern Ireland. The six counties were given a period for reflection and choice. They might explore the ground of unity, and seek, by negotiation with the Free State, additional amplifications and guarantees of the local autonomy which was theirs by the statute of 1920.[2] But if they should decide to maintain their separation from the Free State and their existing connexion with the United Kingdom, they must resign themselves to a rectification of their boundaries in accordance with the decision of a specially constituted Boundary Commission. In either event, the Ulster leaders had the worst of the argument. They had insisted upon their separate status. They had also claimed that the territorial limits defined in 1920 were an inseparable part of those 'existing rights' which the British had agreed to respect. On both these issues they were rebuffed. However, once again there was an opposition between theory and practice. In practice, so later events proved, the 'existing rights' remained intact.[3]

[1] The 'Ulster month' was postponed by Section I (5) of the Irish Free State Agreement Act of 31st March 1922 (12 Geo. V, ch. i). This was an act to give force of law to the articles of agreement for a treaty between Great Britain and Ireland; but the sub-section declared that it should not be deemed the act for ratification referred to in article 11 of the treaty. Section 5 of the Irish Free State Constitution Act of 5th December 1922 (13 Geo. V, ch. i) laid it down that this should be treated as the act of ratification from which the month referred to should run.

[2] Article 15 mentioned some of the heads which might be included in negotiations for safeguards to satisfy Northern Ireland, and gave in advance the form of law to any agreement which might be reached.

[3] Undoubtedly the Irish delegates, and particularly Collins, believed—and thought that Lloyd George shared their belief—that by means of the Boundary Commission the Irish Free State would gain such a large increase of territory that Northern Ireland, in all probability, would be unable to maintain her separate existence. See Pakenham, *Peace by Ordeal*, pp. 274–5, 323, 346, 386, and *Treaty Debate*, p. 35.

The statement of Lloyd George in the House of Commons gave some cause for

Revolutionary Irish nationalism had thus gained formal recognition of its claim to speak for a united Ireland. Had it also gained recognition of its claim to *de jure* sovereignty? Throughout the negotiations leading up to the agreement, the British government had avoided all words and actions which would imply this recognition. But what of the form in which the agreement was recorded? What of the word 'treaty'? Are not treaties agreements between sovereign authorities? The Irish representatives, it was true, accepted for the future, on behalf of Ireland, the status of a dominion. Here there was no ambiguity. But what was Ireland's status at the moment of this acceptance? Here the English failed to achieve their customary precision. Here the jurists still disagree. The Irish government, say some, was never more than a *de facto* revolutionary authority which had partially established itself; the form and style of a treaty, therefore, represented merely a concession to Irish sentiment.[1] The treaty, others say, when read in the light of British elucidations of it, implied 'that *in statu nascendi* the new Irish State had been recognised as a sovereign entity'.[2] British statesmen gave evidence of some uneasiness and some uncertainty when they were pressed on this issue. Mr. Churchill invited the House of Commons to think chiefly of the future, when Ireland's position with regard to treaties would be that of Canada, Australia, and other dominions. The description of the present instrument as a treaty, he said, connoted 'the closing of an episode'.[3] But what kind of episode? Government spokesmen deprecated excessive probing. 'In my opinion', declared the Attorney-General, 'this is not an occasion for constitutional pedantry.' Yet the controversy raised two important questions.

misgiving, but did not quench these hopes. See Hansard, *House of Commons Debates*, vol. cxlix, 16th December 1921, col. 314–15. The actual wording of the treaty, however, established no single principle whose operation was bound to fulfil the expectations which had been raised. Article 12 provided that the Boundary Commission, if Northern Ireland's withdrawal from the Free State should make it necessary to erect it, would be composed of three persons, one to be appointed by the government of the Irish Free State, one to be appointed by the government of Northern Ireland, and one, the chairman, to be appointed by the British government: and that the Commission should delimit the boundaries 'in accordance with the wishes of the inhabitants, so far as may be compatible with economic and geographic conditions'. Here was a second principle to check the operation of the first. See below, p. 162, note 1.

[1] Cf. Philip Noel Baker, *The Present Juridical Status of the British Dominions in International Law* (Longmans Green, 1929), p. 319.

[2] Kohn, *Constitution of the Irish Free State*, pp. 56–9, and references.

[3] Hansard, *House of Commons Debates*, vol. cli, 2nd March 1922, col. 620. Cf. Professor Berriedale Keith, *Letters on Imperial Relations*, No. 22. In this letter (10th December 1921) Professor Keith maintained that the official description of the instrument implied the recognition of Ireland 'as a sovereign Power'.

'The first is whether the Irish Republic, which in Ireland is considered to have been one of the parties to the Treaty, was an international entity and would therefore come into existence again were the Treaty abrogated. The second is whether treaties made between members of the British Commonwealth are international or domestic documents.'[1]

These doubts sprang from the form of the agreement only. In the substance of it the British successfully avoided any recognition of Dáil Éireann. Articles 17 and 18, which provided for the transition from the existing situation—of which there was no agreed definition—to the future dominion constitution, and for the acceptance and ratification of the signed instrument, allotted to Dáil Éireann no part either in the process of transition or in the process of acceptance and ratification. On the British side, future procedure was easy and clear. His Majesty's government would hand over to an Irish provisional government, whose constitution was provided for in article 17, the necessary powers and machinery. His Majesty's government would submit the present instrument to the approval of parliament, and thereafter would secure the legislation necessary for its ratification. It was thus the destiny of the Articles of Agreement for a Treaty between Great Britain and Ireland to become the schedule to a British act of parliament.[2] The moment of ambiguity, surely, might now pass into oblivion. The legal processes of British monarchy resumed their normal march—towards a fulfilment which, it must be confessed, would have seemed in 1922, if it had been prophesied then, fantastically unwelcome and paradoxical.[3]

Regarded from the Irish point of view, the transitional articles of the treaty created an awkward situation, having regard to the theory maintained in the recent past. To a section of the Irish nationalists

[1] Mansergh, *The Irish Free State: its Government and Politics*, p. 42. By registering the treaty at Geneva the Irish showed that they regarded it as an international instrument. The British protested that in their view the Covenant of the League and conventions concluded under the League were not intended to govern the relations *inter se* of various parts of the British Commonwealth. The Irish in their turn protested that in their view article 18 of the Covenant imposed on them a clear and unequivocal obligation to register the treaty. See League of Nations, *Treaty Series*, vol. xxvii, 1924, pp. 449–50. Underlying the British view was anxiety lest disintegration of the Empire might come through the full action of international law being admitted into Empire relationships and driving out the constitutional law of the British monarchy.

Generally speaking, there was in 1922 a tendency on the British side to minimize the treaty element in the complicated processes of the Irish settlement. Ten years later the British were laying great stress on this element. See below, pp. 321–2.

[2] Irish Free State (Agreement) Act, 1922 (12 Geo. V, ch. 4).

[3] See particularly *Moore* v. *Attorney General of the Irish Free State* (1935: 51 T.L.R.) as revealing implications of the Statute of Westminster, 1931.

these articles seemed to compel a definite denial of the national theory, and to make a breach in the loyalties on which the theory rested. The lawful authority in Ireland was Dáil Éireann. The negotiators sent to London were sent by Dáil Éireann and were responsible to Dáil Éireann. The treaty which the delegation had brought back from London contained no mention of Dáil Éireann. The treaty was to be submitted for approval, not to Dáil Éireann, but 'to a meeting summoned for the purpose of the members elected to sit in the House of Commons of Southern Ireland'. If approved, the treaty was to be ratified by some body whose composition was not specified.[1] The British government was indeed surrendering within the twenty-six counties what was left of the administrative machinery which it had controlled since the Act of Union, but it was not making this surrender to Dáil Éireann. Under article 17 it would transfer to a provisional government, chosen by 'members of parliament elected for constituencies in Southern Ireland since the passing of the Government of Ireland Act, 1920', the powers and machinery necessary for the discharge of its duties pending the constitution of a parliament and government of the Irish Free State. But Saorstát Éireann claimed to possess already a parliament and government. Saorstát Éireann knew nothing and would admit nothing about 'Southern Ireland' and the members elected for its 'House of Commons'. These belonged to the jargon of usurping British legalism; they meant nothing to the rightful Irish nation. From now on, therefore, the signatories of the treaty found themselves in a dual position. Undoubtedly they must secure the support of Dáil Éireann, the authority on whose behalf they claimed to have acted. But they must also call into being that other assembly, whose authority was necessary, according to the treaty, during the transitional period of the immediate future. They brought the treaty back to Dáil Éireann, which on the 7th January 1922, after two weeks of bitter debate, accepted it by a majority of seven. The meeting of members elected to sit in the House of Commons of Southern Ireland was held on the 14th January, and those present accepted the treaty unanimously. Only the majority-party of the Dáil and the four members chosen by Trinity College attended. The fifty-seven members of the Dáil who had refused to vote for the treaty would not recognize a body

[1] Irish ratification of the treaty is contained in the Constitution of the Irish Free State (Saorstát Éireann) Act, section 2: 'The said Constitution shall be construed with reference to the Articles of Agreement between Great Britain and Ireland . . . which are hereby given the force of law.' This Act (no. 1 of 1922) became in Irish theory the basis of the constitutional law of the Free State. Section 2 of the Act was repealed in 1932. For further discussion see Chapter VI, Section II, below.

which by definition was a denial both of Irish sovereignty and Irish unity.[1] It is said, with perfect truth, that the second Dáil never ratified the treaty. Ratification was the work of the body known as the third Dáil. Approval of the treaty, which article 18 laid down as a condition precedent to ratification, was a dual process. The second Dáil approved it by a majority-vote. By this act of approval it sanctioned also that other process of approval which the treaty itself enjoined.

During the months of transition to the new constitution of Saorstát Éireann there was also, as regards administration, a similar duality. After the Dáil's vote approving the treaty Mr. De Valera resigned his presidency. On the 9th January a motion for his re-election was defeated by 60 votes to 58. On the 10th January 1923 Arthur Griffith was elected as President by the pro-treaty majority, the opponents of the treaty having left the Dáil. Both before his election and after it Mr. Griffith pledged himself to keep the republic in being until such time as the establishment of the Free State was 'put to the people, to decide for or against'.[2] As President of Dáil Éireann, Griffith chose a ministry which the Dáil accepted. But at the same time Griffith accepted responsibility for the constitution of a provisional government according to article 17 of the treaty. Griffith himself refused to complicate his position further by accepting membership of the provisional government, which otherwise coincided very closely with the ministry approved by Dáil Éireann.[3] The provisional government was constituted under the leadership of Michael Collins on the 14th January, and two days later the British handed over Dublin Castle to it.

In form, dual government continued until the 9th September 1922, when Mr. Cosgrave, who had succeeded Michael Collins as head of the provisional government, announced to the third Dáil the end of the dual system. In practice, the provisional government had from the beginning shouldered the responsibility for ruling. It had a double mandate: a direct mandate from the assembly named in the treaty, and an indirect one from the Dáil itself, granted by the majority vote for the treaty. It also possessed the machinery and

[1] It did not, like the Dáil, formally purport to represent all Ireland. One should realize, however, that it was not identical with the parliament of Southern Ireland contemplated by the Act of 1920: e.g. it was not bicameral, nor was it summoned by the Lord-Lieutenant, nor did its members take the oath enjoined in that act.

[2] *Treaty Debate*, pp. 400 and 411.

[3] The members of the new Dáil ministry were: Arthur Griffith, Michael Collins, Gavan Duffy, E. Duggan, W. T. Cosgrave, Kevin O'Higgins, Richard Mulcahy. The members of the provisional government were: Michael Collins, W. T. Cosgrave, E. Duggan, P. Hogan, F. Lynch, J. McGrath, Eoin MacNeill, Kevin O'Higgins.

the powers which the British had handed over to it. Obviously, the real responsibility and the real power belonged to it. Its task was a twofold one: first, to prepare the constitution of the Free State, and secondly, to maintain conditions of peace and order which would make it possible both to obtain a vote of the Irish people upon the treaty settlement, and at the same time to bring into being a representative body with power to adopt the constitution. Article 17 of the treaty allotted to the provisional government for the completion of its task a period of twelve months from the date when the treaty was signed.

The price paid for achievement was civil war. The cleavage between the supporters of the treaty and its opponents was too deep to be bridged by majority decision. On the 9th December 1921, when Mr. De Valera announced to the Irish people his disapproval of the treaty, he also pleaded with them not to depart from the 'definite constitutional way of resolving our difficulties'. Assuredly, the constitutional method which he had in mind was decision by Dáil Éireann. Even after the vote for the treaty and the rejection of the motion to re-elect Mr. De Valera as President, there seemed some ground for hoping that the minority would still undertake the task of constructive opposition, in order 'to get the best out of that treaty'.[1] Events soon proved that this hope was a delusion. The revolutionary upheaval was not yet ready to subside. The principle of indefeasible republican right opposed itself to the majority principle. Early in the debate on the treaty Erskine Childers raised the question 'whether this assembly shall, or even can, surrender its independence'.[2] In the end, a large section of the opponents of the treaty took the ground that the Dáil had no power to subvert the republic. This section, therefore, refused to accept either the vote on the treaty or the processes which had led to the establishment of the provisional government. That government was in its eyes an 'unlawful authority'. Gradually there emerged a complete theory in justification of republican resistance to the provisional government, and to the elected assembly which might thereafter purport to establish a constitution for the Irish Free State, and to exercise authority in its name. The second Dáil, according to this theory, possessed authority grounded upon three principles: the existence of the republic, the sanctity of national independence, and the territorial integrity of Ireland. It possessed no authority to deny these principles. The second Dáil had not voted—it could not

[1] See Mr. De Valera's speech of 9th January, *Treaty Debate*, p. 38.
[2] Ibid., p. 37.

have voted—for a treaty which subverted these principles. Its vote had been merely a vote against war. Moreover, the second Dáil had never been dissolved. Despite the pretence of democratic elections, the second Dáil, whether in its numerical completeness or in an ideal purity achieved by the exclusion of those members who had been false to their oath, remained and must remain the sovereign authority over Ireland.[1]

Behind these theories were guns. The guns were ready to go off, it must be admitted, before the theories were elaborated in their final symmetry. The men with guns had no very great respect for the second Dáil, even in the idealized form of its purification from the contaminating participation of the faithless majority. The unsubtle militarist mind was quite willing to solve all problems by a dictatorship of the Irish Republican Army. The I.R.A., it was pointed out, was in existence before the Dáil; and, as a condition of accepting the jurisdiction of the Dáil, it had insisted on all members taking the oath of allegiance to the republic.[2] In this statement there was some distortion of historical fact, for the original autonomy of the Irish Volunteers dated from a time anterior to the republican declaration of independence issued by Dáil Éireann. Putting back the clock would restore the army's freedom from political control, but in logic it would also remove the army's republican label. The angry republicans in the army were not, however, concerned with these niceties of logic and historical accuracy. Their purpose was to defy the provisional government and to prevent it from establishing the Free State by the processes provided for in the treaty. They regarded themselves as a lawful power and trustees of the undying republic. Their method was force. When the Dáil thought better of its promise to permit a convention of the army, the republican section held a conference of its own and announced the organization of 'executive forces' to defend the republic.[3] In April these forces established themselves in the Four Courts and organized themselves

[1] For examples of these arguments see the pamphlet *By What Authority*, which, from the extreme republican point of view, traverses the events from the vote on the treaty to the June elections and the attack on the Four Courts. The differences as to principle and expediency within the republican ranks, the relativity of some of the theories in the light of a changing political situation, and the difficulty of harmonizing the wishes of political and military leaders, are brought out in some letters captured and published by the Free State government. See the *Correspondence of Mr. Eamon De Valera and others*, Dáil Éireann, P.P. 1, 1922.

[2] See the pamphlet *The Responsibility*.

[3] Cf. *By What Authority*: 'The control of the Republican Army was taken out of the hands of the men who would risk even Civil War to surrender the independence of their country.'

for action throughout the country. At the same time they threatened to open a border-war in the north; for they held it their duty to fight until the English were expelled from Ireland.

Throughout the first half of 1922 the provisional government, led by Michael Collins, felt itself compelled to proceed by a series of improvisations and compromises. The government believed itself bound to honour the signature of the treaty and to honour the acceptance of it by vote of the Dáil and by vote of the assembly stipulated in the treaty. The government was also desperately anxious to secure from the Irish people a free vote which would contain the people's verdict on the treaty and would permit the people's representatives to proceed with the constitution of the Free State. It also cherished the hope that a successful prosecution of these tasks might induce the people of the six counties to think very seriously before they exercised their right of petitioning for separation from the Free State.[1] But overshadowing even these preoccupations was the dread of civil war. War between old comrades was in itself a hateful prospect; and it contained the danger of anarchy which might give the pretext for a second British occupation and thereby ruin all that had already been achieved. To avert this danger Collins felt himself compelled to smudge the issue which he desired to place before the Irish people. On the 20th May he agreed to a pact with De Valera by which the pro-treaty and the anti-treaty parties should present themselves to the Irish electors as a 'national coalition panel' in accordance with their existing strength in Dáil Éireann.[2] At the same time there was an explicit agreement that 'any and every interest' would be entitled to take part in the elections. The agree-

[1] Collins prepared the ground by an agreement with Sir James Craig which aimed at restoring peaceful conditions on the border and in Belfast, and at securing, in this atmosphere of restored peace, a meeting during the 'Ulster month'. In this meeting the statesmen would seek agreement on the conditions necessary for a united Ireland, or, if this failed, they would seek agreement on boundary revision. See 'Heads of the Agreement between the Provisional Government and the Government of Northern Ireland, 31st March 1922' in the *Irish Year Book*, 1922, p. 258. The republicans bitterly attacked Collins for this agreement.

[2] The terms of the agreement are in the *Irish Year Book*, 1922, p. 259. The most important articles are: Article 1: 'That a National Coalition Panel for the third Dáil, representing both parties in the Dáil, and in the Sinn Féin organisation, be sent forward on the ground that the national position requires the entrusting of the Government of the country into the joint hands of those who have been the strength of the national situation during the last few years, without prejudice to their present respective positions.' Article 2: 'That this coalition panel be put forward as from the Sinn Féin organisation, the number for each party being their present strength in the Dáil.' Article 3: 'That the candidates be nominated through each of the existing Party Executives.' Article 4: 'That any and every interest is free to go up and contest the election equally with the Sinn Féin panel.'

ment had at last secured the chance of a democratic pronouncement, which the militarists had tried to stop. In a speech at Cork on 14th June Collins welcomed the competition of other groups. Thereupon he was accused of betraying the 'national coalition panel'. Alternative readings of the pact were made the basis for alternative interpretations of the June elections. According to one interpretation the people of Ireland showed their will by reducing the anti-treaty faction to the number of 36 in a house of 128. According to the other interpretation, the national union pact won 94 seats against the 32 seats secured by its interloping opponents.[1]

Collins treated the election as a vote in favour of the treaty. Common sense will support his judgement. But revolutions are made by qualities which are more exalted and more violent than common sense. The appeal to common sense as the regulative virtue marks the end of a revolution. Collins, indeed, believed that in the interests of Ireland the revolution must now be ended. His opponents believed that for the sake of Ireland the revolution must continue. In these circumstances a clash was inevitable. It began at the end of June, when the provisional government ordered an attack on the Four Courts.

The events of the civil war, its bitterness, its waste of leaders and destruction of comradeship, do not come within the scope of this survey. We are concerned only with those convictions and attitudes which have affected the relationship of Ireland to Great Britain and the British Commonwealth. It was the view of the British government, emphatically and insistently expressed, that the Irish provisional government must honour the treaty by taking action against the minority who were attempting to wreck it. It was the view of the opponents of the treaty that the provisional government was re-establishing the authority of the King in Ireland 'with an economy of British lives'.[2] It was the view of the provisional government that it was defending the position which the revolution had won. 'If order could not be maintained,' declared Collins, 'if no national government was to be allowed to function, a vacuum would be created, into which the English would be necessarily drawn back.'[3] Kevin O'Higgins asserted that the right of the people 'to found a State on the basis of the Treaty which had been signed by their plenipotentiaries and endorsed by their Parliament had to be vindi-

[1] The election figures were: pro-treaty party, 58; anti-treaty party, 36; labour, 17; farmers, 7; independents, 6; Trinity College, 4.

[2] The republicans were able to quote this phrase from a speech of Lord Birkenhead's.

[3] Quoted Beaslai, *Michael Collins and the Making of New Ireland*, vol. ii, p. 395.

cated without question'.[1] Which view was right? The republicans were right on the issue as they stated it, for they were in truth resisting the monarchical constitution of the British Commonwealth. Collins and O'Higgins were right on the issue as they stated it, for they were in truth fighting for the life of an Irish state founded upon democratic suffrage. A second question must therefore be asked. Which statement of the issue was better designed to elicit relevant truth and to serve during that time of crisis the higher interests of Ireland? The answer to this question will vary with the particular temperaments and loyalties of individuals. Until the future has produced some consensus of opinion among Irishmen, the student who comes from outside may be forgiven if he makes no pronouncement. It is better to return to themes which lend themselves to more objective treatment. And first, the constitution of the new state demands elucidation.

The constitution was drafted under conditions of uncertainty and disorder, and it bears some marks of this origin.[2] But its lack of a single coherent principle is more deeply rooted. It would not be enough to say that the constitution of the Irish Free State, like the constitutions of the Dominions, contained the forms of monarchical authority and the substance of national sovereignty. This would be a partial and misleading statement. The constitution of the Irish Free State contained not only the substance, but also the dogmatic statement of national sovereignty. Article 1 of the constitution declared the Irish Free State (otherwise called Saorstát Éireann) to be 'a co-equal member of the community of Nations, called the British Commonwealth of Nations'. Article 2 asserted: 'All powers of government and all authority legislative, executive and judicial in Ireland, are derived from the people of Ireland, and the same shall be exercised in the Irish Free State (Saorstát Éireann) through the organisations established by or under, and in accord with, this Constitution.' Throughout the constitution there was a sustained effort to work out the implications of this principle of Irish popular sovereignty.

'The constitution', says Dr. Kohn, 'was a most comprehensive and,

[1] Kevin O'Higgins, *Three Years Hard Labour* (Address delivered to the Irish Society of Oxford University, 31st October 1924). 'In Ireland in 1922', he said, 'there was no State and no organised force. The Provisional Government was simply eight young men in the City Hall, standing amidst the ruin of one administration, with the foundations of another not yet laid, and with wild men screaming through the keyhole.' They had 'not yet cleared the blood from their eyes'.

[2] A rather heterogeneous constitutional committee collected for study a large number of advanced and new democratic committees and produced a number of drafts, from which the Saorstát's constitution had to be put together.

in spirit, essentially republican constitution on continental lines. It had the characteristic dogmatic ring of all constitutions which embody not the legislative crystallisation of an organic development, but the theoretical postulates of a revolutionary upheaval. It mocked the time-honoured empiricism of the British constitution by the enunciation of basic principles and the formation of dogmatic definitions. It postulated fundamental rights. It defined in detail the scope and the functions of the several constitutional powers. It reduced to precise terms the conventional rules of the British constitution. Its archaic symbols had to be introduced, but their meaninglessness for Ireland was writ large on every page. The monarchical forms paled into significance in the light of the formal enunciation of the principle of the sovereignty of the people as the fundamental and the exclusive source of all political authority.'[1]

In short, the new constitution did not merely combine the phrases of monarchy with the reality of national sovereignty; it actually opposed the phrases of national sovereignty to the phrases of monarchy. It jostled together two symbolisms. By external tests it might be judged to approximate to the dominion model; but a closer examination would reveal a conflict of principle reminiscent of the constitution of Louis Philippe's France. There was, however, this difference between the constitutions of the Irish Free State and the July Monarchy: that whereas, under the latter, the principles of monarchical authority and popular sovereignty started their conflict on fairly even terms, under the former, popular sovereignty dominated the life of the Free State from the very beginning.

The British government had consented in advance to the general plan of this document. The provisional government, after it had initiated the work of constitution-making by appointing, in January 1922, the drafting committee, had to make a decision on a question of procedure and tactics. Admitting as it did that the constitution must be within the bounds laid down by the treaty, would it be better to present the draft constitution to the British government first, and to the Irish constituent assembly second, or would it be better to reverse this order? The provisional government decided that the constituent assembly would gain in security and freedom if it knew in advance the precise limits within which it must move. There was some legal disputation as to these limits, and the British demanded some modifications in the early drafts of the constitution; but the draft which the provisional government published in June

[1] Kohn, *Constitution of the Irish Free State*, p. 81. Generally, for an admirable juristic analysis of the constitution and for an examination of its working, see respectively the books cited by Kohn and Mansergh.

1922, on the eve of the elections, had been passed by the British government as being in conformity with the terms of the treaty.[1] When the provisional government, now under the leadership of W. T. Cosgrave, presented this draft to the constituent assembly in September, it allowed non-party discussion except on those articles which were necessary to keep the constitution in conformity with the treaty. These it made a question of confidence.[2]

The name 'constituent assembly' requires some explanation, and raises again difficult and controversial questions as to the origin of the Free State. Once again there is a divergence between British and Irish theories as to the origin of the state. The British parliament, as has been seen, had quite quickly closed the moment of ambiguity implied in the signature of the Articles of Agreement for a Treaty. The normal processes of constitutional monarchy had been resumed by the passing of the Irish Free State (Agreement) Act on the 31st March. Collins had pressed for this Act as a witness of British willingness to keep faith in ratifying the treaty, and the first sub-section of the Act provided: 'The Articles of Agreement for a Treaty between Great Britain and Ireland set forth in the schedule to this Act shall have the force of law as from the date of the passing of this Act.' The second sub-section legalized the transfer to the provisional government, by orders in council, of the powers and machinery referred to in article 17 of the treaty.[3] It went on to enjoin the dissolution of the Parliament of Southern Ireland, and the holding of 'an election of members for the constituencies which would have been entitled to elect members to that Parliament'.

> 'The members so elected [the sub-section continued] shall constitute the House of Parliament to which the Provisional Government shall be responsible, and that Parliament shall as respects matters within the jurisdiction of the Provisional Government, have power to make laws in like manner as the Parliament of the Irish Free State when constituted.

[1] It was also published as a British white paper, Cmd. 1688 of 1922. The original draft discussed in London was not published. It is known that among alterations on which the British insisted was the insertion, in article 65 of the draft (article 66 of the constitution), of the clause safeguarding the right 'of any person to petition His Majesty for special leave to appeal from the Supreme Court to His Majesty in Council or the right of His Majesty to grant such leave'. This right, which was valued as a safeguard to minorities, and which existed in Canada, was held by the British government to be implied in the treaty. See p. 332. It is also known that the British insisted on inserting the parliamentary oath in the constitution.

[2] Since the anti-treaty party would not take its place in the assembly when it met in September, the labour party, with a membership of seventeen, filled the rôle of opposition.

[3] See Statutory Rules and Orders, 1922, no. 315. *The Provisional Government (Transfer of Function) Order, 1922,* 1st April 1922.

In all this there was no mention of a constituent assembly. The Act provided for a body which might well be called a provisional parliament. The representatives of Irish constituencies who assembled in September 1922 did not exclude this British view of their status and powers. But they placed their British title after their native Irish titles as third Dáil and constituent assembly of the Irish nation.

> 'Dáil Éireann'—so ran the preamble to the Constitution of the Irish Free State (Saorstát Éireann) Act—'sitting as a Constituent Assembly in this Provisional Parliament, acknowledging that all lawful authority comes from God to the people, and in the confidence that the National life and unity of Ireland shall thus be restored, hereby proclaims the establishment of the Irish Free State (otherwise called Saorstát Éireann) and in the exercise of undoubted right, decrees and enacts as follows. . . .'

The constituent assembly had done its work. But the constitution of the Irish Free State was not yet in existence. British authority still had a part to play. The last article of the constitution provided for 'the passing and adoption of this constitution by the constituent assembly and the British parliament', and for the announcement of its passing and adoption by Royal Proclamation not later than the 6th December 1922, which was the day fixed by the treaty to mark the term of the provisional government's authority. The British parliament duly passed a confirmatory statute 'to provide for the constitution of the Irish Free State'. The Royal Proclamation was duly issued on the 6th December.

The constitution of Saorstát Éireann was now legally established. But what was its legal origin and foundation? Did it derive from the action of the constituent assembly or from the action of the imperial parliament? In the complexity of the processes which have been sketched there is material for unending juristic controversy. It is impossible here even to suggest the subtleties of this controversy.[1] But we may perhaps anticipate one of its characteristically paradoxical outcomes, which became apparent later. The Irish judicial interpretation, by treating the constituent assembly as the legal source of the constitution, tended in some degree to retard and hinder the evolution of the constitution away from the treaty. The British legal interpretation, by treating British statute as the legal source of the constitution, led later in logic to the conclusion that the powers conferred by the Statute of Westminster on the Irish Free State implied legal authority to eliminate the treaty from the municipal law of the Irish Free State.

[1] For an approach to them see Kohn, *Constitution of the Irish Free State*, part ii and part v, ch. x.

By way of provisional explanation of what has just been said[1] some inquiry is necessary into the legal relation of the treaty to the constitution. How did the treaty become part of Irish municipal law? The answer is contained in clause 2 of the Constituent Act, and also in article 50 of the constitution itself. Clause 2 ran as follows:

> 'The said Constitution shall be construed with reference to the Articles of Agreement for a Treaty between Great Britain and Ireland set forth in the Second Schedule hereto annexed (hereinafter referred to as "the Scheduled Treaty") which are hereby given the force of law, and if any provision of the said Constitution or of any amendment thereof or of any law made thereunder is in any respect repugnant to any of the provisions of the Scheduled Treaty, it shall, to the extent only of such repugnancy, be absolutely void and inoperative and the Parliament and the Executive Council of the Irish Free State (Saorstát Éireann) shall respectively pass such necessary further legislation and do all such other things as may be necessary to implement the Scheduled Treaty.'

This clause was recited in the preamble to the British act of parliament which adopted the constitution. Article 50 of the constitution, which dealt with the processes of constitutional amendment, laid it down that amendment must be 'within the terms of the Scheduled Treaty'. Yet this same article contained the gap through which the treaty was later thrust out of its position within the constitution as supreme law of the Irish Free State, overriding the constitution itself and all subsequent amendments to it. In its original form, article 50 provided that all amendments to the constitution must first pass through the ordinary legislative channels and thereafter be submitted to a special referendum. As a result of the debates in the constituent assembly, provision was made to postpone for eight years the referendum as a necessary process in constitutional amendment. During these eight years the ordinary legislative channels would alone suffice.[2] In 1929 the period of amendment without referendum was extended for another eight years.[3] In 1932 De Valera's majority in the Dáil turned this unchecked amending power against the treaty, in its aspect as Irish municipal law invested with overriding force over the constitution. The Constitution (Removal of Oath) Act repealed section 2 of the Constituent Act, and deleted

[1] For fuller explanation and discussion see Chapter VI below.

[2] During the Cosgrave period it was held that amending Acts had to be specified as such. After 1932, when De Valera came to power, ordinary legislation without specification was thought sufficient.

[3] Amendment No. 16, contained in Act No. 10 of 1929.

the restrictive clause of article 50 which confined constitutional amendment 'within the terms of the Scheduled Treaty'.

The result was to open up a new period of uncertainty with regard to the constitutional foundations and future of Saorstát Éireann. The previous ten years, during which the state was under the control of the Cosgrave administration, had given to the outer world an impression of legal and political stability which was all the more powerful because of its contrast with the prevailing instability of Europe. The Irish Free State appeared to be unshakably founded upon the treaty. It does not fall within the scope of this survey to record in any detail the internal history of the state during these years. The government resolutely established its authority *de facto*, which by 1925 was sufficiently strong to survive even the destruction of those hopes with respect to Northern Ireland which had played so large a part in securing the treaty's acceptance.[1] The *de jure* existence

[1] See p. 148 above, note 3. There was delay in constituting the Boundary Commission which was legally binding on the parties to the treaty as the result of Northern Ireland exercising the option of withdrawing from the Free State. The delay was partly due to the preoccupation of the Irish Free State with establishing its authority and to the British delay in taking the final legal steps to implement the constitution of Northern Ireland enacted in 1920. See The Irish Free State (Consequential Provisions) Act, 1922, passed on the same day as Irish Free State (Constitution) Act. It was partly due to the desire of the conservative and labour governments of the United Kingdom to reach an agreed settlement which would render the commission unnecessary. See correspondence contained in Cmd. 1928 of 1923 and Cmd. 2155 of 1924. The British government took throughout the view that 'the Treaty, by reason of the statutory force with which it was invested by Act of the Imperial Parliament in which Northern Ireland is represented, is, in the view of His Majesty's Government, binding on the government of Northern Ireland' (ibid., dispatch of Mr. J. H. Thomas, 23rd May 1924). The government of the Irish Free State, while maintaining that the treaty was binding *qua* treaty, took note also of the different British interpretation which also admitted its binding character with regard to the north. See Mr. Cosgrave's speech of 12th August 1924, reported in *The Times*, 13th August 1924. The government of Northern Ireland, however, took the view that it was not bound to appoint its representative to the Boundary Commission. The British government thereupon sought to elicit the legal position by means of several questions referred by His Majesty to the Judicial Committee of the Privy Council (ibid., pp. 26, 27). As the result of the answers given, the government secured from parliament The Irish Free State (Confirmation of Agreement) Act (14 & 15 Geo. V, c. 41). This act confirmed the agreement made with the Irish Free State whereby, in the event of Northern Ireland still refusing to appoint its commissioner, power of appointment should be exercised by the British government. Thus the commission was constituted. Its investigations continued for a year. But in November 1925, when its report was about to be published, Professor MacNeill, the representative of the Free State, resigned. By a leakage to the press the general tenor of the commission's forthcoming report had become known—that there would be no substantial transfer of territory, but small modifications on both sides. Thereupon the three governments met in conference, and, on 3rd December 1925, made a new agreement, being 'united in amity', and 'resolved mutually to aid one another in a spirit of neighbourly comradeship'. The agreement revoked the powers conferred on the Boundary Commission and left the territory of

of Saorstát Éireann, thanks to the treaty, at last achieved that external recognition which revolutionary nationalism alone had been unable to win. Looking back upon the chaotic ambiguities of the revolutionary struggle, the legally constituted authority of the new state classified them, for its own purposes, by precise legal interpretation. The legislature and the courts defined in law the signification of the assemblies which had succeeded each other—first Dáil, second Dáil, third Dáil.[1]

With a schismatic legalism which in the end became pathetic, those members of the second Dáil who had voted against the treaty refused to accept any of these established facts. There was, they maintained, no Irish Free State. There had been no constituent assembly. There had been no third Dáil; nor could there be a fourth Dáil or a fifth. They, the second Dáil, still remained the living sovereign authority of the undying Irish republic. As late as 1928 a remnant of them were still posturing in their secret, solemn, pseudo-constitutionalism. But they were a dwindling sect. They could barely muster the quorum enjoined by the dead constitution which they posed as maintaining—twenty members of the Dáil out of one hundred and twenty-eight. The Irish of the dispersion were forgetful of them. The Irish Republican Army no longer recognized their authority.[2] In 1926 De Valera himself separated from them. The robust national reality of the Irish Free State, imperfect though it was, killed the cloudy make-believe of the second Dáil. To the physical-force men the Republic became what it had been after Easter 1916—a memory and an ideal for which they were ready to fight and kill. Their uncompromising realism saw in the Irish Free State that very enemy which Irish patriots had so often defied in the past—an administration backed by

Northern Ireland as it was by the Act of 1920. It contained substantial financial relief for the Irish Free State—notably from the debt and pension obligations contained in article 5 of the treaty—for which the British taxpayer paid the price. On the Irish Free State side there were granted some smaller financial adjustments. Finally, the agreement abolished the Council of Ireland, which had hitherto survived from the Act of 1920, and provided inter-parliamentary machinery between north and south as a means of handling common interests in the present, and perhaps preparing unity in the future. In the future, matters demanding the action of both authorities would have to be handled by negotiation between the two governments.

The agreement was confirmed by the British parliament (15 & 16 Geo. V, c. 77) and by the Oireachtas (No. 40 of 1925).

[1] Cf. the Interpretation Act, 1922.

[2] See the very revealing documents discovered by the police of the Irish Free State in 1928 and published by Mr. Cosgrave's government in 1930 (P. no. 202)—especially pages 34–5. See also the letter of congratulation from the second Dáil to the United States government on the Kellogg Pact printed, as a pamphlet (Dublin Stationery Office, 1929).

guns and by courts of law. De Valera's more intelligent realism now saw in the Irish Free State what Collins had seen in the treaty and the constitution—an arena of opportunity in which Ireland might struggle towards her ideal. The ideal had not changed. But the tactics of struggle might change.[1] In 1927, forty-four members of De Valera's new party, Fianna Fáil, were returned by the electors. They took the oath prescribed by the constitution so that they could fight for their immediate objective, which was the removal of the oath from the constitution. The two divergent theories which had come together at the Sinn Féin Conference of 1917 had found again at last a common ground. But it was not the old ground of party unity; it was the new ground of agreed constitutional procedure which permitted them to renew their struggle according to the rules of Saorstát Éireann.

So the entry of De Valera and his followers into the Parliament of the Irish Free State brought a moment of stability more complete than any which Ireland had known since the first Dáil declared the independence of Ireland in January 1919. But this moment of stability prepared new instabilities, not merely for Ireland, but for the British Commonwealth of Nations, of which Ireland was a member. What was the cause? It will be discussed in a later chapter of this book. But it may be deduced even now from the narrative of the treaty negotiations and the civil war, which has already been given. Men differed, it may be said, about little things. Lloyd George threatened Ireland with 'immediate and terrible war' unless her spokesmen would accept common citizenship in place of reciprocal citizenship, an empire membership in place of an empire association, the Crown in the Irish constitution instead of the Crown uniting the associated nations of the British Commonwealth. These also were the issues which ranged Griffith and De Valera in opposite camps and drove half of the republican fighters back into the hills. 'Practical men' may protest that there is not very much to choose between the oath contained in Document No. 2 and the oath contained in the treaty. But that little was sufficient to cause a civil war in Ireland. It had already sufficed to cause an ultimatum from Great Britain to Ireland. If De Valera had been merely 'a practical man', he would have safeguarded Irish unity by accepting the Crown where the treaty placed it. If Lloyd George had been merely 'a practical man', he would have sought the appeasement and good will of a united Irish people by accepting the Crown where the Irish

[1] Even in 1922 De Valera was ready to envisage this possibility. See his letter of 7th September 1922 in Dáil Éireann, P. no. 1, 1922, p. 8.

proposals placed it.[1] But it would be naïve to abstract the rationalist and utilitarian element from the many-sided totality of history, and to employ this element alone in explaining events and personalities. The history which lay behind the events chronicled in this chapter was charged with conflicting emotions, memories, and loyalties, and these were arrayed against each other in conflicting symbols.

[1] As early as 16th June 1922 a purely practical outlook manifested itself rather astonishingly in the question asked by an eminent authority on constitutional law: 'Is not the Constitution of the British Commonwealth of Nations elastic enough to include a Republic?' See Keith, *Letters on Imperial Relations*, p. 34.

CHAPTER IV

INDIA AND RACE EQUALITY

I

India joins the Conference

The development of the imperial conference, during the war, had been marked by one striking deviation from the normal order. That order assumed self-government as an indispensable qualification for admission to the conference circle. Self-government was the principle of growth which, without much planning, had shaped the form and functions of the conference. The first conference of 1887 had been a gathering representative of the whole British Empire; but a few years afterwards the self-governing colonies, without waiting for a lead from Great Britain, separated themselves out as a peculiar society and held a conference of their own at Ottawa. The principle underlying this separation was not formally discussed; it was taken for granted, and the imperial conference without very much fuss constituted itself as an inner circle of communities privileged to manage their own affairs. The members of this inner circle were jealous of their freedom, which they were progressively enlarging, until at last it became a status of equality with Great Britain. In this way the 'peers' of the British Empire separated themselves from its subject communities. It became fashionable in some quarters, after the war, to draw a hard line between the British Commonwealth, which was the community of the fully free, and the British Empire, which included also the subject peoples. The idea was not a new one. It was present in the mind of an Australian political leader who said, long before the war, that the Australians were 'citizen-subjects' of the British Empire, whereas the Indians were 'subject citizens'.[1] The same idea found expression at the 1907 Conference, when a high official of the India Office attended to speak on a matter which vitally concerned Indian interests and sentiment:

> 'Mr. Asquith: "Sir James Mackay wishes to say something, and he represents India."

[1] *Commonwealth Debates* (1901), vol. vii, col. 4631. He was the labour party leader, Mr. Watson, later for a few months prime minister. It is interesting to note Professor Keith's opinion that self-government should not have been made a qualification for membership of the imperial conference, thus excluding India. See A. Berriedale Keith, *The Governments of the British Empire* (Macmillan, 1935), p. 181.

'Mr. Deakin: "Not in the sense in which we represent our countries. He speaks for the British Government."

'Mr. Asquith: "He speaks for the Secretary of State."'

A colleague of the Australian Prime Minister harped on the same theme with a crude arrogance. Let India raise her standard of living: let her pay a fair wage: then and not till then could she invite comparison 'with all other white people of the self-governing Colonies' (*sic*). As things were, the speaker said, India was in a totally different category, and the Conference need pay scant attention to the arguments brought forward on her behalf.[1]

This churlishness was fortunately not typical of the manners of dominion statesmen in their dealings with India's spokesmen. At the 1911 Conference, for example, Sir Joseph Ward disclaimed any feeling of superiority on the part of New Zealanders towards 'our fellow British subjects' in India. He willingly admitted that Indians had 'a right to the fullest consideration upon the score of race', and that their pride in their civilization was no less deep and worthy of respect than that of the self-governing Dominions. Unfortunately, in their immigration laws and in their shipping legislation and in their treatment of resident Indians, the Dominions had not succeeded in achieving the ends at which they aimed without doing grave offence to Indian sentiment. The questions at issue will be considered a little later. At present it is necessary to insist only on the central fact of the intense irritation caused in India by dominion policies which seemed to be based on an offensive assumption of racial superiority. Lord Crewe said in 1911 that this was the sole issue which united seditious agitators and the loyal representatives of moderate Indian opinion. He pointed out that the issue was bound to become still more troublesome in virtue of the 'growing tendency to apply principles of self-government to India'. Meanwhile, the British government constantly found itself in the invidious position of having to listen to appeals from one part of the Empire against another. Would it not be possible to achieve direct understandings between the Dominion and Indian governments which would free the home government of this disagreeable duty? The home government had a right to ask that the Dominions should so frame their policies as 'to avoid wanton injury to the self-respect of non-European British subjects'. The Dominions had a duty to contrive that their domestic

[1] Cd. 3523 of 1907, pp. 294, 325. The matter under discussion was a clause in an Australian shipping bill, which had been reserved, restricting preference to British goods carried on British ships manned by white labour. About this time Indian pride was offended by a press vulgarity suggesting that Australia would send troops to 'keep order' in the event of trouble in India.

policies should not unnecessarily create embarrassment in the administration of India. Otherwise, there was no hope of a truly united Empire.

> 'However close the connexion and however perfect the understanding between the Mother Country and the self-governing Dominions, we are not a united Empire unless that understanding spreads to some considerable extent also to that vast part of the Empire of which, of course, India is the most prominent division, but which also includes all the Crown Colonies which are inhabited by the various native races.'[1]

From the argument of Lord Crewe in 1911 and from the ensuing discussion it would be possible to deduce the lines on which—ideally at any rate—a reconciliation of dominion interests and sentiment with those of India, and the consequent achievement of a deep and strong imperial unity, might be achieved. India would continue to progress towards self-government. The Dominions would negotiate directly with an Indian government closely in touch with Indian opinion. Those negotiations, while recognizing the right of each community under the Crown to determine the elements of its own population, would sweep away all suggestion of racial arrogance and establish the principles of equality and reciprocity between India and the Dominions. In the end, perhaps—though in 1911 it would have needed an inspired leap of the imagination to reach so far—India would achieve political equality with the Dominions. She would qualify in the usual way for admission to the imperial conference. She would join the inner circle of the privileged.

Only six years later, Indian representatives were welcomed at the Imperial War Conference. The welcome was enthusiastic. The spokesmen of Great Britain and of each Dominion in turn vied with each other in their friendly and flattering tributes to India. The Canadian Prime Minister moved, and the New Zealand Prime Minister seconded, that the necessary steps should be taken to modify the resolution of 1907 fixing the constitution of the imperial conference, so that in future India might attend it as of right.[2] At a single stride India appeared to have reached the inner circle. How had she qualified for admission? Not in the ordinary manner. Her

[1] Imperial Conference Papers 1911: *Memorandum by the India Office.* Cd. 5745 of 1911, pp. 394 ff., and Cd. 5746–1, No. XXIII.

[2] Cd. 8566 of 1917, pp. 10, 22. The Australian Prime Minister was prevented by an election struggle from attending the conference; his assent was to be obtained before the next conference. The Indian representatives at the 1917 Conference were the Maharajah of Bikanir and the late Lord Sinha; the latter became afterwards a member of the British government as Under-Secretary for India, and was government spokesman in the House of Lords during the passage of the Montagu-Chelmsford reforms.

political status was far below that of a self-governing Dominion. She had qualified by her extraordinary services to the British Empire. In the words of Mr. Austen Chamberlain, 'she had bled herself white at the beginning of the war to supply the deficiencies of the Empire in troops, arms and guns'. She had achieved the equality of a comrade-in-arms. In the deliverances of dominion spokesmen there is not the slightest trace of racial self-consciousness or political exclusiveness; their references to India glow with a genuine warmth and friendliness. It is true that they found some difficulty in reconciling India's subordinate political status with the principle of equality which they affirmed to be the basis of the Empire's constitution. The Dominions, they declared, were 'autonomous nations of an Imperial Commonwealth'; India they could only describe as 'an important part of the same'. But they were willing to assume that the 'important part' of the Commonwealth was already treading a path leading towards the same goal which the 'autonomous nations' had already achieved. The admission of India to the conference, which should normally have been the sequel to Indian self-government, was a recognition of the fact that self-government was India's destiny. It was, so to speak, a payment in advance which India had earned by her extraordinary services. India, declared the Prime Minister of Newfoundland, had 'established the right to be here'; her future progress would confirm that right. 'There can be no question in the mind of any one who has studied what is going on in India, that India can ever go back to where she was, and that in the near future a wonderful development is going to take place there. . . .'[1] Four months later, on 20th August 1917, an announcement of the Secretary of State for India in the House of Commons confirmed this prophecy.

> 'The policy of His Majesty's Government' [declared the Secretary of State] '. . . is the increasing association of Indians in every branch of the administration and the gradual development of self-governing institutions with a view to the progressive realization of responsible government in India as an integral part of the British Empire.'

It was true that the Secretary of State added a caution against undue impatience. Progress in this policy could only be achieved by successive stages; the British government and the Government of India, on whom lay the responsibility for India's welfare and advancement, must judge 'the time and measure of each advance'. Nevertheless, His Majesty's government had decided that substantial steps in advance should be taken in the immediate future. This is not the

[1] Cd. 8566, p. 120.

place to inquire in detail how this pledge was fulfilled. As a sequel to the declaration of August 1917 occurred Mr. Montagu's visit to India, the publication of the Montagu-Chelmsford report, and the Government of India Act 1919. Indian opinion regarded these reforms as the beginning of a process which would fulfil the promise implied by the admission of India to the imperial conference, and by her admission, in company with the Dominions, to the League of Nations.

> 'I cannot fail to remember' [declared Mr. Srinivasa Sastri at the Imperial Conference of 1921] 'that the position we occupy here is not comparable by any means to the position occupied by our colleagues from the Dominions. They are called here by virtue of their being Prime Ministers. We come by nomination from our Government. We realise that that marks a great difference in our status, although not in the privileges to which we have been admitted at these meetings. We hope that next year, or the year after, our successors, who will take our place here, will come by a better right. The person who represents in the place of His Highness[1] more than one-third of British territory in India will probably be chosen by the Chamber of Princes by election, and the man who takes my place may likewise be elected by the Central Legislature of the land. We have not yet acquired full Dominion status, but we realize we are planted firmly on the road to the acquisition of that status.'[2]

Thus the year 1917 saw established, and the following years saw reaffirmed, the 'form', the principle of development, which was to reach completion with India's equality in the British Commonwealth of Nations. But the 'matter', the actual conditions in which that principle must strive to realize itself, soon proved to be stubborn. There was intractable material in the British parliament, in India, in the imperial conference itself. The resignation in 1922 of Mr. E. S. Montagu, the Secretary of State for India, revealed the extent to which India's present international status, in default of present self-government, was illusory. Mr. Montagu, as official

[1] This was His Highness the Maharao of Kutch, who had a traditional connexion with the emigration problems to be considered later: since for centuries Kutch's subjects had emigrated to East Africa and carried on business there.

[2] Cmd. 1474 of 1921, p. 33. Cf. Cmd. 1988 of 1923, pp. 86, 90, 108, 111, 118. The Australian and New Zealand prime ministers assert emphatically in 1923 that India is no longer a dependency, but a component part of the British Commonwealth and a complete equal at the imperial conference. The Free State representative asserts more realistically that the Indian delegates are not yet 'on a equality with the rest of us, because they are not here in a representative capacity'. There is, he says, an anomaly in India's presence at the conference which will disappear only when India has self-government. It needs to be pointed out that the Indian representatives at the conference are still nominated. (1936.)

spokesman for the Government of India, published Indian criticisms upon the proposed treaty of peace with Turkey. Mr. Montagu, as a member of the British government, was held to have violated the principle of cabinet solidarity and was forced to resign. It thus became apparent that India, despite the fine show of her place in the imperial conference and her membership of the League of Nations, had in the last resort no deciding voice of her own. The Government of India was overlooked by the India Office, and the India Office was 'a subordinate department of His Majesty's government at Whitehall'. On crucial matters, the British cabinet must decide what India would be permitted to say.[1] The incident revealed the danger of a policy which had granted the forms of status before it had granted the substance; it might easily find itself paying in disillusionment and rebellious impatience the price of a momentary appeasement and enthusiasm.

Within India, the process of shifting the foundations of government so that they should rest 'on the confidence of the people of India',[2] encountered formidable obstacles. If it were to be effective, Mr. Montagu had reflected, the process should be swift;[3] but it was not possible to make it swift. In addition, events were soon to reveal some defects of quality in the political leadership of India. More important, from the point of view of the present argument, were the defects of quality which had already been revealed among Englishmen resident in India. Oratory at the imperial conference emphasized the British Empire's mission of assuaging the bitterness arising between European and Eastern peoples, and guiding into the path of free co-operation a relationship which otherwise might develop in conflict.[4] But Mr. Montagu, during his Indian journey, discovered that the racial exclusiveness and arrogance of the English community were a root cause of the government's troubles.[5] The Amritsar shootings and humiliations of 1919 uncovered an abyss of racial insolence and racial resentment which threatened catastrophe to the great design which the British Commonwealth had dared to plan in 1917. General Dyer, the officer responsible for the shootings, affirmed before a commission of inquiry

[1] *J.P.E.*, vol. iii, pp. 302–5. Dewey, *The Dominions and Diplomacy*, vol. ii, p. 136.

[2] Edwin S. Montagu, *An Indian Diary* (Heinemann, 1930), p. 326. Also pp. 51, 62.

[3] Op. cit., 21st April 1918. On the Montagu-Chelmsford report—'It will, however, be completely out of date unless we proceed with the scheme quickly.'

[4] Cmd. 1474, pp. 13, 15, 16, 39.

[5] Montagu, op. cit., passim, e.g. at p. 4: 'Again I say that the social question, the fact that the civil servants are willing to work with the Indians but not to play with them, the fact that the Boxwallah will have nothing to do with them, has really brought the present political situation upon us.'

that his object had been, not merely to disperse a dangerous crowd, but to produce 'a sufficient moral effect from a military point of view not only on those who were present, but more especially throughout the Punjab'. This was the doctrine which the British had denounced as Prussianism. 'Are you going to keep your hold on India', cried Mr. Montagu in the House of Commons, 'by terrorism and racial humiliation and frightfulness . . . ?' Would Englishmen dare, demanded Lord Birkenhead in the House of Lords, to apply General Dyer's principles in Winnipeg? British rule, he pleaded, could not stand for one set of principles in Great Britain and the Dominions, and for another set of principles in India. But the House of Lords did not agree with him. General Dyer was subjected to discipline, but he became a martyr-hero to a section of the press, a large faction in the House of Commons, and a majority of the House of Lords. The agitation in the press and parliament of Great Britain, and the corresponding agitation in India, revealed depths of racialistic *hubris* and humiliation which made the platitudes of imperial conference oratory —India's devotion to the King-Emperor, the Empire's noble mission of interpreting to each other the East and the West, and all the rest of it—sound like empty hypocritical humbug.[1]

Even at the imperial conference itself, the hopes of 1917 found no easy or speedy fulfilment. Undoubtedly a most promising beginning had been made in 1917 in the search for a better understanding between the Dominions and India.

> 'The Imperial War Conference,' [declared the much-quoted 'reciprocity resolution' of that year] 'having examined the Memorandum on the position of Indians in the Self-governing Dominions presented by the Indian representatives to the Conference, accepts the principle of reciprocity of treatment between India and the Dominions and recommends the Memorandum to the favourable consideration of the Governments concerned.'[2]

From the point of view of the Dominions, this resolution represented a distinct gain. For it contained India's official endorsement of the

[1] See the report of Lord Hunter's committee, Cmd. 681 of 1920, p. 30, for General Dyer's statement, and especially chapters 3, 5, 11. A summary of the British debates is in *J.P.E.*, vol. 1, pp. 598 ff. The treatment of General Dyer (retirement on half pay and no further employment in India) was debated in the Commons on the India Office vote. In the Commons the voting was 230 to 129 for the government. The Lords (129 to 86) deplored the treatment of General Dyer as 'unjust to that officer, and as establishing a precedent dangerous to the preservation of order in face of rebellion'. The *Round Table*, vol. xii, p. 618, commented on the Amritsar episode: 'To the Indian, and the higher his character the stronger his indignation, the events of 1919 were the brand of subjection burnt into the living flesh.'

[2] Cmd. 8566, pp. 7, 117–22, 159–62.

principle, already admitted by the British government, that the Dominions had the right to restrict or to prohibit the entry of Indian immigrants. Eighty years previously, Lord John Russell had instanced immigration as a matter which of necessity must remain subject to imperial control; the reason was obvious, for immigration-restriction must affect both foreign relations and relations between different parts of the British Empire. In the early fifties of the nineteenth century, nevertheless, the Australian colonies initiated policies of restricting the entry of Asiatics. Their restricting acts, aimed first at the Chinese, were extended gradually until they affected also the Queen's subjects in India. The legislation of the colony of Natal in the nineties was directed primarily against British Indians. The legislation was reserved, and, after discussion, was amended to eliminate *nominatim* exclusion; Natal attained her end by means of an education test. This was the method which Mr. Chamberlain urged upon the Australian colonies (whose restrictive bills had similarly been reserved) at the Conference of 1897. He very firmly requested the Australian colonies 'to arrange a form of words which will avoid hurting the feelings of any of her Majesty's subjects'. At the same time, he sympathized with their determination to protect their communities against an influx of people 'alien in civilization, alien in religion, alien in customs, whose influx, moreover, would seriously interfere with the legitimate rights of the existing labour population'.[1] Australia and New Zealand found in the education test the means of satisfying both their own communities and the British government, although the latter had to reject their ideas of the amount of protection necessary for them, when these expanded to a penalization of British ships which employed Indian sailors in their waters.[2] Canada restricted Indian immigration by a different method—by legislation empowering the Governor-General-in-Council to exclude 'any speci-

[1] C. 8596 of 1897, p. 113. The writer is indebted to Professor Eric Walker for information about a letter from Mr. Gandhi to Mr. W. P. Schreiner, which has a direct bearing on the matter in the text. The letter is in the unpublished *Schreiner Papers*, and was written on 17th August 1909 when both men were in London fighting the South Africa Act. Gandhi complained bitterly of the Transvaal Immigration Law which banned 'Asiatics as such' and was 'an affront to a whole race', and declared that there would be no justification for making it the law of the future Union. He cheerfully admitted that the education tests of the Cape, Natal, and Australia were well understood and could be accepted. Mr. Gandhi explains his position in his book *Satyagraha in South Africa* (Madras, Ganesan, 1928), pp. 138–40.

[2] Cd. 3523 of 1907, p. 315, Cd. 5745 of 1911, pp. 136 ff., 279, 394 ff. On the unfortunately named 'White Australia' policy, see Hancock, *Australia*, chap. iv, or, for a full and scholarly treatment, with bibliography, Myra Willard, *History of the White Australia Policy* (Melbourne University Press, 1923).

fied class of immigrants' or 'immigrants belonging to any race deemed unsuitable to the climate or requirements of Canada'. Canadian legislation also insisted on continuous voyage from the country of emigration—thereby virtually excluding Indians, who were compelled to change ship at Hong Kong—and prescribed a minimum amount of money which immigrants from different countries must possess. The amount fixed for Indians was £40. These measures were effective in protecting Canada from an 'influx', and at the same time they were not objectionable to Indian sentiment, except in so far as the 'gentleman's agreement' with Japan gave to Japanese immigrants an advantage over Indians.[1] In South Africa there were special problems which must be considered later. In general, it is important to stress the fact that the British government offered no opposition to the restrictive legislation of the various dominions. The principle of this legislation was endorsed at the Conferences of 1907 and 1911. Lord Crewe in 1911 dismissed the argument

> 'that every subject of the King whoever he may be or wherever he may live has a natural right to travel or still more to settle in any part of the Empire. His Majesty's Government, [he declared,] fully accept the principle that each of the Dominions must be allowed to decide for itself what elements it desires to accept in its population. The extreme contention urged by some Indians, though not by those entitled to speak with responsibility, that membership of the British Empire shall entitle any British subject to reside where he chooses, is disposed of by acknowledged political facts.'

This declaration was sufficiently reassuring to induce the New Zealand Prime Minister to withdraw a resolution which asserted that, in order to preserve imperial harmony, 'every race should be relegated to its own zone'. Nevertheless, it was far more reassuring to hear from the lips of the leader of the Indian delegation, on the occasion of India's first attendance at an imperial conference, a similar declaration, and to hear this declaration emphatically reiterated on the occasion of her second attendance. For in 1918 Sir S. P. Sinha moved a resolution which contained these words:

> 'It is an inherent function of the Governments of the several communities of the British Commonwealth, including India, that each should enjoy complete control of the composition of its own population by means of restriction on immigration from any of the other communities.'

[1] This legislation is well summarized in Cd. 5746–1, No. XXIII. Cf. Keith, *Responsible Government in the Dominions*, vol. ii (1928 edition), chap. iv.

This principle the Imperial Conference reasserted, again on Indian initiative, in 1921 and again in 1923.[1]

It is desirable to pause for a little in order to reflect upon the meaning of these reiterated declarations. They embodied a theory of imperial citizenship which appears highly paradoxical, and which certainly is in marked contrast with the theory generally adopted by other empires of the past and of the present. The British Commonwealth turned its back on the ideal of a cosmopolis, which was the ideal of two great contemporary empires, the Union of Soviet Socialist Republics and the French Empire. Let us postpone, for the time, consideration of the Soviet example,[2] and content ourselves with working back from modern France to ancient Rome. The French Empire professed allegiance to the ideal of a common citizenship which opened to all who were sharers in it, irrespective of their race and domicile, the highest careers for which their talents might fit them, anywhere within the Empire's boundaries. The French Empire professed to offer to all its subjects the great boon of *la civilisation française*. For the French, throughout the nineteenth century, remained on the whole faithful to the theory of their first revolution, which had expressed itself in the Declaration of the Rights of Man and in the attempt to transform Haytian negroes, at a blow, from slaves into citizens. Their theory had affiliations with the Stoic conception of the natural equality of all men, which had been the philosophical foundation of citizenship in Rome's imperial cosmopolis. The movement in the Roman Republic and Empire was from variety of status to a common status. Citizenship extended outwards from Rome to Italy and finally to the provinces beyond Italy. Claudius, according to a satire penned by Seneca, had made up his mind to see every Gaul, German, and Spaniard, wearing the toga. Vespasian extended Latin rights—which were the half-way house to citizenship—to all Spanish cities. Perhaps because of the more rapid and thorough spread of the Latin tongue in the west, full citizenship was extended there more quickly than in the east. But Caracalla finally instituted a common status of citizenship for all the peoples throughout the whole Empire without exception.[3] The Empire was now conceived

[1] Cd. 8566 of 1917, p. 117; Cd. 9177 of 1918, p. 195; Cmd. 1474 of 1921, p. 35; Cmd. 1987 of 1923, p. 8; Cmd. 1988 of 1923, p. 81.

[2] This is considered in Chapter VIII below.

[3] The writer is indebted to Mr. A. J. S. Jones of All Souls College for an advance proof of his article 'Another Interpretation of the "Constitutio Antoniniana"', shortly to be published in *Roman Studies*. The article criticizes the restrictive interpretations previously held and argues that citizenship was granted without exception. The main object, it is suggested, 'was the simplification of law and administration by the abolition of a distinction which had long ceased to correspond with the facts'.

as a world community with a common nationality. 'We are all one people', wrote the poet Claudian, on the eve of the Empire's fall.[1]

Within the British Commonwealth, the movement during the past half century has been in a contrary direction—from the ideal of a single political nationality to the ideal of a variety of nationalities. The implications of this movement, in so far as the communities of European descent are concerned, will be discussed in another chapter.[2] Here it need only be noted that the multicellular conception of citizenship within this section of the Commonwealth has not extended so far as to impede the free movement of individuals, or to hinder the exchange of one local nationality for another. But between these communities of European origin and the rest of the Empire, a barrier has been set up. The most surprising and significant feature of this novel development has been the fact that the races against whom the barrier was raised have accepted and even approved the raising of it. It might be argued that India's approval of the principle of immigration restriction, reiterated at four successive imperial conferences, was merely opportunist, the measure of her relative weakness and political dependence, the unconvincing utterance of moderate politicians who were bound in the long run to be repudiated by their countrymen. Yet these politicians repeatedly claimed that the disabilities of Indians within the British Empire comprised the one issue on which classes and masses, graduates and illiterates, moderates and revolutionaries, were agreed. They themselves were not at all moderate in their upbraiding of some of the Dominions. Why did they spare Australia and New Zealand, whose uncompromising resolve to keep themselves 'white' was so frequently reproved by shocked liberal idealists in Great Britain? Could it be that there was some element of error, or of irrelevance, in the philosophy of these idealists?

Their philosophy was akin to that of the French; but it was power-

[1] Claudian, *de Consulatu Stilichonis* (c. A.D. 400), l. 150 (on Rome):

> Haec est, in gremium victos quae sola recepit,
> humanumque genus communi nomine fovit
> matris, non dominae, ritu: civesque vocavit
> quos domuit . . .
> . . . .
> quod cuncti gens una sumus.'

Cf. the lines of Rutilius Numationus (c. A.D. 417):

> 'fecisti patriam diversis gentibus unam:
> profuit iniustis, te dominante, capi.
> dumque offers victis proprii consortia iuris,
> urbem fecisti quod prius orbis erat.'

(I am indebted for these quotations to my colleague Professor J. O. Thomson.)

[2] See Chapter V and Supplementary Chapter. The reader will observe that 'political nationality', not 'personal nationality', is the subject of the present discussion.

fully reinforced by the evangelical fervour peculiar to England. It was the alliance between the rationalist doctrine of the rights of man and the Christian teaching of love for man which overthrew the slave trade and slavery. Could any union of thought and emotion be better fitted to satisfy in the dependencies of a great empire the demands of human dignity, and to promote the harmony of diverse peoples within a common system of right? In India, this philosophy and this piety found expression in a famous clause of the Charter of 1833:

> 'No native of the said territories, nor any natural-born subject of His Majesty, resident therein, shall, by reason only of his religion, place of birth, descent, colour, or any of them, be disabled from holding any place, office, or employment under the Company.'

The same thought and feeling inspired Macaulay's famous minute on education written in the same year:

> 'It may be that the public mind of India may expand under our system until it has outgrown that system, that by good government we may educate our subjects into a capacity for better government, that having become instructed in European knowledge, they may, in some future age, demand European institutions. . . .'

How easy it would be to interpret the last century of Indian history solely in the light of these pronouncements, to ascribe to the virtue which is contained in them everything which stands to Great Britain's credit in her dealings with India, to accuse her forgetfulness or denial of them as the cause of all her failures. It would be easy for a liberal Englishman to systematize history in this way—but not so easy for an Indian. For the pronouncements exemplify not only the generous faith of nineteenth-century idealism, but also its insensitiveness. Indians will share the opportunities of the British, if they prove themselves capable of becoming like the British. They will receive European institutions, as a reward for their progress in European knowledge. . . . Is there no other knowledge?[1]

The philosophy of nineteenth-century liberalism, whether it was preached in churches and chapels or in circles of enlightened rationalists, combined a noble fervour for the brotherhood of man with a profound indifference to the anthropological and historical individuality of the communities in which men actually lived. It was distorted and impoverished by an unconscious philistinism which

[1] Cf. the Maharajah of Alwar at the Imperial Conference of 1923: 'The solution, I firmly believe, will not be in grafting Western principles of government on to the East with a stroke of the pen. Already many old bottles have cracked into which this new wine has been poured.' Cmd. 1988, p. 90. (Perhaps it is needless to say that the writer is not at present taking up a position with regard to specific political controversies about the constitution of India.)

ignored all values except those of bourgeois European society, which it assumed to be of universal validity. In theory it may be criticized because of its abstract individualism. In practice it suffered from a squint which made it slow to detect the evils of industrialism. With the best intentions in the world, it tolerated, it even encouraged, the ruthlessness of an acquisitive society. Its abstract theory of human rights became the natural ally of an abstract political economy. The isolated individual was translated into the mobile labour-unit. In the name of human equality he was endowed with the 'right' of being uprooted from his own civilization and dumped in the unlovely fringes of western capitalistic society. The nineteenth-century liberals were slow to see anything objectionable in sweeping Bantu away from their lands to live in compounds and work in mines, or in transporting Indians from their homes to labour in the plantations of Fiji and Natal. Without any twinges of conscience—for did not labour naturally seek its market ?—they played their part in creating the problem of 'white capital and coloured labour'.

It was as 'coloured labour' that British colonists in the nineteenth century came to know their fellow subjects in India.[1] The system of 'indenture', under which Indian labourers were imported, was the sequel to the abolition of slavery. The great act of abolition was passed in 1833; in 1834 the sugar-colony of Mauritius, where the planters believed themselves to be threatened with ruin, led the way in procuring Indian 'coolies'. Sturdy abolitionists in England suspected the reintroduction of slavery under another name. Brougham, Fowell Buxton, and others, secured in 1840 the appointment of a commission to investigate the system of indentured labour. Three members of the commission recommended its discontinuance: the fourth member recommended its continuance with safeguards. The House of Commons, by 113 votes to 24, accepted the minority recommendation. Throughout the next three generations there flowed to the colonies a steady trickle from India's vast reservoir of labour: between 1842 and 1870 Mauritius received 351,401 indentured labourers; British Guiana 76,691; Trinidad 42,519; Jamaica 15,169. Natal, a late arrival in the Indian labour market, had by 1870 received only 6,448. But in 1884 Natal's Indian population was 27,000; in 1891 it was 35,000; in 1921—ten years after the export of indentured labour to this province had been prohibited by the Government

[1] The facts in this paragraph are taken chiefly from the *Report of the Committee on Emigration to the Crown Colonies and Protectorates*, Cd. 5192 of 1910. Professor Erickson, of the University of Illinois, is preparing a complete history of Indian indentured labour. A bibliography by Mr. Evans Lewin, containing many titles on the subject, was published by the Royal Empire Society in 1926.

of India—it was 140,000. In the last decade of the nineteenth century, the Indian population of Natal actually outnumbered the European population. The problem of South Africa's relations with India had been created.[1]

The British Government and the Government of India, who were jointly responsible for this system, were slow to perceive that it could give rise to any problem. The swelling protests of colonial democracy and Indian patriotism irritated, but hardly disturbed, a complacency which took for granted the rights of men and capitalists. Lord Salisbury, when he was Secretary of State for India, was anxious that the policy of exporting coolies should be pursued more vigorously. In 1875 he invited the Government of India to take a more active part in their recruitment. He argued that this would confer a great benefit on the colonies, which needed labour, and on India, which contained too many people. And the labourers might rest assured that, when they had served their indentures, they would be 'in all respects free men, with privileges no whit inferior to those of any other class of Her Majesty's subjects resident in the Colonies'. But might they rest assured of this? Lord Salisbury's statement was generally true of Mauritius and the West Indian islands, where racial origin was irrelevant as a qualification for civil and political rights, and where the theory of the natural equality of mankind was working itself out in the most logical way, that is, by making these communities a 'melting pot' of diverse races.[2] But in those colonies of European settlement which enjoyed responsible government or were aspiring to it, Lord Salisbury's promise was entirely without grounds. It was a growing awareness of this fact, and a growing realization of Indian resentment against the indenture system, which made the Government of India more prone to caution than the Secretary of State. In his reply to Lord Salisbury, the Viceroy remarked that the people were 'prone to regard with the utmost suspicion the acts and motives of their foreign rulers'. The Government of India was unwilling to take upon its shoulders any direct responsibility for recruiting; in the future, as in the past, it would base its action upon the principle of freedom of contract; it would continue to supervise the terms of contract in the interests of fair play, but otherwise would remain 'purely neutral'. But in the course of time pure neutrality became an impossible position. A long dispatch of December 1908

[1] By restriction of Indian migration the Europeans thereafter recovered a preponderance over the Indians.

[2] There was therefore no 'Indian question' in these colonies (see Cd. 1988 of 1904, pp. 98, 129)—and since this chapter is a study of conflicting ideals and policies, they will not come directly under review.

laid bare the growing uneasiness of the Government of India at the position of Indians overseas. The self-governing colonies of the Empire, and particularly the colony of Natal, had repudiated the promises of racial equality which British statesmen had made to Indian emigrants on the Empire's behalf. And was it not the accepted destiny of all colonies to become self-governing? The Government of India was already afraid that in East Africa the antagonism of white colonists to the Indians might create 'similar problems to those which have had such deplorable effects in South Africa'. The argument of this dispatch advanced steadily towards the conclusion that the indentured-labour system was creating such problems for the British Empire that its abolition was imperative. But the argument swerved away from this conclusion; the theories of the rights of man and the mobility of labour stood in the way.[1] Even after Indian patriotism had made the issue one of national honour, even while the national leaders were attacking the indenture system as a badge of helotry and humiliation, the Government of India continued to regard it merely as a commercial transaction between individuals, and drew comfort from the conclusion of the experts that 'its advantages have far outweighed its disadvantages'.[2]

The Indian leaders and their English supporters refused to accept this comforting assurance. They pointed out that the method of recruitment led to fraud of the worst kind; that relatives of recruited labourers were frequently given a cash payment, and a higher one for a woman than for a man; that, roughly, there were five men recruited for every woman, and that the discrepancy of sexes on the plantations led to immorality, suicide, and murder. They also pointed out that this system of 'semi-slavery'—as Sir William Hunter called it—degraded Indian honour abroad.[3] They declared that the indenture system had forced upon India a violent and unnatural intercourse with the outer world. From the time of Buddha until about A.D. 1000 there had existed a period of natural Indian expansion, both commercial and cultural; thereafter Hinduism had withdrawn within its own frontiers, in order to preserve its

[1] The correspondence paraphrased above may be found in Cd. 5192 of 1908.

[2] *Report to the Government of India on the Conditions of Indian Immigrants in Four British Colonies.* Cd. 7744 and 7745 of 1914–16. The colonies were Trinidad, British Guiana, Jamaica, and Fiji. The conclusions are in Cd. 7744 at pp. 322 ff.

[3] The writer has particularly in mind the investigations of Rev. C. F. Andrews and Mr. W. W. Pearson in Fiji towards the end of the War. These investigations had a marked effect, not only on the Government of India, but on public opinion in Australia. A lady representing the Australian National Council of Women, Miss Garnham, continued Mr. Andrews' inquiries, and the writings of Rev. J. W. Burton appealed to a wide Australian public on behalf of the Fiji Indians.

cherished observances from the impact of the expanding Mohammedan world.[1] This self-withdrawal had not affected the trading enterprise of low-caste Hindus nor that of Mohammedans, and there was a natural tendency towards its disappearance in the later nineteenth century. India might have looked forward to taking an honourable place in the commercial and cultural intercourse of nations. But her natural development had been anticipated and violently distorted by the interests of colonial capitalism, which regarded her merely as a reservoir of cheap labour. The Government of India's policy with regard to indenture had never been accepted by Indian national feeling, and as soon as this feeling became politically articulate it violently attacked the system, which meant to Gandhi and Gokhale and Malaviya exactly what slavery had meant to Clarkson and Wilberforce. A resolution was passed unanimously in the Indian legislative council early in 1910, on Mr. Gandhi's motion, calling upon the Government of India to terminate the system as regards South Africa unless it were able to secure satisfactory assurances from General Botha's government with regard to the treatment of the Indian population. The assurances were not forthcoming, and in 1911 Indian labour emigration was closed to Natal. Early in the following year Mr. Gokhale moved a resolution for the complete abolition of indentured labour emigration. The Government of India did not accept the resolution, which, however, secured the support of all the unofficial Indian members. But in 1916 a resolution to the same effect passed the legislative council. The system was suspended by regulation in 1917, and this action was confirmed by the Emigration Act of 1922. Already, on 1st January 1920, every Indian in the colonies still serving under indenture had been set free. That day is India's 'Abolition Day'.[2]

The historical sketch given in the preceding paragraphs should suffice to make clear the reasons for India's concurrence in the reciprocity resolution of 1917 and her reaffirmation of the principle underlying this resolution at succeeding imperial conferences. It is also clear why the force of Indian protest was directed, not against Australia and New Zealand, which had rigorously restricted Indian immigration, but against Natal, which had stimulated it.[3] If only

[1] Hindus were not allowed to cross *Kala pani* ('black water'). Raja Rum Mohan Roy was one of the first to break through this restriction.

[2] The author is indebted to Mr. H. S. L. Polak and Rev. C. F. Andrews for expositions which have made it possible for him to appreciate the intensity of Indian feeling with regard to indentured labour.

[3] It will be pointed out below that Natal sought simultaneously to restrict Indian 'immigration' and import Indian 'labour'.

the labour democracies of Australia and New Zealand had realized the true position, they were not resisting, but were supporting, the demands of Indian nationalism. Australian and Indian idealists were fighting the same enemy, which was capitalistic acquisitiveness masking itself under the rights of man. The position of Indian patriots, owing to the perversion of natural development which had been inflicted upon India, was a complicated and difficult one. They had to resist simultaneously immigration-promotion policies which implied Indian inferiority, and immigration-restriction policies which implied the same inferiority. Sir Tej Bahadur Sapru was thinking of the former when he protested in 1923 that there ought to be '. . . . no emigration from India outside on any conditions whatever. We do not want our nation outside India to appear as a nation of coolies. We have had enough of that.'[1] India's tendency was to withdraw, as she had withdrawn in an earlier period of her history, from an outside world in which her people had suffered degradation and pain.[2] But the tendency did not run to extremes. In those countries to which Indian immigration had been a natural and not a perverted movement, such as East Africa, India was disposed to resist violently any interference with the existing rights of her people. At the same time she was ready to acquiesce in the immigration-restriction policies of the self-governing Dominions, provided that India herself possessed equal rights to restrict immigration from them. Her demand was for equality; but the content of this equality was very different from that which had been intended by the liberal theory of the nineteenth century. It was not the equality of abstract individualism, the equality assumed to belong to isolated individuals in a cosmopolis; but rather the equality of historically diverse communities living together in a wider community of rights and duties. The new theory might indeed be put in a phrase: 'Equal rights for diverse communities.' The theory was only tentatively formulated; it was implied rather than stated; but it corresponded closely to India's historically conditioned mood, and to the existing phase of development in the British Commonwealth of Nations.

> 'You have received' [said Sir Tej Bahadur Sapru to the prime ministers of the Commonwealth] 'a rich inheritance of independence

[1] Cmd. 1988, p. 81.

[2] It is relevant to mention the growing feeling in India that the country has suffered by costly western standards which she cannot afford, and the growing criticism of the practice of sending abroad large numbers of Indian students on the ground that they do not necessarily bring back qualifications commensurate with the amount spent on them, or attitudes adapted to India's traditional scheme of life.

and self-government in your territories. I am still aspiring to it. I hope my aspirations will be realized very soon, and then, like you, I shall be jealous of any outside authority imposing its will upon me in my affairs.'[1]

It is now possible to return to the narrative of events in the imperial conference. On one of the most momentous of all possible issues between India and other members of the Commonwealth there was, as we have seen, agreement. Immigration-restriction was a right inherent in the status of each self-governing community of the Commonwealth. From the point of view of the British Dominions, India's acceptance of this principle in 1917 and at three successive imperial conferences was an extraordinary gain. But India, on her part, expected from the Dominions definite contributions to that 'better understanding' which the Conference of 1917 anticipated. After the central issue had been disposed of by a repudiation of the notion of unfettered movements of population within a cosmopolitan empire, there still remained two other issues of considerable importance. The first of these concerned the rights of individuals travelling from India to other parts of the British Commonwealth without any intention of permanent settlement. The nations of the British Commonwealth, although each one intended to determine the elements of its own population, had no intention of stagnating in isolation from each other. Their spokesmen assumed that students, merchants, and tourists would by their activities promote the mutual advantage and understanding of India and the other communities under the British Crown. But, in most of the British Dominions, Indians of these classes had laid upon them the onus of proving—possibly to crude and unsympathetic civil servants—that they were not members of the prohibited class. Lord Crewe had in 1907 voiced the complaint of Indian gentlemen that they could not set foot in some of the Dominions 'without undergoing vexatious catechisms from petty officials'.[2] At the 1918 Conference, Sir S. P. Sinha proposed that the passport system should be used reciprocally between India and other British countries as a means of endorsing rights of

[1] Cmd. 1988, p. 83. In effect the control of migration has actually been transferred from the India Office to the Government of India. An Emigration Standing Committee of the Indian Central Legislature has been in existence for several years in an advisory capacity to the member of the Government of India in charge of the Department of Education, Lands, and Emigration. Under the proposed new constitution emigration and immigration are not reserved matters.

[2] Cmd. 5746–1, p. 272. They were sometimes liable to suffer affronts even after they had passed the officials. When Mr. Gokhale visited South Africa in 1912, even the special precautions taken by men of intelligence and goodwill did not entirely save him from insulting treatment by ignorant persons.

visit and temporary residence. The Conference accepted the proposal, and future conferences were spared from any perplexities on this vexatious matter.[1]

The second subordinate issue was intrinsically more serious, and was permitted by constant irritation to swell to prodigious dimensions. This issue concerned the rights of Indians who were actually resident in other British countries. General Smuts had expressed the hope in 1917 that India's acceptance of the immigration policies of the Dominions would make it easy for them to satisfy her wishes for better treatment of Indians who already possessed dominion domicile.

> 'In South Africa' [he said] 'there has been this fundamental trouble, that the white community have been afraid of opening the door too wide to Indian immigration. . . . I have always felt sure, that once the white community in South Africa were rid of the fear that they were going to be flooded by unlimited immigration from India, all the other questions would be considered subsidiary and would become easily and perfectly soluble.'[2]

As regards the other Dominions, this anticipation of the South African statesman proved itself to be generally correct. Discussions at the Conferences of 1921 and 1923 revealed little or no cause of complaint against New Zealand and Australia. In New Zealand the rights of Indian residents were in every respect equal with those of other citizens: 'My fellow countrymen', said Sir Tej Bahadur Sapru, 'can live there among the New Zealanders as fellow-citizens in honour.' In Australia, Indian residents were excluded from the franchise in the Commonwealth and in two states; they were also subject to discrimination with regard to pensions and—in certain states—in one or two branches of economic activity. But the government of the Commonwealth professed its eagerness to grant a speedy equality.[3] In Canada the problem was rather more intractable; for the Dominion government, although its intentions were benevolent, lacked the resolution to exercise its constitutional right of compelling British Columbia, which contained the great majority of a scanty Indian immigration, to conform to the standards of the other eight

[1] Cd. 9177 of 1918, pp. 195, 248. Mr. Sastri, during his visits to the Dominions after the 1921 Conference, declared that this matter was now settled to Indian satisfaction. Cf. *Round Table*, vol. xiii, pp. 175–6.

[2] Cd. 8566, p. 1119. This was before the publication of the 1921 census which disproved the exaggerated statement as to the increase of Indians in South Africa.

[3] Cmd. 1987, p. 19. Cmd. 1988, pp. 77, 107–12. In 1925 the Commonwealth admitted Indians to the franchise. Keith, *Responsible Government in the Dominions*, p. 815. The States, with the exception of Western Australia, have done the same.

provinces.[1] But it was against South Africa that the Indians launched their most bitter complaints. In 1917 General Smuts had raised expectations which he was not able to fulfil. Public opinion among the European population of South Africa, so far from permitting the government to ameliorate the condition of Indians resident there, demanded that new restrictions should be imposed upon their freedom. Public opinion in India was no longer content to accept specific satisfactions for specific grievances, but began to demand complete equality in active citizenship between the Indian and European inhabitants of the Union. The quarrel between India and South Africa invaded the harmony of three successive imperial conferences, and at last ended in deadlock. The quarrel was about the rights of no more than eight score thousand Indians—a few grains of India's multitudinous progeny.[2] But it was the kind of quarrel which wrecks empires.

At the Imperial War Conference of 1918 the Indians showed their first sign of impatience. India had done her part, they said, in seeking a better understanding; it was time for the Dominions to do theirs. A list of Indian grievances laid stress upon the oppressions inflicted by South Africa—economic discrimination in land laws and the granting of trade licences, offensive railway regulations, denial of the municipal franchise. India, her spokesman also hinted, might by her progress in representative government qualify her children abroad for full political rights.[3] At the 1921 Conference the hint became a demand. Mr. Sastri moved a resolution which, while it reiterated the right of each British community to control the composition of its own population, asserted that there was an incongruity between India's position as an equal member of the British Empire and the existence of disabilities upon British Indians lawfully domiciled in some other parts of the British Empire. The resolution claimed for these Indians 'all the rights of citizenship'. In India, said Mr. Sastri, the treatment which this resolution received would be regarded as 'the test by which the whole position must be judged'. The Conference passed the resolution with a rider affirming South Africa's

[1] British Columbia feared that if the Indians were given the franchise the far more numerous Chinese and Japanese would also claim it. In some respects the Indian position was inferior to the Japanese, which had concluded with Canada an agreement to limit immigration. Indians in British Columbia did not until after 1923 possess the privilege of Indians in South Africa, of bringing in one wife and her children (being minors).

[2] The 1921 census showed 161,339 Indians in South Africa. Most had been born there.

[3] Cd. 9177, pp. 245–7. The disabilities complained of did not exist in the Cape Province.

dissent from it, and an additional rider affirming India's grievance against South Africa.[1] In this resolution the unanimity rule of the imperial conference became a fiction which emphasized the fundamental conflict between two members of the Commonwealth. Some months later a New Zealand commentator shrewdly summed up the situation—'If the people of India will not stay in the Empire unless they are granted full equality, and South Africa will not stay in if they are, there is a tough proposition ahead of the Empire.'[2]

Two years later, at the Conference of 1923, the conflict reached a pitch of intensity which would have involved the rupture of diplomatic relations between India and South Africa, had they not been joined in a constitutional system under the British Crown. Sir Tej Bahadur Sapru and His Highness the Maharaja of Alwar, speaking for India, complained of an indignity which 'cuts to the quick our national pride and our new consciousness', 'which permeates and sours our whole outlook in regard to Imperial partnership'. They complained of a loss of *Izzat*, of a diminution of their own worth in their own eyes, of an affront to their self-respect and honour. 'Nothing hurts more', said the Maharaja, 'than the loss of *Izzat*. . . . It is that one word which is the keynote of half the troubles of the world.' Sir Tej translated the conception of *Izzat* into a homely metaphor when he said that he was fighting as a subject of King George for a place in his household, and that he would not be content with a place in his stables. Addressing General Smuts, he said that if the Indian problem in South Africa were allowed to fester much longer, it would pass beyond the bounds of a domestic issue and become 'an issue of foreign policy of such gravity that upon it the unity of the Empire may founder irretrievably'.[3] General Smuts refused to yield. India, he retorted, could not have it both ways; if she were a member of the Commonwealth she could not make her grievances an issue of foreign policy, and if she did make them an issue of foreign policy, she could not claim for Indians the privileges of the Commonwealth. His argument, as it proceeded, might have invited from Indians the counter-retort—'Were the privileges of the Commonwealth worth claiming?' The status of a British subject, he said, did not confer rights of citizenship within the member-states of the British League of Nations. The common Kingship was the binding link between the parts of the Empire; it was not a source

[1] Cmd. 1474, p. 8.

[2] *Round Table*, vol. xiii, p. 296. The writer was commenting on an indiscreet passage in a speech of Mr. Sastri's, delivered in New Zealand during his tour of the British Commonwealth after the 1921 Conference.

[3] Cmd. 1988, pp. 81, 83, 84, 91.

from which private citizens would derive their rights. 'They will derive their rights simply and solely from the authority of the State in which they live.'[1] Softening his argument a little, he fastened on the Indian claim to the franchise: the status of a British subject did not carry with it the right to vote in any and every British community. 'There is one British citizenship over the whole Empire . . . but we must not derive from the one British citizenship rights of franchise.' The Indians, in short, had no case in constitutional law.[2] And to their plea of *Izzat* General Smuts replied with an argument of necessity. Once South Africa granted the suffrage to Indians, she would have to go farther and grant it to natives; and that would be the end of her western civilization. 'So far as South Africa is concerned, therefore, it is a question of impossibility. Sir Tej and his colleagues say, quite rightly, that for India it is a question of dignity. For South Africa, for white South Africa, it is not a question of dignity, but a question of existence, and no government could for a moment either tamper with this position or do anything to meet the Indian point of view.' Here was deadlock. 'We are up against a stone wall', said General Smuts, 'and we cannot get over it.'

The preceding narrative has sketched a series of episodes in the long quarrel between India and South Africa, but only from the angle of political debate in the imperial conference. To understand these issues in their concrete reality, it will be necessary to make a short excursion into South African history.

II

India and South Africa

It was suggested in the previous section that the honest liberalism of the nineteenth century, with all its great gifts of vision and sym-

[1] Ibid., pp. 138–40. The Indians answered 'You cannot . . . have two kinds of citizenship in the same Empire, a higher and a lower'. But General Smuts's argument had been anticipated by Sir Wilfrid Laurier in 1911 (Cd. 5745, p. 407): 'They [Indian residents] have all the rights of British citizens, but there are to the exercise of these rights certain conditions attached, which are matters of municipal and local regulation.' There are some unresolved contradictions in General Smuts's utterances at this conference, e.g. pp. 138–40 and p. 116. Did *all* rights derive from the 'State in which they live', or only franchise rights? If all rights had a local origin, did the status of British subject mean anything at all to an Indian in South Africa? Was there in fact such a thing as British citizenship? The reader gets the impression that General Smuts cautiously retreated to his first position—the franchise. Cf. p. 132. The Home Secretary tried to straighten out the confusion by distinguishing imperial nationality and local citizenship. But he was not present at the debate.

[2] On this Sir Tej Bahadur Sapru commented (Cmd. 1988, p. 85): 'Nobody has doubted that constitutional right (i.e. of South Africa to fix its franchise) but there are limits to that constitutional right, limits which are prescribed by prudence.'

pathy, had sometimes a tendency to squint, and even to wink an eye. Reflection upon one significant fragment of Indian history, the painful episode of indentured labour, showed how misleading it would be to credit to the liberal philosophy all the good which British rule has wrought in India, and to ascribe all the evil which it has wrought to a denial of that philosophy. Would a similar inquiry into South African history reveal a similar patchiness in the record of the liberal idea of European duty towards the Bantu people? The inquiry must be postponed to a later volume of this book; the present section will give merely a preliminary view of the difficult country to be explored. It takes its departure, not from England, but from India.

But first it may be useful to recall a not uncommon interpretation of South African history. According to this interpretation, the idealism of the English people heroically set itself the task of dealing in justice and love with Hottentots and Bantu. An ordinance of 1828 put free coloured persons on a footing of civil equality with Europeans. The great Act of 1833 brought freedom to the slaves. The constitution of 1852 permitted in Cape Colony no barrier which would exclude from the fullest functions of citizenship any subject of Her Majesty on the ground of his race or colour. A belief in human rights which derives equally from the rationalist philosophy of the eighteenth century and from its evangelical revival seems to repeat itself in an unbroken series of professions and promises. 'There shall not be in the eyes of the law', declared Sir George Napier when he annexed Natal, 'any distinction or qualification whatever founded on mere distinction of colour, origin, language, or creed; but . . . the protection of law in letter and substance shall be extended impartially to all alike.' And Rhodes at the end of the nineteenth century reiterated the principle which underlay the liberal franchise of Cape Colony: 'Equal rights for every civilized man.'[1] How easy it would be to found upon these professions a simple interpretation of 'complex South Africa'. It would be easier, by far, than the corresponding

[1] The full note which Rhodes wrote on the edge of a newspaper was as follows: 'My motto is, equal rights for every civilized man south of the Zambezi. What is a civilized man? A man whether white or black who has sufficient intelligence to write his name, has some property or work, in fact is not a loafer.' With regard to the 'civilization' franchise of the Cape, the writer now asks a question which he cannot yet answer: whether it was qualified by the assumption—which appears in a dispatch written by Sir Alfred Milner in 1904 (Cd. 2239, p. 25)—that only a tiny minority of 'natives' would be admitted to 'white privileges'? In 1929 there were only 15,780 natives on the electoral roll of the Cape: in 1931 there were only 12,271. See Ifor L. Evans, *Native Policy in Southern Africa* (Cambridge University Press, 1934), p. 14. The Cape franchise which was abolished in 1936 had in fact never been exercised except 'by the merest fringe of the impending mass'. (*Round Table*, vol. xiii, p. 57.) This does not imply that the natives did not highly value it.

interpretation of Indian history. For this time the drama need not be found in a struggle between the better and worse selves of Englishmen. Englishmen need have no worse selves. The Boers could most adequately fill that rôle. . . . England's missionaries and her beneficent capitalists uphold the banner of 'equal rights for every civilized man'. The Boers maintain the principle that black people are slaves by nature. They write that principle into the constitutions of their seceding republics. 'The people', declare the Transvaal folk in their Grond-Wet of 1858, 'desire to permit no equality between coloured people and the white inhabitants, either in Church or State.'[1] For the dramatically minded historian this declaration is a godsend. South Africa's racial history almost writes itself. The white peoples gather under their opposing banners; upon the issue of their struggle hangs the fate of the oppressed. The Boers are the oppressors, the British are the deliverers. . . . But suppose the historian were an Indian? The stirring simplicities of South African history would rearrange themselves. The Boers, it is true, would retain their rôle as single-minded champions of the inequality of races. Gandhi has recorded President Kruger's reply to a deputation of Indians who came to him to plead for just treatment of Indian traders:

> 'You are the descendants of Ishmael and therefore from your very birth bound to slave for the descendants of Esau. As the descendants of Esau we cannot admit you to rights placing you on an equality with ourselves. You must rest content with what rights we grant to you.'

Gandhi, while he criticizes the bigotry of this reply, seems to find some pleasure in contemplating its candour.[2] Among the British he found a more virulent intolerance unrelieved by candour. Viewed from the Indian angle, it is the British section of the white population of South Africa which has been the arch-enemy of human equality. It was among the British colonists in Natal that the Indians first tasted humiliation and woe. It was the British traders of Johannesburg and the Transvaal townships who most bitterly hounded the Transvaal government to their persecution.

But perhaps only the colonial British were guilty. May it not be possible to interpret the history of South Africa's racial problems as a struggle between the Christian and liberal principle of human equality, to which the British government and people are in general faithful, and the un-Christian, irrational egoism of the colonists, both British and Dutch? Such an interpretation would retain the

[1] G. W. Eybers, *Select Constitutional Documents illustrating South African History* (Routledge, 1918), p. 364.

[2] Gandhi, *Satyagraha in South Africa* (Madras, 1923), p. 56.

dramatic simplicity of the hero-and-villain theme, and would conclude with the lamentations of a despondent but unblemished virtue. . . . The narrative will reveal how far this interpretation can be sustained.

It is time to take up the story of Indian migration from the South African end. White capital and Indian labour together built the fortunes of Natal. But the white men assumed that the fortunes were for their sole enjoyment. They very soon took up the position that it was the perpetual rôle of the Indians to be labour; nothing more. The Indians, naturally, had a different idea of what constituted a desirable future. The entry of tens of thousands of indentured labourers began to produce its natural result in the development of a more diversified Indian community. From Mauritius came a solid trader, Sheth Abubakar Amod, to do business among his compatriots on the Natal plantations. The trader prospered, purchased land, extended his enterprise to supply the simple wants of native Africans. The rumour of his prosperity spread from Natal to Mauritius and India; other traders entered with their servants to share his good fortune. Thus there began a new kind of Indian settlement.[1] At the same time, considerable numbers of labourers who had completed their indentures remained as 'free Indians'. They, too, sought to make a living by trade—usually on a petty scale—or by service, or by the cultivation of fruit and vegetables. In short, they began to compete as free men in the ordinary activities of the community. According to the official theory of the indenture system, this was a most desirable development: India permitted the export of labourers under contract in order that they might better their condition. According to the liberal theory propounded in British South Africa—the theory of 'equal rights for every civilized man'—the development should have been very welcome. It was surely a matter for congratulation that the Indian labourers should begin to struggle up the ladder of economic opportunity which would some day—no doubt a very distant day—bring them to the level of 'white privileges'. But the South Africans, when they realized what was happening, consigned their theory to perdition.[2] There was too big a crowd of Indians jostling for places on the lower ranks of the economic ladder. The white settlers believed that the Indians, in their struggle to ascend, would thrust their way into positions which

[1] By the end of the Great War about fifty thousand Indians—nearly one-third of the Indian population of Natal—belonged to this class.

[2] Or it might be said that they appealed to the 'reservation' referred to in the note on p. 188.

should be reserved for Europeans. For the Indians had a far less expensive standard of living than the Europeans, and therefore a greater power to thrust and cling. And what would be the fate of the unfortunates who were pushed from their foothold? A dominant race which had built its homes precariously on the broken ground of African society could not even ask such a question without feeling a shiver of panic. The dizzy eminence of the white man's position in South Africa could be measured, and sometimes was measured, by the depth of the abyss into which he must hurtle when he lost his foothold on the heights. There were 'poor whites' in Natal before the Indians began to prosper there. The dominant race dreaded that Indian prosperity would multiply them. It is possible that their fears were unreasonable. It is possible that their conception of their own self-interest was short-sighted, and that the Indian problem was presenting to them a challenge which some day they would be compelled for their own good to face.[1] Whether or not this was true, their history had not equipped them for the necessary painful effort of economic and social self-criticism. It had on the contrary plentifully endowed them with fears and prejudices. The Indian became to them a new kind, a more dangerous kind, of 'native'. In their justification it may be urged that they were not really in contact with Indian civilization, but chiefly with the broken and ragged edges of the lowest class in that civilization. In their condemnation it must be said that it was by their own will that these human fragments of India existed on South African soil; it was their own action which had created those immoralities of plantation life and that insanitary squalor in the cities, which so appalled them.[2] They postured as the defenders of European civilization in South Africa; but their policy offended against the highest standards of that civilization in treating other human beings merely as means. Their policy aimed simultaneously at maintaining the supply of Indian labourers who were so useful to white capitalists, and at excluding or expelling from Natal the Indians who had risen or were likely to rise to a status higher than that of a human instrument. For their own purposes, they were simultaneously excluding Indians who possessed wealth, education, and

[1] The *Report of the South African Economic and Wage Commission of 1925* (U.G. 14, 1926) laid stress on the gap between a small number of white workers paid artificially high wages and a large number of under-paid natives. The commission considered this system inelastic and dangerous to all: it reported a growing proportion of 'poor whites'—and this class since then has greatly increased.

[2] Gandhi, *Satyagraha in South Africa*, p. 40, on the indentured labourers—'how they broke through all the restraints which religion or morality imposes, or, to be more accurate, how these restraints gave way, and how the very distinction between a married woman and a concubine ceased to exist among these unfortunate people'.

careful sanitary habits—the tests of civilization on which they commonly laid stress—and choosing the poorest, the dirtiest, the most illiterate. And they were doing their best to send these people back to India in their original condition. By a system of discriminatory taxation their legislature endeavoured to compel labourers either to reindenture themselves for a further period, or to leave the colony. The British government offered no opposition to the content of the colony's anti-Indian legislation; but it protested against the form of it when the legislature grounded its measures on differences of race and colour. It was this formal adoption of racial discrimination which stirred up opposition in another quarter, with effects upon the Empire's future which are still incalculable. In 1894 a young Indian barrister called Gandhi happened to be in South Africa on legal business. He began his political career with a struggle against the principle of racial discrimination embodied in a franchise bill which was introduced into the Natal legislature in that year.[1]

In his early South African days, Gandhi might well have thought himself a humble champion of the principles which the British government was fighting to establish. It was still possible with some plausibility to dramatize racial policies in South Africa as a struggle between the enlightenment of the British government and the prejudices of the local European population, both British and Dutch. The British government, although it felt itself unable to alter the content of Natal's anti-Indian legislation, eliminated from the Franchise Act and from the Immigration Restriction Act all offensive phraseology. And it was vigorously defending the rights of Her Majesty's Indian subjects resident in the South African Republic. These Indians, who were mostly of a higher standing than the Madrassi labourers who predominated in Natal, were forbidden by a law of 1885 to own fixed property; they were compelled to register at a high fee if they wished to trade; they were compelled to accept segregation in bazaars. The British government protested against

[1] Gandhi, *Satyagraha in South Africa*, p. 50. Natal received responsible government in 1893. The first immigration restriction act finally became law in 1897. Discriminatory taxation dates from 1895, when an act imposed an annual tax of £3 on labourers who failed to return to India or to reindenture. In 1903 the tax was extended to girls over 14 and boys over 16. There is a full summary of the anti-Indian legislation, in a context of reproving comment, in Keith, *Responsible Government in the Dominions*, chapter IV, § 4. Cf. R. L. Buell, *The Native Problem in South Africa* (Macmillan, 1928), vol. i, pp. 24–8.

On Mahatma Gandhi, British readers may be referred to two books by Mr. C. F. Andrews, *Mahatma Gandhi, his own story*, and *Mahatma Gandhi at work* (Allen & Unwin, 1930 and 1931). These are authorized *résumés* of the two volumes, not easily procured, *My Experiments with Truth* and *Satyagraha in South Africa*.

this legislation on the ground that it infringed the London Convention of 1889 between Great Britain and the South African Republic. Arbitration relieved the tension caused by this issue, but did not end it.[1] Till the very eve of the South African war, British ministers continued to denounce to British audiences the enormity of President Kruger's treatment of the Queen's Indian subjects. It was an offence against human equality. It was an affront to British dignity. It was, in short, a just cause—though certainly not the only just cause nor the chief one—of war. Indians within the Transvaal and outside it might be excused if they hoped for great things from a British victory. The Indians of Natal, inspired by Gandhi, demonstrated their loyalty as British subjects by organizing an ambulance corps. But the end of the war brought them bitter disillusionment. Before long their complaints were assailing the ears of British administrators in the conquered republics and of the distant authorities in London.

> 'What the Indians pray for is very little. They ask for no political power. They admit the principle of restricting cheap labour, no matter from what source it may come. All they ask for is freedom for those that are now settled, to trade, to move about, and to hold landed property without any hindrance save the ordinary legal requirements. And they ask for abrogation of legislation that imposes disabilities on them because they wear a brown skin.'[2]

They asked, in fact, that the British administration in the Transvaal should be true to the professions and promises which the British government had made. The very reverse happened. The old laws of the Transvaal remained on the statute book. The new British officials enforced them with unprecedented efficiency. A specially constituted Asiatic department of the administration in Pretoria exercised its ingenuity in closing every gap through which Indians without right of domicile might slip into the Transvaal. To this end, the department planned a new system of registration which included, among other things, identification of Indians by their finger-prints. Gandhi, in recording his view of these events more than twenty years after they had occurred—he happened then to have leisure for reflection and writing in Yeravda jail—took particular pains to stress the fact that it was not the Boers, nor yet the South African British, but the responsible English administrators and their very intelligent

[1] C. 7911 of 1895. *Papers relating to the grievances of Her Majesty's Indian subjects in the South African Republic.* Cf. C. 7946 of 1896.

[2] Cd. 2239 of 1904, p. 21 (quotation from a memorial of the British Indian Association of Johannesburg).

English advisers, who were the chief contrivers of offence and insult to the Indians, and who were therefore the unwitting authors of that new experiment in human resistance to wrong which has made the story of the small Indian community in South Africa a fundamental chapter in the history of modern India.[1]

Gandhi's reminiscences[2] should be read in conjunction with the blue books issued between 1904 and 1908. These reveal the thoughts of the administrators whom Gandhi accuses, and throw a vivid light on the complications of the struggle whose history he narrates. A letter from the Lieutenant-Governor of the Transvaal, written on 13th April 1904, illuminates the mental habit of an official who exemplifies perfectly, in his struggle to see what is right and to do it, the qualities and limitations of his nation and class.[3] The Lieutenant-Governor is torn between his consciousness that it is dishonourable for Englishmen to break their word, and his conviction that on this particular issue it is impossible for them to keep it. 'Promises have been made without knowledge or perception of the consequences involved in their fulfilment.' A barrier to fulfilment is the intense feeling of the European population of the Transvaal. The feeling may be irrational: it is none the less a force to be reckoned with. It has behind it the whole weight of South African memories. . . . It is, moreover, rooted in economic necessity. The existence of a vast mass of Africans excludes white men from unskilled labour: the entry of a 'horde'[4] of Asiatics threatens to drive them out of all the activities intermediate between unskilled labour and the small number of high directive and professional occupations. . . . South Africa is one of the few countries inhabitable both by Asiatics and Europeans, and its future racial character is at stake. 'If the redemption of the pledges means that in fifty or a hundred years this country will have fallen to the inheritance of the Eastern instead of the Western populations, then from the point of view of civilization they must be numbered among the promises which it is a greater crime to keep than to break.' . . . There is no need to paraphrase and quote any further. The Lieutenant-Governor has begun by stating the case of the Europeans in South Africa, he has gone on to appreciate it, he has ended by making it his own. In all probability there was not a single English administrator in the two conquered

[1] Gandhi, *Satyagraha in South Africa*, ch. x. Gandhi is particularly bitter in his attack on Mr. Lionel Curtis.

[2] See the conclusion of footnote on p. 192.

[3] The letter is printed in Cd. 2239 of 1904, pp. 28 ff.

[4] Actually the number of Indians in the Transvaal was somewhere between 11,000 and 13,000.

republics whose thoughts did not flow through the same channel. Lord Milner and 'Lord Milner's young men' and Lord Selborne all accepted the South African point of view. They quoted with approval the South African contention that 'there is hardly any mistake a young country may commit which cannot afterwards be amended and undone except a mistake in the elements of population'.[1] When pressed by others, or by their own consciences, they admitted a formal breach of faith, but alleged in condonation of it supervening impossibility and *salus populi*. They also alleged a conflicting promise. Britain had pledged herself to grant self-government to the Transvaal and the Orange River Colony. It was therefore the duty of British administrators not to abate the reality of this self-government by pretending to decide in advance issues which must ultimately be decided by the South African communities.[2] Their thought was—one thing at a time. Their very idealism made them ruthless. It fastened on the high project of appeasement between Afrikaner and Briton; it hardened them to exact from the Indian minority part of the price. Perhaps some of them believed that justice and goodwill, when they had been tested and proved within practicable limits, would take courage from their own achievements. If these virtues should now inaugurate a new era in the relations between English and Dutch, an understanding of the true foundations of this appeasement might in some future day inspire those who had been blessed by it to extend its blessings to others.[3]

Whether or not these conjectures of motive are well-founded, the fact is clear that the local British administration had both in word and deed repudiated those principles of justice to which the British government had appealed on behalf of the Indians in the Transvaal. Would the British government endorse this repudiation? Would the Indian community submit to it? Gandhi and his associates were prepared to go to considerable lengths to allay the fears of the Transvaal Europeans. They were willing to submit, as a voluntary act, to a new registration of Indians lawfully resident in the Trans-

[1] Cd. 3308 of 1907, p. 3. Dispatch of Lord Selborne, 9th June 1906.

[2] Ibid. Lord Selborne had made this promise in a speech of 5th October 1905. He refers in his dispatch to a pledge 'in some cases explicit, but in all cases implied, that the solution of the fundamental questions of the country should, as far as possible, be left over until the time when, through the medium of responsible government, they should discuss these questions face to face with the imperial authorities'.

[3] The same line has been taken recently by Mr. Lionel Curtis in discussing the Protectorates. Other parties to the discussion maintain that too high a price may be paid for unity between Afrikaner and Briton. See Margery Perham and Lionel Curtis, *The Protectorates of South Africa* (Oxford University Press, 1935), and p. 284 below.

vaal, complete with passes of identification, photographs, and finger-prints. This, they argued, should suffice to allay all fear of an influx of unqualified Indians. But the British administration insisted on achieving its purpose by stringent legal enactment, and to this end drew up the Asiatic Law Amendment Ordinance of 1906. This the Indians determined to resist. On the 11th September 1906 a large gathering of the Indian population of Johannesburg assembled in a Jewish theatre hired for a meeting of protest. The date of the meeting has some importance, for it was then that a new principle and method of struggle came into being among Indians. Europeans called it passive resistance. The Indians were not satisfied with this name. Gandhi had described how he chose one more akin to Indian conceptions.

> 'Truth (Satya) implies love, and firmness (Agraha) engenders and therefore serves as a synonym for force. I therefore began to call the Indian movement "Satyagraha", that is to say, the Force which is born of Truth and Love or non-violence.'[1]

Twenty years later *Satyagraha* proved itself to be the most baffling and dangerous weapon with which Indians resisted British rule in their own country. In 1906 it rallied Indians in South Africa to a more resolute struggle than any which they had yet attempted.

But first they appealed to the British government. The Colonial Secretary, Lord Elgin, had to face a deputation sent by the Indians of South Africa and strongly supported by prominent Englishmen. The troublesome Gandhi himself came from South Africa to speak for his community. 'Under the ordinance', he declared, 'the British Indian is assumed to be a criminal.' Lord Elgin replied to the deputation with the polite but inconclusive remarks which are in order on occasions of this kind. The British government would not commit itself on so important an issue without serious deliberation. But the deputation, to its great joy, learnt by a cable received on the voyage home that Great Britain would abide by the principles which she had professed. A dispatch of Lord Elgin to Lord Selborne, dated 29th November 1906, contained the refusal of the government to accept at present the Asiatic Law Amendment Ordinance.

Here, surely, the issues at last became clear to the dramatizing historian. He has failed to write this chapter of history with Britons acting in the heroic rôle and Boers playing the part of villains; for Britons acted even more offensively towards the Indians than did the Boers. He has failed to interpret it as a struggle between unjust

[1] Gandhi, *Satyagraha in South Africa*, p. 173, and chap. xiii passim.

colonists and upright English administrators; for the administrators identified themselves with the colonists. But at last the enemies and the champions of human equality have grouped themselves under their opposing banners: on the one side are ranged South Africa's Britons and her Boers and her English administrators; on the other side stands the British government, faithful, despite all assaults upon its constancy, to its promises and its principles. . . . Unfortunately, not even this interpretation can be sustained. Lord Selborne had cause to complain that the Secretary of State had by his previous attitude virtually endorsed a policy which he now reversed; but the reversal was nothing more than a self-righteous gesture, for it was accompanied by private assurances to the representatives of the Transvaal that the British government would not oppose the wishes of the colony when these expressed themselves in an act of the legislature shortly to be erected. Indeed, within a few months of the return of Gandhi from London, the Transvaal received responsible government; and the Asiatic Law Amendment Ordinance reappeared almost unchanged as Act No. 2 of 1907. Attached to the Act was the suspending clause which the constitution demanded. Lord Elgin, having considered the Act, informed the Governor of the Transvaal that His Majesty's government still retained its opinion upon the principle contained in it, but did not feel justified in resisting the general will of the colony. The measures, admitted Lord Elgin, were the same; but they had behind them 'a very different weight of authority'.[1]

This pronouncement illuminates from a different angle the principle of self-government which was transforming the British Empire into a Commonwealth of Nations and which was, by common consent of all statesmen, the secret of all virtue and strength. Decentralization, said General Botha a few years later, had done wonders. The Indians of South Africa would not have agreed with him. They complained that the principle of colonial or dominion autonomy was swallowing up other principles which had given the British Empire its moral unity.

> 'I contend' [declared an Indian member of the House of Commons] 'that the grant of autonomy does not carry with it the right to undermine the noblest traditions of the British Constitution and the pledges of the Crown in respect to the rights and liberties of subjects of the King belonging to other portions of his Dominions. . . . The Imperial con-

[1] All these transactions may be followed in *Correspondence relating to Legislation affecting Asiatics in the Transvaal*, Cd. 3308 of 1907, and in *Further Correspondence*, Cd. 3887 of 1908.

nexion is dissolved into a figment if His Majesty's Ministers are unable to protect Indian subjects in all parts of the British dominions.'[1]

There is truth in this indignant protest; nevertheless, it needs to be critically examined by the historian, and even by the reformer. This narrative has already made it clear that those 'noblest traditions of the British Constitution', to which the Indian politician appealed, were partly responsible for creating the unlovely muddle in South Africa. The formal liberty of a British subject to accept any contract anywhere in the British Empire was not substantial freedom when it herded uprooted Indian labourers into the fenced compounds of Newcastle in Natal. If it should be argued that the theory of individual rights which saw nothing objectionable in this uprooting was also resolute and consistent in claiming 'equality' for the uprooted ones, the answer must be made that the resolution and consistency expressed themselves chiefly in gestures. Principles have to prove themselves, not merely by reiteration in speeches and sermons and review articles, but by their energy in actual life. The principles which the British government professed wilted when they had to face a test in the concrete realities of South African society. Nothing in the end seemed to be left of them except the virtuous deprecation of a liberal Colonial Secretary in London. One is tempted to ask whether virtue enunciating general propositions at a distance is virtue at all. One is tempted to urge that ultimately there was more hope for the Indians in South African prejudice than in English posturing, for the latter was abstract and formal, whereas the former was bound to get knocked about by facts. But perhaps it is better to avoid a premature summing-up and to continue the narrative, which may well make it clear that all these oppositions are too sharp, and that the struggles of principles, so far from being at an end, was continuing in complications even harder to dramatize than they had been hitherto, and with subtleties which derived partly from the new technique of the evolving Commonwealth, and partly from transformations which the principles themselves were undergoing. Nor need it yet be assumed that these transformations signified the decadence of the principles; they might, on the contrary, prepare a more realistic and effective statement of them.

The next episode in the history of the Indians in South Africa is

[1] Cd. 2239, p. 8 (Sir M. Bhownaggree in 1904). Professor Berriedale Keith expresses a similar point of view: the British government, he says, should have taken measures to secure the elementary rights of Indians before it granted self-government (*Responsible Government in the Dominions*, pp. 826, 827). Schreiner, thinking chiefly of the Bantu and the Coloured People, made the same criticism when denouncing the 'fundamental weakness' of the Vereeniging settlement.

comparatively free from complication. The retirement of the British government had for the time made the issue a straight one between the legally constituted colonial authority and the local Indian community, which could not resist effectively without going outside the law. It was, of course, a central point in the conception of *Satyagraha* that the laws of men, when they were unjust, should be resisted in the name of the higher law of God. Gandhi has told at length the history of Indian resistance. His story is at times discursive and is full of picturesque detail, but it fixes the reader's attention, perhaps unintentionally, upon the contrasted personalities of Gandhi himself and of General Smuts. Was General Smuts a man who broke faith? Gandhi raises the question repeatedly. Once or twice he has second thoughts which lead him to question his first assumption of General Smuts's crookedness.[1] But his narrative is in general an indictment, not only of South African injustice, but of a South African's falseness. His book is indispensable material for history; but it has few of the qualities of a disciplined and imaginative work of history, which indeed it does not pretend to be. Such a history has not yet been written, and the writer of it, even if he may command the whole range of contemporary material, will find it a delicate task to compose a just narrative. Pending the appearance of this very desirable work, the student of to-day must be content, as before, to look in the blue books[2] for a useful corrective to Gandhi, and to look from time to time into his own mind to make sure that impressions are not hardening unreasonably into judgements. Chronicle, for the time, must serve in place of history. The struggle continued without a break until the provisional settlement contained in the Indian Relief Act of 1914. In its earlier phase it was a continuation of the resistance which the Indians had offered to the British administrators of the Transvaal. The Asiatic Law Amendment Ordinance had now become the 'Black Act'; the *Satyagrahis* deliberately disobeyed its provisions and forced situations which compelled the authorities to send them to gaol. When the Transvaal legislature passed the Immigration Restriction Act of 1907, Gandhi felt justified in using

[1] Gandhi, *Satyagraha in South Africa*, especially at p. 291. The charges against General Smuts are (1) That in 1907 he promised to repeal the Asiatics Registration Act (No. 2 of 1907) after Gandhi had offered voluntary registration instead of registration under the Act, and that he broke the promise. See ibid., pp. 229–42, 301–2. (2) That in 1912 he promised Gokhale to secure the removal of the £3 tax imposed in Natal on ex-indentured labourers, and broke the promise. See p. 200 below, and notes. These charges cannot be proved on printed evidence. The death of many of the witnesses makes it impossible to decide the issue by personal testimony.

[2] Cd. 3387 of 1908, Cd. 4327 of 1908, Cd. 5579 of 1911, Cd. 6283 of 1912–13, Cd. 6940 of 1913, Cd. 7111 of 1914, and Cd. 7265 of 1914.

Satyagraha to oppose this measure also. The establishment of the Union of South Africa did not at first alter the tactics of struggle inside South Africa, for the laws of the provinces remained in force. The Union, however, planned to supplement them by a general immigration act, and this became the target for outside criticism. The Union naturally enhanced the privileges and responsibilities of South Africans in the inner circle of the British Empire. A new technique in the ordering of relations between different governments of the Empire began to have some effect upon the destinies of Indians in South Africa. Written protests from the Government of India to the British Colonial Secretary, who no longer possessed any real power over South Africa,[1] gave place to the first tentative experiments in direct inter-governmental negotiation. In 1912 the Union government accepted a visit from the Indian statesman Gokhale. The immediate effect of this visit was not to ensure a settlement, but to intensify the crisis. Gandhi heads the chapter in his book which records the events succeeding Gokhale's visit with the words—'Breach of Pledge'. Gokhale believed that he had secured from Generals Botha and Smuts a promise that the £3 tax on ex-indentured labourers, which had existed in Natal since 1895, would now be removed. In 1913 General Smuts denied that this promise had been given. Thus there were two conflicting interpretations of an imprecise agreement.[2] But Gandhi believed that he now had just cause to widen the objectives and deepen the force of the *Satyagraha* movement, which for a considerable time had been sustained by a minority of devoted Indians and their European friends.[3] The centre of the struggle now shifted from the Transvaal to Natal, and the indentured labourers were called to fight as *Satyagrahis*. An unexpected event gave an unparalleled emotional stimulus to this

[1] As late as 1908 Morley, as Secretary of State for India, invited the Secretary of State for the Colonies to persuade the Transvaal government 'to remove the impression, now widely prevalent in India, that British Indian subjects lawfully resident in the Transvaal are exposed to vexatious treatment, and that His Majesty's government is unable to protect them.' Cd. 4327, p. 8.

[2] Gandhi, *Satyagraha in South Africa*, p. 408. Cf. p. 414, where he says that Gokhale 'supposed' that the £3 tax would be taken off. See also note 1 on p. 199.

[3] Gandhi says that when the struggle was at its height there were, from no more than 20,000 Indian literates, 3,500 subscribers to *Indian Opinion* (ibid., p. 223). But in 1912 he told Gokhale that the maximum number of resolute *Satyagrahis* was about 66, and the minimum 16. The movement owed much, not only to these resolute Indian supporters, but also to a few European supporters—notably to Mr. H. S. L. Polak, who from 1905 onwards was in the centre of the struggle and has continued for more than thirty years his unflagging support of the rights of Indians in the British Empire. Other supporters were Mr. A. H. West, Miss Sonja Schesin, and Mr. Kallenbach, who put 'Tolstoy Farm' at the disposal of the *Satyagrahis*.

final effort. A judgement of Mr. Justice Searle, of the Cape Supreme Court, in March 1913, had the appalling effect of invalidating Indian marriages and of bastardizing Indian children on a wholesale scale. 'As if unseen by any one,' reflects Gandhi, 'God was preparing the ingredients for the Indians' victory and demonstrating still more clearly the injustice of the Europeans in South Africa. . . .'[1]

On the 6th November 1913 Gandhi led a band of over two thousand 'pilgrims', nearly all of whom were strikers from the Newcastle coal-mines, towards the border of the Transvaal. To cross the border was a breach of the immigration laws of the Transvaal, and it was Gandhi's plan to win justice by compelling the authorities to enforce the law upon so large a company of willing sufferers that its iniquity, and therefore its weakness, would become flagrant in the eyes of the whole world and even in the eyes of the European community of South Africa. This is not the place to record the dramatic episodes in which Gandhi's plan unfolded itself—the stages of the pilgrims' march, the arrests of leaders, the deportation of the main body to Natal, the new strikes everywhere among the labourers, the transformation of compounds into prisons, the rising excitement in South Africa, the growing indignation in India, where on the 24th November the Viceroy proclaimed the people's 'deep and burning sympathy' with their fellow countrymen in South Africa. These are but some of the sensational scenes in an action which was working to its close. 'The Union government', observes Gandhi, 'had not the power to keep thousands of innocent men in jail.' *Satyagraha* could claim a victory which was won not merely by its own direct impact against entrenched authority, but by its power in calling forth the action of others on a ground of principle—India acting by protest, Great Britain acting by protest and persuasion, the conscience and imagination of South Africa acting against South African prejudice and callousness. The South African statesmen nerved themselves for an effort to break free from the imprisonment in which the fears of the European population had bound them, and to win the power to do justice. They prepared the way by appointing an Indian Enquiry Commission, before which Sir Benjamin Robertson, an Indian civil servant, was deputed by the Government of India to give evidence. The Commission prepared the way for a settlement.

> 'We have to realize' [it reported] 'that the indentured Indians have been brought here to serve our own needs, that for better or worse the majority of them have come to stay, and that in the interests of good

[1] Gandhi, *Satyagraha in South Africa*, p. 419.

government it is desirable to remove as far as possible any causes of irritation.'[1]

Both before and after the commission reported there were interviews and correspondence between Gandhi and General Smuts. The upshot of these negotiations and of the Commission's report was the Indian Relief Act,[2] which satisfied the Indians on those immediate issues—such as the annual £3 tax on ex-indentured labourers in Natal, the registration issue in the Transvaal, and the validity of Indian marriages—which had been the object of the *Satyagraha* struggle. The Act, nevertheless, fell far short of a final settlement. With regard to the administration of existing laws, General Smuts accepted the principle put forward by Gandhi that they should be administered 'in a just manner and with due regard to vested rights'. But there was still on the statute book legislation which the Indians regarded as an infliction, although they had not opposed it by *Satyagraha*. In letter to General Smuts dated 30th June 1914 Gandhi reserved the right of his countrymen to raise these issues at some future time. 'Complete satisfaction', he declared, 'cannot however be expected until full civic rights have been conceded to the Indian population.' General Smuts, on the contrary, demanded that the Indians should accept what had been conceded to them 'as a complete settlement of the controversy'. These clashing declarations were ominous of future trouble. And yet there were also good grounds for hoping that the measure of the appeasement now achieved would broaden and deepen. Gandhi publicly accepted the Immigration Regulation Act which the Union parliament had passed in the previous year. He publicly declared that the Indians in South Africa had no political ambitions. And he expressed the not fantastic hope that the Europeans of South Africa, reassured on these two most vital issues, 'would see the justice and indeed the necessity' of meeting the moderate wishes of a relatively inconsiderable minority on South African soil.[3] He himself, after doing so much to link the histories of South Africa and India, returned at last to his own country. Within South Africa the Indian question for some time slumbered. When it was revived on the occasion of India's welcome to the Imperial

[1] Cd. 7265, p. 29.

[2] Act No. 2 of 1914.

[3] In a private letter Gandhi gave an important definition of 'vested rights' which was forgotten. 'By vested rights I understand the right of an Indian and his successors to live and trade in the township in which he was living and trading, no matter how often he shifts his residence or business from place to place in the same township.' See *Report of the Asiatic Land Tenure Act Commission*, (U.G. No. 7, 1934) Part I, p. 12. This report contains a useful survey of the historical origins of the land problem in the Transvaal.

War Conference, it was revived in an atmosphere of comradeship and hope. But this atmosphere, as we have seen, was soon darkened by conflict.

For the reopening of the conflict, the end-of-war neurosis was perhaps partly responsible. Boom and slump, insecurity and anxiety, shook the white South Africans into a panic and a search for scapegoats. There had been no population inquiries since the census of 1911; rumour flew in Natal that Indians were outstripping Europeans by a prodigious increase.[1] It was believed in the Transvaal that there was a widespread evasion of the provincial immigration laws. In both provinces the cry was raised that the white man's living was in danger. The undertaking given in 1914 to respect the 'vested rights' of Indians was remembered, but was subjected to niggling and restrictive interpretations which in the end involved a repudiation of the pledge and an offensive against Indian livelihoods. In the Transvaal the *status quo* had been upset in 1918 to the advantage of the Indians by a magistrate's decision extending their rights in the matter of trading licences. But in the following year a municipality obtained a legal injunction which had the effect of bringing into operation a hitherto ignored provision of the Gold Law of 1908 which forbade Indians to reside on proclaimed land. Almost all the Rand was proclaimed land. The Indian community in the Transvaal was faced with complete ruin. In 1919 a select committee listened to the complaints of both parties. The Europeans, as so often before, advanced the argument of economic necessity; the Indians, as usual, demanded not law but justice. The European view prevailed. Parliament, by passing the Asiatics Land and Trading Amendment Act, barred for the future the grant of new trading licences to Indians, and made impossible for the future their evasion of the old Transvaal law which forbade them to own fixed property.[2] But the panic was not stilled. There were frenzied demands for compulsory segregation of Indians and compulsory repatriation. The government en-

[1] The Lange-Robertson Commission which reported in 1921 refers to wild statements by the South African League, e.g. that the country was in danger of becoming an 'annexe to India'. The Commission showed that in fact the Indian population was increasing more slowly than the European. In Natal it was decreasing, and an Indian superiority of numbers had given place to a European superiority.

[2] It should be stated that the 'evasion' was merely nominal, and had in the first instance been suggested by the Transvaal government itself. It became a practice well known to the government for a trusted European to become the nominal owner on behalf of an Indian real owner, who was protected by registering a mortgage against the property for its full value, a mortgage not being in law 'fixed property'. An equally accepted alternative was the registration of private companies, whose members were, e.g. the Indian real owner and his wife, and which enjoyed in law a separate legal *persona*.

deavoured to stave off this clamour by appointing a commission and by quoting the moderate terms of its report. General Smuts appealed for patience, balance, and the 'long view'.[1] But he went to the Imperial Conference of 1921 imprisoned by the violent passions of the people whom he represented. There he met Indians who were similarly imprisoned by the lacerated pride and the impatience of their people. The Montagu-Chelmsford reforms were barely launched, the Amritsar humiliations were still smarting, Gandhi was in India preparing for a new *Satyagraha* struggle, Congress was demanding *swaraj*. Indian nationalism strained at the limitations which Gandhi had accepted in 1914. Gandhi had then excluded any future demand of political rights for the Indian community in the Transvaal. The Indian speakers at the 1921 Conference claimed a full equality which would include the right of franchise also. The open clash between South Africa and India at the Imperial Conference of 1921 brought new fuel for the passions of the South African white community. It was the province of Natal which aimed the next blow against the Indians. Provincial ordinances of 1922 and 1923 forbade them to purchase or lease land belonging to municipalities—a restriction which was of most serious hurt to the Indians in Durban. Every new action which was now taken, almost every new word which was uttered, increased the tension between South Africa and India. It was at the 1923 Conference—when the Kenya controversy also was at its height—that the Indian delegates affirmed their loss of *izzat*; it was at this Conference that General Smuts declared: 'For South Africa, for white South Africa, it is not a question of dignity, it is a question of existence. . . . We are up against a stone wall, and we cannot get over it.' It seemed to Indians that the South Africans were making of this stone wall a hateful prison-compound to ruin and degrade their compatriots. Legislation against the Indian community continued. Natal in 1924 and 1925 passed measures to deprive Indians of the municipal franchise. The Transvaal municipalities introduced further restrictions on the granting of trading licences to Indians. The government of the Union could not resist the violent current of prejudice and panic.[2] In 1924 General Smuts

[1] e.g. at the party conference of December 1921 (*Round Table*, vol. xii, p. 446). South Africans, he said, were now paying for the sins of their fathers—they should try gradually to reverse what had been done—but for their own sake and that of the Empire they should not force matters. The Lange-Robertson Commission had declared against compulsory repatriation and segregation, but had supported them as voluntary policies.

[2] The Smuts government had in fact twice vetoed the Natal act depriving Indians of the municipal franchise. In 1925 General Hertzog's government accepted the

brought forward a Class Areas Bill, which authorized the establishment of separate trading and residential areas for persons other than natives who possessed common racial characteristics. This meant segregation, which for the Indians was ruin and humiliation. General Smuts had by now been swept far from his undertaking of 1914 to respect 'vested rights'. But General Smuts was denounced by the nationalist opposition for his moderation and pusillanimity. In 1924 he fell. General Hertzog, who succeeded him, introduced a far more stringent measure of segregation, and with it a prohibition against the entry of the wives and children of Indians lawfully domiciled in South Africa.[1] The Bill was intended, said General Hertzog grimly, 'to supplement . . . the inducement which is held out to Indians to leave the country'.

But the Bill was never passed. It must again be left to the historian of the future to trace and to interpret the operation of those forces, which in India, in South Africa, in Great Britain, and generally in the inner circle of the equal nations of the British Commonwealth averted at the last moment a land-slide of racial conflict which would have demonstrated the failure of the Commonwealth to preserve under stress any vestiges of moral unity. It may be that the future historian will discover some connexion between the satisfaction in 1926 of South Africa's misgivings about her status in the Commonwealth, and her acceptance in the same year of equal negotiations with Indian representatives. For it was not only Indians who were jealous of their *izzat*. The intensity of the white South African's passions on the Indian question sprang, it is true, ultimately from his feeling of insecurity amidst the vast native majority in his country; but it was perhaps exacerbated by the feeling, however unjustified, that South Africa's subordinate status in the British Empire was somehow or other responsible for an intolerable complication of her racial problems. If this were so, the reassurance which General Hertzog brought back from the 1926 Conference would give a feeling of liberation. And certainly, the conviction which the Nationalist leaders gained at last in that year, that South Africa could fulfil her destiny most adequately and most honourably within the British Commonwealth, must have stimulated them powerfully to do their utmost to appease a quarrel which was becoming a scandal and a reproach to the Commonwealth. But these

Boroughs Ordinance, which provided that in future no one should be enrolled for municipal elections who did not possess the parliamentary franchise.

[1] The Areas Reservation and Immigration Registration (Further Provision) Bill, to take effect in 1930.

tentative interpretations, and the story of the negotiations which won General Hertzog from his reluctance to meet an Indian delegation, must not be pursued here.[1] A Round Table Conference between South African and Indian delegates met behind closed doors in Capetown on the 17th December 1926, and concluded its labours on the 11th January 1927. On the 21st February the Minister of the Interior announced in the South African parliament that the governments of the Union and of India had come to an agreement with each other. This agreement was announced by identical statements in the two legislatures, and by laying on the tables of each mutually approved summaries of the conclusions arrived at. This method of procedure avoided the necessity of formal parliamentary ratification which a formal contract would have demanded. The governments were not prepared to run unnecessary risks with a public opinion which might easily be inflamed to destroy what they had achieved. They had taken a stride ahead of public opinion. In South Africa this was particularly true. Yet the prospective gains of appeasement were so great that the South African legislature accepted what had been done almost without protest.

The most important heads of the agreement were as follows.[2] Both governments reaffirmed 'their recognition of the right of South Africa to use all just and legitimate means for the maintenance of western standards of life'. The government of South Africa recognized that Indians domiciled in South Africa, who were 'prepared to conform to western standards of life, should be enabled to do so'. For those Indians in the Union who desired to avail themselves of it, the government of South Africa would provide a scheme of emigration to lands where western standards did not prevail. The Government of India, on its side, would undertake to receive with care Indians who accepted the opportunity of repatriation. The government of South Africa, in the expectation that this agreement would reduce the difficulties with which it had been faced, would proceed no farther with the Areas Reservation and Immigration and Registration (Further Provision) Bill. Both governments would keep in touch in the future in order to watch the working of the agreement and to exchange their views upon it. In addition, the Government of India, on the request of the government of South Africa, would appoint an

[1] It should, however, be noted that the Round Table Conference had been prepared by the visit of an Indian delegation to South Africa in 1925 and the visit of a South African delegation to India in 1926. Thus, after so many years, was the Suez Canal bridged!

[2] The full text of the agreement can be readily consulted in Buell, *Native Policy in Africa,* vol. i, pp. 155–9.

agent in the Union 'in order to secure continuous and effective co-operation between the two governments'. These were the leading headings of the agreement. In the detailed notes and proposals as to ways and means for carrying its principles farther into effect there was everywhere evidence of a realistic good faith which did not ignore the difficulties which might still arise.

> 'It is difficult' [the joint communication stated] 'for the Union government to take action, which is considerably in advance of public opinion, or to ignore difficulties arising out of the constitutional system of the Union, under which the functions of Government are distributed between the Central Executive and the Provincial and minor local authorities.'

Nevertheless, the document proceeded to affirm the Union government's willingness to undertake a variety of enterprises—to put pressure for reform on the administration of Natal, where was the chief centre of trouble; to take steps for an investigation by public health authorities into sanitary conditions around Durban; to adhere to the principle of equal pay for equal work; to consider, when the time should come for revising trade licensing laws, suggestions propounded by the Government of India for the restriction of the discretionary power of local authorities; to consider the provision of facilities for higher education, with hostel accommodation for Indian students at 'The South African Native College' at Fort Hare in the eastern Cape Province. Scattered among these detailed clauses were phrases which betokened qualities of human imagination which had hitherto been absent in official South African policy towards the Indians—'a happy family life', the 'uplift of the Indian community', were affirmed to be desirable ends.

In general, the agreement testified to a real effort on the part of India and South Africa to bring to bear on their joint problem the principles of the reciprocity resolution of 1917. That resolution had pointed both to the future and to the past. It expressed, so far as the future was concerned, the ideal of equality, in legal power and in mutual respect, between diverse communities. This was the ground for recognizing that these diverse communities possessed the right to fix the elements of their own populations. But this mutual avowal of future policy did not suffice for the settlement of present issues. As a result of a different attitude held in the past, there were already one hundred and sixty thousand Indians in South Africa. The profession of an agreed ideal for the future was irrelevant to their situation. The reciprocity resolution therefore sought to apply to their condition the ideal generally professed at the time of the immigrations. This was the ideal of 'equal rights for all civilized men'. But here South Africa had failed to do her part. This was the root cause of the angry recriminations of the following ten years. Yet in 1927 the Indian delegates, instead of reiterating their demands for mere justice, exercised imagination and charity. They recognized that the fears of Europeans in South Africa, however unreasonable they might appear, could not be argued away. They recognized that the Indian problem was more acute in South Africa than in the other dominions because the number of Indians was greater there, and because the Indian community was concentrated in one or two localities, the great majority in Natal. They recognized the fact that immigration restriction had not allayed alarm. They were therefore ready to agree to proposals for lightening this load of numbers, not merely by the negative method of restriction on entry, but by the positive method of voluntary repatriation generously assisted by both governments.[1] The South Africans, on their part, thereupon endeavoured to achieve an equal degree of imagination and generosity in applying the formula of equal rights for all civilized men. They confessed, in effect, that this ideal was a sham unless it carried with it a determined effort to create for all men the condition which would make it possible for them to achieve the material supports and the cultural aids to life included in the western idea of 'civilization'.

There were irreconcilables both in South Africa and in India who attacked the agreement as a betrayal of principles and of human rights and interests.[2] It was possible that the ground won for mutual respect and friendship might not in the future be held. And yet a rot had been stopped. Standards essential to the survival of the British Commonwealth as a community capable of commanding respect and loyalty had at the last minute been saved.

When viewed in the perspective of a long and bitter history, this agreement, notwithstanding its obvious shortcomings, was worth all the optimistic oratory about the union of East and West in the British Empire which had been so popular at the end of the war. And once again, as long ago when zealots were pursuing the end of an appeasement between Briton and Boer in South Africa, there were some who dared to hope that goodwill would still take strength from each difficult and partial achievement.

'In bringing this agreement about' [wrote the *Cape Times*] 'the Union government has done good service to South Africa, to the world,

[1] India, as has been stated, promised after-care of repatriated Indians; the South African government promised their passages and a bonus of £20.

[2] Gandhi himself accepted the agreement.

and to the cause of the Empire. The friendship of India is a moral and material asset that South Africa will never regret possessing; she has shown the world that it is possible for East and West to meet and talk and understand, even when vital issues are concerned. . . . In solving her share of a problem that is destined in various forms and guises to be one of the most vital and difficult that mankind will have to face in next 100 years, South Africa has vindicated her young nationhood and taken her place among the advanced peoples of the world. It is, too, let us hope, a happy augury for the manner in which she will yet be given grace and wisdom to handle a still greater problem and one in respect of which she will again find herself the agent of mankind—the Native problem.'[1]

But the men who preach peace and goodwill have sometimes too quick an eye for the happy auguries they desire to see. Optimism was now running too fast.

III

Indians in Kenya

It was not only the South Africans whom Indian orators arraigned at the Imperial Conferences of 1921 and 1923. The British government itself was the target of their bitter attacks. For the British government directly controlled Kenya, where a vigorous Indian population claimed equality with the Europeans, and was denied it.[2] No other humiliation, declared the Maharaja of Alwar in 1923, so deeply seared the pride of India as did this denial. It was galling, not merely in itself, but because of the source from which it came. 'Kenya', he pointed out, 'is not a self-governing Dominion, but is a colony administered by the British government.'[3]

The Indians laid stress upon the difference of political status in order to keep the East African issue separate, so far as possible, from the South African issue. But were these issues separate in fact? There was a disposition in European imaginations, and even in a few Indian ones, to leap from immediate grievances, fears, and ambitions, into vague and vast visions of a momentous contest

[1] Quoted Buell, *Native Policy in Africa*, vol. i, p. 28. The *Round Table*, vol. xvii, pp. 627 ff., commented similarly that the agreement, although it left many things untouched, marked 'a new plane of vision'. 'It is a step forward from the attitude of mere race and colour prejudice to a frank recognition of human needs and aspirations.' And as to technique—'The Conference was an experiment in inter-Dominion relations, and it has set a precedent for the future.'

[2] The 1921 census showed the following population in Kenya: Europeans, 9,651; Indians, 22,822; Natives, something under 3,000,000

[3] Cmd. 1988, p. 93; cf. p. 98. The Secretary of State for the Colonies emphatically accepted the responsibility.

between East and West, of which all Africa was the stage. Africa's modern empire-builders had the habit of thinking in continental dimensions. The historian, by following them in this habit, may find the clue not only to their achievements, but also to their illusions and extravagances. Rhodes prophesied a British linking of the Cape and Cairo, and he achieved a thrust of British power north across the Zambesi. From Livingstone on the Zambesi to Nimule on the Nile the distance along a straight line is 1,600 miles. Slightly to the east of this line stretches the so-called 'broad backbone' of highlands which run from South Africa to the borders of Abyssinia. The disciples of Rhodes in South Africa marked these highlands as the road by which white settlement must advance.[1] In East Africa there were already other disciples of Rhodes, equally faithful to what their local leader called 'the white ideal'.[2] The war simplified the picture in which this white idealism saw the pattern of its future. For the war obliterated German East Africa. It seemed now far easier for Kenya Colony to 'radiate her civilizing influence southward to meet the civilizing influence radiating northward from Rhodesia'.[3] The area which was calling for this civilizing influence was a million square miles—little less than the area of India. Dizzy imaginations dreamed of this territory as 'white man's country'—not, certainly, a country peopled everywhere by white men, but a country governed and guided from centres where white men had deeply rooted themselves.

But the war, while it removed the complications of divided European sovereignty, added complications of a graver kind. One of these complications was a shaken faith among the people of Great Britain in the virtues of 'the white ideal'. In western Africa, where climatic conditions were unfavourable to European colonization, a new and contrasted idea of the relationship between western civilization and the natives of Africa had already taken shape; and this idea, which had originated among a creative minority, was now spreading widely among politically minded people in Great Britain.[4] The new

[1] See General Smuts, *Africa and Some World Problems* (Oxford University Press, 1930), Lecture II, and Amery, *The Forward View*, p. 252. It has, however, been pointed out by J. H. Oldham, *White and Black in Africa* (Longmans, 1930), that the high country more nearly resembles 'a chain of islands' than a 'broad backbone'.

[2] The phrase is Lord Delamere's. See Elspeth Huxley, *White Man's Country* (Macmillan, 1935), vol. ii, p. 204. The East African Economic Commission which reported in 1919 included a chapter individually submitted by one of its members, Mr. E. Powys Cobb, arguing for a 'Dominion of Middle Africa' from which Indians would be excluded.

[3] Huxley, op. cit., vol. ii, p. 199.

[4] The 'West Coast policy' was well established before the war. The publication of Lord Lugard's *Dual Mandate* (Blackwood, 1922) did much to bring it into prominence, and the dispute between Lord Leverhulme and Sir Hugh Clifford in 1924 dramatized it before the English public.

SOUTHERN AND EASTERN AFRICA: ALTITUDE

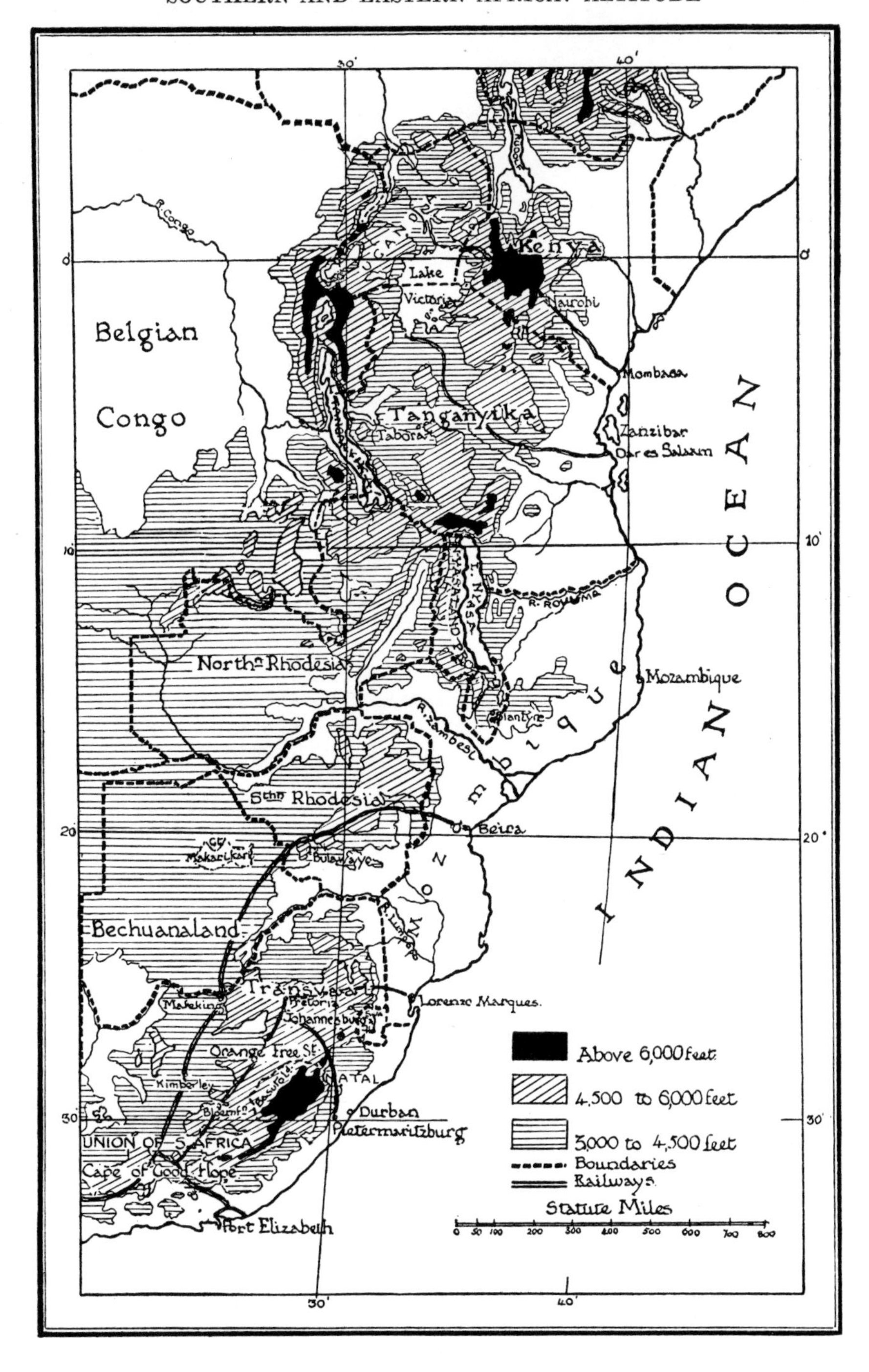

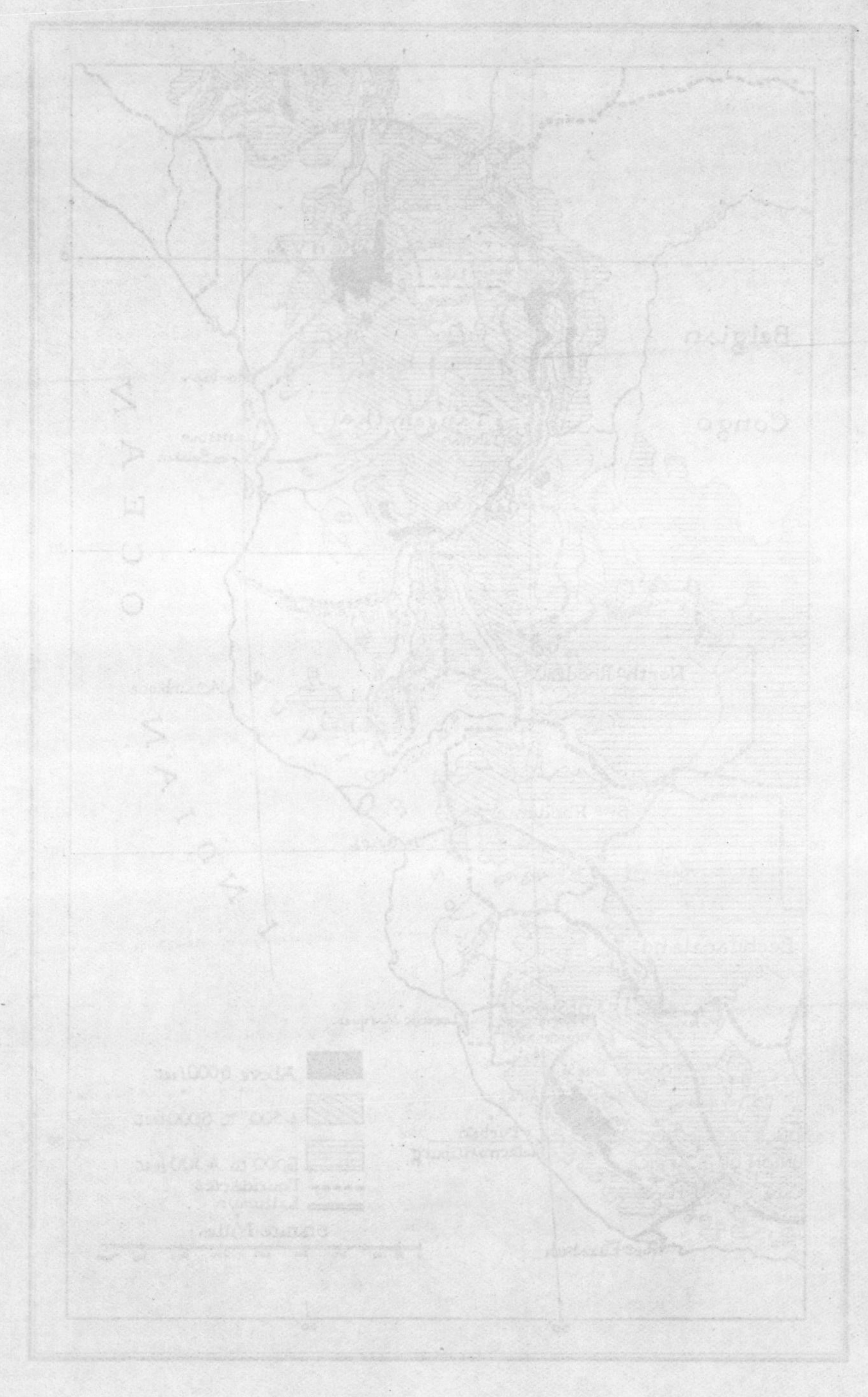

liberal idealism showed a strong tendency to break with the old, and to denounce the intrusion of European colonists into 'black man's country'. The colonists of Kenya therefore appealed to the traditions of Livingstone and Rhodes, and proclaimed it their first task 'to kill the spread of the West Coast policy to the East'.[1] In this task they looked to South Africa for support. They looked for the same support in their resistance to Indian aspirations. This was the second insufferable complication of their ambitious racial strategy—that Indians should claim with them an equal share in the British Empire's civilizing mission. Beneath the Indian plea for equality they thought that they detected a will for domination. They thought that the Indians were fighting to supplant them as the destined masters of Africa. Their alarm was nothing new to South Africans. As early as 1904 the Lieutenant-Governor of the Transvaal had found it 'difficult to conceive any question more momentous than the struggle of East and West for the inheritance of these semi-vacant territories'.[2] In 1904 this was not, perhaps, a very convincing picture of actuality; but in 1918 it looked more plausible. India, too, had fought through the war. Indian troops had helped to win East Africa. India's nationalist pride demanded compensations in East Africa for affronts inflicted elsewhere. To India's responsible statesmen this compensation meant merely equal rights for Indian subjects of the Crown; but to irresponsible zealots it meant a good deal more. The Indian spokesman at the Imperial War Conference of 1917 demanded merely 'the unrestricted opening to Indian business of any territory acquired from the enemy in East Africa';[3] the English head of a Moslem college went farther and claimed for India dominion over the territory which her troops had helped to conquer.[4] In so far as Indian nationalism allowed itself to be attracted by proposals of this kind, it was setting forth along a new path: no longer content to advance a claim of equal rights for its nationals abroad, it was hankering after the profit and prestige supposed to be associated with the privilege of possessing colonies. It was urging India to join other late-comers among modern nations in the colonial scramble. The erection of Tanganyika into a mandated territory did not at first deflect these ambitions. The East Africa Indian Congress, meeting at Nairobi in November 1919, passed a resolution requesting the League of Nations and the mandatory power 'to preserve the said territory for the

[1] Huxley, *White Man's Country*, vol. ii, p. 204.
[2] Cd. 1684 of 1904, p. 32.
[3] Cd. 8316 of 1917, p. 161.
[4] Sir Theodore Morison in *The Nineteenth Century*, vol. viii, pp. 430–41.

purpose of Indian colonization'.[1] The same reckless enthusiasm dreamt of 'the annexation of this African territory [Kenya] to the Indian Empire with provincial government under the Indian Viceroy'.[2] There was no substance in these dreams. They meant little more than an angry rejoinder to the racialist visions of the Europeans in East Africa. Mr. Gandhi and other responsible leaders in India condemned them from the very beginning, and they soon died a natural death. The Indian leaders in Kenya and Tanganyika retreated quickly to ground more easily defended. They rescinded their resolution calling for special privileges in Tanganyika: they declared that they desired nothing more than equal treatment for all sections of His Majesty's subjects.[3] But they had already inflamed the racialism of their European antagonists. They had given occasion for the accusation that their moderation was merely tactical, and that their plea for equal justice masked a craving for domination. Zealots of the 'white ideal' returned with new fervour to their large-scale maps. Was Kenya to be the northernmost link in a chain of white settlement stretching from the Cape to the Abyssinian frontier, or was it to be 'a funnel through which an Asiatic flood would pour into Africa and filter down the eastern territories, lapping against the foundations of a western political and economic system . . .' ?[4] Merely to ask this question was to forge a new link of sympathy between Kenya and South Africa. It united these two widely separated scenes in the unity of a single drama. The handful of British settlers in the Kenya highlands—and there were settlers from the Transvaal there too—looked to the South Africans as examples, as friends, perhaps as champions and defenders. The South Africans on their part were ready to look upon the Kenya settlers as a frontier post of their own civilization. This linking of South Africa and Kenya had little historical substance; it was as yet nothing more than a disposition of mind which coloured historical and political interpretation. Yet within the ten years which followed the war it tended more than once to acquire a solid substance. Even in 1923 the separate Indian

[1] Resolution quoted in Sir Benjamin Robertson's report, 4th August 1919, Cmd. 1312, p. 3.

[2] Speech of Mr. Jeevanjee, quoted Huxley, *White Man's Country*, vol. ii, p. 121.

[3] Cmd. 1312, p. 6. In August 1919 Lord Milner had promised to consider the possibility of establishing in Tanganyika an Indian agricultural settlement. The Government of India was advised by the provincial governments that settlers were not likely to be forthcoming, and was advised by Sir Benjamin Robertson that the conditions for settlement were unpromising. The Indians in East Africa and the Government of India itself in the end rejected the scheme on principle also; they sought, not privilege, but equality.

[4] Huxley, *White Man's Country*, vol. ii, p. 142.

problems of South Africa and Kenya converged and fused in the imperial conference discussions. General Smuts asserted that the demands of the Indians in Kenya had had 'a very bad effect' in South Africa.[1] What concern had the Union of South Africa with the troubles of a British Crown Colony? None at all, except on the theory that African racial policy was indivisible.

It is time to turn from the romantic geography of the racial idealists to a more sober lesson in chronological history. Whatever the hotheads on each side might say, the Indians in East Africa were fighting a defensive battle, and they were losing it. The Government of India, as far back as 1908, had in an official dispatch expressed anxiety for their future.

> 'Fears have already been expressed,' [it said] 'that when the country is actually granted self-government, the antagonism of the white colonists and the Indian traders and settlers may result in similar problems to those which have had such deplorable effects in South Africa.'[2]

From the Indian point of view, these effects would be still more deplorable than anything which had been suffered in South Africa. For in East Africa the Indians had very much more to lose. It was not they, but the British settlers, who were the late arrivals in East Africa. The connexion between Indian enterprise and the eastern coast was centuries old. The European settlers, when confronted with this historical fact, laid stress upon the word coast.[3] The Indians, they affirmed, never penetrated inland until they found an easy way as camp-followers in the wake of European enterprise during the last decade of the nineteenth century. It was men of British stock who had done the tough work of pioneering. The Indians, therefore, had no just claim to equal profits and equal privileges. But the Sanderson Commission, which in 1910 gave some attention to this argument, quoted in rebuttal of it the testimony of a great East African pioneer, Sir John Kirk. 'But for the Indians', Kirk had said, 'we should not be here now.'[4] It was Indian merchants who had opened the

[1] Cmd. 1988, p. 113.

[2] Cd. 5193 of 1910, p. 11, dispatch of 10th December 1908.

[3] They also asserted that the Indian activity on the coast was disreputable; e.g. Lord Delamere: 'They never pioneered Kenya. They financed and provided arms for the Arab slave trade.' Huxley, *White Man's Country*, vol. ii, p. 145. But see Winston Churchill, *My African Journey* (London, 1908), p. 49.

[4] Cd. 5193, p. 239. For a similar and more recent judgement see *Gazette of India, Extraordinary*, 24th June 1935, quoting a dispatch of the Governor of Uganda which testifies to the valuable services of Indian traders, performed in the early days sometimes at risk of life. The technique of Indian penetration in Africa was wholly peaceful: it would repay historical examination.

avenue of commercial penetration which led to British rule. Indian labour, no less than British capital, had played an indispensable part in the construction of the Uganda railway. Indians were still playing an indispensable part in the service of that railway and in the commercial activities radiating from Nairobi. 'In short,' Kirk had concluded, 'drive away the Indians, and you may shut up the Protectorate, I think.'[1]

It was easy for the European settlers, contemplating the brilliance of their own services to Kenya's development, to forget the part which the Indians had played. In 1897 there were but a few scattered Europeans in the Kenya highlands. But within less than a decade there had grown up a strenuous and masterful community of settlers. In 1902 the British government began positively to encourage British immigration. Settlers adventured to Kenya from Great Britain, from South Africa, even from far-distant New Zealand. These settlers were the best pioneering stock. They brought with them the courage, the acquisitiveness, the ruthlessness, the persistent experimenting audacity of their civilization. Some of them brought capital. They brought the plants and animals of other lands. They came to East Africa with the faith and the will to subdue its soil and rule its people. They came with the conviction that they were bringing civilization to East Africa. Their transforming energy introduced a new control in a society where Indian enterprise had introduced merely a new influence. They made themselves—it is the phrase of one of Kenya's governors—the power-house of East Africa.[2] Quickly they sent down roots in their new soil, and quickly they began to think of it as a country destined to be under their dominion. In 1906 they secured from the Secretary of State for the Colonies a statement which they interpreted as a pledge that no settler not of their race should secure land in the Kenya highlands. Two years later they secured another statement which they interpreted as a confirmation of that pledge.[3] Very soon they began to grow restless under Colonial Office control, which cramped and checked their impatient energy. They remem-

[1] Cd. 5193, p. 238.

[2] Sir R. Coryndon. Cf. *Report of the Commission on Closer Union of the Dependencies in Eastern and Central Africa* (Hilton Young Report), Cmd. 3234 of 1929, 'an immense fund of energy introduced into these territories.'

[3] Lord Elgin asserted that it was not in accordance with the principles of British rule to put legal restrictions on any section of the community, but that as 'a matter of administrative convenience', grants in the highlands would not be made to Asiatics. Effective restrictions were in fact imposed on the transfer of land to Indians by the 'veto clause' of the Crown Lands Ordinance of 1915; but this left unchanged the *legal* principle asserted by Lord Elgin. See *Indians in Kenya*, Cmd. 1922 of 1923, para. 8. See also below, p. 234.

bered those 'inalienable rights' of self-government which other colonies enjoyed. Their claim to take a share in policy was first admitted in 1915, when they were allowed to elect representatives to a specially instituted war council. In the following year they received a promise that their claim would be acknowledged in the normal constitution of the colony so soon as the war was won. A committee set to work to frame proposals. The upshot was a new constitution of the colony, which was announced in February 1919. The Europeans were given two seats on the executive council, and were represented by eleven elected members on the legislative council. The right of franchise was a European privilege in which Indians, to say nothing of Africans, had no share. The legislative council still retained a majority of nominated members; but the next step, surely, must lead to a majority of elected Europeans. In politics Kenya seemed to be moving rapidly along the road which would make it white man's country. The British government was at this time encouraging a new immigration of demobilized soldiers. British public opinion had not yet been swept away by the current of reaction against the colonizing ideals of the nineteenth century. In Kenya it had as yet hardly occurred to anybody that 'the West Coast policy' was a real menace to 'white ideals'. As for the Indian claims, these seemed still to European settlers to be an irritating, but not very alarming, impertinence. The colonists confidently took the offensive against the Indians. Quoting the report of a distinguished sanitation expert, Professor Simpson,[1] they demanded complete residential and commercial segregation of the Indian populations in the towns. They demanded also a barrier against Indian immigration. They asserted in disparaging terms the contrast between themselves, the missionaries of civilization, and the Indians, whose influence upon African natives they denounced as degrading and corrupting.[2] They did not doubt that the future was theirs. Indian fears that the bitterness of their South African experience might repeat itself in circumstances far more humiliating were justified by the general trend of events between 1900 and 1920, and particularly by the most recent events. In Kenya the Indians had very much more to lose than they had in South Africa. They seemed to be in danger of losing almost everything.

The Indians of Kenya, nevertheless, enjoyed certain strategical

[1] The Report was published in 1913.

[2] e.g. in some notorious paragraphs of the Economic Commission (consisting of two officials and six settlers) which was appointed in 1917 and reported in 1919. 'Physically the Indian is not a wholesome influence because of his incurable repugnance to sanitation and hygiene. . . . The moral depravity of the Indian is equally damaging to the African . . .' and so on.

advantages which encouraged them resolutely to defend the broken line of their status and to launch a counter-attack to recover the ground which they had lost. They possessed, first of all, the support of the Government of India. British statesmanship was attempting the momentous task of winning the active consent of Indian nationalism to India's membership of the British Commonwealth, and the Government of India repeatedly insisted in the most forcible terms that this endeavour was being jeopardized by Indian nationalist resentment at the affronts which twenty-five thousand Indians in Kenya suffered at the hands of ten thousand white men. So the India Office came into action against the Colonial Office. The Indians of Kenya enjoyed a second strategical advantage through the erection of the conquered German East African colony into the mandated territory of Tanganyika. For the mandate established a standard. It affirmed first of all the principle that the interests of the native Africans were paramount. Thereafter it affirmed the principle of equal opportunity for all members of the League of Nations, of whom India was one. The mandate did not guarantee political equality; but, honestly interpreted, it barred the surrender of political power to a resident minority who might use it for an exclusive racial interest. The terms of the mandate, it may be noticed, raised the question of closer political union in East Africa, a question with which both the native and the Indian controversies were destined to become entangled. The mandatory power was authorized to constitute the territory into an administrative union with the adjacent territories under its sovereignty or control.[1] It might have been argued that the merging together of all East African territories which were under British rule would help the Indian cause by swamping the political influence of the Kenya Europeans. Indian opinion, however, feared that the result would be the reverse. It feared that the political influence of the Kenya Europeans would spread over the whole East African field, and that the exercise of this influence would soon destroy the guarantee of economic equality. 'Experience elsewhere has shown', declared the Government of India, 'how easy it is to subvert nominal equality by administrative action. We need only recall the exclusion of Indians from the uplands of Kenya "as a matter of administrative convenience".' The Government of India, therefore, demanded that it should be consulted before final arrange-

[1] Article XI. The statement appears to be plain; but there has been a great deal of controversy about it, and as a result nobody seems quite to know whether the mandatory power really has the right of incorporating Tanganyika with Kenya and Uganda or not.

ments were made for the administration of Tanganyika, and it affirmed the principle 'that it was not desirable, during the period of tutelage, that the government should in any way be controlled by alien settlers, of whatever nationality'.[1] This principle the mandatory power was ready to accept. The régime established in Tanganyika was, on the whole, satisfactory to Indian opinion. Indians envisaged a future in Tanganyika which would compensate both their interests and their pride for the barriers raised against them in Kenya.[2] But Kenya, they did not forget, ought still to offer to them the British Empire's atonement for the wrongs inflicted on them in South Africa. There was also Uganda, where the European and Indian business communities were on good terms with each other.[3] With regard to these three territories Indian policy was closely co-ordinated. It sought, first of all, to defend the principle of equality in Tanganyika, and to trust Indian enterprise to improve the position of Indians there. Secondly, it demanded that Uganda must remain in principle one with Tanganyika, and not become one with Kenya. Thirdly, it intended to cite Tanganyika as a model to which Kenya also should assimilate its policy. The mandated territory must set a standard for all East Africa.[4]

To this design the European settlers in Kenya offered a stubborn resistance. They fought to hold the ground which they had won and to win the new ground which would make them the masters of Kenya's destiny. They pressed upon the government of Kenya, which in its turn pressed upon the Colonial Office. The Colonial Office had then to meet a counter-pressure from the India Office, behind which was the Government of India, driven by the angry storms of Indian nationalism. The conflict concentrated itself for a time in debate between the two departments of state; then it spread outwards again through report and controversy in parliament and the imperial conference, until it once again dispersed itself unhealthily in the rancour and recrimination of demagogic rhetoric and press

[1] Letter from the Government of India to the Secretary of State for India, 10th February 1921. Cmd. 1312 of 1921, p. 7.

[2] Sir Benjamin Robertson reported in 1920 that there were 20,000 Indians in Tanganyika. They practically controlled the retail trade, they got most of their supplies from Indian merchants, they were already acquiring large estates, the climate suited them. Also they were in friendly relations with the Europeans. He thought their future very promising.

[3] Cmd. 1311 of 1921, p. 9. The Government of India, in a dispatch of 21st October 1920, mentions the agreement of Europeans and Indians in the report of the Uganda Development Committee, even on the burning question of segregation.

[4] Ibid., p. 10. 'It seems to us an impossible position that Indians in a British colony should be subject to disabilities to which they cannot be subjected in an adjoining mandated territory.'

polemics. While the dispute was at its height Kenya was resentfully enduring the after-war slump, aggravated locally by a disproportionate collapse in the price of her exports, by heavy government expenditure, and by an altered currency.[1] Amidst this turmoil the British government had to make a policy. No wonder it found it hard to steer a straight course.

On the 21st May 1920 a dispatch from Lord Milner to the Governor of Kenya laid down decisions upon the chief subjects of controversy. Only on one matter, immigration, were these decisions acceptable to the Indians. The dispatch assured them that there would be no immigration restriction of such a kind as to place Indians at a disadvantage with other immigrants. But it also reasserted the exclusion of Indians from the Kenya highlands. It admitted their right to share with the Europeans the privilege of elective representation on the legislative council. But it offered them as a separate community only two elected members to counterbalance the eleven elected Europeans who had recently been added to it. It offered them a similarly inferior position on municipal councils. It also asserted the principle of race segregation for residential areas and, wherever possible, for commercial areas. Moreover, although the dispatch did not mention this, Lord Milner, without consulting the India Office, had taken steps to apply the same principles, *mutatis mutandis*, to the Uganda Protectorate.

The Secretary of State for India remonstrated. His protests were reinforced by an emphatic dispatch from the Government of India.[2] This dispatch expressed regret that Uganda, where Indians and Europeans had lived side by side in a happy relationship, should have been dragged into the East African controversy. 'As things now stand,' it argued, 'the Indians in Uganda fear that disabilities to which they have not hitherto been subjected, will now be imposed upon them.' But the dispatch was chiefly concerned with the task of rebutting the principles of policy which Lord Milner had asserted in Kenya. It denounced the decisions with regard to communal franchise, racial segregation, and land ownership. Accepting the necessity of maintaining an official majority on the legislative council in order to safeguard the interests of the natives—which, as Lord Milner had confessed, were sometimes forgotten in this controversy—it expressed the conviction that the only reliable safeguard for Indian

[1] The writer cannot enter into a discussion of the movements of the Indian rupee and its effects on currency policy in Kenya. This is a complicated matter which has been simplified for purposes of political controversy in Kenya; but not in Uganda, although Uganda experienced the same vicissitudes.

[2] Cmd. 1311. Dispatch of 21st October 1920.

interests was adequate Indian representation on the council. In opposition to the Milner plan of communal representation heavily weighted in favour of the Europeans (Europeans 11 members: Indians 2) it demanded 'a common electoral roll and a common franchise on a reasonable property basis *plus* an educational test without racial discrimination, for all British subjects'. The same system of representation, the dispatch argued, should be followed in the municipalities.[1] The neglect of Indian well-being by European municipal councillors was in large measure responsible for the insanitary conditions which were used as an argument for segregation. The Government of India attacked both commercial and residential segregation. The former was irrational and impracticable, and would, in practice, mean nothing more than the reservation of the best business sites for Europeans. The latter would similarly mean the allocation of the best sites to Europeans, and it would be regarded in East Africa and India, no matter what Lord Milner's personal motives might be, as the infliction of a racial stigma. The ends which Lord Milner professed to have in view—'social comfort, social convenience, and social peace'—must be sought by a more efficient and more just municipal administration. In the highlands, a kind of rural segregation already existed for the benefit of European ownership. In handling this matter, the Government of India advanced the familiar argument that Lord Elgin's original restriction upon the grants of land to Indians 'as a matter of administrative convenience' had not been intended to prevent the transfer of properties for which Indians were prepared to bid. But now there was a veto upon private purchase. Moreover, the reason alleged for this veto—that Indians had in the lowlands opportunities from which climatic conditions debarred Europeans—did not exist in fact. Even in the lowlands a severe discrimination was in practice exercised against Indians in favour of European planters. The Government of India was inclined to agree with Lord Milner that Indians would not thrive in the highlands, but it deduced from this belief a very different inference of policy. 'If then, as Lord Milner suggests,' it neatly argued, 'the issue in Kenya Colony is merely a question of climate, we would urge that it be left for the climate to decide.' The long dispatch closed with an appeal to general principles. It appealed to the principles set out in the Covenant of the League of Nations; and to the standard which

[1] The municipal council of Nairobi consisted of 1 nominated official and 12 elected Europeans. Lord Milner proposed to add to it 3 elected Indians. The Government of India desired (*a*) an increase of Indian members elected on a common roll and a common franchise organized by wards, (*b*) an increase of nominated members to act as a safeguard against the predominance of any single community.

Great Britain, as mandatory power responsible to the League, was upholding in Tanganyika. It appealed also to the imperial conference, and to the reciprocity resolution which India had accepted in 1918 'for the sake of imperial unity'.

This powerful attack from India shattered Lord Milner's Kenya policy. As a white paper published in 1923 very mildly said, the dispatch 'reopened the whole question'.[1] Lord Milner himself retired in January 1921, and the uncertainties of British policy in Kenya were increased by a series of changes in the direction of the Colonial Office; within a few years Lord Milner, Mr. Churchill, the Duke of Devonshire, and Mr. Thomas were in turn responsible for policy. The question of Indian rights in Kenya remained open to blasts of passionate advocacy which drove British policy hither and thither in hopeless confusion. If the issue had been decided by declarations of general principle, the Indians would have won a resounding victory. The third report of the standing joint committee of Lords and Commons on Indian affairs accepted in 1921 'the general principle which the Government of India have laid down, namely, that there is no justification in Kenya for assigning to British Indians a status inferior to any other class of His Majesty's subjects'.[2] The Imperial Conference declared in the same year, with South Africa alone dissenting, that there was 'an incongruity between the position of India as an equal member of the British Empire and the existence of disabilities upon British Indians lawfully domiciled in some other parts of the Empire'. But the British government had not counted the cost of putting its principles into practice in Kenya colony. It tried to persuade the European colonists to be docile, to be reasonable. It instructed the Governor of Kenya to seek pacification by a round table conference of Europeans and Indians; when this failed, it called him to England to work out an agreed settlement through discussions at the Colonial Office. But the Governor carried in his pocket a document setting forth the 'irreducible minimum' of the white men's demands—and this 'irreducible minimum' demanded more even than Lord Milner's declaration had conceded. The British government then struggled to achieve a settlement over the heads of these intractable colonists. An inter-departmental committee of the India Office and the Colonial Office, consisting of the two Under-Secretaries of State, the Honourable Edward Wood, M.P.,[3] and Earl Winterton,

[1] *Indians in Kenya*, Cmd. 1922, p. 5.

[2] House of Commons Paper 1921, No. 177.

[3] Mr. Wood subsequently became Lord Irwin and a Viceroy of India, and later Viscount Halifax.

M.P., actually came to an agreement. Their report recommended a common electoral roll and a non-discriminatory property and educational test, together with practical arrangements which would result immediately in a 10 per cent. Indian electorate and give the Indians four seats in the legislative council as against seven (or alternatively eleven) European seats. It rejected segregation. It reported against immigration restriction. Thus on three of the crucial issues it declared against the European claims. On the fourth issue, that of the highlands, the two under-secretaries agreed to differ. The Government of India accepted this agreement, although not without reservations for the future. The Secretary of State for the Colonies accepted it. The British cabinet accepted it. But the white settlers of Kenya prepared to kidnap the governor and to set up a rebel government.[1]

The British government now found itself face to face with that most embarrassing and dangerous kind of sedition which calls itself loyalty. The rebellious settlers adopted the motto 'For King and Kenya', and generally ended their seditious councils of war by singing 'God Save the King'. At the same time they proclaimed 'the sacred right of resistance', sent a delegation to South Africa, and hinted at a Kenya–South African republic. They calculated that the British government would wilt when it reflected that 'there might be music to face in Pretoria. . . .'[2] The ways of loyalty are sometimes strange. But they are not unpredictable. The Canadian loyalists who in 1847 assaulted the King's representative in the streets of Montreal, the Ulster loyalists who proclaimed their readiness to 'kick the King's Crown into the Boyne', and the Kenya loyalists who in earnest or in bluff threatened the danger of a new Boer War and the disruption of the British Commonwealth, were all of them examples of the same political phenomenon.[3] All of them manifested the pride, fear, and resolution of an 'ascendancy' threatened with the loss of its privilege and power. All of them easily assumed, and intensely believed, that their own interest was an imperial necessity. They

[1] These plans are sympathetically described in Huxley, *White Man's Country,* and unsympathetically by W. McGregor Ross, *Kenya from Within* (Allen & Unwin, 1927), chapters xx–xxii. For the European settler standpoint see also Lord Delamere and Mr. Archer, *The Indian Problem in Kenya,* and E. Powys Cobb, *The Thermopylae of Africa* (Nairobi, 1933); on the other side, Norman Leys, *Kenya* (Hogarth Press, 1926).

[2] Huxley, *White Man's Country,* vol. ii, pp. 138–9. The Kenya deputation to South Africa also got into touch with Southern Rhodesia, which then was receiving the enviable prize of self-government.

[3] See above, pp. 20, 95–6, and below, pp. 424–5. One might also choose some examples from the history of Natal where there has more than once been talk of secession, e.g. during the trouble with the imperial government after the Zulu revolt of 1906.

were loyal to an Empire which they fashioned in the image of their own prejudices. If the Imperial Crown should make itself the symbol of principles and procedures inconsistent with the 'irreducible minimum' on which they took their stand, then they were prepared to resist its authority by force. This is the breaking-point of any constitutional system. It is a breaking-point which even the most stable commonwealth must reach when the loyalties of religion or race or class are felt so intensely as to forbid a compromise which would save the wider loyalty which comprehends and transcends these narrower ones. In mid-nineteenth-century Canada, the wider loyalty triumphed. In the Irish crisis which erupted on the eve of the war, the victory of the narrower loyalty shook the constitutional system of the United Kingdom. It seemed in 1922 as if the defiance of a few thousand colonists in Kenya would shatter the advance 'from force to persuasion' which was the only principle by which the British Commonwealth could in the long run endure. His Majesty's government was not prepared to coerce its rebellious subjects in Kenya on the basis of the Wood–Winterton proposals. On the other hand, Mr. Sastri gave warning that, if the Indians were rebuffed, he would not predict what would happen in India.[1] There had now been a continuous crisis extending for almost three years. The Indians had rejected the Milner proposals. The Europeans had defeated every proposal made since then. The bitter antagonism of two tiny communities in a country where both were aliens had repercussions extending far beyond Kenya: it created a deadlock between two of His Majesty's Departments of State; it dragged into controversy the governments of India, Great Britain, and South Africa; it threatened an irreconcilable quarrel which must one day make inevitable a schism in the British Commonwealth. It had become impossible to achieve a settlement of the dispute on a basis of agreed justice, for the warring communities held conflicting ideas of justice.

Why had affairs come to such a pass? The European settlers accused the Indians, and the Indians accused the Europeans, and the compromise-loving people of placid England accused both parties. Why must they be unreasonable? Why must they make trouble? The new idealism which was coming quickly into fashion turned angrily and virtuously against the white settlers. The present writer

[1] Huxley, *White Man's Country*, vol. ii, p. 146. Mr. Andrews has told the writer that Mr. Sastri, dangerously ill in London during the critical discussions of 1923, 'at the crisis of his illness said to me in agony, "If Kenya is lost, all is lost".' The 'all' which Mr. Sastri dreaded to lose was India's loyal membership of a Commonwealth standing for the reconciliation of nations and religions in a system of law and freedom. Surrender to racialism would prove the Commonwealth a sham and kill Indian loyalty.

does not feel called upon to defend them; but neither does he feel called upon to join their accusers. He has criticized their naïve ideas of imperial policy and their quite inadmissible conception of imperial loyalty. But he is not disposed to reprove their naughty manners. It did not cost stay-at-home Englishmen anything to exchange one idealism from another; but it was painful and it might be costly for the Kenya colonists to move from the world of Cecil Rhodes into the world of Lord Lugard. And had they been given fair notice to move? The 'white ideal' still appealed to the British government in 1919, when it encouraged a new immigration of settlers into the Kenya highlands. The old assumptions of colonial autonomy were surely in its head in 1915, when it admitted settler representatives to the war council. The same assumptions surely dictated the Milner proposals of 1920. Was it not natural that the Kenya settlers should imagine themselves advancing towards the same end which their fellows in Southern Rhodesia were even then rapidly approaching? How could they be expected to understand that their idea of empire, which in 1915 was accounted noble, and in 1920 was still a respectable orthodoxy, must be deemed in 1923 to be tainted with sin? If the historian feels himself obliged to deal out praise and blame, let him deal out a fair share of blame to the pharisaism which is always so stiffly virtuous when other people pay the price of virtue, and to the muddle-headed weakness which refuses to think out its policy on a basis of principle but waits till it is pushed into just dealing.

The British government at last summoned up sufficient resolution to impose on both parties a compromise. The compromise was not 'a settlement'. It nevertheless saved for the future the possibility of a settlement which the two warring communities in Kenya might yet achieve, perhaps after a struggle as long as, or longer than, that which French and English had waged in Canada. This struggle, like that earlier one, would be not merely a struggle between two races, but a struggle by both races with the problems which beset them separately and together on a difficult soil. In East Africa the problem which would most closely beset them was that of their relationship to the natives of the soil. This truth was stressed by the white paper which the British government issued in July 1923. The white paper corrected the distorted perspective of Kenya controversies, reducing the Indian-European conflict to the moderate proportions which properly belonged to it. That was its chief merit.[1]

[1] Cmd. 1922. The white paper was issued after consultation with deputations of Europeans and Indians from Kenya and the Rev. Dr. Arthur to put the native view. There were also three representatives from India.

The white paper rediscovered the vast majority of Kenya's population, namely the native Africans. It is true that Europeans and Indians had frequently made perfunctory references to the primary interests of the African; but in practice they had fought their sectional battles with little thought of his existence. The Colonial Office also had allowed its interest to be switched from the African population to the noisy rivalries of two small immigrant communities. It now made a resolute effort to recover perspective.

'Primarily' [the memorandum asserted] 'Kenya is an African territory, and His Majesty's government think it necessary to record their considered opinion that the interests of the African natives must be paramount, and that if, and when, these interests and the interests of the immigrant races should conflict, the former should prevail. Obviously the interests of the other communities, European, Indian, or Arab, must severally be safeguarded. Whatever the circumstances in which members of these communities have entered Kenya, there will be no drastic action or reversal of measures already introduced, such as may have been contemplated in some quarters, the result of which might be to destroy or impair the existing interests of those who are already settled in Kenya. But in the administration of Kenya His Majesty's government regard themselves as exercising a trust on behalf of the African population, and they are unable to delegate or share this trust, the object of which may be defined as the protection and advancement of the native races.'[1]

The resolute assertion of these principles prefaced announcements which dashed the pretensions of both parties. First of all, the Europeans were plainly told that in no conceivable future would Kenya become 'white man's country' in the South African sense—a country in which the resident white minority would hold political power and control the destiny of the African population.

'It has been suggested' [said the memorandum] 'that it might be possible for Kenya to advance in the near future on the lines of responsible self-government, subject to the reservation of native affairs. . . . His Majesty's government cannot but regard the grant of responsible government as out of the question within any period of time which need now be taken into consideration. Nor, indeed, would they contemplate yet the possibility of substituting an unofficial majority on the Council for the government official majority.'[2]

The principle of trusteeship, it was now asserted, barred the way to responsible or even representative government based upon European predominance. The other principle of respecting the established rights of immigrant communities, honestly interpreted, barred three

[1] Cmd. 1922, p. 9. [2] Ibid., p. 15.

of the five demands which the white men had tabled as their 'irreducible minimum'. They had insisted on racial segregation in the towns, immigration restriction, and a European monopoly of the right of franchise. His Majesty's government flatly rejected the policy of segregation between Europeans and Asiatics. It declared that immigration restriction on racial lines was contrary to British policy and that immigration restriction of any kind would be contemplated only in extreme circumstances. It upheld the Indian right to the franchise. In future the European community would continue to elect 11 members to the legislative council; the Indian community would elect 5, the Arab community would elect 1. On other issues also European exclusiveness received a check. In particular, the principle asserted in the Wood-Winterton report that Indians and Europeans should be equally eligible for nomination to the executive council—personal capacity constituting the one qualification—was maintained.

The European community in Kenya was abashed and angry at these decisions, but decided for tactical reasons to conceal its dissatisfaction.[1] The Indian community, on the other hand, made no attempt to hide its violent resentment against the white paper. It is only necessary to change the point of view to see that Indian pretensions had been dashed even more completely than those of the Europeans. For the Indians were demanding abstract justice. It was denied them. Some of their fears were allayed. They would not be called upon to submit to the humiliation of segregation. There would be no racial barrier, direct or indirect, to Indian immigration. But there still remained a barrier against them in the Kenya highlands. An historical summary of this old dispute rejected all the Indian arguments, and concluded with the decision that 'the existing practice must be retained as regards both initial grants and transfers'.[2] The promise to set aside for Indian settlement an area in the lowlands (if this could be done without infringing on native reserves) did not soothe Indian indignation; for the question had become one of prestige. The Indians had rejected all ideas of reciprocal rights for separate communities, and had raised the principle of equal rights for individuals in a single community in which Indians and Europeans were fused. Because of this principle they bitterly attacked the franchise decisions. It was not enough for them to have a vote on a wide communal franchise. They demanded a common roll on which European and Indian voters—even a reduced number of Indian

[1] Huxley, *White Man's Country*, vol. ii, p. 155.
[2] Cmd. 1922, pp. 15–17.

voters—would man for man count as equals. This equality had been granted them in the Wood-Winterton report. It was now withdrawn. The white paper argued persistently for the communal system. This system made possible a wider Indian franchise than would otherwise have been established. It permitted the immediate grant of electoral representation to other communities which were ripe for it, notably the coastal Arabs. It provided a framework into which African native representation could be fitted in due season. Practically, it was the only system which would work in a country where communal loyalty was stronger than the common loyalty.[1] In India itself, for this very reason, it had been necessary to establish a system of communal representation.[2] All these arguments made no impression upon the Indians. Communal representation emphasized their separateness, which they had been made to feel, and felt, as inferiority; and it condemned them to be perpetually in a minority.

In India itself there was a violent agitation against the British government's decisions. The Indian legislative assembly passed in a day all stages of a bill which provided that immigrants into India from British possessions would enjoy 'no greater rights and privileges' than those which the possessions granted to Indian immigrants.[3] Angry voices, issuing from the leaders of 'moderate' Indian opinion, denounced 'the advancing spirit of South Africa', and asserted that the people of India were no longer equal members of the British Commonwealth, but 'helots in a Boer Empire'. There was talk of boycotting the coming imperial conference. Instead, all parties and sections of Indian public opinion called on India's representatives at the conference to protest with all their might against the injustice which the British government had perpetrated in Kenya. The delegates protested with passion. The Maharaja of Alwar made in debate one particularly telling thrust. The Colonial Office, he said, had based its case upon the trust which Great Britain held on the African native's behalf. Was it not grotesque that a country held in trust for its inhabitants by Great Britain should during the period of this trust be saddled with a franchise given to somebody else? What would happen when the natives awoke from their slumber and found themselves compelled to reckon with those who had established interests in their country 'not under trust, but under a franchise'?[4]

[1] Cmd. 1922, p. 12. In Kenya, said the white paper, 'no candidate, European or Indian, could stand as the advocate of the other race without sacrificing the support of his own'.

[2] In India, however, it was on religious, not racial, lines.

[3] See *Immigration into India Act, 1924* (Government of India Act, No. 3 of 1924).

[4] Cmd. 1988, p. 93. The Maharaja was logically consistent, for the Indians would

To these taunts the British government could offer no logical answer. It might, perhaps, have offered instead an historical explanation. It might have confessed that the implications of trusteeship were becoming clear to it only after it had permitted the growth of interests likely to interfere with the exercise of that trusteeship. It might have explained that projects of white settlement in Africa, which had been acceptable to Merivale and Livingstone and nineteenth-century idealism, had only of recent years become unattractive to the idealism of a new generation. Reading between the lines of the 1923 memorandum, one gathers the impression that the Colonial Office would have been ready enough to expunge both Indians and Europeans from the page of its Kenya complications, if only wishing could have done it.[1] But wishing has no power to undo what the past has done. It was not possible to undo the settlement of the highlands, which only a few years previously had seemed a splendid enterprise; nor was it even possible to revoke the recent grant of franchise. It was not possible to arrange in a scheme of abstract justice the complicated conflicting interests of Africans, Indians, and Europeans. The best that might be hoped for was a decision which would moderate the conflicts which had arisen from haphazard policy in the past and raise a standard of justice towards which the communities in Kenya might struggle in the future.

> 'It is not to be expected that issues so grave can be composed to the immediate satisfaction of the several interests concerned,' [the memorandum of 1923 concluded] 'but His Majesty's government believe that the decisions now taken, resting as they do on the broad basis of the British trusteeship for the Africans, provide an equitable adjustment of those interests.'

IV

Review

It is necessary now to attempt a sketch of the recent history of Indian-European controversies in South Africa and Kenya, and to attempt a general view of these controversies in the light of the central problem of Indian nationalism and India's relation to the

have accepted equality on a basis of no franchise, either for Indians or Europeans. But they were prepared to accept neither (1) Europeans first and the rest nowhere, which was the implication of the 'irreducible minimum' programme: nor (2) Natives first, Europeans second, and Indians third, which with some justification they believed to be the implication of the white paper.

[1] Cmd. 1922, p. 9: 'Whatever the circumstances in which members of these communities have entered Kenya. . . .' Cf. Huxley, *White Man's Country*, vol. i, p. 98, quoting Lord Peel, 'I think the best solution of this trouble is to buy you all out . . .', and p. 191, quoting Mr. Ormsby-Gore, 'I personally regret the history of the colony.'

British Commonwealth. This is a difficult task. The historian is too close to his subject; he cannot see the clear shape of events which are still shaping themselves. Even in the separate restricted histories of Kenya and South Africa, Indian and European relationships still tend to move in jerks which make it difficult to detect the rhythm of their progress, which one day will become discernible. Moreover, in both these countries the Indian question is a minor theme in the general pattern of racial issues. The native African theme is dominant. But while on the one hand the study of the African theme is in the scheme of this book still premature, on the other hand the Indian theme is not easily detached from the composition where it belongs.

In Kenya, the white paper of 1923 did at any rate serve the purpose of establishing the dominance—the word then used and thereafter much discussed was 'paramountcy'—of native African interests. Before 1923 it had been generally assumed that 'white civilization' was in Kenya the measure of all things. This assumption the Indian community had violently assailed on the ground that the principle of the British Commonwealth demanded equality between individual members of European and Indian civilizations when these met on the common soil of a British colony. The Indians attacked the claim of the Europeans to rule alone. The question implied throughout years of passionate controversy was—'Does the future in Kenya belong to the Europeans, or does it belong to the Indians, or does it belong to both together?' The declaration of 1923 laid it down that *the* future, as the phrase had hitherto been understood, belonged neither to the Europeans nor to the Indians. It belonged to the Africans. Kenya, one might perhaps say, was 'black man's country' in which, nevertheless, the European and Indian communities, in virtue of their established interests, possessed, each of them, *a* future. This announcement of policy, if it were seriously intended and honestly accepted, must have a deflating effect on the passions of the immigrant communities. By lowering the value of the prize for which they had believed themselves to be struggling, it must lessen the motive for violent struggle. If, for example, responsible government was just round the corner, there was every motive for the most violent dispute on the principle of parliamentary representation. If, on the other hand, due performance of the British trust made it essential for the government to retain a nominated official majority on the legislative council, then the principle of representation became less important than some practical scheme which would assure both Indians and Europeans that their interests and convictions would with due weight be impressed upon a government standing above their clamour.[1]

Unfortunately for Kenya's peace, the clarity of the 1923 pronouncement was smudged by changes in the political direction of the Colonial Office and changes in the governorship, by the incessant coming and going of investigating committees, and by the overproduction of printed material by His Majesty's Stationery Office.[2] Little shifts or hesitations in British policy were distorted by nervy imaginations in Kenya into violent oscillations or abrupt reversals. The European community, in particular, remained uncertain whether it should regard the declaration of paramountcy 'as a threat of injustice, which it is right to resist, or as a pious declaration, which was never intended to be taken seriously'.[3] The declaration of paramountcy was contained in four carefully balanced sentences whose clarity could hardly have been improved upon. But the colonists seemed incapable of reading all four sentences together. Their very first reading had been in all probability their most careful and accurate one. In their fight with the Indians they had for tactical reasons taken the high ground of native interest, and they were alarmed that the British government should so purposefully take them at their word. 'They had rubbed the magic lamp of native interests,' writes Lord Delamere's biographer, 'but the Djin who suddenly materialized before them had a nasty look, not at all the obedient servant they had hoped to see.'[4] They very soon persuaded themselves, however, that the Djin had gone tamely back into his bottle. The interpretations which British politicians placed rather too lavishly on the paramountcy doctrine encouraged them to conclude that the doctrine did not after all mean very much. In the first place, there were refinements upon Lord Lugard's phrase of the 'dual mandate'. English statesmen slipped from the 'dual mandate' to the 'dual policy', which they defined as 'the complementary development of native and non-native communities'.[5] The wishes of the colonists at once fathered the thought that the 'complementary' principle obliterated the idea of European subordination implied by the principle of African paramountcy. In the second place, there were refine-

[1] Cf. *Joint Committee on Closer Union in East Africa* (House of Commons Paper, 1931, No. 156), vol. i, p. 41.

[2] Ibid., p. 13: 'There can be little doubt that the rapid succession of a number of commissions of inquiry and government white papers has resulted in a feeling of uncertainty among various sections of the community in East Africa.'

[3] Cmd. 3234 (Hilton Young Report), p. 40.

[4] Huxley, *White Man's Country*, vol. ii, p. 155.

[5] *Report of East Africa Commission* (Ormsby-Gore Report), Cmd. 2387 of 1925, pp. 22 and 23.

ments upon the notion of trusteeship. Why should Englishmen at home bear the entire burden of the sacred trust? Was it not fantastic to imagine that those Englishmen actually in Africa were free of the obligation? 'The trusteeship lies really', declared the Ormsby-Gore Commission, 'upon the shoulders of every man and woman of our race in Africa. It is in very truth a white man's burden, and all Europeans in Africa must share in the work.'[1] As a statement of the duty of every European man and woman living in Africa, this was the most admirable Christian idealism. But the Kenya colonists did not choose to interpret it merely as a beautiful sermon on their individual duty. They interpreted it as a removal—as yet only a tentative removal, but one full of hope for their future—of the barrier raised so firmly in 1923 against their advance to political power. If they shared the trust, then it was logical that they should share its administration. Before long their leaders were pressing for powers which would have made it possible for them, although they did not state the matter thus, actually to vary the terms of the trust.[2]

The prize of political contest in Kenya seemed to be regaining its old value; it was therefore natural that European and Indian rivalries should lose little of their old animosity. Moreover, the geographical range of political action seemed likely to extend itself. About 1925 the question of federation or closer union between the East African colonies, which since the war had been intermittently in the heads of British statesmen, came definitely to the forefront. The European settlers of Kenya, led by Lord Delamere, were quick to imagine an opportunity of achieving 'the solidification of the white ideal'. The civilizing influence of Kenya would radiate southward to meet the civilizing influence radiating northward from Rhodesia. A combination of colonies would be able to diminish Colonial Office control and kill the West Coast policy. Lord Delamere dreamed of a monster federation stretching from the borders of Abyssinia to the Zambesi, and comprehending the six colonies of Kenya, Uganda, Tanganyika, Nyasaland, and the two Rhodesias. In a series of unofficial inter-colonial conferences at which he was both organizer and host, he endeavoured to fire the delegates of the other colonies with his own dreams of 'a central African dominion'.[3] But the cautious leaders

[1] Cmd. 2387.

[2] It was the Hilton Young Commission which pointed out that association of the immigrant communities in the trusteeship for the natives 'must not give them power to vary the terms of the trust'. Cmd. 3234, p. 7.

[3] Southern Rhodesia, which enjoyed responsible government, did not participate, and Uganda was not represented until the third and last conference. On the idea of a 'Dominion of Middle Africa' see above, p. 210.

of Northern Rhodesia were unwilling to dilute their country, which was 'whiter' than Kenya, in the 'black north'.[1] They were also unwilling to share the vexations of Kenya's Indian problem. Lord Delamere resigned himself therefore to the prospect of achieving his vision by stages, beginning with the closer union of the three East African colonies. Even this more moderate ambition was grounded upon an assumption which was soon proved to be too sanguine. But at this time the Europeans of Kenya imagined that the Colonial Office had already decided upon a policy of closer union, and they believed that they could exact a price for their support of this policy. The price which they demanded was a majority of elected European members in the legislative council. If events turned out as they anticipated, they would reap a double advantage. They would establish their political future as masters in Kenya. They would at the same time penetrate the surrounding provinces with their Kenya point of view.[2]

The questions at issue between Europeans and Indians were, it is obvious, subordinate to the question of European-African relationships, and were at the same time inextricably interwoven with that larger problem. Because of this, the Indian community in Kenya found itself, virtually in its own despite, fighting on the ground of the white paper of 1923. The Indians had not accepted the specific decisions of that document with regard to the highlands and the electoral system. They were indeed abstaining from the exercise of the communal franchise which had been granted to them.[3] But their circumstances compelled them to applaud the declaration of paramountcy, which barred the erection in Kenya of a white oligarchy. Inevitably they became the allies of Colonial Office control against the demands of the European colonists. Inevitably also they opposed the closer union proposals because it was in fact impossible to detach them from their association with the 'white ideal' and consider them merely on grounds of strict administrative and economic convenience. They were, of course, supported in their resistance by the neighbour-

[1] The Hilton Young Report (p. 27) gave the following figures of European population: Uganda, 1,752; Kenya, 12,529; Tanganyika, 5,274; Nyasaland, 1,716; Northern Rhodesia, 5,581. These figures have to be considered in relation to the native population. Whereas the proportion of Europeans to natives in South Africa is 1 to 4, and in Southern Rhodesia 1 to 20, in Kenya it was about 1 to 200, and in Eastern and Central Africa generally about 1 to 400. For Mr. Amery's view of the political future of the 'broad backbone' see *The Forward View*, p. 259.

[2] For a general account of the unofficial conferences see Huxley, *White Man's Country*, vol. ii, pp. 199 ff.

[3] Not till 1931 did the Indian community elect its five representatives, and these were under pledge not to take their seats.

ing Indian communities of Tanganyika and Uganda, which, although not entirely satisfied with their own status, were horrified at the prospect of being assimilated to Kenya.[1] Until the publication of the Hilton Young Report in 1929 there seemed to be real ground for their fears.[2] But that report marked a definite turn in the flow of the tide. It refrained from the temptation to consider the project of closer union in isolation from the context of policy, and it reaffirmed in unambiguous terms the paramountcy of native interests, subject to the qualification, which was explicit in the 1923 pronouncement, that paramountcy must not mean the destruction of the interests, already established, of the immigrant communities.[3] It firmly rejected any constitutional changes which might lead towards responsible government, as the Kenya settlers understood that phrase. Responsible government, it declared, implied representative institutions resting upon 'the basis of a single homogeneous community'. It could not come in Kenya until the natives themselves were able to share in the responsibility.[4] Here was a frank answer to the question which was continually being begged in Kenya's controversies—What is Kenya? Who are the people of Kenya? 'We, the people of Kenya,' the colonists had continually challenged, 'demand our inalienable rights of self-government.' The majority report of the Hilton Young Commission declared in unmistakable terms that the European settlers were not the people of Kenya. The people of Kenya had not yet formed itself; but the paramount element in the formation of the future must be the native African element. Side by side with this element were 'the immigrant communities'—a designation which the Europeans bitterly rejected. And well they might. On the one hand, it destroyed their picture of Kenya as white man's country served by a numerous accessory population of dependent Africans. On the other hand, it introduced into a very different African picture the complication of a second community sharing with the Europeans their immigrant status. This complication the Europeans had tried persistently to shove aside as an unpleasant confusion in their Kenya design. But the shape of things

[1] e.g. appendixes to *Report by the Rt. Hon. V. S. Srinivasa Sastri regarding his Mission to East Africa* (Delhi, Government of India Press, 1930). In Uganda, with a population of 1,874 Europeans and 11,564 Indians, two Europeans and only one Indian were nominated to the legislative council. In Tanganyika the Indians demanded three additional nominated representatives.

[2] The white paper, *Future Policy in regard to Eastern Africa*, Cmd. 2904 of 1927, seemed to them (perhaps as a result of careless reading) to foreshadow closer union without the safeguards which they demanded.

[3] Cmd. 3234, especially p. 40.

[4] Ibid., pp. 83–4.

was now once again altered and distorted for them. The native African became the centre of the picture. The Indian's proportions expanded to equal the shrunken proportions of the European. The Hilton Young Commission carried the logic of this rearrangement even into the vexed question of the franchise. Not content with reaffirming the central doctrine of the 1923 pronouncement, it went back beyond this pronouncement and resurrected from the Wood-Winterton recommendations the Indian principle of a common roll. A saving caution prompted it to doubt whether the necessary agreement could be obtained immediately; a common roll, it nevertheless asserted, was 'the ideal to be aimed at'.[1]

The commission did recommend a series of steps to be taken in the direction of closer union; but these recommendations were clearly overshadowed by its pronouncements on policy. The Secretary of State for the Colonies, Mr. Amery, attempted to press forward with the administrative scheme, and for this purpose dispatched to East Africa the permanent Under-Secretary of State.[2] But the scheme had now been detached from its original context. Europeans supported a modified form of it only half-heartedly; Indians opposed it with renewed confidence. Before long the Europeans dropped the scheme altogether. Two new white papers issued by Lord Passfield in 1930 convinced them that the Colonial Office, now that it was under labour direction, was their inveterate enemy. There was nothing new in these white papers.[3] In substance they were a repetition of the Hilton Young Report. This perhaps was the trouble. They forced into the faces of the Kenya settlers a simplified reproduction of that unwelcome picture. Perhaps, too, a strain of unimaginative rectitude which might be detected in the two white papers led the overwrought colonists to espy in them menaces which they did not in fact contain. It took the patient, simple clarity of the parliamentary joint committee which reported in 1931 to make it clear to them that no new assault upon their established rights was intended. After eight years of manœuvres, illusions, and alarms, the 1923 principles—from which His Majesty's government had in fact never definitely departed—were emphatically and precisely reaffirmed.[4]

[1] Cmd. 3234, p. 210. (For the dissenting report of the chairman, see pp. 244 ff.)

[2] Sir Samuel Wilson. See *Report by Sir Samuel Wilson on his Visit to East Africa*, Cmd. 3378 of 1929; cf. Amery, *The Forward View*, p. 257.

[3] *Statement of the Conclusions of His Majesty's Government as regards Closer Union in East Africa*, Cmd. 3574 of 1930, and *Memorandum on Native Policy in East Africa*, Cmd. 3573 of 1930.

[4] Even on the question of the common roll the joint committee in effect returned to the 1923 pronouncement. While it was unwilling to prejudge the question for the

It was at last clear, therefore, that the place of the European-Indian dispute was only on the wings of the Kenya stage. This did not mean that the bickering was over. It arose, for example, on the question of the highlands, following upon the report, published in September 1934, of the Kenya Land Commission. The chief task of the commission was to remove from the minds of the African natives and their friends in England the fear that their interests and rights on their own soil would be in the future encroached upon. But the commission's terms of reference also empowered it to define the area known as the Kenya highlands, in which persons of European descent were 'to have a privileged position in accordance with the white paper of 1923'. The Commission, after deciding upon a moderate area of 16,700 square miles,[1] recommended that the boundaries of this area should be safeguarded by order-in-council, so that the Europeans, no less than the Africans, should in the future be free from the feeling of insecurity. The British government was in no hurry to act on this suggestion; but in the Indian legislature there were protests against this proposal to consecrate privilege, and, it was alleged, extend it.[2] It was believed that the British government, in accordance with an unpublished recommendation of the Morris Carter Commission, was contemplating an order-in-council which would incorporate a legal prohibition against sale or lease, to any person of colour, of land in the defined European area. Such an order-in-council would have embodied a change in the declared principle of British policy, for it would have translated the existing administrative discrimination into a recognition in law of the colour-bar principle. It would have been a repudiation of the theory of colonial rule to which the British Empire appealed in order to justify before other nations its great possessions.[3] It would also have convinced India that her claim of racial equality could never win its way against the opposition of a white colonial minority. The statement of these dangers proved sufficient to avert the policy which would have entailed them. On the 9th July 1936 the Secretary of State for the Colonies announced in the House of Commons that two new orders-in-council would be issued, one defining native reserves,

future, it considered that the common roll 'would be impracticable under present conditions' (p. 41).

[1] *Report of the Kenya Land Commission* (Morris Carter Commission), Cmd. 4566 of 1934, part iii, ch. ix. On the one hand the tendency had been to argue a restriction of the highlands to 1908 limits (the Indian figure was 11,000 square miles); and on the other hand expand them to include any land suitable for European settlement.

[2] e.g. debate of 27th March 1935, reported in the *Manchester Guardian*, 28th March 1935.

[3] See Lord Lugard's letter in *The Times*, 27th May 1936.

the other defining the boundaries of those parts of the highlands which were to be set aside for non-native occupation. But there would be nothing in either order imposing legal disabilities against Indians, or against any person on grounds of race, colour, or creed. The position would remain as the white paper of 1923 had defined it.[1]

Meanwhile, the perspective in which men viewed the Kenya scene continued to change. Indian anxieties, no less than European ones, were tending to fasten less upon the future relations between the rival immigrant peoples than upon their future relationship to the native African people. It was action initiated by Tanganyika, hitherto regarded as the standard of justice in East Africa, which sharpened these anxieties. In order to lessen the impact of an 'economic blizzard' upon native well-being, the government of Tanganyika early in 1932 introduced schemes of 'orderly marketing' designed to raise prices, improve quality, develop diversified production, secure to producers quick returns in cash, and foster native co-operation. The governments of Uganda and Kenya followed suit. The Indians in East Africa were alarmed at this new policy whose effect certainly was to press heavily upon small Indian traders. The Government of India thereupon sent to East Africa an investigator whose report pleaded for the old order of *laisser-faire*, and alleged the existence, or at least the possibility, of a European plot against the Indian community. But this allegation did not occupy a central position in the report. The substance of the report, together with the governors' comments on it, made it clear that the new order to which many Indians must with discomfort accommodate themselves was based primarily upon calculations of native interest, and not upon European malevolence and prejudice.[2]

The economic blizzard was beating with equal fury upon the

[1] Hansard, *House of Commons Debates*, vol. cccxiv, 9th July 1936, cols. 1441–3 and 1460–9. Indian opinion expressed relief that there would be no legal discrimination, but still protested against the continuance of administrative discrimination.

[2] The documents are printed in *The Gazette of India, Extraordinary*, 24th June 1935. The same expert (Mr. K. P. S. Menon) reported much more strongly on the injustices suffered by the Indian trading community in Zanzibar. The burden of his accusation was that some European competitors of the Indians, with the connivance of some officials, had used the pretext of protecting Arab cultivators in a deliberate attempt to ruin the Indian community, and this in an island where the Indians had preceded even the Arabs and had developed the clove trade for generations. The complexity of the situation in Zanzibar is indicated by the fact that Arab cultivators themselves have recently (1936) revolted against the methods of official administration in the coco-nut industry, and also that British merchants unexpectedly joined hands with the Indians in demanding an investigation into the clove industry. At the time of writing the results of that investigation are not yet available. The author is aware that conditions in Zanzibar are very relevant to the problems dealt with above, and regrets that he is not sufficiently well informed to handle them adequately.

European colonists. The world was entering upon a phase in which there was little effective demand for the products of the Kenya highlands. During a long succession of years after 1930 the majority of settlers could hope only in very good seasons to make a profit on only one export crop, coffee. They did not possess the advantage which has repeatedly been of decisive strategic importance in the development of European settlement in Africa, namely, a mining industry which both built up colonial resources through international exchange and provided a local market for a diversified agricultural economy.[1] Anxious observers of their plight began to compare it with that of the Boers before the days of Kimberley, or with that of the Rhodesians imagined to be without their mines. Necessity was forcing into the forefront a new method of approaching Kenya's problems. During the first decade after the war the controversy had dealt almost entirely with justice. Frequently the appeals to justice had masked a battle of interests and passions, so that the historian who reads these appeals is compelled to handle sceptically the arguments of right propounded on both sides, and to examine words, not only to discover what they say, but to discover what they conceal. Frequently, too, the notion of justice which was in men's minds—and particularly in the minds of distant Indians and Englishmen—was highly abstract. From 1929 onwards public opinion began to deal with the concrete historical reality of the situation in Kenya. This did not mean that the standard of justice was lowered. The widely-read report of the Hilton Young Commission eloquently affirmed 'the primary purpose of political institutions, namely, the achievement of social justice'.[2] But the commission did a good deal to bring justice down to earth. It investigated not only the rights of the various communities in Kenya, but their capacities and opportunities. And if its report removed towards the wings of Kenya's stage both the European and Indian communities, this resulted not merely from arguments of abstract justice, but from a forecast of the prob-

[1] Smuts, *Africa and Some World Problems*, Lecture II, and Cmd. 3234, pp. 15, 23. It may be relevant here to give the occupational statistics of the Kenya Indians according to the 1931 census (Colonial Office No. 12149, *Report on Census of Non-Natives*, 24th April 1931, by C. F. Spencer). Of a total Indian population of 39,644, agriculture employed 120, commerce 9,868, domestic service 675, government 780, railways 1,670. The total European population in 1931 was 16,812. The comparative percentage rates of increase since 1911 were:

	Europeans	*Indians*
1921 . . .	204	115
1931 . . .	429·5	272·6

The Europeans gained proportionately more quickly both by natural increase and immigration.

[2] Cmd. 3234, p. 90.

able future of these communities in East Africa. The Commission believed that both the Europeans and the Indians had exaggerated their future prospects. It pointed out that the area open to European settlement was comparatively small. Despite 'the immense fund of energy' which European settlement had introduced into Africa, it must be looked upon—for climatic, economic, and social reasons—as 'still in the experimental stage'.[1] The Indians also had rendered indispensable services to East Africa, but they would have to face in the future 'competition from both sides'—from Europeans who were being forced into occupations which Indians had hitherto monopolized, and from Africans forcing their way upwards into the same occupations. The Commission believed that the Indians would succeed in keeping for themselves a useful place in East Africa, but it considered that economic forces were already operating to check Indian immigration and would operate more strongly in years to come. The years which immediately followed the publication of these opinions seemed strongly to justify them. Indeed, circumstance no less than statesmanship appeared to be mitigating those exaggerations which had inflated the importance of Kenya's European-Indian problem during the years which followed the war. Racial justice in Kenya was no less desirable in 1935 than it had been in 1923. The guidance and control of the British government was no less necessary. But it was becoming clear that more would have to be demanded, and perhaps more would be forthcoming, from the intelligence and goodwill of the actual people who were facing in Kenya the lessons of a difficult experience.

In South Africa, intelligence and goodwill on the whole succeeded in maintaining the ground which they had gained by the Capetown agreement of 1927. That agreement was more like an armistice than a treaty. It did not contain even in outline the heads of a solution for all problems. The proportions of the racial question in South Africa were altogether different from its proportions in Kenya; for South Africa might with far greater justification be called 'white man's country'—a country in which Europeans were both economically and politically in the saddle, a country in which their civilization might survive, although not without stress, even without native support.[2] It was a country where the ruled races did in substance have to accept the position of accessories to the civilization of their rulers. The Indians in most parts of South Africa had to bear hardships in comparison with which the inequalities of Indians in Kenya

[1] Ibid., pp. 18–25.
[2] This opinion is expressed in the Hilton Young Report, Cmd. 3234, p. 32.

—although these more greatly stimulated the protests of Indian nationalism—were almost negligible. In Kenya there was a controversy about the principles of the franchise. In three of the four South African provinces Indians enjoyed no parliamentary franchise at all. Only in two of the South African provinces had they ever enjoyed a municipal franchise, and in one of these provinces, and that the more important, their right was disappearing.[1] Their problem was in essence that of a voteless community trying to gain a living in a society where the voters believed themselves menaced by Indian competition. That problem made itself felt in various forms of pressure. There were the restrictions on Indian freedom of movement between the provinces. There was the lack of legal security in the Transvaal for the Indians whose businesses were on land occupied in contravention of the Gold Law of 1908.[2] There was the constant uncertainty and anxiety about trading licences; in this matter municipal authority, which very often was prejudiced against the Indians, was only in part checked by provincial oversight—also likely to be prejudiced—by the government of the Union, and by the courts. There were abuses of sanitation and bad conditions of housing and of bazaar organization in those places where municipal neglect of Indian interests manifested itself. None of these grievances, anxieties, and hardships was directly removed by the Capetown agreement of 1927.

That agreement, nevertheless, marked a great step forward and brought to the Indians hope that these and similar grievances would in the future be considered in a new spirit. The government of the Union announced its intention of undertaking a positive policy to improve Indian conditions, and of pressing the other constitutional bodies in South Africa to do the same. This policy might be expected to mitigate the rigours of existing law; it might even be expected to create an atmosphere in which changes in the law to the benefit of Indians would become possible in the future. In return for India's

[1] The Indians enjoyed the parliamentary franchise in the Cape where, however, there were only 1,471 Indian voters. They had enjoyed it in Natal until Act No. 8 of 1896 was passed. This Act debarred from the franchise men whose male ancestors came from countries which had no representative institutions. They could be placed on the roll by special leave of the government of the day. In 1934 there were only thirteen voters in Natal out of an Indian population of 163,400. The Provincial Ordinance No. 3 of 1926 in Natal barred further Indian enrolments for the municipal franchise.

[2] For the complexities of this matter the reader may be referred again to the earlier chapters of the *Report of the Transvaal Asiatic Land Tenure Act Commission* (U.G. No. 7, 1934) and particularly to its clarification of the important difference between the laws (*a*) on the statute book, (*b*) as administered in practice, and (*c*) as occasionally interpreted in the courts.

promised co-operation in a scheme of voluntary subsidized emigration designed to reduce the less easily assimilable Indian element in South Africa's population, the South African government promised a strenuous effort to help those Indians who remained to conform to western standards. And the agreement authorized the Government of India to maintain in South Africa an Agent who would watch over Indian interests and be able to jog the memory of the Union government if it should show signs of forgetting or postponing its undertaking.

A perusal of the annual reports issued by the Government of India's Agent in South Africa leaves on the whole an impression of moderate progress. If there had been hopes that the Capetown agreement would lead to a sudden and sensational transformation of the whole Indian question, these certainly were disappointed. There was, in the first place, no notable rush by Indians to claim the assistance offered them should they wish to emigrate 'to India or to other countries where western standards are not required'. At the beginning there was indeed a modest exodus averaging about 2,000 persons a year;[1] but in 1932 the two governments, re-examining the position in the light of five years' experience, recognized that the possibilities of assisted emigration to India were practically exhausted owing to the economic and climatic conditions of India and to the fact that 80 per cent. of the Indian population of the Union was now South-African-born.[2] It was therefore necessary to undertake the not very hopeful enterprise of looking about for something to supply the place of that part of the 1927 agreement which was India's chief contribution to appeasement.[3]

The South African contribution to appeasement invited in several respects the cynical comment of disillusionment. In the first place, the trend of events in South Africa was tending to lay still further

[1] The figures of assisted emigration under the agreement are:

	Indian born	*Colonial born*	*Total*
1928 . . .	1,669	1,808	3,477
1929 . . .	658	670	1,328
1930 . . .	567	445	1,012
1931 . . .	973	988	1,961
1932 . . .	1,094	1,594	2,688
1933 . . .	776	717	1,493
1934 . .	adults 764	adults 200	adults 964

The rise of the figures in 1932, the year in which the two governments recognized that the scheme had no future, was doubtless due to the depression. The comparatively high figure of African-born emigrants was due to the fact that the Indian-born took their African-born children with them.

[2] *Council of State Debates*, 5th April 1932, p. 319.

[3] See below, pp. 242–3.

stress upon the political inferiority of the Indian population. In 1930 the Hertzog government carried a bill giving votes to white women throughout the Union. This measure created the odd situation that in the Cape and in Natal, where there was no adult male suffrage, the women's suffrage was wider than the men's. The Franchise Act of 1931 therefore established universal suffrage for European men. The result was to emphasize the gap between the privileged and unprivileged, the 'active' and the 'passive' citizens of South Africa. The Indians remained on the wrong side of a newly emphasized barrier. They had plenty of evidence, too, of the practical disadvantages of political inferiority. The 'white labour' policy of the Hertzog government was reducing the public employments open to them at a time when they were suffering from technological unemployment and also from the effects of economic crisis.[1] Nor was the government willing at first to include them in its plans of unemployment relief. These were for the benefit of Europeans only. When at last the government adopted a more humane policy and consented to make a grant in aid of municipal relief works which would benefit Indians, the ungenerous haggling of the Durban municipality, within whose jurisdiction the greater part of Indian distress was concentrated, delayed further the urgently needed alleviation of Indian distress.[2] It was indeed the municipalities, and particularly the municipality of Durban, from which the Indian community had usually most to fear. This accounts for Indian opposition to the extension of Durban's municipal boundaries, an extension which would increase from 17,000 to 66,000 the number of Indians subject to the jurisdiction of these unkind city fathers. The municipality was contemplating the expenditure of half a million pounds on roads and housing within the newly incorporated area, and in this expenditure the Indians, who outnumbered the Europeans almost by three to one, would have not the slightest say. 'Not one Indian voter', reported the Government of India's Agent in South Africa, 'will be added to the roll.'[3]

The Indians of Durban alleged a deliberate attempt on the part of the municipality to drive them from their shops in the richer and pleasanter parts of the city into the more squalid quarters. The smaller Indian community in central Transvaal also had reason to fear the municipal authorities. In 1931, for example, the Pretoria city council drew up a set of rules for the Asiatic bazaar which

[1] *Annual Report of the Agent of the Government of India in South Africa for the Year ending 31 December 1931*, para. 32 (with figures of reduction of Indians in railways and police in the Cape and Natal).

[2] Ibid., para. 30; *Report for 1932*, paras. 19 and 20; *Report for 1933*, para. 23.

[3] *Report for 1931*, p. 14.

increased the existing insecurity of the holders of stands and in other respects closely imitated the rules made for native locations under the Urban Areas Act. In the same year the Transvaal provincial council passed a new licences control ordinance whose effect was to remove existing safeguards against the arbitrariness of municipal authority in the issue of licenses. 'It places the livelihood of an unrepresented community', reported the Indian Agent, 'in the hands of men who in certain cases are or may be their commercial rivals, and it takes away the right of appeal to a court of law.'[1] On another matter of fundamental importance to Indian economic security, the government of the Union adopted a policy which with reason occasioned the greatest alarm. The Transvaal Asiatic Tenure Bill, introduced into parliament early in 1931, threatened to establish at last a correspondence between law and practice in the matter of Indian land occupation, not by liberalizing the law, but by abolishing in wholesale fashion those tolerated practices by which in fact its rigours had been mitigated.

But it is time now to look at the other side of the picture. The 1927 agreement had recognized standards of humanity and justice to which the Indian community could appeal, and it had established on South African soil a representative of the Government of India whose duty it was to remind South African authorities of these standards. His presence was not in vain. His representations to the Pretoria city council secured a postponement in the publication of the bazaar rules, some immediate alterations in their content, and a promise of consultation in the future. His efforts secured also the reservation by the Governor-General-in-Council of the Transvaal Licences Control Ordinance. They also secured from Dr. Malan, Minister of the Interior for the Union, an agreement to postpone the Asiatic Tenure Bill pending a new conference between the Government of India and the government of the Union.

That conference was held in Capetown from the 12th January to the 4th February 1932. On the 5th April the two governments announced simultaneously their satisfaction with the past working of the Capetown agreement and their intention to continue their co-operation 'in the common object of harmonizing their respective interests in regard to Indians resident in the Union'. They would walk in that better path of friendliness where they had set their feet in 1927. In one respect they admitted a need to modify their joint programme. For the scheme of assisted emigration, which had reached the limit of its possibilities, they agreed to substitute

[1] *Report for 1933*, p. 13.

co-operation in a colonization scheme designed to settle in other countries Indians both from South Africa and from India. Their intention was to investigate together the possibilities of this new scheme, and to associate with their investigation a representative of the Indian community of South Africa. Except in this matter, their 1927 agreement stood without modification. The government of the Union would 'continue to adhere to its policy of uplifting the permanent section of their Indian population'. And the Government of India would continue to maintain in South Africa an Agent whose presence had 'admittedly proved most helpful alike to the Indian community in South Africa and to the promotion of friendship between the two countries'.[1]

It is not possible to follow in any detail the later phases of an important question which still awaits competent specialist investigation and which has of necessity been treated rather sketchily in these pages. In general, it is true to say that the 1932 agreement, like its predecessor, led both to some disillusionment and to some solid satisfaction. The Transvaal Licences Control Ordinance, which had been reserved as a result of the representations of the Agent of the Government of India, came into operation in the winter of 1932. The Agent, however, reported that the courts might after all be able to play some part in mitigating the dangers likely to arise from it.[2] The Asiatic Land Tenures Act was passed with modifications designed to meet Indian objections. The Act denied to Indians the rights of occupation and ownership of land in the mining areas, but empowered the Minister of the Interior to exempt them from the restrictive provisions of the law in respect of occupation. This practical mitigation of the Act did not remove the intense Indian dislike and dread of its principle. At the 1932 meeting of the South African Indian Congress there was talk of fighting the Act by passive resistance. Leaders of the Transvaal Indians, nevertheless, organized themselves to co-operate with the commission appointed by the Union government to report to the Minister of the Interior on the principle and detail of the exemptions to be granted; and the Commission, presided over by Mr. Justice Feetham, began its task in a manner which gave promise of just and humane decisions.[3]

The plan of an investigation undertaken jointly by the governments of India and South Africa into the prospects of Indian colonization hung fire. The Union government decided on its own account to

[1] *Council of State Debates*, 5th April 1932, vol. i, no. 16, pp. 318–21.
[2] *Report of the Agent of the Government of India in South Africa for 1932*, p. 9.
[3] Ibid ,pp. 4–8; *Report for 1933*, pp. 7–12.

undertake a preliminary investigation, and invited the South African Indian Congress to nominate a representative to serve on the investigating committee. This invitation caused a split in the Indian community, which had already been deeply divided on the issue of co-operation with the Land Tenure Commission. The radical members of the Congress would have nothing to do with a scheme which they denounced as an attempt to deprive them of their birthright in South Africa; the moderates insisted that they should not let slip their first opportunity of co-operating as a community with the South African government. The radicals seceded from the Congress and formed 'the Colonial-Born and Settlers Indian Association'.[1] Yet the report of the colonization committee, when it appeared, belied their disillusioned forecasts; for it definitely repudiated the alleged plot to solve the Indian problem in South Africa by shovelling out of the country Indians who wished to remain in it.[2]

The student of European-Indian relations in South Africa should take care not to confine his attention to statutes and ordinances and governmental commissions and the long-drawn-out struggle between legal right and natural justice. Underlying all immediate controversies were deeper issues. The chances of racial harmony in the future depended not merely upon this act of parliament or that judicial decision, but upon the moral and social progress of the South African community, including the Indian population which history had made a part of that community. Progress of this kind, if it occurred, would some day express itself as progress in positive law. And progress of this kind was occurring. There were economic changes whose tendency must be to moderate the persistent European fear of suffering defeat in a battle of social standards along racial lines. The census returns made it clear that there was no fear, even in Natal, that the Indian population would swamp the European. The tendency was in the other direction.[3] There were, again, occupational changes in the Indian population which contained in themselves perplexities, but also hope. Indian employment was decreasing on sugar plantations, mines, and railways. Partly as a result of native pressure from below, the Indians were raising themselves in the

[1] *Report for 1933*, p. 8.

[2] *Report of Indian Colonization Enquiry Committee for 1933–1934* (U.G. 23—1934). The tone of the report is rather academic, but it investigated colonization projects on the assumption that the intention of the 1932 Agreement was to pursue 'a colonization scheme' as 'primarily an Indian scheme for the benefit of India's surplus millions', giving opportunities to South African Indians to participate, and help the venture by their experience.

For note 3 see p. 244.

occupational scale.[1] It was true that they were encountering as they rose the obstacle of the 'white labour' policy. Yet they were establishing themselves in factories where the wages board secured for them equal rates of pay with European workers; and they were playing an equal part with European workers in some of the trade unions.[2] Co-operation between the European and Indian populations was growing also at other levels of society. The reports of the Government of India's Agent in South Africa contain increasingly frequent references to the courtesies paid by European officials and by European society to the Agent personally; they also record a rising standard of manners as between the European and Indian communities.[3] There were many signs that both the South African government and also prosperous members of the Indian community were playing a steady part in raising Indian standards towards the 'western' level which the Capetown conferences had agreed to be necessary. Between 1927 and 1933 Indian enrolment in the schools of Natal almost doubled itself. The opening in 1930 of the Sastri school in Durban provided for the first time a place of secondary education for South African Indians. In 1934 they secured, together with the coloured community, their first opportunity of secondary education in the Transvaal. Their community life was beginning more fully to enrich itself with educated leaders who, having graduated either in South Africa or abroad, began as teachers or doctors to

[3] The figures by provinces are as follows:—

Province	*Year*	*Europeans*	*Indians*
Cape	1911	582,377	6,606
	1921	650,609	6,498
	1931	749,231	6,500
Natal	1911	98,114	133,030
	1921	136,838	141,336
	1931	177,440	163,400
Transvaal	1911	420,562	10,048
	1921	543,485	13,405
	1931	696,120	15,500
Orange Free State	1911	175,189	106
	1921	188,556	100
	1931	205,375	100

[1] Some details are given in the report of the Colonization Enquiry Committee (U.G. 23—1934).

[2] *Report of the Agent of the Government of India in South Africa for 1931*, p. 17. The Furniture Workers' union had an Indian majority. An attempt at separate Indian and European unions in the catering trade had broken down, and the single union had an Indian secretary. The Indian influence was present, though not as yet strong, in the typographers' union and in others.

[3] e.g. *Report for 1933*, p. 2: 'It is worth noting that at many of the places visited, particularly in Natal, dinners and lunches were given in the leading hotels to which for the first time Indians were admitted as guests on an equal footing with Europeans.'

serve their own people.[1] Without progress of this kind, there could never be substantial equality between Indians and Europeans. Given a continuance of this progress, there was surely ground for hoping that substantial equality and a growing friendliness would prepare the way for formal equality and a real partnership in pursuing the common good of South Africa. Perhaps there were few individuals in South Africa who openly proclaimed this hope or consciously framed it even in their own minds. But some such hope was implicit in the first agreement between the governments of the Union and of India. By that agreement the Government of India had accepted the facts of South Africa's individual historical evolution and had laid aside its rôle of a prosecuting counsel arraigning human iniquity at the bar of eternal justice. The government of the Union, for its part, had accepted certain principles of justice as the goal towards which South African history must struggle.

In 1936 the parliament of the Union took a notable step forward in the legislative recognition of these principles. It passed the Transvaal Asiatic Land Tenures Act Amendment Bill, thus admitting Indians to the right of land ownership in the Transvaal, a right which had been denied them since 1885. This new Act was the sequel to the report of the Feetham Commission which has been already mentioned.[2] After an investigation undertaken with painstaking fairness the commission had submitted detailed recommendations with regard to the exemptions to be granted from the statutory restriction upon the occupancy of land in the Transvaal. When the bill to give effect to its recommendations was introduced, the Agent of the Government of India intervened and reopened the question of land ownership. Before the second reading, the bill was referred to a select committee which not merely accepted the principle of exemption for purposes of occupation, but suggested that the right of ownership should also be given to Indians in those areas where their right of occupation was to be recognized. In view of the fact that barely one hundred Indians lived outside the areas for which exemption had been recommended, this was a far-reaching proposal. It was incorporated in the act passed by the legislature, which also cancelled all contractual re-

[1] For education see especially ibid., pp. 17–19. In 1932 and 1933 five South African Indians returned to practice in their own country after having graduated in medicine overseas; in 1932–3 two Indians graduated in arts at the University of South Africa and took teaching posts in Sastri College. The writer has not intended to suggest that before 1934 there were no educated men in the Indian community in South Africa. His point is that it was now becoming possible for Indians to get advanced education within South Africa instead of having to go abroad for it.

[2] *Transvaal (Asiatic) Land Tenures Amendment Act* (No. 30 of 1936).

strictions in title-deeds and entrusted to the minister effective powers to secure, even over the heads of local authorities, a satisfactory standard of civic amenities. This legislation was an encouraging send-off to the goodwill delegation of the Union of South Africa, which was then about to sail for India. It was also the first definite refutation of those gloomy prophets who had insisted—with apparent justification hitherto—that the improvement in the economic and social status of the Indians would have no effect upon their legal position. It seemed now as if civic equality for the Indian community in South Africa was not, after all, an altogether hopeless dream.

The government of the Union and the Government of India were trying to lead the European and Indian communities of South Africa along the road of appeasement. There was indeed no certainty that they would reach their goal. That measure of progress which English and French in Canada, Afrikaners and British in South Africa, had achieved already in a similar journey, lay far ahead of them. Indians and Europeans were starting their pilgrimage with so much heavier a burden of injustice inflicted and suffered. They might falter; they might, after a short struggle forward, sink down to rest in a dull complacency. They might quarrel about the stages of their journey. The Indians might rebel because they found the stages too short and slow, the Europeans might grow nervy and violent because of the Indian demand for haste. Almost certainly they would find every now and then that they had lost their true path. For the lights which men follow in journeys of this kind are their own fallible ideas of justice. Without a theory of right no single step may be taken; yet theories mislead as well as lead. The theory of the natural equality of mankind guided the courage and kindness which destroyed slavery; but it also became a mask behind which an acquisitive society accumulated labour-units and destroyed personality. Historical content drained itself away from this theory; too often it became a proposition of abstract intellectualism seeking to impose itself upon the rich variety of human life. By reaction the idealists began to demand respect for the rights of historically diverse communities, only to find that this ideal too was made the excuse for terrible oppressions. The Germans perverted it into a racialism which aimed at driving the Jews back into their ghettos. In South Africa and East Africa it might easily be used to justify racial segregation hardening itself into an oppressive caste system. Yet the British Empire has never, since that disastrous time when it split on the rock of a juristic concept, surrendered to any single formula purporting to contain the entire explanation of its complex being and purposes. It has proceeded tentatively, adapting theories rather than scrapping them, reinterpreting the old in terms of the new and criticizing the new in the light of the old. It has recognized circumstance, the individuality of place, the changing limits of the possible, the varying pull of interests and the different colours of men's minds. Its ethics have been experimental.[1]

Opportunism devoid of principle is the perpetual danger which besets these tactics. But the very diversity of the British Commonwealth is some defence against this danger. The English have their own rallying point in a standard of orderly fair play, the heritage of many centuries of evolving freedom. The other communities associated with the English in the Commonwealth of Nations can appeal to this same standard in protest against English malpractices. The American revolution began as a vindication, against the English, of English principles of self-government. The British in Canada demanded the assimilation of their constitution to that of Great Britain. The French in Canada rejected the racial implications in which the doctrine of assimilation entangled itself. They demanded British liberties as a defence of their French nationality. In South Africa the Afrikaners—having learnt by experience the disposition which the British not infrequently manifest to evade payment on their own moral I O U's—formed the habit of making the British write their principles down in black and white in public documents. Their tough persistence beat the British back with the stick of British principle. But by doing this they left it open to others to belabour with the same stick both Afrikaner backs and British ones. The Indians were the first to use this opportunity. At the Imperial Conference of 1923 Sir Tej Bahadur Sapru chastised with a will both British and South African politicians. 'We judge you', he said, 'by a standard which is admittedly very high.' And he went on to argue that his victims had no possible way of excuse or escape. For the standard was their own.[2]

The writer is aware that he has been permitting himself to indulge in the dangerous habit of lofty and optimistic speculation. It is true that he has not woven this pattern of an idea merely out of his own sanguine imagination; the materials of the pattern belong to the very stuff of the history which he has narrated. But in the same stuff there exist also the materials for a very different pattern. The Indian

[1] In this and the following paragraph a distinction is implied between an intellectual theory or hypothesis, of which a community may make use, and this community's disposition of mind and heart, its idea or ethos. The writer believes the distinction a valid one, but he must leave the exact statement of it to the philosophers.

[2] Cmd. 1988, p. 75.

question after all occupies a subordinate place among the racial problems of South Africa, and the answer to it must depend in large measure on the manner in which those other problems are met. Will South Africa evolve a new caste system based on the social and spiritual segregation of its races? And will the Indians and the coloured people accept a caste superiority over the natives as compensation for their caste inferiority to the white people? Or will all the more lowly races join with each other to oppose their white masters? Or, finally, will the Indians be granted sufficient resolution and sufficient encouragement to continue their struggle for equality? Whatever answer the future may give, the Indian community has the opportunity of playing an important part, either as teachers of submission, or as leaders of revolt, or as mediators between races struggling within a single territory to realize a juster and more subtle unity than that of the national state.[1] The last alternative is the only one that is consistent with the ethos of the Commonwealth of Nations, whose ideal of equal rights for diverse communities is not qualified by the reservation that these communities must be separated from each other by the sea. But is not the last alternative altogether beyond the South African possibilities? If some of the writers on the native question are to be believed, it is.[2] According to the foregoing survey of the Indian question, it is not.[3] But it must be admitted that the Indian approach to South Africa's racial complexity leads only to its fringes; a more direct approach along the main road of South African history will have to be attempted in a later volume.

It will also be necessary to seek a more direct approach to India's history. It was at the Imperial War Conference of 1917 that Indian nationalism first found official utterance in a setting of dignified equality. Because this nationalism fastened upon the unequal treatment of Indian emigrants as the immediate obstacle to be over-

[1] See Edgar H. Brookes, *The Colour Problems of South Africa* (Lovedale Press, 1934), pp. 32 ff.

[2] See, for example, Leonard Barnes, *Caliban in Africa* (Gollancz, 1930), and *The New Boer War* (Hogarth Press, 1932).

[3] It may be relevant here to refer to the progress of the Indian community in Fiji. The Rev. C. F. Andrews, revisiting Fiji in 1936 after an interval of twenty years, found a transformation which was 'amazing'. In the same year the Secretary of State for the Colonies, despite an agitation from a section in Fiji for reversal to a nominated legislative council, announced a reconstituted legislative council in which Indian representation was raised to an equality with European. The Indians, however, still had demands to make: it is odd to note that these included not only election on a common roll, which had been denied to the Indian community in Kenya, but also representation by a member on the executive council; in this matter they appealed to the Kenya practice.

thrown in the struggle for status, it has been necessary to follow into Africa the story of India's relations to the Empire. But this immediate preoccupation of Indian nationalism, although it was a natural one, distorted to some extent the realities of India's situation. India had reversed the accustomed order of political evolution under the British Crown, by acquiring a status among the nations before her own national unity was surely grounded on self-government. The spokesman of the Irish Free State at the Imperial Conference of 1923 pointed this out with the authority of one whose people had learnt by bitter struggle that status is the result, and not the cause, of freedom. The Indian representatives, he said bluntly, were not yet in fact on an equality with the other members of the conference. 'If I were an Indian, putting myself in their position, I would recognize that this hypersensitiveness about their treatment outside of India arises really from the fact that they have not, so far, reached the degree of self-government that the rest of us have reached.'[1] The Indian spokesmen questioned the phrasing of this opinion, but they recognized its substantial truth. If you wish to keep India in the Commonwealth, they said, you must fulfil her aspirations for self-government. You must admit her to a position of equality with the Dominions.[2]

But what was the position of the Dominions? It was rapidly changing. India was demanding a status which was in process of defining itself. The following chapter will be concerned with this process of definition.

[1] Cmd. 1988, p. 118. [2] Ibid., pp. 86, 96.

Note

Population Figures for the Chief Countries of Indian Migration in the British Empire

Kenya (1934)	34,955
Uganda	15,086*
Tanganyika	29,000*
South Africa (1934)	165,731†
Ceylon (1935)	775,000
Federated Malay States (1935)	397,582
Unfederated Malay States (1935)	111,513
Straits Settlements (1935)	125,798
Fiji (1934)	83,289
Trinidad (1931)	137,583
Jamaica	17,725
British Guiana (1934)	136,004
Mauritius (1935)	265,756

* Asiatic population including Arabs and Indians.
† Asiatic population.

CHAPTER V

THE STATURE OF THE DOMINIONS, 1922–1936

I

Diplomatic Separateness, 1922–1926

From the tangled half-explored country which has been traversed in the two preceding chapters the narrative now returns to a well-known road which many careful travellers have trodden hard. Legal commentators have mapped and marked every bend and all the minute undulations of this road, and political speculators have repeatedly surveyed its general direction.[1] What then is left to be attempted by the present Survey? There is still room for some economic map-making, but this must be postponed to a later volume. There is room also for a backward-glancing view of the legal and constitutional landscape, and this will be offered in a later chapter.[2] The present chapter will do no more than point out the main political landmarks, and it will hasten along the familiar road by forced stages.

Events themselves now hastened by forced stages towards an end which at last began to seem clear. Hesitation and uncertainty had remained dominant in the after-war years which we have chronicled in Chapter II: among the Dominions, and within each one of them, contrasted fears and hopes testified to unresolved ambiguities. Was the new status of the Dominions a reinforcement to the unity of the war years, or a dissolvent of it? Among many who thought this unity precious there spread a mood of deepening anxiety. The Prime Minister of Australia foreboded 'a dying illumination'; wistful New Zealanders felt themselves in their own despite being 'unloosed from the silken bond'.[3] But there were others who shared their ideal without sharing their misgivings. The slashing optimism of Mr. Lloyd George interpreted the Conference of 1921 as a proof that the war-time partnership would endure and deepen. In December 1921 he

[1] Readers who regret the highly selective and summary character of this chapter may be referred, for legal aspects, to the numerous publications of Professor Berriedale Keith; for diplomatic aspects to the books quoted in Chapter II by Professors Toynbee and Dewey. Professor C. A. W. Manning has discussed *The Policies of the British Dominions in the League of Nations* (Oxford University Press, 1932) and Mr. K. C. Wheare's *Statute of Westminster* is an excellent short account of the evolution of Dominion Status. Beyond these books there is a voluminous literature of varying merit.

[2] See below, supplementary chapter by Mr. R. Latham.

[3] See above, p. 82.

told the House of Commons that the foreign policy of Great Britain would be from henceforth the joint foreign policy of the British Empire. The instrument of that joint policy would still be the British Foreign Office: that, he said, was inevitable. But all the Dominions would combine with Great Britain to control the instrument. It was an exhilarating vision.

> 'The advantage to us is that joint control means joint responsibility, and when the burden of Empire has become so vast it is well that we should have the shoulders of these young giants to help us along. It introduces a broader and calmer view into foreign policy. It restrains rash Ministers and will stimulate timorous ones. It widens the prospect.'[1]

The vision was a fallacious one. Within less than a year after Mr. Lloyd George's confident pronouncement there came from Canada the first of a quick succession of shocks which made it clear beyond all possible doubt that some at least of the young giants of the Empire desired neither joint control nor joint responsibility, but the very opposite.

Was joint control anything more than a fiction? The Dominions had no opportunity of controlling the events which issued in the Chanak crisis of September 1922. Five minutes before midnight on Friday the 15th September Mr. Lloyd George cabled to them a call to back up British policy by armed force. The call was a melodramatic one; it resounded in the Press; and it was dinning in the ears of the peoples before some of the governments were officially aware of it. The governments and peoples responded variously. Within one hour of the arrival of Mr. Lloyd George's message, the Prime Minister of New Zealand cabled the offer of a contingent: within a few days 12,000 New Zealanders volunteered for active service. The Prime Minister of Australia was hardly less prompt in giving an affirmative response, but he resented the brusqueness of the invitation. The Prime Minister of Canada had greater cause for resentment, for the first intimation of the call from Great Britain came to him from the Press. His reply shattered this melodramatic demonstration of the doctrine of joint responsibility. Responsibility, he answered, belonged to the parliament of Canada. His government was anxious to receive more information, it was ready if necessary to summon parliament; but no Canadian government could commit the country to a warlike expedition without parliamentary authorization. The same doctrine was enunciated by General Smuts, when he returned to Pretoria from Zululand after the crisis had already passed. His chief concern then was to explain away the manner and

[1] Hansard, *House of Commons Debates*, vol. cxlix, 14th December 1921, col. 30.

the matter of the British government's call to arms, a task which that government itself had already attempted. The episode had nevertheless revealed the falsity of Mr. Lloyd George's picture of imperial unity. To his cry, 'Come over and help us', New Zealand had answered 'Yes' with enthusiasm, Australia had answered 'Yes' with resentment and misgiving, Canada had answered 'This is a matter to be considered'. The Canadian theory contradicted that of Mr. Lloyd George at two stages. In the first place, Canada would not admit joint responsibility where there was no real joint control. In the second place, Canada would not accept joint control as a desirable end. The liberal government of Canada admitted no other responsibility save that to the controlling Canadian parliament: its purpose was to extend the old doctrine of responsible government further into the field of foreign affairs, and to disentangle Canadian policy from the imperial policy pursued by the British Foreign Office.[1]

So the 'young giants' had minds of their own. Canada had her own road to follow. The response of Canada to the Chanak challenge announced this; so did the treaty signed at Washington in March 1922. There was nothing unusually important in the substance of the treaty; it dealt with fish, which was no fresh concern of Canadian governments. Comparing the treaty with its predecessors, there are apparent only two novel features; it is described as a treaty between the United States and Canada, and it is attested by two signatures only, one Canadian, one American.[2] The significance of the treaty, which has no doubt been exaggerated, lay in its elimination of the pre-existing forms of British supervision. There was a certain amount of awkwardness in the process. This was due, not to serious resistance on the part of the British authorities, but rather to routine conservatism and a slowness of perception; however, it enabled the leader of the opposition in the Canadian parliament to accuse the government of 'elbowing aside' the British Ambassador.[3] The United States Senate threatened a far more serious awkwardness, for it added a reservation to the effect that 'none of the nationals, inhabitants, vessels or boats of any other part of Great Britain' should

[1] On the Chanak crisis see especially the Canadian House of Commons Debates, 1st February 1923. In general, *J.P.E.*, vol. iv, pp. 268 ff. (Canada); pp. 586 ff. and 619–20 (South Africa); pp. 49 ff. and 141 (New Zealand); pp. 95 ff. (Australia). It is worth noting that the New Zealand opposition maintained the same position as the Canadian government—i.e. that parliament should decide (the voting was 57 to 10 for the government), and the Australian opposition maintained that on issues of war the people must decide by referendum.

[2] *Treaty Series*, no. 18, 1925, Cmd. 2377. The correspondence concerning the treaty is in *Canadian Sessional Papers*, 1923, no. 111.

[3] *J.P.E.*, vol. v, p. 312.

engage in the halibut fishery contrary to the provisions of the convention. 'Any other part of Great Britain!' To the Canadian nationalist it was a most offensive phrase. The Canadian government was ready to legislate to prevent citizens of any other country (including British subjects) from fishing from Canadian bases, and it hoped that this action would satisfy the Senate. The hope was realized, and the treaty was in due course ratified without the amendment. Thus the Canadian government had succeeded in securing from the United States that recognition of its international status of which it had been disappointed when the Senate rejected the Covenant of the League.[1]

The opponents of Mr. Mackenzie King's government denounced this assertion of a separate diplomatic status on the ground that it tended to imperial disruption; at the same time they sought to minimize its extent. They pointed out that the advice to His Majesty at every stage of the treaty-making procedure was transmitted through the British government; there remained, therefore, an effective British control over Canadian diplomacy.[2] The pedants continued to cling to this point for years, and it was not finally disposed of until the Irish Free State eight years later secured its own Great Seal.[3] The British government itself never paid much attention to such a small technicality; its own legal advisers declared that the advice of the Canadian government to His Majesty was in fact direct, and that the British government was nothing more than the channel of transmission.[4] Mr. Mackenzie King on his part was willing to admit the need for caution in working out 'a great constitutional experiment', and to accept the procedure of transmission through a British channel as a convenience which might limit the possibilities of disharmony inherent in separate dominion foreign policies.[5] It was, however, necessary to seek for more positive safeguards. The position had at last arrived which nearly a century earlier Lord John Russell had declared to be obviously incompatible with imperial unity; the King was now acting in his relations with foreign Powers according to the separate and distinct advice which he received from the several equal governments which ruled in his name. What if that advice should conflict?

The Imperial Conference of 1923 attacked the problem. The prin-

[1] Mr. Mackenzie King avowed this objective. *J.P.E.*, vol. iv, p. 810.

[2] Mr. Meighen, *J.P.E.*, vol. iv, p. 812.

[3] See Mr. McGilligan's speech of 23rd July 1931 in Keith, *Speeches and Documents on the British Dominions*, pp. 254, 255.

[4] Mr. Mackenzie King quoted Sir Cecil Hurst's opinion given at the 1923 Conference, in the Canadian House of Commons, 21st March 1924. *J.P.E.*, vol. v, pp. 328 ff.

[5] *J.P.E.*, vol. v, pp. 331 and 506.

ciples which it laid down were clear and simple. For joint control and responsibility it substituted separate control and responsibility. But, in addition to the constitutional responsibility of each government to its own parliament and people, it assumed a moral responsibility of each government to its associates in the Commonwealth circle. The negotiation, signature, and ratification of treaties affecting only one part of the Empire depended on the initiative of the individual government concerned. No part of the Empire could by its action impose active obligations on any other part. For this very reason it was the duty of each government to consider carefully whether its policy was likely to touch the interests of any one of its associates. In that event, it was to inform the government concerned, and give it an opportunity of stating its views and of participating in the negotiation if it should consider that its interests were intimately affected. In short, the right of Commonwealth members to pursue their separate foreign policies was tempered by their duty to harmonize these separate policies by consultation with each other. The arrangements with regard to procedure upon which the Imperial Conference agreed, rested upon an understanding which might be expressed as follows: 'In matters which obviously concern us all we act together as we acted at Paris. In matters which concern us singly each of us may act alone. But it is incumbent on us to remember that what seems to concern only one of us may in practice concern others, and it is our duty to make certain that our separate action does not create trouble or embarrassment for our associates.'[1]

The principle was clearly stated, but it was not to be expected that it should be quickly understood in all its implications or that all the means necessary for carrying it into effect should be quickly provided. The Imperial Conference met while the governments of Great Britain and Canada were at cross purposes over still another issue of foreign policy, and its declaration of principle did not suffice to end their discord. Turkey was again the subject-matter of dispute, but the issue this time was not war-making but peace-making. Towards the end of 1922 there had met at Lausanne a conference to which the Dominions were not invited. The British government nevertheless assumed that they would wish to take the same steps with regard to signature and ratification which they had taken when the other peace treaties were under consideration. The Canadian government replied that it had no complaints to make with regard to the procedure which had been adopted; but that the Canadian parliament must decide the extent to which Canada was bound by the negotiations at

[1] The treaty resolutions are in Cmd. 1987, pp. 13–15.

Lausanne and by the treaty arising from them. To this the British government replied that it was content that the Canadian parliament should consider and approve the treaty before His Majesty was advised to ratify it. The communication was intended to soothe Canadian susceptibilities, but it had the opposite effect because it quite missed the point. At Paris, Canada had been concerned with the process of treaty-making at four stages: she had been formally represented at the conference; her representatives had signed the treaty; her parliament had thereafter approved the treaty; and finally her government had formally assented to ratification by the King on Canada's behalf. Now she insisted that she must share the whole process of treaty-making, or she would take no part in it at all. She had not been invited to send representatives to the conference or to sign the treaty. The implication was that conference and treaty were not her concern. Peace with Turkey was a separate interest of Great Britain, just as halibut fishing in the North Pacific was a separate interest of Canada.[1]

Yet there was a difference. The whole Empire had been at war with Turkey, and the Treaty of Lausanne was ratified in the name of the whole Empire. Canada was bound by the British government's signature and ratification. But how was she bound? According to Mr. Mackenzie King, she was bound in form only. He sought to distinguish 'between the purely legal and technical position in which this Dominion may be placed and the moral obligations which arise under treaties depending upon the manner in which such treaties are entered into'. Was the distinction sufficient? Was it possible to make a neat distinction between legal obligation and moral obligation? So long as Canada retained the will to remain in the Empire, the great issues of peace and war, whether they arose in Europe or the South Pacific or the Middle East, must be of more than technical interest to her. For they affected the life of the Empire itself. If Canada desired complete disentanglement from those issues, she must disclaim legal, no less than moral, responsibility; for the former, despite all protests to the contrary, was always liable to expand into the latter. The opposite state to legal responsibility was the right of neutrality, and it was improbable that the right of neutrality could be effectively established without secession from the Empire.[2] These

[1] *Correspondence with the Canadian Government on the subject of the Peace Settlement with Turkey*. Cmd. 2146 of 1924. Professor Toynbee in *The Conduct of British Empire Foreign Relations since the Peace Settlement* states that the necessities of the international situation made it impossible for the British government to secure separate Canadian representation.

[2] This much-disputed question is discussed below, pp. 280, 304, 307.

were the considerations which led critics of the British government to attack it for failing to face and to beat down the foreign opposition to dominion representation at Lausanne, and for raising this ugly dilemma: either the Dominions must accept the possibility of finding themselves at war in virtue of a purely British act, or they must will neutrality and separation.[1] The same considerations led critics of the Canadian government to declare that autonomy was not enough. There must in addition be positive co-operation 'for the common purposes'.[2] But what were the common purposes? At what point did they emerge from the separate purposes of the individual governments of the Commonwealth? When did the members of the Commonwealth face the outer world alone, and when did they face it together? This was the crucial question. The Canadian government had not attempted to think out an answer to it. Nor was there any urgent need that it should do so, for the answer would depend in part on the form which the outer world took; if it took the form of an all-embracing, law-abiding community of states, would it be any longer an *outer* world? Might not the lesser citizenship of the British Commonwealth dissolve into the larger citizenship of the universal league? Ideas such as these were in some men's minds. But in the minds of others the outer world was hardly present at all. The Canadian government itself was not thinking primarily of foreign relations, but of intra-Commonwealth relations. The international problems of the British Commonwealth interested it chiefly because of their effect upon national status within the Commonwealth. 'We were simply seeking to maintain', declared Mr. Mackenzie King, 'that equality of status which had been gained, and which we have been in the habit of asserting, as between the self-governing Dominions and the Mother Country. . . .'[3]

The Canadian government was able to view foreign affairs chiefly in their secondary effects upon the internal constitution of the British Commonwealth because it was sheltered from their direct impact; the British government felt the direct impact and was therefore prone, whether by negligence or necessity, to relegate to the background the question of intra-Commonwealth relationships. It was negligence rather than necessity which accounted for the British labour government's action in recognizing the U.S.S.R. without first consulting the Dominions.[4] There was, on the other hand, some

[1] See Sir Edward Grigg's speech of 6th June 1924, *J.P.E.*, vol. v, p. 406.

[2] *J.P.E.*, vol. v, p. 508 (Mr. Meighen).

[3] Speech of 9th June 1924. Keith, *Speeches and Documents on the British Dominions*, p. 333.

[4] See Mr. Bruce's statement of 10th October 1924, *J.P.E.*, vol. v, p. 78.

element of necessity in its acceptance of a conference on the Dawes reparations plan without ensuring separate representation for each dominion. Mr. J. H. Thomas said later that it was impossible to turn the conference into a mass meeting, and Mr. Ramsay MacDonald pleaded with the Canadian government to recognize the urgent need of seizing the opportunity of a settlement which would bring appeasement. On this issue the Canadian government was accommodating, and the Dominions were represented by a panel system in the British Empire delegation; the separate representation which had been theirs at Versailles they had to forgo. Was this consistent with the principle of equality? Must the constitution of the British Commonwealth repeatedly distort itself to fit existing international procedure? Why should not international procedure be modified so as to fit the new constitution of the British Commonwealth? These questions were asked both in Great Britain and Canada.[1]

To the persisting awkwardness and irritation which arose from these recurrent questions of status there was added at this time the disappointment and anger of the Dominions at the labour government's reversal of the preference policy which had been recommended by the Imperial Economic Conference of 1923. Both on the political and the economic side the basic causes of friction were political; but it was tempting to account for them by pointing to deficiencies of machinery. In June 1924 Mr. Ramsay MacDonald sent to all the Dominions a cabled dispatch which proposed a sub-conference to report upon necessary improvements. The dispatch contained a variety of suggestions; but, said Mr. MacDonald, the British government had quite an open mind and was merely exploring the situation. After six months of discussion by cable the project fizzled out. It had, however, evoked from Australia a practical suggestion which the Commonwealth government quickly followed up by action. The imperial conferences, said Mr. Bruce, were a sufficient means for harmonizing the general trends of policy; but they could not provide for urgent and unforeseen questions. If the convention of consultation was to be effective in such circumstances, there was indeed need for improved machinery. To provide this, Mr. Bruce urged a closer liaison between the Foreign Office and the dominion governments, and he suggested as the first means of securing it the establishment by each Dominion of a Foreign Office branch in its High Commissioner's Office, with a man of high quality in charge of it.[2]

[1] Notably by Mr. L. S. Amery and Mr. Mackenzie King. The full correspondence is in *Canadian Sessional Papers*, 1924, no. 309.

[2] Mr. Bruce's extremely able dispatch of 16th July 1924 is worth careful study

The Australian lead was followed later by the other dominion governments. Mr. Bruce's logic was indeed irrefutable: if, as everybody admitted, the separate policies of His Majesty's governments were to be harmonized by consultation, there must of necessity be effective means for consulting. But supposing consultation failed to achieve harmony? Supposing the separate foreign policies of the Dominions and Great Britain failed to dovetail into an agreed common policy? Differences of circumstance and purpose might be so fundamental that mere machinery could not bridge them. Canada provided again a good illustration of this possibility. Her policy was strongly influenced by the deep-seated continental isolationism which determined the policy of her powerful southern neighbour. Her reluctance to undertake active obligations in Europe had been apparent in the Chanak and Lausanne episodes. But by entering the League she had accepted written obligations which on paper appeared more exacting than any which she owed to the Empire. This was for her a displeasing situation; with energy and with some success she set herself the task of modifying it.[1] In this task both the leading parties of Canada were in agreement. Indeed, the difference between the two parties on the main issues of foreign policy were probably less than the speeches of their leaders suggested. Both were agreed in desiring disentanglement from European dangers. Mr. Mackenzie King pursued this aim by minimizing Canada's active obligations both to Great Britain and to the League. Mr. Meighen desired a more active collaboration with Great Britain, in order that Canada and the other Dominions might draw her away from European commitments 'along a line which more suited Great Britain, as a world Empire'.[2]

But supposing that it should prove impossible for Great Britain to disentangle herself from Europe after the North American fashion? At this time and for many years to come the immediate issues were discussed in connexion with a far-reaching debate on high politics.

in its entirety. See *Consultation on Matters of Foreign Policy and General Imperial Interest*, Cmd. 2301 of 1925, no. 5.

At this point the reader may be referred to Mr. Gerald Palmer's book, *Consultation and Co-operation in the British Commonwealth*. This book covers the subject in all its details and the present Survey will therefore not discuss it at length.

[1] For four years prior to 1923 Canada had sought for the deletion or modification of the territorial guarantee contained in Article X of the Covenant. In 1923 the League Assembly voted an interpretative resolution (Persia alone dissenting) which took into account 'the political and geographical circumstances of each state' and laid it down that 'no Member should be under the obligation to engage in any act of war without the consent of its parliament, legislature, or other representative body'.

[2] Speech of 9th June 1924 on Lausanne Treaty. *J.P.E.*, vol. v, p. 508. This was very much the attitude of the New Zealand government. See its arguments on the Protocol in Cmd. 2458 of 1925, nos. 8 and 13.

The Canadian view of international relationships had some relationship to the 'two hemispheres' theory which had expressed itself in the Monroe Doctrine and the United States policy of neutrality. The opposing conception of a 'League to enforce peace', although it owed much to America's war-time idealism, had its deepest roots in European experience and thought. According to this conception, the policy of neutrality had been proved by events to be fallacious; all wars were potentially world wars and peace was therefore indivisible: the negative policy of national isolation must give way to a positive policy of universal security under collective guarantee. The British labour government attempted in 1924 to carry this conception a stage further forward by supporting the attempt of France and her friends to 'close the gap in the Covenant'. But the Geneva Protocol was alarming both to the dominion governments[1] and to the conservative party in Great Britain. For Great Britain also had her tradition of insular 'disentanglement'—modified, it is true, by her interest in the European balance of power and particularly by her concern with its effects upon the Low Countries. Would the labour government of Great Britain have persisted in its support of the Protocol even if this had meant parting company with the Dominions on a fundamental conception of policy? In rejecting the Protocol, Mr. Baldwin's government probably followed its own inclination, but it was also powerfully moved by its desire to keep a common front with the Dominions. Canada might congratulate herself that she had done something to direct Great Britain along a line which 'more suited her as a world Empire'—and more suited the Canadian desire for disentanglement.[2]

All the same, Great Britain found it impossible to maintain the common front. In western Europe, at least, she was obviously entangled by history and geography, and her conservative government felt itself compelled to apply in western Europe the policy of guaranteed security which her labour government had sought to universalize.[3] At Locarno, Great Britain gave a precise military

[1] For a résumé of the attitude of the Dominions to the various security projects which have issued from Geneva see Manning, *The Policies of the British Dominions in the League of Nations*. The unanimous rejection of the Protocol by the Dominions is documented in the white paper, Cmd. 2458.

[2] It is not implied that Canada's attitude on this issue was more decisive than that of any other Dominion. The most vigorous attack on this 'mischievous' document came from New Zealand. e.g. '. . . Apart from the form of expression, the intention and effect of this document is not in accord with common sense, however much it may accord with visionary doctrines.' (Cmd. 2458, p. 14.)

[3] In idea the League was universal; but all the Dominions in their opposition to the Protocol made much of the fact that three Great Powers, the United States, Germany, and Russia, were outside the League.

guarantee with a geographical limitation. But that geographical limitation did not induce the Dominions to share the guarantee. Article 9 of the Treaty of 16th October 1925 ran as follows: 'The present Treaty shall impose no obligation upon any of the British Dominions, or upon India, unless the Government of such Dominion, or of India, signifies its acceptance thereof.'[1] No other government of the British Commonwealth accepted the obligation.

In the House of Commons Mr. Lloyd George denounced this breach in the Empire's diplomatic unity.

> 'I thought one of the achievements of the war was that it had unified the Empire, had brought the Dominions into the orbit, as it were, of our foreign policy, and that we should have the advantage of knowing that whatever happened to us in the future would be as a result of a policy they were just as much responsible for as we were.'

If Mr. Lloyd George did in truth still think this, he had been strangely blind to the lessons of Chanak and Lausanne. Throughout the past three years Canada had given constant and unmistakable proof of her resolution not to be drawn into the orbit of Great Britain's policy. At the time of the Lausanne Conference the British government had been taken aback by Canada's insistence that a large issue of peace and war was merely a local British interest. Now it found itself compelled to act in a manner which gave colour to that assumption. It was impossible, declared Sir Austen Chamberlain, to wait on the Dominions.

> 'The affairs of the world do not stand still. . . . I could not go, as the representative of His Majesty's Government, to meeting after meeting of the League of Nations, to conference after conference with the representatives of foreign countries, and say, "Great Britain is without a policy. We have not been able to meet all the Governments of the Empire, and we can do nothing." That might be possible for an Empire wholly removed from Europe, which existed in a different hemisphere. It was not possible for an Empire the heart of which lies in Europe, . . . and where every peril to the peace of Europe jeopardises the peace of this country.'[2]

The only moral which Sir Austen Chamberlain drew from this separateness of British policy was the need of a conference between Great Britain and the Dominions. But what would the conference aim at? The Imperial Conference which met in October 1926 did not oppose, but recognized, the principle of separate responsibility. 'We felt', it said in its report, 'that the governing consideration

[1] Keith, *Speeches and Documents on the British Dominions*, p. 356 and note.

[2] Hansard, *House of Commons Debates*, vol. clxxxviii, 18th November 1925, cols. 520-1.

underlying all discussions of this problem must be that neither Great Britain nor the Dominions could be committed to the acceptance of active obligations except with the definite assent of their own Governments.' The conference further elaborated the rules agreed upon in 1923 for treaty-making, in order to bring them into complete conformity with this basic principle. But at the same time it reinforced the rules which were designed to remind the separate governments of their responsibility one to another. It sought to buttress the convention of consultation against all possibility of misunderstanding or oversight.[1] While asserting the separate responsibility of the Commonwealth's members, it was mindful of the 'special relationship' in which they stood to each other. Both in the procedure of treaty-making and in the form of the treaties to be made, that special relationship was symbolized by the Crown.[2]

The verbal clarity of this statement left nothing to be desired, and yet the deeper issues still remained obscure. What was the cause of this obscurity? The report admitted differences in function between Great Britain and the Dominions, but its major premiss was their equality of status. This premiss was a secure foundation for a theory of constitutional relations within the Commonwealth. Was it equally useful as a viewpoint of international relations outside the Commonwealth? In international relations stature counts for more than status. The status of sovereignty in international usage, like the degree of doctor in university usage, is a label which covers wide differences of capacity. Great Britain and the Argentine Republic are both sovereign states; but it is not possible to deduce from this fact anything of high importance for the issues of peace and war in the world. And was it possible to learn any important lesson in international politics from the declaration of the Imperial Conference that both Great Britain and New Zealand were free to conduct their own foreign policies? The substance of those policies was likely to be so different. According to the theory of equal status, the Locarno policy was a local interest of Great Britain alone. But its intention was to under-pin the League of Nations and thereby to strengthen the peace system of the whole world. In fact, it was bound to concern

[1] e.g. not the negotiating government, but its associates in the Commonwealth, were in the future to be the judges of whether a negotiation affected them. Notification of proposed negotiations, therefore, must be circulated as a matter of routine. The negotiating government on its side might conclude that silence meant consent.

[2] Cmd. 2768 of 1926, pp. 20–7. There is a full discussion in Toynbee, *The Conduct of British Empire Foreign Relations*, pp. 83–110. Compare Keith, *Responsible Government* (2nd edition), pp. 908–18, 1231–5, and Corbett and Smith, *Canada and World Politics*, pp. 153 ff.

the whole British Commonwealth. Article IX of the Locarno Treaty, which exempted the Dominions and India from the obligations undertaken by Great Britain, rested upon the conception of 'passive belligerency'. This conception was in substance a restatement of Sir Wilfrid Laurier's doctrine of colonial autonomy.[1] It was a precarious conception, because it was applicable only in favourable circumstances; other circumstances could be conceived in which the Dominions would be forced to choose between real separation from Great Britain and a real sharing of her dangers and responsibilities.

Nevertheless, the Imperial Conference of 1926 was probably wise in leaving these questions unanswered. The question of status presented itself out of the experience of the preceding years and demanded an immediate answer; the underlying question already engaged the attention of publicists, but did not yet excite the peoples. In all probability no answer would be given until events framed the question as a challenge. Perhaps when that challenge came the Dominions would have grown strikingly in stature, and their 'local' foreign policies, like those of Great Britain, would be interlocked with the greater issues. If that were so, the question would be clearer. But the Conference of 1926 was content not to search the future too closely. It simply declared its faith that, although each Dominion must remain the sole judge of the nature and extent of its co-operation, no common cause would thereby be imperilled. It did not attempt to define the common cause.

II

Equality and Appeasement, 1926–1936

In its work of tidying up the confusion which had been apparent in the British Commonwealth's foreign relationships during the previous four years, the Imperial Conference of 1926 was guided by a very strong committee which comprised all the prime ministers and heads of delegations together with the Foreign Secretary and the Dominions' Secretary of the United Kingdom. Lord Balfour was the committee's chairman. Its report, following the terms of reference, dealt not merely with diplomatic problems but with a variety of questions affecting the internal order of the Commonwealth. All these questions it answered in the light of a governing principle which it expounded with suppleness of thought and distinction of language.

It has indeed become fashionable to approach the 'Balfour Report' with a reverential awe which might possibly be due to some pre-

[1] See above, pp. 38, 50.

eminent religious document. Commentators have expounded the texts of this scripture with theological ingenuity and rapture. Philosophers have discovered in it a universal principle valid for the government of all mankind.[1] It may be so. But doctrinal speculation of so rarified a character is fortunately not a function of this Survey, which may pursue its humbler task of elucidating the development of a specific human association, the British Commonwealth, amidst the changes and chances of this mortal life. Viewed from this angle, the Balfour Report is impressive not merely for its philosophic imagination but for the sharpness of its insight into actual circumstance. It was, first and foremost, finely accurate description. With admirable economy of words it cut through the thickets of legalism and skirted the marshes of vague moralizing, and revealed the British Commonwealth as it was in the year 1926. It revealed also the direction of the road along which the British Commonwealth had passed, and the immediate end which that road was now approaching. Its insight was historical.[2] It described not merely the form but the motion of a community. The principle of motion which it professed to discern was the same principle which Mr. Asquith had acclaimed in the Imperial Conference of 1911: Liberty operating within Unity. But in the fifteen years which had passed since Mr. Asquith's declaration, Liberty had outgrown the shelter of imperial sovereignty within which it had been nurtured. Liberty, in its maturity, revealed itself as Equality. The Balfour Report recognized that Liberty and Unity were now reconciled through the free association of equals. 'Equality of status,' it declared, 'so far as Great Britain and the Dominions are concerned, is thus the root-principle governing our inter-imperial relations.[3]

The Report is memorable not only for its descriptive ability but for its political shrewdness. In the delicate adjustment of human relationships some men gain from experience and philosophy the wisdom which others laboriously seek by specialist studies. Perhaps it is not fanciful to discern in the suave and confident phrases of the Balfour Report a method akin to that of psycho-analysis. It exorcised something which might have been called, in a jargon fashionable at the time, the inequality-complex. In Europe and in Asia a thwarted passion for equality was threatening to destroy the unity whose foundations had been laid in the nineteenth century by the dominant technique and theory of the western world. The same passion, had

[1] e.g. Coatman, *Magna Britannia*, pp. 73–83.
[2] See especially Cmd. 2768, p. 14, para. 4.
[3] The Liberty-Equality-Unity theme has been already handled on p. 4 above.

it been resisted and repressed, might have shattered the unity of the British Commonwealth. The representatives of Canada and South Africa and the Irish Free State came to the Imperial Conference of 1926 resolved to strike a blow for equality. They found no adversary to receive the blow. 'Equality', the Balfour Report in effect declared, 'is yours and ours already. Equality is the rock on which our Commonwealth rests. There are, it is true, some surviving relics of the old unequal order. Let us inspect them one by one. And then let us take the trouble to remove them. This is an immediate task in which we can all work together.'

The Report itself in one or two deft touches illustrated the technique of redecoration which would be sufficient to reveal the true structure of a Commonwealth founded upon equality. It suggested an alteration in the title of His Majesty the King in order to meet 'the altered state of affairs arising from the establishment of the Irish Free State as a Dominion'.[1] It declared that the governor-general of a Dominion occupied in all essential respects the same position in relation to the administration of public affairs in the Dominion as His Majesty the King occupied in Great Britain, and it gave directions for removing those usages of procedure which were reminiscent of a time when governors-general had been regarded as agents of the British government or the Colonial Office.[2] Its recommendations with regard to treaty procedure recognized the equal autonomy of Great Britain and the Dominions in the sphere of foreign affairs. It asserted the principle that appeals to the Judicial Committee of the Privy Council should not be determined otherwise than in accordance with the wishes of the parts of the Empire primarily affected, although it qualified this principle by the assertion that consultation and discussion ought to precede changes in which other parts of the Empire were concerned.[3] It dragged into the light a series of surviving inequalities in the operation of dominion legislation. Some of these—notably the practices with regard to disallowance and reservation—it disposed of in principle,[4] by recognizing that it was the right of each

[1] *Report*, p. 15, para. (*a*). For the ensuing act and proclamation see Keith, *Speeches and Documents on the British Dominions*, pp. 170, 171 and note.

[2] In this year a secretaryship of state for the Dominions had been established as an office separate from the secretaryship of state for the Colonies; though for the time being Mr. L. S. Amery (whose competence had done a great deal to clear up the muddles of the previous years) combined the two offices. For previous trends in this direction see above, p. 49.

[3] On this issue alone did the impulse to equality meet some resistance, due perhaps to pressure from the political minority in the Irish Free State which imagined the appeal to be a safeguard of its rights. See below, p. 369.

[4] With the qualification (*Report*, p. 17)—'. . . apart from provisions embodied in

dominion government to advise the Crown in all matters relating to its own affairs, and that in consequence it would not be in accord with constitutional practice for His Majesty's government in Great Britain to tender advice to His Majesty in any matter appertaining to the affairs of a Dominion against the views of the government of that Dominion. It also placed on record the principle that 'legislation by the parliament at Westminster applying to a dominion would only be passed with the consent of the dominion concerned'. But it recognized that the enunciation of general principles was not sufficient to adjust to the new order of equality such complex matters as the uncertain territorial limitation upon dominion legislation, and the merchant shipping legislation of the Empire. It recommended that these matters should be referred to expert committees for report leading to future action. This recommendation (although no doubt it was inspired by nothing more subtle than plain common sense) was a masterpiece of practical reason. For the impatient passion for equality should not be too abruptly appeased. To do this may well breed incredulity and the persistence of a restlessness all the more dangerous because it has no rational end. The Balfour Report brought a deeper appeasement by insisting that there was still work to be done. The end was near: one more effort, a common effort, and it would be won.

It will not be necessary in this chapter to chronicle in any detail the processes of technical adjustment which followed the direction agreed upon by the Conference of 1926. This would involve a tedious repetition of work which has already been effectively done by other writers.[1] A later chapter will survey the legal and constitutional results achieved between 1926 and 1936. At present a different objective will be pursued. Not the manner and matter of constitutional statement, but rather the interweaving of nationalist aspiration and constitutional statement in a relationship of reciprocal cause and effect, will be the main theme of the narrative.

The theme is an elusive one, and where so many separate nationalisms are under review it is impossible to avoid a considerable degree of over-simplification. Each Dominion possessed its peculiar individuality, and in each individuality there were complex and contradictory elements. No doubt it is to some extent misleading to speak

constitutions or in specific statutes expressly providing for reservation.' The specific statute which the Report had in mind was the Colonial Stock Act, 1900. In 1934, when the Union repealed clause 65 of its constitution (containing the disallowance provision) it entered into agreement with the British government to safeguard the original loan contracts by a process of notification and binding itself to accept British protest. This was confirmed by British and South African legislation.

[1] See note on p. 250 above.

of 'the public opinion of Australia' or 'the feeling of New Zealand'. Roughly it is true to say that Australia and New Zealand were satisfied with the facts of freedom and equality, and indifferent or even opposed to the persistent preoccupation of their associates with the forms. They had not demanded the Balfour Report but acquiesced in it. New Zealand was content that the governor-general should remain the channel of communication between Wellington and Downing Street. Neither Australia nor New Zealand adopted the Statute of Westminster. It was in many respects natural that their national patriotisms should grow outwards into an imperial patriotism, instead of seeking to segregate themselves. But in both Dominions, and particularly in Australia, nationalism had also anti-imperialist associations. The ideology of social democracy in Australia had in origin been anti-aristocratic, and in development had become anti-capitalistic. Imperialism, according to Lenin, was the last stage, the monopoly stage, of capitalism. This dictum had very little relevance to the problems which the Balfour Report discussed: the bond between Great Britain and the Dominions was not 'imperialistic' in Lenin's sense. Imperialism, nevertheless, vaguely suggested enormities of exploitation of which London was the centre, and was a useful epithet of denigration to fling at the conservative classes and parties who professed most loudly their affection for Great Britain. The conservatives, on their side, were quite ready on occasion to brand their political opponents as disloyalists. Thus there was a tendency for the opposing class-parties to take up different attitudes towards British Commonwealth affairs. One party tended to assert a monopoly of 'Our Empire'. The other party gathered to itself memories of Irish wrongs, wisps of pacifist idealism, and reflections of a communist-tinged intellectualism. In neither case did these tendencies give more than a colouring to the sturdy texture of realistic nationalism which was common to all Australian parties. The parties which opposed labour had not the slightest intention of sacrificing Australian interests to Great Britain; the labour party had not the slightest intention of jeopardizing Australia's connexion with Great Britain. But, speaking generally, the labour party was sceptical of the oratorical fervour which some of its political adversaries were wont to lavish on the British Commonwealth; it manifested a disposition not to commit itself too deeply to an association of dubious virtue. Its attitude of relative aloofness had some affinity with the far more deeply rooted aloofness of Canadian nationalism.[1]

[1] To supplement this extremely impressionistic sketch see W. K. Hancock, *Australia* Benn, 1930), especially chapter iii.

In all the Dominions allowance must be made for hesitations of this kind. The world, it must be remembered, had, during the period under review, two centres of experiment which in varying degree fascinated forward-looking idealism. Moscow or Geneva, or both of them, might produce something of greater moment to humanity than the British Commonwealth of Nations. The liberal movement which had been dominant in the western world since the French Revolution, not yet realizing the magnitude of overthrow which was sweeping against it, cherished new visions of perfectability. Not only in the Dominions, but also in Great Britain—and indeed far more in Great Britain—these new visions threw into relief the imperfections of the British Commonwealth. To some idealists, and particularly to youthful ones, these imperfections appeared to be a deep-seated disease: empires were incurable. Even if it were granted that the British Empire was in truth transforming itself into a commonwealth, it still remained comparatively unattractive as an object of idealism; for the good may be the enemy of the best. Perhaps the most noteworthy quality of this prevalent mood was its disinterestedness. This was sincere and generous; but it also assumed too optimistically a security which seemed to offer unlimited freedom of choice. Events might prove this freedom illusory. Perfection might recede: the good itself might be in danger. If this should happen, the mood of disinterestedness, so far as it meant an illusory detachment, would have to pass. A mood of more intimate attachment, a mood of membership or of 'belonging'—whether to nation, commonwealth, or class—would in all probability take its place.

The feeling of security was not fundamentally shaken before 1931, the year in which the British parliament completed its part in removing the last scaffoldings of sovereignty which obscured the proportions of a commonwealth founded upon equality of status. While that feeling of security lasted, its tendency was probably to encourage the centrifugal operation of the nationalisms within the British Commonwealth. This happened not merely because there was no strong pressure of outward danger to maintain the 'joint responsibility' which had been the ideal of Mr. Lloyd George and the Imperial War Cabinet; indeed, it was sometimes argued that the recrudescence of such pressure would have the effect of splitting the Commonwealth.[1] Security operated in another way also: it fostered visions

[1] 'As the great experiment of the British Commonwealth faces the future it is reasonably apparent that its disintegration or permanence reduced to simplest terms, is disintegration in a War World or continuance in a Peace World.' From a memorandum prepared for the unofficial British Commonwealth Relations Conference held at

of peace and justice which were more alluring than the imperfect achievements of the British Commonwealth, but which had not yet embodied themselves in actual institutions capable of demanding complete allegiance. It encouraged a critical attitude towards the actual, without creating a spirit of sacrifice resolute enough to run risks in order to actualize the ideal. Democratic idealism in Canada, for example, was prone to contrast the limited ends of the British Commonwealth with the theoretically universal ends of the League of Nations; but when faced with Article X or Article XVI of the Covenant it was quick to make all necessary reservations for the safeguarding of Canadian sovereignty.[1] In these circumstances, a universalist ideology reinforced the patriotism of the prairies, and in the division of loyalties Canadian nationalism was the residual legatee.

Canada was the first Dominion in which the war-time government was driven from power by the opposition. The liberal government of Mr. Mackenzie King was strongly supported by the two chief centres of nationalism highly suspicious of imperialist entanglement—provincially minded Quebec and the continentally minded prairies.[2] It has been shown in the preceding section how Mr. Mackenzie King's government took the lead in asserting dominion autonomy in the field of foreign relations, and thereby created problems of adjustment which were faced by the Imperial Conferences of 1923 and 1926. To the Conference of 1926 the Canadian government brought other demands.[3] At this conference, too, it had the support of other Dominions which had moved into the attacking phase. At the previous conference the representatives of the newly created Irish Free State had been content to watch and follow; but from now on they were ready to lead the march towards equality. In South Africa, the nationalist party had been in power since 1924. Its leader, General Hertzog, frankly told the Imperial Conference that its business was to hasten the transformation of an Empire, which South African

Toronto in 1933. See A. J. Toynbee (ed.), *British Commonwealth Relations: Proceedings of the First Unofficial Conference on British Commonwealth Relations* (Oxford University Press, 1933).

[1] This appears repeatedly in the papers prepared for the above conference.

[2] In support of the adjectives used the writer would refer to the speeches of M. Bourassa and the writings of Mr. Dafoe—e.g. his book, *Canada an American Nation.*

[3] Canada demanded a definition of the position of governor-general, following the controversy arising from Lord Byng's exercise of the dissolution power (see Keith, *Speeches and Documents on the British Dominions*, pp. 148–60, and *Responsible Government in the British Dominions*, Part II, c. iii, § 7). The decision of the Privy Council in *Nadan* v. *R.* had also aroused dissatisfaction and controversy on the appeals issue. (1926 A.C. 482. Keith, *The Sovereignty of the British Dominions*, pp. 421–3.)

nationalism still repudiated, into a Commonwealth which would win South Africa's free consent.[1]

There were now three dominion governments demanding complete equality as the price of their appeasement, and in the other Dominions there were parties which had some sympathy with the demand. Would appeasement follow when the price had been willingly paid? The Irish Free State need not here be considered; its case is the crucial one, and will be considered in a separate chapter. In this section the problem will be examined chiefly from the South African standpoint, just as in the preceding section the problem of diplomatic autonomy was examined chiefly from the Canadian standpoint.

There were some obvious similarities in the development of Canadian and South African nationalism. In both countries, two separate national cultures had been brought within the same political framework by the crude method of conquest. In both countries the people of the victorious nation had been forced to admit limitations which obliterated the normal effects of conquest. Conquest was not followed by domination. It obliterated political frontiers but did not erase cultural frontiers. The history both of Canada and South Africa became therefore the history of a reciprocal adjustment of cultures. The essential quality of reciprocity showed itself both in struggle and in partnership. Struggle enforced a recognition of diversity; partnership was based upon that recognition. By struggle the French Canadians and the Afrikaners won from the British respect for their individual ways of life. The common way of life which they were willing to share was British in its origin; but this origin was transcended by the acceptance of separateness in cultural loyalties and of community in the loyalty to a shared territorial home. There are some who say that this transcending of British origins revealed the true British philosophy, which is not British in any racial sense.[2] Regarded from a narrower political standpoint the process gave a peculiar complication to the action of nationalism. At every stage in Canadian and South African history the problem of the imperial relationship was interwoven with the problem of inter-racial or inter-cultural relationship. Lord Durham had recognized this in 1838. Recognition of it in 1867 was the foundation stone of the Dominion of Canada. Recognition of it in 1926 was still essential to an understanding of Canada's constitutional problems.

[1] See above, p. 53.

[2] See a lecture given by Professor F. Clarke, *Quebec and South Africa. A Study in Cultural Adjustment* (Oxford University Press, 1924). To this short lecture the writer owes more than to most of the long books.

By that time the 'attacking phase' of French-Canadian nationalism had passed.[1] The aim then was to conserve the rights and privileges of French-Canadian Quebec, which the British North America Act had secured 'as firmly as law can secure anything'. It was the nationalism of British Canadians which was then disposed to attack as badges of unequal status the appeal to the Privy Council and the processes of constitutional amendment by British act of parliament which the constitution of the Dominion enjoined.[2] But to these formal limitations upon Canadian autonomy the province of Quebec clung, believing them to be a substantial safeguard of its rights and privileges. This issue might sometimes appear to be one between Great Britain and Canada; in fact it was an issue between Canadian British and Canadian French.

Although there is an essential similarity between the national histories of South Africa and Quebec, there are also important differences. Cultural distinction in South Africa was not identified, as it was in Quebec, with a distinction of religion. In protecting his individual way of life the Afrikaner could not, like the French Canadian, fortify his spirit by calling to mind his membership of the Universal Church which valued him. But the Afrikaner had less need of such protection. His community was not surrounded, as Quebec was surrounded, by people of another faith and origin and culture. Dispersion for the French Canadians meant the acceptance of an alien manner of life; for the Afrikaners it meant an extension of their own way. The French in Canada were pre-eminently a self-segregated people: the Afrikaners in South Africa lived side by side with the British throughout the Union.[3] Moreover, they were the majority. Cultural adjustment could not therefore be sought on a federalistic basis, and, in the decisive compromise, forbearance and moderation would be no less due from the Afrikaners towards the British than from the British towards the Afrikaners.

But the British conquest, which in Canada had been achieved at one blow in the eighteenth century, was not completed in South Africa until the beginning of the twentieth century. When General Hertzog's party achieved power in 1924, memories of that conquest

[1] There were signs in 1936 that it might be reopened. See *The Times*, 27th March 1936.

[2] See J. S. Ewart, *The Kingdom of Canada, Imperial Federation, the Colonial Conferences, the Alaska Boundary, and other Essays* (Toronto, 1908), passim.

[3] Five-sixths of the province of Quebec is still French; about half a million French live elsewhere in Canada, and nearly twice that number in New England. In South Africa there is a relative provincial concentration of the Afrikaner population in the Orange Free State, and of the British population in Natal; but neither province is really comparable with Quebec.

still rankled, and Afrikaner nationalism was still in its 'attacking phase'. Seen in perspective, the Union may be regarded as obliterating the conquest in the same sense in which federation obliterated it in Canada. But it was not easy to catch the clear perspective of events which had moved so rapidly and with such a violent displacement of loyalties; moreover, to gather the fruits of the Union must be a long harvesting.[1] The nationalist party had attacked General Botha and General Smuts on the ground that they were too slow in establishing the real cultural equality and the real national independence which, according to their professions, the Union guaranteed. The two demands, for equality between Afrikaners and British on the soil of South Africa, and equality of status between South Africa and Great Britain, were interwoven. Afrikaner pride saw in the latter the sign and symbol of the former.

On his return to South Africa after the Imperial Conference of 1926, General Hertzog declared that equality of status was now admitted. If South Africa now remained within the British Commonwealth, this was by her own free will. The moment seemed propitious for a deepening appeasement. Instead, there soon flared out a violent controversy between Afrikaners and British.

An educationist with a long South African experience has illuminatingly described 'the extreme sensitiveness of the social and spiritual texture' which controversy can so easily tear.

> 'The ground on which educational processes must work, the cultural material through which the educator operates, are all intensively alive and palpitating. They are penetrated through and through with historic memories, with glowing passions, and with intimate personal and group loyalties. The most innocent and colourless procedures may acquire a sudden significance under such conditions. All unwittingly and with the best intentions teacher and administrator may raise a storm and the lightnings begin to play. It is not perversity or mere quarrelsomeness or factious self-assertion which charges the electric atmosphere. It is just history.'[2]

If the lightnings can play so easily in the schools, how much more easily can they be made to flash in the constituencies. And history on the platform will arouse an incomparably greater storm than

[1] The linguistic and literary revival of Afrikaans followed rather than preceded the effort of political nationalism. The first attempt, round about 1860, was not very successful. In the bi-lingual clause of the Act of Union, not Afrikaans but Dutch was contemplated. Dutch was the language of the Reformed Church. The first complete translation of the Bible into Afrikaans did not appear till 1935. But long before this, Afrikaans had come into its own as a language of literary expression.

[2] Clarke, *Quebec and South Africa. A Study in Cultural Adjustment,* p. 6.

history in the classroom. The controversy which now swept South Africa dealt with history in its simplest form, history in symbols. In 1925 the Minister for the Interior, Dr. Malan, had introduced into parliament a nationality bill containing provision for a national flag. The government put the bill forward with a provision that a committee of all parties should consider the design of the flag. The committee split on the issue of including or excluding the Union Jack. Representatives of the South Africa party demanded its inclusion; representatives of the nationalist party refused it. To one section of the South African people the Union Jack signified defeat and an alien domination; to the other section it signified 'a partnership in all virtue' between the generations and between the countries. One section or the other felt itself being forced to make a symbolic surrender of its memories and loyalties. The government tried to find a compromise in a neutral design which recognized only the South African present: four bars for the four provinces of the Union. In this design there was no repetition of the old *Vierkleur*, nor was there anything to suggest recognition of the Crown or the Commonwealth relationship. The British section would not make a surrender and call it neutrality. In reply to its storm of protest the nationalist government announced that it would suspend the bill for the present and again seek for agreement; but in 1927 it would proceed with the bill whether agreement had been found or not. There were more committees and commissions and further compromises and delays. Having made one proposal which was professedly based upon ignoring past history, the government made another which professed to recognize past history. A new design included both the Union Jack and the old republican flags. British sentiment rejected this proposal on the ground that it relegated to an obscure position in the national flag the symbol of the Commonwealth partnership. The South African party insisted that no symbol must be accepted which did not command the substantial support of all sections of the people. The government nevertheless carried through the House of Assembly the bill embodying its flag proposal, although the bill provided that the Union Jack might also be flown as an emblem of the Commonwealth partnership. The Senate rejected the bill. The government planned a joint session to end the deadlock, and if necessary a referendum. This could only mean the imposition of the majority's will amidst conditions of the most bitter strife. Was the strife necessary? Might not South African heraldry be regarded as 'a thing indifferent', on which British and Afrikaners might agree to differ? In October 1927 the two parties agreed upon a compromise. They gave up the attempt to secure agreement on the design of a single flag. They agreed that South Africa should in the future have two flags of equal symbolic meaning: the Union Jack to symbolize the Commonwealth loyalty, the South African flag to signify the national loyalty.[1] The compromise might be criticized on the ground that loyalties which were interwoven in the minds of many South Africans should not be symbolized on separate flagstaffs. But the essence of the compromise consisted in the readiness of each side to sacrifice theoretical harmonies in order to secure practical goodwill. Both parties realized the absurdity of buying a symbol of national unity at the price of national division. Paradoxically, the two separate and equal flags testified to the victory of a common will.

The possibilities of a general compromise within South Africa were increased by the thoroughness with which the work recommended by the Conference of 1926 was being carried through. In 1929 there met in London the expert conference to which had been assigned the task of reporting on the operation of dominion legislation and merchant shipping legislation.[2] The report of this conference, which was adopted in substance by the Imperial Conference of 1930, formed a bridge between the declarations of 1926 and the Statute of Westminster. The experts considered that their task was strictly limited to applying those principles of 'freedom, equality, and co-operation' —which had stood the test of 'the most trying conditions' and had been authoritatively recognized in 1926—to those special cases where law or practice still remained inconsistent with them. They reviewed these inconsistencies one by one and pointed out the appropriate means of removing them. Disallowance and reservation, they agreed, were not in accord with existing constitutional practice; where they found a statutory expression in dominion constitutions they might be removed by dominion legislatures alone, if these possessed sufficient power, and in other cases by co-operation between the dominion legislature and the legislature of the United Kingdom. The uncertain position with regard to the extra-territorial operation of dominion legislation would, in the opinion of the conference, best be cleared up by means of a declaratory enactment made, with the consent of the Dominions, by the parliament of the United Kingdom.

[1] The narrative given above shows that this compromise, for which Mr. Tielman Roos deserved especial credit, had been foreshadowed in the previous proposal.

[2] *Report of the Conference on the Operation of Dominion Legislation and Merchant Shipping Legislation*, Cmd. 3479 of 1929. In 1926 two separate conferences had been contemplated. The report is written in clear language intelligible to the layman and may be recommended as the best short review of the whole position. Wheare, *The Statute of Westminster*, chapters v–vii, may be consulted simultaneously.

The restrictions contained in the Colonial Laws Validity Act had once served a useful purpose in securing uniformity of law and co-operation on various matters of importance; but these desirable ends must henceforward be secured by methods based upon the principle of equality. The experts therefore recommended an enactment of the parliament of the United Kingdom declaring that the Colonial Laws Validity Act should cease to apply to any law made by the parliament of a Dominion, and providing against the possibility of a restoration of the old common law doctrine of repugnancy. There remained the problem arising from the existence of a legal power in the parliament of the United Kingdom to legislate for the Dominions. An act of parliament abolishing this power would be subject to repeal by a succeeding act of parliament. But in British constitutional practice convention counted for no less than command. The report recommended that both in the preamble of the proposed Statute and in an enacting clause the constitutional position should be affirmed that no law hereafter made by the parliament of the United Kingdom should extend to any Dominion otherwise than at its request and with its consent.

The general result of adopting these recommendations would be to remove all doubts as to the full legislative powers of the parliaments of the Dominions. This would open the way for co-operation to secure in essential matters the coherence and uniformity which had been achieved hitherto by the legislative supremacy of the United Kingdom. With regard to merchant shipping, the report applied, with considerable attention to detail, the general principles which it had affirmed, and submitted the heads of an agreement between Commonwealth members, which would achieve the end hitherto secured by imperial legislation.[1]

The principle of equality was developed by the report to its logical end; but equality still operated within unity. It was in its references to the Crown that the report particularly emphasized the principle of unity. As the freely associated members of the Commonwealth were united by a common allegiance to the Crown, it followed that the laws relating to the Throne and the Royal Style and Titles were matters of equal concern to all. The report recommended that this position should be recognized in a convention similar to that which had in recent years controlled the theoretically unfettered powers of the parliament of the United Kingdom to legislate on these matters. The convention should be placed on record in the proceedings of the

[1] The Imperial Conference of 1930 approved a draft agreement, for the terms of which see Cmd. 3717, pp. 32–7. It came into force on 10th December 1931.

next imperial conference and should appear in the preamble of the proposed act of parliament of the United Kingdom, in the following terms:

> 'Inasmuch as the Crown is the symbol of the free association of the members of the British Commonwealth of Nations, and as they are united by a common allegiance to the Crown, it would be in accord with the established constitutional position of all the members of the Commonwealth in relation to one another that any alteration in the law touching the succession to the Throne or the Royal Style and Titles shall hereafter require the assent as well of the Parliaments of all the Dominions as of the Parliament of the United Kingdom.'[1]

In South Africa, the lightnings of a subsiding storm quivered momentarily around this paragraph. The report in its entirety was thoroughly satisfactory to General Hertzog. It was General Smuts, forgetful of his usual political shrewdness, who raised an old issue of theoretical controversy which was naturally tending to become unimportant and stale. General Smuts laid stress upon the recommendation with regard to the succession and the Royal Style and Titles as disposing once for all of the question of secession. The principle of common action in this regard on the part of all members of the Commonwealth, he argued, negatived the unilateral withdrawal of any member of the Commonwealth. But General Hertzog would not consent to an interpretation of free association which denied the freedom to withdraw from the association. The result of General Smuts's intervention was to call forth an amendment, which was carried by a party vote, to the resolution adopting the report. The report was adopted subject to the condition that section 60 should not 'be taken as derogating from the right of any member of the British Commonwealth of Nations to withdraw therefrom'.[2] When General Hertzog set out for the Imperial Conference of 1930, he carried with him a mandate from the South African parliament to bring this reservation to the attention of the Conference. He was, however, content that the reservation should be 'duly noted'. It did not appear on the records of the Conference.[3]

It is unnecessary here to record the last stages of the activity at the Imperial Conference and in the various parliaments of the Commonwealth, which culminated in the passage through the parliament of the United Kingdom of the Statute of Westminster, 1931.[4] The

[1] Section 60.

[2] *House of Assembly Debates*, 20th May and 22nd May, vol. xv, cols. 4420–80 and 4571–81.

[3] See *Round Table*, vol. xxii, p. 455.

[4] The preparation of the Statute of Westminster, its content, and its particular

effect of the Statute, generally speaking, was to 'make clear the powers of dominion parliaments' in the sense of the principles enunciated in 1926. In the future, dominion parliaments would be competent to legislate with regard to those matters of dominion concern which had hitherto been regulated by legislation of the imperial parliament. They would also have the power to repeal existing imperial legislation on the same matters. They would have full power to make laws having extra-territorial operation. They would have the most formal assurance that legislation of the parliament of the United Kingdom would apply to them only at their request and with their assent. These were the general enactments contained in the Statute. In the circumstances of some Dominions, and particularly those Dominions with federal constitutions, the parliament of the United Kingdom still remained an essential vehicle for the expression of dominion will. The Canadian provinces, for example, were unwilling to surrender the safeguard of the existing processes of constitutional amendment contained in the British North America Act. By the will of Canada, Australia, and New Zealand clauses were inserted into the Statute of Westminster, which placed their constitutions beyond the range of the powers which the Statute conferred upon dominion parliaments. Australia and New Zealand also secured the insertion of a section stipulating that the powers which the Statute conferred on their parliaments should not belong to them until those parliaments had adopted the sections which conferred the powers; moreover, they might at any time revoke their action of adoption. These two Dominions were satisfied with their existing freedom, and, so far from seeking the enhanced status which the Statute offered them, their chief concern was to prevent that status from being foisted upon them.[1] Only the Irish Free State and the Union of South Africa adopted in their fullest extent the powers which the Statute made available. In both countries the governments gave explicit assurances that these powers would not be used in defiance of existing moral obligations. In the

application to each dominion, are all admirably dealt with in Wheare, *The Statute of Westminster*. It may be noted here that the principle of appointing governors-general by the King on the direct advice of the dominion governments was accepted by the 1930 Conference. (Cmd. 3717, p. 27.) This time it was the Australian labour government, ranging itself with the Dominions which demanded appeasement through recognition of their national claims, which most urgently pressed the claim. Its sequel in the Irish Free State is dealt with in the next chapter.

[1] See Section 10 of the Statute, which applies to Newfoundland as well as to Australia and New Zealand. For a reasoned argument in favour of the adoption of the Statute by Australia see article by Professor K. H. Bailey in *Australian Rhodes Review*, No. 1. Its forthcoming adoption has since been announced.

Irish Free State these obligations were primarily external; in the Union they were internal. The government of the Irish Free State assured the British government that it regarded the Articles of Agreement for a Treaty as a mutually binding instrument which could only be altered with the consent of both parties.[1] The South African government made in parliament a statement of comparable import with regard to the 'entrenched' clauses of the Act of Union. The existing rule which provided that the Cape franchise, the equality of English and Dutch as official languages, and certain other matters could only be removed by a two-thirds majority of the members of both houses, remained as a 'moral obligation of the parliament and the people to respect the basic principle in our constitution'.[2]

It was an oft-repeated argument of General Hertzog's that the formal recognition of South Africa's equal and mature national status would bring forth the fruits of contented membership in the British Commonwealth, and appeasement between the two European peoples of South Africa. Those Dominions and those parties which viewed with misgiving the destruction of the old forms of imperial unity accepted in good faith the promise of new forms and a new spirit. The time had now come when the promise would be tested.

The period of comparative prosperity and security in which the legal redefinition of the British Commonwealth had taken place was now closing. In every political society, economic crisis now tested the adequacy of the existing order to produce a degree of unity sufficient for resolute leadership. In some countries the difficulties and dangers of this time revealed dissensions deep enough to split the state and to make leadership impossible except by the way of party violence; in other countries parties drew together sufficiently to establish leadership on the basis of majority consent. In South Africa the reaction to economic distress threatened for a time to follow the old lines of 'racial self-defence'.[3] Apprehension of such a relapse into dissension provoked in turn an incomparably stronger reaction in favour of national concentration. The Union discovered in the crisis that its unity was more securely grounded than it had known.

The nationalist government, in fending off its economic and political difficulties, placed great hopes in the Ottawa Conference. The South African delegation, under the able and fair-minded leader-

[1] See pp. 331 ff. below.

[2] The safeguards to amendment of the constitution in these matters are contained in section 152 of the Act of Union. See *House of Assembly Debates*, vol. xvii, cols. 2736–63.

[3] *Round Table*, vol. xxiii, pp. 438–9.

ship of Mr. Havenga, did indeed make excellent use of the opportunity.[1] Along the road of economic policy South Africa moved towards a closer accord with Great Britain. Mr. Havenga cited South Africa's agreements at Ottawa as a proof of the liberating effect of the Commonwealth's political transformation.

> 'The Conference', he declared, 'has perhaps greater significance for the Union than for any other member of the Commonwealth of Nations. It marks the close of an era and a justification of the constitutional changes which commenced in 1926 and for which the Union of South Africa was largely responsible. It is the refutation of those doctrinaire theorists who advocated a federal Empire and could not visualise co-operation except in an atmosphere of domination and compulsion. . . .'[2]

All the same, nationalist sensitiveness continued for a short time to limit economic co-operation. It was in part responsible for the government's reluctance to follow Great Britain's example in departing from the gold standard. Would not this be a sign of economic subordination? The real interests of South Africa proved themselves stronger than such scruples, and in December 1932 the government relieved the reserve bank of its obligation to redeem in gold.

Three months later the impetus towards national concentration, which Mr. Tielman Roos had liberated, resulted in a coalition government in which General Smuts served as the lieutenant of General Hertzog. The new government was sworn in on the 31st March 1933, and in the May elections was returned with 138 avowed followers in a House of Assembly numbering 150. There were in addition 6 independent members who supported the coalition. For all practical purposes the government seemed to have the backing of an almost unanimous House. But, whereas General Smuts's followers had unanimously endorsed the coalition, a large section of General Hertzog's supporters had 'accepted' it without 'approving' it. Their acceptance had secured their election on the coalition panel. But their withholding of approval developed into definite opposition when their leader proceeded from a coalition of parties towards a real fusion. And there had already been opposition from the other quarter.

In order to prepare the way for fusion, a final effort of constitutional definition was necessary. Nationalists must be assured that the

[1] Mr. Havenga's policy at Ottawa had been to oppose measures of increasing inter-Empire trade at the expense of world trade but rather to foster inter-Empire trade by lowering tariffs. He secured important agreements with Great Britain and Canada. This involved securing release from the most-favoured-nation treaty made with Germany in 1928.

[2] *Round Table*, vol. xxiii, p. 450.

title-deeds of South African equality were indeed beyond question. 'The status of the Union of South Africa as a sovereign and independent state' must not rest merely upon declarations of imperial conferences and an act of the British parliament, but upon legislative enactment of the Union itself. The Act to provide for the declaration of the status of the Union of South Africa,[1] which the coalition government passed through parliament in 1934, implied the theory that the sovereignty of the Union was self-derived. Section 2 of the Act reasserted the theory—propounded centuries previously in Irish controversy—that acts of the British parliament extended to South Africa only when they were re-enacted by the South African parliament. In accordance with this doctrine, Section 3 provided that the Statute of Westminster, which was set forth in the Schedule, should be deemed to be an act of the parliament of the Union and construed accordingly. Section 4 declared:

> 'The Executive Government of the Union in regard to any aspect of its domestic or external affairs is vested in the King, acting on the advice of His Ministers of State for the Union, and may be administered by His Majesty in person or by a Governor-General as his representative.'

The section proceeded to affirm that any reference in the South Africa Act and in this Act to the King should intend the King acting on the advice of his ministers of state for the Union, but it qualified this declaration with the phrase 'save where otherwise stated', and explicitly safeguarded the power of the governor-general to dismiss ministers.[2] Other sections abolished the reservation of bills, deleted the words 'of the United Kingdom of Great Britain and Ireland' from the oath of allegiance to be taken to His Majesty, and as qualification for membership of parliament deleted the phrase 'a British subject of European descent' and substituted for it the phrase 'a person of European descent who has acquired Union nationality'. In deference to protests made during the debates, there was, however, included in this last section a reference to 'domicile as a British subject' as one of the ways by which the necessary qualification could be acquired. The government showed itself, indeed, anxious to meet the objections of those who feared that the prerogative of the Crown and their own status as subjects of the Crown were being impaired. Its spokesmen asserted repeatedly during the debate that the present legislation did not go beyond the Statute of Westminster.

[1] *Act to provide for the declaration of the Status of the Union of South Africa; for certain amendments of the South Africa Act, 1909, incidental thereto, and for the adoption of certain parts of the Statute of Westminster, 1931.*

[2] This proviso was inserted in response to criticism in debate.

In order to conciliate the parallel fear that the powers and even the existence of the provinces of the Union were in danger, it safeguarded them in a special act.[1] Its programme of constitutional definition included in addition one more act, the chief objects of which were 'to provide for the King's acts as head of the executive of the Union', and for 'the use of the Royal Seals in connection therewith'.[2] This Act supplemented Section 4 of the Status of the Union Act, which declared the executive government, both in domestic and external affairs, to be vested in the King acting on the advice of his ministers of state for the Union. It provided the Union with its own Royal Great Seal and Signet, and it underlined the provision that the governor-general might act on behalf of His Majesty. Its effect was to remove all limitations upon the delegation of the King's executive power. Under its provisions, it would be entirely in order that while the King's ministers in Great Britain were advising him to declare war, his ministers in South Africa should be advising his representative there to declare South Africa's neutrality.[3]

Generally speaking, this South African legislation carried to a conclusion in legal definition the 'Sister Kingdom' theory which had originated in Ireland, played an important part in the early stages of the struggle for American independence, and come once more to the fore in the recent history of the British Commonwealth.[4]

General Smuts appealed to the House to accept this legislation as a final statement of constitutional freedom, and to pass it 'as the charter of liberation from the mischievous constitutional doubts and fears of the past'.[5] All doubts, however, were not resolved. General Smuts still maintained that South Africa had no constitutional right of neutrality and secession; General Hertzog continued to assert the opposite. From this point of view the Status of the Union and the Seals Acts were made the object of conflicting interpretations. But the two parties were content to regard these differences as unimportant. General Hertzog had publicly written to General Smuts—'As to the divisibility of the Crown, the right of neutrality, and the right of secession, they are matters on which we differ.'[6] He was content that the controversy should rest there. In a similar spirit, the republican controversy was put on one side as a matter of subordinate importance in which liberty might be allowed to tender consciences.

[1] U.G., no. 45, 1934. [2] U.G., no. 70, 1934.

[3] See especially Section 6 of the Act. The interpretation given in the text is that of Professor Keith. See *Letters on Imperial Relations, Indian Reform, Constitutional and International Law, 1916–1935* (Oxford University Press, 1935), nos. 108 and 109.

[4] See above, pp. 11, 101.

[5] *The Times*, 12th April 1934. [6] *Round Table*, vol. xxiv, p. 664.

The programme of principles upon which the two parties agreed as the basis of their fusion dealt with this issue in the following paragraph:

'The maintenance is affirmed of the existing relationship between South Africa and the British Commonwealth of Nations and co-operation between its members, subject, however, to there being no derogation from the status of the Union and no assumption of external obligations in conflict with its interests.

'While the party stands for maintenance of the present constitutional position, none will be denied the right to express his individual opinion about, or to advocate his honest convictions in connexion with, any change of our form of Government.'[1]

The second sentence, although in form it tolerated any form of constitutional advocacy, became known as 'the republican propaganda clause'. Its aim was to quieten the consciences of those old fighters who, while they were content that their party should now affirm loyalty to the Commonwealth, were loath to disavow their former adherence to the republican idea. The declaration, for all its verbal inconsistency, is striking testimony to the progress of appeasement in South Africa. Republicanism itself was now taking its place among 'things indifferent'. Men could think differently about it, and still work together to serve a South African nation within the British Commonwealth.

But not all men. What was acceptable to the former nationalist Prime Minister, General Hertzog, was unacceptable to his former Minister of the Interior, Dr. Malan. Between May and December 1934, General Hertzog and Dr. Malan fought in party meetings throughout the Union for the allegiance of the nationalist rank and file. Dr. Malan was supported by *Die Burger*, the only Afrikaans newspaper in the Cape Province, and *Die Volksblad*, an Afrikaans newspaper in the Orange Free State. Motor lorries conveyed from meeting to meeting bands of enthusiastic 'Young Nationalists', dressed in yellow shirts and black caps,[2] to defend against the weary surrender of tired politicians the sacred cause of Afrikaans culture and South African independence. The rebellion of Dr. Malan was unable to detach the Orange Free State, which remained firm in personal allegiance to General Hertzog, but it detached the majority of Cape nationalists. When fusion was finally accomplished in December 1934, General Hertzog brought into it a party which had lost its militant left wing. General Smuts, similarly, had lost his militant right wing. Just as Dr. Malan's followers were unable to

[1] Clause 2 (*c*) and (*d*) of terms of fusion published 5th June 1934 (*Cape Times*, 6th June 1934).

[2] *The Times*, 26th May 1934.

accept old enemies as allies and to affirm that the existing position of South Africa in the British Commonwealth was a status to be defended and that republicanism was merely to be tolerated as a thing indifferent;[1] so the followers of Colonel Stallard could not accept the leadership of a government which both in its legislation and its party programme had tolerated, if it had not affirmed, the heresies of a divisible crown and neutrality and secession. The English-speaking majorities in Natal and the eastern districts of the Cape Provinces had long been alarmed both for their cultural privileges[2] and for their rights as subjects of an imperial crown. They were, potentially, an Ulster within the Union, just as Dr. Malan's nationalists were potentially a Sinn Féin party. But between the two extremes there stood a large majority which was determined to maintain 'the constitution which divides us least'. A more hopeful parallel than that of Unionism and Sinn Féin would be that of the Elizabethan compromise, which, although it failed to achieve a 'comprehension' of the whole nation, nevertheless staved off the civil dissensions which rent other nations, and, as its roots deepened and its fruits ripened, grew into a wider unity resting on no totalitarian order but on the recognition of diversities.

The present writer cannot venture to prophesy which of these parallels will be closer to the future course of events. He is indeed acutely conscious of the speculative vagueness and the uncertain interpretations which are unsatisfactory characteristics of what he has already written. 'Equality and Appeasement', the two themes to which he committed himself in the title to this section, cannot be commented upon with a lawyer's precision nor measured with a statistician's accuracy. Yet a narrative which ignored these themes would be like *Hamlet* without the Prince of Denmark. The writer is quite certain that in this South African inquiry he has made mistakes, and perhaps bad mistakes, because he has had perforce to rely (as he did not have to rely when treating similar themes in the Irish chapters) upon the printed word. Yet he believes that it is better to make mistakes than to shirk the attempt.

[1] Gestures are significant, and it is worth recording that on 24th January 1936 Dr. Malan seconded a motion of condolence with the King, Queen, and Royal Family on the death of King George: but walked out of the House with his followers when General Hertzog moved a motion of congratulation and loyalty to King Edward. *The Times*, 25th January 1936.

[2] The interpretation of the bilingual rule exacting a command of both languages from civil servants had in fact given a marked temporary advantage to Afrikaners; for whereas practically all Afrikaners knew English, many English-speaking people, notably in Natal, had never bothered to learn Afrikaans. On the language-in-schools question see Clarke, *Quebec and South Africa. A Study in Cultural Adjustment.*

The interpretations of the chief South African leaders can, at least, be given as a matter of exact record. Dr. Malan prophesied that, despite the party fusion, 'the struggle against Imperialism would be as fierce as ever, but the spirit of young South Africa would win'.[1] General Smuts prophesied that the vendetta between Afrikaner and British zealots would in the future appear petty in comparison with the issues which the whole South African nation would have to face. Speaking on the Status of the Union Bill he said:

> 'Whether it is neutrality or secession or any one of these things, they will be decided not by legal documents nor by the phraseology of a bill like this, but by the ordeal of facts, of great events which might shake not only this country but even the world. But sufficient to the day is the evil thereof. We must leave these things alone.'[2]

General Hertzog similarly prophesied that domestic dissensions would be overshadowed by pressure from the outside. Speaking on the Abyssinian crisis, he foreboded 'one of the bloodiest and cruelest periods the world has ever known. . . . Yet we hear from the opposition that we should regard Great Britain as our enemy, as if we are not going to have enough enemies. And we must do this to a country which has handed us our freedom to use as we think fit!'[3]

Dr. Malan's antithesis between South African nationalism and British imperialism might be useful propaganda, but it would not stand historical criticism. Accepting provisionally the vagueness of the words employed, the historian may point out that South African nationalism, even in its embryonic form and in the days of colonial dependency half a century earlier, was already developing its own imperialism.[4] In South-West Africa, which Union troops had conquered and which the Union government was now administering as a 'C' mandate, the sovereign and independent state of South Africa was faced with a problem no less 'imperial' than that of any other state which was responsible for the government of dependencies. There were also signs that the problem might possibly bring South Africa into direct dispute with the counter-imperialism of a first-class Power.[5]

South African nationalism also had a racial intensity which im-

[1] *The Times*, 6th June 1934. [2] *Round Table*, vol. xxiv, p. 671.

[3] *Round Table*, vol. xxvi, p. 183.

[4] This may be documented from the Angra Pequena negotiations between Lord Granville and Bismarck in the early eighties of last century. There is ample material in *Die Grosse Politik*, vol. iv.

[5] The demand for colonies was becoming fashionable. In August 1936 the Polish Foreign Office stated officially that it would put forward Poland's claim to colonies in South America or South Africa. *Manchester Guardian*, 1st August 1936.

pelled it to declare its concern for European supremacy throughout the African continent.[1] But when a second Great Power established European supremacy in Abyssinia by the resolute use of military and air power, South Africans felt themselves threatened in their security.[2] The shelter behind which the old legalistic controversies had been debated seemed now to be collapsing.

There was one other controversy to which reference may be made in a closing paragraph. This was not a controversy involving the relations of sovereign governments, but a controversy involving the relation of human individuals. Its protagonists for more than a century had been evangelical Englishmen and calvinistic Afrikaners. Its subject had been the destiny and rights of the native Africans. Have the events which have been chronicled in this section any bearing upon this controversy? It has been asserted that every instalment of appeasement between Englishman and Afrikaner has been bought at the expense of the native African.[3] Such an assertion raises an issue no less momentous than any which has hitherto been investigated; but the investigation of it must for the time being be postponed.[4]

III

The Common Cause

Equality of status between Great Britain and the Dominions within the Commonwealth necessarily implied their equal status in the society of nations. The 'inward' and 'outward' aspects of dominion status, although for purposes of exposition it was possible to stress now one aspect and now the other, formed parts of a single reality. In practice, dominion nationalism generally concentrated on the 'inward' aspect, and was disinclined to think out clearly the full meaning of equal status in a world of sovereign states. Even the Report of the Inter-Imperial Relations Committee of 1926 avoided a thorough probing of this issue. It asserted without qualification the doctrine of responsible government, in external no less than in internal affairs. It reiterated the principle that neither Great Britain nor the Dominions could be committed to active obligations except

[1] Here the statements of Mr. Pirow are particularly illuminating, e.g. to the Imperial Press Conference, 1935. *The Times*, 6th February 1935.

[2] See the account of the Abyssinian crisis in section iii of this chapter.

[3] e.g. the various books of Mr. Leonard Barnes. In relation to the fusion it will be necessary to consider particularly (*a*) the 1935 agreement with regard to the Protectorates, (*b*) the Native bills passed by the Union parliament in 1936.

[4] An approach to the question was prepared in Chapter IV. The question will be more systematically considered in Volume II.

with the definite assent of their own governments. It declared that each Dominion must remain the sole judge of the nature and the extent of its co-operation. In all these affirmations the interpretation of equality was separateness—separate responsibility, separate decision, separate action. According to the logic once used by Lord John Russell, this meant disruption.[1] But in the minds of Lord Balfour and the other members of the committee there was another logic, the paradoxical logic by which General Botha had once acclaimed decentralization as the way of unity.[2] By 1926 decentralization had almost run its full course; the political will of the Commonwealth was distributed among the Commonwealth's several equal parts; but—'. . . no common cause will thereby be imperilled'.

What were the grounds of this belief? No doubt it rested essentially upon an interpretation of past experience, upon an assumption that the theme which had been dominant in the Empire's history from the time of the Durham Report until the Great War would still continue to repeat itself. The Balfour Committee translated this interpretation of history into a teleological affirmation sufficiently far-reaching to justify unlimited faith in the Empire's future. 'The British Empire is not founded upon negations. It depends essentially, if not formally, on positive ideals. Free institutions are its life-blood. Peace, security, and progress are among its objects . . .' This affirmation might be true, it might in the long run be decisively true; but it did not explain precisely how six equally responsible governments could in the immediate future so conduct their separate foreign policies as to imperil no common cause. What had the committee to say with regard to this pressing practical problem? It pointed to the existence of three distinct facts, by whose operation the principle of equality, which had at first expressed itself as separateness, found a new expression in membership. The first fact belonged to an order assumed to be permanent; this fact was the Crown, which symbolized the 'special relationship' existing between all members of the Commonwealth. The second fact belonged to an order which was in process of decline, but which nevertheless was important now and would remain important for a considerable time to come; this fact was the difference of function between Great Britain and the Dominions. The third fact belonged to an order which was in process of development; this fact was the system of consultation and co-operation which was growing up between the members of the Commonwealth.

So the Imperial Conference of 1926 recognized and blessed the fact

[1] See above, p. 23. [2] See above, p. 2.

of separateness in the faith that it would be overruled for the common weal. Was this faith well grounded? It was an orthodoxy which was challenged, either openly or covertly, by opposing heresies. There were many people, particularly in the Australasian Dominions, who rejected the comforting doctrine that the way to unity lay through separateness; at the end of that road, they believed, was a miserable disintegration. There were many others, particularly in the Irish Free State and South Africa, who gave a contrasted emotional colour to the same interpretation. Their ideal was separation unqualified by any special relationship between members of a still-surviving Commonwealth. To them the declaration of 1926 was another stage in 'the march of the nation' towards an absolute separation from Great Britain and the British Commonwealth. The optimism of the Balfour Report rested upon the assumption that the gospel of the Commonwealth would prove itself sufficiently vital to convert these heretics. Was this assumption valid? A strict examination of historical evidence cannot as yet provide the answer to this question; the period under review is too short. It is possible merely to chart the trends of tendency, with the warning that what appears at short view to be the main line of the curve may later reveal itself, to the more distant view which will one day be possible, as nothing more than a deviation from the main line.

With this reservation, it already seems possible to assert that separateness has made greater inroads into the 'special relationship' symbolized by the Crown than the orthodox doctrine asserted in 1926 was prepared openly to anticipate. The Balfour Report laid particular emphasis upon the value of the Crown in treaty-making procedure. All treaties were to be in the name of the King; the Commonwealth was composed of many nations, but would present itself to the outer world as one contracting party. Thus there would be avoided in the future that separate designation of the different parts of the Commonwealth which had been permitted in some treaties of the post-war years. Was this an effective contribution to the unity of the Commonwealth, or was it merely a fiction which masked the waning of that unity? The model form of signature appended to the Balfour Report seemed to admit the interpretation that the same King contracted separately for the separate parts of the Commonwealth. The Report also affirmed that full powers for the negotiation and signature of treaties should be issued on 'the advice of the Government concerned'. In accordance with this principle, plenipotentiaries of the Union of South Africa, with full powers from His Majesty, signed in 1928 a treaty with the German

Reich 'for and on behalf of the Union of South Africa'.[1] In the same year Canada objected to the implication, which it espied in the draft treaty with Egypt, that His Majesty was contracting in general, and not merely for Great Britain and its dependencies. All this was implicit in the report of the Inter-Imperial Relations Committee and in the previous developments which the report summed up. It did not touch directly 'the symbol of the special relationship'. But what reality lay behind the symbol? What did the special relationship amount to? Did it for example possess any precise meaning which modified the international action of Canada or South Africa in such a way as to preserve 'the diplomatic unity of the British Empire'? The safeguard on which legal specialists had laid such stress—namely that full powers to negotiate and sign were contained in an instrument under the Great Seal, whose issue depended on action of the British government—disappeared in 1932, when first the Irish Free State, and a few months later the Union of South Africa, acquired Great Seals of their own. This new departure also had significance for the final and formal moment of treaty-making, namely the act of ratification, which was effected under the Great Seal. Already, in ratification, there has been a drift from the formal unity of the practice which had been endorsed in 1926. The practice then was that, in treaties imposing obligations on more than one part of the Commonwealth, ratification, after it had been agreed upon by consultation, should be effected by a single act delivered under the Great Seal. But the Kellogg Pact for the Renunciation of War was ratified by six separate acts simultaneously delivered,[2] and the Naval Treaty of 1930 was ratified in a separate act on the part of the Irish Free State. From 1932 onwards, those Dominions which chose to provide themselves with Seals of their own could still further emphasize their separateness. It was becoming apparent that the symbol of the Crown could be employed to support a theory and programme of separation, as well as to support the theory of 'the special relationship' and the ideal of unity. It depended upon the point of view from which the Crown was regarded, upon theories of indivisibility or divisibility, upon refinements of juristic interpretation and metaphysical subtleties about the one and the many.[3] Beyond question the trend in the processes of treaty-making which

[1] See above, p. 278, note 1.

[2] The ratifications of the Irish Free State and Canada were delivered by their Ministers in Washington; the other Commonwealth ratifications were delivered by the British Ambassador.

[3] These matters are handled with liveliness and subtlety by Professor W. Y. Elliot in *The New British Empire*, chapter i.

has been described in the present paragraph gave much support to the contention that the King had become juristically six separate persons.[1]

> 'It appears idle' [wrote an eminent Australian lawyer in 1932] 'to pretend that "the principle of the diplomatic unity of the British Empire" has not already been departed from, or that the arrangements which now exist belong merely to constitutional usage and not to international relations and law.'

At the time of the Lausanne controversy, the Canadian Prime Minister had argued that Canada was not morally, but only legally bound by a treaty of major importance made on the advice of His Majesty's government in Great Britain; there would in the future be ample material for arguing, in similar circumstances, that a dominion was not even legally bound. Assuming the existence of a desire still to preserve the unity of the Commonwealth by effecting the convergence at a common point of the separate foreign policies of the King's separate governments, the strain upon the dexterity of these governments, and upon their sense of responsibility, must be exceedingly grave. Exceedingly grave, too, might be the strain upon the King himself, if he should in a matter of vital importance receive conflicting advice from the different governments which had the right to approach him directly. It is true that the South African legislation of 1934, which has been described in the previous section, established a procedure by which this last difficulty could be avoided. But in doing so, it opened a road by which the Union of South Africa, while still professing to act in the name of the King, could withdraw altogether from the circle which was supposed to mark the 'special relationship' between Commonwealth countries, and try her fortune amidst the shifting partnerships and rivalries of international relations at large.

It would, however, be premature to press to a final conclusion an argument which rests upon facts of a special category and upon interpretations which are matters of controversy. Perhaps it is sufficient merely to point out the ease with which this argument, failing the action of restraining circumstances, might be pressed in fact to the conclusion of imperial disruption. The interest therefore shifts to the nature and power of the restraining circumstances. But the shift must be a gradual one; it is necessary first to view the 'special relationship' from still another angle. Has it been the tendency of this relationship to dissolve itself into general inter-

[1] e.g. Mr. P. McGilligan's speech in the Dáil, 17th July 1931, printed in Keith, *Speeches and Documents on the British Dominions*, p. 245.

national relationships in such a manner as to obliterate the system of public law peculiar to the Commonwealth, or to destroy the possibility of building up such a system? In establishing themselves as international persons, have the Dominions become nothing more than international persons to Great Britain and to each other? A minister of the Irish Free State, discussing in the Dáil the implications of the report of 1926, asserted definitely that there were limits to the merging of intra-Commonwealth rights and obligations in general international rights and obligations.

> 'The exact nature of the relationship outside the common bond' [he said] 'is undefined; but it is naturally felt that League treaties and conventions cannot be taken as applying completely, as to all their articles, between them (the members of the Commonwealth) as if there were no special relationship whatever.'[1]

In two important matters, commerce and naval strength, international practice has commonly assumed that the British Commonwealth is a single unit.[2] In the attempts made since the war to strengthen the foundations of a law-respecting international community, the British government, supported by the majority of the Dominions, has been persistently anxious to preserve the 'special relationship' between members of the Commonwealth, interpreting this to mean that they would not submit to international jurisdiction disputes among themselves, but would find their own means of settling them. This anxiety showed itself most clearly in the discussions with regard to the Optional Clause of the Statute of the Permanent Court of International Justice. At the Imperial Conference of 1926 it was agreed not to accept this clause without further discussion. When in 1929 there came to power in Great Britain a labour government pledged to accept the clause, efforts were made to find a common formula of acceptance for Great Britain and all the Dominions. Before the discussions were complete, the delegation of the Irish Free State at Geneva signed the clause without any reservation whatever. The delegations of the other governments

[1] Mr. Desmond Fitzgerald, quoted in Manning, *The Policies of the British Dominions in the League of Nations*, p. 14.

[2] *Per contra*, the treaty of 1928 between the Union of South Africa and the German Reich admitted the most-favoured-nation principle without qualification. See also W. P. M. Kennedy and H. J. Schlosberg, *Law and Custom of the South African Constitution* (Oxford University Press, 1935), p. 399. The Irish Free State's attitude of separateness on the naval issue (see pp. 390–1 below) culminated in the statement of her representative at the Naval Conference of 1936, that the Irish Free State had no concern with the treaty as she possessed no navy and had no intention of possessing one.

of the Commonwealth signed later with identical reservations, and the British Foreign Secretary added this formal statement:

> 'Disputes with other members of the British Commonwealth are excluded because the members of the Commonwealth, although international units in the fullest sense of the term, are united by their common allegiance to the Crown. Disputes between them should therefore be dealt with by some other mode of settlement, and for this provision is made in the exclusion clause.'[1]

The South African government was willing, as a matter of convenience, to accept this statement of policy; but it held as a matter of principle that disputes between His Majesty's separate governments were justiciable before the Permanent Court. The Irish Free State was uncompromising on the issue of its international personality; but in practice it was not unwilling to discuss 'some other mode of settlement' of disputes between Commonwealth members. This discussion took place at the Imperial Conference of 1930. The reservation of intra-Commonwealth disputes which all the Commonwealth members save the Irish Free State had attached to their acceptance of the obligatory jurisdiction of the Permanent Court of International Justice, and the public assertion of the British Foreign Secretary that some other method of settling such disputes should be found, made it a matter of some urgency to establish a special procedure for the Commonwealth. The rapid progress towards the Statute of Westminster increased this urgency, for it forecast the final disappearance in the near future of the old forms of legal adjustment, and pointed to the possibility that even the Statute of Westminster itself, which was to be the foundation of the new order, might become matter for conflicting interpretation. In view of these circumstances, the Imperial Conference of 1930—the Irish Free State included—agreed 'that some machinery for the solution of disputes which may arise between the members of the British Commonwealth is desirable'. But the machinery which it recommended was primitive in comparison with the Permanent Court at the Hague, and the obligations which the members of the Commonwealth were willing to accept towards each other fell far short of those which they had already accepted towards states which did not share their 'special relationship'. They rejected for their own society the idea of a permanent tribunal. They rejected the principle of compulsory jurisdiction, which they had accepted in justiciable disputes with other nations. All that they agreed upon

[1] League of Nations 10th Assembly, *Journal*, p. 194, quoted in Manning, *The Policies of the British Dominions in the League of Nations*, p. 293.

was the means for establishing a tribunal in the event of both parties to a dispute voluntarily agreeing to submit the dispute to its decision. The complete inadequacy of this half-way agreement was proved when Mr. De Valera succeeded Mr. Cosgrave and acted on a contrary view of the Free State's legal obligations to Great Britain. This was the first occasion when the need for a legal decision arose. But Ireland refused a Commonwealth tribunal and Great Britain refused an international tribunal. The law was ousted. What light did the dispute between His Majesty's governments in Great Britain and the Irish Free State throw upon the theory of a 'special relationship'? This theory was itself the central object of controversy. It has been said: 'Where there is a society there must necessarily be a law, and where there is a law there must, or at any rate there should, be some authority competent to declare the law.'[1] The dispute between the two governments really turned upon the issue whether the British Commonwealth of Nations was a society at all. In substance, Mr. De Valera's position seemed to rest on the assumption that Ireland belonged to no other legal society than the general society of nations.

The record, therefore, so far at least as the 'marginal members' of the Commonwealth are concerned—if the phrase may be used, without any reproachful intent, to indicate reluctance to accept the implications of the theory of a special relationship—shows, so far as it has been examined, a marked inroad of separateness upon unity. But the record has dealt hitherto chiefly with forms and doctrines. It is time to pay rather more attention to the substance of this separateness, to consider its extent and its limitations and the nature of these limitations. This aspect of the problem may be approached in the first place by considering the exercise made by the Dominions of the right of legation, which had admittedly belonged to them since 1920. The right of legation had of course its formal side, and here, too, the movement was towards separateness. The careful distinction between matters relating only to a Dominion, and all other matters, which was asserted when the first appointment of a Dominion Minister to a foreign capital was made,[2] was allowed later on to become blurred. The original robust phrase safeguarding the diplomatic unity of the British Empire was later on attenuated by a gloss which mildly explained that it meant consultation in matters

[1] Toynbee, *British Commonwealth Relations*, p. 110. Cf. generally pp. 107 ff. and 196 for a treatment of the problem of a tribunal, which is discussed also in the Supplementary Chapter to this volume. The subject is discussed in relation to the special conditions of Ireland in Chapter VI below.

[2] Cmd. 2202 of 1924 (appointment of Irish Free State minister at Washington).

of common concern. In the communications informing foreign governments of the appointment of dominion representatives to their capitals, the separate instance of His Majesty's separate governments came to be openly acknowledged.[1] In all this the drift of tendency was in exact accord with the developments in treaty-making procedure. But we must now consider the actual exercise which the Dominions made of their separate powers. We must examine the extent to which they exchanged diplomatic representatives with foreign states, and the nature of the treaties which they made.

Up to the present time (1936) the following dominion legations have been established:

Canada:	At Washington.
	,, Paris.
	,, Tokyo.
South Africa:	At the Hague and Brussels.
	,, Rome.
	,, Washington.
	,, Berlin and Stockholm.
	,, Paris and Lisbon.
Irish Free State:	At Washington.
	,, the Holy See.
	,, Paris and Brussels.
	,, Berlin.
	,, Madrid.

These three Dominions also maintain a counsellor (Canada) or a representative (South Africa and the Irish Free State) at the League of Nations in Geneva.

This is the full extent of the diplomatic representation of the Dominions outside the Commonwealth. Looked at from the point of view of Australia and New Zealand, who have not exercised the right of legation, it may seem a good deal. It may seem, at any rate to the timid and the conservative, that South Africa and the Irish Free State and Canada have ventured far along the difficult and dangerous path of separate diplomacy. But let the contrast be made with Great Britain. Great Britain maintains abroad fifty-three missions, thirteen of which are embassies. She has political representation in every capital, and consular representation in every

[1] Compare in all these points with the appointment of Irish Free State minister to Berlin in 1929. Keith, *Speeches and Documents on the British Dominions*, p. 446.

important city. Controlling this far-flung and finely meshed representation abroad there is at home the portentous organization of the Foreign Office with its ten specialist departments. There is in addition the Department of Overseas Trade, which belongs half to the Foreign Office and half to the Board of Trade. Compared with the universality of Great Britain's diplomatic activity, South Africa and Canada and the Irish Free State are seen now to have made but a few short and spasmodic excursions into the territory of diplomatic activity. The difference of function, to which the Balfour Report referred, begins now to impress itself heavily.

How does the Commonwealth of Australia, which has appointed and received no diplomatic representatives, obtain information from abroad and carry on negotiations with foreign countries when its interests render this necessary? The British government places at Australia's disposal the entire organization which it maintains. How does the Dominion of Canada do its business with countries in which it has no representation? Canada depends on precisely the same service. The contrast therefore between those Dominions which have exercised the right of legation and those which have not is in some degree a misleading one. The contrast might with equal truth be stated as one between Great Britain, which performs the diplomatic function on a world-wide scale, and the other members of the Commonwealth, which either do not perform this function at all, or perform it in a very limited degree. In Vienna, Moscow, and Nanking, all the Dominions are on exactly the same footing. They get their information through the Foreign Office and the Dominions Office. If one of them should wish to present a communication in Vienna or Moscow or Nanking, the British representative will present it 'at the instance' or 'request' of the Dominion concerned. But whereas in commercial or technical matters this procedure is followed in the ordinary course of routine, in 'matters of general and political concern' a procedure is followed which ensures that there shall be consultation.[1]

Enough has been said to indicate the manner in which equality of status between Great Britain and the Dominions must, in their international action, be modified of necessity by their inequality of stature. But it is reasonable to suppose that this inequality will be progressively reduced. As between Great Britain and such a Dominion as Canada the inequality may in some distant future disappear altogether.[2] The Balfour Report stated that for a considerable

[1] See p. 301 below.

[2] Differences of stature may be equated, rather crudely, with differences of

time to come the major responsibility in foreign affairs must remain with Great Britain; but it did not anticipate the indefinite continuation of this situation. It is therefore all the more necessary to turn from the order which, however gradually, is in process of decline, and to consider the order which is in process of development. In support of its affirmation of belief that no common cause would be imperilled by the complete extension of responsible government into the realm of foreign affairs, the Report of 1926 placed the greater emphasis, not on the still-surviving difference of function, but on the still-growing system of co-operation.

It appears to be generally accepted that the fears which afflicted conservative souls when the right of legation was first claimed by a Dominion have hitherto been belied by events. Indeed, the presence in a foreign capital of representatives of several of His Majesty's governments is considered to be a useful means of consultation and co-operation. The resultant harmony, of course, is conditional upon the existence of the will to co-operate and upon the absence of adverse factors which might thwart that will. Obviously, there could be no co-operation between the representatives at the Vatican of the United Kingdom and the Irish Free State during the dispute between the United Kingdom and the Holy See about Maltese affairs.[1] The presence at a foreign capital of separate representatives of a number of His Majesty's governments may in abnormal circumstances help to advertise to the world a conflict of policy between these governments; it will hardly, however, be the cause of that conflict. Conversely, under normal conditions of goodwill, their presence may be

population. The 'white population of the Empire' was not, however, being very rapidly 'redistributed', as the following totals show:

Great Britain		*Australia*	
1911	41,126,040	1911	4,455,005
1921	43,176,521	1921	5,435,734
1931	44,937,444	1935 (estimate)	6,724,305
Irish Free State		*New Zealand*	
1926	2,971,992	1911	1,008,468
1935 (estimate)	3,033,000	1921	1,218,913
		1935 (estimate)	1,485,046
South Africa (total population)		*Canada*	
1911	5,973,394	1911	7,206,643
1921	6,928,580	1921	8,787,949
1935 (estimate)	8,600,300	1931	10,376,786

The movement of deceleration tending towards stagnation was appearing, with some time-lag, in the Dominions as well as in Great Britain. This subject will be dealt with in Volume II.

[1] On Malta see below, Chapter VII, section i.

an additional factor in securing the convergence of policies to a common end; it will hardly, however, be the chief factor. The mechanism and method of co-operation must be sought for primarily in the capital cities of Great Britain and the Dominions.

For a detailed and accurate description of the system, the reader may be referred to a handbook already published by the Royal Institute of International Affairs.[1] It is unnecessary in this Survey to cover ground which has been so thoroughly investigated; a few paragraphs must suffice for the main outlines. The basic principle of co-operation was clearly set forth by the Imperial Conferences of 1923 and 1926, in the rules which they adopted for treaty-making. Those rules have been described above. They limited the separateness implicit in the doctrine of equality by correlating, with the rights which equality conveyed, the obligations which it imposed. Each member of the Commonwealth had the right to do its own business in the world; each member had equally the right to demand that it should not be embarrassed or endangered by a careless exercise of the same freedom by a fellow member; each member was therefore under the obligation to inform its fellow members of the policies which it was pursuing, to listen to their observations, and if necessary to consult with them for the purpose of harmonizing conflicting intentions. In order that this system should work it was essential that the various governments should be furnished with ample information of each other's policies, and should establish the organizations necessary for the digestion of this information. Difference of function to some extent simplified the problem; Great Britain possessed a world-wide organization and Great Britain handled the most momentous issues of policy; the first line of development (whose early beginnings have already been described)[2] was to secure a stream of information from London to the dominion capitals. The Foreign Office was, of course, the great reservoir of information; after 1926 the Foreign Office branch of the Dominions Office became a channel—the necessity of which was sometimes questioned—through which much of the information passed. In the capitals of the Dominions, departments of external affairs expanded slowly—too slowly, it was often said; their function was to sift and focus the information received, so that it might be of use to ministers. But 'arid facts are not information', and the communication of facts from a distance had to be supplemented and in large measure supplanted by the direct communication of facts to dominion representatives

[1] Palmer, *Consultation and Co-operation in the British Commonwealth.*

[2] See Chapter I, section iv, above (p. 50).

of sufficient standing and experience to know what they wanted and to get it, and of sufficient capacity to appreciate the facts in their proper perspective and to convey their meaning to the governments at home. Australia was the first Dominion to take effective measures for this purpose; in 1924 the Australian government established an External Affairs' branch of the High Commissioner's Office in London, under the direction of an officer who rapidly vindicated the utility, and indeed the necessity, of the system. The other Dominions have since adopted the same system in principle, although there are differences of detail. The general tendency of observers is to favour the appointment of high commissioners who are themselves capable of performing these quasi-diplomatic functions.[1] In recent years the aspect of reciprocity has come increasingly to the fore. The representative of a Dominion in London is useful not merely for receiving and transmitting the information and views which his government should possess, but for conveying from his government the information and views which the British government should possess. Moreover, the British government has felt the need to have its own accredited representatives in dominion capitals, so that here too 'arid facts' may be translated into understanding. This has become all the more necessary since the governors-general have ceased to act as the channels of communication between the British and Dominion governments. A feature of the system at present developing is therefore the reciprocal appointment of high commissioners between Great Britain and the Dominions. The most notable gap in the symmetry of the system is the paucity of representation between Dominion and Dominion. The 'network of contacts' runs from a centre to various points of the circumference and back again: it does not link the points on the circumference. But the growth of this linking also is frequently prophesied.[2]

[1] See Toynbee, *British Commonwealth Relations*, pp. 68–71. The development of the High Commissioner's status and functions has completely vindicated the original Canadian proposal of 1879, to which the British government demurred (see p. 29 above).

[2] Intra-Commonwealth quasi-diplomatic representation is at present as follows:

I. *Representatives of the Government of the United Kingdom in:*

Canada:	High Commissioner for His Majesty's government in the United Kingdom.
	Trade Commissioners (2 in Montreal, 1 each in Toronto, Vancouver, and Winnipeg respectively).
Australia:	High Commissioner for His Majesty's government in the United Kingdom.
	Trade Commissioners (1 in Sydney and 1 in Melbourne).
New Zealand:	The Governor-General.
	Trade Commissioner (in Wellington).

Information cannot be rigidly separated from consultation; the one merges into the other. The most satisfactory form of consultation is face-to-face discussion between the responsible heads of governments, but of necessity this can only occur rarely. It occurs at imperial conferences, and the records of the various conferences show their concern with matters of foreign policy; for example, in 1923, following upon the Corfu incident, a general discussion on the League of Nations: in 1926 discussions on Locarno, the Optional

Union of South Africa:	*High Commissioner in the Union of South Africa for His Majesty's government in the United Kingdom.
	*His Majesty's High Commissioner for Basutoland, the Bechuanaland, and Swaziland.
	Trade Commissioners (in Capetown, Durban, and Johannesburg respectively).
Irish Free State:	Trade Commissioner (in Dublin).
Newfoundland:	The Governor.
Southern Rhodesia:	The Governor.

II. *Representatives of the Dominions in the Commonwealth:*

Canada:	High Commissioner in the United Kingdom.
	Air Liaison Officer in the United Kingdom.
	Trade Commissioners in the United Kingdom and in New Zealand (Auckland).
	†Agent-Generals for the Canadian Provinces of Quebec and British Columbia, in the United Kingdom.
Australia:	High Commissioner in the United Kingdom.
	External Affairs Officer in the United Kingdom.
	Liaison Officers for Defence (3) in the United Kingdom.
	Agents-General for individual Australian states in the United Kingdom (6).
New Zealand:	High Commissioner in the United Kingdom.
	Trade Commissioner in the Commonwealth of Australia (Sydney).
	Trade Commissioner in the Dominion of Canada (Toronto).
Union of South Africa:	High Commissioner in the United Kingdom.
	Trade Commissioner in the United Kingdom.
	Trade Commissioner in the Dominion of Canada (Montreal).
	Trade Commissioner in British East Africa (Nairobi).
Irish Free State:	High Commissioner in the United Kingdom.
Newfoundland:	Trade Commissioner in the United Kingdom.
Southern Rhodesia:	High Commissioner in the United Kingdom.
India:	High Commissioner in the United Kingdom.
	Trade Commissioner in the United Kingdom.
	Agent-General for the government of India in the Union of South Africa (Capetown).

* These two High Commissionerships are at present held by the same officers, but the offices are quite distinct, even to the extent of having different precedence, uniforms, office staff. See Palmer, *Consultation and Co-operation in the British Commonwealth*, pp. 30–1.

† Office to be abolished. See *The Times*, 5th September 1936.

Clause, and mandates: in 1930 discussion on mandates, the General Act, and disarmament. But the imperial conferences have a variety of preoccupations, they meet but rarely, and moreover the principles of foreign policy can be separated only with difficulty and perhaps with danger from the continuous development of policy amidst changing situations. In 1917 the need for more continuous contact was recognized and in some degree met by accepting the principle of direct communications between prime ministers; the development of the means of communication has progressively increased the possibilities of this form of contact. Yet discussion by means of wireless telephony remains a poor substitute for discussion across a table, and the continuity and effectiveness of consultation depends in large measure upon the system of inter-governmental representation which has just been described. There remains, however, considerable difference of opinion as to the character and functions which should belong to the representatives whom the dominion governments maintain in London. Should they have a 'political' or an 'ambassadorial' character? The first idea has found its most complete expression in the plan, which has on more than one occasion been put forward, of establishing in London resident ministers to represent the dominion governments. The intention behind this suggestion is to make the consultations which take place in London as authoritative and binding as they can possibly be made without trenching upon the principle of responsible government. The same desire for continuity, responsibility, and practical effectiveness in consultation may be illustrated by a further suggestion which has been made: namely that the representatives of the Dominions in London should form with British representatives a committee which would not only prepare business for the imperial conference, but which would also perform without interruption 'staff and intelligence' work for the governments of the Commonwealth in the sphere of foreign affairs. A committee of this kind, it has been said, would perform functions analogous to those of the committee of imperial defence and might indeed be called the committee of foreign affairs. But the trend of development has been running in a different direction. The general preference, expressed perhaps most emphatically in Canada, is for representation through non-political high commissioners of eminent diplomatic capacities, enjoying a tenure of office independent of ministerial changes. As for the suggested committee of foreign affairs, it stirs up immediately—and so does every other suggestion of similar tendency—all that repugnance to centralization, or even the appearance of centralization, which has been sufficiently illustrated in the first section of this chapter, and in the earlier chapter which revealed its vigorous existence in the period of Sir Wilfrid Laurier before the war.[1]

It is obviously impossible to get very far in the discussion of organization without probing into the purposes which organization exists to serve. Between the man who would advocate the establishment of a committee of foreign affairs and the man who would abhor the proposal there lies a deep difference of judgement and feeling—if not about 'the common cause', at any rate about the common need. Roughly speaking, one individual opposes the establishment of joint machinery because he is afraid that his Dominion may be implicated in a joint policy; the other individual favours its establishment because he believes that the implication exists already in virtue of the Commonwealth membership. The opponents in the debate appeal eagerly to the philosophies and the moralities: 'parochialism' and 'oecumenicalism' face each other in opposing battles.[2] All too frequently, it must be confessed, the parochialists and oecumenicalists snatch at each others' weapons and march to the attack behind each others' standards. It will be well to withdraw for the time from this vast and confused struggle; skirting the much disputed heights of philosophy, let us, so far as we can, pursue our inquiry into 'the common cause' along the humdrum path of history. The official records must still have something more to say about those things which are, in fact, done and planned in common, and those which are not. We need not at the moment seek to know whether or not the ultimate purpose of the Commonwealth 'must be found, and is to be found, in the moral or spiritual sphere'.[3] If indeed it should be proved that the British Commonwealth is the Divine Idea on Earth, or if the opposite should be proved, that certainly would be a most valuable demonstration. Yet it would still remain not entirely unprofitable to examine the form of the British Commonwealth as it stands on this day, the 10th September 1936.[4]

[1] In addition to Palmer, *Consultation and Co-operation in the British Commonwealth*, see for a full and satisfactory elaboration of this paragraph Toynbee, *British Commonwealth Relations*, pp. 62–8. See also above, Chapter I, section iv.

The analogy with the Committee of Imperial Defence is not altogether a happy one: its composition depends entirely upon the British Prime Minister; and dominion ministers have made very little use of the privilege of attending extended to them in 1911.

[2] See Toynbee, *British Commonwealth Relations*, p. 22.

[3] op. cit., p. 53.

[4] See Sir Thomas Smith, *De Republica Anglorum* (ed. L. Alston, Cambridge University Press, 1906), p. 146: 'I have declared summarily as it were in a chart or mappe . . . the forme and government of England . . . not in that sort as *Plato* made his common wealth, or *Zenophon* his kingdome of Persia, nor as *Syr Thomas More* his

What in fact have been the matters which the Dominions have treated as matters of separate concern? Are all other matters the separate concern of Great Britain, or are some of them matters of common concern? These are clarifying questions. To prepare an answer to the first question, let us consider the nature of the agreements or treaties made by the Union of South Africa with foreign Powers. In 1928 the Union signed with the Portuguese government the Mozambique Convention, which dealt particularly with the recruitment of labour in Portuguese territory. In 1931, by an exchange of notes with the Japanese consul in South Africa, it agreed to relax its immigration regulations in favour of Japanese entrants. In 1928 it made with the German Reich a treaty of navigation and commerce, which, among its other provisions, offered to Germany the most-favoured-nation treatment accorded to 'any other state'—a new form of words which included states members of the Commonwealth. This gave Germany a right to share all preferences which might in the future be granted to states within the British Commonwealth; and South Africa was as a result compelled to obtain release from the engagement before she could implement the Ottawa agreements. There remains one other instrument of significance for this inquiry—the Paris Peace Pact of 1928, to which, as has already been pointed out, the Dominions were distinct parties. The British government, in becoming a party to this pact, had made reservations specifying various areas which were indeed outside the juristic boundaries of the British Empire, but the integrity of which was judged a necessary part of the Empire's defence.[1] The South African parliament expressly safeguarded itself from any imputation that it was bound by these British reservations.

The substance of these various instruments was undoubtedly important; but it was a noteworthy feature of all of them that they did not impose upon South Africa 'active obligations'. None of them contained engagements which would necessitate discussion between the authorities responsible for the Union's external affairs and those responsible for its defence. With the exception of the Kellogg Pact, which because of its universality and its content of undefined morality possessed for many of its signatories no precise

Utopia, being feigned common wealthes, such as never was nor never shall be, vaine imaginations, Phantasies of philosophers to occupy the time and exercise their wittes; but so as Englande standeth and is governed at this day the xxviij of March *Anno* 1565, in the vij year of the raigne and administration thereof by the most vertuous and noble Queen Elizabeth, daughter of King Henrie the eight. . . .'

[1] Cmd. 3109 of 1928. Elliott, *The New British Empire*, p. 226, speaks of 'the roving Monroe Doctrine' of the British Empire.

significance, none of these instruments dealt with matters of 'general and political concern'. Was it possible to classify foreign affairs into two distinct branches, the first containing all matters of 'general and political concern', and the second all other matters? Was it further possible to restrict separate action to the second category only? The report of the 1930 Imperial Conference showed a tendency towards this principle, although it uttered no explicit affirmation of it. The Conference agreed it to be desirable that the second category of foreign affairs should be so far as possible defined, and that the definition should include 'such matters as, for example, the negotiation of commercial agreements affecting exclusively a dominion government and a foreign Power, complimentary messages, invitations to non-political conferences and requests for information of a technical or scientific character'. It was considered proper that in handling such matters dominion governments (where they did not possess ministers accredited to the heads of the foreign states with which they wished to deal) should make direct use of the appropriate British ambassador or minister, presumably without any obligation of consultation. In matters of general and political concern, however, dominion governments, even when they were compelled for reasons of urgency to communicate direct with a British ambassador or minister, should communicate simultaneously with the British government. The British representative, on his part, would, if practicable, await a telegram from His Majesty's government in the United Kingdom before taking any action. These recommendations, it is true, covered only one form of diplomatic activity; but they implied generally a certain amount of progress in defining, if only negatively, those matters which must fall within the sphere of common concern.[1]

Common concern, however, did not necessarily mean common responsibility. South Africa doubtless had been kept fully informed about the proposed British reservations to the Kellogg Pact; she would have been entitled to complain of a breach of the conventions agreed upon in 1923 and 1926 if she had not been kept informed. But the South African parliament expressly disclaimed responsibility for the policy contained in the reservations. Similarly, the Imperial Conference of 1926 recorded its unanimous approval of the Locarno treaty; but none of the approving Dominions undertook that definite adherence which alone, under article IX of the treaty, would place positive responsibility upon their shoulders. Perhaps the most far-reaching and the most impressive illustration of this divergence

[1] Cmd. 3717 of 1930, pp. 29–30.

between matters of common concern and matters of common responsibility is afforded by the subject of defence. Emphatically, defence was a matter of common concern, and successive imperial conferences agreed that it was so. The Imperial Conference of 1923 reported in considerable detail upon the subject. It declared that each part of the Commonwealth should be primarily responsible for its own defence, but it also asserted that adequate provision must be made for safeguarding the Empire as a sea-Commonwealth. It specified some of the areas where this provision was most essential, notably the central highway through the Mediterranean and the Red Sea. But it did not say whose responsibility it was to keep this highway open. Even when it affirmed the vital interest of Australia, New Zealand, and India in the establishment of a naval base at Singapore, it did not affirm or even suggest that these communities had any responsibility to share the burden of establishing or defending the base. Later imperial conferences probed no deeper into this issue. The assumption was that the people of Great Britain would continue to bear the burden of general maritime defence. Difference of function was here taken for granted.[1]

Amidst these imprecisions, the design of the Commonwealth's defence policy appeared to trace itself in widening circles. There was the inner circle of the home defence of each member; this circle was firmly marked; responsibility—although not an exclusive responsibility—was affirmed; it lay *primarily* upon the individual member. There was a wider circle which marked the special interests of special members—for example in Singapore; but special interest was not equated with special responsibility. Finally there was the outer circle of the common interest, such as the common interest in maintaining as a minimum standard of the Empire's maritime strength equality with the strongest foreign Power, and in providing for this purpose adequate naval bases and fuelling stations in order that the navy might be able to act wherever any part of the Empire was threatened. Here, as in general foreign affairs, the major responsibility was assumed to lie upon Great Britain. What the Dominions did accept was not responsibility, but co-operation of a kind which would enable them in varying degrees to assume responsibility if they should so choose. In air defence, for example, the Conference of 1923 laid down the principle of maximum uniformity in organization, training, and equipment, and the Conference of 1926 recommended the mutual exchange of air-force officers and units. This was essen-

[1] See particularly the 1923 and 1926 Conferences, Cmd. 1987, pp. 16–17, and Cmd. 2769, pp. 34–6.

tially the application to the junior service of the technique which had been elaborated in the Laurier–Haldane epoch, which has been surveyed in the first chapter of this book.[1] This technique had been vindicated during the Great War, and since then there had been no backsliding; on the contrary, co-operation had if anything become, through long practice, more effective.[2] But was the method which on the whole had been appropriate to the circumstances of 1911 equally appropriate to the circumstances of 1931? In two respects there had been some change in the situation. The Dominions had achieved equality of status, Great Britain had diminished in stature. This diminution was relative, not merely to the Dominions, but to foreign nations. Air power had immeasurably reduced Great Britain's domestic security, and the challenging naval power of other nations had diminished her ability to keep open the ways of the sea-Commonwealth. In the light of these facts it might in course of time appear that the system of common concern unsupported by common responsibility belonged, not to any eternal order of dominion self-government, but to a phase in which this order was still in process of outgrowing the old colonial immaturities; it might further appear that the persistence of this phase, with all its creative possibilities and achievement, had been conditioned by the commercial and maritime predominance which Great Britain had built up in the nineteenth century and which she was destined to lose, or share, in the twentieth.

Let us test these suppositions by considering one definite example —the position of the naval establishments at Halifax and Esquimalt in the Dominion of Canada. The Canadian government possesses complete control over these establishments; this is a natural application of the principle of Dominion self-government. But the Canadian government accords to the Admiralty such rights as are judged necessary for the efficiency of the Royal Navy in western Atlantic waters; this is a natural application of the principle affirmed by Canada, as by all other members of the imperial conference, that general naval defence is a matter of common concern, and that to ensure its efficient performance, bases and fuelling stations must be supplied. Here, then, are two practical deductions from two recognized principles. But are both deductions logically inevitable? And can it be taken for granted that they will not come into conflict? The Canadian doctrine of responsible government, applied to the

[1] See above, pp. 44–6.

[2] A fuller treatment will be found in *The British Empire: a report on its structure and problems by a study group of members of the Royal Institute of International Affairs.* (Oxford University Press, 1937), published simultaneously with this volume.

question of defence, maintains that the Canadian government and parliament will on each occasion decide whether or not Canada will be involved in war.[1] It is a doctrine of responsibility *ad hoc*, as opposed to a doctrine of responsibility assumed in advance or at long range. Such a doctrine is always popular with constitutional countries enjoying shelter; it has been persistently popular in Great Britain. It does not, however, belong to the essence of responsible government. Great Britain did not cease to be a constitutional democracy when her government, with the approval of her parliament, accepted the long-range obligations of Locarno; nor did France surrender her system of responsible government at the moment when she signed the pact of mutual assistance with Soviet Russia. The Canadian doctrine does not sum up the complete and irrefutable theory of responsible government, but is rather a special application of that theory made possible by the special circumstances of Canada. At the present period of her history there are combined in those circumstances a complete equality of national status and a degree of national security which is abnormal and highly enviable. It is at present unlikely that Canada will be involved in war to defend her territorial integrity or her most immediate vital interests.[2] At the same time she possesses the right to announce on each occasion whether or not she will consent to be involved in a war to defend the common interests of the Commonwealth. What does this right imply? In 1914 and 1924 it meant no more than a right of passive belligerency; in 1934 it could with some cogency be interpreted as a right to neutrality. Theoretically at any rate it would be possible for Canada to adopt—admittedly by stages of great difficulty—powers comparable with those embodied in the South African legislation of 1934; and thus to furnish herself with the means of withdrawing, by apparently constitutional processes, from a state of belligerency in which other members of the Commonwealth were involved. If, however, the opposite state to belligerency—the state of neutrality—were to be effectively asserted, the Canadian government would be compelled to refuse to the Royal Navy the services of Halifax and Esquimalt. Then at last there would be revealed a fundamental contradiction between the doctrine of separate responsibility and the doctrine of the common cause. The individual responsibility of Canada (but the phrase begins to sound ironical) would make it impossible for Great Britain to perform that very function which

[1] For the origins and development of this doctrine see above, pp. 37–8 and pp. 251–2.

[2] See H. F. Angus, 'Canada and Naval Rivalry in the Pacific' (in *Pacific Affairs*, June 1935).

Canada herself had joined in declaring to be a matter of common concern.[1]

At this conclusion to the argument the reader may perhaps remember Burke, and cry out against so much logic and so little sense. Perhaps he would do better to upbraid, not logic, but the lack of it. For surely there was an inner contradiction in a theory which—partly by statement and partly by implication—asserted both the common duty to provide, and the individual right to withhold, the naval facilities necessary to a Commonwealth which

[1] The constitutional position of Canada, Australia, and New Zealand with regard to naval defence is in general similar. All of them maintain naval forces of their own. The naval bases in their territory are completely in their control in every respect, and the Royal Navy has no rights or property in them. At the same time, the relations between the Royal Navy on the one hand and the dominion navies on the other are of the closest. Exchanges of ships and of personnel take place between them, and there are statutory provisions for placing units of them under a single command when in company with one another, and assimilating their disciplinary control. This, however, is by agreement *ad hoc*. Similarly, provided this close co-operation continued, the Royal Navy would be offered any dockyard facilities it needed in dominion naval bases, on suitable financial arrangements; but it could not claim them of right.

The position of the Irish Free State and of the Union of South Africa does not conform to that of the three Dominions mentioned above. The difference arises largely from the fact that neither of these Dominions possesses, or intends to possess, naval forces of its own. The position of the Irish Free State as a result of the Treaty and the currents of politics is discussed in the following chapter. The position of the Union is as follows. Up to 1921 the imperial government retained the property of the lands and buildings of the naval base of Simonstown, and also retained responsibility for their defence. By agreement in that year it transferred to the Union government the freehold of the lands and buildings, 'with a servitude registered against it in favour of the Admiralty as perpetual user for naval purposes'. This agreement was contained in an exchange of letters and subsequently was embodied in the Admiralty Lands Agreement of 23rd June 1930. Statutory provision for the taking over by the Union Government of War Department lands and buildings had been made in the Defence Endowment Property and Account Act, No. 33 of 1922. At the same time there was transferred to the Union government responsibility for the land-defence of the naval dockyard at Simonstown. The Union government gave an assurance that it would maintain the functions of Simonstown as a naval link in the sea communications of the British Empire, and that it would for this purpose consult with the Admiralty. Should the charges of maintaining an adequate state of defence be greater than those which the Union government would be prepared to pay from a domestic point of view, the imperial government would be ready to consider bearing part of them.

The position was thoroughly discussed in the debates on the Status of the Union Bill, and the correspondence of 1921 appears in Hansard. (See *House of Assembly Debates*, 22nd April 1934, cols. 2570 ff.) The spokesmen of the government made it clear that the new legislation in no way affected the position of the navy in South African waters, which was a fact 'like Table Mountain'. It may at first appear strange that a dominion which has gone farther than Canada in defining its sovereign international status should accept more precise obligations towards Great Britain. But the narrative has made it clear that the 'free hand' does not follow as a logical result from 'sovereign independence', but follows rather from the accident of geographical situation.

was linked by the sea? It might be that the contradiction was merely superficial and temporary, that the confusion was of the familiar kind through which free men and free nations must always struggle to reach a clear view of changed situations. Yet the confusion, while it lasted, could not fail to be embarrassing. Whereas the over-simplified logic of Edmund Burke's generation had produced, as its characteristic political vice, arrogance, the confused logic of the maturing twentieth century seemed likely to produce the hardly less dangerous vice of timidity. How was it possible for the statesmen of the British Commonwealth to pursue resolute policies unless they had some assurance that the doctrine of individual responsibility would not, in a time of danger, be invoked against the doctrine of common concern? They might indeed have disregarded these doctrinal contradictions if they had been able to believe that they sprang merely from incoherent thinking, which clearer reasoning would in time dispel. But they could not fail to be aware that the theoretical confusion had deeper roots in conflicting emotions and in opposed calculations of interest. Only in New Zealand was there an almost unchallenged alliance between sentiment, interest, and the doctrine of the common cause. In Australia the same alliance was predominant, but was challenged by sections of the labour party. In South Africa interest and sentiment were to some degree opposed; interest was affirming with increasing urgency the need of common action for defence, while sentiment still remained divided, the old fighting nationalism still spurning the appeasement offered by South Africa's mature national status within the refashioned British Commonwealth. In Canada, on the other hand, an overwhelming predominance of sentiment accepted with satisfaction the readjustments which had culminated in the Statute of Westminster; but sentiment and calculation alike urged a considerable section of the people to state at a minimum Canada's obligations to the Commonwealth. The 'common cause' appeared to all New Zealanders as a life-line; but to many Canadians it appeared as a lure enticing them from their regional security. Sentiment as well as calculation divided articulate students of foreign policy (and no doubt the inarticulate masses as well) into champions of 'regionalism' and advocates of 'co-operation'. No wonder, therefore, that there was confusion in the theoretical statement of obligation. The confusion sprang from a natural and deep-seated desire to make the best of two worlds.[1]

[1] There is ample documentation for this paragraph in the report of the Toronto Conference (Toynbee, *British Commonwealth Relations*), which is especially illuminating on the topic of 'regionalism' and on the complexities of Canadian public opinion. See

In an attempt to resolve all these ambiguities, a third world was called into existence. Everything was put upon the League of Nations. The separate lines of policy, which had no fixed point of convergence within the British Commonwealth itself, were produced beyond the bounds of the Commonwealth into the sphere of international action, converging at Geneva. His Majesty's six several governments might well despair of keeping their foreign policies in line if they had severally to double and twist after the perplexing chances of shifting diplomatic circumstance; but their separate decisions would surely become predictable and harmonious so soon as they were governed by a code. The Covenant of the League, liberally supplemented by pacts of peaceful intent, seemed to supply that code. In origin, the League was very far from being a merely British creation; but after the latter-day transformations of the British Commonwealth it seemed—while still serving its primary purpose—to satisfy that Commonwealth's particular needs. In principle, if not in detail, the League system seemed to provide in advance for the main contingencies of foreign policy. Individual responsibility within the British Commonwealth could not bring disharmony, so long as each national unit of the Commonwealth remained loyal to the identical obligations which each had assumed. The Covenant, supplemented by the Paris Peace Pact, appeared to lay even the bogy of neutrality.[1] The possibility of disharmony between policies aiming at the security of the Commonwealth as a whole, and policies aiming at the regional security of its most sheltered members, seemed to be dissipated by the magic of 'collective security'. The League appeared to offer a generous shelter which covered the whole Commonwealth and each of its associated nations. It offered also a rallying-point, not only for the Commonwealth's diverse interests, but for its diverse political idealisms. The ardent parochialists, who protested that their duty was to their own nation only, might perhaps be persuaded that the League, which existed for the sake of each separate member-nation, existed therefore for the sake of their nation. The ardent universalists, who admitted a duty to their neighbour but admitted it only on the heroic scale, without any inner intimate ring of neighbourhood, were willing to promise to the League what they would not promise to the Commonwealth. The ardent imperialists, who felt in their hearts that the nearer duty was

also *The Times*, 21st April 1936, for a letter by J. M. MacDonald dividing Canadian opinion on foreign policy into three groups of indeterminate size—'the 100 per cent. North Americans' (including most of the French and foreign elements), 'the imperialists', and the 'collectivists'.

[1] See Toynbee, *British Commonwealth Relations*, pp. 179 ff.

the one which mattered, realized with their heads that the larger obligation to the League could be made to include the more intimate obligation to the Commonwealth. In each of these groups there was insincerity. But in each of these groups there was also sincerity. There were men who held Dante's creed, at once intimately parochial and grandly universal. These men believed in the reciprocal value and necessity of communities which in themselves were wholes and which were also parts of larger wholes ascending hierarchically until they were completed in a universal unity.

So for a time it seemed that the diverse and sometimes discordant voices of the Commonwealth might be harmonized in a choir praising in one benedicite the Nations and the Commonwealth and the League. Prominent men assembled in unofficial conference at Toronto in 1933, and did homage to 'the ideals for which both the Commonwealth and the League of Nations stand'. The Commonwealth, they declared, was 'not a political but a moral entity'; it was 'a microcosm of the League and a valuable one'. The League, they said, was but 'the application on the international plane of the principles which our own experience and history have gradually evolved as the guiding lights of the Empire'. Both the Commonwealth and the League, they asserted, were 'great voluntary organisations for many purposes established with the same object, and indeed to a very large extent on the same principles and the same model'. The hymn of praise rolled on; now it was the League which was glorified, now it was the Commonwealth; at one time it was humanity, at another time it was the chosen British people. 'The Empire is significant', an Australian declared, 'because it shows not what Englishmen are but what human beings can be.'[1]

Yet there were still discords; nationalists fearful of being dragged from their shelter, and imperialists fearful of being committed beyond their interests and their strength,[2] refused to sing in tune. Was the League system, an Australian sceptic asked, an aspiration or a fact? If it was no more than an aspiration, the problems of the Commonwealth could not be solved by the interdependence of the Commonwealth and the League.[3]

In 1935 and 1936 events raised this question more insistently than it had ever been raised before. There will be set out below an abbreviated chronology of the Abyssinian crisis as it affected the

[1] Toynbee, op. cit., pp. 13, 40, 47, 53, 141.

[2] For a systematic exposition of this point of view see Hon. R. S. L. Amery, *The Forward View* (Bles, 1935).

[3] Toynbee, *British Commonwealth Relations*, p. 175.

policy and opinion of each Dominion and of India. The main phases of the crisis may first be recalled. Throughout the summer and early autumn of 1935 the League of Nations made feverish though belated attempts to resolve the crisis peacefully. In September 1935 His Majesty's government in the United Kingdom took the lead in insisting that it must be resolved in accordance with the League code. On the outbreak of war in October, the League declared Italy to be the aggressor and recommended the imposition of economic sanctions against her. The Italian government replied to these economic sanctions by counter-sanctions, and announced that it would reply by acts of war to any further sanctions which, in its opinion, had directly or indirectly the character of acts of war. In December the British Foreign Secretary and the French Prime Minister propounded a peace plan which offered to Italy direct possession of about one-third of Abyssinian territory and indirect control of another third. The Dominions were not consulted about this plan, but they were 'so far as possible kept informed'.[1] The plan was generally repudiated by public opinion in Great Britain, the Dominions, and the member-states of the League. The Foreign Secretary resigned. No new sanctions were imposed against Italy, the war continued, and in May the Emperor of Abyssinia fled from his capital which the Italians occupied. In June the British Foreign Secretary announced in the House of Commons that His Majesty's government had decided that there was no longer any utility in continuing sanctions against Italy. The Prime Minister said a few days later that the fullest possible information as to the views of the British government had been given to the dominion governments, which would themselves announce their decisions on the subject of sanctions to their own parliaments, or at Geneva.[2]

The abbreviated dominion chronicles will now be given.[3]

Australia

31st August 1935: The Federal cabinet declared that Australia would support Great Britain's policy to the fullest possible extent.

24th September 1935: In a debate in the House of Representatives the Prime Minister declared that Australia's policy was close co-operation with Great Britain in her efforts for a settlement of the dispute and in maintaining League principles. The deputy leader of the labour party urged withdrawal from the League and asked parliament to declare that it would not support sanctions or war.

[1] Hansard, *House of Commons Debates*, vol. cccvii, 18th December 1935, col. 1727.

[2] Ibid., vol. cccxiii, 18th June 1936, col. 1203.

[3] The references, except when otherwise stated, are to *The Times*, and the dates given are those of announcements in *The Times*.

27th September 1935: The New South Wales labour council decided, after a stormy debate, to support a policy of neutrality and to define defence as 'resistance to actual attack'.

17th October 1935: Australia accepted in principle the recommended sanctions.

19th October 1935: The leader of the Lang labour group declared that if Australia did not intend to fight for sanctions she should not undertake to enforce them.

2nd November 1935: A bill to impose sanctions was introduced. H.M.S. *Sydney* was placed at the disposal of the government of the United Kingdom and proceeded to Gibraltar.

4th November 1935: The Federal cabinet asked Mr. W. M. Hughes to resign on the ground that he had written in a recently published book, 'Sanctions are either an empty gesture or mean war'. (Despite this Mr. Hughes had declared himself whole-heartedly in support of the imposition of sanctions against Italy.)

29th November 1935: The All-Australia Trades Union congress protested against the imposition of sanctions by 78 votes to 41, but by a large majority defeated a proposal for a general strike in the event of war.

7th February 1936: Mr. Hughes rejoined the cabinet, after writing to the Prime Minister a letter in which he expressed a belief in such sanctions, other than military sanctions, as might tend to prevent or hamper aggression. He also affirmed his conviction that a strong British Empire was essential to the effective functioning of the League and to world peace.

Canada

11th September 1935: During election speeches Mr. Bennett (conservative) said that Canada would not be embroiled in any quarrel where the rights of Canadians were not involved, and Mr. Lapointe (liberal) declared that nothing at stake in Abyssinia was worth the sacrifice of a single Canadian life.

30th October 1935: The Prime Minister stated that the government had no doubt that it was expressing the overwhelming conviction of the people of Canada in declaring its continued and firm adherence to the fundamental aims and ideals of the League of Nations and its intention to make participation in the League the corner-stone of its foreign policy in the general field.[1]

1st November 1935: The government declared its intention of taking immediate steps to ensure the imposition of sanctions agreed upon by the League against Italy.

4th November 1935: The Canadian delegate to the committee of eighteen (Mr. W. A. Riddell) proposed that coal, oil, iron, and steel should be added to the list for embargo so soon as it appeared that the principle

[1] *J.P.E.*, vol. xvii, p. 268.

of embargo was being sufficiently accepted to make its application to these materials effective.

2nd December 1935: Mr. Lapointe (acting Prime Minister) stated in the Canadian House of Commons that the proposal to add oil to the list for embargo was not a Canadian proposal but was made by the Canadian delegate as a personal suggestion.

7th December 1935: Referring to the Hoare–Laval plan, the *Winnipeg Free Press* said: 'Somehow it is impossible to reconcile a stroke so brilliantly unscrupulous and so diabolically effective with plain-speech, honest-face Stanley Baldwin.'

19th June 1936: The Prime Minister (Mr. Mackenzie King) announced in the House of Commons that the government would support the raising of sanctions and instruct the delegates at Geneva accordingly.

India

30th July 1935: A huge gathering of Calcutta citizens condemned the attitude of Italy to Abyssinia and regretted the inability of 'imperialist powers' to keep the peace.

18th September 1935: Sir Philip Chetwode said in the Council of State, 'If we go to war, we wish to go with India behind us'.

2nd October 1935: Mr. Subdas G. Bose, President of the Congress Committee of Bengal, commented on this statement in a letter to the *Manchester Guardian*. He said that if India were to be behind Great Britain, Great Britain must first demonstrate her moral superiority over Italy by giving up bombing frontier peoples and by conceding a great (but not complicated) measure of self-government to India. Otherwise, if India were forced into a war against her will, 'non-violent non-co-operation would be the result'.

19th October 1935: Lord Zetland (Secretary of State for India) expressed the opinion that if war took place there would be time to consult Indian public opinion as to the part to be played by Indian troops . . . but so far as he could judge the whole sympathy of India was for Abyssinia.

21st May 1936: An Abyssinia day was observed in India as a condemnation of the Great Powers for their failure to assert the authority of the League and as an expression of sympathy with the Abyssinians.

Irish Free State

24th August 1935: Mr. De Valera, President of the Executive Council, announced that decisions of the Irish government on the Abyssinian question could be taken independently of Great Britain on each point, and would be determined by a desire to see the League function as an effective guarantee of peace.

17th September 1935: Speaking in the Assembly of the League, Mr. De Valera declared that the present crisis was a final test of the League. If the sovereignty of the weakest state were unjustly taken away, the foundation of the League would crumble into dust. It would then be far better for the old system of alliances to return. The Irish nation had of its own choice entered into the obligations of the Covenant and would fulfil them in the letter and in the spirit.

7th October 1935: Speaking at Ennis, Mr. De Valera opposed the suggestion that he should have bargained with the British government over the question of Irish support for the League. It was a question of duty, and one could not properly bargain about doing one's duty.

20th June 1936: In a debate in the Dáil, Mr. De Valera said that until recently he had agreed that the League's power of coercion should be intensified. He was now certain that if the League were to be reformed in such a manner that it could reinforce economic sanctions by military sanctions against an aggressor, the Free State would not fulfil its obligations.

New Zealand

23rd August 1935: The Prime Minister (Mr. Forbes), speaking in parliament, said that if Great Britain were involved in war New Zealand would be also. If war broke out parliament would be summoned.

20th September 1935: Mr. Forbes said that New Zealand would stand by her obligations under the Covenant. The testing time of the League had come.

17th October 1935: The New Zealand cruiser *Diomede* was detailed for special service under the Admiralty.

22nd October 1935: The Prime Minister, announcing in parliament that New Zealand had agreed to put into effect certain sanctions in accordance with the decision of the League of Nations, said that the leaders of the labour party had been called into conference by the cabinet and had given their approval of the decision.

7th March 1936: The Prime Minister expressed the opinion that there should be a conference of representatives of various parts of the British Commonwealth to determine a united course of action for future economic and defence policy.

4th July 1936: The New Zealand delegate speaking in the League Assembly said that New Zealand was in favour of maintaining sanctions but would abide by the decision of the Assembly.

South Africa

13th August 1935: General Smuts (deputy Prime Minister), speaking at Capetown, said that if the League failed, Europe would again be divided into hostile camps. A great conflict in Africa must raise anxious feelings between black and white races.

11th September 1935: The Prime Minister (General Hertzog) said that the League must do its duty. South Africa had in the past never been unduly concerned about invasion, and there had been a time when she was prepared to get rid of the British fleet. To-day the position was different; if South Africa forsook her friends and sent them away she must look after her own defences.

14th September 1935: The South African delegate in the League Assembly (Mr. te Water) said that South Africa was deeply moved by policies threatening a new partition of Africa, which was fraught with danger to the adventuring nations, to the black peoples of Africa, and to the white civilization, now after centuries of trial and sacrifice firmly and beneficently established in South Africa. If the crime of training the teeming black races of Africa for war were permitted, and if Europe used Africa for its own purposes, . . . the people of South Africa firmly believed that armed Africa, in its due and patient time, would arise and overthrow the white invader, and revert to the black barbarism which it had been their difficult task to penetrate and enlighten.

19th September 1935: Dr. Malan, leader of the opposition, stated that in his opinion South Africa should exercise her right of neutrality.

10th October 1935: The Union government instructed its delegate at the League to support whatever action was taken against Italy.

14th October 1935: Mr. te Water, in the committee of eighteen, proposed that the heads of diplomatic missions should be withdrawn from Italy.

25th October 1935: South Africa announced that she would put all the sanctions voted by the League into force against Italy, thus being the first state to have taken this decisive step.

30th October 1935: Dr. Malan said that his party stood behind the League but if membership were not to South Africa's advantage and threatened to draw her into war, she would withdraw. He believed that the British Empire was at the root of the Union's troubles and that the Empire connexion should be broken.

7th December 1935: A conference of chiefs, headmen, and teachers, natives of Natal and Zululand, passed a resolution expressing sympathy with Abyssinia, and another appealing to the Union government to hold its hand from abolishing the Cape native franchise. They felt that Great Britain, in coming forward to defend Abyssinia, had lived up to the traditions of the spacious days of Queen Victoria, and the Cape native franchise was a living symbol of those traditions.

19th December 1935: Opinion in South Africa, as shown in the press, &c., was opposed to Hoare–Laval proposals.

1st–3rd February 1936: Debate in the House of Assembly on Dr. Malan's motion asking the government to state its intention of avoiding any steps which might widen the scope of the dispute, and to affirm generally that with the exception of defending itself if attacked, South Africa would stand aloof from every war. In opposing the motion General Hertzog asserted the necessity of fulfilling South Africa's obligations to the League, whose action at this moment was a real defence of South African independence against a real menace to it. General Smuts affirmed the two cardinal points of South African foreign policy to be collaboration with the British Commonwealth and effective membership of the League. The motion was lost by 98 votes to 14.

27th April 1936: The Minister of Defence (Mr. Pirow), in announcing extensive new defence plans, said that, apart from any moral obligation to the League, South Africa was absolutely free to make her own decisions on all issues of peace and war. But this freedom did not mean that there would be no contact between South Africa and Great Britain in military matters.

17th June 1936: General Hertzog, addressing the House of Assembly, said that South Africa would not run away from her obligations under the Covenant whatever other nations might do.

2nd July 1936: The South African delegate at Geneva opposed the raising of sanctions.

Considered as a whole, this chronicle of the policy of the nations of the British Commonwealth in a decisive crisis demonstrates both the failure of the League, and the failure of the Commonwealth to resolve through the League its own problems. The chronicle contains material for many interesting analyses which readers may themselves pursue. A few points only will be raised here. It is first of all apparent that the harmonies acclaimed at Toronto in 1933 had been imagined rather than achieved. It had too frequently been assumed that an effective society of nations had already been established, or that it was on the eve of being established. The cost had not been counted. It had not been realized that in order to establish the rule of law the nations would have to pass through the phase of the hue-and-cry, which is a very dangerous phase unless the law-defying persons are without exception puny and timid wrong-doers. It was perhaps not impossible to turn the League from an aspiration to a fact; but to do so there must be some surrender of sovereignty, or at least the acceptance of unlimited liability for certain defined purposes. The Abyssinian crisis showed that the insistence on limited liability, which was one cause of uncertainty in the British Commonwealth, was at the root of the weakness of the League. The manifold blessings which the League seemed to offer could not be bought on the cheap. It now became apparent that a confused Commonwealth could not solve its problems by turning them over to a confused League.

It is, in the second place, interesting to note that—excepting perhaps in New Zealand—the same hesitations and divisions reproduced themselves in Great Britain and all the Dominions. Throughout the Commonwealth there raged the controversy which had disturbed the early Christian Church, as to whether force was, or was not, justifiable. The Church had in the end answered and closed this controversy by its doctrine of *bellum justum*. But the peoples of the British Commonwealth made no conscious decision; they failed to realize that in certain circumstances peace and justice become contradictories. Judged by their own standards, they drifted finally into a peace bought by the sacrifice of justice.

To correct the doctrinaire flavour of this summary judgement,[1] it is necessary to refer, in the third place, to the interests and emotions which lay behind the doctrinal disputations. In general it may be said that the crisis revealed nothing new. The various Dominions and the various political parties in them acted along the lines of the policies whose development has already been sketched in this chapter. Some readers may have been surprised by the Irish Free State chronicle Mr. De Valera was throughout conspicuous among the Commonwealth's statesmen for clarity and straightforwardness. The next chapter will perhaps show that his action was exactly in accord with the idea which he consistently held of the Free State's position and obligations. The other impressive chronicle is the South African one. It reveals acute anxiety about racial relationships throughout the whole African continent—an anxiety which a 'crown colony chronicle' for all Africa would have done much to justify.[2] It reveals also a preoccupation with the territorial security of South Africa, which was rapidly being forced from its accustomed shelter. In the hands of Mr. Pirow, the Union's department of defence had already during the past few years been taking a novel prominence before the South African public.[3] And effective defence necessitated active co-opera-

[1] The writer has dealt more fully with this theme in the *Contemporary Review*, May 1936.

[2] See, for example, a letter of Sir Hesketh Bell in *The Times*, 25th October 1935, drawing attention to outbursts of racial feeling in the West Indies and elsewhere. The African natives knew only that white men were killing black men with the object of taking their land. . . . It was of urgent importance that British subject-races should be thoroughly persuaded of the British Empire's complete dissociation from Italy's unjustifiable action. . . .

[3] For example:

May 1934: Mr. Pirow announced in the House of Assembly a five years' defence plan, which would achieve:

- (*a*) a total of 56,000 'reasonably' trained men and a national reserve of 100,000 riflemen, with stocks of arms and equipment;
- (*b*) coastal defence through harbour fortifications and a sufficiently large land force (with bombing aircraft and mobile batteries) to prevent landing at unfortified spots;
- (*c*) defence of the mercantile marine by aircraft squadrons. (*J.P.E.*, vol. xv, pp. 927 ff.)

November 1934: Mr. Pirow declared that South Africa's policy was to make her defences strong enough to beat off anything under large-scale naval attack. There would be air squadrons at all big ports; fixed defences would be modernized and have mobile batteries attached. The aim of South

tion with Great Britain. There was a shifting of South African emphasis. National independence, which had so long been assumed to be a problem of intra-Commonwealth relations, now began to reveal itself as a problem of international relations. This change had an immediate repercussion on intra-Commonwealth relations; it brought into the foreground the matters of common concern. In Mr. Pirow's mind these matters were primarily air services, military equipment, and improved facilties for the British navy in South African waters. The 'common concern' was becoming more precise and more tough. But what about the 'common cause'? In the oratory of imperial conferences and in the pious expositions of professors the common cause had been expounded in a loftier, if vaguer, manner. To the evangelists of the British Commonwealth of Nations, the ideal of 'the government of men by themselves' had, whether intentionally or not, implications of racial equality—developing slowly, it might well be, through 'trusteeship'—which found no echo in Mr. Pirow's speeches.[1] Was this symptomatic for the future?

African defence policy was the provision of land and air forces capable of dealing with trouble not only in the Union but as far north as the Limpopo. (*The Times*, 10th and 13th November 1934.)

May 1935: The Prime Minister, General Hertzog, in debate on the status of the Union legislation, said that the freedom of his people and country depended on the British navy, which meant exactly the same to South Africans as to Englishmen. (*The Times*, 15th May 1935.)

April 1936: Mr. Pirow declared in the House of Assembly that recent events on the African continent had called for the revision and extension of the defence plan put forward by him in May 1934. Among further measures proposed were:

1. the provision of a training scheme which in 5 years would produce 1,000 pilots and 3,000 mechanics;
2. formation of an anti-tank battalion capable of being transported 500 miles in 48 hours by non-fighting aircraft;
3. formation in 5 years out of civil aircraft of 12 squadrons of high-speed multi-engined bombers with 5 machines to each squadron.

He also said that coastal defence was still governed by the 1928 agreement with the committee of imperial defence. An extension of the programme in Capetown was under consideration. The Union's obligations with regard to the Simonstown base would be carried out in spirit and letter.

Freedom of choice in issues of peace and war was a cardinal point of the government's programme, but it did not mean that there would be no contact with Great Britain in military matters. (*The Times*, 28th April 1936, and *J.P.E.*, vol. xvii, p. 627.)

Mr. Pirow's pronouncements on the return of German colonies may be collated with these announcements on defence. In 1935 he declared himself generally in favour of this action: in 1936 he asserted that the Italian success in Abyssinia made the presence of Germany in Africa more than ever desirable. But he ruled out the handing back of German South-West Africa by the Union and the handing back of Tanganyika by Great Britain as contrary to South Africa's interests and quite inadmissible. (*The Times*, 15th and 17th July 1936.)

[1] A well-informed writer in the *Spectator*, 12th June 1936, seems to summarize

Would the vision of the good life fade in the struggle for mere life? Had the evangelical ardours of conference and lecture room signified no more than the lucky man's smugness, the millionaire's uplift? In short, would the Commonwealth, under external pressure, turn itself again into an Empire, shedding in the process those parts which found it safer to be out of the Empire than in it? It had been prophesied at Toronto in 1933 that the members of the Commonwealth, should the collective system break down, might find themselves at the mercy of their regional situations. If this should come to pass, the Abyssinian crisis might in the future be regarded as the first clear chart of the regional tides; they would sweep Australia, New Zealand, and South Africa closer to Great Britain; they would sweep Canada into the North American distance: whether they would sweep Great Britain and Ireland into conflict or partnership no man could prophesy.

But all this is speculation. In a world of many inventions, regional situations themselves were far from being static, and calculations of *raison d'état* based on an attempted realistic appreciation of them ran great risk of being proved short-sighted by events. A longer-sighted realism might well conclude that it would be dangerous to allow the immediate regional situations to dominate foreign politics. Enlightened self-interest might thus find itself in agreement with the emphatic belief, which on the whole predominated throughout the Commonwealth, that the Commonwealth relationship must in all circumstances be maintained. It might even find itself in accord with the desire to persist in the attempt—admittedly far more formidable than had been realized in the optimistic nineteen-twenties—to interpenetrate the Commonwealth-order with a world-order based upon similar principles.

It is not, however, the writer's intention to conclude this chapter with soothing phrases to comfort yearning perfectionists. On the evidence which has been presented, no positive summing-up of the chapter is possible. Once again it must be insisted that the perspective is too short. One cannot stand far enough away from this history. If it were possible to do so, what would be the verdict? Would it be the verdict which historians pass to-day on the Germany of the late fifteenth century? There one can see the political disintegration of a society—a misfortune for Germany and also for Europe,

fairly the spirit of Mr. Pirow's pronouncements on African native questions: 'He wants to garrison white civilization in the Union against the possibility of black attack.' Consideration of these questions is postponed to Volume II: neither praise nor criticism is implied at present.

as three generations of violent German protest against this distant past have made plain to the modern world. Some of the causes of Germany's disintegration—distracting national complications as in Bohemia and Hungary, a stagnation of population, an extreme decentralization—may seem to be operating in the British Commonwealth to-day. But the present writer would not be prepared to press an analogy which in so many other respects does not fit. Equally attractive as an analogy, but perhaps equally uncertain, is the whole tradition of English history—the priority of custom to command, the priority of society to politics, the pervasiveness of influence, the dislike of elaborate organization, the love of local life, the dangerous habit of waiting on the event, or, if a more reassuring phrase be preferred, 'the gift for being only just in time'.

It would be legitimate to use these two contrasting analogies as tentative clues, but they would lead to an investigation which would be much wider and more elusive than the constitutional and political themes which have been handled in this chapter. It would be necessary to inquire not merely whether there is a common cause, but whether there is a common way of life. And it would be necessary to search for the manifestations of this common way of life in other fields besides the political one.[1]

It would appear that the late Lord Balfour had it in mind to undertake such an inquiry. A few weeks before his death he wrote on a piece of paper the following headings:

> 'Whence comes the cohesion of the Brit. Emp.?
> 1. Patriotism. Loyalty. Custom.
> 2. Religion. Race. Pride in various manifestations. Habit. Language.
> *Mere* law is the weakest of all bonds.'[2]

Some of Lord Balfour's headings—loyalty and race, for example—lead into complicated matters, as the present volume shows. But Lord Balfour believed that the complicated matter was pervaded by a simplifying unity. The famous document of 1926 which is associated with his name attempted no analysis of this unity but emphasized its monarchical symbolism. The phrases in which the Balfour Report affirmed the significance of the Crown were reiterated at the Conferences of 1929 and 1930, and passed almost unchanged into the

[1] To Professor W. Y. Elliot's head of *idem sentire de republica* we might add, as another head, *manners*—in a broad sense of the word. The author should perhaps state here that in using the phrase 'common way of life', he does not intend anything so portentous as a 'civilization' peculiar to the British Commonwealth, since that obviously does not exist.

[2] See *The Times*, 14th December 1936; letter from Mrs. Blanche Dugdale.

preamble of the Statute of Westminster. That Statute was the culmination of a long period of legal restatement. The new statement lacked the unambiguous clarity of the old one. But it contained something more than 'mere law'. The 'established constitutional practice' which the Statute of Westminster affirmed belonged to the general categories enumerated by Lord Balfour, which suggest, perhaps rather too fervently and too indiscriminately, the psychological roots of the thing which students of British institutions call 'convention'.

In the crisis which ended with the abdication of King Edward VIII in December 1936 it was the 'established constitutional practice' which the Statute of Westminster recorded, rather than the 'mere law' which it enacted, that guided the action of Great Britain and the Dominions. Or perhaps it would be truer to say that Great Britain and the trans-oceanic Dominions, while abiding scrupulously by 'mere law', directed their legal action towards maintaining the convention set out in the preamble of the Statute—namely, that they were all equally concerned in the Crown as the symbol of their 'free association' in the Commonwealth of Nations. It would have been easy for them to act separately and discordantly. Some of them had refrained from adopting the Statute of Westminster; to others of them it applied; one of them had reiterated it by local legislation which underlined and expanded the national independence which it recognized. But all of them, with the exception of the Irish Free State, availed themselves of the constitutional practice which permitted the old imperial sovereignty to act as the obedient servant of dominion self-government. The crisis was swiftly resolved. Public opinion throughout the greater part of the Commonwealth, which had of late been shaken out of its old complacency, was now in the mood to comfort itself by contemplating this striking reaffirmation of the Commonwealth's monarchical symbolism.[1]

This symbolism was not, however, affirmed in the Irish Free State. The next chapter must follow Lord Balfour's clues of loyalty, religion, race, language, custom, and pride into an environment where their first impulse was one of separation rather than unity.

[1] The complicated legal aspects of this transaction are fully dealt with in the Supplementary Chapter, section 3, and the appendix to that chapter. For the special Irish significance of it see pp. 387–90 below.

CHAPTER VI

IRELAND UNAPPEASED

I

The Return of Mr. De Valera

'The Irish Free State is a coequal member of the Community of Nations forming the British Commonwealth of Nations.' This was the first article of the constitution which the second Dáil, sitting as a constituent assembly, adopted in 1922. Ten years later this principle of coequality, reaffirmed at the Conference of 1926 and thereafter worked out in detail, was the accepted foundation of the imperial constitution. Yet Ireland remained unappeased. In 1932 the constituencies of the Free State returned to power a party which professed a deep dissatisfaction with the country's existing status. Was this dissatisfaction beyond healing? Was the clash between Irish nationalism and the Commonwealth irreconcilable? Perhaps it is too early to answer. But it may be possible to find in a narrative of events the approach to an answer.

The men who took charge of the government of the Free State in 1932 were the same men who had repudiated the Free State in 1922. What were the grounds of their opposition in 1922? They then launched a twofold accusation against Griffith and Collins and their followers. These men, they said, had betrayed Irish right by surrendering the sovereign indivisible republic. And they had let themselves be paid in false coin. They had gulped a promise which would be proved a sham. Though they might flatter themselves that their mutilated Ireland would have the effective freedom which Canada enjoyed, events would reveal their blindness. Granted that dominion status in Canada had meant the end of British dominion, dominion status in Ireland would mean the perpetuation of it. . . . To the pro-treaty party, these accusations came as a challenge. They admitted that the treaty was a compromise. They maintained that it was a necessary compromise and on the whole a fair one. They accepted limitations. They recognized the Crown. They would bow to the decision of the six northern counties, whatever that decision might be. They were ready to lower their gaze to the ground at their feet, to bend their thought away from the perfect Irish state laid up in heaven to an imperfect Irish state which would be fashioned on Irish soil here and now. Instead of the flawless vision and the unending struggle, they offered to the Irish people a new fact, an organized self-governing state. This actual state, they insisted, would be an instrument in the hands of the Irish nation, it would work, it would be real: it would, moreover, be the new road, the only true road, towards the ideal.[1] Facing their enemies, Griffith and Collins accepted the appeal to facts. They died before facts had vindicated them. The Cosgrave government redeemed their pledges. It could not expect tolerance from Mr. De Valera and his followers; it had to face their armed opposition. In the face of this opposition, it set up the state.

This work of state-building had two aspects, one external, the other domestic. The external aspect has been dealt with in the preceding chapter; it was the vindication of article 1 of the constitution, the 'implementation of coequality'. Mr. De Valera himself was willing at last to confess that events under this head had refuted his accusations and prophesies.[2] The British did in fact keep faith. The Irish did in fact find in the community of the Commonwealth—and particularly among the South Africans and Canadians—a guarantee and a support of their expanding rights. They did from the very beginning possess the very powers which Canada possessed, and they advanced with Canada in every step which she took forward. The Irish Free State achieved an international personality. On this the Cosgrave government insisted with a strictness which the British government believed to be overstrained.[3] But the Cosgrave govern-

[1] The best expression of this view-point came from Deputy P. Beaslai on 3rd January 1922 (*Treaty Debates*, pp. 176 ff.). 'What we are asked is, to choose between this Treaty on the one hand and, on the other hand, bloodshed, political and social chaos, and the frustration of all our hopes of national regeneration. . . . The trouble is that many Irishmen, bred in this hateful atmosphere of foreign occupation and foreign ascendancy, have never visualized freedom. . . . They have not dreamed of the great work of national reconstruction, of healing the wounds, of substituting healthy natural food for poison. . . .'

[2] e.g. speech in the Senate 1st June 1932. *J.P.E.*, vol. xiii, p. 773: 'As a result of the 1926 and 1930 Imperial Conferences, said the President, he thought that the Twenty-six Counties . . . had practically got into the position—except only that instead of being a Republic it was a Monarchy—which he aimed at in 1921 for the whole of Ireland. He confessed that advances had been made which he did not believe would be made.'

[3] The British government did not oppose the assumption by the Free State of the right of legation, which Canada had been recognized as possessing since 1922. But it resisted the Irish contention that the fundamental basis of its relations with the Free State was to be found in international law, maintaining instead that a special law and procedure governed the relations of members of the Commonwealth *inter se* (see pp. 149–50 and 290–1 above). This theory developed gradually. In 1922, when the British government questioned the registration of the Treaty at Geneva, it did not in set terms deny that its basis was to be found in international law. It would seem in retrospect that it was no fixed or clearly thought out principle which prompted

ment insisted with equal strictness upon the obligations and the limitations which it considered to be binding upon the Free State as an international person. It felt itself engaged in honour to maintain with an equal firm consistency both the rights which the treaty guaranteed, and the limits which it imposed. This consistency was not only of the letter but of the spirit. To enlarge her rights, the Irish Free State had made the fullest use of the conventions of the Commonwealth's constitution, particularly of the imperial conference procedure and the accepted method of friendly consultation. Mr. Cosgrave's government believed that the Free State could not in fairness employ a contrary method to break through the limitations which had been accepted and which still survived. Not without an austere pride, the Cosgrave party took its stand upon the treaty. But their opponents remained dissatisfied. Accepting at last what the treaty had yielded, they still denounced it for what it had withheld.

In domestic affairs, as in its relations with fellow members of the Commonwealth and of the League, the Irish Free State under Mr. Cosgrave's guidance sought to demonstrate the capacity of Irishmen to pass the most stringent tests of political capacity and respectability. But what were those tests ? It counted for something that this new period of Irish history coincided with the effort of the community of western Europe to reorder its life in accordance with the guiding ideals of the nineteenth century, which had been challenged from one side by the German Empire and were now being challenged from another side by Bolshevism. There were in the western air sentiments of orthodoxy which it was unfashionable to question. The world had been made safe for democracy, which now might face with confidence its historic task of reconciling order and liberty. Nation and state were fused with each other, yet each national state was bound, sometimes legally and always morally, to respect those fragments of other communities which found themselves of necessity separated from their own brethren and compelled to share an alien life.[1] In economic affairs the old orthodoxies of the nineteenth century were predominant. After the swollen expenditure of the war, after the improvised state socialism, after the blockade, the cry now was for a return to 'normality'—for a paring of govern-

the objection to registration. Perhaps it was natural pride and inability so soon to make a great adjustment of thought. The *inter se* theory became explicit some time later, and was promoted enthusiastically as one way of maintaining diplomatic unity.

[1] Articles 86 and 91 of the Treaty of Versailles use the following precise phraseology: 'persons belonging to racial, religious, and linguistic minorities', and 'inhabitants of a country who differ from the majority in race, language, and religion'.

ment expenditure and a return to private enterprise and a reopening of the channels of trade.

These were the ends which the Cosgrave government pursued with a proud resolution. It was not enough for this government to create out of chaos an Irish state; the new state must prove itself under every head to be a model state. In face of armed resistance and the persistent disease of political assassination, it vindicated—when necessary with a scientific ruthlessness[1]—the Abraham Lincoln conception of democracy. It established the rule of law grounded on the principle of majority decision. At the same time it safeguarded by an exemplary impartiality and tolerance the rights of the law-abiding minority. Its budgets were models of careful prudence. It kept taxation low, and it directed the incidence of taxation upon those shoulders best able to bear it. Its tariff policy pleased the orthodox by limiting its aim to a gradual growth of Irish industry, which would not smooth the path for inefficiency, nor burden the consumer and the farmer.[2] It set under way with hitherto unprecedented efficiency and speed the last phase of land purchase, and at the same time it speeded up the war against the inefficiencies which too easily beset a peasant agriculture. It emphatically improved the quality standards in stock-raising. Its success in reorganizing the production of butter attracted Danish investigators to the study of Irish methods. Its faithful observance of economic law provoked the admiration of the professors. The practice of the Irish Free State demonstrated to perfection the principle of comparative costs: how sensible it was to import maize for stock feeding and to clear a handsome profit from the exported animal products! The channels of trade flowed full, and private enterprise flourished with a wealth-creating vigour which was stimulated, not trammelled, by watchful government departments.... In short, the new Irish state measured up to all the orthodoxies which were prevalent at the time of its foundation. Unfortunately for the founders, there arose before long throughout western society a widespread popular revolt against these orthodoxies.

[1] Cf. *Il Principe*, c. xvii: 'E intra tutti i principi, al principe nuovo è impossibile fuggire il nome di crudele, per essere gli stati nuovi pieni di pericoli.' In its use of punishment the Cosgrave government adopted on the whole the exact means necessary to its willed end of setting up the state, with the result that the effect was in the long run merciful.

[2] The general principle aimed at was a remission of taxation equivalent to the duty imposed, with a view to avoiding an extra cost to the community. About twenty manufacturing industries were assisted by tariffs: the principal ones were boots and shoes, wearing apparel, woollens, furniture, soap and candles, bottles, confectionery, bodies for lorries. The tariffs ranged from 15 per cent. on boots to 33⅓ per cent. on wooden furniture.

The Irish Free State under Mr. Cosgrave was the objective, the unemotional, scientific, intellectual state. Throughout Europe, and not least in Ireland, people were beginning to tire of this kind of state. They wanted more emotion and more drama. The political artists were pushing aside the political scientists. The party state was challenging the neutral state. In Ireland people were getting weary of their government's very virtues. They were tired of hearing Mr. Cosgrave called the just. It did Mr. Hogan no good to be labelled the best minister of agriculture in Europe. Besides, the achievements of the Cosgrave government were winning for it dangerous defenders. The bankers, the country gentlemen, the Protestants, the old unionists, spoke of it with grudging toleration, if not with approval. They almost forgave the green pillar-boxes and the Soldier's Song. The people no longer found these symbols thrilling. It became easier for the government's enemies to attack it as unnational. A growing section of the middle classes attacked it as unhelpful. Tariffs can be so scientific that they do not protect. A double drive to raise quality and keep down costs is not always the quickest way to win the hearts of farmers.[1] Had not the heirs of Arthur Griffith a quicker and more dramatic economic programme? Sinn Féin had promised a self-sufficing Ireland. There was no sign of its appearance. The Irish economy still rested on the export of cattle and the import of manufactures. There was a heavy import of wheat and maize as well. Why could not Ireland grow her own food for man and beast? There persisted in the popular mind a firm conviction that the decay of tillage was the cause of the depopulation of Ireland.[2] The Cosgrave government ignored this conviction. But there was a great future for any political leader who would raise the cry of 'Speed the Plough'. Farmers and townsmen alike were waiting for a leader who would bring them into the promised land of economic nationalism.

Mr. De Valera was plainly cast to be the chosen leader. But

[1] There was an Irish Farmers' Protectionist Union. Within the Farmers' Union itself there was a strong Protectionist faction, which felt the attraction of Fianna Fáil when the Union affirmed Free Trade (*Irish Times*, 26th March 1927). Protectionism seems to have been strongest in barley-growing areas.

[2] There is no real foundation for this belief. The percentage decline in rural population has been much the same in all the twenty-six counties since 1841, while the percentage declines in tillage and increases in cattle have differed widely. See a valuable paper by R. C. Geary, *The Future Population of Saorstát Éireann* (Statistical and Social Inquiry Society of Ireland, 29th November 1935), especially the table on p. 24. See also *Agricultural Statistics, 1847–1926* (published by the Department of Industry and Commerce, 1928), p. lx. The whole question is fully discussed below in section iii of this chapter.

Mr. De Valera seemed debarred by his past professions from seizing the opportunity. He had denounced the treaty as a surrender. Upon the treaty his opponents had built the Free State. He had denied the authority of the Free State. He had denounced its constitution as a usurpation. How then could he join the constitutional struggle? When he fought the election of 1923, he appealed for a popular verdict against the Free State. He could hardly appeal for a mandate to govern it. But the Free State would continue to be governed. This was the fact which the Cosgrave government had unshakably established. The only way to oust the Cosgrave government was to recognize what it had achieved. Only a constitutional party, accepting the authority of the Free State, could hope to direct that authority to other purposes. Under the pressure of these necessities Mr. De Valera's party narrowed and concentrated its attack. Its object became not the entire constitution but the oath, which excluded honest republicans from playing their full part in the constitutional struggle.[1] If the oath were removed, the State might become the possession of a united people instead of the monopoly of a party. The constitution itself seemed to offer a method by which the oath might be removed. Article 48 made provision for constitutional amendment by the processes of the initiative and referendum. It was only necessary to secure the signatures of seventy-five thousand voters in order to set the machinery in motion. In 1927 Mr. De Valera's new party, Fianna Fáil, initiated by this procedure an amendment to delete from the constitution article 17, which imposed the oath. The amendment, had it been carried by a referendum of the people, would in all probability have been declared unconstitutional in the courts; for the constitution act provided that the constitution must be construed with reference to the treaty within the limits of which amendment must also be confined. It was unlikely that the judges, who were sworn to defend the constitution, would agree with Mr. De Valera against both the British and the Irish government that the oath was not mandatory in the treaty.[2] The political danger, nevertheless,

[1] Mr. De Valera proposed to the Sinn Féin Convention of 9th March 1926 that republicans should promise to enter the Free State legislature if the oath was removed. He lost the motion, resigned his presidency of Sinn Féin, and thereupon organized the Fianna Fáil party. Mr. Patrick Belton anticipated the action of this party by entering the Dáil on 26th July 1926, having taken the oath.

[2] In 1927 Mr. De Valera published an opinion signed by three lawyers supporting his argument. But the argument received a very limited amount of approval, and Mr. De Valera soon dropped it in 1932. By then the Statute of Westminster had given stronger grounds for the removal of the oath.

was extreme. Mr. De Valera's attack in the constituencies coincided with the assassination of Kevin O'Higgins. All parties and sections disclaimed responsibility for the assassination. But the Cosgrave government decided to take resolute measures to broaden the basis of the state. It made up its mind to force Mr. De Valera's party to take its stand unequivocally on constitutional ground. It secured from the legislature, which still possessed constituent power,[1] the abrogation of article 48. This prevented the turmoil of republican assault upon the oath. The government then amended the electoral law by inserting a provision which demanded from each candidate a written engagement that he would, if elected, take the oath.[2] Mr. De Valera's party was now compelled to choose between a final renunciation of electoral propaganda and a definite acceptance of the existing constitutional procedure. It was a choice between futility and imperfection, between a political purity signifying impotence and a political activity admitting limitations. Mr. De Valera chose activity. By an apparently unequivocal act he at last accepted the Free State, oath and all. Yet the manner of the act implied a reservation. He took the oath as an 'empty formula'.[3]

How is this transaction to be interpreted ? To the uncompromising republicans the interpretation presented no difficulty. 'Recognition of the Free State—with or without an oath—is treason to the republic.'[4] Griffith was a traitor when he brought back the treaty of surrender. Collins was a traitor when he headed the provisional government. Cosgrave was a traitor when he set up a pretended constitution for the so-called Free State. De Valera was a traitor—so logic insisted against sympathy—when he entered the parliament of the Free State. Another comrade had fallen from the faith. . . . This the Fianna Fáil party stoutly denied. They were still republicans. But they admitted the logic of the stricken field. They had a duty to the Irish people. The people needed peace and unity. They could

[1] Under article 50; cf. pp. 161–2 above.

[2] Electoral (Amendment No. 2) Act, 1927.

[3] Briefly, the chronology is as follows:

June: Election which split the constitutional majority among five parties.
1st July: Removal of oath petition published with 75,000 signatures.
10th July: Assassination of Kevin O'Higgins.
20th July: Public Safety Bill introduced.
Bill to remove initiative from constitution.

The Electoral Amendment Act was also introduced in July. The Fianna Fáil party entered the Dáil on August 16th. Mr. Cosgrave dissolved before the end of the month and was returned in a stronger position in September. Both the big parties gained at the expense of the smaller ones.

[4] Pamphlet by Mary McSwiney, *The Republic of Ireland* (Cork, Lee Press Printing Works), p. 34.

win these blessings only on constitutional ground. The oath was a stumbling-block before conscience. Fianna Fáil took the oath so that it might achieve the removal of the oath. Thereafter constitutional action would be open to everybody. All the republican parties could then join with Fianna Fáil in securing from the people a mandate to use the legal processes of the Free State to re-make the constitution. . . . This, said Mr. Cosgrave's party, was not honest. If the oath was only an empty formula, why had Mr. De Valera refused to take it years before? Why had he denounced it for causing a schism in the nation? It was always in his power to end the schism by uttering the formula. In fact, allegiance existed independently of the oath. The Crown was in the constitution of the Free State. The Free State was a member of the British Commonwealth of Nations. These things were fundamental. Either one accepted the Free State, or one did not. If one did, one accepted also the agreement upon which the Free State was founded. That agreement left plenty of room for the enlargement of national rights, but it also determined the method of the enlargement; and the limitations which it imposed remained binding until by the accustomed method of adaptation they were transcended.

Which of these interpretations is to be selected? To accept any one of them would mean joining the prosecution or the defence. The historian who is not an Irishman will not, it is hoped, be blamed for evading this entanglement. Let the interpretation be sought, perhaps a little timidly, along another path. Let it be admitted that revolutions have a rhythm of their own. According to their various dispositions, men join revolutions and emerge from them at different stages. The rhythm of the Irish revolution was running down. Political reality was killing political romance. A new fact, the imperfect Irish state, was killing the old dream of establishing here and now the perfect Irish commonwealth. Collins and his friends had entered the world of fact before the end of 1921. In the next few years Cosgrave shaped the state. In 1927 De Valera crossed from the revolution to the state. But there was some hesitation and ambiguity in his crossing.[1] He left behind him in the world of revolutionary romance reproachful comrades. The stalwarts of the Irish Republican Army still proclaimed a mystical oneness between the Irish people and the undying republic of Ireland. On behalf of the republic, which was the only lawful allegiance, they claimed the right to shoot anybody exercising political authority either in the

[1] e.g. *Dáil Debates*, vol. xxviii, 14th March 1929, col. 1400: 'Those who continued on in that organization which we have left can claim exactly the same continuity that we claimed up to 1925.'

Free State or in Northern Ireland.[1] Their theory made the revolution perpetual. Mr. De Valera understood the futility and the savagery which this wild romanticism threatened. He was ready now to defend the principle that no other authority than the existing state had the right to use force and inflict death.[2] But at the same time he promised to alter the forms of the state so that they should no longer be a provocation to revolutionaries and a justification of their defiance. Was it possible to satisfy the republicans without attacking the foundations of the state? Was it possible to placate the revolutionaries and at the same time observe the treaty? At one moment Mr. De Valera suggested that he would merely take what the treaty in fact allowed: in the next breath he implied that the treaty could not bind the people of Ireland.[3] Like other chieftains, who in other countries of Europe were at this time fighting their way to power, he showed an ambiguous face. He had passed from revolution to the state: was he planning to use the state to reopen revolution? It is easy—our generation knows it well by experience—to work through a constitutional system towards the destruction of that system.[4]

Once again interpretation dissolves into uncertainties. Perhaps it is wiser not to attempt to wring too much from a commentary on words, but to return to a chronicle of events in the hope that they may reveal more clearly the answers to fundamental questions. The reaction which followed the assassination of Kevin O'Higgins gave to the Cosgrave government a new lease of power which ran out in 1932. All this time the Fianna Fáil propaganda was gaining ground. It 'lowered the hurdle' sufficiently to attract the main body of unappeased political nationalism without too greatly frightening ordinary people. It demanded a mandate to delete the oath from the constitution; but it promised that there would be no fundamental republican recasting of the constitution until the people had been again consulted. It attacked the treaty as a *Diktat*; but it announced no intention to repudiate the treaty. On the contrary, it argued that the existing agreements between Great Britain and the Irish Free State

[1] Cf. the present constitution of Oglaigh Na h-Éireann (Irish Republican Army). Its object is to uphold the sovereignty and unity of the republic of Ireland: its method is primarily 'force of arms': it is ready to 'delegate' its power to a *de facto* civil republican government if one should be set up.

[2] e.g. his speech in the Dáil 15th October 1931, and his speech at the Wolf Tone demonstration of 1931, quoted in *Round Table*, vol. xx, p. 145; also the official party programme of October 1932, cf. *Round Table*, vol. xxii, p. 372.

[3] Cf. p. 336, below.

[4] See Warner Moss, *Political Parties in the Irish Free State* (Columbia University Press, 1933), p. 29, for some contradictory statements on this issue of constitutional observance.

enabled the latter legally to seize more advantages than the Cosgrave government had claimed. Most welcome of all to the farmers was the news that the land annuities were not due to Great Britain, and that a Fianna Fáil government would not pay them. The political programme expanded into a campaign all along the line for a robust economic nationalism. Protection for manufacturers, protection for tillage, would make a prosperous, busy, lightly-taxed, self-sufficing, independent Ireland. This was the core of the programme.[1]

The Cosgrave government could offer nothing of comparable appeal. It was very gravely preoccupied with the fundamental task of protecting public order, threatened in its latter years by a serious recrudescence of revolutionary activity. Its efforts to protect the state culminated in the military tribunal legislation of 1932, which by constitutional amendment inserted Article 2A into the constitution—a long chapter of precautions and penalties overriding the fundamental individual rights which the original constitution guaranteed. Was this, demanded Fianna Fáil, the Cosgrave party's much vaunted respect for law and liberty?[2] Surely there must be another road to peace. There was, moreover, the world depression. Mr. Cosgrave sought escape from it by the old paths. On the eve of the elections of March 1932, he made a sharp untimely gesture of orthodoxy by announcing a reduction in the salaries of teachers and civic guards. It was magnificent, but it was not politics. The electors rejected the leader who for ten years had controlled the state. Yet they were still hesitant. They gave Mr. De Valera a majority which depended on Labour support.[3]

[1] As set out by the Ard Fheis of Fianna Fáil, October 1931.

[2] The underlying point, that a constitution meant to be rigid had become extremely flexible, and that the intended limitation by fundamental law of a non-sovereign legislature had never come into operation, is dealt with below.

[3] The position before the elections was:

Government parties		*Opposition parties*	
Cumann na nGaedheal	65	Fianna Fáil	56
Independents	11	Labour	10
Farmers	6	Independent Republican	1
Independent Labour	2		
National League	1		
	85		67

The following were the results of the elections:

Government parties		*Opposition parties*	
Cumann na nGaedheal	56	Fianna Fáil	72
Independents	13	Labour	7
Farmers	4		
	73		79

For continuation of note 3 *see next page.*

II

The Dispute

In 1932, when Mr. De Valera assumed power, the legal possibilities of the situation were considerably larger than they had been in 1927, when he took the oath as an empty formula. They had been enlarged by the Statute of Westminster. But to what extent had they been enlarged? As to this, there was sharp difference of opinion.

When the Statute of Westminster was debated in the House of Commons, the right-wing conservatives wished to amend it so as to exclude any authority in the legislature of the Irish Free State to repeal, amend, or alter the Irish Free State Agreement Act, or the Irish Free State Constitution Act, or so much of the Government of Ireland Act as continued to be in force in Northern Ireland. To this amendment Mr. Winston Churchill gave powerful support. He announced that he had been advised on high technical authority that the bill would confer upon the Irish Free State full legal power to abolish the treaty, at any time when the Irish legislature might see fit to do so. If the imperial parliament passed the bill which was before it without inserting into it the proposed amendment, it would be leaving itself without legal protection against the bad faith and the ill will of some future Irish government. The most learned of imperial constitutional authorities disagreed with Mr. Churchill. It was true, Professor Keith wrote, that the Irish legislature would have power under the Statute of Westminster to repeal the treaty and the constitution *qua* British statutes. But the treaty was embedded in the constitution of Ireland and given the authority of fundamental law. Irish lawyers, who had consistently argued that the constitution derived from the sovereign Irish people, could hardly accept British legislation as annihilating the limitations which the constitution imposed.

Note 3 continued.

The elections of the following year (January 1933) gave the following results:

Government parties (Supporters of Mr. De Valera)		*Opposition parties*	
Fianna Fáil	77	Cumann na nGaedheal	48
Labour	8	Independents	8
		Independent Labour	1
		Centre Party	11
	85		68

There is an excellent table giving results for all parties (abstentionist as well as constitutional) from 1923 to 1933 in Moss, op. cit., p. 23.

> 'The Parliament of the Irish Free State was deliberately created by the Constituent Assembly as a body of limited powers. . . . The judges of the High Court and of the Supreme Court are subject to the Constitution (Article 69) and they are sworn to uphold the Constitution.'

But this was not all. The treaty had validity apart from the fact that it was embedded in the fundamental law of the Irish Free State. It had the legal character of a signed agreement which had been ratified by the legislatures of the two countries. There was, it must be admitted, a difference of opinion as to the exact legal status of the agreement. The Cosgrave government had never varied from their position that it was a treaty in international law. The British government had sought persistently to deny or evade this contention. 'But', said Professor Keith, 'the British government in 1921 and ever since has regarded it as at least an inter-imperial compact binding on both sides, and this obligation ought to be described as legal.' He carried the argument still further. It did not belong to legislatures to conclude and terminate international agreements. Even if there should be no restriction upon the legislative power of the parliament of the Irish Free State, this would not mean that an act of the legislature could remove a legal obligation binding the state externally. At most, the legislature could force the government to commit a breach of the law.[1]

The President of the Executive Council of the Irish Free State made a prompt and practical contribution to the discussion. On 21st November 1931 Mr. Cosgrave addressed a letter to Mr. Ramsay MacDonald which was decisive in causing the defeat of the proposed amendment to the Statute of Westminster. '. . . We have reiterated time and again', declared Mr. Cosgrave, 'that the Treaty is an agreement which can only be altered by consent.'

Despite this declaration, the precise effect of the Statute of Westminster upon the treaty remained for some years a matter of controversy. The British government was justified in accepting Mr. Cosgrave's letter as an affirmation, in the name of the Irish Free State, of the binding character of the treaty. But in what sense was it binding? And what was the precise content of the obligation which it imposed on the Irish Free State? Here there was room for differences of opinion. With regard to the first question, it has been already shown that the British government had been unwilling to

[1] *Journal of Comparative Legislation*, 3rd series, vol. xiv, p. 107, cf. p. 256, and Keith, *Letters on Imperial Relations*, No. 75. Cf. R. Gallopin, *Le Conflit anglo-irlandais* (Paris, 1935). The most relevant passages from the debates on the Statute of Westminster can be consulted conveniently in Keith, *Speeches and Documents of the British Dominions*. See ibid. p. 302 for Mr. Cosgrave's letter.

accept the contention propounded from the beginning by the Free State government, that the treaty was in the strictest sense an engagement in international law. Even if that contention were now accepted, there still remained a second cause of ambiguity, namely, the doubt whether 'international law' was, in the strict sense of the word, law. This doubt was widely prevalent among English lawyers, many of whom had absorbed Austin's teaching that there was no 'positive international law' but only 'positive international morality'. In accordance with this teaching, government spokesmen in the debates on the Statute of Westminster thought it sufficient to emphasize the *morally* binding character of the treaty. But did this affirmation define with sufficient precision the character of the treaty obligation? With regard to the content of the obligation, the British interpretation was certainly not imprecise; on the contrary, it showed in succeeding years a marked tendency to rigidity. It maintained, in effect, that the Irish Free State was debarred from the enlargements of dominion status achieved since 1922 whenever the limitations which existed at that date were written into the treaty. For example, the British government maintained that the Irish Free State had no power to abolish the appeal to the Privy Council, although the Free State government believed that it possessed this right, even prior to the passing of the Statute of Westminster.[1] It was finally decided by the Judicial Committee of the Privy Council in 1935 that the Statute of Westminster had conferred the right.[2] After this decision, it was clear that many of the British protests against many measures of Mr. De Valera's government had possessed no sure foundation in English law.

Since it was the Cosgrave government which had given the pledge of 21st November 1931, it will be as well to state the views of this government as to the meaning of the pledge. These views, so far as the present writer is capable of interpreting them, can be found both in the record of the Cosgrave party when it was in power, and in the arguments which it advanced after it had passed into opposition. They were maintained with a notable consistency. First, they started from the postulate of Irish lawyers that the treaty did not, in the Irish Free State, derive from an act of the British parliament. Doubtless they recognized that legislation inconsistent with the Colonial Laws

[1] It was reported in the *Manchester Guardian* of 31st January 1930 that Mr. McGilligan was contemplating legislation to abolish appeals. The question is summarized at length in the note on p. 370 below. Long before the 1935 decision of the Judicial Committee Professor Keith argued that the Statute of Westminster empowered the Free State to abolish appeals. *Journal of Comparative Legislation*, 3rd series, vol. xiv, p. 108.

[2] See below, p. 372.

Validity Act might be regarded by British judges as not forming part of the legislation of the Irish Free State. The Colonial Laws Validity Act was 'the sword of contingent validity' which might be wielded against Irish Free State legislation—but only by British courts and only within the scope of their judicial sway. That sword the Statute of Westminster struck from the hands of British judges. It no longer left it possible for them to pronounce legislation of the Irish Free State invalid. But, in this context, it did only that. The treaty was still there. It might be carried out in the spirit and in the letter; it might be modified slightly or radically by the contracting parties; it might be broken by one of the contracting parties. All that was accomplished by the part of the Statute of Westminster which referred to the Colonial Laws Validity Act was this: that, if a breach did occur, British judges could no longer rule the breach by the application of the Colonial Laws Validity Act, and pronounce invalid any results of the breach in so far as they flowed over inside the jurisdiction of the English courts.

The Statute of Westminster did, however, touch the treaty in another way. It affected status. The treaty worked in the main through status; it assured to the Irish Free State the same status as the Dominion of Canada. But the treaty operated also by way of definite and distinct stipulations. Sometimes a stipulation might be so closely connected with status as to leave it uncertain whether the stipulation was, so to speak, a demonstration, not meant to be complete and exhaustive, of status, or whether it was a limitation imposed and accepted in disregard of, or in defect of, status. At other times a stipulation was obviously unconnected with status. The harbour and other defence provisions contained in the treaty were precise stipulations whether they were in accord with status or not. The liability for the public debt was also precisely stipulated. Allegiance, on the other hand—using the word loosely—was bound up with status. In so far as anything in the treaty—or, via the treaty, in the constitution—derived from status, it was open to a Saorstát government to make revision in accordance with the new position. It was not limited by the previous content of the word Dominion. The Saorstát possessed the same status as the Dominion of Canada, whatever the content of that status might be. The boundaries, however they might be drawn in detail, were declared in 1926 to be proper to 'autonomous communities . . . equal in status, in no way subordinate to each other . . . and freely associated as members of the British Commonwealth of Nations'. By the same declaration, the Dominions were 'within' the Commonwealth, and 'united by common allegiance'. The status of autonomy and equality had not swallowed up allegiance. But, unless there was a breach of allegiance, or unless there was a departure from some precise stipulation, there could not be said to be any breach of the treaty. Moreover—to return to the first point—if a breach should occur, it would be no longer open to any British court to say where and what the breach was, or to order it to be repaired, or to pronounce the Saorstát as persisting in constitutional illegality.

The legal position taken up by the Cosgrave party would appear to fit very well with the legal position as clarified by the decision of the Judicial Committee in 1935. But it must be remembered that the controversy between the Irish Free State government and the British government was conducted for three years in a legal fog. It must also be remembered that legalistic difference was not the root cause of the controversy. It was rooted in nationalist opposition. Mr. De Valera was attacking a position which the British government was trying to hold. The fog which impeded the defence was favourable to the assault.

Mr. De Valera's return to power signalled an immediate stir in the camp of Irish nationalism. The government at once released the imprisoned republicans. It suspended the activity of the military tribunal. It took a part in republican celebrations and parades. But there was moderation in its fervour. It would remove the oath; thereafter it would demand the obedience of republicans to the Free State. Thereafter it would vindicate the principle: 'One government and one army.' The leaders of the I.R.A., and civilian chieftains like Miss Mary McSwiney, were not so easily wheedled. Oath or no oath, the Free State remained in their eyes what it had always been, a usurping authority. Their intransigeance made it all the more necessary to win the rank and file and to impress upon the masses that the change of government signified a new thrust for Irish freedom. The political atmospherics of Ireland showed all those signs of electrical disturbance—soon to become so familiar in Europe—which prelude the unilateral action of unappeased nationalism. In a series of public pronouncements Mr. De Valera let the people know that he intended to assert Irish rights without asking leave of Great Britain He intended first of all to remove the oath from the constitution and to cut off the payment of land annuities.[1]

British statesmen began to reply to these pronouncements. They began to warn and to lecture. Mr. De Valera neither flinched nor

[1] See *The Observer*, 21st February 1932; *Manchester Guardian*, 16th March 1932; *New York Times*, 18th March 1932.

blushed. At last, on the 22nd March, the Secretary of State for the Dominions elicited from the High Commissioner of the Irish Free State a statement of his government's position with regard to the oath.[1] The statement opened with the legal proposition that the oath was not mandatory in the treaty. But it continued in a series of affirmations which led progressively further from purely legal argument. The constitution was the people's constitution and the people had an absolute right to modify it as they chose. The people had now spoken. They regarded the oath as a relic of medievalism and an intolerable burden. It had been the fundamental cause of all the civil dissension in Ireland and it made impossible friendly relations with Great Britain. It was a conscience test unparalleled in treaty relationships between states. It was a test imposed from outside under threat of immediate and terrible war. The argument which had opened with a legalistic contention with regard to the interpretation of the treaty had by now swept into a vehement attack upon the treaty itself. Mr. De Valera was now on the ground of indefeasible national right. He was challenging the *Diktat*. He was once again the anti-treaty chieftain of 1922. What did this mean? It meant a break from the policy of fulfilment. It implied a breach in the continuity of self-definition which had guided the Irish Free State from the time of its foundation until that moment. Yet Mr. De Valera was speaking as Minister of External Affairs in the Irish Free State. He was speaking through the established diplomatic representative of the Free State in London. He was President of the Executive Council of the Irish Free State. He held power by the same title which had justified Mr. Cosgrave's power. This title he was ready to invoke against the irreconcilable revolutionaries. There was, therefore, in his position and policy a continuity with the immediate past, as well as a breach of continuity. Which would count the more?

As soon as Mr. J. H. Thomas had received the statement from the High Commissioner of the Irish Free State, he informed the House of Commons of its substance. He denied the legal argument that the oath was not mandatory in the treaty. He denied the much more alarming contention that an election and a change of government could wipe out an agreement hitherto regarded as binding. 'I do not know any party in the House', he said, 'that has ever subscribed to

[1] *Papers relating to the Parliamentary Oath of Allegiance in the Irish Free State and the Land Purchase Annuities*, Cmd. 4056 of 1932. The Irish White Paper (P. No. 650) gives, in addition, a note from Mr. Dulanty confirming the points of his statement in a rather fuller form than that given to it by the British summary.

the policy that a bargain or treaty between two sides could with impunity be repudiated by one.' The historian must distinguish between the directly relevant and the possibly irrelevant implications of this general statement. As there were legitimate differences of opinion about the meaning of the treaty and the Statute of Westminster, the statement was not necessarily relevant to all the actions of which the British government complained. It was, however, relevant to the immediate political situation which the British government had to face; for the Irish Free State government, in its statement of 22nd March, had in the most sweeping and emphatic manner denied the doctrine pronounced in November 1931 by Mr. Cosgrave on behalf of the state—'that the Treaty is an agreement which can only be altered by consent'. Mr. Thomas applied the principle of change by mutual consent to the annuities dispute no less than to the dispute about the oath. So far, the Irish government had made no official communication about the annuities. A question from the British government gave Mr. De Valera an occasion for stating his intention. From then onwards the two disputes ran parallel, with the annuities question gradually taking the first place. It will, however, be convenient to deal with these issues separately, and in the order of their emergence into official controversy.

Mr. De Valera replied on the 5th April to Mr. Thomas's dispatch of the 23rd March. In his reply he made no attempt at all to defend the legal argument which he had originally advanced.

> 'Whether the Oath was or was not "an integral part of the Treaty made ten years ago" [he now declared] is not now the issue. The real issue is that the Oath is an intolerable burden to the people of this State and they have declared in the most formal manner that they desire its removal.'

This was sufficiently clear. Treaty obligation, if it existed, must give way to *vox populi*. *Vox populi* swelled angrily in Mr. De Valera's dispatch. The observance of the treaty imposed no equality of sacrifice on Great Britain and Ireland. Great Britain had forced the treaty on Ireland. It had cost the British nothing. It had enhanced their prestige throughout the world. For Ireland it had meant the perpetuation of British domination. It had meant the outrage of partition. Even in the area of the Free State, it permitted the British to keep maintenance parties in some of the principal ports. It allowed them to claim in time of war or strained relations rights which, 'if granted', would make a mockery of Ireland's right to neutrality. . . . Sentence after sentence of this dispatch virtually denounced the treaty. But the denunciation never made itself explicit. Instead of a plain declaration, there came always a new burst of indignation.

> 'To England [repeated Mr. De Valera] this agreement gave peace and prestige. In Ireland it raised brother's hand against brother, gave us ten years of blood and tears, and besmirched the name of Ireland wherever a foul propaganda has been able to misrepresent us.'

Mr. De Valera was infusing into his diplomatic communications the emotional vehemence which had for years been let loose in the Irish party struggle.

The controversy was becoming totalitarian. Mr. J. H. Thomas replied that it was now apparent that the oath and the annuities questions were merely a part of a far wider issue, which was nothing less than a repudiation of the settlement of 1921 as a whole. It was not merely a question where lawyers might dispute and quibble over legal points. It was an announcement by one party of its absolute right to free itself of an engagement binding upon two parties.[1]

Yet again one is compelled to ask whether Mr. De Valera's words had to be given a very precise meaning. They read like a rousing appeal to Irish national feeling rather than a communication to the British government. They may perhaps have accurately expressed his ultimate intentions, but they went far beyond his immediate programme. To remove the oath from the constitution did not necessitate such a widely ranging argument. Mr. De Valera himself was content to employ in the Free State parliament arguments which were more moderate and more strictly relevant. The purpose of the bill which he introduced into the Dáil on the 21st April was twofold: first to remove the oath, and secondly to expunge from the Constitution Act and from the constitution itself the provisions which made the treaty fundamental in Irish municipal law. Mr. De Valera argued that these provisions were an abnormality and an unnecessary abnormality: his bill therefore did not conflict with the treaty, but merely put the treaty in its proper place.[2] As for the removal

[1] Cmd. 4056, p. 6. In the same month (April) the Prime Ministers of Australia, New Zealand, and South Africa appealed to the President of the Executive Council of the Irish Free State to observe the conventions which generally regulated the conduct of Commonwealth members in their relations with one another. Mr. De Valera rebuffed these approaches. General Hertzog, replying, disclaimed any intention to express an opinion on the merits of the dispute. He said that he hoped merely 'to promote the chances of a satisfactory solution of the dispute, a matter of interest to all of us'. It is interesting to note that the labour party in New South Wales cabled to Mr. De Valera and Mr. Ramsay MacDonald a message of sympathy with the Irish people in its 'fight for self-determination'. For these interchanges see *The Times*, 2nd, 4th, 5th, and 9th April 1932.

[2] There is, of course, nothing 'improper' about making treaties, already binding

of the oath, a fair interpretation of the status of equality which the Free State had achieved could not deny this right to the legislature. For the treaty secured to the Free State the rights which the other Dominions possessed, and these rights had expanded to a point where they could abolish their parliamentary oaths if they chose to do so. In all this there was none of the emotional defiance which had been the mark of Mr. De Valera's communications to the British government; he was now speaking the language of reasoned political discussion and legal argument. His legalism, indeed, refined itself almost excessively. He had to meet the argument that in repealing section 2 of the Constitution Act he was violating the treaty as a whole, because in this section the legislative ratification of the treaty was contained. He countered by the argument that the only legislative ratification which the treaty enjoined was that of the British parliament. A French writer who is not indisposed to give some weight to this contention nevertheless says of it 'il ne manque pas d'un certain cynisme . . .'.[1]

It is now quite clear—although it was by no means agreed at the time—that Mr. De Valera had in strict law a very strong case for his Removal of Oath Bill. If it be granted that the oath and allegiance are not so bound together that the refusal of the one is destructive of the other, and if the oath is regarded not as a stipulation but as resting upon status, it is easy to justify its removal.[2] In any case, British courts had no power to declare its removal invalid. But it must be remembered that the legal position had not yet been cleared up by judicial decision. The British government discovered only in 1935 that some of the legal arguments which it had used confidently had no validity. It therefore continued for some time to fire bad ammunition in the legalistic conflict.[3] The opposition

internationally, part also of municipal law. The American constitution enjoins this, as Mr. De Valera's critics pointed out.

[1] See *Dáil Debates*, especially 27th April 1932 and 19th May 1932. And Gallopin, *Le Conflit anglo-irlandais*, pp. 87 and 88. Gallopin maintains that ratification by usage may remain undisturbed despite the disappearance of formal ratification.

[2] Professor Keith came round to this point of view. The treaty secured to the Irish Free State equal rights with Canada: Canada, indeed, could not by straight legislative act abolish the parliamentary oath, though she could set in motion the necessary imperial legislation. South Africa could abolish it by an act. *Journal of Comparative Legislation*, 3rd series, vol. xiv, pp. 254–6, vol. xv, p. 263, and *Manchester Guardian*, 14th June 1932. For the argument about 'status' and 'stipulation' see above, p. 333. In Ireland, however, the bill was attacked on the ground that it was inconsistent with the constitution as 'the fundamental law' of the state. A few years later the High Court opened a similar argument in the Ryan case.

[3] Thus Mr. Thomas (Hansard, *House of Commons Debates*, vol. cclxxxi, 14th November 1933, col. 726) and Lord Hailsham (Hansard, *House of Lords Debates*, vol.

in Dáil Éireann attacked the Removal of Oath Bill from stronger ground. It did, indeed, traverse the legality of the bill in substance; but it concentrated its attack upon the procedure. After the Irish Free State had achieved so much by observing the convention of consultation, it was ungracious and unwise to snatch at more by a violation of that convention. What was thus seized would not be securely held. A purely legalistic action of a unilateral character would cause dissension in Ireland and dissension between Ireland and Great Britain. The articles of agreement had expanded into a code of constitutional association; by tearing up this code the Irish Free State endangered its own title-deeds. Senator Douglas argued that the obligation to consult on all matters of common concern remained the one fundamental bond between the members of the Commonwealth, a bond which in no way restricted the freedom or offended the dignity of any member. Both houses of the legislature, he said, would have been willing to pass resolutions against the oath in order to give the government authority to secure its removal by agreement. Why had the government chosen to act with such unnecessary brusqueness? It was this line of thought which determined the Senate's amendment to the bill. It added a clause providing that the abolition of the oath should not take effect until an agreement had been reached with Great Britain, and until the Dáil had ratified this agreement. It also deleted clauses 2 and 3 of the bill, which removed the treaty from its place of supremacy in the constitutional law of the Irish Free State. This action blocked for a time the road which the Fianna Fáil government had determined to follow. It was only after the dissolution of January 1933 and the return of the government to power that the unamended bill became law by vote of the Dáil alone.[1] This vote at last cleared the way for whatever constitutional refashioning of the Free State Mr. De Valera planned to achieve. An account of his plans and achievement under this head will be attempted later on.

It will be convenient now to take up the narrative of the land

xc, 6th December 1933, col. 335) challenged three constitutional amendments (Amendments Nos. 20, 21, 22) introduced by the Free State government in 1933—one conferring on the Executive Council the power, hitherto vested in the Crown under Article 37, of formally recommending appropriation; the second deleting article 41 (withholding of assent and reservation); the third terminating the right of appeal to the Privy Council. All these amendments were at once judged by Professor Keith to be definitely within the powers of the Free State. *Journal of Comparative Legislation*, 3rd series, vol. xvi, p. 138.

[1] According to the deadlock provisions of Article 38A of the constitution. For a fuller summary of the debates on the bill see Kohn, *Constitution of the Irish Free State*, pp. 373–86.

annuities dispute. But this narrative will create a wrong impression if it is given more than a provisional isolation; it must constantly be borne in mind that the financial quarrel was set in the context of a vehement nationalistic assault upon the association with Great Britain, as this had been accepted during the previous ten years. The monarchical symbolism which the treaty settlement had recognized was attacked, not only by removing the oath, but by removing the Governor-General who was considered to be identified with the previous régime. In effecting this removal Mr. De Valera employed, with some brusqueness, powers which belonged to the status of the Irish Free State as this had expanded under the treaty. But it would be naïve to imagine that the nationalist impulse which Mr. De Valera's party represented was content merely to exploit to the full the expanded treaty status. It was aiming at a different status. Mr. Dan Breen reminded the Dáil that during the war with England he had made an attempt on the life of Lord French. He said that he did not try to kill Lord French in order to make room for James MacNeill or anybody else, but in order to kill the last link of British supremacy in the country.[1]

The attack on the payment of the land annuities, which had been in the forefront of Mr. De Valera's electoral propaganda for many years, strengthened with the alloy of interest the shining metal of resurgent Irish right. Ireland, according to this propaganda, claimed no more than was justly hers; as on the issue of the oath she denounced an affront to her honour, so on the issue of the annuities she rejected an unjust distraint upon her goods. On the eve of the 1932 election the Cosgrave government had sought to meet this propaganda by issuing a closely reasoned statement by the Attorney-General analysing the history and nature of the land annuities, and showing that their payment was legally and morally binding. The statement was endorsed by five leading counsel. In haste, the Fianna Fáil party published a contrary statement with seven legal signatures to prove that payment was not legally or morally binding. This was the burden of a series of pronouncements made by Mr. De Valera immediately after his accession to power. On the 23rd March the

[1] See *The Times*, 11th July 1932, for the correspondence between the Governor-General, Mr. James MacNeill, and Mr. De Valera. Mr. James MacNeill had on his own authority issued the correspondence for publication. See *J.P.E.*, vol. xiii, p. 768; *Journal of Comparative Legislation*, 3rd series, vol. xiv, p. 258. The removal of the Governor-General, before his term, on the direct advice of the Free State government to the Crown, was, according to Professor Keith, entangled with 'a deliberate policy of discourtesy'; but was constitutionally a logical result of the conference resolution of 1930. The installation of Mr. Buckley in a suburban villa on a reduced salary did not, of course, meet Mr. Dan Breen's point.

Secretary of State for the Dominions formally challenged these pronouncements. The Irish Free State, he said, was bound by 'the most formal and explicit undertaking' to continue payment. What, inquired Mr. De Valera in his reply of the 5th April, was this formal and explicit undertaking? His government was aware of no such undertaking. . . . The Cosgrave government had in its statement laid stress on two undertakings. The first was the financial agreement dated 12th February 1923; the second was contained in the 'Heads of the Ultimate Financial Settlement between the British Government and the Government of the Irish Free State', dated 19th March 1926. But neither of these agreements, according to Mr. De Valera, was binding.

It is quite impossible within the scope of this chapter to give a complete account of this financial dispute. The white paper alone runs to sixty-three closely printed pages, and since then mountains of controversial argument have been piled up.[1] The argument continues, but there is still no adjudication. Probably there never will be an adjudication. On the whole, it seems in the circumstances best to describe the brawl without saying very much about the booty. Yet something must be said.

The land annuities recall to mind one of the successful policies of the later period of the Union. The policy sought to make the Irish farmers, who for centuries had been tenants on the land, the owners of it. It first took legislative form in the 'Bright clauses' of the Landlord and Tenant (Ireland) Act of 1870. It continued through a series of acts up to 1909. Broadly speaking, there were two phases of this legislation: from 1870 to 1889, when purchase was financed by issues of money from the Exchequer of the United Kingdom or from the Local Loans Fund; from 1871 to 1909, when purchase was financed by the issue of stock. It was only the payments under the second head which were in dispute, for the Free State had been finally released of any obligation under the first head by the comprehensive agreement of 1925, which, to compensate for the disillusionment over the boundary, relieved it from the liability with regard to the public debt of the United Kingdom set out in article 5 of the treaty. In the British view, and in the view of the Free State government under Mr. Cosgrave, the land annuities under the legislation of 1891–1909 were not part of the public debt of the United Kingdom.

[1] The white paper is P. No. 579. Cf. the *Fianna Fáil* pamphlet; *Dáil Debates*, passim; Henry Harrison, *The Strange Case of the Irish Land Purchase Annuities* and *Spotlights on the Anglo-Irish Financial Quarrel*; Gallopin, *Le Conflit anglo-irlandais*; also the text of the agreements referred to above and of the conference referred to below (Cmd. 4184 of 1932). The newspaper material is voluminous.

They were payments from the Irish purchasers to the stockholders. At the same time, the state was deeply concerned in the transaction. Public authority intervened to provide machinery and to give a guarantee. The machinery of collection was the Land Commission, originally an instrument of United Kingdom authority. Payments were made into a land-purchase account; a deficiency in this account was made up immediately by the consolidated fund, and thereafter by a guarantee fund which was composed of receipts from certain taxes in Ireland and of sums destined for the execution of public works in Ireland. But the ultimate obligation rested upon the Irish tenant-purchaser.

Until the Fianna Fáil party began to put forward a different theory, this view of the facts was generally accepted. Yet it was not unnatural that the liquidation of the Union and the emergence of the Free State out of revolution should produce a number of ambiguities. In Northern Ireland local finance was only partially disentangled from United Kingdom finance; between the Free State and the United Kingdom there was a complete disentanglement. Northern Ireland continued to bear her share of the public debt, and in addition paid an imperial contribution; but Northern Ireland retained the land annuities. Was the Irish Free State in a worse position? Mr. Cosgrave's government certainly did not think so. That government did not doubt that in taking over the machinery of the Land Commission[1] it took over also the liability to collect and transmit the land annuities. Transmit them to whom? It would have been open to it to dispense with the British National Debt Commissioners and set up its own machinery to manage the land stock and apply the annuities to the stockholders' interest and to sinking fund. It had no desire to pay for this unnecessary machinery. These were the considerations which he had in mind, so Mr. Cosgrave has stated repeatedly, when he made the agreement of 1923. He thought he had made a good bargain—he had saved for the state a heavy administrative cost, and bonus and excess stock charges as well.[2] The liability remained what it had always been. He had not created it, he had merely admitted it. The same thing was true of the Blythe–Churchill agreement of 1926, which also admitted the liability. It did not create the liability. It was there already; it was recognized, for example, in section 12 of the Land Act of 1923. The

[1] On 31st March 1923, according to Article 79 of the constitution. As the controversy developed, attention focused also on the Provisional Government (Transfer of Functions) Order of 1st April 1922.

[2] *Dáil Debates*, 26th June 1923, col. 2479.

Cosgrave government did not dream that it had cause to reproach itself. On the contrary! It had aimed at the real objective. It had secured in 1925 an agreement which wiped out all liability for the Free State's share of the debt of the United Kingdom. In virtue of this achievement it was able to hand over to its opponents, when they took office, a state whose financial position was unique, whose total public debt was less than a single year's revenue.

Mr. De Valera in effect accused the Cosgrave government of its failure to realize that it had made a still better bargain than that on which it prided itself. For seven years, this accusation implied, the government had been innocently paying a debt from which by its own action it was free. For the land annuities—so Mr. De Valera and his legal and journalistic champions sought to establish by a minute criticism of British legislation and administrative practice[1]—were, in fact, a part of the public debt of the United Kingdom from which Ireland had been completely released by the 1925 agreement. What of the agreements of 1923 and 1926 which admitted the liability to pay the annuities? These agreements, unlike the 1925 agreement and the treaty itself, had not been ratified by the Dáil: they could not therefore be regarded as binding on the state.[2] Moreover, it was untrue to say that these agreements, incomplete and invalid as they were, simply recognized a pre-existing liability. The Government of Ireland Act had extinguished the liability both for Southern Ireland and for Northern Ireland. And even if it should be admitted—but it was not admitted—that this act never came into force in Southern Ireland,[3] it was still impossible to argue that the burden of the annuities could be shifted on to the Free State by the casual process of transferring the functions of government. The burden was never

[1] Harrison maintains this most vigorously of all, and is followed by the French writer Gallopin.

[2] The question is argued in the papers contained in Cmd. 4184. Keith admits some force in the non-ratification argument from the point of view of international law, seeing that side by side with the unratified agreements were ratified ones. In constitutional law (to which in other aspects of the controversy the British government was appealing) he says that it is quite clear that the executive cannot usurp the functions of the legislative and bind the country to pay money. He cites the Ottawa Conference agreements, and sums up: 'The conclusion seems unavoidable that the effect of a government compact under the common law of the British Commonwealth is merely to impose an obligation to seek Parliamentary moneys necessary to implement the mis-called secret agreement' (*Journal of Comparative Legislation*, 3rd series, vol. xv, p. 118).

[3] In fact the act provided that its various provisions were to come into operation on an 'appointed day'. For Northern Ireland the appointed day for the operation of the financial provisions was fixed as 22nd November 1921 (*Statutory Rules and Orders 1921, No. 1696*, 9th November 1921). For Southern Ireland the day was never fixed.

there, except in the form of a contingent liability for a share of the public debt of the United Kingdom. And this liability had been expunged in 1925.

These are the main issues in the dispute. It is a dispute between Irish lawyers, a dispute between Irish political parties, a dispute between successive Irish governments, a dispute between Mr. De Valera's government and the British government. The writer of this Survey has not been appointed arbitrator. It would be presumption on his part to attempt a judgement on the legal issues, and he conceives it to be his task to treat them merely in the context of the whole political conflict. He holds himself free, however, to trace the current of conflict through its legalistic eddies, and to draw attention to those contradictions in verbal statement which are so frequently the mark of combats which originate not in logic but in impulse.

It was the impulse of the British government to be shocked and indignant and to use strong measures which would bring Mr. De Valera to his senses or bring about his fall. It believed that it held an overwhelming advantage owing to the dependence of the Irish economy on the English market, and it intended to use this advantage both in the dispute about the treaty and the dispute about the annuities. In a statement to the House of Commons on the 11th May Mr. Thomas made it clear that the removal of the parliamentary oath would be met by an economic counter-stroke. It would, he said, be unreasonable to make further agreements with a government which had already repudiated an existing agreement. Here was an announcement to Mr. De Valera's government that it had nothing to hope from Great Britain at the Ottawa Conference. The announcement, in fact, went farther; for if the two governments failed to make an agreement at Ottawa, the Irish Free State would lose on the 15th November the existing 10 per cent. preference provisionally granted to Commonwealth countries under the Import Duties Act 1932. In Dublin Mr. De Valera retorted that no threats would bend the will of the Irish people. The removal of the oath was a domestic matter. The retention of the annuities was a legal right: if the British government thought differently, let it submit a claim. At the same time, Mr. De Valera informed the British government privately that he would be ready to receive British ministers in Dublin. Perhaps after all, it seemed, he might be willing to consider the British government's point of view. A milder mood ensued. On the 8th June Mr. J. H. Thomas and Lord Hailsham conferred with Mr. De Valera in Dublin. On the 10th June the conference was continued in London. Its avowed purpose was to discuss 'the difficulties which have arisen between this country and the Irish Free State with regard to negotiations connected with the Ottawa Conference'. In fact, the discussion at these two meetings had ranged over a much wider ground. At the first meeting Mr. De Valera had frankly revealed his 'ultimate aim'—the unity of Ireland, the recognition of Ireland as a republic, some form of association with the British Commonwealth, and recognition of the King as head of the association. It was the old programme of Document No. 2. But Mr. De Valera 'quite fairly and frankly stated' that he had not at the last election received a mandate to give effect to this programme. With regard to the immediate difficulty, he said that he was anxious to discover a *modus vivendi*. The second meeting in London failed to discover one. Each side restated its point of view. The British representatives then advanced a proposal which their liberal critics had been repeatedly urging. They suggested that the financial dispute should be submitted to the arbitration of a tribunal composed according to the recommendations of the Imperial Conference of 1930. This proposal Mr. De Valera refused. He said 'No'. He said 'The dice would always be loaded against Ireland'.[1]

On the 1st July £1,500,000 was due from the Free State in payment of land annuities. The British government began to study the measures which it would take in the event of payment being withheld. At the same time the discussions about arbitration continued.[2] They achieved no result. To His Majesty's government in the United Kingdom it was a 'point of principle' that the tribunal should be composed entirely of members of the British Commonwealth. It appealed to the resolution of the Conference of 1930. The government of the Irish Free State was unable to accept this 'artificial restriction on the personnel'. It ignored the resolution of 1930. That resolution had indeed been left extremely vague. It did no more than recommend that a tribunal should be constituted after a certain fashion in the event of two governments wishing to submit some justiciable issue to its decision. It imposed no obligation. Mr. De Valera's rejection of 'artificial restriction', although its brusque phrasing and

[1] Statement by Mr. J. H. Thomas in the House of Commons (Hansard, *House of Commons Debates*, vol. cclxvii, 17th June 1932, col. 685). Professor Keith had taken the government to task for not offering arbitration by a tribunal of the kind contemplated in the 1930 resolution. Sir Stafford Cripps had taken the same attitude, while regretting that something better than this *ad hoc* body had not been established in 1930. But this was not through lack of will in Great Britain.

[2] For the correspondence see Cmd. 4116 of 1932 and, for a fuller statement, the Irish white paper P. No. 829.

the political context in which it was set marked a departure from the spirit of Free State policy in recent years, did not mark a breach in the theory which the Free State had always propounded. With great consistency the Free State had rejected the *inter se* doctrine and had maintained that it had the right to invoke international law and international procedure should it so desire. In practice, it had recognized with increasing readiness that its intimate association with the other members of the Commonwealth under the Crown did make other procedures appropriate.[1] But now there had come the most abrupt reversal and challenge. It would surely have been too much to expect that the British government even for the sake of an immediate success should consent to throw in the hand which it had thought it worth while to play ever since the treaty.[2] The British government sincerely believed that a principle of importance for the cohesion of the whole Commonwealth was in question. Nevertheless, its persistency on this 'point of principle' proved to be incompatible with strict consistency of argument. At one moment, for example in the matter of ratification, it was appealing to the doctrine of international law; at the next it was denying the propriety of international procedure.[3] The fervour of its appeal to the sanctity of treaties might always be challenged by the reminder of its reluctance ten years ago and on many occasions since to admit that the articles of agreement signed in December 1921 *were* a treaty.[4]

On the 6th July Mr. J. H. Thomas appealed earnestly to Mr. De Valera not to let the possibility of a friendly settlement of the land annuities question break down on this one point of form. But

[1] The present writer is convinced that the full truth about the Commonwealth tribunal will never be grasped until the discussions of the 1930 Conference are published in full. In general, however, the position has been explained above (see pp. 290–1 and 321). It would appear that the British government, in accordance with its deductions from the theory of the special relationship, desired a Commonwealth tribunal of a representative type for which definite rules—procedural and otherwise—were to be drawn up. No other government of the Commonwealth appears to have shared this desire. The proposal eventually adopted would seem to represent a wish to be insincerely receptive of an idea on which the British set great value, rather than to any appreciation of the usefulness of the idea. As for the treaty and constitutional matters in general, the Cosgrave government, remembering its disillusionment over the Boundary Commission, did not regard them as suitable for legal interpretation. They did, on the other hand, positively regard them as matter for negotiation.

[2] Mr. Lansbury and Lord Parmoor sided with Mr. De Valera and advocated an unrestricted tribunal (*The Times*, 10th August 1932).

[3] Cf. *Journal of Comparative Legislation*, 3rd series, vol. xv, p. 117.

[4] Thus on 17th June 1932 Sir Stafford Cripps spoke of the 'so-called treaty': it was an *agreement*; the Sovereign could not make a *treaty* with himself, i.e. there had been no Republic of Ireland to make the treaty. These views derived naturally from ambiguities insisted upon ten years earlier.

was it a true assumption that a will to peace was being thwarted merely by stubborn principle in a matter of detail? It is significant that Mr. De Valera had on the 2nd July introduced an additional stipulation that the prior approval of the Oireachtas should be obtained for any agreement as to the acceptance of arbitration, the constitution of the tribunal, and the issues to be submitted to the tribunal for arbitration. In this very dispatch he had already enlarged these issues to include bonus and excess stock under the Land Acts of 1903–9, pensions and compensation to ex-members of the Royal Irish Constabulary, civil and judicial pensions, and a number of other items. It might perhaps have happened that, even if the British government had accepted the tribunal as Mr. De Valera wished to define it, Mr. De Valera would then have continued to lengthen the list of items with the intent to prevent the arbitration taking place. It will be seen later that he showed an emphatic readiness to widen rather than to narrow the objects of dispute. A definite statement with regard to intentions is impossible, but it is a not improbable interpretation that Mr. De Valera was at that time resolved in any event to unsettle rather than to settle the Free State's relations with Great Britain. The time had come for beginning a new stage in 'the march of a nation'.

Before the controversy about the tribunal had come to its close, 'economic war' had already opened. The 1st July came and the annuities were not paid. The British immediately introduced ways-and-means resolutions preparatory to a bill which would give the Treasury general powers to recoup itself to the extent of the sums withheld. On the 6th July the text of the Irish Free State (Special Duties) Bill was issued. On the 8th July the delegation of the Irish Free State sailed to Canada for the Ottawa Conference. Would not the British government hold its hand until the delegation should learn at Ottawa the price which it would have to pay for this quarrel? Would it not wait until the family gathering of the Commonwealth had attempted conciliation? Members of the opposition made this plea and found support from conservatives whose constituencies were specially interested in the Irish trade. But Mr. Thomas answered that there was nothing to be gained by 'dragging other Dominions into a dispute which did not affect them'. Obviously, he hoped for victory by rapid and dramatic action. 'The lull', he said, 'would strengthen the position of Mr. De Valera.'[1] There was no lull. The bill was hurried through Parliament.[2] On the 12th July the Irish Free State (Special Duties) Order was laid upon the table of the

[1] *The Times*, 9th July 1932. [2] 22 & 23 Geo. V, c. 30.

House of Commons. It imposed duties of 20 per cent. *ad valorem* on Irish live animals, butter, eggs, cream, bacon, pork, poultry, game, and other meat of all kinds. The retort from Dublin followed quickly. On the 13th July Mr. De Valera gave notice of the Emergency Imposition of Duties Bill, enabling the government to impose duties by order of the executive council. 'The British people are going to feel this economic war just as much as we are,' said Mr. De Valera. Before the end of the month duties of about 20 per cent. were already in operation against British coal, cement, iron and steel goods, which together made up about one-third of the import trade with Great Britain.[1]

The Irish retort surprised by its moderation. *The Times* referred to the new duties as 'tentative', and still hoped for reconciliation.[2] Two new attempts were made to this end. The first originated in a collaboration between the Irish and the British labour parties which took place early in July; the plan was, that instead of an arbitration tribunal there should be a commission of inquiry whose findings should be limited to the facts and should not possess the character of an award.[3] Mr. Ramsay MacDonald favoured the plan and Mr. De Valera came to London to discuss it; but the discussion broke down at the very beginning because the two governments failed to agree about the situation which was to be maintained pending the constitution of the commission and the presentation of its report.[4]

The second attempt at a settlement was by direct negotiation in a conference which met in London on the 14th and 15th October. The statements submitted for this conference contain perhaps the shortest and best summary of the conflicting attitudes in the financial quarrel. The memoranda on the side of the Free State[5] illustrate the vehemence of the nationalist impulse, which was converting the different technical arguments into a far-reaching arraignment of

[1] *Emergency Imposition of Duties Act No. 16* of 1932. *Emergency Imposition of Duties (No. 1) Order*, 1932.

[2] *The Times*, 27th July 1932.

[3] The idea was put forward by Mr. Norton (Irish labour party) but was thought to have originated with Sir Stafford Cripps. See *Manchester Guardian*, 18th July 1932. A similar method had been adopted successfully in a dispute between France and Italy in 1912 and again between Germany and Holland in 1915.

[4] The British maintained that there were three possible means of ending the dispute: (1) to arbitrate; (2) to negotiate as if the dispute had not started, i.e. the Free State would hand over the annuities pending settlement and the British would take off the duties; (3) to negotiate from the present position, i.e. the Free State would still retain the annuities and the duties would still remain in force (*The Times*, 5th August 1932). Mr. De Valera demanded that the duties should be taken off while the Free State retained the annuities. In September he offered to pay the annuities into the Bank of International Settlements pending decision; but the British maintained that this made no difference in principle. At this time the annuities were already being paid into a suspense account.

[5] Cmd. 4184.

Great Britain. Already, in July, Mr. De Valera had added to the original dispute about the annuities six new items of dispute.[1] He now had a longer bill to send in. He resurrected the old claim of compensation for a century of over-taxation under the Union, and the claim for a share of the assets of the former United Kingdom.[2] He claimed compensation in consequence of Great Britain's departure from the gold standard. He claimed a share of the road fund of the United Kingdom. He had more claims to make under the headings of coinage, currency, and half a dozen other items. And before the end of the conference another and quite unlimited counter-claim showed signs of raising its head—a counter-claim based on 'the circumstances surrounding the confiscation and tenure of Irish land'.[3] So Mr. De Valera laid upon the negotiating table the trump card of 'the conquest'. That trump was bound to shatter the game of negotiation.

It is customary in political no less than in commercial negotiations for the bargaining parties to state at the outset what they hope to win, and then gradually to narrow the gap between their opposing claims. In the negotiation which has been described this did not happen. The explanation probably is that the annuities dispute, real though it was, was only part of a much larger conflict. The documents quoted have made it clear that, to Mr. De Valera, the surrender of Ireland's financial right, which he accused the Cosgrave government of perpetrating, was but part of the larger national surrender of 1922. And so the small battle which was now opening was part of the larger battle for the indefeasible right of the 'ancient nation'. The British, reacting, also nursed an angry consciousness of violated right. Had not the government of the Free State given them assurances? Could these be wiped out by an election? They felt that Mr. De Valera was determined to repudiate a fair bargain; to this fair bargain and to the generous honouring of it, he owed the very powers which he was now ungenerously using to discredit and destroy it. They felt that a growing friendliness was being wantonly destroyed. They felt that their trust had been deceived and abused. It was significant and of evil omen that the old anger and the old fears began to express themselves in debates which purported to discuss the technicalities of a financial obligation. Mr. J. H. Thomas

[1] He had not, however, as yet withheld payments under these heads.

[2] Article 5 of the treaty had provided that Ireland's proportionate liability for the public debt of the United Kingdom should be determined 'having regard to any just claims on the part of Ireland by way of set-off or counter-claim'. The liability was wiped out in 1925. Mr. De Valera now argued that this did not wipe out the counter-claim.

[3] Cmd. 4184, p. 19.

harked back to the 'coercion of Ulster'. Mr. Lloyd George remembered the submarine menace and 'our poor ships'.[1] Englishmen and Welshmen, like Irishmen, can be swept by their memories into emotional storm. It was now their mood to have done with fruitless conciliation and to hit back hard. They had little doubt that their blow would be successful.

In Dublin, Mr. De Valera's government raised the cry of national self-defence. It was ready for the struggle. It welcomed it with a grim exhilaration. The British, cried Mr. De Valera to a crowded gathering in College Green, were forcing Ireland to do in a short time what she was determined to do in any event. The British would feel this economic war just as much as the Irish. But the Irish would find through the struggle their own true future. 'Every day's distress here at the start will mean a day of prosperity in the future. It will mean a proper national economy in the future.'[2]

The revival of the old quarrel with England had created for Mr. De Valera the atmosphere of emotional fervour which he needed for launching a drastic experiment in economic nationalism. This experiment will be examined in the following section. The method of investigation will now be a different one; instead of a narrative of succeeding situations, the reader will be offered a survey looking backward from the summer of 1936.

[1] *The Times*, 18th June 1932.

[2] Ibid., 29th July 1932; cf. *Manchester Guardian*, 14th July 1932.

Note

*Payments withheld by the Government of the Irish Free State, 1932**

	£
Bonus and Excess Stock under the Irish Land Acts (payment due in December 1932)	134,500
Royal Irish Constabulary Pensions (monthly payments made up to and including May 1932)	1,000,000
Civil Pensions (monthly payments made up to and including April 1932)	60,000
Judicial Pensions (quarterly payments made to July 1932)	20,000
Local Loans Fund Annuity (half-yearly payments due July 1932 not paid)	600,000
Works Annuities:	
(1) Telegraph Acts (quarterly payment due June 1932 not paid)	16,000
(2) Public Offices (Dublin) Act (payment due 22nd May 1932 not paid)	13,200
(3) Railways (Ireland) Act and Marine Works (Ireland) Act (annual payment due September 1932)	10,000
	1,853,700
Land Purchase Annuities (in 1931)	2,976,590
	£4,830,290

* Statements by Mr. Thomas, Secretary of State for the Dominions (Hansard, *House of Commons Debates*, vol. cclxviii, 4th July 1932, col. 49), and by Mr. Elliot, Financial Secretary to the Treasury (Hansard, *House of Commons Debates*, vol. cclxiv, 21st April 1932, col. 635).

III

Economic Nationalism

The nature of the Irish economy throughout the latter half of the nineteenth century and even as late as the third decade of the twentieth century might almost be said to belong to a world without frontiers. Freedom of activity on a world-wide scale had first of all the most striking effects in the fundamental matter of population. In 1851 the population of the twenty-six counties was 5,112,000: in 1926 it was 2,972,000. Every decade since 1841 had marked progressive depopulation, although the rate of this depopulation varied at different periods. What was its cause? It began as a flight from poverty; but it continued for a different reason. From the time of the famine until about 1880 the chief cause of emigration was hunger or hopelessness at home. Thereafter its chief cause was the attraction of opportunity abroad. The standard of living in Ireland was now rising at a faster rate than the standard of living in England. An Irish expert, surveying the past century, has expressed the opinion that it rose in that period 'from one of the lowest to one of the highest in Europe'.[1] The natural rate of increase of the population, owing chiefly to a low marriage rate and the increasing age at marriage, was decelerating towards a low level. The opportunity within the open frontiers of the United States and the British Empire, and indeed of Great Britain herself,[2] drew from Ireland her small

[1] R. C. Geary, 'The Future Population of Saorstát Éireann and Some Observations on Population Statistics' (*Journal of the Statistical and Social Enquiry of Ireland, 1935–6*), p. 31. The present paragraph is based chiefly on this paper together with *The Census of Population*, 1926, vol. x.

[2] A table on p. 20 of the *Census* of 1926, vol. x, shows that between 1841 and 1926 the immigration from Ireland into Great Britain had been about half that to the United States. The *Preliminary Report of the Census* of 1936 contains statistics

British Retaliation, 1932–6†

Net Receipts from Duties charged under the Irish Free State (Special Duties) Act, 1932, *including any duties levied under the Import Duties Act*:

1932–3	1933–4	1934–5
£2,462,618	£4,372,622	£4,533,094

(years ended 31st March)

The receipts in 1935–6 were approximately £4,782,000. According to an Irish calculation (quoted in *United Ireland*, 2nd May 1936) the amount collected by the British government in the three complete years 1932–5 was £14,661,920; the amount withheld by the Saorstát government was £14,531,668. This left a balance of £130,252 in favour of the British government.

† 26th Report of the Commissioner of H.M. Customs and Excise for the year ended 31st March 1935 (Cmd. 5014 of 1934).

natural increase, and far more. Irish emigration may have begun in despair, but it continued in hope. Within Ireland the young man might hope to better his condition; but in the United States or Canada he might hope to better it still more. The prosperity of kinsmen who were thriving across the seas became an irresistible magnet to many who remained at home. From the lands of great opportunity friends and relatives beckoned; they did more; they sent help so that the stay-at-homes might follow them.[1] The accessibility of distant countries came to be looked upon as a permanent blessing of Irish life. 'Connemara children', it was said, 'are born with their faces towards the West.' Out of every 100 of the young people in Connaught who in 1911 were between the ages of 15 and 19, 53 had in 1926 migrated from the province and the great majority of them from the country. In 1921 no less than 1,817,457 persons who had been born in Ireland were living in the United States or Great Britain or elsewhere in the British Empire. Their number was equivalent to 43 per cent. of the population of Ireland in 1926.[2] No other country in the contemporary world has even approached so vast an emigration.[3] The movement of population may indeed be regarded as part of the movement from country to city which occurred throughout western society in this age; but the cities which received the great Irish influx were outside Ireland.

The Irish who stayed at home depended in equal measures upon a frontierless ordering of things; but whereas for the export of people all North America and all the British Empire were open, for the export of goods the free market of Great Britain was sufficient. This freedom, which had of course been part and parcel of the Union,[4] continued throughout the first decade of the Irish Free State. Its existence had the consequence of an unhindered response in Ireland to the operation of the force of supply and demand. From 1870 onwards the world consumption *per capita* of wheat was taking a downward course; the *per capita* consumption of meat was moving upwards. The main tendency of grain prices was to decline; but the prices of cattle, butter, bacon, eggs, and other live-stock products

showing the volume of emigration to Great Britain in recent years; and the probable trend of emigration in the future is discussed in an article by Dr. George O'Brien in *Studies*, December 1936.

[1] Geary, op. cit., p. 24: 'In the quota years of emigration to the United States, when the Saorstát was so generously treated, it is understood that 95 per cent. of emigrants' fares were paid by relatives in the United States. This is "attraction" with a vengeance.'

[2] *Census*, 1926, vol. x, p. 20.

[3] No other country; but on the exodus from Europe between 1933 and 1936 of the scattered Jewish nation, see Chapter VIII, section ii, below.

[4] With slight exceptions until 1825, when the 'Union Duties' were repealed.

remained persistently favourable. The European grass-lands still enjoyed a natural 'shelter'—it was not yet the day of refrigeration—which European plough-lands had lost. Tillage had never played a predominant part in the Irish agricultural economy. Even in 1851, the peak year, it had amounted to less than 35 per cent., as against 65 per cent. in Denmark to-day. Yet even so there was room for adjustment to the pressure and stimulus of the latter part of the nineteenth century. Tillage gave place steadily to pasture.[1] Ireland procured the bulk of her wheat and stock-feeding mixtures from countries which possessed greater natural advantages for cereal culture, and which were deprived by distance from enjoying the full advantage of the unlimited British market for live-stock and live-stock products. The Irish economy concentrated upon this advantage. Its developing prosperity depended upon the continued absence of any economic frontier shutting it off from Great Britain. This, at any rate, was the prevalent economic view.

Sinn Féin propaganda, it is true, had from its earliest beginnings presented the issue in a different light. That propaganda had an ancestry in the eighteenth century, when Swift and Berkeley had denounced Ireland's servitude to British protectionism. In the nineteenth century conditions were different; 'infant industry' countries within the British Empire and outside it were struggling to escape from their subservience to the British free-trade system. According to Arthur Griffith, Ireland's part in the Union did not even permit her to make herself an 'infant industry country'. She was perforce a neglected pastoral province of Great Britain. He wanted her to use political freedom, when she had won it, to build up an economic frontier behind which she might fashion her industrial life as a national unit. But nowhere in his writings does the idea occur that the frontier might become reciprocally restrictive. Perhaps this is not to be wondered at. France depended both upon her own protected market, and upon the open British market for quality goods. The moderate success of Australian protectionism in increasing and diversifying industrial production would have been impossible without the open British market for wool and wheat and metals.[2] Griffith wanted a barrier against British industrial production: it never entered into his calculations that the British might in their turn erect a barrier against Irish pastoral production.

[1] This fact has little relevance to depopulation. See note on page 324. Irish emigration was actually greater in 1850–4, when crop yields were the highest on record, than in 1845–9.

[2] See *The Australian Tariff* (Report by a Commission of Five Experts, Melbourne, 1929).

Between 1932 and 1935 Great Britain built up a formidable barrier against the Irish Free State. Because of the unsettled dispute, Ireland lost the opportunity of making a preferential agreement at Ottowa. This meant that her exports to Great Britain, with certain exceptions,[1] became subject to the 10 per cent. *ad valorem* duty under the Import Duties Act 1932. There were in addition the special duties first imposed in July of the same year and afterwards increased. At the end of 1935 the most important tariff restrictions upon Irish trade, taking into account both the general 10 per cent. duty and the special duties, were as follows:

Live cattle . . .	Rates varying from £1 5*s*. to £6 according to the age and class of the beast.
Butter	40 per cent. *ad valorem*.
Bacon	40 per cent. *ad valorem* or 16*s*. per cwt. whichever was the greater.
Eggs	40 per cent. *ad valorem*.
Horses	40 per cent. *ad valorem*.
Sheep	10*s*. a head.
Mutton and Lamb . .	10*s*. a carcass.
Poultry (dead) . .	From 4*d*. to 5*d*. per lb. according to class.[2]

These tariff impositions were a severe blow to the Irish economy; but quota restriction was a still severer blow. This came into force as against Ireland on the 1st January 1934. It meant a complete prohibition of Irish beef and veal, a 50 per cent. restriction—on the the 1933 figures—upon fat cattle, and a 100 per cent. restriction upon store cattle. Some mitigation came out of the coal-cattle pact of January 1935, whereby the Irish quota under all heads was increased by 33⅓ per cent. The cement-cattle agreement of 1936 brought a further mitigation.

The British government asserted that the quantitative restriction derived entirely from British agricultural policy: it had nothing at all to do with the Anglo-Irish dispute. This profession may be compared with Mr. De Valera's often-repeated statement that the economic war was compelling him to attempt more quickly what he would have chosen to attempt and been compelled to attempt in any event. Altogether apart from the economic war, there existed in Great Britain forces making for a restriction of Irish imports, and there existed in Ireland forces working to secure a greater independence of the British market. Was it sound for the Free State to continue to build up its economic structure in the same degree as in the past upon the produce of its grass-lands exported to Great

[1] The important exemptions affecting Ireland were live quadruped animals, meat, hides and skins, and wool.

[2] Some of these have since been reduced.

Britain? In the nineteen-twenties the whole world was becoming conscious of the advance of agricultural protectionism in Europe. The wheat-exporting countries were the first to become awake to the menace. Italy's *battaglia di grano*, initiated in 1925, was a dramatic advertisement of closing markets. The price of meat sustained itself for a time after wheat prices had begun to collapse, but by 1930 the reduced purchasing power of continental markets was causing a rush to the British market which threatened not only a collapse of the price but also the possibility of British import quotas. There were signs of an interruption—to say the least—to the security which the grass-lands had enjoyed for more than half a century. At the same time, improvements in transport and refrigeration had reduced the advantage which Ireland's grass-lands had once enjoyed over competitors because of their proximity to the British market. The Cosgrave government had done something to strengthen the Irish economy for the difficult times which might be coming. Not only had it improved the competitive vigour of the traditional production; it had also through the beet industry taken the first step towards agricultural protection; it had instituted a tariff of moderate height and extent; it had established a large system of electrification. Its policy had gently guided the Irish economy in the direction of a greater diversity. But did not the situation which opened out in the early thirties demand more drastic treatment? The depression in America violently cut short emigration; for the first time since the famine the Irish population began to increase.[1] The prices of animals and animal products sank catastrophically. And then Great Britain followed the restrictive policies of other countries. Even had there been no change of government in 1932, many of the measures which have been taken since then would still have been necessary. Nevertheless, the change of government had economic consequences. Great Britain's economic retort to Mr. De Valera's policy aggravated the situation by placing the Irish producer at a competitive disadvantage with his rivals. How far was this disadvantage compensated by the atmosphere of militant fervour favourable to drastic measures of economic nationalism? The question is relevant to a political rather than an economic analysis. It will not be pursued here; nor will any attempt be made to measure the relative strength of the various forces which pushed Ireland towards economic change.

[1] The method which the United States adopted to check immigration was to refuse consular visas to persons who were likely to become public charges or who had not secured work or promise of work prior to their arrival in the country. In practice this confined immigration to persons of private means. Apart from consular restriction, reports of conditions in the United States were a sufficient deterrent.

The immediate struggle counted for something. The old Arthur Griffith doctrine to which the Fianna Fáil party paid homage counted for something. The appetites of lobbying interests counted for something. The fears, hopes, and calculations of departmental experts counted for something. For the purpose of considering in their entirety the policies of economic nationalism, it will be convenient to look at them chiefly from the experts' point of view: without, however, falling into the error of imagining that the experts were their sole architects.[1]

An indication of the impact of the various adverse forces with which the De Valera government had to grapple may be found in some figures of Irish exports:

Total exports, in £000's

	1929	*1931*	*1933*	*1934*	*1935*	*1936* (10 months)
To United Kingdom	43,466	34,944	17,940	16,422	17,991	16,654
To other countries .	3,338	1,332	1,129	1,152	1,624	1,553

Exports of live animals in £000's

1929	*1931*	*1933*	*1934*	*1935*	*1936* (10 months)
19,695	18,328	7,512	6,115	7,316	7,361

Exports of cattle: numbers exported

1929	*1931*	*1933*	*1934*	*1935*	*1936* (10 months)
774,733	765,952	589,862	511,103	668,176	604,799

Exports of cattle, in £000's

1929	*1931*	*1933*	*1934*	*1935*	*1936* (10 months)
13,449	12,670	6,055	4,258	5,376	5,321

The 1929 figures show the high level before the depression. The 1931 figures show the impact of world depression mitigated by the strong position still held by Irish live-stock in the British market. The figures of the following years show the impact of the various blows weakening the Irish position in the British market itself. Only in 1935 is there some relief, arising out of the coal-cattle pact in January of that year. Generally speaking, the Irish Free State suffered a 59 per cent. fall in the value of its exports in a period in which Great Britain suffered a 49 per cent. fall.

[1] Materials from the Irish Free State *Statistical Abstract*, and the monthly *Trade Statistics*: the *Quarterly Statistical Bulletin* issued by the Currency Commission: the excellent annual report and periodical surveys in the *Economist*: regular articles in the *Round Table* and occasional articles in the *Economic Journal*. The agricultural policy of the Free State is analysed at length in an obituary notice of Mr. Patrick Hogan by Dr. George O'Brien in *Studies*, September 1936. Students of the economic life of the Saorstát will await with impatience the report of the Banking and Currency Commission now taking evidence at great length.

Out of this situation arose a whole series of interwoven problems. Fundamental was the plight of the pastoral export industry, which for generations had been basic to the Irish economy. Its collapse threatened a drastic shrinkage of purchasing power, employment, and general economic activity. Was it possible to arrest the process of collapse? Was it possible to find compensation in other activities for what had been lost? What specific remedies of subsidy, protection, and government activity should be applied? What would be the cost of these remedies? How would the cost balance with the advantages? The experimental response to these various challenges could not be altogether at haphazard: there was another objective indicator of the immediate economic problem which helped to define it and to set limits to the choice of possible solutions. It was an inescapable necessity that the Saorstát should remain solvent on its general international account. If, on the one hand, a portion of the national income from export was lost, the nation must make a reduction in its payments for imports. If, on the other hand, there were certain imports—for example coal and petroleum and tea—which it was quite impossible to sacrifice, the nation must at all costs maintain exports sufficient to pay for them.[1] A source of strength to the Free State in this situation was its position as a creditor nation. Here it enjoyed an advantage which was in marked contrast to the burden laid upon other primary producing countries, such as Australia, whose basic industries were at this time taking a similar heavy punishment.

The following figures indicate the situation with regard to the balance of payments:

	Total imports (net)	*Total exports in £000's*	*Excess of imports (amount)*	*Percentage of external trade*
1924	67,586	49,721	17,866	14·9
1933	35,208	18,439	16,768	30·6
1934	38,771	17,574	21,197	37·2
1935	37,023	19,615	17,408	30·4
1936*	32,363	18,208	14,155	27·9

* 10 months.

In the good years—the war years had been particularly good years—Ireland had built up strong investments in Great Britain. To the interest from these investments must be added as heavy

[1] At present peat is not an alternative—not even an expensive alternative—to coal for industry. But in announcing in May 1935 the government's intention to spend £200,000 on the mechanical cutting of peat, Mr. S. Lemass expressed a hope that it might be made the source of electrical energy. (*Weekly Irish Times*, 23rd May 1936.)

items in the country's invisible exports, remittances from emigrants, pensions paid by Great Britain to persons resident in Ireland, and receipts from tourists and the sweepstakes. There are, however, no generally agreed figures as to the extent of the invisible exports.[1] The practical question which economists asked during the bad years was whether the invisible items sufficed to make good the deterioration on the visible account? Had the Irish Free State begun to drain away its capital assets abroad? It was extraordinarily difficult to give a precise answer to this question. Materials for tentative calculation were contained in section V of the *Quarterly Statistical Bulletin* issued by the Currency Commission. These figures suggested that a constantly favourable balance of total payments had changed into a net shrinkage of funds amounting to about 16 per cent.

Excess of Free State outside assets over debits (in round figures)

Quarter ending 31st December	1932:	£88,000,000
,, ,, ,, ,,	1933:	£82,000,000
,, ,, ,, ,,	1934:	£75,000,000
,, ,, ,, ,,	1935:	£74,000,000

It would be a mistake to build too much upon these figures. The point of them in general is the reminder that the Irish Free State possessed substantial reserves which made easier difficult adjustments in its economy.[2] At the same time any marked depreciation of these reserves would be a danger signal. The invisible assets of the Free State were in some degree precarious: pensions would diminish; the stopping of emigration would dry up emigrants' remittances; economic and political insecurity might frighten interest-receiving residents out of the country. Pressure on the total balance of payments might then have to be met by a drastic reduction in the standard of living.

The Free State government and its expert advisers did not too greatly alarm themselves with fears of this kind. But of necessity they had in their heads the factors which have been indicated in the foregoing tables. They had to take account of the shrinkage of Irish exports and the strain upon the balance of payments. In view of these conditions, how could they adjust the economy of the Irish

[1] A writer in *The Economist* (vol. cxix, pp. 116–17) diffidently calculated a net income from invisible exports of £10,000,000.

[2] For a novel and deliberately ironical proposal for the use of these reserves see Joseph Johnson, *Nemesis of Economic Nationalism* (P. S. King, 1934). Assuming that the Free State wished to win the 'economic war', he argued that it was foolish to subsidize export on which the British government levied duties. Consistency demanded that this target for British blows should be withdrawn. The external assets should be systematically recalled to finance a plan of home development.

Free State to a changing world, and at the same time make it stronger and more in keeping with the aspirations of nationalism?

Generally, they answered these questions with the words, 'Produce more at home'. The actual protective policies which they adopted sought to reduce imports from abroad by increasing and diversifying both agricultural and industrial production. At the same time, they sought by the use of bounties and the opening of alternative markets to keep flowing the reduced stream of traditional exports. They also sought to give additional support to employment and purchasing power by means of public expenditure. Sentimental and political considerations cut across their economic planning. It was, for example, desirable to distribute through the constituencies the benefits which tariffs conferred. Political expediency and nationalistic sentiment agreed—but economic calculation did not always agree—in favouring small holders, and even very small holders.[1] National sentiment also demanded that an attempt should be made to prevent English capital from insinuating itself into a strong position behind the Irish tariff wall.

Little can be said here of the policy on its industrial side. The Irish Free State was rapidly transferred from a low-tariff country into a high-tariff country. The official import list published by the government in January 1936 contained 1,974 categories of goods: of these over 1,000 were subject to tariffs. The tariff rates were generally high, large classes of imports being taxed around 40 per cent., 50 per cent., 60 per cent., 75 per cent., and a few even at 100 per cent. or even more. In addition to tariff protection, the government adopted a system of quota limitation or absolute prohibition, mitigated where necessary by licence to import pending the establishment of the home industry.[2] It also took a step towards state capitalism by establishing the industrial credit corporation to help the launching of new industries, such as the production of cement and industrial alcohol. The act gave to the Minister of Finance power to underwrite new companies and to take up shares in the event of a deficiency of public subscriptions. Its intention was to compensate for the lack of underwriting companies and issuing houses in the Irish Free State. To assess the general economic results

[1] The Department of Agriculture puts the minimum economic size of a farm with average quality land at 30–40 acres: with the best land it puts it as low as 20 acres. The Land Commission works on lower estimates. An example of the influence of national sentiment on land policy worth mentioning is the establishment of Irish-speaking colonies from the Gaellacht on grass-lands subdivided in the old fattening country of the east.

[2] See *Control of Imports Act*, No. 12 of 1934.

of this industrial policy would necessitate an effort of economic analysis which would be complicated and controversial and probably still premature. But the policy produced quick visible results in substituting Irish-made products for a wide range of imported articles.[1]

It is easier to measure the more definitely drawn boundaries of achievement and possibility in the field of agricultural policy. The desire to contract the production of the grass-lands, for which the external market had been narrowed, and the desire to relieve the pressure upon the balance of payments, co-operated with the sentimental disposition to turn land back from pasture into tillage. But there was no prospect at all of external markets for the products of Irish tillage. The possible extent of the change over was therefore limited to the capacity of the home market.[2] Home production might in varying degrees supplant the importation of wheat, animal feeding stuffs (notably maize), sugar, fruit, and vegetables. Possibly—by a higher consumption of milk and light beer—the bill for tea imports might be reduced. These were the chief possibilities.

In this programme of supplanting imports by home production wheat took the first place. The Fianna Fáil party had made wheat a symbol.[3] Wheat was associated in the popular mind with a large and thriving population; the decline of wheat was associated with the emigrants' sorrows. A toughness contributed by science made out of sentimental longings a practicable policy; new processes of drying sodden grain in the mills lifted the anxious apprehension of wet harvest weather.[4] Here was the answer of a small wet country to the achievements of dry farming which in the last two generations had made the fortune of wheat growers in the wider fields of the new countries. To sentiment and science the government added a tax upon the consumer. It secured legislation enabling it to fix a standard price for home-grown wheat and to require the millers to purchase all the millable wheat produced in the country. The difference between the standard price fixed by the state and the average market price was at first paid out of public funds. Between 1933 and 1935 the

[1] Cf. *The Economist*, vol. cxxi, p. 1116, for a table showing decline in various imports. Paper, footwear, cardboard, leather, hats, gloves, clothes, and cheap cloth are leading items.

[2] This was increasing numerically, since the cessation of emigration, at the rate of about 20,000 persons a year. Expert opinion anticipated a low and decreasing rate of increase, cf. Geary, *The Future Population of Saorstát Éireann*, passim.

[3] The majority report of the Economic Committee of 1928 had pronounced against the artificial encouragement of wheat.

[4] The harvest weather in the early years of the new wheat policy was in fact persistently good.

deficiency payments were from 6*s.* 4*d.* to 8*s.* 11*d.* a barrel. In 1935 the system of standard prices was changed to a system of minimum prices. According as the wheat acreage tended to grow, the amount payable out of public funds tended to increase. Direct subsidies from public funds ceased in 1936, and the increased cost of the wheat scheme went directly on to the consumer of flour and bread by the plan of fixing the price which millers paid for the wheat. What expansion of acreage did this policy achieve? In the harvest year September 1933 to September 1934 the Irish Free State grew only 10 per cent. of the wheat which it consumed. In the harvest year 1934–5 it grew 25 per cent. In the harvest year 1935–6 it grew about 33⅓ per cent. The land under wheat increased from 26,000 acres in 1932 to 163,000 acres in 1935. Those in charge of the enterprise refused to admit that there was any limit to its expansion this side of complete self-sufficiency. That would mean that an annual saving approaching £3,000,000 on imports had been achieved. It would mean that 650,000 acres had been converted from pasture into tillage; or, allowing for a threefold rotation of crops, three times that number of acres.

There were other grain crops which the Saorstát might grow instead of importing. Legislation provided for the admixture of home-grown grain with all maize meal sold for animal feeding; the proportion was fixed from time to time at a level calculated to absorb any surplus of oats or barley or other grain which might remain on the home market after general demands had been supplied. The objective aimed at was to eliminate the entire importation of maize, maize meal, linseed, cotton-cakes, and other feeding-stuffs. That would save an annual payment of about £1,500,000. It might turn over to tillage 320,000 acres, a figure which again could be multiplied because of the rotation of crops.[1]

There was also sugar. The factory established by the Cosgrave government at Carlow had made possible the protected cultivation of beet. With an eye to a strategic dispersal of the benefit the De Valera government established additional factories in appropriate sites. The method of protection was both to tax and to control imports, and to remit duty on home-manufactured sugar, so that the

[1] The actual acreage for oats and barley was:

Crop	*1931*	*1935*	*Change*
	acres	*acres*	*acres*
Oats . .	622,799	614,116	8,663 decrease
Barley .	115,735	138,650	22,915 increase

Irish manufacturer might pay a remunerative price for the crop.[1] In 1928 the Free State had spent £1,438,000 on sugar importation; in 1934 it spent only £506,000—although the fall in value was greater than the fall in quantity. In that year the country was growing four-fifths of its requirements, and very soon it would be supplying them completely. Sugar cultivation, however, transferred a smaller acreage from pasture to tillage: 10,000 acres had been sufficient to supply the original Carlow factory; 57,000 acres were under cultivation in 1935; the expansion still to be achieved would hardly extend beyond 20,000 additional acres. There was, too, a certain amount of crop substitution in connexion with sugar cultivation; while the beet acreage was increasing, the acreage under turnips, mangolds, and potatoes was decreasing, although not proportionately. There was a further extension of tillage to be hoped for through the cultivation of fruit and vegetables, and here there was an additional £400,000 of imports to supplant. The government encouraged fruit and vegetable culture by tariffs, and imposed a quota on the importation of onions. With greater caution it set itself to foster also the cultivation of Irish tobacco. The 800 acres under tobacco in 1935 were a small beginning in an attempt where the vehemence of the consumer's preference might for once prove itself stronger than the impulses of economic nationalism.

The ministers and officials responsible for these efforts were doubtless ardently aware of the successes already achieved and those which were within reach. An outside observer, however, must be equally conscious of the limits to success. Assuming that every objective was completely obtained, the total saving on imports—which even in the depression years had remained nearer £40 millions than £30 millions—would be no more than about £5 millions. The transfer to tillage, by the most optimistic estimate, would hardly affect more than 15 per cent. of the fields of the Irish Free State. Even in 1851, when the population of the twenty-six counties was over 5 millions, and when grain culture was at its maximum, the amount of land under wheat, corn, roots, and green crops was no more than 3½ million acres, leaving 8½ million acres to pasture. Even then Ireland was predominantly a stock-raising country. Taking the conditions as they existed in 1935, it was plain that policy could merely shift the margins of the economy, it could not change its basic character.

[1] In October 1934 the excise duty of 2*s.* 4*d.* per cwt. was put on sugar and the customs duty brought up to 8*s.* 8*d.* In May 1935 both customs duty and excise duty were increased by 2*s.* 4*d.* per cwt. They stood then at 21*s.* and 4*s.* 8*d.* respectively. In the Finance Bill of 1936 they were reduced to 8*s.* 8*d.* and 2*s.* 4*d.* respectively.

The pastoral industry remained fundamental. Nothing save a great disaster could alter this fact.

It was the policy of the government during this particular time of stress to keep the pastoral industry alive by means of state assistance. In the early days of the 'economic war', the Minister for Industry and Commerce had suggested that this state assistance was but a temporary expedient to compensate the victims of the war and to ease the process of transition.[1] But, if the possibilities of transition were themselves limited, policies which were more than temporary expedients would have perforce to be adopted to keep the pastoral industry in health. It would seem that the Minister of Industry and Commerce became increasingly conscious of this necessity.[2] However this may be, the system of bounties in the period under review was on the whole efficacious in countering the British duties which otherwise would have completely ruined the export trade; although of course bounties could have no effect in restoring that portion of the trade which was irrevocably cut off by quota limitation. The chief bounties were as follows:

Live cattle (over 2 years)	20*s*. per head.
Creamery butter	Not exceeding 27*s*. per cwt.
Other butter	Not exceeding 23*s*. per cwt.
Bacon	12*s*. per cwt.
Eggs	2*s*. to 1*s*. 7*d*. per great hundred according to grade.
Turkeys (dead)	3*d*. per lb.
Other poultry (dead)	3½*d*. per lb.
Horses	20 per cent. *ad valorem*.

The total bounty payments in the year 1935–6 amounted to £2,273,000. In the estimates of the following year they were considerably reduced.

Other expedients were adopted to save from ruin that large part of the Irish economy which received the direct impact of the blow from outside and which could not find immunity by a transformation. The government pursued a search for new markets. Belgium made a bargain which gave to Ireland a quota for horses and butter. Spain gave to the Free State a quota for eggs in return for a quota for oranges.[3] There were agreements of small importance with South Africa and Canada. There was an agreement with Germany, whereby the Reich agreed to import Free State products in a ratio of 1 to 3 of

[1] Mr. S. Lemass quoted in *The Economist*, vol. cxvii, p. 1235.

[2] Mr. Lemass in 1935 defined policy thus: (1) concentration on home production; (2) limitation of export surplus to the capacity of external markets; (3) so far as possible confine purchases abroad to buyers of Irish products.

[3] The Free State found some difficulty in securing payment.

the value of German sales to the Free State: in April 1936 Irish negotiators improved this bargain to a ratio of 1 to 2. These trade agreements served a useful purpose in relieving the depressing effects of an unsaleable surplus; yet their comparatively small achievement served only to emphasize the overwhelming importance to the Irish economy of the British market.

Exports from the Irish Free State: Percentages

	1932	*1933*	*1934*	*1935*	*1936* (10 months)
To United Kingdom	96·3	94·0	93·6	91·2	91·5
To foreign countries	2·9	4·8	4·9	7·8	7·4

It was the cattle trade which received the heaviest blow. The British quota threw back on to the Irish market 150,000 fat cattle, which amounted to a 100 per cent. increase of supply into Ireland. While the price was held up for the cattle admitted into Great Britain and those which could be smuggled across the northern frontier, the price of those which had to be disposed of in the Saorstát fell to calamitous levels. The government, adapting economic necessity to its political and social policy, instituted a scheme of free beef for the poor. This scheme may come to be regarded by the social historian as one of the first examples of 'marrying health to agriculture'—that is, of helping farmers and improving nutrition by the same measure. But the scheme had to be modified because of its cost.[1] Other measures, such as a bounty on the export of hides, and encouragement for the killing of calves—satirical farmers called it 'the slaughter of the innocents'—hastened a direct and drastic reduction of the herds. The farmers themselves responded to economic stimulus and pressure by turning increasingly from the production of beef to the production of milk and butter. A source of meat supply which during the Great War had been of peculiar value to Great Britain was being dried up, and this at a time when Great Britain was becoming increasingly conscious of the dangers which might arise from too great dependence on trans-oceanic sources of supply.

Some of the social effects of the new economic policies tended towards the unexpected. The government had deliberately chosen to show special favour in relieving the dairy, bacon, and poultry industries, on the ground of the greatest good of the greatest number; in these industries larger numbers of small producers were engaged. Political and social, no less than economic views, rendered the dominant party not unwilling to leave the larger producers, the 'ranchers', to bear the heavier burdens and losses. Undoubtedly this happened at

[1] *Birmingham Post*, 23rd April 1936.

first. But the larger farmers of the east were thereafter able in some measure to pass on the loss to the smaller farmers of the west who supplied them with store cattle. Many of the larger farmers were able in addition to share the advantages of protected wheat and beet growing. It was often the smaller 'mountainy' farmers, whose land was completely unsuitable for tillage, who bore the heaviest loss.

The gloomy forecasts of the opposition party and the professional economists were also in large measure belied; or, at the least, fulfilment of their prophesies was postponed.[1] They had prophesied quick catastrophe as a result of the drying up of purchasing power. But purchasing power was to a very welcome degree sustained. What the small peasant family lost in sales it often made up by employment of one sort or another on community utilities. Pensions, public works, a large housing scheme, and the protection of industrial and some branches of agricultural activity, vigorously sustained employment and purchasing power.[2] Whether or not there was an increase of unemployment was a matter of dispute.[3] Undoubtedly there was a burden upon the finances of the Free State:

Surplus or Deficit, in £000's

1930–1	*1931–2*	*1932–3*	*1933–4*	*1934–5*	*1935–6*
−902	−1,640	−1,141	−1,321	−2,432	−505

Net National Debt

1931	*1932*	*1933*	*1934*	*1935*	*1936*
15,136	16,157	14,077	24,502	25,505	19,263*

* Changes in accounting make comparability difficult.

Yet, if these figures reveal a burden, they reveal also that it was a comparatively light one. The state which Mr. De Valera inherited from Mr. Cosgrave was almost free of public debt. The community was cushioned from the dangers which might have threatened the new economic policy by its strong creditor position. Those dangers might become serious later; they did not seem to be immediate in 1936. In that year there was a marked improvement in the position of the public accounts.

More significant at the moment than the burden falling visibly

[1] Most gloomy was Johnston, *Nemesis of Economic Nationalism*. Cf. his article in the *Economic Journal*, September 1934, on 'The Purchasing Power of the Irish Free State Farmers in 1933', and another article in the *Nineteenth Century and After*, February 1936. Both articles contain a great deal of interesting fact.

[2] See some figures in *The Economist*, 2nd May 1936, p. 247.

[3] *The Economist*, taking three alternative indices (unemployment insurance, health insurance, census of production), showed by each varying increases of unemployment. Contrast the conclusions of the *Report on the Trend of Employment and Unemployment in the Saorstát* (P. No. 1852).

upon the taxpayer was the less measurable burden imposed upon industry. The costs and benefits arising from policies of economic nationalism are matter for delicate and complicated calculation, and no such calculation has been undertaken for the Irish Free State.[1] Yet some signs may be mentioned of the growing costs. The protection of tillage had by the end of 1935 imposed a direct and visible cost upon the live-stock industry; whereas in Northern Ireland the cost of maize meal was £6 a ton, in the Irish Free State the cost of the equivalent mixture was £7 10*s*. a ton. The cost was bound to rise, with the continuing success of the tillage policy, perhaps to the height of £9 a ton. More generally, industry was paying a cost for agricultural protection (for example, in wheat and butter); the agricultural community was paying more for a wide range of industrial products; the whole community, whether urban or rural, was paying the cost of protection both in town and country. The cost of living index in the Free State at the end of 1935 stood at 140 as against 125 in the United Kingdom. The special and highly appreciated advantage of cheap meat was in large measure being paid for by the destruction of capital assets, and could not be expected to continue indefinitely. Rising costs must tend to pile up against the export industries, and in this there was a threat to economic health. Either prosperity or depression was liable to create difficult problems. Depression would have the disastrous effects on purchasing power which economists had been prophesying. Prosperity was inseparably bound up with imports, which were both one of its causes and one of its effects. The progress of a diversified economy necessitated the importation of raw materials, machinery, petroleum, and similar commodities. If that progress caused a rising standard of living, there would be an increased importation of tea and other consumption goods. And what if the real terms of trade changed to the disadvantage of the Saorstát? She would then have to increase her exports in order to secure the things she needed, unless—like some contemporary nations—she was prepared to accept the self-sufficiency of defiant poverty.

The aim of this section has not been to attempt an expert analysis of the whole problem of economic nationalism in the Irish Free State. The materials for such an analysis have not been sufficiently sifted, nor is the present writer qualified for a task of close statistical and economic reasoning. He believes, however, that the general description of tendencies which he has offered corresponds to the facts and

[1] e.g. no calculation of comparable thoroughness to that on the Australian Tariff. See note on p. 353.

that it is strictly relevant to his main study. The economic effort which Mr. De Valera's government undertook had a remote ancestry in the economic oppressions and discontents of eighteenth-century Ireland, and a more immediate parentage in the teaching of Sinn Féin. Its programmes corresponded with the political programmes; expressed in terms of popular oratory, they aimed to break the shackles binding Ireland to Great Britain; the end pursued was independence. Mr. De Valera's government might claim to have pursued that end with resolution. It might also claim—though its opponents would challenge such a claim—to have succeeded rather more than the majority of contemporary states in meeting the difficulties and dangers of a troubled time. But its very successes were bound to make it increasingly critical of the indiscriminate propaganda of the emotional inexperienced nationalists. Of necessity, the government tempered nationalist aspiration with economic calculation. There were still visions to follow, but there were also statistics to consult. Some visions dissolved. Possibilities took their place. The possibilities brought their own exhilaration, perhaps a more sober, sharper exhilaration. Plans of limited achievement which will be grasped here and now are to some minds more satisfying than dreams of limitless perfection some day.[1] The dreams of boundless wheatlands became a plan for 650,000 acres under wheat: this was the furthest boundary of achievement, this therefore was its goal. Similarly, the poetic vision of a self-sufficient Ireland became the plan for a different Ireland—an Ireland which would indeed be economically independent, but whose independence could realize itself only through interdependence with Great Britain.

This is the basic fact which the inquiry has revealed. In the years which have been under review Great Britain and the Irish Free State deliberately inflicted economic damage upon each other.[2] That damage, undoubtedly, was not light. Yet it had not been able to

[1] But there is an Irish saying, 'The far-off hills are green'.

[2] Two tables are given without comment to suggest the British loss:

Imports into Irish Free State: Percentages British and other Countries.

	1929	*1932*	*1933*	*1934*	*1935 Apr.-Dec.*	*1936 Jan.-Apr.*
From United Kingdom	77·2	75·8	70·0	66·8	54·3	55·2
From other countries	20·0	18·2	22·6	27·3	33·8	33·6

N.B.—Up till April 1935 imports were classified by countries of consignment: after that by countries of origin. About one-fifth of the imports coming from the U.K. in 1932, 1933, and 1934 were re-imports.

Percentage of total British Exports taken by the Irish Free State.

1929	*1931*	*1932*	*1933*	*1934*	*1935*
4·8 (4th)	7·8 (2nd)	7·1 (2nd)	5·2 (5th)	4·9 (5th)	4·7 (6th)

do more than scratch the grapplings binding the two economies together. According to the current phraseology, the Irish Free State was a 'dissatisfied' state; it resented its status, it claimed as of right the elimination of a frontier, its nationalism was unappeased. Yet, like every other state, the Irish Free State had objective interests which its rulers were constrained by necessity and duty to serve. There was room for differences of interpretation, there was bound to be some imperfection of knowledge and some deviation from the exact line; but objective fact imposed bounds beyond which deviation was inconceivable, so long as policy was in the hands of men who had a genuine and rational concern for the well-being of their country. The unappeased nationalism of the Irish Free State was directed against Great Britain. The interest of the state—or at any rate the interest of the state as an economic structure—demanded friendship and collaboration with Great Britain. Great Britain on her part had a powerful economic interest in friendship with the Irish Free State. But of overwhelming importance was her political interest in a friendly and associated Ireland, for this was vital to her security and independence.

Political interest, however, is not so capable as is economic interest of relatively exact and agreed measurement. It is easily and commonly distorted into violent emotional affirmations and clashes and one-sided impositions of power. This perhaps had been at the root of the long bitterness between England and Ireland. And, if it was now encouraging that there was a growing awareness of a community of interests, this awareness remained disquietingly incomplete. On the Irish side it was chiefly awareness of economic fact. The English were chiefly preoccupied with political fact as they saw it. With increasing frequency Mr. De Valera stated that it was possible for Great Britain and Ireland to come to an understanding on the basis of their shared interests. But did he admit the validity of the strategic interest which was dominant in the minds of British statesmen? At any time from the beginning of 1935 it would have been possible to settle the economic dispute. The British were not willing to separate the economic dispute from the political one. There were perhaps some signs that the political situation was slowly developing towards a point at which at least some temporary adjustment might become possible. There were, on the other hand, signs which might suggest the opposite. And even if the more optimistic reading of the signs was true, there remained the time factor. To be safe, reconciliation should come soon. The possibilities of a slow sheltered growth might be ruined by a storm bursting in from outside.

IV

Politics

The last section attempted to measure in some rough fashion the achievements of economic nationalism in the Irish Free State, and to mark the probable limits of achievement. Far less must be attempted, it is quite certain, in a section dealing with politics. The measurement of political facts is even more difficult than the measurement of economic facts, especially when the political facts must be viewed from close at hand. The mountains of to-day are so frequently the mole-hills of ten years hence. These mountains or mole-hills are, moreover, far too numerous; so that the contemporary chronicler falls almost inevitably into the double offence of distortion and prolixity. Yet he must not shirk his task. Perhaps a severe selection may mitigate the prolixity, and there may be some defence against distortion in a method of inquiry which will examine tentatively and in turn the more important points of view from which selection may profitably be made.

The point of view of the British government was reiterated in ministerial statements delivered from time to time in parliament between 1932 and 1936. Usually there was more emphasis than exactness in these pronouncements. The old confusions about the legal nature of the Articles of Agreement for a Treaty, the legal origins of the constitution of Saorstát Éireann, and the relation of the Statute of Westminster to both these instruments continued for some time to make a fog.[1] Generally speaking, the British government tried to clarify the issues by a rough simplification of them. In the meetings of June 1932 Mr. De Valera had frankly stated that his ultimate aim was an Irish republic, in association with the British Commonwealth of Nations and recognizing the King as head of the association. The Secretary of State was quick to espy in every new move of the Irish Free State government that breach of law which he believed to be inseparable from its final purpose. The discussion in the House of Commons on the Free State act abolishing the appeal to the Privy Council, and on two other acts which at the same time whittled away the monarchical symbolism of the constitution, illustrated very well the British attitude.[2] The

[1] See above, Chapter IV, section iv, and Chapter VI, section i.

[2] These Acts have already been referred to on p. 339. It may be convenient here to summarize the history of the appeal so far as it concerned the Irish Free State. It had been doubted by lawyers in Great Britain as well as the Free State (e.g. by Professor Keith) whether the treaty made mandatory provision for the appeal.

legislation, said Mr. Thomas, constituted a further breach of the treaty. Its significance was a progressive elimination of the Crown from the constitution of the Irish Free State. Its tendency was towards the setting up of an all-Ireland republic partially associated with the British Commonwealth of Nations. Any proposal of this

Article 66 of the constitution contained the contradictory assertions that the decision of the Supreme Court of the Free State should be 'final and conclusive' and not 'capable of being reviewed by any other Court Tribunal or Authority whatsoever', and also that nothing in the constitution was to 'impair the right of any person to petition His Majesty for special leave to appeal from the Supreme Court to His Majesty in Council or the right of His Majesty to grant such leave'. Kevin O'Higgins stated in the Dáil that the practice agreed upon in discussions held in 1922 corresponded to that observed in the case of South Africa, and that an appeal would lie only in cases where international issues were raised (*Dáil Debates*, vol. xiv, 27th January 1926, col. 116). This view was upheld in the early applications for leave to appeal, and the applications were dismissed. Lord Buckmaster declared that 'as far as possible finality and supremacy are to be given to the Irish Courts' (*Hull* v. *McKenna*, 1926 I.R. 409). This practice was, however, reversed in a case of 1925. The Free State government regarded the decision to admit the appeal as a breach of the understanding reached in 1922, and before the appeal was heard carried legislation to affirm its view of the law in despite of any contrary decision which might be given. The petitioners then withdrew the appeal. (See Keith, *Responsible Government in the Dominions*, p. 1090.) At the same time the Free State government did not oppose the admission of an appeal involving the interpretation of Article X of the treaty (*Wigg and Cochrane* v. *The Attorney-General of the Irish Free State*). The decision was confessed to be a bad one; and arrangements were made for a rehearing of the case by the Judicial Committee under a special reference. The Irish Free State authorities objected to this procedure, and, although the Judicial Committee came to the conclusion that the previous decision was in substance right, declined to accept it. The issue was settled thereafter by agreement under which the United Kingdom government undertook to pay the cost of the benefits resulting from the Judicial Committee's decision. The right of the Privy Council to grant leave of appeal was challenged in 1930 in the case of *Performing Rights Society* v. *Bray District Council*, and was upheld: though the decision was again forestalled by legislation of the Irish Free State. In practice, therefore, the right of appeal was ineffective. Judgement had been given in only two cases and in neither had it taken effect. In 1926 the Irish Free State representatives secured a declaration from the Imperial Conference that it was 'no part of the policy of His Majesty's government that questions affecting judicial appeals should be determined otherwise than in accordance with the wishes of the part of the Empire primarily affected'. At the same time the conference declared that changes in the existing system which raised issues primarily affecting one part but also affecting other parts of the Commonwealth should not be effected without consultation. This was a barrier of convention to unilateral abolition of the appeal; but it is apparent from the debates in the Dáil that the Cosgrave government believed that it would be able to secure British agreement for removal of the appeal in the future—the 'newness' of the treaty being an argument for present delay. It also believed that it had British benediction of its system of negativing the appeal while it formally remained. In 1930 it raised the question again at the Imperial Conference, and after that it pressed for a special agreement for the abolition of the appeal. It was the hope of reaching agreement which induced the Cosgrave government to refrain from abolishing the appeal by legislation. It claimed to possess the power, but it preferred to use if possible a different method.

kind would be 'totally unacceptable' to His Majesty's government in the United Kingdom. It would be inconsistent with the declaration of the Imperial Conference of 1926, which made free association under the Crown the fundamental constitutional principle. Upon this basis the Irish Free State was free to manage its own affairs. Upon this basis she enjoyed great privileges; but the privileges carried with them responsibilities. It was the desire of the British government to see the Irish Free State take her part as a member of the British Commonwealth, not grudgingly, but of her own free will, accepting both the responsibilities and the privileges.[1] This declaration invited a retort. Supposing the Irish Free State professed herself willing to forgo the privileges, would she then be released from the responsibilities? Supposing she felt herself unable to play her part ungrudgingly and of her own free will in the British Commonwealth, would the Commonwealth then relieve her from a grudging and compelled membership? Had the government of Great Britain—so Mr. De Valera inquired in a dispatch of 30th November 1933—at last brought itself to recognize Ireland's right 'to exist as a distinct and independent nation'? Had it realized 'the evils of a forced association'? Had it made up its mind 'not to treat as a cause of war or other aggressive action a decision of the Irish people to sever their connexion with the Commonwealth'? These questions extracted from the Secretary of State an answer stiff with rectitude. His Majesty's government in the United Kingdom did not accept Mr. De Valera's interpretation of past history nor of the present connexion founded upon the treaty settlement. It did not therefore see any grounds for answering questions founded upon that interpretation. It was unable to believe that the Free State government contemplated the final repudiation of treaty obligations in the manner suggested, and therefore did not feel called upon to state what attitude it would adopt in circumstances which it regarded as purely hypothetical. In conclusion, Mr. Thomas sought to prove the fact of Irish freedom by appealing to 'that free intercourse on equal terms with the other members of the British Commonwealth which the Irish Free State have enjoyed under the Treaty Settlement, culminating in the Statute of Westminster'.[2]

But what did the Statute of Westminster mean to the Irish Free State? Precisely this was the immediate question. There has already been some discussion of the question in section i of this chapter.

[1] 14th November 1933. *J.P.E.*, vol. xv, pp. 48, 49.

[2] Hansard, *House of Commons Debates*, vol. cclxxxiii, 5th December 1933, cols. 1457–61, contains the correspondence.

The Irish treaty and the Irish constitution were contained in British acts of parliament, and the Statute of Westminster empowered the legislature of the Irish Free State to alter British acts of parliament. It therefore empowered it—so Mr. Churchill had argued during the debates on the statute—to alter the constitution and the treaty. The labour opposition in Great Britain advanced the same argument. Mr. De Valera used the same argument. The British government, on the contrary, tended to minimize the British parliamentary aspect of treaty and constitution—though once it had been at pains to stress them—and to emphasize the character of the treaty as a contract which could only be altered by mutual agreement. The Statute of Westminster, declared Lord Hailsham, was 'of course in the case of the Irish Free State . . . conditioned by the terms of the treaty under which the Irish Free State was granted the *status* which it enjoys'.[1] This argument, if pressed to an extreme, would make the enlargement of dominion status by the Statute of Westminster illusory whenever the more restricted status of 1922 was written into the Irish treaty.[2] Its immediate purpose was to prove the illegality of three amendments to the Free State constitution. But the argument did not come altogether well from that party to the treaty which in its early days had resisted the Free State's attempts to give to the treaty full value in international law.

A decision of the Privy Council on the 6th June 1935 made it impossible for the British government to persist in the argument, at least in those legal implications which Lord Hailsham had given to it. The Privy Council had to consider whether the Constitution (Amendment No. 22) Act 1933, amending article 66 of the constitution so as to terminate the right of appeal, was valid. The substance of its judgement is contained in the following paragraph:[3]

> 'The position might be summed up as follows: (1) The treaty and the Constituent Act respectively form parts of the statute law of the United Kingdom, each of them being parts of an Imperial Act. (2) Before the passing of the Statute of Westminster it was not competent for the Irish Free State Parliament to pass an Act abrogating the treaty

[1] Hansard, *House of Lords Debates*, vol. xcviii, 25th July 1934, col. 1077. According to the argument sketched on p. 333 above, it was incorrect to say that the statute was 'conditioned' by anything. It was a direction to British judges and a direction on legal grounds only.

[2] According to the same argument, the only restrictions upon the enlarged status must depend upon 'stipulations'—the extent of which and the breach of which were not to be defined and 'sanctioned' in a British court.

[3] *Moore and Others* v. *Attorney-General for the Irish Free State*, 1935 A.C. 434. 51 T.L.R. On the substance of this case as it came before the Supreme Court of the Irish Free State see 1934 I.R. 44 and *Journal of Comparative Legislation*, vol. xxiv, pp.

because the Colonial Laws Validity Act forbade a Dominion Legislature to pass a law repugnant to an Imperial Act. (3) The effect of the Statute of Westminster was to remove the fetter which lay upon the Irish Free State Legislature by reason of the Colonial Laws Validity Act. That Legislature could now pass Acts repugnant to an Imperial Act. In this case they had done so.'

The Board went on to say that it expressed no opinion

> 'on any contractual obligation under which, regard being had to the terms of the treaty, the Irish Free State lay. The simplest way of stating the question was to say that the Statute of Westminster gave to the Irish Free State a power under which they could abrogate the treaty, and that, as a matter of law, they had availed themselves of that power.'

Legal critics complained that the judgement confused two things: the existence and validity of a treaty as between the parties, and the legislation necessary for enforcing the treaty. They denied that the Free State legislature could possess a power to abrogate the treaty (since both in English and Irish law the treaty-making power belonged to the executive); it could possess only the power to annul the effect of the treaty as municipal law of the Free State.[1] But the British government had to face the fact that the particular legal position which it had occupied against Mr. De Valera was now completely untenable. It did not find it easy to reorganize its defensive line. It could hardly appeal from English legal theory of the Irish constitution, now so forcibly but embarrassingly asserted, to the contrary theory of it maintained in the past by the Irish courts. Nor could it now reverse completely its own earlier opposition to Mr. Cosgrave's insistence on the unqualified international nature of the treaty, and at the same time improvise an un-Austinian theory of international law. The only ground upon which it could still stand was 'positive international morality'. A legal power, the attorney-general maintained, did not confer a moral right; 'there must be some obligations that are binding other than legal obligations[2]'. The

119 ff. The case, which dealt with fishery rights in Lough Erne, raised very interesting questions of Brehon law and the establishment of English law in Ireland.

[1] Cf. Professor Keith in *Journal of Comparative Legislation*, vol. xxiv, pp. 271 ff., and *The Spectator*, 21st June 1935.

[2] Hansard, *House of Commons Debates*, vol. ccliv, 10th July 1935, cols. 455–6. Sir Thomas Inskip said also: 'Up to the Statute of Westminster we were the only Parliament that had the power to alter the Treaty. After the Statute of Westminster, of course, we continued to have the power as well as the Irish Free State.' The position now, he continued, was that both parties, instead of one, were under a moral obligation not to make unilateral use of their legal powers. This was consistent with his argument of 1931, quoted and criticized on p. 332 above.

government had to resign itself to the fact that British courts could not invalidate the action of the Irish Free State if it chose to sweep away all the forms and processes of monarchy recognized in the treaty, including the office of governor-general. But it tried to make some provision against such a contingency and against that final contingency, which now seemed so much nearer, of a seceding Irish republic. On 10th July 1935 Mr. J. H. Thomas spoke in very general terms about the sanctity of treaties, the disastrous effects upon Free State nationals in Great Britain which the setting up of a republic would entail,[1] and the opposition of the British government to such action. 'We are not going to be a party to,' he said, 'and we will take every step we can to prevent, Southern Ireland going out of the British Commonwealth.' Was this a threat of force? Sir Stafford Cripps interpreted it thus, but Mr. Thomas interjected: 'No. I said I would be no party to doing anything that would drive her out.' Sir Thomas Inskip tried to efface the impression that a political threat had been delivered. 'Even if the Irish Free State were to go out of the Empire,' he said, 'I do not suppose that after the first irritation we should find it difficult to be on friendly terms with them.' But, in answer to Mr. Churchill, he denied that it was his intention to reduce the force of what the Secretary of State had said. But what exactly had the Secretary of State said? Where did the government stand? The tendency of the debate was to create the impression that an unwelcome event was drawing nearer, and that the British government was determined not to define in advance its attitude to that event. Freedom-loving apostles of the new British Commonwealth told the world that in no circumstances would Great Britain use force against an Irish Free State which decided to secede;[2] but the British government had made no declaration to this effect. Unionists continued to denounce the dismemberment of the Empire. Realists insisted that the government must not pledge itself in advance to accept an act which in its unforeseeable political context might be a threat to the safety of Great Britain. The government itself, partly perhaps for this reason, partly perhaps in accordance with its long-practised shyness of any theoretical pronouncement upon the right of secession, said nothing more. It left the course of future British policy towards the Irish Free State uncertain and obscure.

It also left the initiative with the government of the Irish Free State. It is easy to point out, from the British standpoint, the con-

[1] He greatly exaggerated these effects, according to Professor Keith. See *Letters on Imperial Relations*, No. 85.

[2] e.g. Professor Coupland, *The Empire in These Days*.

tradictions of Free State policy. The assurances given by the Free State in 1931 that it recognized the treaty as a mutually binding agreement had played a decisive part in the debates on the Statute of Westminster. The Free State now felt itself at liberty to ignore the contractual aspect of the treaty and to insist on the statutory aspect only. Mr. De Valera's advent had created a breach of continuity which—if it is held that a government may speak for the state and not merely for a passing majority in the state—amounted to a breach of faith. The new government took advantage of every power which had accrued to the state by its predecessor's policy, and at the same time felt itself unbound by its predecessor's pledges. The government was thus enabled to denounce the shame of Ireland's unfree title-deeds and to exploit a freedom of unilateral action which by these legal title-deeds, and by no others, was virtually unlimited. Both to the British government, and to the opposition led by Mr. Cosgrave, and to the rigid republicans, this policy seemed unfair in the extreme.

The policy, however, must also be viewed in the light of the assumptions of the Fianna Fáil party and of the majority of nationalistic voters whose adherence this party had secured. In their view Mr. De Valera's government was continuing the fight for freedom by methods appropriate to the occasion. They were not chiefly concerned to justify themselves in face of the protests which came from England; they were chiefly concerned to ward off the accusations of the militant republicans. They had to prove their loyalty to the separatist ideal. From this point of view it becomes plain that the upbraidings of the British government were useful and perhaps even necessary to them. The Cosgrave government had grounded itself on the assumption that the treaty settlement was an honourable one, and upon the further assumption, which had grown out of the experience of expanding Irish rights, that the Saorstát's relations with Great Britain and the other nations of the Commonwealth were normal and friendly relations. The Fianna Fáil party rested on the assumption that the treaty was for Ireland an ignominious surrender and for Great Britain a perpetuation of the conquest by other means. The war for Irish freedom was therefore still being fought. But there were two ways of fighting, the way of the lion and the way of the fox, and in present circumstances the second method had the greater advantage. Most certainly the Fianna Fáil party would not have stated its position by such a cold analysis. But it would have contended—and the result is the same—that it was justified in using the weapons which British law placed in its hands and at the same time denying the validity of any law which was not wholly Irish. Its policy was the continuation of struggle by other means.

But to what end? Mr. De Valera had realized in 1922, and he was realizing now from his experience as responsible head of the Irish Free State, that the destinies of Great Britain and Ireland were in many ways interlocked. In the winter of 1922–3 he had been ready for association with Great Britain and the other nations of the Commonwealth, but he had not been willing to accept the terms of the association as the British insisted on defining them. Instead of the common Crown and common allegiance, he had demanded reciprocal citizenship between original and independent nations; instead of 'membership' of the Commonwealth, he had demanded 'external association' with it. He had indeed fought the civil war—as civil wars must perhaps be fought—under the more inspiring, the more understandable banner of the perfectionist zealots. But those days were now long past, conditions were now totally different; neither the crude methods in which these old comrades persisted nor the unreal simplicity of their ends could be acceptable to a statesman who must measure against present possibilities and future contingencies the real needs of the community for whose well-being, material and spiritual, he had accepted a heavy responsibility. His earlier programme of external association might not fit the opportunities of 1932 or 1936. What might have been conceded to the English then might be too much to offer them now. Yet perhaps it might satisfy. What the English had then refused might now be taken from them by means of the weapons which they had surrendered into Irish hands, and something like the settlement which had been sketched in Draft Treaty A and Document No. 2 might after all fit the possibilities and the needs of the new times.

Such an interpretation, which must of course be recognized as highly speculative, is consistent with the words and acts of the De Valera government between 1932 and 1936. Facing the party which had supported the treaty and which was pledged to the principles of co-operation and consultation with the Commonwealth nations by which the treaty rights had been enlarged, Mr. De Valera insisted that the state remained unfree and that adherence to the old methods was a sign of its servitude. If Ireland was free, he asked, why was Cobh being held, and why were the British maintaining parties of troops on Irish soil? Was it with the will of the Irish people that the six counties were cut off from the rest of Ireland?[1] If Ireland

[1] Speech on final stage of the bill to abolish the Senate. *Dáil Debates*, vol. lii, 25th May 1934, cols. 1850–80.

was free, what was the meaning of those threatening declarations made from time to time by British statesmen? Were they not trying to tie Ireland to constitutional forms which she disliked? Ireland had been invaded, and had struggled against that invasion for over seven and a half centuries. The British were still trying to insist on their pretended right to tell the Irish what they must do. It was obvious that if the Irish did not get the form of government they wanted, some power from outside was preventing them. The conquest had not yet been undone.[1] . . . But the conquest had been in large measure undone. On this Mr. De Valera insisted with equal emphasis. Ireland, he declared, was free in part.[2] It was his answer to the doctrinaire republicans. If it were not true, his was a usurping un-national government which had no authority to defend public order against the patriot army which was continuing the seven centuries of struggle against alien and usurping rule. In reply to the upbraidings and threats of the revolutionary republicans, Mr. De Valera repeatedly appealed to the free choice of a democratic community by whose authority the state possessed one government and one army. He promised that before his government completed its term of office it would bestow upon the community a constitution which would be 'Irish from top to bottom'.

> 'We are at the moment [he said] very nearly being completely free. The only thing that is not now done with the will of the people is that a foreign King, as I call him—a foreign King because, if the people were free, they would not select him—signs some letters of credence in cases where representatives are sent to a foreign country.'[3]

If the chief blemish upon freedom was the monarchical symbolism injected into the people's constitution, Mr. De Valera's claims were justified. Long ago, Mr. Cosgrave's government had justified the claim of the defenders of the treaty that those forms could not impede the fact of self-government won for the Irish Free State. Mr. De Valera had done more; he had used the fact to wipe out the forms. It no longer belonged to the representative of the Crown to make formal recommendation of appropriations. It was no longer within his formal power to withhold assent to Bills or to reserve them. The parliamentary oath of allegiance had been abolished. The appeal to His Majesty in Council had been abolished. Irish citizenship had

[1] See a special press interview in the *Daily Telegraph*, 3rd April 1935.

[2] Speech of 25th May 1934, quoted above.

[3] Speech at Ennis, 30th June 1935. The passage about the 'foreign King' was quoted with indignation by Colonel Gretton in the debate of 10th July 1935. See Hansard, *House of Commons Debates*, vol. ccciv, col. 406.

been defined by an act of the Oireachtas in a manner which took no account of British theories of a common status founded upon allegiance. Although the office of governor-general still for the time survived, it no longer survived in the dignified trappings of monarchy, and each transient occupant of the precarious office might be removed, as he might be appointed, on the decision of the executive council.

Of these signposts along the road of Irish freedom only one need now invite a short pause for inspection. The Irish Nationality and Citizenship Act 1935[1] perhaps revealed more clearly than any other measure the direction in which the road was leading, even if it did not reveal the road's end. Legislation was becoming immediately necessary because the new economic ordering of things sought to limit the effective control of industry to Irish nationals.[2] But Irish nationality had never been satisfactorily defined. It had rested merely upon a vague reference in the treaty and upon a very incomplete article[3] of the constitution. The oath of allegiance stipulated in the treaty, which referred to the 'common citizenship of Ireland with Great Britain', had now been abolished. The treaty itself had lost its force in the municipal law of the Free State. Article 3 of the constitution, while provisionally and inadequately defining citizenship, provided also that at some future date 'the conditions governing the acquisition and termination of citizenship in the Irish Free State should be determined by law'. That determination had never been made. As a result, thousands of children born since 1922 and thousands of returned emigrants were not in law Irish citizens. Their only statutory status was under the British Nationality Acts of 1914 and 1918, if indeed these acts were still in force in the Irish Free State. The legislation of 1935 now repealed these Acts 'if and so far as they were ever in force in the Irish Free State'. It proceeded to provide for Irish nationality generally in the manner of the British legislation, adding, however, provisions, which progressive opinion had for long demanded, abrogating the doctrine that marriage automatically affects the citizenship of a woman who marries a non-citizen. The part of the measure which provoked most controversy was that which substituted for the 'common citizenship' of which the treaty had made mention arrangements for recognizing 'reciprocal citizenship' between Saorstát Éireann and other countries. Mr.

[1] Act No. 13 of 1935. The Bill was ordered to be printed on 27th June 1934, it was introduced into the Dáil early in November, and was considerably amended in the Senate and Dáil before it passed.

[2] Cf. *Control of Industries Acts*, 1933 and 1934.

[3] Article 3.

De Valera explained to the Dáil on the 19th December 1934 that henceforward no person who was of Irish nationality would be regarded by Irish law as a British subject. He added that it would be an impertinence for the British to continue to speak of Free State nationals as British subjects. This was in answer to Mr. Thomas, who had announced that the bill did not purport to, and could not in any case, deprive any person of his status as a British subject. For this announcement Mr. Thomas claimed high legal authority.[1] But the doctors differed. It was pointed out at the time[2] that the bill as originally presented *did* purport to eliminate from Irish law the status of a British subject, by repealing the Acts of 1914 and 1918, and also that the bill was later amended with the intention to exclude the possibility of British status under the common law. Even if the effectiveness of this exclusion were doubted, it was clear that one provision of the measure was effective: its naturalization provisions made possible the creation of Irish nationals who would not be British subjects. It would not be possible to issue passports to these persons in the name of His Britannic Majesty.[3] With regard to the central question of common status, Professor Keith believed that there would be a conflict of views, and lamented that there was no Commonwealth tribunal to resolve the conflict. Looking back now on the Nationality and Citizenship Act one must place by its side the Aliens Act which was passed immediately afterwards.[4] This Act defines an alien as a person who is not a citizen of the Irish Free State, thereby including British subjects. But it also empowers the executive council to exempt the citizens, subjects, or nationals of any country from any provision of the Act or of any order issued under the Act. Citizens, subjects, or nationals of all parts of the British Commonwealth did in fact receive prompt exemption.[5]

Plainly, this legislation is a systematic and literal elaboration of the theory first put forward by the Irish delegation of 1922 in Draft Treaty A. It is permeated with the ideas of 'external association' as against 'membership', and of 'reciprocal citizenship' as against 'common citizenship'. 'Not a single line or comma of this bill', Mr. De Valera had asserted in the Dáil, 'would be altered if a Republic was declared for the whole of Ireland to-morrow.'[6] And

[1] Speech at Derby, 1st December 1934; *The Times*, 3rd December 1934.

[2] By Professor Keith, *Journal of Comparative Legislation*, 3rd series, vol. xvii, pp. 115 ff.

[3] Observation in the *Round Table*, vol. xxv, p. 374.

[4] No. 14 of 1935.

[5] *Aliens (Exemption) Order*, 1935. *Statutory Rules and Orders*, 1935, No. 80.

[6] *Dáil Debates*, vol. liv, 28th November 1934, col. 410.

yet the situation remained complicated. The Statute of Westminster, which recognized the authority of the Free State legislature to repeal British statutes in so far as they were part of the law of the Free State, declared in its preamble[1] that the Crown was the symbol of the free association of the members of the British Commonwealth of Nations and that these were united by a common allegiance to the Crown. Mr. De Valera had appealed to the conclusions of the Imperial Conference of 1930 with regard to nationality; but that conference had recognized allegiance to the Crown as 'the basis of the common status possessed by all subjects of His Majesty'. The Conference of 1926 had made a similar pronouncement. So long as the Irish Free State remained within an association which had accepted the Crown as its symbol, could it merely by its own protesting legislation evade the consequence of common status founded upon allegiance, which was a recognized principle of the association? It might be said that these were the infinitely wearisome and endlessly arguable technicalities of lawyers. Then why not cut the argument short once and for all? It might take two members of the Commonwealth, or perhaps all of them, to untie the knot of a common status.[2] But one member might cut the knot. Why did not the government of the Irish Free State renounce allegiance to the Crown and so end the argument? Why did it not take the only way to certainty, the declaration of a republic? The question was thrown at Mr. De Valera repeatedly by his opponents in the Dáil, and particularly by Deputy MacDermot. Mr. De Valera's answer was always the same. There were immediate dangers and obstacles against which it would be insane to rush. Never again must there be a débâcle as in 1921. When they declared a republic, they must be in a position to make their declaration effective.[3]

What were these dangers and obstacles? In seeking an answer to this question it will be worth while to change the method adopted above of keeping close to particular events and particular statements and working outwards from an exposition and criticism of these towards a general view of the developing situation. It will be worth while to stand farther off and look for a general pattern in events, running the risk that the pattern which is discerned may turn out

[1] Mr. Churchill, however, had pointed out in the debate that the preamble had no legally binding effect.

[2] Professor Keith in the *Journal of Comparative Legislation*, loc. cit. Those who wish to follow further the legal arguments as to the inadequacy of the Free State legislation to destroy the common status of British subjects may be referred particularly to Mr. Costello's speeches in the Dáil.

[3] Speech of 25th May 1934, cited above, p. 376.

to be too formal and may in practice be badly broken up by events still to come. Standing aside in this way, the observer will perceive not only the obstacles raised by Great Britain, but also others which existed in Ireland itself, both in Northern Ireland and even in the Free State.

The obstacles raised by Great Britain were naturally the ones on which Mr. De Valera laid most stress, and little more need be said about them. In the circumstances of the time it was hardly conceivable that Great Britain would send another Black and Tan expedition to beat down a seceding Irish republic. It was probably unlikely that Great Britain would employ even intensive economic 'sanctions', and it was certain that British spokesmen exaggerated the automatic damage to Irishmen living in the Commonwealth of secession by the Irish Free State. Still, the final act of political severance might well produce, now or later, economic results which would be extremely damaging. And the refusal of the British government to state in advance what its reaction would be undoubtedly kept within the field of possibility dangers which even a united republican Ireland might hesitate to confront.

But there were also the obstacles arising from the disunity of Ireland. Both in Ireland and outside it the opinion was frequently expressed that the nationalists would have to choose between republicanism and unity: that they could not have both.[1] The official opposition to Mr. De Valera's government accepted the argument that republicanism and unity were incompatible; and chose unity. It might with some justice have been retorted that unity seemed an unlikely prospect anyhow. But the Fianna Fáil party would never confess this, it would never surrender its ideal of an all-Ireland republic. Irish patriotism is pre-eminently patriotism of place: Armagh, the Glens of Antrim, the 'four green fields' are inextricably interwoven with the national sentiment. But was there a genuine correspondence between the desire of national sentiment and the direction of nationalist policy? Might not the continually receding mirage of the republic one and indivisible perpetuate a pursuit in which the provisional and the undefined would continue to be accepted and even welcomed? Might not a republic of the twenty-six counties still be pushed away because it was not the Republic of Ireland? But when would that come? Certainly, there were no signs that Mr. De Valera's policy was creating a union of hearts between North and South behind the republican banner. The gulf of partition

[1] It is interesting that the French writer Gallopin, who generally sums up on Mr. De Valera's side, comes to this conclusion.

was deepening. Even in sport the separation became almost absolute. Politically, the rejection by the Saorstát, one by one, of the monarchical symbols, provoked in the governing majority of the North a fiercer will to hold them and to flaunt them. Economically, the protectionist policies of the Saorstát were cutting the six counties off from Ireland and convincing them, if they had ever needed to be convinced, that both their agricultural and industrial interests could only thrive in the larger economic unit of the United Kingdom. The same policies were creating in the twenty-six counties a vested interest for the perpetuation of partition. Would the new industries established there welcome the prospect of extinction for the sake of Belfast? Did Irish nationalism really desire industrial domination from the north? Did it, in fact, will the 'All-Ireland Republic', or did it wish merely to keep dreaming of it?

The psychological obstacles to a union of North and South were no less formidable than the economic ones. The Fianna Fáil party, while it sincerely declared that it ruled out the use of force against the North, flattered itself by repeating that the North would soon 'come to its senses' and join the rest of Ireland if only Great Britain would 'stand aside'. This definitely was an illusion. The real fact to be reckoned with was not partition but the northern will for partition. This was but the obverse of the northern will for union with Great Britain. To talk of Great Britain 'standing aside' had no meaning when the majority in the north would go to the last extreme to prevent Great Britain tearing herself from them or thrusting them out. To talk of the north 'coming to its senses' was to forget

> The hard cold fire of the northerner
> Frozen into his blood from the fire in his basalt.[1]

The Protestant north was inflexible. It did not allow itself to become entangled in the mental barbed wire of political theorizing and legalistic controversy. It asserted its will. To Irish dominionism and Irish republicanism alike it opposed the conception which it had inherited from the 'ascendancy' and the union—the conception of the development of the British Isles as a single political, economic, and strategic unit. It took what measures it deemed necessary to defend itself and its ideal. English liberals discovered to their horror that these were not the measures of British legal and parliamentary convention, but the measures of a garrison.[2] But argument and pro-

[1] From *Belfast*, by Louis MacNeice, a poet of Ulster origin.

[2] See *Report of a Commission of Inquiry appointed to examine the purpose and effect of the Civil Authorities (Special Powers) Acts (Northern Ireland) 1922 and 1933*, published in 1936 by the National Council of Civil Liberties. For the reply of the govern-

test had no effect upon the Orange rulers in Ulster. Only a fighting creed and a will no less intractable than theirs might break or shake them. Communism might provide that creed and that will and a fanaticism strong enough to efface the existing sectarian fanaticism which divided the workers. It might be that Mr. Peadar O'Donnel, the missionary of a united workers' republic, was the only revolutionary leader who knew what he wanted and knew the purchase-price of what he wanted. But what impression could the gospel of a workers' republic make against the embattled property and Protestantism of Ulster, or, for that matter, against the entrenched property and Catholicism of the Irish Free State?

If, as English liberals complained, the Civil Authorities (Special Powers) Acts of 1922 and 1933 had transformed Northern Ireland into a police-state, the amending Article 2 A had imposed upon the constitution of the Irish Free State a transformation of similar character, if not quite of similar extent. The Cosgrave government had secured this amendment from the legislature, and the De Valera government on coming to power deemed it advisable to suspend and not to surrender the operation of the amendment.[1] It discovered later on that it could not do without the special powers which Article 2 A conferred. Indirectly, the military tribunal for which the article made provision was the occasion of a more fundamental extension of the powers of The State *versus* Man. Out of its operations arose the whole question whether there was or was not a fundamental law limiting the actions of state authorities. The original constitution, in the manner of continental democracy, had explicitly affirmed the rights of man and of the citizen. But it had left a loophole for amending the processes of amendment, and when this had been achieved the rights of man and of the citizen might be amended out of existence. That was the purport of a decision of the Supreme Court in December 1934.[2] The decision affirmed the power of the

ment of Northern Ireland see the *Weekly Irish Times*, 30th May 1936, and Northern Ireland, *House of Commons Debates*, 26th May 1936, col. 1766. The Prime Minister denounced the report as a grossly biased publication similar in tendency to the propaganda for an all-Ireland Republic—'To this I need hardly say the loyalists of Ulster will never agree.' But the report was a document of English liberalism, not of Irish republicanism. Among its authors was a former Principal of Somerville College, Oxford.

The writer must here confess, what the reader has doubtless observed, that the two chapters on Ireland in this volume suffer from the lack of a thorough treatment of the North. Such a treatment would have to be grounded on a complete historical and sociological investigation which has not as yet been undertaken.

[1] *Constitution* (*Suspension of Article 2A*) *Order 1932*, 18th March 1932.

[2] *The State* (*Ryan and Others*) v. *Lennon and Others*, I.R. 1935, pp. 170 ff. The arguments and the judgements in this case, both in the High Court and the Supreme

legislature to alter the constitution at its will: it left in the constitution nothing 'fundamental'. It should be remembered that the normal checks which in Great Britain and in the Dominions tempered the apparent omnipotence of an elected legislature were at this time being abolished in the Irish Free State. Recently in New South Wales a governor had taken his stand upon the law and had dismissed a premier whom he judged to have gone outside the law; the incoming premier had taken responsibility for the governor's action and the electorate had emphatically endorsed it.[1] In the United Kingdom the King possessed normally a regulative function which in practice was likely to be more important than that of a governor in an Australian state. Since the Imperial Conference of 1930, the authority of the governors-general had in all the Dominions, at least potentially, lost something of that monarchical aloofness which it had been the intention, four years earlier, to give it.[2] In the Irish Free State the office of governor-general now hardly counted for anything at all. Moreover, the Senate, after taking a long time in dying, came to an end in May 1936.[3] No checks at all, either of institutions or of law, were now left upon the transitory majorities of single chamber. Would a majority which was in possession allow itself to be transitory? Would it not succumb, now or later, to the temptation to perpetuate its power? Was not the Irish Free State already far along the road, familiar in ancient Greece and in contemporary Europe, which led from democracy to dictatorship?

These questions were asked in the Irish Free State. Nevertheless, although in theory Mr. De Valera had finally cleared the road to the party-state, in practice he showed no serious intention of leading his party along it. Conditions in Ireland seemed favourable to the continuance of a two-party or multi-party system. Was this because something healthy in the British legal and parliamentary tradition had rooted itself in Irish soil? An observer from the North reflected, perhaps a little naïvely: 'The strange thing is that many in the South have understood the real principles of the British Empire of to-day

Court, contain perhaps the most illuminating commentary on the evolution of the constitution of the Irish Free State and carry the matter beyond Dr. Kohn's fine exposition.

[1] Comparative implications are discussed in the *Journal of Comparative Legislation*, 3rd series, vol. xiv, pp. 258 ff.

[2] The appointment in 1930 of an ex-Chief Justice as Governor-General in the Commonwealth of Australia was followed in 1936 by the appointment of an ex-minister as Governor-General in the Union of South Africa.

[3] Immediately afterwards the government appointed a commission to report upon the constitution of a second chamber alternative to the one abolished. In September 1936 the commission presented a report which testified to much diversity of opinion.

much better than they do in the North.'[1] Mr. De Valera had shown courage and astuteness and conviction in his struggle to lead the Irish Free State from force to persuasion. He had in 1932 been pliant but not completely yielding towards the militant republicans; in 1933 and 1934 he had withstood General O'Duffy's half-Fascist attack and had seen its collapse; in 1936 he seemed to have won for public authority the backing, against revolutionary violence, of the vast majority of opinion in the Irish Free State. The authority of the state seemed now to rest upon a broader basis of consent than had ever before supported it; this strengthened state Mr. De Valera might one day hand over to his constitutional opponents, as they had handed over an established state to him. It even seemed not impossible that the militant republicans might in time be drawn into the constitutional processes of the state. Protesting that they would never follow the road which Fianna Fáil had taken ten years earlier, they took in 1936 what seemed to be the first step along it.[2]

The interpretation of movements in opinion is the most baffling and deceptive of enterprises; it would be folly to make summary judgements here. Even more would it be folly to attempt from the outside the interpretation of a complex and controversial personality. Yet one can at least perceive a logic in the series of circumstances with which Mr. De Valera's personality has become entangled. Deeper than his commitment against partition (for he had persistently repudiated the use of force to end it); deeper, too, than his commitment to the republic (for he had many times protested that he was no doctrinaire), was Mr. De Valera's commitment to the cause of union among the nationalists of Ireland. The controversies about the part which he had played in 1922 were hardly relevant; for if there was something to be said for the contention of his friends that he had striven then for the unity of the national forces, it was natural that he should still strive for it; and if there was something to be said for the contention of his enemies that he had then destroyed

[1] W. S. Armour, *Facing the Irish Question* (Duckworth, 1934), p. 252.

[2] In close touch with the I.R.A., the organization Cumann Poblacht Na Éireann was formed. Its constitution professed allegiance to the republic of 1916; its object was to proclaim the republic and break the connexion with England and the British Empire. Its elected candidates would not enter the usurping Dáil, but would form a lawful assembly to which others would be attracted. Mr. De Valera's followers had once professed the same intention.

The De Valera government, while continuing its policy of winning the militants to constitutional methods, showed increasing firmness against the irreconcilables. Following a series of assassinations in 1935 and 1936, the I.R.A. was proclaimed an illegal association by a government order of 19th June 1936.

unity, it was natural that he should seek now to establish a different interpretation. It was in any case inevitable that he should be haunted by memories of civil war. This he recognized as the greatest possible evil.[1] He was bound, therefore, to follow a course of action which would be sufficiently forthright to attract all but the irreconcilable republicans and yet be sufficiently moderate to prevent a flight of all prudent citizens into Mr. Cosgrave's camp. Whether or not (as has here been suggested) these tactics were in accordance with his own temperament and principles, they were certainly in accordance with the interest of his party. Fianna Fáil fought unceasingly with the Irish Republican Army for the possession of the martyrs and memories of Easter Week and the struggles of 1919–23.[2] At the same time it had the support of the capitalist interests grouped behind economic nationalism. It was, in addition, still able to adopt with considerable success the role of the poor man's party. But in this role it was coming unceasingly under fire, and leaders of militant republicanism saw an opportunity of reviving the old alliance between the national and the social revolution.[3] At the prospect of such an alliance the Church and both the great political parties raised the cry of communism. Fianna Fáil, no less than Fine Gael,[4] was bound by its structure to oppose Mr. O'Donnel's way to the all-Ireland republic.

These were some of the political complexities amidst which Mr. De Valera was compelled to move in his search for 'the government that divides us least'. Only some of the political elements have been exhibited, and these have not been weighed and measured; yet

[1] Speech of 25th May 1934 quoted above; cf. a speech identical in tone of 23rd June 1936. *Weekly Irish Times*, 27th June 1936.

[2] The press of the Irish Free State before and after the Easter celebrations of each year may be consulted for illustrations of what has been rudely called 'a body-snatching competition' and what might with more dignity be called the battle of the Lily and the Torch. The Irish Republican Army, whose emblem is the Easter Lily, has tried to appropriate to itself the memories and martyrs of 1916, 1921, and 1922. '... They died for the Republic. We will accept nothing less.' But Fianna Fáil has called on patriots to 'Honour the Men of Easter Week' by wearing a torch. However, the period of free competition in processions and celebration was closed in June 1936 when the government declared the I.R.A. an illegal association and as an immediate sequel prohibited a Wolf Tone gathering at Bodenstown.

[3] Significant was the offer of the I.R.A. to intervene on the side of the workers in the transport strike of the spring of 1935 (*The Times*, 25th March 1935). Equally significant was the arrest which followed of seventy prominent members of the I.R.A. (*The Times*, 30th March 1935). Developments of this kind can best be followed in the papers of the left which appear and disappear (e.g. those with which Mr. O'Donnel has been connected—the *Republican Congress*, the *People*, &c.). A good deal of fact is contained, with much anti-communist comment, in the pamphlet, *Can Ireland go Communist?*, by Professor Hogan.

[4] The Fine Gael party had declared for membership of the Commonwealth.

enough has been revealed to suggest a third answer to the question asked above: Why did not Mr. De Valera cut the knot of confusion and uncertainty by an act of secession from the Commonwealth? The strain might have been too great upon the unity of the community for which he was responsible. On the one hand, the act might have unleashed the revolutionary left; on the other hand, it might have had damaging repercussions which would provoke the revolt of formidable conservative forces. The chief 'sanctions' against uncompromising separatism were, perhaps, internal ones.

In the circumstances, it seemed in 1936 that those prophets were most likely to be right who anticipated that the new constitution, 'Irish from top to bottom', which had been promised, would eliminate the Governor-General and in most other respects leave things rather as they were.[1] The Free State had already travelled most of the road which Mr. De Valera had wanted to take during the treaty negotiations and the early days of the Sinn Féin split. Little remained to be done to shape the constitution so that the theory of external association might fit its facts.

The crisis of the monarchy in December 1936 speeded up the work of constitutional remodelling, and illustrated at the same time its necessarily tentative and provisional character. On the 10th December, members of the Dáil were summoned by telegram to meet at 3 p.m. on the following day, 'for the purpose of considering, in connection with the proposed abdication of His Majesty King Edward VIII, proposals for the amendment of the Constitution and other legislation'. The government placed before the Dáil two bills, which it proposed to push through the Dáil by guillotine procedure. The general effect of the first bill would be to remove the Crown from the internal constitution of Saorstát Éireann.[2] The effect of the second bill would be to recognize the Crown in the sphere of its existing action in external relations, so long as the other nations of the Commonwealth continued to recognize it as 'the symbol of their co-operation'.[3] Mr. De Valera declared that the government was

[1] *Manchester Guardian*, 20th April 1936. On 24th June 1936 Mr. De Valera definitely announced in the Dáil that the new constitution would provide for an elective head of the state.

[2] *Constitution* (*Amendment No. 27*) *Bill*, 1936. It amended articles 2A, 12, 24, 41, 42, 51, 53, 55, 60, 68. It abolished the function of the Representative of the Crown in executive government; in the appointment of ministers, judges, the special tribunal; in legislation, in the assent to bills, and in the summoning of the Dáil. The bill left the *office* of governor-general for the time being in existence, but functionless.

[3] *Executive Authority* (*External Relations*) *Bill*, 1936. Mr. De Valera explained its contents thus: 'We propose to continue the King for the functions which he in fact

prepared to take responsibility for the second bill only when it had secured the first. He asserted emphatically that an alteration in the constitution of the state was a matter which concerned 'ourselves alone'. Nevertheless, it was necessary, so long as the Irish Free State remained associated with the states of the British Commonwealth, that she should take 'common action, or rather concerted action . . . in the matter'. Constitutionally and legally, Edward VIII would remain King in the Irish Free State until his abdication had been decided upon by Parliament.[1]

The opposition attacked both the method and substance of the government's action. It agreed that legislation was necessary to resolve the crisis; but it argued that the proposed legislation did not resolve the crisis. It did not provide for the abdication of King Edward. Instead, it changed the functions of the kingship. It altered the constitution in a manner which was obscure but possibly far-reaching. The government had promised that the people would be given the opportunity for a considered verdict upon constitutional change; that promise it was now breaking. It was a 'parody of parliamentary practice' to alter the fundamental law of the state 'under a guillotine resolution in about five hours'. That was not the way of democracy, but of dictatorship.[2] Why had there been no consultation between parties, as in Great Britain?[3] And why had there been no consultation with the other States of the Commonwealth? 'How have we kept our word', Mr. Costello asked, 'with those Dominions which helped the representatives of the Irish people to achieve their freedom in the Imperial Conferences of 1926 and 1929 and 1930?'[4]

The opposition argued that the government was clinging with its left hand to the tow-rope of the Commonwealth, while it waggled the republican flag with its right.[5] The bills would not enlarge the freedom of Saorstát Éireann. The actual powers of the state would not be increased one whit: they could not be, for they were already complete sovereign powers. The change in symbolism, nevertheless,

directly exercises and for these only.' Of the two bills together he said that they eliminated fiction from the constitution. 'What is happening is that from the King are being taken away any functions internal, either direct or indirect, in the Administration of the Government and in the internal Executive of the country, and we are retaining the King for those purposes for which he was used hitherto.' *Dáil Debates*, 11th December 1936, cols. 1279, 1280.

[1] Ibid., cols. 1231–4.

[2] Ibid., cols. 1245, 1285, 1348.

[3] Ibid., col. 1261. This point was made by Mr. Davin for the Labour party.

[4] Ibid., col. 1299.

[5] Ibid., cols. 1268–9. [Dr. O'Higgins.]

was a serious matter. It was a clear breach of the Treaty.[1] It was also a breach of the principle of association in the Commonwealth, whose members accepted the Crown as 'an integral part of the State'.[2] The President had announced that article 1 of the constitution, which asserted the Free State's membership of the Commonwealth, remained in force. But suppose the nations of the Commonwealth thought otherwise? Suppose they decided to reject a member who rejected the rules of their association?[3] The British Commonwealth, like any other association, had the right to lay down its own rules of membership. Did the government know what the reply of Great Britain would be? Did it even know what was the extent and what were the limits of its own proposals? The opposition argued that the Constitution Amendment Bill removed the King from the constitution, but not from the state.[4] It pointed out that neither of the two bills dealt with the immediate issue, the abdication of King Edward. 'Surely the position is', declared Mr. McGilligan, 'that to-morrow night we will have in this country apparently a Governor-General without function, Edward VIII King, but without function, and the new King with a limited function.'[5]

The government admitted the force of this last criticism, and on the 12th December it introduced into the second bill an amendment making explicit provision for the abdication of King Edward.[6] The opposition welcomed this amendment, and was not prepared to divide against the bill. But another amendment moved by Mr. Costello emphasized the divergence of interpretation and feeling between Mr. Cosgrave's followers and Mr. De Valera's. The amendment proposed to describe the Crown in the words accepted by the nations of the Commonwealth—'as the symbol of their free association'—instead of in the words employed by the bill—'the symbol of their co-operation'. Mr. De Valera offered a compromise. He

[1] Ibid., cols. 1287–90, 1389. Mr. McGilligan pointed out that the argument employed for the Removal of Oath Bill, namely that the oath was not mandatory in the treaty, could not possibly be applied to the office and functions of the Governor-General.

[2] Ibid., col. 1316—a very clear argument by Mr. Desmond Fitzgerald, and col. 1366, for General Mulcahy's emphatic acceptance of monarchical symbolism.

[3] Ibid., col. 1293. Mr. Costello—'We do not know the repercussions.' There were many complaints that Mr. De Valera had given no account of the reception by the British of his communication, some time earlier, of his intentions with regard to the removal of the Governor-General from the constitution.

[4] Ibid., col. 1253, and 12th December, col. 1409. Professor Thrift emphasizes that both bills deal with the functions, not with the entity, of the King.

[5] Ibid., col. 1357.

[6] Ibid., col. 1389. Mr. De Valera admitted in effect that for twenty-four hours Ireland has had a different king from the other nations of the Commonwealth.

would substitute the word 'association' for the word 'co-operation'. But he would not accept the whole phrase—'free association'.

Mr. McGilligan: 'What is the objection to the word "free"?'

The President: 'I am not certain that in all cases it is free.'[1]

On that note of doubt this chapter may fittingly conclude. It records a fact—the influence of past centuries of Irish history, persisting in the new era of the Commonwealth of Nations. The student of Irish history will not feel any surprise at this persistence. On the contrary, he would have felt surprise if fifteen years of the Commonwealth relationship had been sufficient to wipe out the associations of centuries, with their penal laws, their plantations, and their oppressions. It is not sufficient, for the understanding of modern Ireland, to study only the records of the Irish Free State. Still less is it sufficient to study the debates between the two chief parties in the state. For there are other elements in Ireland which have not shared in the new political experience. The six northern counties are not represented in the Dáil; the militant republicans are absent. But both these elements must of necessity enter into the calculations of national idealism and statesmanship. In a country so divided by its past, both recent and remote, the search for 'the government which divides us least' must be both cautious and patient.

It may also prove true that this search must go hand in hand with the search for Anglo-Irish friendship, itself a matter demanding patience. And, if the Irish have the right to demand of the English that they should study past history, the English, in revenge, may fairly demand of the Irish that they should study present geography. The chief danger to the future of the two peoples in 1936 seemed to be the rapid impetus of events, which might forestall the efforts of history and geography to come to terms with each other.

The treaty contained provisions based upon strategical interdependence. Mr. De Valera had more than once attacked these provisions. He had denounced the presence of British maintenance parties in Irish forts. He had declared that no Irish government could retain the confidence of the Irish people if it granted to a British government the rights which the treaty permitted it to claim in time of war or strained relations.[2] Here was an issue which might cut through all the legalisms and turn the battles of theory into a struggle for mere life. The Privy Council decision of 1935 made it clear that Irish legislation abolishing the defence clauses of the treaty would not be invalidated in British courts. But

[1] *Dáil Debates*, 12th December 1936, col. 1487.

[2] *The Times*, 8th June 1935.

the British government and people would be likely to regard it as a breach of the treaty and a threat to the safety of Great Britain. In the War of 1914–18 the navy depended upon Irish harbours as bases for operations necessary for the defence of the trade and food supply of the British Isles. Without the use of these harbours it could not have conducted the anti-submarine struggle upon which the outcome of the war depended. The development of air power since 1918 had multiplied the dangers which threatened the British Isles and had still further emphasized the strategic importance of the Irish coast in a struggle against blockade and starvation. The symbols and loyalties and theories of the English and the Irish might have shattering effects in a world which geography and invention made so dangerous. Even in the past, the fact of struggle for security in a world of conflict had lain very close to the root of struggle and suffering in Ireland. And in 1936 the world which had failed to build upon the League of Nations showed all the signs of collapsing again into conflict.

In continental newspapers there had been speculations on the possibility that Ireland might serve as a spring-board for an attack upon Great Britain. Mr. De Valera denounced these speculations. He said that he would never permit the Irish Free State to be used by foreign Powers as a base for attack upon Great Britain.

> 'I have been making that statement in almost identical terms since 1917 [he declared]. I made it from a hundred platforms in the United States during the years 1919–20. A free Ireland in times of common risk could be for Great Britain only a friendly Ireland, and would be a surer safeguard to Britain's security than could possibly be an Ireland in subjection, for an Ireland in subjection could only be a hostile Ireland.'[1]

The statement bore the stamp of sincerity, as indeed the earlier statements had done. But was the sincerity supported by a knowledge which had counted the cost? The treaty had anticipated an arrangement by which the Irish Free State should take over her own coastal defence;[2] but neither Mr. Cosgrave's government nor Mr. De Valera's had made any move to do so. Moreover, coastal defence was useless unless it was co-ordinated with naval defence and air defence. Friendliness between Great Britain and Ireland had strategical implications no less definite than its economic implications. In all the utterances of Mr. De Valera, none contained greater hope for the future than the two words, 'common risk'. But if the words were to mean anything, there must be community of purpose before the common risk became immediate common peril.

[1] Ibid. [2] Article 6.

Looking back upon these years of dispute between Great Britain and the Irish Free State, the writer feels that their experience reveals the strength of the objective facts working for the interdependence, the co-operation, and in the end for the reconciliation of the two countries. Economically and politically each of them had so much power to harm the other; yet neither could inflict this harm without doing extreme damage to itself. The two countries would remain inseparably bound, even if they were bound in a mutually inflicted ruin. Given a newly created friendship between them, all things were possible. A friendship which should extinguish for ever all fear of conflict between them could not fail to bring with it the fruits of appeasement between North and South. Yet would Great Britain and Ireland discover the secret of friendship? Or would they discover it in time?

CHAPTER VII

THE MEDICINE OF THE BODY POLITIC

I

Three Islands

In the decade which followed the Great War it was frequently assumed that 'the government of men by themselves'—which by vigorous assertion or tacit consent was generally taken to be the central principle of the British Commonwealth[1]—was destined to realize itself not only inevitably but rapidly. The British Commonwealth was pictured as a 'procession' of communities passing through the crown colony stage to representative government and finally to responsible government.[2] Ireland, India, Southern Rhodesia, and Ceylon might hold different places in the procession; but all of them were moving forward towards the same end. This was an inspiring conception, and undoubtedly it exercised considerable influence upon policy. But before very long inspiration began to flag a little. Some of the foremost members of the procession showed an inclination to break out of its ranks altogether; to many eager nationalists, for example in Ireland, the right of self-government meant the right of secession. Must the principle of the Commonwealth involve acquiescence in the dissolution of the Commonwealth? There were, on the other hand, other communities which seemed unable to keep pace with their fellow marchers in the procession. The movements of these communities were reminiscent of the children's game of snakes-and-ladders. After getting a certain distance, they found themselves being sent back to the starting-point.

India, it was generally agreed, was the great test of the Commonwealth principle. The very attempt to realize the principle in India was proof of a belief in its universal validity; self-government was not merely a privilege for Europeans. At the same time there were present in India both the difficulties which have been mentioned. On the one hand, there existed among nationalist Indians widespread impatience and resentment at the slow pace of the procession, and among some of them there was a disposition to reject as a fraud any instalment of self-government which fell short of full independence.

[1] The most vigorous attempt at systematic assertion is to be found in Lionel Curtis, *Civitas Dei* (Macmillan, 1934). Cf. Coatman, *Magna Britannia*.

[2] See A. E. Zimmern, *The Third British Empire* (Oxford University Press, 1926), passim.

On the other hand, there were fears—which, although they were voiced chiefly among Englishmen, were not necessarily disingenuous—lest the pace of the procession, even as it had been fixed, might be too hot for India's three hundred millions, and might throw into confusion and strife the communities into which that vast mass of mankind was divided.

The Indian problem is too large to be faced at this late stage of a volume; means must be found of approaching it in the next volume by the economic path. The present chapter will instead consider three islands whose histories are interesting in themselves and of some value in relation to the central question of Indian government and indeed of government throughout the Commonwealth. If we are hardy enough to regard the Commonwealth's experiment as the adventure of an idea, we surely must also be resolute enough to face those elements of surprise, bafflement, and discomfiture which are mingled with the triumphs of every adventure. Is it possible by reflection on experience to recognize the conditions which make for success and those which make for failure, and to frame policies accordingly? Of the three islands whose circumstances will now be examined, only one, Ceylon, seemed in 1936 to be keeping the place assigned to it in the Commonwealth procession. The other two, Newfoundland and Malta, had fallen out of the march. For the purposes of this section Malta is of these three islands the most significant, and will be considered at the greatest length.

The experiment of self-government in Ceylon appears a venturesome one when viewed in the light of that island's history. For more than two millenniums Ceylon had been an absolute monarchy.[1] The British, in the early years of their occupation, had shown no disposition to regard themselves as missionaries of the Commonwealth idea; so far were they from introducing self-governing institutions that they allowed the 'village republics', whose free functioning in the immediate matters of peasant life had tempered the autocratic form of society, to fall into decay. Not until the second half of the nineteenth century did the British attempt to revive village self-government and to establish municipal government in the larger towns. The central government of Ceylon, when the Great War began, was still crown colony government of a strict type: there was an official majority on the legislative council, and of the ten unofficial members of the council only four were elected. A movement towards associating the people with the government was nevertheless under

[1] *Report of the Special Commission on the Constitution of Ceylon* (Donoughmore Commission), Cmd. 3131 of 1928, p. 5.

way, even though this movement had not reached an advanced stage in practice. In the minds of the people of Ceylon, the movement was leaping far ahead of practice. Before the war was over a body called the Ceylon National Association was demanding a four-fifths majority of territorially elected members on the legislative council, an elected speaker, financial control for the legislature, and a half share for its elected members of places in the executive council. The ultimate aim was national autonomy on the dominion model.

But was Ceylon a nation? The Ceylon National Association represented chiefly one section of the Ceylon people, the low-country Sinhalese.[1] It was customary to classify the five million inhabitants of Ceylon by communities. There were, for example:

(1) 3,300,000 Sinhalese, amongst whom the 1,200,000 inhabitants of the ancient kingdom of Kandy held themselves to some extent apart from the Sinhalese of the plain.
(2) 540,000 Ceylon Tamils, living for the most part in the northern and eastern plains, whose ancestors had come from southern India, but who were now an integral part of the Ceylon people.
(3) 312,000 Mohammedans, of whom some were descendants of Arab traders who had settled in Ceylon, some were descendants of Arabs from India, and some were Malays.
(4) 700,000 Indian Tamils, who had been introduced in recent times as plantation labourers but who for the most part would remain as a permanent part of the population.[2]
(5) The small but important community of burghers, who were of Dutch descent.
(6) The still smaller community of Europeans, about 11,000 in number, who played a dominant part in the economic life of the island.

The classification which has been given is the classification adopted by the Donoughmore Commission. It will be observed that this classification injects the criterion of religion into a classification primarily racial. Another classification, adhering strictly to the racial principle, would divide the Mohammedan population into Indian Moors, Ceylon Moors, and Malays.[3] The main point is, how-

[1] The Tamils had at first joined in the Ceylon National Association but before long seceded from it.

[2] In 1936 a motion was tabled in the State Council asking for immediate legislation 'to repatriate the non-Ceylonese who, by securing for themselves employment which the Ceylonese are capable of undertaking, have caused unemployment among the Ceylonese'.

[3] This other classification was adopted in 1922 by the governor of Ceylon. Cmd. 1809 of 1923, p. 16. The Donoughmore Commission itself reported a desire of the Malays for separate communal representation. (Cmd. 3131, p. 94.)

ever, that classification by communities along lines which are in general perfectly distinct is quite unavoidable. This fact was bound to dominate the problem of constitution-making in Ceylon. When the loyalties and affections of numerous sections of the people attach themselves primarily, not to the territory and the territorial collectivity, but to some separate racial or religious community, then the attempt to establish 'government of men by themselves' is likely to end in the government of the weaker communities by the stronger ones.

This, at any rate, was the idea behind the constitution which the British government granted to Ceylon in 1920. The constitution rested 'on the recognition of the fact that the population of Ceylon is not homogeneous, and that the social structure is founded on a communal basis'.[1] The legislative council was composed of 14 nominated official members and 23 elected members—11 of whom were elected by territorial constituencies, and 8 by 'communities'. The intention was to secure representation for every community, and to secure such a balance as would safeguard even the smallest community—provided it had the support of the official members—from the necessity of submitting to the will of the others. But this device inevitably placed the smaller communities in the invidious position of joining with the official members to impede the advance in political power which the majority of the people of Ceylon demanded. The Ceylon National Association asserted that the British were using the communal argument as a pretext to perpetuate their own autocratic control. The new legislative council evinced no interest in any subject except the shortcomings of the new constitution, and a majority of the elected members—a majority composed entirely of Sinhalese[2]—demanded, in the name of 'homogeneity and progress',[3] an enlarged legislative council in which the official members would be reduced to less than one-seventh of the whole, and the great majority of elected members would represent, not communities, but territorial constituencies. In answer to this demand, the Secretary of State for the Colonies sought to effect a compromise.[4] It was this compromise, embodied in the constitution of 1923, which the Donoughmore Commission investigated six years later.

[1] Cmd. 1809, No. 1.

[2] Ibid. For the proposed reforms there were 12 votes, all Sinhalese; against them were all the official votes and 11 unofficial votes, the latter comprising all the non-Sinhalese unofficial members and one Sinhalese unofficial member.

[3] Cmd. 1906 of 1923, pp. 7, 13.

[4] Cmd. 2062 of 1924, No. 3 (dispatch of the Duke of Devonshire).

The Donoughmore Commission viewed the constitution of 1922 and the attempts which had been made to work it as an experiment in political education which had gone all awry. It denounced two radical mistakes in the régime of the preceding six years: the first was 'the divorce of power from responsibility', the second was the 'canker' of communal representation.[1] The first failing it treated with a magisterial severity reminiscent of Lord Durham's report on Canada. The unofficial members, who were not responsible for the conduct of public business, enjoyed an overwhelming majority in the legislative council; the official members, who were responsible, were in a permanent minority. Sitting in a row on the government bench, they were an irresistible target for the elected members to aim at. It had been the hope of the British government that the constitution would train the politicians of Ceylon in the art of political co-operation; the elected members had virtual responsibility for legislation and it was they who controlled the public purse; it was the intention to initiate them into the practical business of state affairs by the institution of select committees. Select committees had been instituted with a vengeance; in a house of 49 members there were no less than 55 *ad hoc* select committees; a single deputy might be serving on 10 or 12 of them. In default of definite responsibility there was an indefinite and unlimited interference with the business of government. Real power fell into the hands of the finance committee of the legislative council; the executive council was devitalized, the position of the governor himself was both impotent and humiliating, all the standards of efficiency and moral courage in government were rotting away. The only remedy which the Donoughmore Commission saw for the existing disease of anaemic administration and feverish politics was to place power and responsibility in the same hands. Either the clock must be put back, and power must be taken from the elected representatives, or it must be put forward, and responsibility must be given to them. The Commission favoured the second course. But, despite the fact that it had in diagnosis so closely followed the teaching of Lord Durham, it was unable to imitate the grand simplicity of Lord Durham's remedy. It recommended that the elected representatives should be granted 'as great a degree of responsibility for the management of the affairs of the island as is compatible with a system which must inevitably fall somewhat short of full responsible government'.[2] Why must the remedy inevitably fall short of full responsible government? The report alleged the inexperience of the politicians of Ceylon and the small constituency

[1] Cmd. 3131, pp. 18 ff., 39, 90 ff.

[2] Cmd. 3131, p. 67.

which they represented, but above all it alleged the intensity of communal feeling.

> 'It is almost true to say [it argued] that the conception of patriotism in Ceylon is as much racial as national, and that the best interests of the country are at times regarded as synonymous with the welfare of a particular section of its people. If the claim for full responsible government be submitted to examination from this standpoint, it will be found that its advocates are always to be numbered among those who form the larger communities and who, if freed from external control, would be able to impose their will on all who dissented from them.'[1]

In short, the virulence of the second disease which the Commission believed to afflict the body politic of Ceylon prevented it from recommending the simplest and most natural remedy for the first disease.

The Commission, however, believed that the malady of communalism would in some degree prove susceptible to an improved treatment. The method adopted in greater or less degree in all constitutions of the past had been to accept the existence of the separate communities as a given fact, and to recognize this fact in the representative system in such a way that each community would feel that it possessed a political defence for its rights. It had been hoped that communal representation would drive out fear; that each community, knowing itself to be secure, would learn to co-operate with its fellows for the common good of the whole island and people; and that the habit of co-operation would in time produce a larger loyalty, which would not cancel, but which would transcend, the nearer communal loyalties. The Donoughmore Commission reported that these hopes had been disappointed. Instead of moderating communal interests and passions, communal representation had aggravated them. Its results had been to freeze into immobility the divisions which Ceylon had inherited from the past, and to thwart the vigorous action of those present forces whose natural tendency it was to dissolve the old divisions. So far from attenuating communal self-consciousness, communal representation was intensifying it to such an extent that new communities were discovering their need for political recognition.[2]

> 'We have come unhesitatingly to the conclusion [the Commission declared] that communal representation is, as it were, a canker on the body politic, eating deeper and deeper into the vital energies of the

[1] Cmd. 3131, p. 31.

[2] For example, the Malays had withdrawn from the Mohammedan community and were demanding separate representation as a racial community. Cmd. 3131, p. 94.

people, breeding self-interest, poisoning the new growth of political consciousness, and effectively preventing the development of a national or corporate spirit.'

Communal representation must therefore be swept away. The new constitution must not acknowledge, but must ignore, Ceylon's separate racial and religious histories. It must recognize only the common territorial history; it must express the 'unifying tendencies' of modern society and 'the modern principle of political equality'. The communities must be made to accept a 'merging in the general electorate'. In order that the merging should be thorough; in order, too, that the modern principle of political equality should be able to express itself forcibly, the electorate must be emphatically enlarged. The Commission rejected property qualifications, it even rejected a literacy qualification, and recommended that the electorate should be enlarged from the existing 200,000 male voters to a figure of almost 2,000,000 voters—1,200,000 men and 650,000 women.[2]

If the existence of the communities could be ignored in the electoral system, why could it not also be ignored in the constitutional system considered as a whole? If the communities could so easily be put on one side, what remained of the case against responsible government, which rested chiefly upon a recognition of their existence? The problem was one of degree. The Commission recognized in practice that constitution-making could not obliterate the existence of the separate communities, nor could it put an end to their sectional political action. But it might do a great deal to render their sectional action more difficult and to render easier and more attractive their collaboration in pursuit of the common weal of them all. The report of the Commission is interesting, not as a theoretical exposition of communalism in general, which it does not offer, but rather as a resourceful essay in practical tactics with reference to the actual communal problems of a particular territory. It regarded communalism in Ceylon as the enemy of the common good of Ceylon, and it attempted so far as possible to out-manœuvre the enemy. The enemy was strong enough to thwart the hope of responsible government. It was strong enough to render desirable special recognition of the rights of the numerically smallest community, the Europeans, and the vesting in the governor of special powers to protect the rights of

[1] For the analysis of communal representation and the franchise recommendations, ibid., pp. 30–1, 42, 74, 80–99. To overcome the problem of the large number of illiterate voters after these recommendations were accepted, the device was adopted of allotting each candidate a colour, and arranging that each voter should cast his ballot paper (unmarked) into a box painted with the colour of the candidate he favoured.

every threatened minority.[1] But the enemy was not, in the Commission's judgement, strong enough to thwart a notable step forward in repairing the first weakness of the state, which was the divorce of power from responsibility. The recommendations of the Commission under this head show a refreshing readiness to break free from the traditional stereotyped forms of British colonial policy and to express the reality lying behind the forms in new institutions appropriate to the 'realistic requirements' of a new situation in an individual and peculiar society.[2] Holding fast to its central conviction that power must be equated with responsibility, the Commission sought to realize it by a fusion of legislative and executive activity in the representatives of the people, so that executive action might always command the necessary legislative and financial support, and legislative action might grow out of executive experience. The fusion of the two activities was to be embodied in an institution called the State Council, which would sit both in legislative and executive session. In its executive aspect the State Council would divide itself into seven committees, whose elected chairmen would be ministers with departmental responsibility. Three other ministers—the officers of state—would form with the chairmen of the seven committees the Board of Ministers; these three ministers would be responsible for the general political departments of government, but their function would be advisory rather than directive and they would not possess the right to vote on the Board of Ministers. It is not possible here to set out at length the carefully considered details with regard to the relation of a minister to the Board of Ministers, of a minister-chairman to his committee, of a committee to the State Council, of the governor to the whole system. Although each difficulty seemed to be provided for, the proposed constitution might appear to be dangerously complicated in comparison with the proved simplicities of responsible government. But the complexities would appear legitimate ones and many of the uncertainties would be dissipated if a comparison were made with the London County Council. The Commission was in fact seeking to adapt to the conditions and needs of Ceylon the experience of the great municipalities, which, freed from the distractions of high politics, had been able to adapt their organization and energies to the pressing problems of social welfare. It believed that the people of

[1] The governor was to have power to nominate unofficial members up to 12, of whom not more than 6 were to be Europeans. In his instructions there would be included an explicit prohibition against assenting to legislation imposing special penalties or granting special favours to any particular community or religion.

[2] Cmd. 3131, pp. 19, 45; a protest against slavish imitation of the British constitution.

Ceylon needed most this training in the actual, and that practical responsibility in affairs which most immediately touched the common good of all would build up in them a commonwealth loyalty capable of harmonizing their separate communal loyalties. This widening of loyalty was the indispensable preliminary to self-government on the usual parliamentary model.

What the Donoughmore Commission therefore recommended was not merely a large transfer of political power but a large experiment in political education. The recommendations were accepted by the British government. At the time of writing (1936) the new system of political education has been in operation for more than five years. What results have been achieved? Opinions are conflicting. On the one hand, it is argued that there has been a decline in administrative efficiency and political morality. It is said that communal selfishness shows no signs of disappearing, that it dominates politics as much as it ever did, the only difference being that the weaker communities are deprived of self-expression and the means of self-defence. These allegations are, on the other hand, flatly denied, and the state of Ceylon to-day is asserted to be an immeasurable improvement on its state under the old constitution.[1] The present writer has not the special knowledge which would qualify him to decide between these opposing arguments. But he is inclined to give the benefit of the doubt to the constitution which is now having its innings. At the very least, there has been no proof of a collapse comparable with that which closed the innings of its predecessor. One may perhaps sum up the constitutional history of Ceylon since the end of the Great War by recurring to the borrowed metaphor which was used earlier. After a period of indecisive straggling, Ceylon strode forward to an advanced place in the procession of self-government, and up to the present she has kept that place.

Another island, Newfoundland, has had during the same period a surprising experience and a very different one. Newfoundland was Great Britain's oldest colony, and Newfoundland had achieved the status of a Dominion. She had not indeed achieved the international status enjoyed by her far more powerful sister-states in the imperial conference circle,[2] but she was nevertheless in the van of the proces-

[1] For an attack on the report of the Donoughmore Commission, and particularly on its recommendations to extend the franchise and extinguish communal representation, see Sir Ponnambalam Ramanathan, *Memorandum* (London, 1930). Present controversies are reflected in an article and correspondence in *The Times*, 24th March, 8th April, and 5th May 1936.

[2] A Newfoundland politician once referred to his country as 'a mouse invested with the trappings of an elephant'.

sion of self-governing communities. But in 1933 she consented to take a humble place at the very tail of the procession. In an address presented to His Majesty, the two houses of the Newfoundland parliament prayed that the Letters Patent of 1876 and 1905, which were the legal basis of Newfoundland's self-governing institutions, might be suspended, and that new Letters Patent might be issued in order to provide for the temporary administration of the island by a commission of government of six persons, three to be drawn from Newfoundland and three from the United Kingdom. The Commission of Government, presided over by His Excellency the Governor, would take the place of the old institutions of responsible government and would be vested with full legislative and executive authority. His Majesty's government in the United Kingdom would exercise supervisory control over the Commission, and would assume general responsibility for the finances of the island until such time as it might become self-supporting again, and would in particular make such arrangements as might be deemed just and practicable with a view to securing to Newfoundland a reduction in the present burden of the public debt. It would be understood that as soon as the island had again become self-supporting, responsible government, on the request of the people of Newfoundland, would be restored.[1]

This address was the preliminary to the Newfoundland Act, 1933, by which the imperial parliament substituted for the old order of responsible government a new order of rule by governor-in-commission. The address itself was the outcome of the report of a royal commission over which Lord Amulree had presided, and it repeated the chief recommendations of that commission. The reader who wishes to examine in detail the reasons which induced the people of Newfoundland to accept so drastic a diminution of their status within the British Commonwealth must consult the report of the Amulree Commission.[2] Generally speaking, the report reveals the failure of British institutions in Newfoundland to meet the challenge presented by Newfoundland's natural environment and historical situation. The failure was due, partly to the magnitude and difficulty of the task with which institutions had to grapple, and partly to a degenera-

[1] Newfoundland Act 1933 (24 Geo. V, ch. 2), First Schedule. The resolution that the humble address be presented was passed unanimously in the legislative assembly; in the legislative council two members abstained.

[2] Cmd. 4480 of 1933. In addition to this report, see *Papers Relating to the Report of the Royal Commission*, Cmd. 4479 of 1933, *Memorandum on Proposed Financial Resolution*, Cmd. 4481, and the act cited above. Also *Report by the Commission of Government on the Economic Situation of 1933*, December 1934, Cmd. 4788 of 1934, and subsequent reports.

tion of those institutions. One has to imagine an island rather smaller than England and rather larger than Ireland, with a population of less than 300,000 persons scattered over six thousand miles of coast-line, and distributed, partly owing to the ancient controversy over fishing rights between France and Great Britain,[1] chiefly in those regions which are least hospitable to agriculture. One has to imagine this community depending for its livelihood on a single uncertain industry, the cod-fishing industry. One has to imagine an almost medieval primitiveness of organization in this industry, and a vicious credit system which sapped the security and independence of the fishermen and poisoned commercial and social relationships. These were the problems of economic geography and social organization which it was the duty of government to tackle; the crying need of Newfoundland was a thorough modernization of its basic industry, both in its technical and financial aspects, and the fashioning of a more diverse economy. Responsible government proved itself in-capable of attempting any serious action to meet this need. Perhaps the distorted scale of political action—the disproportion between the size and difficulty of the country and the population which was living in it—lay at the root of the failure. The Amulree Commission did not conceal its opinion that Newfoundland would have fared better as a province of the Dominion of Canada. But in the late eighteen-sixties, when the continental Dominion would have welcomed New-foundland, signs of returning prosperity and the tactical mistakes of Newfoundland's own advocates of federation encouraged her people to decide for the old order of separate autonomy. During the bad times of thirty years later the people of Newfoundland would probably have welcomed admission to the Canadian federation, but this time it was Canada which held back. Left to her own devices, Newfoundland oscillated between depression and unstable prosperity. Instead of grappling with the real economic problems of the country, its successive governments erected a superstructure of social and administrative organization on shaky foundations. The two decades before the war were a period of 'extravagant and reckless optimism'.[2] In the twelve years which followed the war 'the public debt of the island, accumulated over a century, was . . . more than doubled; its assets dissipated by improvident administration; the people misled into the acceptance of false standards, and the country sunk in waste

[1] Also because of the historic connexion between Newfoundland and Europe. This had favoured the concentration of the British population on the eastern side of the island which was less suitable than the western side for land settlement.

[2] Cmd. 4479, p. 30.

and extravagance'. The onset of the depression 'found the country with no reserves, its primary industry neglected and its credit exhausted'.[1]

In the opinion of the present writer it was the overwhelming difficulty of the challenge presented by nature and history, rather than the degeneration of political life, which was the primary cause of collapse in Newfoundland. But the second phenomenon is the one relevant to the theme of this chapter, and at the risk of distortion it must now be abstracted from the whole complex of Newfoundland's difficulties. The Amulree Commission—whether or not with exaggeration the present writer is unable to say—was unsparing in its condemnation of inefficiencies and dishonesties which had reached scandalous dimensions.

> 'There is general agreement [the report affirmed] that a process of deterioration, which has now reached almost unbelievable extremes, may be said to have set in about a quarter of a century ago. . . . However this may be, there is no doubt that, some years before the war, politics in Newfoundland underwent a process of "modernization", which was responsible for the introduction of methods foreign to the British tradition.'

Those methods were the 'spoils system' in public appointments, corruption in granting contracts and in securing favours for political supporters and constituents,[2] and personal enrichment through politics. Things had reached such a pass, the Commission declared, that the electors preferred to vote for candidates who openly pursued their own fortune at the public expense. 'They [the electors] argued that, if a man proved himself capable of using his political opportunities to his personal advantage, he would be the better equipped to promote the advantage of his constituents: an honest man would only preach to them.'[3]

There is one aspect of this political degeneration which curiously links the problems of Newfoundland with those of Ceylon. It is the religious or sectarian aspect.

> 'It might have been expected [the Amulree Commission reflected] that the influence of the Churches, so strong in Newfoundland, would have acted as a check to political malpractices. It is clear from our investigations that this has not been the case. . . . For members of successive

[1] Cmd. 4479, p. 43.

[2] Institutions of local government were of negligible importance, with the result that political society in Newfoundland exemplified the combination, always sinister, of extreme paternalism and extreme localization.

[3] Cmd. 4480, p. 82.

administrations have been led, consciously or unconsciously, to place the interests of particular sections of the Church before the good of the country as a whole.'[1]

In the latter part of the nineteenth century, sectarian dissension was expressing itself with such vehemence in politics that, in order to mitigate its effects, the leaders of the various denominations agreed that 'all religious parties should be fairly represented in the arrangement of an administration and in the distribution of offices'.[2] In this way there was injected into the system of responsible government something which might be described as conventional communal representation. The Amulree Commission was ready to believe that without this strange convention the fever of sectarianism might have been even more frantic; yet it could not fail to denounce the unhealthy effects of the remedy. '. . . If a member of one denomination obtains a contract from the government, then members of the other main denominations must be selected for some compensating favour.' The same corrupting and expensive necessity dominated the procedure of civil service appointment. In short, the divisions of the Christian Church in the isolated British community of Newfoundland were hardening into a parody of oriental communalism.

It is not necessary to inquire whether the Newfoundland Act of 1933 aimed, as some of its socialist critics asserted, at saving the investments of British bondholders, or whether it was a noteworthy example of the solidarity of the British peoples and the vitality and resourcefulness of British institutions.[3] For the purposes of this objective and rather cold-blooded analysis, the act may best be regarded as administering to a sick society the medicine of the constitution, which is authority. Its passing was accompanied by many protestations that this medicine would not become Newfoundland's daily food, and by expressions of confidence in the capacity of the sick community to recover and to resume its natural motion as a self-governing dominion. But the point which must here be stressed is that Newfoundland did become sick, and that the medicine was administered. Temporarily at least, a community of British stock had found British institutions of self-government beyond its capacities and unsuited to its needs.[4] In view of this experience, there is

[1] Cmd. 4480, p. 88. Also pp. 14, 75.

[2] Ibid., p. 14. The chief denominational groups were Anglicans, Roman Catholics, and the United Church of Canada.

[3] For typical discussion on the Act see *The Times*, 22nd November 1933 and 7th and 13th December 1933; the *Manchester Guardian*, 22nd November and 22nd December 1933; the *Financial News*, 24th November 1933.

[4] It is worth recalling that some years previously the same medicine of government by commission had been applied to the city of Sydney.

no call for exaggerated surprise at the failure to establish similar institutions in a community of very different origins, traditions, and temperament—the community of Malta.

Malta, the third island to be studied in this section, has a greater significance for the present inquiry than have either of the other two. It may seem wilful to say this. For Malta is surely abnormal. There is surely no other community in the British Commonwealth whose domestic disputes are entangled so inextricably with the shattering controversies which divide principalities and powers. The petty politics of the island become suddenly oecumenical, awakening the slumbering thunders of the medieval Papacy. They blow upon the smouldering rivalries of two modern empires, whose sea-communications intersect where fragile-seeming Malta lies low in the sea, a British fortress twenty-two minutes by air from an Italian bombing base.[1] Is it fair to expect self-governing institutions to root themselves in a territory exposed to such fierce gusts blowing from outside? Are constitutions appropriate to battleships?[2] The answer is that the Maltese people demanded responsible government and the British parliament granted it. In granting it, it was but expressing the political philosophy dominant at the time, which insisted that 'the government of men by themselves' was a principle of general validity. It would be no compliment to this philosophy to prove it by easy examples and to test it only in fair weather. The question also arises whether fair weather is the normal condition of this world and this age. Which is abnormal, the scattered isolation of the Newfoundlanders or the crowded insecurity of the Maltese? Both are too exaggerated to be typical; but in the universe of the British Commonwealth Malta is both exceptional and microcosmic. For it is in a distracting and dangerous world such as Malta knows rather than in the sheltered tranquillity which envelops Newfoundland, that the Commonwealth of Nations has to work out its experiment and achieve its destiny.

The experiment of planting British institutions in the stony soil of Malta did not suddenly originate in the enthusiasms of a world made safe for democracy. Throughout the nineteenth century there had been recurring attempts to get Malta moving forward in the procession from crown colony government towards responsible government. There had also been recurring failures. 'It would be

[1] The writer, when travelling to Malta in September 1935, was given this twenty-two minutes estimate by an Italian airman in Sicily, who obviously took great pleasure in imparting the information. This has not been checked.

[2] The phrase 'a constitution for a battleship' is Mr. Winston Churchill's. See Cmd. 1474 of 1921, p. 37.

almost possible to plot a graph of the constitutional history of Malta during the last hundred years showing the rise and fall of constitutions modelled alternatively on the principle of benevolent autocracy and that of representative government.'[1] In the years which followed the Great War there was no change in the plan of the graph; the only difference was that its zigzags became more sudden and steep as the *tempo* of action and reaction in Malta became more violent.

In 1919 Malta represented in miniature the nationalisms which were challenging and distracting a victorious and tranquillity-craving empire. In India the National Congress was agitating; in Ireland Dáil Éireann was organizing a struggle for independence; Malta had her National Assembly. There were impassioned speeches, there were riots, there was military repression, there was constitution-making. But the struggle of Maltese nationalism was not so resolute and bitter as that of Ireland or India or Egypt. This comparative mildness was due not merely to a difference in scale—to the fact that Malta was a territory equal in area to the Isle of Wight with a population no larger than that of Portsmouth.[2] There was also a difference in quality. Whereas the self-conscious literary expression of Irish nationalism linked past and present and interested the masses, the literary or journalistic expression of Maltese nationalism in 1919 emphasized the separate culture of a bourgeois class. Dáil Éireann expressed itself on formal occasions in a language which had once been the vulgar and the literary tongue of Ireland and which still survived among the peasants of the Gaeltacht; the Maltese National Assembly expressed itself on every occasion in a language which the vast majority of the people had never acquired. The reader who consults to-day the dreary rhetoric, the interminable wandering resolutions of *L'Assemblea Nazionale di Malta* will find in them stale repetitions of the eloquence of mid-nineteenth-century Italian liberalism, belated and self-conscious *quarantottade*.[3] Sixty years

[1] *Malta Royal Commission*, 1931. Cmd. 3993, p. 9. The chairman of the commission was Lord Askwith.

[2] The population of Malta and Gozo at the 1931 Census was 234,563.

[3] *L'Assemblea Nazionale di Malta, 26 Febbraio 1919—27 Maggio 1921, Processi verbali e altri documenti* . . . (Malta, Stamperia del Governo, 1923). The Assembly was a numerous body composed as follows: 31 representatives of the clergy, 5 representatives of the nobles, 23 representatives of the professional classes, 9 representatives of the commercial class, 21 representatives of the labouring class, 16 representatives of the press, 23 representatives of committees and associations, chiefly literary and scientific, 76 representatives of 'Circles' (cf. the history of Italy's 48), 7 representatives of religious-educational bodies, 53 representatives of musical and philharmonic societies, 8 representatives of dramatic leagues. The reader must use his imagination in interpreting these figures and must not imagine a very 'corporative' institution.

earlier, had the circumstances been different, oratory of this kind might have swept a passive Maltese people into the Italian state, there to undergo without pain the process of Italianization. But the accident of British naval predominance in the Mediterranean, which was itself one of the actual historical conditions of the nineteenth-century *Risorgimento*, closed Malta to the *Risorgimento*'s expanding sphere of action. England was Italy's strong friend, and the Italianate bourgeoisie of Valletta had no desire to be redeemed into the Italian Kingdom. To the president of the National Assembly which met in February 1919, England was 'the mother country'. The nationalism of the assembly, in its formal declarations, expressed in the Italian tongue the abstractions of nineteenth-century liberal political philosophy which had culminated in the doctrine of self-determination. Behind these abstractions there was the impetus which came from the economic reaction following the war—a reaction which Malta, a great naval station, felt with particular intensity. There was also the natural and proper pride of the Maltese people, who did not desire to leave the British Empire, but demanded a share in its privileges and honours. This was a demand to which the British government was readily sympathetic. Amidst so many uncompromising nationalisms it was a relief to find one which was placable. Two days after the bloodshed of 8th June 1919 there arrived in Malta a new governor, Lord Plumer, who at once took measures to elicit from the Maltese leaders a statement of the constitutional changes which they desired. With the encouragement of Lord Plumer, the National Assembly submitted a draft constitution in August 1919. The draft constitution provided for nothing which was not very British—a bicameral legislature and responsible government in local affairs, with continued imperial control of affairs which affected Malta as a fortress. This was diarchy, which British publicists at that very time were expounding as a system appropriate to the needs of India. In November 1919 Mr. L. S. Amery visited Malta and announced that the British government was ready to grant to the Maltese 'full responsible control of their purely local affairs', reserving to itself control over Malta as 'as Imperial fortress and harbour'.

> 'Malta received the happy and auspicious announcement . . . with feelings of boundless joy which found expression in a spontaneous and most imposing popular demonstration of love and loyalty to the Mother Country . . . amidst the most enthusiastic cheers for their beloved King, the strains of the National Anthem sung by thousands of loyal hearts, and the flutter of the glorious British flag side by side with the National Colours.'[1]

[1] Cmd. 3993, p. 13.

After this day of drama there followed a year and a half of busy delay. The careful wisdom of the Colonial Office, supplemented by Maltese helpfulness, produced at last a constitutional structure which in its elaborate ingenuities was no less lovely than the most perfect of the paper edifices which the constitution-makers of Europe were in those years proudly erecting. The local affairs of the island were 'to be regulated as nearly as possible by the constitutional practice obtaining in like matters in Our United Kingdom'.[1] To this end the governor would be advised by a responsible ministry composed of a dozen departmental heads. The ministry would be responsible to a legislative assembly of 32 members, elected on a literacy and a low property franchise. To check the errors and impatience of the assembly there was an unusually impressive senate: 7 general members to represent age, wealth, and education; and 10 special members to represent specified classes or orders—the clergy, the nobles, the university, the chamber of commerce, the trade union council. But unfortunately it turned out that Malta did not possess a trade union council. The constitution contained all the most approved provisions for resolving deadlocks between the two houses of the legislature. To guard against electoral corruption, it entrusted to the court of appeal the power of deciding on the right of any member of either house to hold his seat.[2]

So much for the Maltese government—the local side of the new constitutional order. The sphere of the Maltese Imperial government was defined, both negatively in the Constitution Letters Patent, and positively in the simultaneously issued Letters Patent constituting the Office of Governor. The constitution enumerated certain restrictions on the legislative authority of the Maltese legislature. Sections 40 and 57 reserved from its authority the established linguistic order of the community, with English the first official language of administration, Italian the official language of the courts, and Maltese in possession of such 'facilities' as were due to 'the language of popular intercourse'. Section 56 reserved the established order of religious toleration. Section 63 reserved a civil list. Section 41 reserved all matters 'touching the public safety and defence of our Empire and the general interests of our subjects not resident in Malta'; and, without prejudice to this general reservation, it enumerated such

[1] Section 54 (5), referring specifically to the relations between governor and ministry.

[2] The relevant documents—the Constitution Letters Patent and the Letters Patent constituting the Office of Governor, together with the important series of Amending Letters Patent which will be referred to in the following narrative—are printed in the appendix to Cmd. 3993.

specific matters as the control and discipline of the armed forces, defence of the island and compulsory acquisition of property necessary for this purpose, aerial matters, cables, wireless, docks, general foreign trade, immigration, naturalization, censorship, passports, and treaties. Section 68 reserved to the Crown full power and authority to revoke, alter, and amend sections 40, 41, 56, 57, and 63.[1] All the powers which were withheld from local control, with the exception of the last-cited amending power, were conferred on the governor in his imperial capacity by section 12 of the Letters Patent constituting his office, which empowered him to legislate for them by ordinance. In his imperial capacity the governor was assisted by a nominated council. But what would be the position in the not unlikely contingency that some issues would arise which were of importance both to the Maltese government and the Maltese Imperial government? To the Colonial Office constitution-makers this problem was simple. At the discretion of the governor, a joint committee of both sides of the government could be summoned to deliberate on matters of joint concern: this institution was the Privy Council of Malta.

The architectural harmonies of this construction were, nevertheless, deceptive. At first appearance the constitution was frankly in the tradition of the Whig doctrine of assimilation and Lord Durham's wisdom. Responsible government in their local affairs and a line demarcating the imperial sphere which they might not enter; this had been the counsel of the Durham Report and this seemingly was the intention of the Malta Constitution Letters Patent, the only difference being that the line of division was drawn in the actual text of the Maltese constitution itself. But the diarchical dividing line was a smudged and a movable one. Section 41 (1) and section 68, taken together, represented a weakness in the legal foundations of responsible government which might bring the whole structure tumbling down. The first reserved from the Maltese legislature 'all matters touching the public safety and defence of our Empire and the general interests of our subjects not resident in Malta'; the second reserved to the Crown a power of amending certain sections of the constitution, including section 41. In the event, it proved possible to use this amending power to extend the general reservation in section 41 (1) to cover the general interests of all subjects of the King resident in Malta, and, in the event of an emergency attested by the

[1] Apart from these reserved sections, the constitution entrusted the amending power to a two-thirds majority of the total members of both senate and assembly voting separately.

Secretary of State, to confer on the imperial side of the diarchy unlimited authority over local affairs. Thus this impressive constitution proved itself to be a fraud.[1]

In all probability it was an unconscious fraud. Nobody in 1921 could have predicted the strains to which the constitution was to be subjected, and nobody perhaps suspected the jerry-building which its elaborate façade concealed. The intention or the hope doubtless was to establish in Malta the method and the spirit of British politics. Was the hope a reasonable one? The royal commission of 1931 believed it to be part of its task 'to consider the general fitness of the Maltese for self-government'.[2] This is reminiscent of the question raised by an English clergyman who visited the Sicilian parliament which had been established by Bentinck during the English occupation of Sicily in Napoleon's time. The clergyman found the members of parliament kicking and biting each other in a heap on the floor of the chamber, and he asked—'Are these people fit for freedom?' But surely the question might be put in a form less hurtful to southern pride. Are British institutions appropriate to the circumstances and temperament of every non-British people? Was all the paraphernalia of double chambers and deadlock devices and slow-moving democracy, which was wrapped up in the majestic monarchical phraseology of the Malta Constitution Letters Patent, appropriate to the needs of a passionate southern Catholic people, with their urgent problems of poverty and of population and the illiteracy which after a century of British rule was still the general rule? Was not the provision for senatorial representation of a trade union council which did not exist characteristic of the doctrinaire superficiality of the British constitution-makers? Should they not have taken account—as the Donoughmore Commission in Ceylon did at a later date—of the social foundations of political life and the urgent individual problems of 'a peculiar people'?

These criticisms of the constitution would probably not have occurred to any one who studied its working during the first five or six years. In this period a number of parties supporting the ministry in power gradually fused into the nationalist party, of which Enrico Mizzi, editor of the Italian paper *Malta*, became the most prominent,

[1] The nineteenth-century constitutions of Canada or the Australian colonies could of course have been superseded by act of the imperial parliament (see the Newfoundland example above). The Maltese constitution was different in that it contained *within itself* provision for the obliteration of responsible government. The process of obliteration is explained on pp. 419, 426 below: the documents are the Letters Patent of 26th June 1930 and the Proclamation of 2nd July 1930.

[2] Cmd. 3993, p. 6.

though perhaps not the most representative, leader. With the exception of one significant conflict,[1] there was in this period no strain upon the diarchical system. Trouble began with the election of 1927, which returned to power in the assembly the constitutional party, led by Sir Gerald Strickland and supported by the labour party. The election was first of all an unscrupulous one; for the nationalists, in order to arouse the horror of the simple Catholic population, distributed through Malta affidavits which testified that Sir Gerald Strickland was a freemason.[2] To this affront the new government at once replied by searching the houses of ex-ministers for government documents. More serious than the unscrupulousness of the election was its indecisiveness. Secure in the legislative assembly, the new ministry faced a senate which was in a position to block its measures. This was the immediate origin of the distractions which followed. The constitution was running into foul weather.

The events which must now be related were a curious mixture of the petty and the grandiloquent. The labouring mouse of Maltese self-government produced, one after another, the most awe-inspiring mountains. It will be best to let the story unfold in a series of episodes in chronological sequence. The first episode was a prologue introducing the court of appeal, which was destined to play a leading part throughout. Seeking for a majority in the senate, the Strickland government attempted to reconstitute the trade union council, which had been called into existence for the purpose of providing the two senators assigned to it in the constitution. The government asserted that the trade union council had been packed 'with delegates who were not *bona fide* trade unionists': it proceeded to 'unpack' it. The result was the entry into the senate of two labour supporters of the administration. But the opponents of the administration arranged for the matter to come before the court of appeal, which claimed to have full and final authority under section 33 of the constitution to settle all matters connected with elections to the legislature. In a judgement of 5th December 1927, the court unseated the two senators. They declared their intention to appeal to the privy council; but announced that they would refrain from taking their seats until the privy council had granted them leave to appeal.

The second episode introduced into the turmoil of Maltese factions the Secretary of State for the Colonies. The occasion of his inter-

[1] Cmd. 3993 p. 19.

[2] The gentleman who in 1927 was in charge of the electoral propaganda of the nationalist party informed the writer in 1936 that he considered the freemason story unfair and unwise: he himself was ill at the time and had no responsibility for it.

vention was a spectacular Appropriation Bill introduced in March 1928 by the Maltese Prime Minister, who had been raised two months previously to the peerage. The Appropriation Bill provided for an excess of expenditure over revenue amounting to £138,000. In order to meet part of this deficiency, the government planned to spend the whole of the reserve fund which its prudent predecessors had accumulated over a period of years. But the senate amended the Appropriation Bill. The assembly thereupon petitioned His Majesty to 'impart immediate instructions' for the amendment of the constitution in order to secure the supremacy of the lower house in finance. The senate in answer passed a resolution reaffirming its rights under the Constitution Letters Patent as 'intact, integral, and inviolable'. In both houses the voting was on strict party lines. But the Secretary of State, in a spirit either of partisanship or ingenuousness, ignored the conflict of parties and perceived only a 'defect in the machinery of the Constitution'.[1] In form, his intervention relaxed the reservations on the powers of the Maltese legislature, to the extent of permitting it—if it passed a particular law in a particular form—to amend two sections of the constitution by a bare majority of both houses sitting together, instead of by a two-thirds majority of the members of each house. In form, therefore, the amending Letters Patent which were now issued on the responsibility of the Secretary of State were a concession by the Crown to the Maltese legislature, permitting it 'to effect a change which otherwise the Crown might have prevented it from making'.[2] In fact, the British government was intervening in the domestic quarrels of Malta in such a way as to put within reach of one faction a success which it could not hope to achieve without this intervention.

But the Strickland party could not reap the advantage of the intervention until it could pass a particular law through the legislature, and for this purpose it still needed additional strength in the senate. It therefore turned again to the trade union council. The manipulation of this body depended upon the secretary, who under the regulations was also the returning officer. In the end the government got its men. But the legality of their presence in the senate was again questioned, and a second legal duel began. This may be regarded as the third episode of the drama. But before this episode was concluded, a fourth opened. A dispute between the government and the clergy crowded to the back of the stage the dispute about the two

[1] Mr. Amery's communications are quoted in Cmd. 3993 at pp. 27, 28.

[2] Cmd. 3993, p. 145. For this complicated procedure see ch. xi of the report. The Letters Patent of 1928 are printed at p. 199.

trade union representatives in the senate. While the senate affair gradually ripened into a first-rate constitutional crisis, the rapidly rising storm of dispute between Lord Strickland and the ecclesiastical dignitaries of Malta dragged the British government into controversy with the Holy See.

If the two senatorial representatives of the clergy had not voted with the opposition, Lord Strickland's Appropriation Bill would have gone through. Lord Strickland made fruitless representations to the archbishop against the alleged unclerical behaviour of 'political priests', and his supporters voiced their violent complaints in the vernacular press. The representatives of the clergy declared that they could not perform their constitutional duties while they were the object of such attacks; they threatened to abstain from sittings of the senate while the abnormal situation continued.

> 'I take this threat as a declaration of war [declared Lord Strickland]. I am not going to say which priests are the threatening priests. . . . The electors of this country are not women . . . the vote is as yet restricted to the men of Malta, and I trust the men of Malta.'[1]

Trusting to the imperial patriotism of the men of Malta, Lord Strickland discovered an issue of loyalty in an affair which the ecclesiastical authorities declared to be one merely of monastic discipline. The rulers of the Franciscan Conventual Order had commanded the transfer from Malta to Liverpool of a monk who had been judged insubordinate. According to the interpretation of the ministry, this was no mere matter of religious discipline, but victimization by foreigners of a British subject and a supporter of the constitutional party. The ministry made two attempts to assume the role of defending imperial honour and interests; on both occasions the governor had to prevent it from crossing the diarchical line and assuming powers which belonged to the Maltese Imperial government. It was by a more ambiguous procedure that the British government became implicated in the local fight of factions. Lord Strickland secured from the assembly a motion which was reasonable in content, namely, that a humble request should be sent to the Vatican to appoint a fully authorized representative to inquire into the present matter of dispute and kindred questions.[2] The day after this resolution was passed, the Cardinal Secretary of State set forth the Vatican's view of the affair in a note which he presented to the British Minister in Rome. He requested that the British government

[1] Cmd. 3993, p. 32.

[2] *Correspondence with the Holy See relative to Maltese Affairs*, Jan. 1929 to May 1930. Cmd. 3588 of 1931, No. 1.

should give to the authorities in Malta instructions which would ensure that the consciences of Catholics would be no longer troubled. In reply, the British Minister suggested that an Apostolic Visitor should be sent to Malta to make an independent investigation; but at the same time he expressed the view of his government that 'the intense participation of priests in politics' lay at the root of the trouble. This was Lord Strickland's thesis. From now onward the Maltese faction fight was exalted to the dignity of the secular controversy of *regnum* and *sacerdotium*. In the common rooms of Oxford and Cambridge erudite partisans in the majestic struggles of the past plunged eagerly into a present war of pamphlets.[1]

The Holy See dispatched to Malta not an Apostolic Visitor, but an Apostolic Delegate, a dignitary of higher status and powers. He was Monsignor Paschal Robinson; and gratification at an appointment which had been made with tact was expressed both by the British government and the Maltese government and assembly. From now on the diarchical line would appear to have been irreparably smudged. There was no consistent effort to disentangle the local aspect of the controversy from its diplomatic aspect; or, if the effort was made, it missed success. The entry of the British government into the controversy did not cause the Maltese government to withdraw from it. The assembly introduced a bill to confer on the Apostolic Delegate powers to examine witnesses under oath and summon them under penalties; Monsignor Robinson informed the ministers that the bill was unnecessary and inopportune, and that it expressed an erroneous conception of the status of an Apostolic Delegate, 'whose authority does not emanate from any civil law but is derived directly from the Holy See'.[3] Lord Strickland thereupon withdrew the bill. But he submitted the heads of a *concordat* which the Apostolic Delegate regarded as the expression of an extreme Erastian tendency.[2] Did not the Apostolic Delegate's report express an equally emphatic theocratic tendency? It roundly attacked Lord Strickland and expressed the opinion that the Secretary of State should decline responsibility for his politics, or compel him to modify them, or find some way of eliminating him from the political life of Malta.[3] On the 2nd July the Cardinal Secretary of State conveyed to the British Minister, not Monsignor Robinson's report, but

[1] See a letter by Professor Zulueta in *The Times*, 1st July 1930, and Mr. G. G. Coulton's pamphlet, *Malta and Beyond* (Simpkin Marshall, 1930).

[2] Cmd. 3993, p. 43.

[3] Monsignor Robinson's report is Document No. XII in *Exposition of the Malta Question with Documents* (Vatican Poliglot Press), a not completely satisfactory translation of the original Vatican White Book of 1930.

an *aide-mémoire* based partly on this report and partly on other information gathered 'on the spot'. The gist of the *aide-mémoire* was that Lord Strickland was not *persona grata* to the Holy See. The Minister gave a copy of the document to Lord Strickland, who published it.[1] The controversy became even more vociferous. The acrimonious diplomatic wrangle between His Majesty's government and the Holy See echoed, and was echoed by, the taunts and counter-taunts of the Maltese factions. The British government declared that it was 'incompatible with the existence of friendly diplomatic relations between the Holy See and themselves that the former should treat as *persona non grata* a Minister exercising executive functions in British territory in virtue of the Constitution of that territory'. His Majesty's government could not 'suffer themselves without expostulation to be exposed, in the person of an executive Minister in one of the British Colonies, to such a slight'. They would submit neither to this nor to the other interferences with the constitutionally elected government of a British colony. If the actions of this government had been illegal, legal remedies lay open to aggrieved persons; if they had been inexpedient, the remedy lay with the electorate. . . .[2] The Holy See, replied the Cardinal Secretary of State, had not interfered and had no intention of interfering with the constitutional government of a British colony. It was a party-leader in this colony who was interfering in a 'purely religious domain'. If, in a diplomatic document addressed to His Britannic Majesty's government, the Holy See had declared Lord Strickland to be a *persona non grata*, this showed no disrespect towards the government of a British colony, but simply stated the truth 'from a religious point of view'.[3] Obviously, the diplomacy of the two Powers could now do nothing more than emphasize the irreconcilable opposition of the two points of view. We need not follow in detail the latter phases of the correspondence. It ended with a superb rumble of medieval Papal thunder. 'The Holy See has always held and still holds that the two complete societies, ecclesiastical and civil, are constituted by God himself. . . .'[4]

Malta itself had already felt the shock of head-to-head collision between the opposed doctrines. The British government had attempted to secure a calming of the atmosphere sufficient for holding elections. It sponsored an undertaking given by Lord Strickland not

[1] The 1931 Commission reported: 'It does not appear that this document should have been published during the course of negotiations.' Cmd. 3993, p. 46.

[2] See especially dispatch of 8th August. Cmd. 3588, No. 12.

[3] The *pro-memoria* of 10th August 1929. Cmd. 3588, No. 13.

[4] Ibid., No. 37 (20th May 1930).

to engage in ecclesiastical controversy during the electoral campaign. The most that could be elicited from the Maltese hierarchy was an instruction to the faithful that they might cry *Viva*, but must not cry *Abasso*.[1] But the ministers complained that the priests were still interfering in politics, and were putting pressure on voters through the confessional. The bishops on their side resented the accusations of the ministers, and on the 1st May 1930 issued a pastoral letter which contained the following injunctions:

> 'And to come to the concrete, and in order not to leave in your souls any indecision. Know therefore, as Catholics:
> (1) You may not, without committing a grave sin, vote for Lord Strickland and his candidates. . . .
> (2) For even stronger reasons you may not present yourselves as candidates in the electoral list proposed by Lord Strickland. . . .
> (3) You are also solemnly bound in conscience in the present circumstances to take part in the elections and vote for those persons who, by their attitude in the past, offer greater guarantee both for religious welfare and for social welfare.'

The pastoral letter went on to declare that the priests were strictly forbidden to administer the sacraments to the obstinate who refused to obey these instructions. In the view of the Catholic Church, these instructions and this sanction had no partisan implications. The bishops, so the Cardinal Secretary of State pointed out, did not condemn the *Constitutional Party*, but only those persons who had been notoriously active in a manner harmful to religion. The Church was defending its flock; it was not interfering with politics . . . . The Governor of Malta took a different view. He summoned the Privy Council of Malta, which consisted of the councils of both sides of the diarchy sitting together, and on the 3rd May 1930 decreed the suspension of the election.[2]

The episode which has just been described, considered not in its oecumenical but in its local significance, was a struggle between two Maltese factions, of which one had secured the backing of His Britannic Majesty's government and the other the backing of the Church Universal. The episode had been an enlivening one; it was now closed. But the faction fight continued with unabated vigour. Nor need it shrink at once to its true parochial dimensions; unable for the time being to merge itself in the majestic conflict of Papacy

[1] Cmd. 3993, p. 52.

[2] Ibid., pp. 33–56. Cf. p. 60 for the Papal Allocution of 30th June 1930: '. . . And in all this no one can ever reasonably see any undue interference or any diminution of freedom . . . freedom is neither lessened nor restricted by the moral law, which but regulates its use. . . .'

and Empire, it discovered a more strictly secular inspiration; from the canon law it turned to the civil law. The court of appeal had not been slumbering. On the 25th June 1930 it delivered a judgement on a case which concerned the validity of the Electoral Act of 1929. In this judgement the Chief Justice reviewed the position of the two senators chosen in 1928 to represent the trade union council. The court of appeal, in exercise of its powers under section 33 of the constitution, had declared their election invalid; yet the two individuals had continued to sit and vote on the plea that they had been granted special leave to appeal to the Privy Council. The Chief Justice stated that an appeal did not stay the execution of a sentence. The two individuals were not legally members of the senate. It followed that 'the votes recorded by them in favour of the proposed law to amend section 42 (3) and section 61 of the Letters Patent of 1921 relative to the Constitution of Malta . . . were given invalidly and were of no effect'. This decision invalidated the long series of acts and ordinances which depended for their legality on the assumption that the conditions for assuming the powers conferred on the Maltese legislature by the Amending Letters Patent of 1st August 1928 had been duly observed. Jurisprudence of a quality which was in large measure strange to British colonial experience[1] had wiped out the results of eighteen months of legislative activity. It had at the very least created 'grave uncertainty appertaining to the laws of the country', and started another furious controversy in which, not merely the ministry and the legislature, but the Chief Justice and the Governor, became the object of violent partisan attack.[2]

The present writer is completely unqualified to express an opinion on the broad legal issues involved in the controversy; nor does he consider it necessary to set forth in any detail the particulars of it. He wishes merely to emphasize the shattering effect of faction upon a badly constructed constitution. The pretentious symmetries of the document of 1921 were now a muddled heap. The only fragment of the constitution which still had relevance to realities in Malta was clause 41 (1), and even this was insufficiently relevant. The clause reserved from the Maltese legislature power to make laws 'touching the public safety and defence of Our Empire and the general interests of Our Subjects not resident in Malta'. It was in virtue of this

[1] The Chief Justice quoted from English cases and treatises and also from Italian authorities on the Civil Law.

[2] The judgement was printed as a pamphlet in the offices of *Malta*, Dr. Enrico Mizzi's newspaper, under the title of 'La Storica Sentenza pronunziata dalla Corte d'Appello in Malta, il 25 Giugno 1930'. For the attacks on the Chief Justice and the Governor, see Cmd. 3993, pp. 72, 73, 77.

reservation[1] that the Governor, having been advised by the Privy Council of Malta that grave disturbances were likely to arise out of the election, had ordered its suspension. But were the local faction fights really a danger to the public safety and defence of the Empire, or the interests of British subjects not resident in Malta? It was at any rate certain that the ordinance suspending the elections would be added to the list of actions to be challenged in the courts of law. The Governor issued another ordinance purporting to validate all acts of the legislature which had received his assent, and all things done under these acts. This ordinance too was certain to be challenged, and had no greater likelihood of surviving the challenge than had any of the measures which it sought to defend. Only the imperial government had power to cut the knot. On the 24th June 1930 His Majesty's government announced in the House of Commons its decision to suspend the constitution temporarily, and to place full legislative and administrative power in the hands of the Governor, while retaining the existing ministry in office. On the 26th June Letters Patent were issued to amend section 41 (1) of the Constitution Letters Patent of 1921, enlarging the provisions with regard to reserved matters contained in that article so that in time of emergency they covered, not merely 'the general interests of Our Subjects not resident in Malta', but also 'the general interests of Our Subjects resident in Malta'. Simultaneously with these Amending Letters Patent, the imperial government issued an Order in Council validating the Governor's ordinances which had been issued from the time of the dissolution of the legislature, and therefore validating, indirectly, the disputed legislation which the Governor had already declared valid by ordinance. The Order in Council also conferred on the Governor increased legislative and executive powers to the extent of the increased reservation of powers. In the opinion of the Askwith Commission this measure was unnecessary, because the Governor already possessed authority to legislate on reserved matters, and therefore 'he could, after the issue of the Amending Letters Patent, legislate for practically everything'.[2]

Politics therefore came to a short pause, with the British government maintaining in office, but not in power, the party of Lord Strickland. For the time being the Governor held powers which were virtually autocratic. This was the situation when the Royal Commission arrived in Malta in the spring of 1931. The narrative which has

[1] And the complementary ordinance power under section 12 of the Letters Patent constituting the Office of Governor.

[2] Cmd. 3993, p. 149. The Amending Letters Patent are printed on p. 201.

been given in these pages is based in large degree on the findings of the Royal Commission. The story which the Commission told in its report was the story of a constitution's failure. But with an optimism which can only be called perverse,[1] the Commission insisted that the story must have a happy ending. The remedy for Malta's ills contained in its recommendations was entirely at variance with the diagnosis of those ills contained in its narrative. 'Our desire', the Commission affirmed, 'is that the constitution should be restored with as few amendments as possible.' A little patching might be done by ordinance of the governor, a little more might be done by Letters Patent; still more patching—for example, a final definition of the trade union council and the fixing of a period beyond which legislation might not be impugned in the courts—would best be done by an act of the imperial parliament. The patched constitution might then put out to sea again. Why should it not have calm sailing? The storms of the past, said the Commission, arose from 'a series of circumstances not likely to occur again'. It could not 'express too strongly' its conviction that a pastoral of the bishops would be 'quite different in tone from the Pastoral of 1930'. Admittedly, there had been in recent years trouble of almost every conceivable kind. But much of it might have been settled 'by reasonable methods, more tact, and fewer personal squabbles. . . '. Surely this begged the whole question. If only the men of Valletta had been of like disposition to the men of Ventnor!

Trying to tread delicately the Commission trod hard on a hornet's nest. The reader must now brace himself to grapple with another universalized issue of Maltese politics. Hard though he may find it to believe, he must accept the statement that this narrative has not as yet handled the most burning matter of controversy. This was the language question. The Commission drew comfort from the fact that neither party had placed this question in the forefront of its electoral propaganda. It reported, however, that both parties had placed it in the forefront of the evidence which they had submitted with regard to Maltese affairs. It admitted that 'language had been made a matter of politics'.[2] Yet it believed that it could make recommendations on the subject as if it were merely a matter of educational technique. It did not indeed suggest any alteration in sections 40 and 57, which guaranteed the existing position enjoyed by English

[1] Lord Askwith said in the House of Lords on 5th May 1936 that the chief object which the Commission had set before itself was to settle the dispute with the Church, which threatened to be a dangerous dispute of an imperial character (*The Times*, 6th May 1936), i.e. its aim was diplomatic.

[2] Cmd. 3993, pp. 116, 121, and Chapter ix, *passim*.

and Italian as the two official languages of Malta.[1] But it did suggest that the use of Maltese, which the constitution recognized as 'the language of popular intercourse', should be permitted in all criminal trials in which the accused person should speak Maltese as the principal language to which he was accustomed.[2] Considerably more important was its recommendation that the system of *pari passu* instruction in schools, which had been established in 1923 with the professed intention of placing English and Italian on an equal footing, should give place in the elementary schools to an improved pedagogical method of teaching English, and English only, through the medium of Maltese. The effect of this on Italian would be to postpone it to the secondary schools, which only a minority of the comparatively small school-attending population of Malta ever reached. The Commission, becoming anxious lest this 'minor point of improvement in education' should be confused with the main constitutional issues, qualified its recommendation by uniting with it a suggestion to take a preliminary sounding of Maltese opinion, in which 'great weight' might be given to the opinion of the legislature. But the British government, without sounding Maltese opinion, and before passing the Act[3] which embodied the constitutional recommendations of the commission, brought into force its language recommendations by the Letters Patent of 25th April 1932. . . .[4] An Italian student of Maltese affairs added to an article which he had just written this postscript: 'England has committed a crime against Italy.'[5]

It is impossible to avoid a discussion of the language question, and unfortunately it is also impossible for a writer who is not a philologist to handle the question exhaustively. The controversy turns largely upon the origin and history of the Maltese language, and is frequently conducted as if this question of scholarship could be solved merely by vehement asseveration. Ardent champions of the language confidently claim for it a Phoenician ancestry, and some of them even declare that it is itself the ancestor of Arabic, Persian, Etruscan, Oscan, or even Greek. Ardent enemies of the language disparage it 'as a poor patois of a lot of bad Arabic'. Fortunately, there is

[1] By making them reserved matters whose amendment also was by Section 68 reserved to the Crown.

[2] Cmd. 3993, pp. 116–17.

[3] Malta Constitution Act 1932, 22 & 23 Geo. v (12th July 1932). Its intention was 'to remove doubts which have arisen as to the validity of previous amending Letters Patent'.

[4] The Letters Patent of 25th April 1932 were brought into effect in Malta by proclamation on the 2nd May. (See *Malta Government Gazette*, No. 7550.)

[5] *Il Giornale di Politica e di Letteratura*, 22nd May 1932, p. 310, article by Signor Benvenuto Cellini.

substantial agreement among scholars, who affirm its close relationship to Arabic—a relationship which even the cultural separation of nearly a thousand years has been unable to obscure.[1] Throughout this long period Maltese has occupied a position which may be compared with the position of English during the century which followed the Norman Conquest. It was the language of the masses of the people, but not the language of the law or of administration or of cultured society. Latin, French, Italian, and English enjoyed at different periods administrative and cultural predominance. But there followed no happy linguistic assimilation. The Maltese peasants and fishermen, it is true, borrowed largely from the Italian vocabulary; and Italian became a second language of many professional people, particularly lawyers. But there was no basis for the claim, born of the hopes of linguistic nationalism, that Maltese was disappearing into Italian.[2]

When the English occupied Malta in 1798, Italian was the language of the courts and of the administration. In the administration the English substituted their own language, but left Italian supreme in the courts. In 1836 Mr. Austin and Sir George Cornewall Lewis, royal commissioners, suggested that Italian should again be recognized as the language of the administration.[3] The thought behind this recommendation was that the inhabitants of Malta should be encouraged to find linguistic unity as an Italian-speaking people, and the main reason advanced was that Italian was of chief service

[1] Professor H. A. R. Gibb has contributed the following note on this point:

'No reputable Semitist of any nationality has ever expressed any different opinion. The philological arguments brought forward on behalf of the Phoenician theory are too trivial to set against the overwhelming weight of evidence of its Arabic origin. The reason for the existence of the Phoenician theory at all is, I believe, a religious one; the objection of the devoutly Catholic Maltese to being identified or connected in any way with the infidels across the straits, and the flattering association of St. Paul's involuntary stay on the island with their profession of Christianity. Be that as it may, the most striking characteristic of Maltese in my opinion is not its basic Arabic vocabulary and morphology, but the relatively slight degree to which Italian influences have disturbed its Arabic linguistic feeling. In spite of the centuries of separation from the living literary and educational traditions of the other Arabic-speaking countries, what modern linguists call the "inner language form" of Maltese is characteristically Arabic, and the structural changes resulting from Italian influences in phonetic system and vocabulary have been made, in all but a few instances, on lines typical of the evolution of Arabic dialects.'

[2] For this claim see Antonio Cini, *La Lingua Italiana in Malta* (Malta, Tipografia del Malta, 1931). But it may be relevant for the writer to mention that, when he consulted the official Maltese version of Cardinal Gasparri's Church Catechism, he was quite unable to understand it and could see practically no trace of Italian, though this was a sphere in which he had expected to see signs of its infiltration.

[3] *Report of Commissioners on Affairs of the Island of Malta, with Correspondence* 3 parts (London, Government Printers, 1838–9).

to trade in the Mediterranean. The British government did not adopt the recommendation. It maintained its original policy, which in course of time became a grievance to Italian nationalism.[1]

According to the interpretation of the twentieth-century propagandists of *italianità*, the English occupation of Malta had withdrawn the island from the process of Italian unification, and the English linguistic policy had arrested the natural process by which Maltese, like Sicilian, was extinguishing itself in Italian.[2] It was to be expected that Italians who held such a view of the manifest destiny of their culture should regard the new educational order contained in the Letters Patent of 25th April 1932 as 'the last phase of the tragedy of Italian', and attack it as an English crime committed against Italy.[3] The existence of this nationalistic propaganda emanating from Rome and Leghorn raises two questions which must be faced. First, was the object of the propaganda merely cultural, or was it also irredentist in the political sense? Secondly, were the Maltese champions of *italianità* loyal subjects of the British Crown? Neither question can be answered with scientific precision. In answering each question, inference and a debatable evaluation of tendency must play a considerable part. To throw a little light on the first question, it may be sufficient to consult a single number of *Il Giornale di Politica e di Letteratura*, a periodical which devotes a considerable amount of space to the affairs of 'Italy beyond the frontiers'. A contributor to this journal who has already been quoted, in criticizing the linguistic recommendations of the Royal Commission of 1931, appeals to the practice of Great Britain in the Channel Islands. He does homage to the aspirations of Malta as *terra commune*, a land Italian in culture and British in political loyalty, a living testimony to Anglo-Italian friendship and understanding.[4] But another contributor in the same issue explains that Italy's present political possession of the South Tyrol is merely the culmination of Italy's past cultural expansion in the South Tyrol, which in the nineteenth century had been impeded by the German language, 'carried outside its natural boundaries'. The present writer is inclined to believe that there are real differences of attitude between individual Italian propagandists of *italianità*, but he does not doubt that the

[1] During the earlier phases of the *Risorgimento* Malta was never a serious object of Italian concern, for very good reasons which have been pointed out on p. 408 above. Yet even in 1848 irresponsible nationalists published maps showing Malta as *terra italiana*.

[2] e.g. Ettore Rossi, 'Il dialetto maltese' in *Gerarchia*, May 1932.

[3] *Il Giornale di Politica e di Letteratura*, Anno VIII, Fasc. IV, p. 308.

[4] Ibid., p. 310: '. . . terra commune, sulla strada di un mare da entrambi solcato.'

propaganda, considered as a whole, has some totalitarian and irredentist implications. What of the partners in this propaganda who are British subjects living in Malta? Their political opponents accused them of disloyalty. But the present chapter has shown the unflagging zest with which actors in the petty politics of Malta sought always to dramatize them into world-shaking issues, and in previous chapters numerous instances have been given of the misuse of the sentiment and symbols of loyalty in the interests of classes or races or parties.[1] The Royal Commission rebuked those persons who were guilty of this unfairness and folly.

> 'The exaggeration tends to provoke resistance, [it said] to create an Italian party, and to cause disunion. It suggests that the people of Malta must be divided into loyal and disloyal subjects of the Crown, an imputation which we do not believe is justified.'

The policy of British rule in the Channel Islands, had it been applicable to the circumstances of Malta, would indeed have been the policy to be desired. But the circumstances were different. In the first place, the solution adopted in the Channel Islands had not been impeded by propaganda with irredentist implications emanating from the territory of a near neighbour. That made a comparable solution for Malta more difficult, although the difficulty was one which would have to be faced by a Commonwealth acting in accordance with its tested principles. In truth, the best answer to an aggrieved nationalism is to remove all reasonable grounds of grievance.[2] But there was another difference of circumstance. French was the language of the people of the Channel Islands; Italian was not the language of the people of Malta, but only one of the languages spoken among Malta's educated bourgeoisie.[3] The attractive ideal which would have made Malta *terra commune* to the British Empire and the Kingdom of Italy, when it was examined, demanded the extinction of the language of the people, which had been stunted by centuries of neglect, but which had nevertheless survived.

The Letters Patent of April 1932 appear, when viewed in retrospect, as a decisive step in the policy of taking Maltese 'out of the kitchen' and attempting to make it a language of administration and literary culture. This process involved pushing Italian out of the position which it had enjoyed previously in the life of Malta. The Letters Patent began the process by giving to Maltese an improved position

[1] See above, pp. 20, 95–6, 221–2.

[2] See C. A. Macartney, *National States and National Minorities* (Oxford University Press, 1934), *passim*.

[3] Even among the educated classes Maltese was spoken generally in the home.

in the courts, although Italian still remained their official language, and by removing Italian from the elementary schools. By doing this it pronounced in advance upon a matter of hot dispute between the Maltese parties. It was surely rather naïve to imagine that this pronouncement would bring peace to Maltese politics and that the patched and restored constitution would work more harmoniously in the future than it had worked in the past.

One forecast of the Royal Commission was immediately falsified. When the election campaign of 1932 opened, the Maltese bishops issued a pastoral letter similar in substance to the one which had caused the suspension of the previous elections. The restored constitution almost foundered at its first launching. As the result of an intense diplomacy, the pastoral was withdrawn and the elections were held. They resulted in a decisive victory for the Nationalist party,[1] which now claimed a mandate to resist the attack on *italianità*.[2] But the recent changes in the linguistic policy were reserved matters which the government and legislature could not directly attack. The ministry attempted in vain to secure from the Secretary of State for the Colonies a relaxation of the reservation. It then sought by indirect methods to circumvent it. This attempt was brought to a close by a proclamation of the Governor of Malta on the 2nd November 1933. The proclamation closed with a bang the latest experiment in 'the government of men by themselves' on Maltese soil. It announced:

> 'The Governor of Malta has found it necessary to dismiss the Ministers, and the Secretary of State for the Colonies being satisfied that a grave emergency has arisen within the meaning of Section 41 of the Malta Constitution Letters Patent, the Governor has assumed powers which, in that event, are vested in him by the Constitution.'[3]

The period between the 2nd November 1933 and the 15th July 1936 has been officially defined as a period of 'provisional govern-

[1] See *Malta Government Gazette*, No. 7483. The poll was a record one: 95·53 per cent. of the electorate as compared with 71·13 per cent. in 1921, 73·38 per cent. in 1924, and 85·69 per cent. in 1927. The nationalists polled 28,906 first preferences and were returned in 21 seats; the constitutional party polled 14,513 first preferences with 10 seats; the labour party 4,221 first preferences with 1 seat. The previous figures for seats were: nationalist party 14, constitutional party 15, labour party 3. The writer has been unable to check the many dramatic stories which are in circulation with regard to the events which caused the withdrawal of the pastoral. Nor can he estimate the extent to which the attitude of the Church accounted for the election results.

[2] e.g. *Il significato del Trionfo Nazionalista nelle ultime Elezioni Generali di Malta e Gozo* (Malta, Stamperia del Governo, 1932).

[3] *Malta Government Gazette*, No. 7824.

ment'.[1] In fact it was strong government by a colonial autocracy: in form it was still government under the Malta Constitution Letters Patent. The actual position was that section 41 (1) of the constitution, as extended by the amending Letters Patent of 1930, had virtually gobbled up all the rest of the constitution. Both of the contending local parties professed dissatisfaction with the situation, and a move was instituted to challenge its legality by legal processes. In 1936 the British government determined to make a clean sweep of the wreckage. Legislation of the imperial parliament restored the Crown to the position which it had held until the issuing of the Letters Patent of 1921—restored to it, that is to say, full power to legislate for Malta by virtue of its prerogative. Explaining the intention of this legislation in the House of Lords, the Earl of Plymouth announced that the government to be set up in Malta would be Crown Colony government. The governor would be assisted by 'an advisory body with a nominated official element'.[2] The wheel had completed its full circle.

The wiping-out in 1936 of a meaningless constitutional fiction had no effect upon the substance of the policy which had been followed consistently in Malta since November 1933. That policy had three aims. The first was to re-establish tranquillity by means of firm government.[3] The second was to raise the Maltese language to the position in administration and culture which Italian had hitherto enjoyed. The third was to convince the Maltese people that strong and efficient government could achieve more for their economic well-being and social happiness than they could hope to gain by the struggle of political parties using and abusing constitutional forms.

It is impossible to do more than mention the enterprises of the government under the third head. They included a vigorous health and hospital policy; extension of agricultural research and agricultural instruction—for example, with regard to the immunization of goats from the infection of *Brucella melitensis*; the improvement of fisheries and the institution of fisheries' councils; a vigorous extension of water, light, and drainage systems, and the improvement of roads; a reorganization of the judicial organization in the interests of speedier justice; and new measures for the preservation and restoration of buildings of historical and aesthetic interest, both as part of a tourist-attracting policy and a policy of improving for the

[1] Hansard, *House of Lords Debates*, vol. 100, 5th May 1936, col. 758.

[2] Ibid., cols. 751 and 752. Also *Malta Letters Patent Act*, 1 Edw. viii.

[3] As examples, see *Malta Government Gazette*, Nos. 7828 and 7833, containing restrictions on the press and on public meetings.

sake of the Maltese people the amenities of their country. All these enterprises were well conceived and energetically pursued. In order to bring the government near to the Maltese people and to compensate in some degree for the withdrawal of the opportunity for the expression of public opinion by the constitutional method, the administration made use of fortnightly press conferences and wireless broadcasting. Crown Colony government was seeking to modernize itself. Yet the experience of Crown Colony government everywhere, and not least in Malta, must surely emphasize its provisional character. It could not, judging from the past, be more than a temporary solution. Following upon a system of responsible government, it could not but be regarded as the medicine of the body politic.

Yet in one important respect the position of Malta, even apart from the defence function which it served in the British Empire, was peculiar. It was a commonplace of contemporary European history that nationalism was a stronger force than parliamentarism. British rule was now appealing to the stunted Maltese nationalism of the masses against the cultural programme which had been championed by the old nationalist party. An ordinance of 1934, to 'provide for the teaching of certain subjects through the medium of the Maltese or English language', removed Italian from the Faculty of Law in the University.[1] The Malta Constitution (Amendment) Letters Patent of 1934 put down Italian from its position as one of the two official languages, and lifted up in its stead the humble language which hitherto had been recognized merely as 'the language of popular intercourse'. 'The English language', ran the amended rule, 'as the official language of the British Empire, and the Maltese language, as the language of the people of Malta, shall be the official languages of Malta.' Maltese now succeeded Italian as the language of the courts. There were some educated men, particularly members of the legal profession, who denounced this change as an affront and a wound.[2] But there were other educated men to whom the change was an exhilarating opportunity; they set

[1] Ordinance No. XXXIV of 1934. About the same time the Statute of the University was remodelled in the sense of a rigid curtailment of its old autonomy. Very large powers were given to the Rector, see *Malta Government Gazette*, Supplement No. xxiv, and compare with the old Statute and Regulations (Malta, Government Printing Office, 1921).

[2] See Enrico Mizzi, *The Constitutional and Language Questions in Malta after the coup d'état of 2nd November 1933* (Malta, 1935), e.g. at p. 43: 'The Italianity of Malta is, for the Maltese who are not renegades or ignorant, an axiomatic truth confirmed by all the moral and material elements which constitute the nationality of a people.' He continues—'The admission of this truth is not and cannot be incompatible with sentiments of dutiful loyalty to the British Crown.'

themselves with fervour to the task of grafting new life into the old stock of the language which had so long been without blossom. And what of 'the people of Malta', the great majority whose daily speech was now to be exalted? It was their enthusiasm or indifference which would be decisive in the contest of loyalties. The spirit of the new call to them was expressed in the text-books which the department of education produced for their children—books of Maltese history, told in the Maltese language, with the Union Jack stamped on the cover. This blending of an ancestral and an imperial patriotism, if it were to be successful, would have to be associated with a double feeling of privilege and duty. The Empire would have to mean something more than a dangerous post in the front line: for example, it would have to mean a reasonable care for the Maltese colonies in other countries, and opportunities of emigration for a congested population.[1] And Malta herself, if she were to command an individual and mature national patriotism, would have to measure up in material well-being and mental vigour to the standards of her Mediterranean neighbours. Was the linguistic revival merely a political improvisation, or would it be pursued with scientific austerity and creative fervour?[2] If not, it would be bound to go stale. And how long would Crown Colony government possess the energy to press forward the effective plans of social amelioration? Could Maltese vigour be harnessed to Malta's problems by some other technique than that which had been tried and found wanting? Could the idea of commonwealth show in Malta some of the versatility which it had shown in Ceylon? All these questions would have to be faced in the future.

For the present, there need be no summing up. One point only must be made now. There was a contrast between the policy of nationality which had emerged from the political struggles of Malta and that which was being pursued elsewhere in the British Commonwealth. In South Africa and Canada the aim had been to treat language as 'a thing indifferent', but in Malta it had become a central article of the State creed. Malta thus conformed to the doctrine of linguistic nationalism which during this period was the orthodoxy of most Mediterranean and Near-Eastern peoples.

[1] 'During the last century the population has doubled, and . . . it is now growing at a net average increase of nearly three thousand a year. During recent years emigration has been largely reduced. . . . If it were not for the high infantile mortality the population, in view of the large families, would increase at a still more rapid rate' (Cmd. 3993, pp. 8–9). As for the Maltese colonies, they are to be found overseas, e.g. in the United States, and all over the Mediterranean, especially in Egypt, where the Maltese number about 20,000, and in Tunisia, where they number still more.

[2] In the early stages of the policy of Maltese revival too little attention was paid to Arabic studies; but there are signs that this error is being corrected.

II

'Communalism' Further Considered

Writing in 1927 Lord Balfour suggested to those enthusiasts who recommended 'the wholesale adoption of British institutions in strange lands' that they should remember not only intellect and theory, but also temperament and character.

> 'Constitutions [he said] are easily copied, temperaments are not; and if it should happen that the borrowed constitution and the native temperament fail to correspond, the misfit may have serious results. It matters little what other gifts a people may possess if they are wanting in those which, from this point of view, are of most importance. If, for example, they have no capacity for grading their loyalties as well as for being moved by them; if they have no natural inclination to liberty and no natural respect for law; if they lack good humour and tolerate foul play; if they know not how to compromise or when; if they have not that distrust of extreme conclusions which is sometimes misdescribed as want of logic; if corruption does not repel them; and if their divisions tend to be either too numerous or too profound, the successful working of British institutions may be difficult or impossible.'[1]

Let us expunge from these observations every trace of tendency, which sensitive spirits may suspect in them, to patronize or pity the less-gifted foreigner. Lord Balfour was but stating the objective truth when he declared that British political machinery presupposed 'a people so fundamentally at one that they can afford to bicker'. Experience has proved repeatedly that the system of alternating party governments will not work either when the parties are chaotic factions or when they are embattled armies. The system of popular election will not work when the people to which governments must appeal is a people fundamentally divided in its values and purposes. When this condition exists, 'institutions of self-government'—to use the common British phrase—become the means by which one section strives to impose its will upon the other; until at last even the shell of the system is likely to be crushed and thrown away.

Attention has already been directed in this volume to a number of communities where, for the reasons advanced by Lord Balfour, self-government has been refused or recalled or doled out in small instalments and with reservations. If, however, these communities are examined, it will be seen that, though they may have received similar treatment, they belong to dissimilar types. For example, in

[1] Preface to Walter Bagehot, *The English Constitution* (The World's Classics edition), pp. xxii–xxiv.

a rough and ready contrast between the political conditions of Malta and Kenya, it would be relevant and reasonably accurate to point out that, whereas Malta was an homogeneous community divided in its own mind, Kenya was an aggregation of several communities—the African, the Indian, the European—each of which might be said to possess its separate mind. Divisions in homogeneous communities may be very acute, particularly when they are interwoven with class antagonisms. They may produce explosions like the wars of religion or the French Revolution or the Spanish war of 1936. But they belong to a different category from the divisions which separate distinct communities existing side by side on the same territory. The phenomenon of schism within the cultural and political unity of a single community was familiar to the city-states of ancient Greece: they gave it a name, *stasis*. The phenomenon of collision or tension between several communities coexisting on a single territory is familiar to the modern British Commonwealth, and a newfangled name has been coined for it—*communalism*.[1]

This name, however, is still employed with some imprecision. Sometimes it is used to denote the recognition of separate communities in a representative system, as when 'communalism' is opposed, whether in Kenya or Fiji or Ceylon, to 'the common roll'. Sometimes it is used to denote not merely the institutional recognition of the communities, but the social fact of their existence. The second usage seems preferable. It is true that communal representation may in certain circumstances (as the Donoughmore Commission

[1] *Stasis* occurred also in medieval Europe: a great literature has familiarized most people with its influence on the history of Florence. In the modern world *stasis* is returning in the struggle of Fascism and Communism, which, like the *stasis* of ancient Greece, has both domestic and 'international' aspects. *Communalism*, on the contrary, was not known in the culturally homogeneous Greek world before Alexander. It was, however, found in the Greek world after Alexander. 'The Acts of the Pagan Martyrs' (Hellenist Anti-Semite Alexandrines who were roughly dealt with by the Roman government) suggest some parallels with the three-cornered relationship in modern Palestine between Jews, Arabs, and His Majesty's government. Also in Palestine the situation before the outbreak of the great Jewish war was in many respects extraordinarily like the present one; only the Jews were then playing the Arabs' part and the immigrant Greeks the Jews' part. It is, of course, possible that the dissensions of a state should reveal simultaneously both *stasis* and *communalism*. Contemporary Spain presents most forcibly the spectacle of a people divided by *stasis*—the conflict of two sections of a single people, separated, one might almost say, not only by the twentieth-century Russian Revolution but also by the eighteenth-century French Revolution and the sixteenth-century Protestant Revolution. Yet interwoven with this division are the national movements of the Basques and Catalonians, which may be regarded as having affinities with communalism. Similarly, the Irish crisis before the War would appear, if attention were focused on Ulster, to be a problem of *communalism*, but as it developed it threatened *stasis* to the United Kingdom considered as a whole.

argued) stimulate communal self-consciousness; but, generally speaking, it is the result rather than the cause of that self-consciousness. The social fact that Hindus and Moslems and Sikhs exist in India is prior to the communal award which has determined their quotas of political representation. The institution of a common roll in Ceylon has not obliterated the communities of Sinhalese and Tamils and Moslems and Burghers, although it has modified and perhaps mitigated their political action. It has been seen that even Newfoundland, which may be regarded as an homogeneous British community, tended to develop, within the forms of constitutional democracy, a system of constructing ministries and making administrative appointments which had in it some tinge of communalism. Northern Ireland has a communal problem which it has smothered rather than solved.[1] Whether or not communalism should be recognized in the constitutional order is a matter of tactics, varying according to the necessities and opportunities of each separate problem. Communalism itself goes deeper than the constitutional order.

It is necessary to consider the communities themselves. What are their characteristics? The search for an exact definition would probably be no more profitable than the dreary attempt to find a formula of 'nationality' which can be stuck like a label on to each member of the variegated band of historical nations. It appears, indeed, as if there exists a close relation between what is known in the British Commonwealth as the problem of communalism and what is known in Europe as the problem of national minorities. In its attempts to deal with these, the Treaty of Versailles very wisely shrank from the attempt to define nationality, and was content to refer to differences of 'race, language, and religion'.[2] It is the same factors which people have in mind when they talk of communalism. It is not necessary that all of them should be present, or that they should be present in equal strength. The Donoughmore Commission expressed the opinion that religious communalism presents the most difficult problems; but this is not necessarily true. The communal problem of India is primarily religious, but the communal problems

[1] The Orange drum in Belfast can start riots which may differ in degree, but do not greatly differ in kind, from those which the Hindu drum can start in Bombay. And manipulation of the municipal electoral divisions in Derry seeks to fend off the possibility of a Catholic majority—a threat which elsewhere might be met by communal representation.

[2] Articles 86 and 91 speak of 'persons belonging to racial, religious and linguistic minorities', and 'inhabitants' of a country 'who differ from the majority of the population in race, language, and religion'.

which have arisen through the emigration of Indians to Kenya and South Africa and Fiji are primarily racial.

It need not be assumed that a communal problem exists wherever communities inhabiting the same territory are distinguished from each other by their separate historical inheritances, whether of race or religion or language or all of them together. Ever since the conquest of 1760, the French of Canada have tenaciously defended their race, religion, and language; but it would be an exaggeration to affirm that Canada is afflicted with communalism. This affliction has been averted by the capacity to which Lord Balfour referred in the passage quoted above—'the capacity for grading their loyalties as well as being moved by them'. Thus it appears that in communalism there is also a strong subjective element. Communalism denotes the existence in one political territory of more than one historically conditioned community. It also denotes the existence within each community of a separate community-consciousness strong enough to stifle or enfeeble the commonwealth-consciousness—that common political loyalty which the state demands in virtue of its claim to be a *communitas communitatum*.[1]

An abstract discussion, however, will not suffice to reveal the force of communalism and the challenge which it thrusts upon statesmanship. It is time to return to the method of investigation by example. The example now to be considered is that of Palestine, which lies outside the area of the British Empire, but does not lie outside the area of British responsibility. His Britannic Majesty is no less responsible for the welfare of Palestine than he would be if it were a 'British possession': he was selected as mandatory by the principal Allied Powers for the purpose of giving effect to the provisions of Article 22 of the Covenant of the League of Nations; and this selection was confirmed by the Council of the League of Nations, which also defined the terms of the mandate. By accepting the mandate, His Britannic Majesty has undertaken an obligation to create the conditions necessary for establishing in Palestine the Jewish national home; he has undertaken to ensure that the rights and position of other sections of the population are not prejudiced; and he has undertaken to secure the development of self-governing institutions. Despite the affirmations which the British government has made from time to time of its conviction that these obligations are not irreconcilable, it has obviously found some difficulty in reconciling them. The inquiry which follows will deal with some of the causes of difficulty which appear to arise from communalism.

[1] The 'totalitarian state' or the 'uni-national state' cannot logically make this claim.

The inquiry must be severely limited. The writer will not attempt to investigate the allegation that a diplomacy of improvisations, followed during the war years, entangled the British government in contradictory obligations to different parties.[1] Nor will he consider the alleged inconsistency between Article 22 of the Covenant of the League of Nations and the terms of the mandate. Nor, again, will he construct a narrative of events since the mandate came into force. That task has already been undertaken in the *History of the Peace Conference of Paris* and in the *Survey of International Affairs*.[2] The present inquiry will follow the method of sociological analysis rather than that of historical narrative. But in this field, too, it must be careful to limit its objective very strictly. It has to be confessed that the materials for sociological study are extremely deficient. This study has a sure foundation only in social history, and the social history of Palestine is still to be written. The Arab life which is now receiving the impact of the western world has not as yet been revealed as it existed before it felt that impact.[3] Moreover, information is lacking even with regard to some of the most important changes and tendencies of the last fifteen years.[4] Finally, the writer must confess that even if the historians and the statisticians had provided the necessary material, he would be prevented both by considerations of space and by his own lack of capacity from making full use of it. A complete sociological investigation of Palestine could only be undertaken by a scholar who, in addition to an adequate equipment of history and economics, had mastery of the Arabic and Hebrew languages. Despite all this, it will be possible to make use of a limited amount of reliable material which is relevant to the problem of this chapter. And if here and there it is necessary to refer to deficiencies of material, this may indicate the heads of investigations which others may pursue.

[1] This, nevertheless, is a matter of prime importance which ought to be definitely cleared up. For an example of the impossibilities which may arise from contradictory promises, see above, Chapter IV, section ii.

[2] H. W. V. Temperley, *History of the Peace Conference of Paris* (Oxford University Press, 1924), vol. VI, ch. i, part iii B, and A. J. Toynbee, *Survey of International Affairs, 1925*, vol. I, part iii (vii); *1928*, part iii B (vi); *1930*, part iii (iii); *1934*, part ii (v).

[3] A study of this subject, with particular reference to Turkey and the ex-Ottoman territories, has been undertaken by Professor H. A. R. Gibb and Mr. Harold Bowen. The first volume of the study will be published in 1937 under the auspices of the Royal Institute of International Affairs.

[4] The mandatory government did not establish a Department of Statistics until 1935. There had, of course, been departmental statistics before this, and extensive use is made below of the 1931 census. But there are still very serious gaps in statistical information.

What are the communities of Palestine ? The reader of newspapers would answer, without hesitation, Arabs and Jews. Yet the mandate contains no mention of an Arab community. In the preamble and in five separate articles it refers to the Jewish people as being historically connected with Palestine, and to the Jewish national home which is to be established in Palestine. But, in contrast with the Jewish people, it refers merely to the 'existing non-Jewish communities in Palestine', 'all the inhabitants of Palestine irrespective of race and religion', 'other sections of the population', 'the various peoples and communities' with their various 'religious interests'.[1] It recognizes, on the one hand, a Jewish community which is a national entity, and, on the other hand, a number of communities (including on occasion the Jewish community itself) which are religious entities.

There was some justification for this classification. On the one hand, European statesmen had some first-hand knowledge of Jewish history; they were aware of the racial and religious unity which had persisted in despite of linguistic division;[2] they were also aware of the unquenchable nostalgia for the land of Israel which had at last found vigorous political expression in the Zionist movement. On the other hand, it was natural that they should tend to arrange their ideas about the existing population of Palestine with the aid of the concepts employed in the Turkish Empire. The 'nationalities' which the Turks recognized were non-Moslem religious communities which did not necessarily possess any racial significance; racial characteristics might indeed be prominent in the Armenian community, but they were difficult to detect in the community of Orthodox Christians. The Empire itself was a Church-State: sovereign power resided in a single Moslem authority with spiritual and secular capacities. The basis of sovereignty, and the basis of the autonomies which sovereignty permitted, was religious confession.[3] The mandatory power inherited the concept of the confessional community. But in two respects the change of sovereignty involved modifications of great practical importance. First, there was with the Jews a very close historical connexion between the religious and national ideas, with the result that Jewish national solidarity was in fact recognized in almost equal

[1] See Preamble and Articles 2, 6, 9. Article 22, which establishes English, Arabic, and Hebrew as the official languages, may be regarded as an indirect reference to an important factor in Arab nationality.

[2] But Hebrew remained the official rabbinical language. Of the three factors, race, religion, and language, race was in the twentieth century the most powerful, strong enough to bind even when religion had been given up.

[3] For a fairly complete and systematic conspectus of the *Millet* system in the later days of the Ottoman Empire, see F. van den Steen de Jehay, *De la Situation légale des sujets Ottomans non-musulmans* (Brussels, 1906).

measure whether recognition made explicit reference to the national home or whether it referred to the religious aspect of Jewish life.[1] In the second place, the change of sovereignty radically affected the status of the Moslem community. Hitherto this community had been identified with the sovereignty itself, but now its position was assimilated to that of the other religious communities which were granted recognition by a sovereign power standing impartially above all of them. Summing up, it may be said that the immediate effect of the change of sovereignty was to emphasize Jewish national solidarity and to contrast with it an unrecognized Arab community divided into Moslems, Christians, and 'Others'. But the ultimate effect of assimilating the legal status of the Moslems to that of the rest was probably to remove an obstacle to the co-operation of all Arabs on a non-confessional basis.[2]

It will be profitable to examine the significance of the legally recognized divisions of the population of Palestine through the eyes of the administrative officials responsible for the enumeration of the people. A census was taken in 1922. One of its chief purposes was to discover the numbers of the various religious communities in order to set up the proposed legislative council, which was to be constituted on a basis of confessional communalism.[3] There was another census in 1931. This census has a far greater scientific value than its predecessor.[4] It employs two chief criteria for tabulating the information gathered about the *de facto* population of Palestine: the criterion of geographical location and the criterion of religious confession.

[1] See the statement of 3rd June 1922 on British policy in Palestine, enclosure No. 5 in Cmd. 1700, at p. 19: 'This community has its own political organs; an elected assembly for the direction of its domestic concerns; elected councils in the towns; and an organisation for the control of its schools. It has its elected Chief Rabbinate and Rabbinical Council for the direction of its religious affairs. Its business is conducted in Hebrew as a vernacular language, and a Hebrew press serves its needs. It has its distinctive intellectual life and displays considerable economic activity. This community, then, with its town and country population, its political, religious and social organisations, its own language, its own customs, its own life, has in fact "national" characteristics.' The organization of a *national* community under the Religious Communities Ordinance is dealt with below on pp. 457–8, and a few exceptional instances are pointed out where the legal recognition of the confession does not correspond with the social fact of nationality.

[2] 'Others' are chiefly Druses. For the constitution of the Supreme Moslem Sharia Council in December 1921 (validated in the Palestine Order in Council 1922) see *Legislation of Palestine*, 1922–1925, vol. ii, pp. 398–402. Although constituted for the management of Moslem Aukaf (pious foundations) and Sharia affairs, the Supreme Moslem Council made itself a focus of Arab nationalism in Palestine, owing both to the personality of its president and the suitability of its constitution for that purpose.

[3] Non-co-operation by the Arabs wrecked the project of a legislative council. See *Papers relating to the Elections for the Palestine Legislative Council, 1923*. Cmd. 1889.

[4] *Census of Palestine, 1931*, vol. i, part i; Report by E. Mills. (Alexandria, 1933).

> 'The tabulation on the basis of religious confession [explains the author of the census report] is founded on a conception which is akin to that underlying that of a *de jure* population. . . . There is a general correspondence between the populations of persons holding an identical faith and the religious communities within the spiritual jurisdiction of a hierarchy maintaining and ordering that faith as a human institution. It follows that these tabulations on the basis of religious confessions are founded on a recognition of the special attachment of persons to the religious institutions recognized as part of the spiritual equipment of the several communities.'[1]

The author goes on to emphasize the difference between Moslems, Jews, and Christians in respect of their traditions, habits of life, standard of living, and other 'functions of population'. He submits that the results of the enumeration are entirely misleading unless they are analysed 'in respect of these component populations'. But may not the results be equally misleading if they are analysed *only* in respect of the legally recognized religious communalism? The reader will have observed that the principle of classification hitherto put forward corresponds exactly in its practical results with the principle adopted in the mandate. The recognition of the Jews as a religious community is equivalent to their recognition as a national community: the recognition of Moslems, Christians, and 'Others' implies the non-recognition of an Arab national community.

But the officer in charge of the census had also received instructions founded on the Palestine Citizenship Order of 1930. He was expected to answer the question: To what governments do persons resident in Palestine owe political allegiance? What are their countries of citizenship? To this question the census report answered that nearly 92 per cent. of the inhabitants of Palestine were of Palestine citizenship. Among the chief communities the percentages of foreign citizenship were as follows: Moslems 1 per cent., Christians 14 per cent.,[2] Jews 38 per cent. The last figure was calculated after allowance had been made for those Jews who had applied for, but had not yet been granted, Palestinian citizenship. The actual number of the Jewish foreign population was 66,000, which was equivalent to 6 per cent. of the total population of Palestine. The fact that so large an element of foreign citizenship existed among the Jewish population did not, however, affect the membership of Jews, whether Palestinian or foreign, in the recognized religious-political Jewish community.

[1] *Census*, vol. i, p. 16.

[2] The Christians included the resident administrative, missionary, educational population, which accounts for the relatively high figure of foreign citizenship among them.

Every Jew belonged to that community unless he took the necessary steps to opt out of it.[1]

With regard to the other communities, the census officer had to take account of an unexpected complication. The actual fact of Arab solidarity had been recognized in the form of an Arab census committee, which was consulted in the same manner as the corresponding Jewish committee. This Arab committee protested against the principle of classification. It maintained that the Jews were being classified, not merely as a religious community, but in reality as a national community, and it demanded the same privilege for Arabs. In effect it argued on behalf of the Arabs: 'You are classifying us as town-dwellers or country-dwellers, as Moslems or Christians, as Palestinian citizens or as persons of foreign citizenship; but in all this you are missing one of the main points. We want to be classified as Arabs.'

The census officer discussed this claim in a section of his report which was entitled 'Nationality within Citizenship'. He explained that in the current and legal usage of the English language nationality was usually held to be identical with citizenship; but he also pointed out that this identification was 'not generally part of the political philosophy of European states'. It was a result of the unusual political history of the island kingdom of Great Britain. In virtue of this history, Englishmen, Welshmen, and Scots found no difficulty in describing themselves as British in nationality. The same phenomenon was true of all but a very small portion of the British Commonwealth. But it was not true of European states whose populations were composed of mixed races. Had the development of Great Britain followed on lines similar to those of central and eastern Europe, it was conceivable that the English concepts of citizenship and nationality would have been similarly disentangled, and that in current and legal usage there would have been a distinction between British subjects on the one hand, and on the other hand 'persons of English, Scottish, and Welsh "nationalities", together with such "nationalities" as might have developed with the Commonwealth'.[2]

The report went on to discuss the changed position of the Moslem community and the special character—religious and at the same time political—of the Jewish community. These matters have been already explained above. With regard to the Arab claim to be classified

[1] *Census*, vol. i, p. 73. On opting out see below, p. 457.

[2] Loc. cit. The British Commonwealth was, of course, already familiar with the distinction between a dominion nationality and the status of a British subject. See p. 74, above, for Canada's nationality legislation, and the supplementary chapter below.

according to 'nationality', its attitude tended to be one of patient expostulation. 'This Arab "nationality"', it said, 'has no legal existence, since there is no Arab community in any formal sense.' It expressed the opinion that 'the vague conception of an "Arab" nationality' was probably the reaction to the existence of a Jewish 'nationality'. It pointed out that declarations of 'nationality' would have no bearing upon the legal status of any community (since the communities were organized on a different principle); nor would they even be a reliable guide for purposes of numerical comparison. Despite all this, it recognized that the demand was proof of 'an awareness, on the part of members of some of the non-Jewish communities, of the possibility of common factors in the aims of the several communities'. And although the classification which the Arab Census Committee demanded would mean 'no more than that a person is an Arab or a Jew according to his own proclamation of the fact', the report itself contained proof that this self-consciousness was deemed to be of importance. It offered the following classifications:

Nationality within Citizenship

	Persons	*Arabs*	*Jews*	*Others*
Total	1,035,821	839,619	174,809	21,393
Palestinian (Settled and Nomad)	949,586	832,999	108,694	7,893

Numbers in each Nationality per 1,000 of the Population

	Persons	*Arabs*	*Jews*	*Others*
Total (Settled and Nomad) .	1,000	810	169	21
Palestinian	1,000	877	115	8

These tables stand out as an exception to the general plan of the 1931 census. A few years later they would not have been considered exceptional. The disturbances of 1936 caused the administration to modify for the time its intention of holding a quinquennial census. Had the census been taken, the authorities would have applied consistently and throughout the principle of classification by nationality, parallel with the religious classification. The same principle is being applied with increasing frequency in inter-censal inquiries. For example, 'vital occurrences' have hitherto been classified under the heading of the religious communities, but it is proposed to classify them in the future under the heading of national declaration also. Migration statistics have since 1935 been classified under the heading: 'Arabs' and 'Jews'. The inference follows irresistibly that the theory of communities which was taken over with modifications from the

Turkish régime does not now adequately reflect the political realities, and is insufficient for purposes of administration. The classification by confessions was the natural one to adopt at the time when sovereignty was transferred, and it still retains some significance;[1] but circumstances have to a very marked degree diminished its importance. The newspaper-reader, who assumes that the periodical explosions in Palestine are due to dissension between Arabs and Jews, is much closer to the truth than the student of documents who, after perusing the mandate and the Religious Communities Ordinance, may be led to the conclusion that the explosions are caused by a religious collision. Communalism in Palestine has its religious aspects, but its most emphatic manifestations are nationalist rather than confessional. The present writer, when he visited Palestine during the disturbed summer of 1936, saw, not a struggle of 'Moslems, Jews, Christians, and Others', but 'two nations warring in the bosom of a single territory'.

An understanding of the challenge which British statesmanship has to face in Palestine cannot therefore be achieved without an analysis of the two national communities. The analysis will be limited to the elucidation of two points which are of very great importance. The first one is obvious, namely, that the problem of communalism is interwoven with a problem of immigration. The second point, which will easily be proved by example, is that there exists an emphatic inequality between the two opposed communities.

Considered generally, the Arab population of Palestine is a 'settled' community and the Jewish population is an 'immigrant' community. This statement may need a little qualification. The Jews never severed completely their ancient connexion with Palestine: throughout the centuries a small remnant remained physically present in the land of Israel, and the modern movement of deliberate re-settlement began, not with the mandate, but three generations earlier.[2] At the end of the war there was in Palestine an estimated Jewish population of 55,000,[3] a considerable proportion of which might fairly be regarded

[1] For example the religious classification illustrates occupational and social differences within the Palestinian community, the Christians being much more highly urbanized than the Moslems and enjoying much greater educational opportunities and equipment. The contemporary history of Syria shows that the confessional classification may have significance for politics also. It suggests that the triumph of the national concept over the religious one in the politics of the Near East is not complete.

[2] Baron de Montefiore in 1835 provided funds for colonization: his example was followed by the Universal Israelite Alliance which founded a school of agriculture about 1870, by Baron de Rothschild who began a more ambitious scheme in 1882, and later by the Jewish Colonization Association.

[3] *Report of the High Commissioner on the Administration of Palestine*, 1920–5, p. 29.

as 'settled'. On the other hand, the Arabs, like the original followers of Moses, were originally immigrants and conquerors. The present Arabic-speaking population of Palestine is a residual population, whose mixed racial character testifies to the long history of the country 'as a meeting-place for migrations east to west and west to east'.[1] The European visitor to a Christian Arab village will be quick to observe features which seem to him to bear the stamp of a crusading ancestry. But the villagers none the less belong to the Arabic-speaking world, which established its culture in Palestine more than ten centuries ago. They are no less deeply rooted in their own way of life than are the inhabitants of an English village. The Arab population, with the exception of the Bedouin, is a settled population of the usual eastern Mediterranean economic type. The Jewish population, however, is not of the ordinary immigrant type. The Jewish immigrants are entering a country where they have deep spiritual roots. They proclaim both that they are Europeans in their civilization, and that they are natives of Palestine returning to their own home.

Between 1918 and 1922 the Jewish population increased from 55,000 to 83,794. Between the census of 1922 and the census of 1931 it increased from 83,794 to 174,610. On the 31st December 1935 it was estimated at 355,000. In 1931 it was 17 per cent. of the total population of Palestine; four years later it was 27 per cent. of the population, which at that date was estimated at 1,308,000 persons.[2]

The Arab population, while it was a diminishing percentage of the total population of Palestine, was steadily increasing in numbers. In accordance with the principle of classification, which has already been explained, the figures are grouped under the headings of the recognized confessional communities. This grouping gives the following results for the years 1922, 1931, 1936.

Estimated Population of Palestine (exclusive of nomads[3] *and of members of His Majesty's Forces)*

Year	*Total*	*Moslems*	*Jews*	*Christians*	*Others*
1922 (census October) .	757,182	590,890	83,794	73,024	9,478
1931 (census November) .	1,035,821	759,712	174,610	91,398	10,101
1936 (30th June estimate)[4]	1,269,965	781,789	370,483	106,474	11,219

[1] *Census*, vol. i, p. 59.

[2] Government of Palestine, Department of Migration, *Annual Report 1935* (Jerusalem, 1936), p. 27.

[3] The Nomadic Bedouin population was estimated at the census of 1922 as 103,331, and at the census of 1931 as 66,553.

[4] Government of Palestine: *Vital Statistics*: *Quarterly Bulletin, No. 2, 1936*. Roughly 80 per cent. of the Christians and 90 per cent. of the 'Others' may be reckoned as Arabs.

The difference between rates of growth between the communities is explained by the different causes of growth. 'Whereas the growth of the Arab population is mainly due to natural increase, immigration is the principal factor in the expansion of the Jewish population.'[1]

The following table gives a general picture of migration between the years 1920 and 1936.[2] It shows the recorded immigrants and emigrants under the headings of Jews and non-Jews. The great majority of the recorded immigrants were persons authorized to enter Palestine as permanent residents. The remainder, who in 1935 numbered 3,804 Jews and 625 non-Jews, entered Palestine as travellers but were later registered as immigrants.

Year	*Recorded Immigration*		*Recorded Emigration*	
	Jews	*Non-Jews*	*Jews*	*Non-Jews*
1920 (Sept.–Oct.)	5,514	202	*	*
1921 „	9,140	190	*	*
1922 „	7,844	284	1,451	1,340
1923 „	7,421	570	3,466	1,481
1924 „	12,856	697†	507†	604†
1925 „	33,801	840	2,151	1,949
1926 „	13,091	820	7,365	2,064
1927 „	2,713	882	5,071	1,907
1928 „	2,178	908	2,168	954
1929 „	5,249	1,317	1,746	1,089
1930 „	4,944	1,489	1,679	1,324
1931 „	4,075	1,458	666	680
1932 „	9,553	1,736	*	*
1933 „	30,327	1,650	*	*
1934 „	42,359	1,784	*	*
1935 „	61,854	2,293	396	387
1936 „	27,909	1,036	773	405

* No statistics of emigration by race were compiled.
† Figures for July to December.
Out of the 2,293 non-Jewish immigrants in 1935 only 903 were Arabs. Separate Arab statistics are not available before 1935.

The above table does not give complete information about the volume of immigration. In addition to the recorded immigrants there was a considerable influx of illegal immigrants, which at its highest (in the years 1932–3) was estimated at 22,400.[3] In the following year the

[1] M. Berenstein, 'Jewish Colonisation in Palestine, I', in *International Labour Review*, vol. xxx, no. 5, November 1934, p. 626. Cf. *Census*, 1931, vol. i, p. 59. The 'actual' Moslem population was practically equivalent to the 'natural' Moslem population.

[2] *Report on the Administration of Palestine and Transjordan for 1935* (Colonial No. 112 of 1936), p. 214, and *General Monthly Bulletin of Current Statistics*, September 1936, p. 4. Classification as Jews, Arabs, and Others was adopted in 1935.

[3] *Administration Report for 1935*, p. 45.

government claimed that it had achieved marked success in reducing the number of illegal immigrants.[1] These fell into two main classes. The larger class was composed of persons who entered Palestine as travellers and remained there illegally. The smaller class was composed of persons who evaded the frontier controls. It is impossible to give statistics about this smaller class. The numbers in recent years of the more important class have been estimated as follows:[2]

Number of 'Travellers' remaining illegally in Palestine

Year	*Jews*	*Non-Jews*
1933	10,376	2,653
1934	2,907	3,022
1935	4,618	3,256

Of the 3,256 non-Jews in 1935, only 1,662 were Arabs.[3]

Looking at these figures as a whole, it is plain that Arab immigration into Palestine is quite inconsiderable compared with Jewish immigration. It would not be necessary to labour this point were it not that statements of a different tendency are sometimes made. The figures of recorded immigration up to 1932, by Mr. Berenstein's calculation, show that non-Jewish immigration amounted to only 9 per cent. of the Jewish immigration. Moreover, the figures of those years, although they are incomplete, make it clear that the emigration of non-Jews frequently exceeded the immigration of non-Jews. In subsequent years there has probably been a net balance of Arab immigration and emigration under this head.[4] The figures given above of travellers illegally remaining in Palestine indicate that there is a noticeable Arab immigration of this class: it is, however, considerably smaller than the corresponding illegal immigration of Jews. In the last and smallest class, the immigrants who evade the frontier controls, there may be a higher proportion of Arabs. The evidence is imprecise and there are conflicting dogmatic assertions. The French authorities have supported the assertion that there is a considerable migration of Hauranese into Palestine. The British authorities in 1934 affirmed that the volume of this migration had been 'grossly exaggerated'.[5] They also insisted on the seasonal character of migration movements from Transjordan. 'No reliable statistics are available', they reported, 'but it is believed that few remain in Palestine

[1] *Administration Report for 1933*, p. 15.

[2] See *Great Britain and Palestine, 1915–1936*. (Royal Institute of International Affairs; Information Department Paper No. 20), p. 63.

[3] Department of Migration, *Annual Report*, 1935, p. 61.

[4] *Great Britain and Palestine*, p. 64.

[5] Permanent Mandates Commission, *Minutes*, 27th Session, p. 47.

permanently. Most seek to make a little capital in Palestine with which to return to Transjordan and to assist their livelihood there.'[1]

Of necessity, therefore, the Palestine Department of Migration is concerned chiefly with the immigration of Jews, in comparison with which all other immigration is inconsiderable. Space is not available here for a detailed analysis of the Jewish immigration; but it will be desirable to refer briefly to a few important considerations. The first of these is the factor of change with regard to the volume of immigration. From 1920 onwards there was a steady inward flow which reached its maximum height in 1925, when there was an immigration of 33,801 Jews. In October of 1925 unemployment began to make its appearance and by May 1927 the official estimate was 8,180 unemployed workers.[2] As a result of this there was from the end of 1925 until 1928 a steep decline in immigration and a rapid rise in emigration, so that in 1927 the Jews leaving Palestine exceeded those entering it by 2,358. By 1928, however, practically all the unemployed had been reabsorbed, and thereafter, despite the retarding effect of the 1929 disturbances, there were rising figures of net Jewish immigration. The census of 1931, surveying the general population increase throughout the whole period since 1922, estimated that if present trends were continued the population of Palestine would double itself in twenty years, the Moslem population in twenty-five years, and the Jewish population in nine years.[3] In the years immediately following the census there was a phenomenal upward leap of Jewish immigration, which in 1935 reached the peak of 61,853 'approved Jewish immigrants arriving'. Between 1933 and 1935 there were 134,540 approved Jewish arrivals, a figure which exceeded the total number (118,378) in the whole thirteen-year period from

[1] *Administration Report for 1935*, p. 50; Department of Migration, *Annual Report*, 1935, p. 21.

[2] M. Berenstein in the *International Labour Review*, vol. xxx, no. 5, p. 628. It should be stated that there did not exist then, and do not exist now, any figures of Arab unemployment which have any value at all. An effective system of registration depends on an effective motive for registration. Jews register through their trade unions and have the motive of unemployment benefit and organization for re-employment. Arab labour is unorganized. The suggestion of the Hope Simpson Report (Cmd. 3686 of 1930), to establish labour exchanges would have no effect on the supply of information unless at the same time a motive for Arab registration comparable with the motive for Jewish registration were supplied. There is also no reliable information with regard to the class of Arab cultivators who are part-time wage-earners. According to the 1931 census this class is larger in Palestine than in any other country. In view of these circumstances it is inevitable that the unemployment question should become the football of political controversy.

[3] *Census*, 1931, vol. i, p. 45. See also graph No. 1 at p. 202 of the Shaw Report (Cmd. 3530 of 1930), which embodies various hypotheses as to the date when the Jewish population might become a majority.

1920 to 1932.[1] In 1936 some tendency towards a decline was apparent, even before the outbreak of the Arab strike or revolt.[2]

At this point the economic inquirer will feel himself impelled to pursue the question of capital importation; but the subject, though of fundamental economic importance, is too large to be handled here.[3] Nor is there space to explain the administrative classification of immigrants, which can easily be discovered by reference to the reports of the Department of Migration. Reference will be made now only to two subsidiary points which are relevant to the accelerated immigration beginning in 1933. There was to some extent a change in its economic composition; a rise in the proportion of 'dependents' from 49·4 per cent. in 1931 to 63·9 per cent. in 1935,[4] and a rise in the proportions of students and members of the liberal professions.[5] There was also some change in the territorial origin of the immigration, which is set out in the following table:

	Proportion per 100 Jewish immigrants coming from all countries in the years		
Country of previous abode	*1922–9*	*1934*	*1935*
All countries	100	100	100
Poland	46	43	46
Russia	20	..	..
Germany	..	16	14
Rumania	6	5	6
Lithuania	5	3	3
United States of America .	3	3	3
Others	20	30	27

[1] Department of Migration, *Report*, 1935, p. 10.

[2] After the revolt, on 5th November 1936, Mr. Ormsby Gore announced in the House of Commons that as a result of existing conditions, economical and political, in Palestine, the labour schedule for the next six months had been fixed at 1,850 instead of 8,000. There was no restriction on capitalist immigrants.

[3] A short and sound introduction to the subject and its sources may be found in Mr. Berenstein's article cited above. There seem to be remediable deficiencies in the sources: for example, it should be possible for the Palestine government to institute banking statistics.

[4] One aspect of the rise in the proportion of 'dependents' was 'a most significant reversal of sex-proportion'. This in turn was associated with the practice of fictional marriages and a Jewish divorce rate of 40 per cent. Ibid., pp. 22, 23.

[5] Ibid., p. 24. 'For instance, the number of immigrant physicians is almost double the number of physicians actually practising in 1931. . . . Again, the number of architects and engineers who have entered the country since the end of 1931 is equal to the number of earners practising these professions in 1931.' The report, while referring to the diversion on a considerable scale of immigrants to new callings, says that there is nevertheless 'an *a priori* expectation that men and women immigrants will usually seek to derive their livelihood from occupations in which they have gained a degree of competence in their countries of previous existence'. It is evident (p. 14) that this does not apply to persons admitted as students, many of whom did

It will be observed that Great Britain is not recorded separately as a country of emigration. It is indeed negligible in calculations of quantity, if not of quality: at the census of 1931 (and certainly there has been no upward movement since then), Jews born in the United Kingdom were only 0·5 per cent. of the total number of Jews born outside Palestine. The figures for Poland and Russia were then 45 per cent. and 34 per cent. respectively. The table given above shows that Jewish immigration from Poland has continued to be little less than half the total Jewish immigration into Palestine, but Jewish immigration from Russia has almost disappeared.[1] The most important fact during recent years has been the rise of German immigration, from a figure which did not justify Germany's inclusion among the chief countries of emigration to a figure which, though still far below the Polish immigration, took second place on the list. The new factor of German-Jewish immigration has a definite connexion with the change in the occupational groups of the immigrants, and particularly with the increase of immigrants belonging to the liberal professions. It also illustrates the truth which the Commissioner for Migration has expressed in the following words:

> '. . . Jewish immigration into Palestine differs from other migration in that it is not solely the response to economic attractions of the country of immigration. No doubt a proportion of Jewish immigration into Palestine does correspond with ordinary migration in this sense; but a proportion of Jewish immigrants comprises those who are attracted to Palestine for reasons of another sort; while yet a third proportion comprises those who have no special interest in Palestine but are repelled from the countries from which they have emigrated. Natural migration is, in effect, the result of the work of the country of immigration conceived as a suction-pump; immigration into Palestine is the result of the combined action of Palestine as a suction-pump and the country of emigration as a force-pump. And it is this fact which gives sufficient reason for any difference there may be between the characters and

not proceed to the institution which had applied for their admission, or else left it shortly to enter the labour market. For measures taken to cope with the overcrowding of liberal professions, see the *Administration Report for 1935*, p. 12, and for further figures on the subject, p. 72.

[1] For a short consideration of the Soviet policy of nationalities, see next chapter. The U.S.S.R. was itself at this time trying to establish in its territories a 'national home' for the Jews. For a critical account of this effort see *Palestine Post*, Jewish New Year Supplement, 16th September 1936. How far the criticism is well-founded, the present writer is unable to say. After he had been informed many times that Hebrew was a prohibited language in the U.S.S.R. (only Yiddish being tolerated) it fell to him as a member of the Birmingham Reference Library Committee to join in acknowledging a gift of six books on Shakespeare, published at Minsk in the year 1936, and printed in the Hebrew language.

attributes of the Jewish immigrant population in Palestine and those of immigrant populations elsewhere; and for supposing that a theory of migration accounting for the phenomenon of migration generally may not account for the phenomenon of migration into Palestine.'[1]

The only parallel in British twentieth-century experience to this extraordinary immigration comes from Canada in the years before the war.[2] But even there the points of contrast are no less striking than the points of comparison. Setting aside altogether the ideological factors, which in Palestine are unique, there is a striking economic and social contrast between the two movements. The immigration into Canada was on the whole an immigration of a specialized occupational character; it was an immigration of labour which was employed in developing the natural resources of a vast country and in the productive use of the capital simultaneously being imported. The 'labour schedule' occupies a prominent place in the Jewish immigration also; but it has already been shown that this immigration contains other strong elements with an altogether different social and economic significance. *Mutatis mutandis*, the Jewish settlement in Palestine is more in line with the Wakefield theory of colonization than with the migration which has actually happened in modern British countries. It is the deliberate transplantation of a complete society represented in all its layers. The Wakefield theory, however, contemplated the transplantation of a complete English society into lands assumed to be empty. Jewish enterprise, like British Protestant enterprise in Ireland during the sixteenth and seventeenth centuries, has to reckon with a country already occupied by a civilized, if less developed, people. It therefore results in the juxtaposition of two separate societies upon the same soil.

[1] Department of Migration, *Report*, 1935, p. 26.

[2] The immigration into Canada during 1911–13 was approximately 1,100,000 in a population of 7,200,000, an average of 5 per cent. per annum. The approved immigration into Palestine during 1933–5 was about 4½ per cent. per annum: adding the considerable illegal immigration, the figure would amount to 5 per cent. per annum—perhaps a shade more, perhaps a shade less. Canada, like Australia, has tended to absorb immigrants by the boa-constrictor method of gorging them and then digesting them with some initial discomfort. Before the war and in the early war period there was in Canada heavy unemployment, which the war and the development associated with it helped to relieve. But comparison with Palestine has limited advantages because of the great differences of circumstances. On the one hand, Palestine gets its capital cheaper and without piling up an external debt. On the other hand, there is no comparison between the size and the natural resources of Palestine and Canada. The occupational distribution of Jewish immigration is also less satisfactory. But the chief point of contrast is the ideological significance of the Jewish immigration and the fact of racial conflict. Under these heads the parallel of seventeenth-century Ireland, rather than that of twentieth-century Canada, suggests itself—to be handled with equal caution.

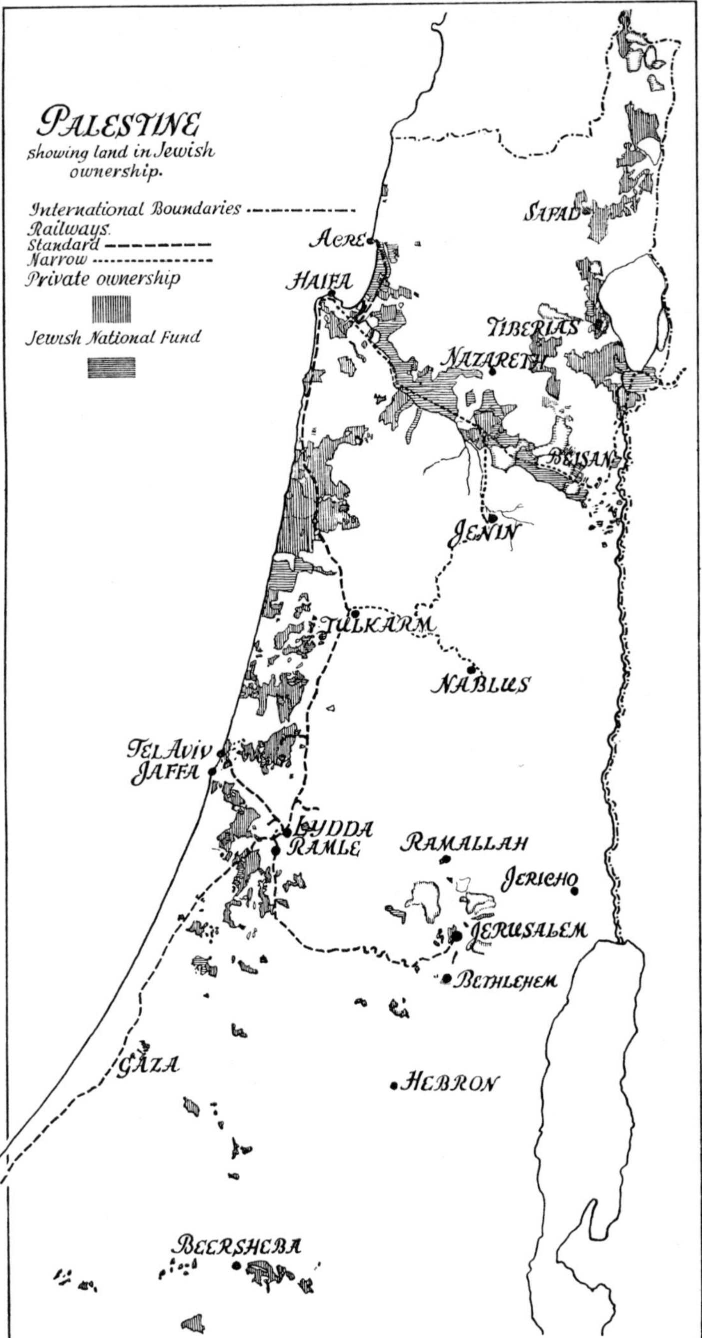

Prepared from the map compiled, with assistance of Government Survey material, by The Palestine Land Development Co. Ltd. (November, 1936). The original was published by permission of the Commissioner for Lands and Surveys, and is reproduced here by courtesy of The Palestine Land Development Co. Ltd.

THE DISTRIBUTION OF NATIONALITIES IN PALESTINE IN A.D. 1937 AND IN A.D. 37

It will be seen that the present Jewish colonies in Palestine are concentrated on the maritime plain and in the depression running inland from the Bay of Acre to Beisen, while the strongholds of the Arabs lie in the hill country of Judah, Ephraim, and Galilee. Nineteen centuries ago, Palestine was divided between two rival nationalities on much the same lines, only with the positions reversed; for at that time the highlands, where the Arabs now are, were held by the Jews, while the lowlands, where the Jews now are, were planted with Greek city-states.

POPULATION DENSITY AND URBANIZATION

The map does not indicate population density and urbanization. At the census of 1931 the urban percentage of the Moslem population was 27, and of the Jewish population, 73·6. Since then the proportion of Jewish town-dwellers to the total Jewish population has increased by 2·2 per cent. (end of 1935).

The study of the relations between two such societies is a most complicated matter and one of the greatest interest to economists and sociologists. Here it must suffice to illustrate only one aspect of the problem as it forces itself upon the attention of administrators. The Arabs represent an oriental community which for about a century has been seeking to adjust and strengthen itself in response to the impact of western society.[1] The Jews in the main[2] represent a cross-section of western society at its highest point of efficiency. As a result there is a *de facto* inequality which at every point of contact between the two societies expresses itself in visible material forms. There are also, of course, in the spiritual texture of the two societies contrasts which may be no less important. There are the oppositions which arise from the particular individual histories and aspirations of the two communities. Oppositions of this kind may give rise to violent psychological disturbances; but they are set on one side here because the material contrasts, although they are not necessarily more important, are capable of being illustrated quickly and convincingly by precise examples.

The first example will be taken from some tables dealing with 'Wages and Hours of Work in Palestine, 1935', made available by the Palestine Department of Statistics. The labour is classified under two headings: European and Asiatic. A certain number of Jews (for example, the Yemenite Jews) are classified under the heading Asiatic; but generally speaking the classification corresponds with the division between Jew and Arab. The tables are very full, and deal with the labour of men, women, and children, in agricultural and manufacturing production, in the building industry, and in government employment. A few typical items dealing with male labour will be selected from each category:

A. *Prevailing Daily Wages (in mils[3]) in Agricultural Employment*

	European labour (Men)	*Asiatic labour (Men)*
Ploughing	250–400	80–120
Orange picking	220–25	120–200
Porterage (carrying baskets) . .	200	80–100
Labourers (general), citrus plantations .	220–25	100–50

(The rates shown in respect of European labour are based on 8 hours' work. The usual hours of work of Arab labourers are: on cereal land, 10–12 hours; in citrus plantations, 8–10 hours.)

[1] One may roughly date the beginning of this effort from the time of Mehemet Ali's rule in Egypt, but the history has yet to be written. See note on p. 433 above.

[2] In 1935 the total immigration from Asia was 5,537.

[3] 1,000 mils = one Palestine £.

B. *Prevailing Daily Wages (in mils) in Manufacturing Industries*

	European labour (Men)	*Asiatic labour (Men)*
Quarrymen, skilled	450–600	200–300
,, unskilled	350–400	100–40
Cabinet-makers, carpenters, skilled	500–600	230–350
,, semi-skilled	350–400	150–200
Locksmiths, fitters	400–700	300–500
Cardboard-box makers	250–500	70–160
Oil pressing and refining	350–400	150–250
Cigarette-makers' assistants	230–300	100–150

C. *Prevailing Daily Wages in the Building Industry*

	European labour	*Asiatic labour*
Masons, skilled	600–700	500–600
,, semi-skilled	400–500	250–400
Concrete workers, skilled	500–600	..
Plasterers, skilled	550–700	250–500
,, semi-skilled	400–500	..
Building labourers	350–400	100–80

(The rates of wages of European workers are based on 8 hours' daily work; the wages paid to Asiatic labour are based on 9–9½ hours' daily work.)

D. *Wages in Government Employment (Minimum and Maximum Wages in mils)*

	European labour	*Asiatic labour*
Mason	350–1,000	200–800
Carpenter for shutter work	250–1,000	200–700
Bricklayer	350–1,000	200–800
Road asphalter	250–500	120–400
General labourers	120–400	70–200
Electrician	250–1,000	250–700

The above figures testify to emphatic inequality between the two communities in the sphere of labour. It would be beyond the scope of the present inquiry to probe too far into the causes of the inequality, but there are obvious connexions between differences in wages and differences in organization. On the Jewish side there is the *Histadruth*, the General Federation of Jewish Labour, which has a membership approaching 90,000 and is one of the most efficient and interesting achievements of industrial unionism in the modern world. On the Arab side there are only a few weak unions. Arab labour, generally speaking, is unorganized labour.[1] The existence on the same

[1] *Administration Report for 1935*, pp. 119–20.

territory of two labour forces, one organized, the other unorganized, one working shorter hours than the other and commanding very much higher wages, of necessity creates the most difficult problems. The General Federation of Jewish Labour has tried to meet these problems by a dual policy. On the one hand, it has sought to protect its own standards—insisting, for example, on a virtual Jewish monopoly of the labour market in Tel Aviv—by measures which are reminiscent of the 'civilised labour policy' in South Africa. Its efforts in this direction have been in accord with the policy pursued in other spheres of Zionist life (notably by the Jewish Agency and by the colonies of the National Fund) of excluding Arab labour altogether.[1] But the General Federation of Jewish Labour has aimed also at encouraging a parallel organization of Arab labour with a view to the levelling-up of standards. National antipathy, however, has proved stronger than the motive of united working-class collaboration, and at the time of writing little of this collaboration is left. The first objective of the *Histadruth*—the civilized labour policy—is alone actively operating.[2]

The General Federation of Jewish Labour is not merely an impressive organization of wage-earners; it includes land-colonists who do not exploit the labour of others; and it undertakes as a co-operative body important enterprises of transport or production. Co-operation is another sphere in which the Jewish community demonstrates its marked advantage in social maturity and efficiency over the Arab community. According to the mandatory power's report for 1935, the total number of functioning co-operative societies was 769, which were distributed as follows:

Jewish	*Arab*	*German*	*Others*
658	74	5	2

The difference in quality was probably even greater than the difference in number: many of the Arab co-operatives were weak and struggling 'thrift societies' in agricultural villages; but Jewish co-operation, whether in finance, in housing, or in agriculture, was vigorous, self-reliant, and resourceful.[3]

[1] The present writer is aware that this policy has roots in nationalist idealism, and it must be understood that he is neither blaming nor praising it.

[2] *Administration Report for 1935*, p. 20. After mentioning that the attempt at parallel organization had won some success at first among the port workers of Jaffa, the report says that resignations became frequent 'as the feelings engendered by the arms smuggling incident overcame the still unformed sense of social solidarity'. Thereafter the 'strike' was a crushing blow to the few surviving efforts of non-national class collaboration. This, however, remains the basis of the Railways and Postal Union.

[3] Ibid., pp. 268 ff. The administration's attempts to foster Arab co-operation

The writer does not wish to imply by this comparison that the Arab community is innately deficient in intelligence or initiative. It has displayed both intelligence and initiative in adapting itself to modern conditions in citrus cultivation, in banana cultivation along the Jordan valley, and in other enterprises. But it has not developed a degree of social efficiency comparable with that of the Jewish community. Wherever one examines the two communities, their *de facto* inequality impresses itself. An examination of banking and finance would reveal contrasts no less striking than those which are indicated by the wages statistics. How far these Arab disadvantages might be remediable through an inner reconstruction of the structure of Arab society would be a matter for a separate investigation.[1] Enough has been said to illustrate the inequality operating in the economic sphere. Let us now turn to the sphere of education. If a comparable inequality is found there, this will serve in large measure to account for Arab inferiority in economic, and also in political, activity. For education is basic to both.

In examining the educational statistics of Palestine for information on the comparative positions of the Arab and Jewish communities, the investigator has to grapple with certain difficulties arising out of the principle of classification. First of all, arrangement under the headings 'Moslems, Jews, Christians, and Others' is still largely employed. With regard to this difficulty, the Commissioner of Migration and Statistics has informed the present writer that for rough purposes the following adjustments are at present satisfactory:

Moslems . . .	100 per cent.	Arab in nationality[2]
Jews	100 ,, ,,	Jewish ,,
Christians . . .	80 ,, ,,	Arab ,,
Others . . .	90 ,, ,,	Arab ,,

It follows that in most cases the numbers of all the non-Jewish communities taken together will exceed by very little the number which might be ascribed to the Arab community. In general it will be left to the reader to make the necessary adjustments.[3] This difficulty has

were the sequel to the Hope Simpson Report and the Strickland inquiry. The 1935 report states that the government has appointed five field organizers to supervise and prepare Arab thrift and co-operative development. Lending to the co-operative societies is organized efficiently by Barclay's Bank.

[1] The investigation might well begin with an analysis of the position of the *effendi* class, about which there is considerable controversy.

[2] Nationality in the sense admitted in the 1931 census: i.e. national declaration.

[3] Within the Christian divisions, schools are sub-divided again by the great branches of Christianity—Orthodox, Catholic, Protestant: and also according to the nations maintaining missionary schools—British, Italian, French, German, Swedish, &c.

reference only to the non-government schools. In the government system classification is on a 'linguistic and racial' principle.[1] There is an Arabic public system and a Hebrew public system. But the word 'public' has very different connotations in the two systems. It is worth while to consider this difference, which will itself supply evidence of inequality and prepare the reader for the evidence contained in the figures given below.

The Arabic public system is in its origin a legacy inherited from the Turkish government. In theory, Ottoman education was gratuitous and compulsory, and Turkish was the medium of instruction. In practice, the schools of minorities received little or no support, and universal elementary education of Moslems never became a reality in any part of the Ottoman Empire. When the British took control of Palestine they substituted Arabic for Turkish as the medium of instruction, and endeavoured to improve the practical efficiency of the educational system.[2] But the administration itself they left untouched. The Arabic public system is, therefore, under the direct administration and control of a government department, and 88 per cent. of the expenditure on it is from public money.[3] The Jewish public system, on the other hand, was created by the Jews themselves, and for many years it was in large measure financed by contributions from outside Palestine. It still receives a grant of £P20,000 a year from the Jewish Agency, and almost 80 per cent. of its budget comes from fees and local contributions. The Jewish community has shown its idealism, its modernity, and its practical efficiency in creating its own system whereby education is given to every Jewish child. Should the government support from the public funds this community enterprise? The question is in some respect similar to the question raised with regard to Catholic education in Great Britain. The early High Commissioners refused financial support; but this attitude was

[1] Department of Education, *Annual Report*, 1934–5, p. 2.

[2] The education estimates were in 1920–1, £E78,000; in 1921–2, £E130,000; in 1922–3, £E114,217; in 1925–6, £E101,392 (= 4·96 per cent. of total estimates); in 1929, £P144,119 (= 6·59 per cent. of total estimates); in 1934–5, £P206,108 (= 6·34 per cent. of total estimates); in 1935–6, £P233,521 (= 4·80 per cent. of total estimates). For graph showing development of all schools since 1922 see Department of Education, *Annual Report*, 1934–5, Table XXVII.

[3] It is the policy of the department to devolve material expenses increasingly on local education authorities. In the case of rural schools the villagers normally provide the land, buildings, and furniture, though the government usually gives a grant towards the cost of new buildings not exceeding half the cost. Sometimes the village will provide an extra teacher. The same policy is beginning to operate in some of the smaller towns, but not in the larger ones. Pupils buy their own books unless they are too poor. In secondary schools the pupils pay £P3 per annum in fees.

later abandoned. If the principle of the grant be admitted, the method of calculating the grant is, in the opinion of the present writer, equitable.[1] The grant is a substantial one; for the year 1935–6 it was fixed at £P36,000; but even so it amounts to no more than about 12 per cent. of the total budget of the Jewish schools. In short, Hebrew education in Palestine is not really a public system at all, but a great voluntary effort of the Jewish community, supported to some extent by public authority. This is true in the sphere of finance; it is equally true in the sphere of teaching and administration. The majority of Jewish schools, embracing about two-thirds of the Jewish pupils in the country, are under the direct control of the *Va'ad Leumi*, the national council of the Jewish community in Palestine. These are the schools which are grouped, in the official reports, under the heading 'Hebrew Public System'; but the public department confines its activity to indirect supervision and general inspection. It has powers of veto—chiefly through control of the budget—which, in practice, are very seldom operative. Thus, in essentials the Jewish community manages its own educational affairs.

Some comparisons with regard to numbers will emphasize the contrast, which has already become apparent in the foregoing general

[1] The government grant to Jewish education is calculated as follows:

(*a*) An estimate is made of the total net expenditure on Arab education in the given year, after deducting revenue from fees, sale of books, &c. Call this figure E (Palestine pounds).

(*b*) Estimates are made of the number of Jewish and Arab children of school-age, i.e. between 5 and 15. All children are included in these estimates whether they are attending school or not. Call these numbers J and A respectively. (It is usually convenient to express the ratio of J to A as a percentage $J : A = P : 100$. At present the ratio of Jewish *children* to Arab *children* is roughly 23 : 100).

(*c*) A grant is then calculated as $E \times \frac{P}{100}$ or, what amounts to the same thing, $E \times \frac{J}{A}$

The government does not pay for each Jewish *pupil* what it spends on each Arab *pupil*, but it pays for each Jewish *child* in the country the same amount that it spends on an average on each Arab *child*, inclusive of all Arab children not attending school. The Jews claim that they pay most of the taxation (a claim very difficult to assess). They also claim that the government should base the grant on what it spends on each Arab child actually attending school. But the method of allocation is considered equitable, as many Arab children are debarred from attending school, especially in the villages, either because the government has not been able to provide a school, or because the accommodation is limited.

The method of calculating the grant has been in operation, with certain minor changes, since 1927. From 1927 to 1933 the grant was calculated on a slightly different basis, the percentage taken being equal to the ratio of the *whole* Jewish population to the *whole* Arab population, instead of the ratio of the school-age populations only. In 1933 the school-age population ratio was adopted as being more equitable.

description, between the higher Jewish educational development and the lower Arab development:

Total Number of Children (Boys and Girls) attending all Schools

	Moslems	*Christians*	*Others*	*Jews*	*Totals*
1920–1	18,126	7,431	..	17,244	42,801
1922–3	20,294	13,722	286	18,535	53,467
1934–5	45,942	19,766	712	52,326	118,746

Making the calculations necessary to re-group these figures under the heads of the two national communities, the figures for 1934–5 are:

Total Number of Children (Boys and Girls) attending all Schools

Arabs	*Jews*
62,396	52,326[1]

What do these figures represent in relation to the total number of children, Arab and Jewish, of school-attending age? Unfortunately, the Department of Education has not yet worked out the exact percentages. But it has been calculated that in 1934–5 the ratio between the Arab and Jewish school-age populations was roughly 100: 21.[2] This means roughly that a Jewish school-age population, which is between one-fifth and one-quarter the size of the corresponding Arab population, produces a school-attending population which is only one-sixth smaller. Virtually it means that no Jewish child goes without schooling and that—to make a rather risky guess—only one Arab child in every four gets any schooling.

So far as possible, every suggestion of praise and blame is being excluded from this analysis. Perhaps this is not altogether possible. Perhaps the writer has been unable to set down with complete coldness, without a trace of the admiration which he feels, the facts of Jewish educational achievement. But it must be emphasized that in setting down the facts of Arab educational inferiority he is not insinuating blame of the Arab community. It must be emphasized in the first place that there is an Arab demand for education which the government has failed to meet. The number of Arab children

[1] The figures are based on Table XXVI of the *Annual Report* of the Department of Education for 1934–5. The translation of the religious-community figures into national-community figures is in accordance with the rough principle explained on p. 450. It may be pointed out that the mandatory power in its annual report for 1935 (p. 132) reaches a higher figure by the rough and ready method of counting all the pupils in the Christian missionary schools as Arabs.

[2] *Administration Report for 1934*, p. 20.

attempting to gain admittance to schools has grown in greater proportion than the number of the school-age population. Only a proportion of the Arab children who seek education are granted it. The figures from 1931 to 1935 are as follows:

Percentages of Applications on behalf of Arab Children to enter Schools (all classes) which were accepted[1]

	Before Expansion Scheme		*After Expansion Scheme*		
Year . .	1931	1932	1933	1934	1935
Percentage .	57	49	62	59	59

In addition to the fact of an unsatisfied Arab demand for education, it is necessary to bear in mind the inheritance of Turkish administration. Still more necessary is it to bear in mind the contrast of the European and Asiatic backgrounds. In education, as in so much else, the Arab community starts some generations behind the Jewish community in the race for modern efficiency. The facts recorded in this inquiry do not necessarily demonstrate superior and inferior intelligence and virtue; but they do certainly demonstrate the *de facto* inequality of two communities at different stages of development.

There is still much more to be learned from the statistics of education. Unclassified aggregate numbers give no idea of the quality of education, which, so far as statistics can reveal it, must be sought in a study of age-groups and classes. Educational efficiency must in large measure be judged according to the period over which education is pursued. That the Jewish community shows an even greater proportionate strength in the earliest years of education is indicated by the following figures with regard to kindergartens:

	Total number of kindergartens (public, assisted, and non-assisted)	*Number of kindergarten pupils registered*
Hebrew	106	5,856
Arab .	234	8,667

A Hebrew superiority which is even more emphatic exists in the higher stages of education. To begin with, there is the Hebrew University, an institution which under humane and far-seeing leadership established its quality in research as a preliminary to establishing itself as a teaching body. In 1935 there were 103 members of the staff, including 22 professors and 29 lecturers. There were 391 students. In addition, Palestinian-Jewish students to the number of about 200 were working in European universities. On the Arab side, there was

[1] Department of Education, *Report*, 1934–5, p. 22.

within Palestine in 1935 a board of studies empowered to hold intermediate and diploma examinations of pass B.A. and pass B.Sc. standard. There were no candidates for these examinations. All Arabs seeking university qualifications sought them outside Palestine: there were, in 1935, 232 Arabs in the higher classes of the American University of Beirut, and about 20 Arabs in British universities.[1] The total number of Arabs achieving a university education outside Palestine—none were achieving it inside—was less than half the total number of Jews achieving it inside the country and outside it. The discrepancy was even greater with regard to agricultural and technical education available within Palestine. Thanks to a magnificent Jewish gift, Arabs as well as Jews possess one first-class agricultural school.[2] In 1935 70 Arab boys attended this school. There were in addition 3 non-assisted Christian agricultural schools attended by 77 boys and 4 girls. On the Jewish side there were 26 boys attending the Kadoorie Jewish agricultural school; 441 boys and 294 girls attending 5 assisted schools; 120 boys and 115 girls attending 4 non-assisted schools. In all, 151 pupils (including 4 girls) attended 4 Arab schools; 996 pupils (including 409 girls) attended 10 Jewish schools. As for technical education, the departmental statistics do not record a single technical school for Arabs; but there were, in 1935, 6 non-assisted Jewish technical schools attended by 463 boys and 42 girls.[3] In secondary education, the Arab College at Jerusalem is the only government school providing a complete course (i.e. up to matriculation standard) for Arab boys.[4] The same school also carries some of its pupils further to be trained as teachers. There are, however, other schools, public and private, which provide a varying amount of secondary school education. The totals are as follows: on the Jewish side, 16 schools with an attendance of 2,480 pupils: for Moslems and Christians, 41 schools with an attendance of 1,540. The translation of this last figure into the appropriate number of Arab pupils would necessitate a larger deduction than usual from the total, because of the comparatively larger number of Christian children included. The existence of a considerable number of missionary schools doing a certain amount of secondary education also explains the discrepancy on the

[1] Ibid., Table XXIII.

[2] The gift of Sir Ellis Kadoorie. The Kadoorie Agricultural School at Tulkarm for Arabs was opened in 1931; the Kadoorie Agricultural School for Jews, on the slopes of Mount Tabor, was opened in 1934.

[3] Department of Education, *Report*, 1934–5, Table XXIII, section v. Of course there is some technical education in ordinary schools.

[4] A full course of secondary education is considered to be four years, leading up to matriculation standard.

non-Jewish side between the number of schools and the number of pupils: many of the schools included have only a handful of pupils at the secondary school stage.[1]

It would be wearisome to carry much farther an analysis which any reader may undertake for himself by a study of the departmental reports. Only one comparison will be added. It will be restricted to the Arabic and Hebrew public system, and will throw light upon the comparative standards attained within these two systems.[2]

Years of schooling	*Grades*	*Arabs*	*Jews*
12 to 13	Higher Training College only	106	79
10 ,, 12	Higher Secondary and Training College		477
8 ,, 10	Lower Secondary	399	960
5 ,, 8	Higher Elementary	1,912	5,543
0 ,, 5	Lower Elementary Cycle	33,648	20,273

The table shows that the Arab school-age population—which in 1935 stood to the Jewish school-age population in the ratio of 100: 21—had a larger number of school-attending children at the lower elementary stage only. The Arabic public system took only 2,355 children into the higher elementary stage, only 445 of them beyond this stage, and only 106 to matriculation standard. If this table be compared with those which have been given above, the demonstration of inequality in the sphere of education becomes overwhelming. On the one side is a community where practically no child goes without some education: on the other side is a community where perhaps three children out of four go without education. On one side is a community with good educational facilities at the bottom and the top, and reasonable ones in the middle; on the other side is a community whose disadvantage in educational quality is apparent everywhere except in the lower elementary cycle.

These facts surely have some bearing upon the comparative backwardness of the Arabs in economic organization, which has already been illustrated. They also have some bearing on the comparative primitiveness of Arab political organization, which will now be briefly demonstrated. But in this regard it is important to remember the legal position which has been explained above—namely, the theory of the state which recognizes autonomous communities on the basis of religious profession, not on the basis of national declaration. The

[1] Department of Education, *Report*, 1934–5, Table on p. 37. Training colleges are included. With regard to missionary schools which engage in a very little secondary education, chiefly at its earlier stages, it may be mentioned that seven German schools had between them only 71 boys and 40 girls in secondary school classes.

[2] Based on Tables VI B and XIII B, ibid.

great majority of Jews have been ready to use this religious definition for their national purposes; indeed, to a large number of Jews the religious and national principles are hardly separable. But the definition which served the purposes of the Jews frustrated those of the Arabs, because it affirmed the separateness of Moslems and Christians.[1] The history of confessional recognition is as follows. Under Turkish sovereignty it had been granted to all non-Moslem communities. By Article 83 of the Palestine Order in Council 1922 it came to embrace the Moslem community also. By the Religious Communities Organization Ordinance 1926, a procedure was established whereby confessional recognition was given important practical effect. The Religious Communities Organization Ordinance permitted any community, which chose to make application, to secure for itself elaborate communal machinery, including the right of taxation.[2] The Jewish community alone made application.[3] The rules which it submitted, and which the government approved, recognized the Congregation of Israel (*Knesseth Israel*) and placed upon the individual Jew the painful obligation of 'opting out of it' if he did not wish to accept its authority.[4] *Knesseth Israel* expresses its community-will in an elective assembly meeting from time to time, and from this assembly the executive body of the community, the *Va'ad Leumi*, derives its authority. It is not necessary to go into new detail to illustrate the

[1] But see note 2 on p. 435 above, dealing with the Supreme Moslem Council as a focus of nationalism.

[2] Article 3. 'Any such Regulations may bestow upon the said Councils or Boards power to impose upon members of the Community contributions or fees for communal purposes which shall be recoverable in the same way as municipal taxes and fees.' (*Official Gazette of the Government of Palestine*, No. 157.)

[3] In addition to the reason given above, the national reason, the Moslem community was inhibited for applying by its theory that the ultimate sovereignty behind ecclesiastic jurisdiction must be Moslem sovereignty.

[4] The Jews, who have exercised their legal right of contracting out, may be grouped in three classes:

(1) The ultra-orthodox Jews of *Agadath Israel*. This organization exists throughout Jewry and its desire to maintain its purity through separateness found expression when *Knesseth Israel* established its elective assembly on the basis of universal suffrage, thus ignoring the traditional strict teaching with regard to the position of women. It desires to control its own affairs—slaughter-houses for meat, burial places, &c. It has no legal recognition from the government. The *Administration Report for 1935* (p. 17) refers to its increasing co-operation with the recognized Jewish community, which indeed contains pious members (the *Mizrachi*) who are hardly less strict in their religion. But negotiations for incorporation have not as yet achieved that aim.

(2) Another class of conscientious ones who contract out are the free-thinkers who will not pay taxes which go to religious courts—which in Palestine have jurisdiction in divorce.

(3) Finally, of course, there is among Palestinian Jewry, as elsewhere, a small minority of tax-shirkers.

important powers which belong to the Jewish community and its executive body; these have already been demonstrated in the discussion of Jewish education, three-quarters of which is administered by *Va'ad Leumi*, under the nominal and very distant supervision of the government department. The Jewish community, in relation to the mandatory power, is in important respects an *imperium in imperio.*

But there is another aspect of the Jewish community, in which its relationship to the mandatory power might almost be termed that of an *imperium ex imperio.* This aspect is typified by the Jewish Agency. The executive offices of the Jewish Agency are in Jerusalem, but there is also an office in London, which is specially charged with the conduct of business between the Agency and the mandatory power. It is difficult to give a simplified picture of the Agency's constitution and activities.[1] The organization in Palestine resembles a cabinet divided into administrative departments,[2] and certainly it performs for the Jewish community in Palestine work which in normal circumstances would belong to the government. But it does not derive its powers from the Religious Communities Organization Ordinance; and although its relations which *Va'ad Leumi* are, in fact, close, they have no basis in local Palestinian Law. The legal basis for the Jewish Agency is in the mandate itself. Article 4 of that document declares that an

> 'appropriate Jewish agency shall be recognised as a public body for the purpose of advising and co-operating with the Administration of Palestine in such economic, social, and other matters as may affect the establishment of the Jewish national home and the interests of the Jewish population in Palestine'.

It will be observed that this declaration does not refer merely to such Jews as happen to be under the jurisdiction of the government in Palestine; it refers to Jews throughout the world, whatever their citizenship. By this article the mandatory power accepted precise obligations towards international Jewry. Certainly it reserved to itself the right of control; but subject to this reservation it recognized the right of all Jews, wherever they might live, 'to assist and take part in the development of the country'. In 1922 it accepted the Zionist Organization, which had territorial divisions in every quarter of the world, as a body which might fittingly perform the functions of the

[1] See *Constitution of the Jewish Agency for Palestine* (The Jewish Agency for Palestine, 77 Great Russell St., London, 1929). This is the constitution of the 'enlarged' Jewish Agency, 50 per cent. Zionist and 50 per cent. non-Zionist.

[2] e.g. departments of colonization, labour, finance, and the 'political department'—a sort of foreign affairs department.

Agency. But Article 4 of the mandate directed the Zionist Organization to secure the co-operation of all Jews, whether Zionists or not, who should be 'willing to assist in the establishment of the Jewish national home'. In accordance with this direction the Jewish Agency came, in the course of time, to be equally representative of two elements—Zionists and non-Zionists. The non-Zionists might be fairly described as persons who are Zionist in sympathy, but who desire to co-operate in the establishment of the Jewish national home otherwise than through the Zionist organization.[1] Among them are many small associations of influential Jews. The Zionists, on the other hand, are members of an elaborate world-wide political organization, which has copied the forms of western democratic constitution-making and which reproduces the characteristic party contests of western political society.[2] It originated as a propagandist body; but, in proportion as the national home has been translated from the realm of aspiration to the realm of fact, the living issues of Palestinian politics have progressively dominated its activities. Yet it still remains an institution of international Jewry, focusing its chief attention on a tiny area of the world's surface.[3] It is beyond the jurisdiction of the political administration in Palestine; indeed, one of its chief concerns is to overlook this administration, and to keep a watchful eye on the policy of the mandatory power. If the British government appears to show a tendency to wander from the straight path which leads to the establishment of the national home, or if it seems to be loitering along this path, the Zionist organization brings into action its extensive resources of propaganda.

The political maturity of the Jewish community might be further illustrated by a study of its parties, which pursue their internal contests without breaking the front of the community in face of the Arabs.[4] It might be illustrated by the unique position which has been enjoyed almost uninterruptedly by Dr. Chaim Weizmann,

[1] See Article 4 of the mandate, and *Constitution of the Jewish Agency for Palestine*, Article 1: '"Zionist" means a person associated with the Agency in the capacity of a member and representative of the Zionist Organization. "Non-Zionist" means a person associated with the Agency otherwise than in the capacity of a member and representative of the Zionist Organization.'

[2] See *Constitution of the Zionist Organization*. At the time of writing (1936) the Labour party has for a considerable period been in the ascendant in Zionist politics.

[3] Ibid., Article 1: 'The aim of Zionism is to create for the Jewish people a home in Palestine secured by public law.' Article 2: 'The Zionist Organisation comprises all Jews who accept the Zionist programme and pay the shekel.'

[4] In the opinion of the writer, the Revisionists, or New Zionists, do not really break the Jewish front. His own inquiries tend to bear out the opinion expressed in the *Administration Report for 1935* (p. 18) that there is a growing co-operation between Zionists and Revisionists. On the other hand this may be a temporary phrase.

virtually the prime minister of world Zionism but depending on the votes of anxious east-European Jews. But enough has been said already to prove the high standard of Jewish effort. It has been shown that, both within Palestine and outside it, the Jews have a particularly advantageous position. The Religious Communities Organization Ordinance has given them inside Palestine a privileged position which the Arabs could not claim without doing violence to their own history and theory. The mandate has given to organized international Jewry a legalized interest in the affairs of Palestine which has some analogies with the legal rights which 'Christendom' used formerly to possess in regard to Christian minorities in the Turkish Empire.[1] But it must be added that the Palestinian Jews and world Jewry have both made exceptionally able use of their exceptionally favourable legal position. The contrast between the Jewish and Arab communities is not merely that between a community which enjoys legal recognition and one which does not enjoy it; there is also a contrast between communities at different stages of political coherence and capacity. In 1923 the Arabs had an opportunity to redress by the weight of their numbers the legal advantage which the Jews enjoyed in virtue of their special recognition in the mandate, but they threw away that opportunity.[2] It may be doubted whether they would have been able to compete with the Jews in using a legally privileged position, even if they had been granted one of comparable significance. After they had rejected the legislative council proposal of 1923, the British government offered them an Arab Agency which it conceived as an equivalent to the Jewish Agency. It is true that this Arab Agency would not in theory have been exactly comparable with the Jewish Agency. The Arabs rejected it on principle.[3] But suppose that an Arab Agency

[1] Bismarck once asked a Russian diplomatist to say what he meant by 'Christendom'. The diplomatist answered, 'Several great powers'. To this Bismarck replied: 'What if they are not in agreement?' *Per contra*, Jewry in relation to Palestine had not the force of 'several great powers'; but did have the force of racial unity. There was a corresponding difference in the 'sanctions' available to it for furtherance of its legally recognized interests.

[2] *Papers relating to the elections for the Palestine Legislative Council.* Cmd. 1889 of 1923.

[3] *Proposed formation of an Arab Agency.* Cmd. 1989 of 1923. It would have differed from the Jewish Agency (1) in having no recognition in the mandate itself, (2) in having no connexion with the Arab community outside Palestine, (3) in being constituted by nomination of the High Commissioner. In rejecting it, the Arab spokesman simply said that 'the Arabs, having never recognized the status of the Jewish Agency, have no desire for the establishment of an Arab Agency on the same basis'. Ibid., p. 10. Historical circumstance probably ruled out the possibility of an Arab equivalent to the Jewish Agency, for the position of the Jewish community throughout the world and its relation to Palestine was unique.

had been entrenched in the mandate, and that its relation to the Arab world outside Palestine had been in theory exactly similar to the relation of the Jewish Agency to the Jewish world outside Palestine? Even then, there would certainly have been important differences in practice. The two worlds were so dissimilar. For the Jewish world outside Palestine was a community commanding great wealth, intelligence, and devotion, and it was prepared to lavish a great deal of these possessions upon Palestine itself. The Arab world outside Palestine had the great advantage of territorial possession and potential military power; but economically and socially its development was less advanced, and, moreover, Palestine was not the chief preoccupation of any one of the political or religious units into which it was divided. As for the Arabs within Palestine, it has already been shown that they were far behind the Jews in economic and educational efficiency.

In the course of years Jewish pressure and Jewish example did something to bring about a modification of the inequality in the sphere of political organization. The census of 1931 has already been quoted as to the effect of Jewish national self-consciousness in stimulating a similar self-consciousness among Palestinian Arabs.[1] The analysis of this heightened nationalism is a complicated task which none but an Arabic scholar could attempt. How far is it a local patriotism, the home-feeling of a people who believe, with whatever justification, that their homeland is being invaded and threatened? How far is it a pan-Arabic movement, struggling for the aspiration of a united Arab state? How far does it reflect Moslem feeling as distinct from Arab feeling? How far is it a growth of recent years? These and other similar questions must be left for others to answer. But, whatever the sources of Palestinian-Arab nationalism, there can be no doubt about its increasing political efficiency. This became marked after 1933, during the years of the upward leap of Jewish immigration. The reports of the mandatory power in these years testified to a growing cohesion among the so-called Arab parties, and suggested that this cohesion was the result of an insistent movement in Arab public opinion.[2] The strike or revolt of 1936 gave ample proof that this was so. For six months the Arab community in Palestine maintained a degree of cohesion and

[1] See p. 438, above.

[2] e.g. *Administration Report for 1935*, pp. 14 ff., gave a summary of the chief parties, which in effect were personal or family followings. The report then mentioned the formation of various organizations for youthful Arab nationalists, and said: 'Towards the end of the year the younger element had gained ground, and were becoming a factor which might challenge the influence of the older Arab leaders.'

organization which in some respects was reminiscent of Ireland in the time of Sinn Féin. The cohesion was none the less impressive because it was not to be found in printed constitutions. At every stage, the advance in effective political unity was made in fact before it was set out in theory.[1]

Strike and revolt are a crude method of redressing the balance; but instances of their effectiveness, in greater or less degree, have already been recorded in this volume.[2] In the particular circumstances of Palestine, strike and revolt, even if they collapsed or were suppressed, might well achieve some measure of success in redressing one further inequality. This was inequality of access to the ear of British democracy. Jewry was represented in every layer of English society—in the Lords and the Commons, in powerful capitalistic organizations and in the labour party, in the press and in the universities. Jews of British nationality had by right a position of equality in the life of the nation which had been entrusted with the mandate, and by their own qualities they had made this position a respected one. The religious traditions of a large section of the English people had made them familiar with the Jewish story, and prompted a spontaneous sympathy with the Jewish aspiration to build their home once more in the Holy Land.[3] There was, indeed, a circle of Arab partisans in England. There was, also, even in England, an anti-Jewish movement. But it was associated in English minds with continental oppressions and masqueradings, and was repugnant to the traditions of insular liberty which were professed by all the political parties and by the overwhelming majority of the British people. The very fact that the Jews were suffering in Nazi Germany was a powerful motive with men of humane sympathy to espouse their cause in Palestine. The Jews could command every means by which an audience could be

[1] After the strike had begun (and it began before it was 'declared') the five parties came together. The Arab Higher Committee combined all religious as well as all political elements. There was the same combination in the 'national committees' which included the whole country in their mesh of organization. Theoretically, the Arab Higher Committee acknowledged responsibility to a congress of the national committees. These committees gave an opportunity of action to the younger men, and their organization was extremely efficient. The writer spent a morning going through the strike-relief accounts of one committee. These were in model order and testified to the successful prosecution of a formidable task.

[2] e.g. the resistance of Ulster to the Home Rule Bill, the resistance of Saorstát Éireann to British rule, and the resistance of the Kenya Europeans to the Wood-Winterton scheme, pp. 96, 221, above.

[3] The experience of the writer as an Australian child was doubtless shared by many English children of his age. He knew the details of Palestinian geography before he knew any other geography, and he was familiar from an early age with the prophecy 'Some day the Jews will return'.

made to listen; they could also command an audience which was disposed to listen. The Arabs, too, raised a cry of bitter woe. Among many of the administrators in Palestine there was a readiness, perhaps an uncritical readiness, to listen to it.[1] But in England their cry, so far from being amplified, dwindled and was almost lost among so many other voices. The Arabs were far away, too far away, too poor, and too unskilled to appeal persistently and effectively to the democracy of Great Britain. But what they could not do through the printed or spoken word they might hope to do by physical protest. It was the same method by which the backward people of the northern and the western counties of Tudor England had sought to gain the ear of monarchs living in the strenuous progressive south. Revolts, strikes, or demonstrations play an intermittent but inevitable part in the system which is called government by public opinion; they are the last resource of the distant or obscure communities who feel that they are forgotten. When, in September 1936, the British government had to postpone the army manœuvres in order to send reinforcements to Palestine, the Arabs might congratulate themselves on winning a prominent place in the attentions of their distant masters, if not in their sympathies. They did, indeed, hope to win a larger measure of British sympathy; but they also hoped to make an effective appeal to British interest. The Jewish community frequently appealed to British interest. Some of its spokesmen offered to perform an imperial function in the eastern Mediterranean.[2] Others reminded the Empire of the services which world-Jewry had rendered to it during the war. Others, who were more rash, threatened the Empire with a formidable enmity unless it made itself the instrument of the Jewish will in Palestine.[3] The Arabs of Palestine, conscious of their kindred with the reviving communities

[1] It is often alleged that large number of British administrators in Palestine have a personal bias against the Jews and in favour of the Arabs. The present writer obviously is unable to discuss this allegation scientifically upon evidence; yet obviously the matter is important. If the allegation is true it would indicate a tendency to mitigate inequality which is both inefficient and mischievous. Inequality can only be redressed by policy grounded upon principle and pursued in a spirit of personal impartiality.

[2] e.g. see the quotations from Lord Melchett, p. 481, below.

[3] Notably the New Zionists, though their threat is politely expressed. e.g. *A Survey of the Revisionist Programme* (London, 1935), p. 9: 'Revisionism is equally remote both from regarding England as the "only" mandatory power possible and suitable, and from "rejecting" Britain as the mandatory. . . . Destiny does not put all her eggs in one basket. But since it is Britain, there is no need to engage in guesswork about other baskets, and least of all before Zionist Jewry has *properly* tried to ascertain whether or not Britain can be induced to adapt its policy in Palestine, fully and unreservedly, to the needs of State Zionism.' These needs are stated on the same page as follows: 'Palestine should cease being an Arab country.'

of Arabia and Iraq, believed that they too had something to offer. They believed that they could play an important part in making or marring the security of the British Commonwealth in an area which it considered vital to its communications. How far there was substance in this contention the present writer is quite unable to say. Nor is he attracted by the exercise of weighing the respective advantages or dangers which might come to the British Empire from the friendship or hostility of Jews or Arabs. Such calculations might appear to be in the spirit of his aloof and seemingly cold-blooded analysis. But his aloofness springs merely from the conviction that the problem of Palestine, which has engendered so much heat, can do with a little cold light. It does not spring from a philosophy of *Realpolitik*. On the contrary, the writer can in the last resort see no other standard for the guidance of British policy than the standard of justice which, as an earlier chapter has shown, it has professed to follow in facing the racial problems which confront it elsewhere.[1] But in Palestine, even more than in eastern or southern Africa, absolute justice eludes its seekers.

It would be a mistake to conclude this section with some moralizing generalities. It is best to sum up what has already been said, and to remind the reader of much that remains to be said by others. It has been shown that there are in Palestine two communities, both of which are predominantly nationalistic in their self-awareness. It has been shown that one community may fairly be called a 'settled' community, the other an 'immigrant' community. It has been shown that the immigrant community enjoys an effective superiority over the settled community in most of the attributes of social efficiency, according to the standards of this time. It enjoys an emphatic superiority in economic power. It enjoys the same superiority in education. In politics it starts with the advantage of specific legal recognition, and it has made the most efficient use of this advantage. It also has the advantage of access to the ear of British democracy. It can bring pressure to bear on the mandatory power both from within Great Britain and also from outside.[2] But here its *de facto* superiority ends. It has wide influence, but no direct power. Its position in a world where other nations possess the soil and the

[1] See Chapter IV, above.

[2] Not merely from democratic countries like the United States. Countries where anti-Semitism is in the ascendant, such as Poland, hope that they will be relieved of many of their Jews by a policy of mass immigration sponsored by the mandatory power. In November 1936 Colonel Beck was reported as raising this matter with the British Foreign Secretary. (*The Times*, 9th and 10th November 1936.)

sovereignty is tragically insecure, harried, and bitter. It is a persecuted nation, a dispersed people. Yet it is this very homelessness, this very weakness, which makes it show a different face to the Arabs. Nowhere but in Palestine does it hope or does it wish to satisfy the natural longing, hard to keep within bounds, to be 'like all the nations'.[1]

It has not been possible in this section to deal with certain important matters which would have to be thoroughly probed in any book which was devoted entirely to the Palestine problem. There has been little said of the inner structure of the two communities—nothing, for example, about the Arab village, or about the *effendi* class, or about Jewish colonization, or about the distribution of Jewish enterprise between city and country. Nor has there been any detailed inquiry into economic relationship between the two communities. Sweeping assertions and prophecies of present and probable future gain and loss are made on each side. The writer is compelled to leave this question entirely unexplored, merely remarking that exact statistical information is lacking under some of the most important heads, and that, even if it were available, the sociological investigator would hardly be likely to see the situation so crystal clear as the propagandists see it.[2] The only thing which is crystal clear is the dominance of national feeling over economic calculation. This renders irrelevant and fallacious every attempt to describe the problem purely in terms of economic

[1] *Like all the Nations?* is the title of a pamphlet published in Jerusalem in 1930 by Dr. J. L. Magnes, then Vice-Chancellor of the Hebrew University. It maintained in detail and with great courage the unpopular thesis that it was better for the national home to be 'poor and small and faithful to Judaism rather than large and powerful like all the nations'. While insisting that the Jews possessed and must possess the right to immigrate, to buy land, and to develop Hebrew life and culture, it argued that neither a Jewish state nor a Jewish majority was essential to the national home. It argued for a legislative council in the present, even though there was an Arab majority, and gave a warning that hurry and a *Wille zur Macht* might destroy the quality of the national home and its historic justification. Its rejection of the plea of Jewish need as a justification for retarding the progress of self-government in Palestine would now have even more point since the advance towards independence in the area of the French mandate has further emphasized the contrast between Palestine and other mandates of the same class within the former boundaries of the Turkish Empire.

[2] For example, the Jews point with justification to the fact that Arab population has increased most in the city and country districts of maximum Jewish enterprise. Some Arabs deny this. Others assert that the increase is associated with proletarianization. The sociological investigator will see evidence of proletarianization in the 'tin-town' at Haifa. It looks like a native location in South Africa. But what is its size? Estimates vary from 12,000 to 6,000. How many of its inhabitants are non-Palestinians? Estimates again vary. The investigator is held up for lack of exact material.

fact, even if that fact were sufficiently accurate in detail and sufficiently wide in its reference. Accurate economic analysis is urgently desirable, not because it will exorcize nationalistic passions, but because it will enable the government to see more clearly through the dust raised by their conflict. At the time of writing (November 1936) nationalism has torn down almost every frail tendril of economic collaboration between the two communities. The beginnings of trade-union collaboration, which were already half-smothered, have now been buried. The Chamber of Commerce at Jerusalem has split in two. Tel Aviv has made ready to establish itself if necessary as a rival port alongside its neighbour Jaffa, like Gdynia alongside Danzig or like Susak alongside Fiume.

What has been the relation of the mandatory power to the warring communities? The detailed narrative of British policy can be studied in the *Survey of International Affairs*. In this book it will be sufficient to consider the main lines of policy in Palestine in so far as they illustrate the tendency of British policy in relation to communal problems generally. Is it possible, by studying not only the Palestine example but other examples elsewhere, to discover any coherent principle which governs or at least influences the response of British statesmanship to the challenge presented by 'two nations warring in the bosom of a single territory'?

It is frequently alleged, either in criticism of the injustice of British rule or as a compliment to its cunning, that the Empire survives by setting one nation against another. *Divide et impera*. Moslems are set against Hindus, Jews against Arabs, the Protestant Irish against the Catholic Irish, the Europeans of Kenya against the Indians of Kenya. British policy, it is said, follows the Machiavellian precept of 'governing by factions'. Perhaps it may be relevant to inquire what Machiavelli did, in fact, say about this brand of policy. He refers to the common saying that Pisa must be held by fortresses and Pistoia by factions. Fortresses, he answers, are of no permanent use to hold a conquered city; if you want to hold it you must either make it your friend or else destroy it.[1] As for factions, they are even more dangerous. They will not enable you to defend your conquest against outward attack, because it will be supported by rebellion from within. The faction which you support will be dangerous to you if it is too strong, for in that event it may dispense with your aid; it will be dangerous to you if it is too weak, for in that event you will have to spend your imperial power in a conflict which, properly considered, is a local conflict outside the sphere of your real interest. Moreover, if you

[1] *Discorsi*, book. ii, ch. xxiv, 'o farsela campagna o disfarla'.

provoke the hostility of a faction in a subject city, you will possibly provoke the hostility of a similar faction in your own city. Machiavelli quotes with approval the historian Biondo, who pointed out that the Florentines, in attempting to divide Pistoia, divided themselves.[1] This comment is extraordinarily apt to the experience of the United Kingdom on the eve of the Great War, when the ancient policy of governing by a faction in Ireland threatened a wider rupture in the United Kingdom.

Machiavelli sums up his argument by judging the maxim to be utterly false which says that conquered communities should be kept disunited; on the contrary, he asserts, it is essential to unify them. It follows that the British, if they do really follow the policy of *divide et impera,* are bad Machiavellians. But is it true that they follow this policy? Undoubtedly they followed it for many centuries in Ireland. They followed it in one of its specialized forms, attempting to hold Ireland by an 'ascendancy' of their own colonists. Machiavelli would doubtless have viewed this experiment with a certain amount of indulgence; for in discussing methods of holding down a conquered province, he includes the planting of colonies. But it is plain that, in his opinion, the efficacy of this method depends upon its thoroughness. He would not have regarded the Protestant minority of Ireland as an adequate foundation for perpetual British rule over an unreconciled nation. It was a half-measure. Machiavelli will admit no half-measures in imperial policy towards conquered nations. You must either exterminate them, he says, or win their consent.[2]

It is plain from the facts which have been recorded in this volume that British policy has advanced since the time of the Tudor and Stuart plantations. According to the disposition of the reader, this change may be regarded either as an advance in humanity or an advance in Machiavellian wisdom. Both elements can be detected in the history of British policy in Canada. The early governors wished to gain the support of the French Canadians against American republicanism; but their humanitarian sympathies were also outraged by the claim of 'a sufficient number of loyal and well-affected Protestants' to ride roughshod over the interests and customs of the French population. The first three generations of British policy in Canada have a startling relevance to the problems which have been considered in this section. British policy oscillated between rival poles: sometimes it grounded itself entirely on respect for the rights of the settled French population, at other times it deliberately set

[1] Ibid., book. iii, ch. xxvii, cf. *Il Principe,* ch. v.
[2] 'o spegnerle o carezzarle.'

itself to swamp and overwhelm the French by a British immigration. But its actual development followed a course which rejected both extremes, and in the end it became clear that this was not merely a compromise, not merely one of those *vie di mezzo* which Machiavelli so disliked. The policy of Lord Elgin was no less positive than the pro-British policy foreshadowed in the proclamation of 1763 or the pro-French policy enshrined in the Quebec Act of 1774. Each of these extreme policies was founded on the same political philosophy, namely, the philosophy of the uni-national state, which became dominant in the nineteenth century. But from the middle of the nineteenth century onwards Canadian development was grounded on a different political philosophy, that of the multi-national state. It is true that the Canadian conditions were, on the whole, unusually favourable to this new conception, which, moreover, was implied rather than stated. It nevertheless regulated political events, and its acceptance lifted Canadian history out of provincial isolation, making it prophetic of a new age, making it relevant to the need, if not to the achievement, of human civilization in the twentieth century.

The same positive and creative political philosophy was implicit in the Vereeniging settlement and in the later development of British-Afrikaner relations in South Africa. Events seemed in large measure to prove its practical efficiency. It became the orthodoxy of the imperial conference. Whereas Lord Elgin had enunciated it with the enthusiasm of a lonely prophet, the orators of the British Commonwealth sang its praises with the fervour of those who are justified by faith. Considerable pains have been taken in this volume to emphasize the limitations of actual achievement, and to criticize the flattering illusions which were cherished by the justified ones. Evangelicalism is sometimes too contemptuous of dogmatic theology, and the enthusiasm of imperial conference oratory left in the air a great deal which might with profit have been embodied in a coherent creed. The British Commonwealth did not think out in all its implications the philosophy of a multi-national community. It followed that as each new problem arose there was uncertainty in practical action, and uncertainty of principle. Despite this, the experience gained in Canada and South Africa profoundly influenced the aims of British policy in other parts of the Empire. The end aimed at was that which Machiavelli recommended—to eschew government by factions and to heal divisions. The writer submits that this aim has been pursued in India; for the communal award was a *pis aller*, and the act of 1935, whether or not its means are appropriate, appears to aim at as much unity as circumstances will allow. The domestic history of India has not, however, been studied in the present volume; so let the examples be taken from material already assembled. The narrative of British policy in Ceylon reveals emphatically that its aim was unity. In Kenya the government aimed in 1922 at a common roll, and only surrendered this aim under pressure. Despite this pressure, policy has steadily resisted the claims of a small European 'ascendancy' to govern the whole community. Responsible government, declared the Hilton Young Report, could not come until the native population of the country was ready to take a share in it. Even in Ireland, where the 'ascendancy' policy had once dominated the whole situation, and where as late as 1914 it had been vehemently maintained by the conservative party, there was by 1921 a definite change. It is true that communalism in Ireland, which as a matter of history has been fostered by Great Britain, split the unity of Ireland and partitioned her into two territories. It is equally true that this partition could not have occurred had not British force been behind the six northern counties. Yet the documents make it clear that the British government acted in this role with reluctance. Lloyd George did what he could to *persuade* Ulster to throw in her lot with Ireland. 'Why will you not be reasonable', the new English statesmanship inquired of Ulster, 'and throw in your lot with the new Irish Dominion?' The question was certainly a naïve one, seeing that the old English statesmanship had spent so many generations in fostering Ulster's 'unreasonableness'. But it was asked.

There is, of course, a difference between a philosophy vaguely held and a policy resolutely pursued, between the desire to achieve a given pattern of social organization and the will to achieve it. British policy was not led by the shallow pseudo-Machiavellian counsellors who thought it clever to govern by factions; its aim was the healing of communal divisions. Sometimes, as in Ceylon, it had sufficient confidence to pursue this aim vigorously. But at other times it made no headway against formidable obstacles. Even on these latter occasions it would hardly be true to say that it governed by factions. The truth is, rather, that, against its wishes, it was governed by factions. In 1921 Mr. Lloyd George would have wished to lead Ulster into a federated Ireland; but he was governed by Sir James Craig, who willed the partition of Ireland. In 1922 the Colonial Office and the India Office agreed on the principle of a common roll for Kenya; but the British government was governed by the Kenya Europeans, who threatened rebellion before they would accept the common roll. The plan of the constitution of Malta aimed at a complete aloofness of the imperial government from the internal affairs of Malta; but the narrative has clearly shown how one faction in Malta made the imperial government its instrument in the Maltese faction-fight. It will be observed that in each of these three examples the phenomenon of 'loyalty', which has been repeatedly noticed in earlier chapters, played an important part in determining events. In 1914 loyal Ulster wrecked home rule; in 1921 loyal Ulster refused to come under Sinn Féin. In 1922 the Europeans of Kenya prepared to fight against British authority in order that they might play the part of loyal British subjects in the Empire's African destinies. In Malta Lord Strickland and other loyal patriots professed their zeal to protect a great imperial fortress against Papal interference and Fascist machinations. No satire is here intended, nor any insinuation of insincerity. The writer is aware that in each of these three instances the subjective emotion of loyalty was immensely strong. But the present analysis is an objective one and is not concerned with personal feelings. It seeks only to relate the personal emotion which calls itself loyalty to the theme of this section—to problems of communalism and the theory of the multi-national polity. Is loyalty to be interpreted in terms of constitutional propriety? The examples of Canada, Ireland, Kenya, and Malta prove that there is no constant relationship between 'loyalty' and the law. Sometimes the 'loyalists' appeal to the law, at other times they defy it. 'Ulster will fight, and Ulster will be right.' Sometimes the 'disloyalists', like Redmond's nationalists, have constitutional propriety on their side; at other times, like the Sinn Féin nationalists, they are in revolt. Whatever they do they still offend 'loyalty', which has a genius for remaining eternally loyal whether it is appealing to the law or defying it. But if 'loyalty' does not mean constitutional duty, how is it to be explained? Can it be related to the phenomenon of political party? This is a more hopeful road of approach. The element of political exclusiveness is common to all the examples which have been examined. Other examples might be sought in the Natal of a generation back, in the dominion party of present-day South Africa, and even in the nationalist party which emerged in Australia during the war. 'Loyalty' is a political commodity which yields the highest returns when it is 'cornered'. Analysis of all the examples would show a common, if not an invariable relation between loyalist profession and the local interest of a section or party. In Kenya, for example, 'loyalty' was interwoven with the claim of twelve thousand white men to dominate more than twice that number of Indians and two and a half million native Africans. But it is not essential to the present argument to prove the existence of a constant relationship between monopolistic 'loyalty' and material interest. The writer is prepared to admit that the association, where it exists, is frequently an unconscious one; he is even prepared to be persuaded that there may be communities where the association is non-existent, or at least of subordinate importance. The essential point that he wishes to stress is the constantly recurring relationship between 'loyalty' and local faction, and the paralysing effect which this tends to have on an imperial policy which is struggling to stand above faction. Lord Elgin was acutely aware of this when he led Canada through the crisis of her history; the argument of the conservative British section, he said, divided the Canadians into two classes, the loyal and the disloyal; this was a monstrous argument which must be repudiated. The Askwith Commission pointed out that the propaganda of the 'constitutional party' in Malta assumed a similar fallacious division, and it added that such a propaganda tended to produce the very evil which it denounced. Similarly, as regards Palestine, Jewish propaganda sometimes attempts to simplify the issue as one between 'the loyal minority and the dissentient majority'.[1] In every instance the tendency of the propaganda is to exclude the majority of citizens, or at any rate an important section of them, from the possibility of good citizenship. 'Loyalty' struggles to express itself in stringent acts of uniformity. The test may vary according to circumstances; sometimes it may follow lines of class, sometimes lines of religion, sometimes lines of race. It is this last expression of the exclusive spirit which is most relevant to the material of the present section. Behind it, consciously maintained or implicitly held, is the theory of the uni-national state. The theory was never more frankly stated than by the British 'loyalists' in Canada. They saw no hope for the British Empire in North America unless the French were 'overwhelmed' by a British immigration. To them English institutions and English loyalty were inseparable from English blood. It was in this sense that one of their leaders declared: 'The Province must be converted into an English Colony, or it will ultimately be lost to England.'[2]

The British Commonwealth has by its acts repudiated the theory of the uni-national state. It will be argued in the next chapter against a German critic that this repudiation, if hesitant and incomplete, is within its limits genuine, and that it is a condition of the

[1] e.g. *Palestine*, vol. xi, no. 36 (3rd November 1936), or no. 42 (9th December 1936—article on 'Jewish Loyalty'). This cleverly written paper is printed by 'The British Palestine Committee', a body about which the present writer has failed to get precise information. The phrasing of the paper is that of the British liberal imperialist; the content is exclusively Zionist.

[2] See p. 20, above.

Commonwealth's survival. Nevertheless, theory tends to lag behind fact, with the result that the end of policy is not clearly perceived until the compulsion of events compels a realization of it. This vagueness in statement of the end tends to produce irresolution in the adoption of means. Kenya affords an excellent illustration. It was only when the local conflict began to poison the imperial conference and to produce unbearable stresses between the governments of India, South Africa, and the United Kingdom, and between the Colonial Office and the India Office, that the British government issued the white paper of 1923. That document recognized at least four communities which possessed rights on the soil of Kenya. It endeavoured to define in a general way the rights of each, and in particular it insisted that the rights of the 'settled' community of Africans were paramount. But the statement was too sudden, and too general, to bring appeasement. Perhaps there was not sufficient conviction behind it. At all events there were signs in the years which followed that the British government was still liable to be driven by the pressure of factions from the road which it had chosen, and even after ten years crammed with commissions, reports, and statements of policy, there still remained some obscurity in theory and practice. The history of Irish policy between 1914 and 1921, which has been told in the third chapter of this book, illustrates the difficulties and hesitations of the transition from one view of policy to the other. In 1914 one of the historic British parties had thrown in its lot with the 'loyalist' section of Ireland. By the summer of 1921 the coalition government of the United Kingdom was prepared to negotiate with Sinn Féin on the basis of a recognition of Irish nationality. Between 1914 and 1921 British policy made the worst of two worlds. It is small advantage to exchange constant subservience to a single faction for constant oscillation from one side to another.

Everything which has been said in the preceding paragraphs could be illustrated convincingly and at length by a narrative of British policy in Palestine. There is time to indicate just one or two of its more important aspects. First, the mandate implies the philosophy of the multi-national state; for it asserts that the establishment of a Jewish national home in Palestine is subject to a guarantee of the rights and position of the people already settled there. This reservation runs right through the mandate. Moreover, the mandate imposes upon Great Britain the obligation of establishing self-governing institutions in Palestine, and this obligation is in the spirit of Article 22 of the Covenant of the League, upon which the whole mandatory system rests. Despite this, the mandate is a hesitating document, in which two systems of thought jostle each other. If it implies the philosophy of the multi-national state, it does so in the form of reservations and exceptions to the philosophy of the uni-national state. If it envisages Palestine as a *communitas communitatum*, it has a clear perception of one community only. It incorporates and expands in detail Lord Balfour's promise (a promise which was itself qualified) to the Jewish nation; but it does not mention any other nation. On the one side is a very definite national home; on the other side are a number of unspecified communities. The experience of Canada and South Africa is written into the mandate, but not in the form of a firmly grasped theory determining the proportions and balance of the document. Rather it is introduced, in this clause and that, to correct the balance of a document which starts by assuming the continental theory of the national state. The mandate rejects this theory, not by a positive counter-statement, but by whittling it away.

From the beginning of British rule in Palestine until the present day, policy has been hampered by a lack of positive precision in defining its principle and end. The imprecision was not merely due to the failure of British statesmen to make the mental effort necessary for embodying British experience in a coherent theory. There was also a particular cause. Behind the hesitations of the Palestine policy were the unco-ordinated improvisations of war-time diplomacy. Again there is a Canadian parallel. The engagements undertaken by the British government between 1760 and 1763 encouraged the settled population of Quebec and the immigrant British community to make irreconcilable claims upon it. In the same way, the Jews and Arabs both alleged that Palestine had been promised to them. Jewish propaganda asserted that Great Britain had promised to the Jews 'rights and privileges in Palestine which shall enable Jews to make it as Jewish as England is English'.[1] Responsible officers of the Zionist organization asserted that there could be only one national home in Palestine, and that a Jewish one; that there could be no equality between Arabs and Jews, but that there must be a Jewish predominance over the Arabs.[2] The Arabs, on their part, denounced the Balfour Declaration as a breach of faith, and refused to admit that the Jews had any national right at all in Palestine. This conflict of claims was the underlying cause of the riots of 1921, and it was not

[1] *Report of the Commission of Inquiry into Disturbances in May 1921* (Haycroft Commission), Cmd. 1540 of 1921, p. 56 (quoting the *Jewish Chronicle*, 20th May 1921.)

[2] Ibid., p. 56, referring to the evidence of Dr. Eder, acting-chairman of the Zionist Commission.

resolved by the publication of the Palestine order in council or by the issue of the mandate in 1922. The Arabs flatly rejected the order in council and the mandate because these documents recognized the Jewish national home. The Jews were less definite in stating their aims. The mandate secured them a national home. The wiser of them were content for the time to leave it at that. Others still insisted that a national home meant a national majority and a national state. In a memorandum of 3rd June 1922[1] Mr. Winston Churchill attempted to clear up the ambiguities, and to state once and for all the meaning of British obligations and the end of British policy. He denied that there was any ground for the 'apprehensions which are entertained both by sections of the Arab and by sections of the Jewish population'. He assured the Arabs that a Jewish national home did not imply the subordination of the Arabic population, language, or culture. He explicitly repudiated the conception of a Jewish state. The Balfour Declaration, he said, did not mean 'that Palestine as a whole should be converted into a Jewish National Home, but that such a home should be founded *in* Palestine'. And he was able to point to a recent resolution of the Zionist Congress to show that Jewry in its official pronouncements was willing to accept the British conception of Palestine as a home 'common' to two peoples, Jews and Arabs. He demanded that the Arabs should accept the same conception. They must recognize the principle of the Balfour Declaration as it was now interpreted. The British government had no intention of departing from this principle. The Jews were in Palestine as of right. The 80,000 Jews who were living there already had all the marks of a 'national' community. It was necessary, if the British government were to fulfil its obligations, that this community should be able to add to its numbers by immigration. The immigration, however, could not be so great in volume as to exceed whatever might be the economic capacity of the country at any time to absorb new arrivals.

The document went on to promise that a committee of the proposed legislative council, to be chosen entirely from the elected members, would have the right to confer with the administration upon matters relating to the regulation of immigration. It denied the Arab assertion that His Majesty's government, during the war, had given an undertaking that an independent Arab government should be estab-

[1] *Correspondence with the Palestine Arab Delegation and the Zionist Organisation*, Cmd. 1700 of 1922, pp. 17–21. This statement anticipated the grant of the mandate to Great Britain, but was nevertheless intended to give the government's interpretation of the mandate.

lished in Palestine. It nevertheless stated the intention of the government to 'foster the establishment of a full measure of self-government in Palestine', and explained that the proposed legislative council would be the next step towards this end. In this, as in every other particular, Mr. Winston Churchill's memorandum clarified the principle underlying British responsibility in Palestine. It rejected the idea, which had been widely held among the Jews, of a Jewish national state. It rejected the idea, which was held almost universally among the Arabs, of an Arab national state. In opposition to both these claims, it gave definite form to the British conception of a state which would embrace two collaborating nations. It pulled together for the first time the central argument of British policy.

But the argument did not reach the hearts of those to whom it was addressed. The Arabs rejected it flatly and immediately. They would have national independence or nothing. As has been shown already, they made the disastrous tactical error (from the point of view of their own real interests) of refusing the legislative council, which offered to them some of the influence due to their numbers and to the fact that their society and culture had been rooted in Palestine for more than a thousand unbroken years. The Jews, on the other hand, showed themselves wiser and more reasonable. The Zionist Organization accepted Mr. Churchill's statement in full when it was issued. But, as the alarms of 1921 subsided, the Jews began to forget their undertaking. They emphasized the rights which it assured to them and slurred over the rights which it ascribed to the Arabs. Some of them openly revived the programme of a Jewish national state, not necessarily an independent state with the right to make peace and war, but a community which would take its stamp from a Jewish majority, 'so that under a democratic rule the Jewish point of view should always prevail'.[1] This amounted to a direct repudiation of the principles accepted in 1922. The majority of responsible Jewish leaders did not countenance this direct repudiation. Dr. Weizmann spoke a different language from that of Mr. Jabotinsky. But the Shaw Commission reported in 1930 a widespread tendency among leaders of the Jewish community to depart from the engagement of 1922 in important particulars. In the first place the commission found 'incontestable evidence' that the Jewish authorities repudiated the doctrine that immigration should not exceed the economic capacity of Palestine, when this doctrine worked against their immigration plans. In the second place, it reported that leaders of important sections of Jewish

[1] *Report of the Commission on the Palestine Disturbances of August 1929*, Cmd. 3530 of 1930, p. 109 (quoting Mr. Jabotinsky).

opinion were now strongly opposed to the development of self-government in Palestine, though this was 'a cardinal element in the programme of policy laid down in 1922'. The report referred to other illustrations which might have been given, and contented itself with citing the claim put forward by the Zionist Organization that the Jewish Agency—contrary to the statement of 1922—should have a share in the administration of the country.[1]

The criticisms of the Shaw Commission were not one-sided. The Jews, said the Commission, had even more reason than the Arabs for a feeling of uncertainty. Their immigration programme had been checked by economic factors for three years; the land which they needed for settlement was acquired only at big cost and the cost was rising. 'Above all, their constructive work once more, after an interval of eight years, has encountered a serious reverse through the murder of peaceful citizens and the destruction of property.' The root cause of the trouble in Palestine was the failure both of Arabs and Jews to appreciate the dual nature of the policy which the Palestine government had to administer.

> 'On both sides the political leaders are pursuing different aims with single-minded vigour. Their activities are directed to one aspect of the question only and obstacles which bar the way to the fulfilment of their aims either are totally ignored or are brushed aside as being of no account. The idea of compromise scarcely exists. In the atmosphere which thus prevails all sight is lost of the difficulties of the Administration and every important decision of the Government is hailed by one side or the other as a failure to carry out the principles of the Mandate. The Government is thus put—in the words of one witness—"in the position of being a target for political criticism when it ought not to be a target for more than administrative criticism".'[2]

In short, both Jews and Arabs were obsessed by the *sacro egoismo* of nationalism; neither would acknowledge the principle by which the British explained and justified their presence in Palestine. The British were partly responsible for this because they had failed to state the principle with sufficient clarity and emphasis. The dual nature of their obligation had indeed been asserted even in the Balfour Declaration, but it had been asserted in such a form and with such an emphasis that the Jews had commonly interpreted that document as a promise to them alone. It had been asserted again in the mandate, but here also the engagements taken to the Jewish community had a more positive ring than those taken to the other

[1] *Report of the Commission on the Palestine Disturbances of August 1929*, p. 14, cf. pp. 106–11.

[2] Ibid., p. 140.

communities. It had been clarified and emphasized by Mr. Churchill's statement of 1922, which the Commission regarded as 'by far the most valuable contribution that has yet been made to the elucidation of the Palestine problem'. But even this statement was too negative. 'It was designed', the Commission said, 'as a corrective to the aspirations entertained among certain sections of Jewry rather than as a definition of the rights of the non-Jewish sections of the community in Palestine.' The Shaw Commission thought it urgent that His Majesty's government should now at last give this definition in positive and unequivocable terms. It should make clear beyond all doubt the meaning which it attached to the passages in the mandate which provided for the safeguarding of the rights of the non-Jewish communities. Yet clarity by itself was not enough. Moral courage and consistency in following a policy were no less indispensable than clarity in defining it.

> 'However clear and explicit the statement of policy may be, uncertainty will remain unless some steps are taken to convince all sections of the people of Palestine that it is the intention of His Majesty's Government to give full effect to that policy with all the resources at their command.'[1]

The Shaw Report took its place at the head of a new and long procession of white papers and blue books, of statements of policy, of letters explaining the statements of policy, of investigating commissions appointed to work out in detail the principles contained in the statements of policy and the letters.[2] The original purpose of all this activity was to establish beyond possibility of challenge the basis of British policy in Palestine—the principle of the shared territorial loyalty, the multi-national state, the *communitas communitatum*, or whatever name is given to the ideal. But the conviction and energy behind this ideal proved itself in practice to be feeble in comparison with the energy, the desperation, which drove forward the conflicting national egoisms of Arabs and Jews. The much-heralded once-and-for-all clear pronouncement on British policy was drowned in the

[1] Ibid., pp. 112, 139, 142, and chapter xi, passim.

[2] This sentence is perhaps guilty of a little satirical exaggeration. The chief documents are: *Statement with regard to British Policy*, May 1930, Cmd. 3582; *Report on Immigration, Land Settlement, and Development*, by Sir John Hope Simpson, 1930, Cmd. 3686; *Statement of Policy by His Majesty's Government in the United Kingdom*, October 1930, Cmd. 3692; Mr. Ramsay MacDonald's letter to Dr. Weizmann, 13th February 1931 (*The Times*, 14th February 1931); and thereafter a series of reports on economic affairs—the French Reports, the Strickland Report, &c. *Great Britain and Palestine 1915–1936*, issued by the Information Department of the Royal Institute of International Affairs, may be consulted for an objective summary of these documents.

shouting of the contending propagandas. For reasons which have been given above, it was the Jewish propaganda which dinned loudest in English ears, until in 1936 the Arabs began to burn and kill.

What, then, emerged from all the reporting and declaring and investigating of these years? A new period, the most dramatic and transforming period, in the history of the Jewish national home. In 1933 an unprecedented immigration began to flow into Palestine. It was accompanied by an unprecedented material progress and financial prosperity. This concurrence led naturally to a shift in the emphasis of the Jewish claim. In spirit there was no change in the tendencies which the Shaw Commission had pointed out. The conception of a dual mandate was pushed still farther into the background. For example, Jewry was now ready for an open and uncompromising opposition to the plan of a legislative council, which the mandatory power was still disposed to pursue. But Jewry also quarried its most effective ammunition out of Mr. Churchill's statement of 1922. The sentence about the economic capacity of the country to absorb immigrants, which the Shaw Commission had reproved it for ignoring, now became its chief weapon. In the letter to Dr. Weizmann, by which Mr. Ramsay MacDonald had appeased the storm of protest which followed the publication of Lord Passfield's white paper in 1930, this sentence had grown into a couple of paragraphs.[1] In official Jewish propaganda it kept on growing until it became the governing instrument of the whole mandate. Article 6 of the mandate directed Great Britain to facilitate immigration 'while ensuring that the rights and position of other sections of the population are not prejudiced'. The Jews were far from repudiating this article. On the contrary, they maintained persistently that the rights and position of other sections of the population were in no respect prejudiced. But what they actually demanded of the mandatory power was that it should facilitate immigration in accordance with the economic capacity of the country to absorb it. To this they added a rider that the economic capacity of the country was capable of absorbing the bulk of the persecuted millions of Jews in Germany, Poland, Rumania, Austria, Hungary, and the smaller countries of Lithuania and Latvia. The rider was usually implicit, but sometimes it was explicit.

The number of Jewish immigrants arriving (excluding the illegal immigrants) was, in 1933, 30,327; in 1934, 42,359; in 1935, 61,854. Even the first of these figures was equal to the number which the Shaw Commission had discussed as the figure demanded by extremists.

[1] *The Times*, 14th February 1931, paras. 13 and 14 of letter.

The Commission had estimated that a Jewish immigration of 25,000 per annum, assuming an equal natural increase among all communities at the rate of 10 per thousand, would give the Jews numerical equality with the Arabs by the year 1948.[1] The immigration figures of 1933–5 therefore made it certain that the Jews, despite their present numerical inferiority, could look forward to becoming a majority in the very near future. This fact dominated the politics of Palestine; everything else became in comparison of trifling importance.

'The economic absorptive capacity of the country' was a partially irrelevant and thoroughly misleading phrase. The Commissioner of Migration made this clear when he laid stress in his 1935 report on the unique character of Jewish immigration. It was not merely an economic venture. In so far as it was economic, it was not entirely, perhaps not primarily, governed by the absorptive capacity of Palestine. It was governed primarily by the expulsive force of other countries and by the non-economic attraction of Palestine. It was the emigration of tortured creatures from Germany and Poland and Rumania. It was a return of the People to the land of Abraham, Isaac, and Jacob. It was a primitive flight from the oppressor. It was the redemption of Israel.[2]

[1] Cmd. 3530, p. 110, and Graph 1 appended to the report.

[2] How did it come about that a phrase originally intended to reassure the Arabs became in the end the chief weapon of the Jews? According to a memorandum kindly furnished to the present writer by the Economic Research Institute, established in February 1936 to conduct practical research for the Jewish Agency, the following points are essential to a proper understanding of the economic capacity of absorption:

(1) Its relative nature. It varies between different countries and different periods. For example, it no longer depends upon basic physical conditions, for agriculture has dwindled in importance and physical conditions can themselves be changed. Again, only history can explain the contrasts in population density between U.S.A. and Europe, Australia and Algeria, Sicily and Palestine, &c. In short, it is not subject to rigid arithmetical measurement.

(2) Five factors chiefly determine absorptive capacity under modern conditions:
- (a) The revolution in agriculture, which has reduced the area of land necessary to support a given population.
- (b) The revolution in industry, which has removed the old factors bringing about localization in favoured districts.
- (c) The shift of emphasis to purchasing power—which immigration increases.
- (d) The provision of capital—which the Jews bring to Palestine under uniquely favourable conditions.
- (e) State action—which in Palestine has been inadequate.

The memorandum argues that between 1920 and 1935 production in Palestine has increased by 281 per cent., while population has increased by 77·5 per cent., and advances other evidence in proof of expanding absorptive capacity.

A very different economic analysis is offered in the *Round Table*, December 1936. The present writer need not involve himself in the economic discussion. It is sufficient to stress the subjective factors. Briefly, the contention of the Economic Research Institute is that the absorptive capacity of Palestine can within very wide limits be determined by the will of the Jews. This shows the manner in which the phrase,

The Jews who followed Moses through the wilderness murmured, quarrelled, and lifted up their conflicting voices; yet a single purpose led them. What purpose guides the Jews who once again are journeying to *Eretz Israel*? A Gentile dare not interpret what is deepest in the heart of Jewry. An historian must judge only by the voices, although they are still conflicting. But there is no mistaking the unanimity and the passion with which this persecuted people cries to be given a home of its own. What does this cry mean for the Arabs, who have had their home in Palestine for more than a thousand years? And what does it signify for the mandatory power, which has pledged itself to do justice between both peoples? What do the Arabs demand of the mandatory power? What do the Jews demand?

The Arabs demand that the immigration be stopped. The Jews demand that it be continued at its present volume, and even increased.

There are exceptions on both sides. It would be wrong to judge by the extremists, who affirm: 'Either the Jews will drive the Arabs into the desert, or the Arabs will drive the Jews into the sea.'[1] There are Jews who speak of Palestine as the common fatherland of Jews and Arabs.[2] There are even a few Jews who believe in this ideal and work for it. The Arabs, unlike the Jews, speak with one voice; and that voice denies that the Jews have rights as a nation in Palestine. Perhaps there are Arabs who would acknowledge the Jewish right, if they were convinced that it did not menace Arab right. But they will not be convinced while the pace of the Jewish influx and its spirit remain what they are. Only a drastic slackening of the pace, a return to the pre-1933 rate, could convince them.

On this issue the Jews will accept no compromise. The voices here

which originally was used by Mr. Churchill to reassure the Arabs in their fears of a Jewish majority and perhaps a Jewish state, has subsequently become the main argument to justify the first, and perhaps to bring about the second. It would be interesting to compare the Jewish interpretation of absorptive capacity with that generally held in the Dominions and the Dominions Office, both in 1922 and 1936. The phrase means something entirely different as used by Zionists and, say, the Development and Migration Commission which was active in Australia in the pre-depression years. The contrast suggests strongly that psychological facts are prior to economic ones in many immigration problems.

[1] The writer is quoting a judgement expressed to him almost in identical words by an Arab and by a Jew. There is a similar tendency, if not an identical meaning, in the assertion: 'Palestine should cease being an Arab country.' *Survey of the Revisionist Programme* (London, 1935), p. 9.

[2] Notably the small body who follow Dr. J. L. Magnes, of the Hebrew University, in the *Covenant of Peace* (Brith Shalom). Dr. Weizmann, who can speak for the Zionist organization, appeals to the ideal of a common fatherland, but at the same time shows no readiness to compromise on the question of immigration, which is the chief cause of conflict between the two communities.

are almost unanimous; it will be sufficient to listen to one which speaks from the high places of industrial life in Great Britain. To Lord Melchett, the policy which permitted a Jewish immigration of over 60,000 in one year is a policy of 'restriction and repression'. He envisages an immigration rising from 100,000 a year to 200,000 a year. He considers that within fifteen years immigration on this scale will have completed its task—the complete evacuation to Palestine of every German Jew, and a large evacuation from Poland, Rumania, Austria, and some other countries. He mentions the transfer of 3,000,000 Jews as a 'practicable proposition' according to his plan.[1] But how does this plan accord with the pledges of Great Britain to the 'existing population'? Lord Melchett enumerates the benefits which the Jews have conferred upon the Arabs, and asserts that although the Arab protests may give the impression of national resistance, they are the work merely of 'a handful of Arab agitators'. He believes that a plan of land-development in Palestine and Trans-Jordan will satisfy the demands of the Arabs, and he promises that the Jewish majority will deal justly with the Arab minority—although this minority is an inferior people.[2] He also has a great deal to offer to the British Empire. He proposes that Jewish soldiers should take over from British soldiers the duty of keeping order in Palestine.[3] He offers Haifa as an imperial naval base and Palestine itself as an imperial air base. But, seeing that the true defence of any region is its population, he offers a garrison of 'several million loyal Jews' to defend the Suez Canal and uphold British imperial power in the Mediterranean and the Near East.[4] This powerful Jewish community in Palestine and Trans-Jordan will naturally enter the British Empire. The Jews demand even now to enter the imperial preference system.[5] . . . What of the mandate? By the time Lord Melchett has finished his imperial argument, very little is left of the mandate. The mandate will have served its purpose—although that purpose is contained neither in its own text nor in Article 22 of the Covenant

[1] Lord Melchett, *Thy Neighbour* (Muller, 1936), pp. 209, 215–17.

[2] At one place (p. 250) Lord Melchett remembers the time 'when the torch of culture and knowledge was kept alight by the harmonious co-operation of Jew and Arab'; but in general he continually stresses Arab inferiority. 'The contributions of the two people to mankind are poles apart' (p. 261). The Arabs object to 'civilised immigration of any kind' (p. 252). They represent the 'revolt of the desert against civilisation'. In relation to the Jews they are as the Red Indians to the English in America, or the natives to the Vortrekkers (p. 224).

[3] Melchett, op. cit., p. 256.

[4] Ibid., pp. 198–202; cf. p. 221: 'If the Empire could rally an army of 500,000 Europeans at this point . . . what a change in the balance of power.'

[5] Ibid., pp. 211–12.

from which it derives. It will have added a Jewish Dominion to the Empire.

Lord Melchett speaks of 'several million loyal Jews'. So the phenomenon of 'loyalty' has appeared again. By carrying a little farther the analysis of this phenomenon it will be possible to pull together the argument of the chapter and relate it to the central theme of this volume. Lord Melchett invites the British Empire to follow the pseudo-Machiavellian precept of governing by factions. He envisages the Jewish community as a majority in Palestine and Trans-Jordan, but as a minority in the larger Arab world. 'Surrounded by a large population of desert Arabs and containing a considerable Arab population of its own',[1] it will be bound by necessity, no less than by gratitude, to uphold British imperial interests in the Arab world. It will, in short, be an Ulster in the Near East; it will be an imperial mission like that of the European settlers in Kenya; it will be like 'that body of English loyalty' planted after the American revolution in Canada.

Placing this conception of a loyal Jewish Palestine beside these other examples, there appears both a similarity and a contrast. Looked at objectively as a pseudo-Machiavellian proposition, there is in the Jewish claim, as in all the others, the 'garrison' assumption. But behind the intellectual proposition there is an altogether different emotional urge. 'The body of English loyalty' planted in Canada was, in its emotions, exactly what it professed itself to be. The title which was given to this community, that of the United Empire Loyalists, was as precise an epitome of actual history as any title can hope to be. Ontario was in fact actually founded by subjects of the King who left their homes in rebellious America rather than surrender the loyalty into which they had been born. Objective criticism of the colonial interests and of the imperial theory which became associated with the emotion of loyalty does not imply a denial of the real existence of this emotion, and its vehemence. No doubt the same emotion exists with equal vehemence among many Zionists of English citizenship. But at the census of 1931 English Jews comprised only 0·5 of the population of Palestine, and it is probable that this percentage has since then been considerably reduced. One does not have to countenance the cruelty and absurdity of political-racialist theories in order to recognize the necessary subjective difference between the 'loyalty' of the Ulster Scot or the United Empire Loyalist, and that of the Polish or Rumanian Zionist. The emotion of the Ulstermen for the symbolism of the British Crown may be

[1] Melchett, op. cit., p. 201.

primitive; it may be exploited by passions and by interests; but it is real. It is impossible that Jews of Polish or Rumanian origin, possibly still retaining their foreign citizenship,[1] can possess the same emotion. It would be positively indecent if 'God Save The King' were sung in Tel Aviv as it is sung in Toronto or Belfast.

Yet this is a matter of subordinate importance. Let it be granted that a real devotion to the British Crown, comparable with that of Toronto or Belfast, might some day grow up in Tel Aviv. The present argument is not primarily concerned with the personal feeling of loyalty. It is concerned chiefly with the communities which allege their particular and exclusive loyalty to the Empire as a barrier to a nearer loyalty—loyalty to their own territorial commonwealth, which embraces and reconciles all its particular communities. In so far as the British Commonwealth has succeeded, it has succeeded by proving that these loyalties, so far from being irreconcilable, are complementary. In so far as it has failed, its failure arises from the persistence of the communal oppositions. The persistent unsatisfactory relationship between Great Britain and the Irish Free State is caused by the survival of the historic religious-national communalism, which expressed itself at last in a partition of Ulster and a partition of Ireland. The loyalty of South Africa to the British Commonwealth, on the other hand, is grounded on the loyalty of the English and Afrikaner communities in South Africa to their Union. The foundation of the Dominion of Canada could not have been achieved unless the British community in Canada had outgrown its original conception of loyalty. Even Lord Durham had assumed that loyalty was the possession and privilege of the British alone. How, then, did the change come about? How was Canadian communalism, which superimposed an unreal division between the loyal and the disloyal upon the real division of race, religion, and language, transcended? What was the process of re-education? In the first chapter of this book and in the present one a good deal has been made of the creative imagination of Lord Elgin. It must now be added that Lord Elgin grasped a chance which others made for him. The appeasement of British and French could not have been achieved by even the most gifted proconsul dispatched to Canada from Great Britain. He could foster that appeasement, he could guide it through difficult places, but he could not of himself create its spirit. That work was done by the Canadians themselves. It was the union between the British radicals of Canada and the French nationalists which gave Lord Elgin his opportunity.

[1] On the retention of their original citizenship by Jews in Palestine, see p. 436, above.

He built with the materials given to him by Baldwin and Lafontaine. Even this statement ascribes too much to Lord Elgin; for Baldwin and Lafontaine and their followers did as much of the building as he. The crucial point in the history of Canada came when a section of 'loyalists' defied the established orthodoxy of 'loyalty'. In men like Baldwin the logic of the British tradition broke away from the accepted shibboleths of British imperialism and confidently set itself to the tasks of a new country. On this ground it was able to establish contact with the French. The same thing happened in South Africa, and might have happened even without the South African war. The same thing has begun to happen in Ireland—although its unfolding has been arrested, and its frustration is symbolized by the partition. In South Africa and in Canada the crucial time came when the 'garrison' widened its vision. Will that time ever come in Ireland? Will it ever come in Palestine?

This is the theory of the British Commonwealth which has been revealed in the narrative of preceding chapters. It is only honest to say flatly that this theory is almost entirely irrelevant to the realities dealt with in the present section. There is something pathetically naïve in the reiterated complaint of the Shaw Commission that neither Arabs nor Jews would understand 'the dual nature of the policy which the Palestine Government have to administer'. 'The idea of compromise', lamented the Commission, 'hardly exists.' How could it exist? One side rejects the mandate altogether. The other side ignores those articles in it which conflict with its zeal for the redemption of Israel. Is there any prospect of a Baldwin–Lafontaine partnership between nationalist Arabs and radical Zionists? The will to partnership does not exist. Arabs and Jews have in their separate turns rejected the first instalments of elective institutions from which might grow the possible instruments of a partnership, if not the partnership itself. A hundred Lord Elgins could not under present circumstances achieve a Canadian reconciliation in Palestine, because they could not find there the materials on which to work. And what has the mandatory power done to create the material and mental conditions from which might grow a will to partnership? The kind of positive work which would be appropriate to the conditions of Palestine is suggested in the following chapter, in a discussion of the problem of nationalities in the U.S.S.R. It would include not a sentimental bias towards the weaker community, but a determined and unceasing war against inequality. Nothing so positive has been attempted in Palestine. At the time when these sentences are being written, another commission of inquiry—a Royal Commission this time—is engaged upon the old task of trying to find a policy in accord with the professed British principles. May its search be fruitful! But, in the period which this volume covers, British principles have been almost completely irrelevant to the realities of Palestine. Both Arabs and Jews regard the issue as one of sheer survival. They may be wrong. But all the suffering and all the hope of Jewry concentrates upon Palestine. Palestine must see again the redemption of Israel. It may see again the tragedy of Israel. On the Arab side as well as on the Jewish side the struggle has tragic vehemence. The native population of Palestine, like the Jewish population, believes itself to be struggling for its home. Neither community believes in its heart that it will be safe in its home unless it is master in it.

The British conception of a home where neither Arab nor Jew shall be master has been irrelevant because it has aroused no effective response among Arabs or Jews. Nor has the British conception been stated with sufficient precision or urged with sufficient conviction or pursued with sufficient realism of means to moderate the desperate passion which drives the two warring communities. British policy has itself been driven. In the summer of 1936, 23,000 British soldiers were administering the medicine of the constitution—administering it, no doubt, as gently as they could—to the struggling Arab majority of Palestine.

CHAPTER VIII

REVIEW

VIEWED from the angle of physical and human geography, the British Empire looks like an untidy aggregation of continental and island territories, of climates and races and religions, thrown together by a haphazard history. The preceding chapters have not sought to conceal this untidiness. Yet the writer would be disappointed if his narrative has proceeded in a series of jerks and jumps. The histories of New Zealand, Kenya, and Ceylon are bound together in a unity, even if that unity is a loose one. In what does the unity consist? There is the fact that in all these countries public acts are in the name of the Crown. This fact symbolizes a unity of constitutional law and convention and technique. But the present volume is not entirely, or even primarily, a constitutional history. And if it is something more than an aggregation of special studies, it is so because the studies are linked in the unity of an historical idea.

The writer has not consciously imposed this idea upon his diverse material with the purpose of drawing it together. He has been led by the idea into the material. He has been led already much farther than he intended; yet he is conscious that he has still very much farther to go. He began his inquiry by reading the published records of the imperial conference. In these records he found the idea of the Commonwealth of Nations taking shape as a fact before it was coined as a phrase. The idea was not hidden away in the back of men's minds; it did not reveal itself merely by implication and suggestion; it was in the foreground, explicit, confident, and challenging. It was asserted emphatically as an interpretation of the past and as a prophecy of the future. 'What are we all?' the statesmen of the British Empire asked each other; and they answered—'We are sister states.' 'We are a league of free nations.' 'We are an imperial Commonwealth of united nations.'[1] In an outburst of self-congratulation which knew no stint the statesmen proclaimed the success of their 'unique experiment in human co-operation'.

It was necessary to investigate so large a claim. Investigation showed that it had some validity as an interpretation of experience in part of the British Empire between the days of Edmund Burke and General Botha. In recording this chapter of history, the writer found that he was able to share the enthusiasm of the men who had

[1] See above, p. 1.

shaped it—of Durham and Howe, of Elgin and Botha, of Laurier and Deakin. There was a satisfying intellectual subtlety and finish in their achievement, for its possibility had been denied in advance by the logic of the schools—a logic which they did not trouble to refute, but which with the most impressive competence they eluded. By insisting on 'the plain common sense of the matter' they deflated the swollen political pretensions of the doctrine of sovereignty, and reduced it to its own proper dimensions as a juristic hypothesis. They proved that the terms empire and liberty were complementary terms, not the opposites of a dilemma. But did they prove this for all time? Was not their success perhaps conditioned by the unusually favourable circumstances of their own passing epoch? The liberty which they worshipped grew into equality. Might not equality swallow up unity? The investigator of this unfinished history found himself recording a growing sobriety of mood. The sanguine orators of 1919 had announced that their Commonwealth possessed the secret of international association in peace and freedom. They had offered their Commonwealth as a model to the world. But the statesmen of 1936 knew that the world had not the least intention of copying the model. They knew that the nations of the Commonwealth were not in the mood to run great risks in order to make their conception the rule of international society. They did not know in certainty what risks the nations of the Commonwealth would be ready to run if their way of life were challenged by danger from without. In short, the experience accumulated between 1919 and 1936 exposed the optimistic illusions which had been prevalent at the end of the war. It would be too much to say that the facts of 1936 were a refutation of the Commonwealth theory of the imperial partnership. But they did refute the universalization of this theory, the translation of it into a model of world government. Or, at the very least, they proved that this universalization was abstract and premature.

The statesmen of the imperial conference made another claim. Relying upon the experience of South Africa and Canada, they asserted that the Commonwealth exemplified the spirit and the technique by which nations, even when they existed together in the same territory, could pursue a common end and serve a common loyalty. This was a claim of great significance to a civilization whose very life was threatened by nationalistic hatreds. But might it not be objected that the tests which the Commonwealth seemed to have passed in Canada and South Africa were very easy ones? In both countries the nations were emigrant communities, detached from the parent stock and free from the explosive compression of crowded Europe. The writer felt that he was bound to investigate a more challenging history. Let the Commonwealth pass the same test in Ireland, before it proceeded to lecture Germans and Poles and Czechs.

Let it pass the same test in India also. The orators of the imperial conference congratulated themselves on their service to humanity in bridging the gulf between Europe and Asia. In welcoming the appearance of Indians in their fellowship, they repudiated emphatically the antithesis between a Commonwealth of equal European nations and an Empire of dependent Asiatic nations. Here was another claim to investigate. Oratory was brought down to earth by a study of the emigrant Indian communities within the British Empire. This study revealed the intense force of Indian nationalism and some of the obstacles which would have to be surmounted before Indians could look forward with pride to equal co-operation with the Commonwealth of Nations.

Both in the chapter dealing with Indian nationalism and in the chapter entitled 'The Medicine of the Body Politic' the writer was conscious of the ambiguities which have gathered round the title, 'British Commonwealth of Nations'. The hair-splitting legalistic commentaries on the title have no importance; but alternative general uses of it sometimes imply opposing political attitudes of very great importance. A sharp distinction between Empire and Commonwealth may symbolize the repudiation of human equality as an ideal. An easy identification of Empire and Commonwealth may symbolize the complacency which refuses to recognize the gap between ideal and fact. In handling the ideas which lie beneath the terminology the writer has attempted to follow, not his own preferences, but the historical evidence.

In precept and to some extent even in practice British policy repudiated the absolute antithesis between the Commonwealth and the Empire. It professed the ideal of 'the government of men by themselves'—not 'the government of British people by British people', or 'the government of Europeans by Europeans', or 'the government of men by Englishmen'. Negatively, it made its position quite plain when it refused responsible government to the British community in Kenya.[1] Positively, it made its position quite plain when it granted responsible government to the people of Malta. But

[1] The grounds of this refusal were most clearly stated in the Hilton Young Report, which said that responsible government could not come until the whole people of Kenya—and especially the native community—were fit to share it. See above, p. 232.

that grant has been rescinded. Chapter VII served the double purpose of illustrating the theoretical universality of the Commonwealth programme, and the actual limitations within which it has had to work. The example of constitutional experiment in Ceylon showed an unusual degree of resourcefulness in grappling with these limitations. The example of constitutional collapse in Newfoundland showed that the difficulties might be too much even for a long-established British community. The example of Malta illustrated the international no less than the domestic complexities amidst which the British conception must attempt to work itself out. The example of Palestine showed the failure of this conception to make any impression upon communities which were passionately absorbed in a struggle for domination or survival. The same example showed also a lack of clarity in the statement of the conception, and a corresponding lack of resolution in willing the necessary means to the end which it implied. This volume has recorded other examples of confusion in political thought and action. It has recorded the contradictory promises made to the Transvaal Indians and the Transvaal Europeans. It has revealed the unresolved contradiction between two orthodoxies of the imperial conference—the orthodoxy of 'the common concern' and the orthodoxy of *ad hoc* parliamentary decision in issues of peace and war. It has pointed out the contradiction between the grant of responsible government to the Europeans of Southern Rhodesia and the almost contemporaneous refusal of responsible government to the Europeans of Kenya. It has emphasized the ambiguities and obscurities of the doctrine of 'paramountcy' which was proclaimed in Kenya. A peroration is not a philosophy, still less a policy; and some of the ideals professed at the imperial conference and in government white papers rang loudly and unconvincingly, like perorations. They had not the firm ring of hard thought or the sharp ring of decided action. The same was true of some academic justifications of the Commonwealth. Was it very helpful to describe the Britannic society as a procession of communities marching purposefully to self-government, when for a hundred years Malta's march had been like Sisyphus purposefully pushing his stone up the hill?

The second volume of this book will break economic ground, first in the Dominions, then in India, then in the Colonies. This investigation may help to reveal more clearly the matter within which the form of the Commonwealth is trying to work itself out. The present volume, however, is not merely formal. Economic fact is not the only material fact. Hard oppositions between ideal and fact have already been revealed. It is time to sum up on this issue. The author believes that he is bound in honesty to make the most explicit avowal of the tendency of his exposition, so far as it has gone. It affirms the reality of the Commonwealth ideal. It affirms that this ideal is not merely British or merely European, but human. At the same time it recognizes a conflict between the ideal and the actual. It recognizes and emphasizes the power of circumstances. The *idea* of the Commonwealth of Nations is confronted both by the nationalism which admits no obligation, and by the *actual* Commonwealth, the mere 'project of a Commonwealth', masquerading as the *societas perfecta*. Between these two extremes lie historical reality, and—this may sound old-fashioned—the possibility of progress.

A friendly German critic, to whom the writer submitted some of his chapters, has challenged the point of view which is implied in them and which has been avowed above. A challenge from the other side is contained in Stalin's book on nationality. It may help the reader to be on his guard against the writer's bias if these challenges are set out here.

The German critic discovers in all the chapters submitted to him an implication which shapes the book and gives it its inner unity; the Commonwealth is in the stage of evolution 'from force to persuasion'. He says that the chapters criticize any premature optimism about rapid advance along the path of this evolution; they show its real difficulties, but they accept it as the real theme of imperial history. The shortcomings of the Empire lie where there is still force and not yet persuasion. The book calls upon the Empire to replace the last remnants of force by persuasion. But what if somebody does not want to be persuaded? What if he does not want to come into even 'a free association'? It is assumed in these chapters that such an individual—for example, a member of the Irish Republican Army—is extremely unreasonable. What is to be done with such a person? It is assumed that he must be subjected to force until he will consent to be persuaded. Whether the fact is recognized explicitly in these chapters or not, force is still present in the Commonwealth. It is accepted as a necessary transitional stage to the paradise of persuasion—just as the dictatorship of the proletariat is a transitional stage to the classless society. Force is not denied, but justified. The new persuasion is based on the old force and justifies it as a mission. But what if people do not accept that justification as valid? What if they wish to stay outside both the force and the persuasion and the entire mission? 'Who gave you', the German asks, 'a right to missionize?'

He follows up this challenge with a second one. The 'mission', he says, is not European, or human, but English. He is willing to accept the force to persuasion theme so far as it affects the 'emigrant Englishman' first discussed in Chapter I; for the force to which the emigrant Englishman bowed was a regulative, not a conquering force; it was, moreover, the force of his own people. For him there was no 'original sin' of force to be 'redeemed' by persuasion as an afterthought. But what of the French Canadians or the Afrikaners? These are non-English and originally non-voluntary members of the Commonwealth. Yet in greater or less degree they have become voluntary members. They have been persuaded. They have become partners in the Commonwealth. Your book, the German complains, appeals to this partnership as proof that the Commonwealth is not merely the expansion of England but a European or human order acceptable to all, derived from general ethical principles. Your book expresses the hope that India and Ireland will also stay in or come into this order, without feeling themselves missionized by alien oppressors, but just out of conversion to a human principle. For does not the Commonwealth recognize national independence? . . . The German doubts whether it does so fully. He distinguishes between a granted or secondary independence and an original or full independence. A study of the South African position might convince him that the distinction was a quibbling one. But it would not affect his main argument. He goes on to submit a more fundamental objection to the theory implied in the volume. Even if it should be admitted that national independence exists in full, the states which possess that independence can co-operate, so he argues, only because they are anglicized in very large degree. The principles of political organization are English, down to techniques like 'Mr. Chairman'. Co-operation is only possible on certain common standards. These standards are English in essence, in spite of all local variations. To deny them is 'being unreasonable', 'not playing the game'. It may be objected that the anglicization is only political, that the Canadian French, for example, are culturally independent although politically they are part of the English system. But where is the border-line between political and non-political? 'To be a gentleman', 'to play the game', 'to keep faith' are non-political values; but Canadian or South African politics depend upon their acceptance. Politics is a function of 'the way of life'; it is not a separable technique. Afrikaners and French Canadians and even constitutionally minded Irishmen have accepted the English way of life. Let its specifically English character be frankly admitted; it becomes a danger to other national ways of life only when it poses as being European or human in an inclusive and general sense.

The German critic concludes by suggesting an alternative view of the British Empire. He agrees that it is not an empire in the simple and crude sense—a region under common sovereign rule. But he insists that it is a region in which the English folk are masters. 'All parts', he says, 'are linked by a community in the presence of Englishmen.' Subject peoples, ruled by migrated Englishmen, form the Empire. Its community consists in the community of race among its ruling class. The subject peoples live contentedly under their rulers because these have brought them within a *pax*; they have brought them order, protection, the means to a good life, a common ethical standard. The leaders of the subject peoples and the 'associate' white peoples can be given a share in the rule, because their stamp has been coined by the English; their ideas of public life, even their ideas of private life—food, clothes, family, sport, hygiene, housing—are English. Where they seem to be separate from the English, they are only a variation from the English. . . . In short, call the thing an Empire and no nonsense. 'The British Empire is a region where the English themselves, or at least their way of life, is paramount.'

If the writer felt himself compelled to choose between this non-universalizing, national-expansionist interpretation of the existing British Commonwealth, and the sweetness and light of the yearning universalizing interpretations, he would choose the former. His narrative of fact has revealed the irrelevance of vague and gushing universalization. Even so, some of the criticisms submitted by his German friend hit home pretty hard against his own work. There is first of all the attack upon 'the force to persuasion' theme. The writer employed the phrase in Chapter IV.[1] He did not intend to imply a pacifist or anarchical political philosophy. He is reluctant to embark at this stage on a theoretical discussion outside his own historical province, and perhaps he will make his point of view sufficiently clear if he says simply that he does not accept force and persuasion as antithetical in society. The chapters which deal with foreign policy have already made it clear that he does not accept force and law as antithetical. He sees the real problem of political history and political science as a problem of *relationship* between force, law, and persuasion. In his view the healthy society is one in which force does not act against the law or outside it, but acts at the bidding of a legal order which is supported by consent. The

[1] See above, p. 222.

moral nature of such an order must be left unexplored here.[1] But in general the writer must admit that his book accepts and 'justifies' force. He accepts it as an historical fact; he 'justifies' it in proportion as it is related to a legal order resting upon consent and upon the values which underlie consent. He recognizes as an historian that the process of 'justification' in human society is a difficult and gradual one. Sometimes it collapses into failure even when it seems securely achieved; sometimes it collapses when it is half achieved; sometimes there appears a lack of capacity or will even to pursue achievement. It must be confessed that the early chapters of this book shortened the perspective unduly. They entered into the history of the British Empire at its most favourable point, when certain of its more favoured dependencies were in fact transforming it into a Commonwealth; when force was, in fact, being 'justified' by consent. The perspective began in some degree to be corrected when the Irish, a nation who had been hammered mercilessly by brute British force, were introduced into the narrative in the third chapter. But it is just at this point that the German critic presses his question. Is it maintained that the Irish must now in all circumstances rest satisfied with a tardy and partial 'justification' of force? Suppose that they cannot so easily break away from their memory of historic wrong? Suppose they wish to keep themselves outside the area of persuasion, as they wished to fight their way out of the area of force? Is force still to be used against them to 'compel them to come in'? To be precise, is not the whole theory of 'free association' a fraud unless it admits the right of free separation?

It will be seen below that Stalin launches the same challenge. The reply to it may therefore be for the time being postponed. But the other challenge which is contained in the German criticism must be dealt with at once. If it be true that the unity of the Empire depends upon its anglicization, and that its 'community' is nothing more than 'the community of race', then the emphasis of this volume is indeed fundamentally wrong.

The writer holds that this time it is his critic who has distorted the historical perspective. He has carried the lines of it so far into a dim background that much of the foreground is invisible and the middle distance is entirely lost. He leaps from the ancient *Völkerwanderung* to the modern *Völkerwanderung*. It is not necessary to be pedantic about his identification of the various emigrant stocks

[1] The writer is not trained to attack the problem philosophically, but he has approached it from the historian's end in a lecture, 'Machiavelli in Modern Dress', published in *History*, September 1935.

of the British Isles with 'the English', for the whole criticism is offered suggestively, not pedantically; 'English' or 'British', it does not very much matter; the assertion in substance is that the British Commonwealth is the possession of a single historical 'folk', asserting everywhere its own separate and distinctive values and manner of life. The weakness of this interpretation is that it depends upon a denial of the historic elements of unity in western society. It assumes that the only formative influences upon the history of Europe have been racial or national influences. It ignores the classical tradition and the Christian Church. Thereby it eliminates the most significant features of the Middle Ages. It may be true that historical investigation has spent a disproportionate amount of energy on the elucidation of the institutional and intellectual elements in European history, to the neglect of the 'natural' elements of family, folk-lore, and village community. But it would be a worse error to rush to the other extreme. The Middle Ages would become quite unintelligible if their history were regarded as nothing more than the aggregate of separate folk-histories. The three-field system, feudalism, towns, canon law, the universities, the crusades, belong to the history of the *res publica christiana*, with which the history of each individual European people is inseparably interwoven. It is impossible to understand even the constitutional history of England merely by studying England. Parliament itself is a European institution.[1] It happens that conditions in the island kingdom were particularly favourable to the development and survival of the local variation of the institution. Admittedly, something more than this also happened. Parliament did indeed develop for centuries as a specifically national institution; it made itself English. But did it thereby make itself for all time exclusively English? How are we to separate those things which are English from those things which are European, or those things which are Italian from those things which are European? Dante is a Florentine; therefore he cannot but be both an Italian and a citizen of the Christian Commonwealth. Not even Queen Elizabeth is 'mere English'; she is a child of the Italian renaissance—that is, of the European renaissance. The expansion of England in modern times has been the expansion of the western world. It is true that the English have brought with them their own machines, their own dress, their own games. But do not

[1] The view that the famous English connexion between taxation, representation, and consent comes not merely from native English genius but from the practice in institutions of the medieval Church has recently been supported by the penetrating scholarship of the late Miss M. V. Clarke. See M. V. Clarke, *Mediaeval Representation and Consent. A study of Early Parliaments in England and Ireland.* (Longmans, 1936.)

Germans use the same machines, wear the same dress, and play the same games? Have these formidable English anglicized the Germans also? Or have the Germans escaped anglicization because they do not say 'Mr. Chairman'?

One has to distinguish between what is universal in origin and national by adoption; between what is national in actuality and universal in potentiality. The writer is not prepared to work out this distinction in a general scheme; but he has to employ it in practice when the evidence which he consults forces it upon his attention. He recognizes in nations as in individuals something which might be called the idiom of personality. This cannot be copied or communicated. But it may act as the vehicle for conveying a general idea which is capable of being expressed in another idiom. This is what happened in Canada in that most interesting and important period between 1763 and 1849. The documentary evidence definitely rules out the theory of anglicization. It shows instead a sort of Hegelian struggle between anglicization and French nationality. There are definite landmarks in the struggle: the capitulations, the proclamation of 1763, the Quebec Act, the Canada Act, the Durham Report, the Union, the joint triumph in 1849 of Lord Elgin, Baldwin, and La Fontaine. The synthesis expressed itself in the federation of 1867. This was not a triumph of the English, but was the coming together of French and English. The coming together did not extinguish French-Canadian nationality, which remained itself, resolved as it had always been to maintain its own way of life.[1]

What the Canadian example does show (and the South African example might be cited to the same purpose) is that the success of the British in handling their imperial problem in Canada depended upon their rejecting the plan of racial and cultural assimilation which Whigs and Tories alike frequently assumed to be inseparable from the plan of constitutional assimilation. But British thought has generally shown a lack of clarity and subtlety and coherence in evaluating the facts of past achievement and the possibilities of future achievement. On the one hand, there has persisted among many Englishmen the simple 'expansion of England' theory of the Empire. This is the theory which the German critic pleads for; but he pleads for it more realistically than do many of its English champions, for he recognizes the 'expansion of England' acting

[1] On the re-emerging tension between French nationalism and the Canadian political system see the *Round Table*, December 1936. The price of federation, like that of liberty, is eternal vigilance.

both through force and through persuasion, whereas they assume, wherever the assumption remains in the least degree plausible, that it acts through power alone. Where the assumption is patently unplausible, they are left without a theory. They are the people who have been portrayed in E. M. Forster's classic novel, *A Passage to India*. But on the other side there are the abstract universalizers of liberal doctrine. They seem to possess an irresistible propensity to generalize the Englishman's 'principles' at large, without realizing that in doing so they are taking for granted the whole rich and stable background of English history. In the field of international relations, even such men as H. G. Wells and Bertrand Russell do this, imagining all the time that they are merely good citizens of the world. Other Englishmen try to assert their 'principles' in the Empire without realizing that what they are really seeking to do is to impose their own national forms, regardless of the historic life and culture and needs of some quite different community. This tendency helps to explain the history of indentured labour, which has been told in Chapter IV. It helps to explain some of the disappointments of educational policy in India. The Englishman has thought it sufficient to transplant, where the need was to translate.

To-day there is a reaction. Systematic studies in anthropology and history, backed by imagination and an increasing desire to understand, are having their effect. There may indeed be danger that the reaction will go too far. There are some things which do not need to be 'translated' from one idiom of life to another, but can be taken over immediately. The English themselves took over in this way the alphabet and arithmetic, and it would be a pity if they were prevented by pseudo-anthropological squeamishness from handing over with the same directness their techniques of hygiene, of nutrition, and of the production which will make improved nutrition possible.[1] Not only sensitiveness, but common sense is necessary in generalizing from the experience recorded in this volume, and, still more, in employing the generalizations as aids to a survey of future possibility. An eminent teacher with wide experience of the problems of nationality and race within the British Commonwealth has endeavoured to express both needs in the phrase 'British with a small "b"'. After surveying the two exaggerations which have been discussed above, he asserts that the time has come 'to draw clearly the distinction between what is locally purely "British" in ... the tribal sense, and what is "british", that is, potentially universal

[1] This is the point of view strongly urged by Professor W. M. Macmillan, for example, in his *Warning from the West Indies* (Faber & Faber, 1935).

and human'.[1] The present writer believes that this distinction has been implicit in a good deal of the history which he has recorded. The distinction, if it is valid, justifies the idea contained in the phrase, 'Commonwealth of Nations'; for it asserts both the real sharing of values and necessities and the real individuality of the nations which share them. It even asserts—what imperialists have often forgotten—the individuality of England. 'Little Englanders' should look into it; they might find something which is not displeasing to them.[2] But the notion of British with anything but a very large B will be displeasing to racialist idealizers of the British Empire. The friendly German critic of these chapters will see in it a new rationalization of the anglicizing 'mission', which in his view needs no 'justification' so long as it is openly grounded on the principle of racial aristocracy. The idea put forward here suggests another kind of 'mission', another kind of 'justification'. These are perverted and alarming words. Let them be translated into contemporary forms of speech. The idea assumes that there is a job of work to be done within the British Empire, for purposes which are plainly human, by the British themselves, and by other nations which are not British. The writer submits again that the idea is not imposed upon history, but arises out of it. With equal emphasis he insists upon the late emergence of the idea into history (it may almost seem like a death-bed repentance)[3] and upon the existing gap between actuality and potentiality.

Communist criticism challenges the potentiality. It asserts that the achievement which is possible for a socialist commonwealth like the U.S.S.R. is impossible for a capitalist commonwealth like the British Empire. The best epitome of the communist argument on nationality is contained in Stalin's book, *Marxism and the National and Colonial Question*.[4] The book is a collection of addresses and articles delivered or written between 1913 and 1935, and the student of these utterances will realize that he must make allowance in his interpretation of them for changes in the political situation and in the alinements of political controversy. He will also understand that

[1] F. Clarke, 'British with a small "b"', in *The Nineteenth Century and After*, April 1936, pp. 428–39.

[2] For a healthy 'little England' feeling, at war both with imperialism and pacificism, see the late G. K. Chesterton's account of his attitude to the Boer War in chapter v of his *Autobiography* (Hutchinson, 1936).

[3] One might almost say that the attempt to hold Ireland by a policy of colonial anglicization persisted from the twelfth century to the twentieth. The policy of the Statutes of Kilkenny, which persisted in various forms into the nineteenth century, stands at the very extreme from the policy adopted in Canada.

[4] Published in 1935 by the Co-operative Publishing Society of Foreign Workers in the U.S.S.R.

Stalin is primarily concerned with racial problems in eastern Europe and Russia, and that he takes of necessity only a distant view of the British Empire. There is nevertheless a most conspicuous coherence and continuity in Stalin's scattered utterances, which always imply a condemnation of the British Empire even when they do not openly pronounce it. It is interesting to observe that the grounds on which Stalin pronounces condemnation are the very grounds on which the German critic is willing to pronounce absolution. Both of them assume that the British Empire consists of an aristocratic nation ruling over other nations. The German admires not only the vigour of the aristocratic nation but also the subtlety with which it masks its force—the skill with which it steers its way between isolation and assimilation, finding in 'association' a device for increasing its strength without diluting its individuality and virtue. But Stalin asserts that in a polity containing many nations the aristocratic principle is bound to break down. Only equality will work. And equality is impossible within a capitalistic order.

Stalin draws a sardonic pleasure from observing the peoples of western Europe caught in the toils of nationalistic antagonism, which for long had been the particular scourge of eastern Europe. It had seemed that the west, thanks to its more fortunate history, was immune from this scourge. In France and England the formation of states had coincided with the formation of nationalities. Nation and state fitted each other. In the east, nation and state did not fit each other. Many nationalities were crowded together within the same state. There they struggled with each other, oblivious of the preaching of the lucky western peoples. But these peoples threw away their good luck. They squandered their advantages of geographical situation and political stability in the foundation of empires. By doing this they transformed themselves into multi-national states. Their expansion, says Stalin, created conditions which made possible a future world economy. But the expansion developed in 'specific forms which were completely at variance with its historical significance'. It did not develop by the collaboration of peoples equal in status, but by the subjection of colonial peoples to European peoples, the exploitation of weaker peoples by stronger peoples. Hence, side by side with the tendency to amalgamation, there arose a struggle for emancipation. The British and French empires found themselves being torn by the same conflicts which destroyed the Hapsburg Empire. Even within their own home-territories, punishment was meted out to them for their *hubris*. Even within the frontiers which they had assumed to be 'natural', the 'ousted nations' rose up in protest or revolt against the 'dominant nations'. In the United Kingdom this was particularly true. Ireland was an English 'plantation', an early overseas colony; the Irish were also an 'ousted' European nation. Nationalism, when it infected the Irish people, infected the masses. What elsewhere was usually a struggle between the ruling classes of the predominant nation and the ousted nation, became in Ireland the rebellion, at once national and social, of a dispossessed people. It was prophetic of judgement to come in Africa and in Asia. The struggle for national equality would become fused with the struggle for economic and social equality. Historical reality had pronounced the doom of the British Empire.

But the multi-national polity which has its centre in Moscow is justified by historical reality. Stalin asserts this with unshakable confidence. The grounds of this confidence need to be described. And in the first place, attention must be given to the right of secession, which Stalin asserts to be the foundation of national freedom in the U.S.S.R. He rejects the cry of 'self-determination' because it is too vague. It can be adapted too easily to the programme of the imperialists. 'We have a better-minted and more clearly defined slogan—the right of nations to political secession.'[1]

Is the cohesion of the many nations combined in the U.S.S.R. really founded upon the right of secession? Fortunately it is not necessary to examine this question on a basis of actual fact; for there is sufficient material for an answer in Stalin's theoretical pronouncements. In the first place, it is evident that he takes up the cry of secession as a propagandist weapon against the 'capitalistic' empires, the empires of Great Britain, France, America, and Japan.[2] He says that the position of the U.S.S.R. is quite different. The right is proclaimed, but social democrats may resist it in certain circumstances.[3] The exercise of the right must be governed by 'expediency'.[4] 'The demand for the secession of the border regions from Russia . . . must be rejected.'[5] On what grounds must the right of secession, which is admitted in theory, be denied in practice? Stalin asserts that it is fundamentally opposed to the interests of the mass of the peoples both of the centre and the border regions. 'It is clear that the political basis of the dictatorship of the proletariat consists mainly

[1] Stalin, *Marxism and the National and Colonial Question*, p. 106 (1921).

[2] Op. cit., loc. cit., 'And inasmuch as we are concerned with colonies which are in the clutches of Great Britain, France, America, and Japan . . . the slogan of the right of peoples to secession is a revolutionary slogan.'

[3] Ibid., p. 19 (1913).

[4] Ibid., p. 64 (1917), cf. pp. 68 ff. (1918).

[5] Ibid., p. 79 (1920).

and primarily of the central, the industrial regions, and not the border regions, which are peasant countries.'[1] The right of secession, it appears, is subject to the dictatorship of the proletariat. When the right conflicts with interest, it behoves the proletariat, and particularly the proletariat of the central regions, to see that it is not exercised. Stalin admits as a general principle that the right is a 'subordinate' one.[2] Subordinate to what? To the interests of the classless society, to the interests of the revolution. The Transcaucasian Tartars cannot be permitted to secede under the leadership of their beys and mullahs; the nations of the border regions cannot be permitted to be independent under the leadership of their bourgeoisie.[3] The apostles of secession have unfettered freedom as nationalists, but they will be shot as revolutionaries. The writer is reminded irresistibly of an episode from his own school-days. A merry master, slashing with his cane at an idle lout, struck a small industrious boy across the face. 'Never mind,' said the master to the small boy, 'I shan't cane you next time you do anything wrong.' Before the lesson was over the small boy was called out to be caned for talking. He reminded the master of his promise. 'I shan't cane you for talking,' the master answered, 'but I shall give you double for impudence.' And he did.

The author will argue later on that Stalin has laid the intellectual foundations for a notable and most significant progress in solving the problems of the multi-national polity. His point now is that this success is not founded upon the right of secession. The right is acclaimed in the U.S.S.R.; but it does not exist there. One is almost tempted to say in contrast that the right exists in the British Commonwealth, but is not acclaimed there. But that would be saying too much. From the point of view of theory, the position of South Africa is the most interesting example. It would appear that South Africa, under the legislation of 1934, would be able by strictly constitutional processes to take a series of steps which would end in secession. Some people, however, argue that there would be a breach of legality before the final act of secession was achieved. On this question of theory General Smuts and General Hertzog agree to differ. But both of them avow that in practice the only barrier to secession is the will of the South African people.

What of Ireland? The German critic who has been quoted above argued from the example of Ireland that 'free association' was a fraud unless 'free separation' was also admitted. Others have made

[1] Stalin, op. cit., p. 168 (1923). [2] Ibid., p. 193 (1924).
[3] Ibid., pp. 18–20, 69–70.

the same point in conversation with the writer, or in comment upon what he has written. They have invited him to pronounce in favour of the right of secession.

Primarily, the writer is an historian, and if he has consented to discuss shortly questions of theoretical right, he has done so only from a feeling of obligation towards the reader. In good faith to the reader he feels bound, so far as he is able, to drag into the light of day the theories which are implied in his historical interpretation, so that the reader may not swallow interpretation and theories together without knowing that he has done so. In particular, it is important for writer and reader to distinguish, so far as possible, between three things: what actually happened, the theory of what actually happened, and the theory of what ought to happen or what some people would like to happen.

What actually happened in 1921 was that the British Prime Minister threatened the Irish representatives with 'immediate and terrible war' if they did not accept allegiance to the Crown and membership of the British Commonwealth of Nations. In act as well as in word Great Britain rejected the right of secession. The theory behind this rejection, in so far as it made itself explicit, was the theory of an indissoluble historical unity which might be largely and progressively relaxed, but must not be completely destroyed. Side by side with this theory was a theory of interest comparable with Stalin's view of the relations between Russia and the border nations. Great Britain and Ireland, it was maintained, lay so close together that they could not become separate strategical units. British statesmen were naturally preoccupied with the danger to Great Britain. But their preoccupation implied a general theory of the historical character of international relationships. It implied Hobbes's assumption that independent nations lived side by side with each other in a 'state of nature', not in a state of law-respecting sociability. It did not imply that this was a matter for congratulation or acquiescence, but that it was a matter which could not be dismissed. The time had not yet come when statesmen could ignore the range of submarines and bombing aeroplanes. Ireland no less than Great Britain had an interest in minimizing the possibility of future collisions with her neighbour. The self-government which the treaty offered to her—here the British argument became a theory of what 'ought' to be—contained the essentials of freedom, and harmonized the rights of nationality with the duties of sociability. This argument a large section of the Irish people rejected. In their eyes the British theory distorted history by ignoring the fact of British violence against Ireland. It distorted the present by ignoring Irish memory of this violence. It distorted the future by ignoring the coming triumph of the League of Nations. These Irishmen did not deny the geographical connexion between Great Britain and Ireland. But they drew different conclusions from it. They argued from their theory of the international harmony which 'ought' to come that no special measures were necessary to ward off collisions between the peoples of the two islands. Or, if special measures remained necessary, these could be discovered without making Ireland a 'member' of the Commonwealth of Nations. They argued from their theory of what had been that Ireland would not find satisfaction in membership. They claimed the right to secede.[1]

Great Britain and the British Commonwealth have not admitted the right to secede. But, since 1922, the position has been greatly altered. The Crown has all but been eliminated from the constitution of the Irish Free State. The treaty has lost its binding force in the municipal law of the Irish Free State. The British government denies that its stipulations have lost their binding force as an international or quasi-international agreement. But it seems likely that the British government would not oppose with violence the promulgation of a constitution for Saorstát Éireann which would embody the programme urged by the anti-treaty party in the Dáil in 1922, provided always that the promulgation of this constitution was not associated with measures which would diminish the power of Great Britain to defend the trade and food-supplies of the British Isles.[2] Nor would the British courts pronounce upon interpretations by the Irish courts of the new Irish constitution. The theory of secession might thus become the constitutional orthodoxy of the Irish Free State. What the author has been invited to do is to declare that the British government and the Dominion governments ought to accept it as the orthodoxy of the British Commonwealth.

He is unable to accept the invitation. In the first place, he is not

[1] Perhaps the summary distorts a little owing to its rapidity. It will be remembered that Mr. De Valera maintained in a letter to Mr. Lloyd George that Ireland could not secede as she had never accepted membership. He insisted upon 'self-recognition'. The idea was held by other people who were not politicians, e.g. by Stephen MacKenna, the translator of Plotinus. See *Journal and Letters of Stephen MacKenna*, edited with a Memoir by E. R. Dodds (Constable, 1936), p. 61: 'I would even now accept this agreement if only it brought us an un-British freedom—just left the question of membership in abeyance, went on the unexpressed assumption that we were members and adherent—though I admit that I wish we were in that case even a little less sovran.' Perhaps the British Commonwealth has since then learnt from South African experience of the nineteen-thirties something of the technique of leaving in abeyance questions of theoretical and symbolic interpretation.

[2] See above, pp. 372–92.

enamoured of theoretical declarations of right. The original constitution of the Irish Free State itself contained such a declaration; and it has been explained above in Chapter VI how empty and meaningless the theoretical rights proved themselves to be. The constitution developed along its own lines in spite of them, thereby reproducing the experience of its continental predecessors and contemporaries. Is there any reason for supposing that a theoretical declaration of the rights of nations would be more relevant or useful than a theoretical declaration of the rights of man? But there is also an objection to the proposed content of the declaration. It is illogical that any society, whether of men or of nations, should begin by postulating the right of its members to secede from it. It is true that two contemporary multi-national communities, the League of Nations and the U.S.S.R., did profess to accept this postulate. But the profession of the U.S.S.R., as has been shown above, was insincere. The profession of the League of Nations was sincere, and was written into the Covenant. Japan and Germany have been within their recognized rights in seceding from the League. But this fact merely emphasizes the weakness of the League as a political society. No political society can hope to flourish if its members can flounce out of it whenever it shows a tendency to fulfil the purposes for which it was created. It should be unnecessary to labour this point, which has been elucidated sufficiently in discussions on the theory of the state. A society or commonwealth of nations differs in essential respects from the state, but it resembles it at least in this: that it implies a philosophy of social obligation. It would be intellectually incompetent or dishonest to rest it entirely upon a philosophy of individual right. Individual right, whether of men or of nations, has its place in every healthy social theory. But its ultimate expression—as resistance, revolution, or secession—cannot honestly be written into the constitution. Like the Whig doctrine of the right of resistance, it lies behind the constitution. It is a moral right which may be invoked against the constitution. It may become a moral duty. But the members of a society who are prompted to exercise it are bound not only by duty but also by necessity to weigh elements of historical circumstance—the vices and (if any) the virtues of the society from which they are seceding, the virtues and (if any) the vices of the society they propose to enter or create, the real good of themselves or of their nation, and the real good of their 'neighbour'—if this word may be taken from Christian teaching to symbolize *some* society to which they cannot but belong, unless they are gods or beasts.

So far as Stalin's criticism of capitalistic empires is concerned, the much-advertised 'right of secession' is a red herring; it is, in Stalin's own word, a 'subordinate' matter. By this he means it is not an absolute right. But Stalin advances other reasons for believing that the U.S.S.R. is bound to achieve the harmony of many nations, whereas the British Empire is bound to be torn to pieces by national conflict. Let it be assumed, for purposes of argument, that there is a hundred per cent. conformity between the practices of the U.S.S.R. and the precepts of Stalin. The precepts, taken by themselves, are a sufficient challenge.

In the first place, Stalin confidently preaches the *participation* of all the nations of the U.S.S.R. in a common task, a common culture, a common belief. He calls upon them all to serve the common proletarian cause, 'to consolidate the alliance between the border regions and the centre', 'to create common spiritual ties'. If this work is to be achieved, the national languages, administrations, theatres, systems of education, so far from being a misfortune, are a necessity and an opportunity.

> 'The Soviet government is not a government divorced from the people; on the contrary, it is the only government of its kind, a government which originated among the masses of the Russian people and which is near and dear to the people. . . . The Soviet government must become no less near and dear to the populace of the border regions of Russia. But to do so the Soviet government must be comprehensible to them.'[1]

One is reminded of the policy of Queen Elizabeth towards Wales. Henry VIII had wished the Principality to enjoy the advantages of becoming 'a member and joint' of the Realm, and to achieve his unifying purpose he had attempted to extinguish the 'singular and sinister usages and customs' of his Welsh subjects. Elizabeth, on the contrary, ordered the Bible and the Prayer Book to be translated into the Welsh language. In Elizabeth's day the unity of the realm rested upon the new religious settlement, and it was desirable that the belief of the Realm should be preached to the Welsh through the only medium in which they could understand it.[2] Once the state comes to stand for a positive doctrine, the languages and usages and customs of its diverse nationalities cease to seem 'singular and sinister'. Is it not right and fitting that 'that most precious jewel,

[1] Stalin, *Marxism and the National and Colonial Question*, p. 83 (1920).

[2] The Tudors did not appreciate the same need in Ireland, probably because the tradition of colonial race ascendancy was too strong. The early Stuarts belatedly translated the Bible into Irish.

the word of Marx'—if one may adapt a phrase of Queen Elizabeth's —should be translated into all the languages of Russia? Is it not proper that all the peoples of the U.S.S.R. should praise Lenin after their several fashions? Stalin presides over a commonwealth of nations held together by a positive theology. Is he not justified in believing that this gives his commonwealth a spiritual unity stronger than any unity which the British Commonwealth can dream of possessing? The British Commonwealth sometimes professes to be an empire of ideas; but the ideas, when one examines them, seem to be subtle, if not elusive—they are ideas about the forms and spirit of procedure, about methods of legal redress and political behaviour, about toleration, moderation, and persuasiveness.[1] They may be ideas which sensitive and intelligent people value highly, but are they ideas which will awaken the fervour of the masses? It is true that the British Commonwealth gives positive value to the idea of nationality. But nationality, unless it expresses itself in the content of some wider principle, tends always to fall into the exaggerations of nationalism, rejecting the obligation of duty to a commonwealth, or to any other society of nations. Stalin, for his part, gives no positive value to nationality, except an ephemeral tactical value. Nationality is to him a means to the end of cosmopolitan communism. He looks forward to 'a single, common culture, both in form and content, with a single common language, when the proletariat is victorious throughout the whole world'.[2] This end is positive enough. But may it not prove itself, when pursued by a tactician less experienced than Stalin, to be too positive? Perhaps the nationalities may lose their joy in a culture which aims professedly at their extinction.

Let it, however, be admitted that the U.S.S.R. enjoys over the British Commonwealth the advantage of possessing the unity of a more definite and positive creed.[3] Stalin claims that it is creating for itself another bond of unity which capitalist empires are forbidden by their very nature from creating—the unity of material condition. Perhaps the most impressive thing in Stalin's essays and addresses is his war against the thing he calls *de facto* inequality. Equality of

[1] e.g. Clarke, *British with a small 'b'*, p. 434: 'Sovereignty of the rule of law, the free action of groups and communities in the life of the whole, individual responsibility for the common good, responsible government, these and other things . . .'.

[2] Stalin, *Marxism and the National and Colonial Question*, p. 261 (1930).

[3] At the present time the contrast in definiteness is probably much greater than that between the definite creeds of Calvinism or the Counter-Reformation on the one hand, and on the other hand indefinite Anglican Compromise of Elizabethan days.

status is acclaimed by the British Commonwealth as the principle which it has realized in part and to which it is professedly striving. Stalin has proclaimed equality of status, but he is not satisfied with it. 'We have proclaimed equality of legal status,' he declares, 'and we are practising it; but equality of legal status, although in itself a factor of the greatest importance in the history of the development of the Soviet republics, is still a long way from real equality.'[1] The real equality at which he aims is equality of capacity and of material reward. He complains that the nations of the U.S.S.R., owing to their separate cultural histories and to the oppressions inflicted on them by the exploiting Russian Empire, are prevented from utilizing their theoretically equal rights. They are the victims of inherited economic inequality—'Eliminated it must be at all costs.'[2] 'The crux of the problem', Stalin repeats, 'lies in the obligation to put an end to the backwardness (economic, political, and cultural) of the nationalities which we have inherited from the past, and to afford the backward peoples the opportunity of catching up with Central Russia politically, culturally, and economically.'[3] With the greatest resolution he attacks the enemies who would resist this enterprise—notably the Great Russian chauvinists and the little chauvinists of the outlying nationalities, which attempt to intrigue themselves into a privileged position and to implicate the U.S.S.R. in a system of government by factions. Are Great Britain and the other nations of the British Commonwealth capable of a similar resistance to the British chauvinists or to the nationalities which dominate locally? Do they possess the will to offer this resistance, or have they even conceived the plan of it? On the limited evidence which has been collected in this volume, there is not much sign of a resolute war on *de facto* inequality. The economy of South Africa still rests upon the assumption that it is desirable to perpetuate the material inequality between Europeans and natives. South African legislation offers a bonus to a white skin. If the Indians in South Africa have been gradually raising themselves towards a position of material equality with the Europeans, they have been doing so, until very recently, by their own efforts, and in the teeth of governmental and municipal opposition. Yet it would be unjust to forget the agreement of 1927, in which the Union government pledged itself to pursue the 'uplift' of those Indians who desired to conform to western standards. Within the British Commonwealth, as in England, new theories fight their way slowly to the front. It may yet happen that the agreement of 1927 may mark the beginning of a new conception of *de facto* equality.

[1] Stalin, op. cit., p. 155 (1923). [2] Ibid., p. 143 (1923). [3] Ibid., p. 103 (1921).

Stalin would deny that this is possible. For to him it is axiomatic that the British Empire, like the other capitalistic empires, is founded on exploitation. It cannot reform itself. It can only be destroyed. It will be destroyed by rivalry with other capitalistic empires blazing into war, and by the suffering of its British and colonial proletariat blazing into revolution. The revolt of the colonies will be like the revolt of Ireland—at once the rising of the depressed class and of the ousted nation.

What would have been the result if the writer had set out to write this volume upon Stalin's hypothesis? He would not have got very far with the volume unless he had been prepared to discard the hypothesis or modify it. It would not have helped him greatly with his sketch of the American revolution, or of the Canadian evolution; nor would it have helped him with his study of the Imperial Conference or the Statute of Westminster. It would not have helped him to enter into the minds of Sir Wilfrid Laurier or Mr. Alfred Deakin or perhaps even those of Mr. Eamon De Valera or Mahatma Gandhi. The writer feels that his volume would have been incomplete if, in deference to an hypothesis, it had been shorn of topics, personalities, and idealisms which are so diverse. Yet he is conscious that his volume cannot pretend to be a finished book about the British Commonwealth. The book will not be finished until Stalin's hypothesis has been tested. The hypothesis may not help very much in explaining the thought and ideals of Mr. De Valera and Mr. Gandhi; but perhaps it may help a great deal in explaining the background in which their minds were formed and their ideals grew. As for the statesmen who attend imperial conferences, it may be discovered that they belong to the exploiting side of the British Empire. In the second volume, therefore, the writer will investigate a different content, and will extend the geographical range of his investigations to include a larger number of colonies. He will not forget that his first task is to construct the narrative of a definite historical period; but he will be mindful of the hypothesis that the idea of the Commonwealth is beyond realization because the ruling races and the ruling classes of the Empire are inextricably implicated in capitalistic profits. Within his period he will investigate the grounds of Stalin's assertion that empire is exploitation, and of Lenin's assertion that empire is monopoly. He cannot yet measure the results which this investigation will produce.

But he believes that a good deal of the interpretation in this volume must stand. It rests upon evidence which he has critically examined, to the limit of his ability.

THE LAW AND THE COMMONWEALTH

By R. T. E. LATHAM

THE LAW AND THE COMMONWEALTH

By R. T. E. LATHAM

I

THE COMMON LAW, ITS NATURE AND EXPANSION

'SIXTHLY', wrote Sir Edward Coke, in a peroration to his report of a great case, 'it appeareth, that the jurisprudence of the Common Law of England is a science sociable and copious: sociable, in that it agreeth with the principles and rules of other excellent sciences, divine and human, copious, for that . . . there should be such a multitude and *farrago* of authorities in all successions of ages, in our books and bookcases, for the deciding of the point of so rare an accident.'[1] This essay is in large measure a study in the sociability and the copiousness of the Common Law in a particular field. The author of this dictum personified the pride of the Common Law in its own integrity and all-sufficiency, in an age when it was still fighting its rivals.[2] That arrogance of the Common Law persists in England to the present day in the unbroken tradition of the courts. For the most part it is a self-regard which coincides comfortably with the neat, logical self-regard of analytical jurisprudence, fortifying analytical theory with the flesh and blood of a living institution. Theory requires that formally the law should never be at a loss for an answer.[3] In practice, says Coke, the Common Law of England never is at a loss for an answer, and that a good one. Jurists may say that law rests on compulsion, but the English judge, taking it for granted that his order will be executed, needs no *fasces*: for him, his robes, which link him directly with Coke and all other lusty English judges, are authority enough.

Other intolerances of the Common Law accord less well with theory. A notable instance is its treatment of statutes. Abandoning the medieval idea that there was a fundamental or immutable law,[4]

[1] *Calvin's Case* (1608) 7 Co. Rep. 1*a*, 28*a*.

[2] It was actually defeated shortly afterwards by its rival, Equity, but Equity rapidly assumed the character and texture of the Common Law, and the Courts of Equity and Common Law were amalgamated in the nineteenth century. In this chapter, unless otherwise indicated, when the Common Law is spoken of Equity is included, but not statute law.

[3] See, e.g., the controversy in international law, whether there can be a 'non-justiciable dispute', discussed in Lauterpacht, *The Function of Law in the International Community*.

[4] As expressed in, e.g., *Bonham's Case* (1610) 8 Co. Rep. 114.

the Common Law recognized the legislative supremacy of Parliament.[1] But to the words of the Parliament whose literal authority it thus recognized it accorded none of that aura of respect and generosity of interpretation with which it surrounded its own doctrines. The courts never entered into the spirit of the Benthamite game, but treated the statute throughout as an interloper upon the rounded majesty of the Common Law. The tendency still persists: the courts show a ripe appreciation of institutions of long standing, whether founded by statute or in the Common Law, but they inhibit themselves from seizing the spirit of institutions and situations which are in substance the creation of modern legislation.[2]

Of international law the Common Law is still less patient: it exists in the English courts only as a presumption to be followed in the absence of a clear rule of municipal law.[3] Further, the Common Law now grows wholly from within. Its last spontaneous 'reception' of a body of alien doctrine was the reception of mercantile law in the eighteenth century.

In short, the modern Common Law has ceased to be 'sociable'. It is impatient of other kinds and systems of law, and does not eagerly claim kinship with moral science or natural reason. Coke justified the Common Law as a system closely conformable to the Law of Nature;[4] his modern successors find the Common Law self-justified. This is not vanity, for popular esteem combines with judicial tradition to give the courts a rare institutional strength. The Common Law is *par excellence* the law of the courts, and its courts have a unique majesty. In the United States, where no parliament has been set over against them as strong after its fashion as they in theirs, the judges have been driven by the traditions of their craft to establish a conscientious judicial tyranny.

This, then, is the nature and quality of the law which has extended itself, in one form or another, over one-third of the world's population and more than one-quarter of its area. In the overwhelmingly greater part of this added field the Common Law operates under conditions vitally different, in one way or another, from the conditions

[1] For a discussion of the exact meaning of this supremacy see pp. 523–4 below.

[2] By repercussion draftsmen tend to concern themselves with minutiae, so that their intention may be manifest in every particular instance to upset the hydra-headed presumptions of the courts in favour of the Common Law. Thus parliament tends to enact the trees, not the wood. A recent instance of the shipwreck of legislation whose general intention was clear is *Rose* v. *Ford*, [1936] 1 K.B.

[3] *West Rand Mining Co.* v. *R.* [1905] 2 K.B. 391; *Rustomjee* v. *R.* 2 Q.B.D. 69; *Mortensen* v. *Peters*, 14 S.L.T. 227. Contrast Art. 6. 2 of the Constitution of the United States.

[4] 'For *jura naturae sunt immutabilia*, and they are *leges legum*.'

of its nurture. It has to mix with alien systems, to cope with unfamiliar institutions, to govern, and even to be administered by, men of strange races, strange loyalties, and strange creeds. How does this very insular product suffer such transplantation? In its new environments does it remain copious, unsociable, and strong? It is the purpose of this chapter to sketch in outline an answer to these questions, in so far as they concern that aspect of the British Empire which is called the British Commonwealth.

The British Commonwealth is only one of two political constellations whose law springs in large measure from the Law of England. The American colonists fought their War of Independence in the name of a not wholly indefensible theory of the Common Law, and Britain took her stand on another.[1] The victory of the colonists resulted in a partition of the Common Law world; but the Americans in their new unit rather exalted than abandoned their Common Law heritage, forging for themselves a federation which fetters policy at every turn by law. Having thus found insistence upon the strictness of the law a two-edged weapon, Great Britain, for the regulation of the Second British Empire, abandoned Declaratory Acts and the strictness of the law in favour of departmental discretion and tacit agreements to let well alone. And when these practices did harden into rules, they became not law but 'convention'.[2]

Meanwhile the law of the imperial relationship, especially that part of it which covered the future Commonwealth, was rusting in comparative disuse. The only great statute of general imperial constitutional law passed in the nineteenth century was the Colonial Laws Validity Act of 1865,[3] and it was occasioned not by any desire of the imperial government to clarify or amend the law, but by the necessity of upsetting the eccentric decisions of a South Australian judge.[4] The courts were a little more active than the legislature, and a couple of dozen leading cases on imperial law might be named. If to these are added the opinions of the law officers of the Crown on colonial subjects,[5] we have all the chief sources of nineteenth-century imperial law. While the Empire strode forward politically, its law stood still. The rules which it needed—for no institution can do without

[1] For accounts of the American and English theories, see above, pp. 6–13; McIlwain. *The American Revolution*; Keith, *Constitutional History of the First British Empire*, ch. xiv; and Kennedy, *Essays in Constitutional Law*, ch. i.

[2] In Dicey's sense of the word, which, originally rather inappropriate, is now irrevocably current. See below, p. 60, for a definition of this sense.

[3] 28 & 29 Vict. c. 63.

[4] Boothby, J., who declared large numbers of colonial statutes invalid for repugnancy to English law.

[5] Some of which are published in Forsyth's collection.

rules of some sort—it formulated in another language and with other sanctions, the language and sanctions of constitutional convention. When, therefore, the Empire became the Commonwealth of Nations, its fundamental law was still in all substantial respects the law of George III, the same law which lost Britain the American colonies.

In 1921 the immersion of a foreign body, the Irish Free State, disturbed the quiet waters of the Conventional Commonwealth. Out of the ferment which it created the Statute of Westminster, 1931,[1] emerged. The Statute of Westminster is all that there is of the Commonwealth in law, and it is not very much. Some institutions—the League of Nations, with which the British Commonwealth is often compared, is a striking example—exist in law before they exist in fact.[2] The British Commonwealth took the law by surprise. This was not remarkable, for it had already taken many of its own statesmen by surprise. Had the Commonwealth in 1931 found its lawgiver, as five years earlier it had found its philosopher in Lord Balfour, the leeway might have been made up. But it did not, and the Statute, however creative in the political sphere, brought a purely negative contribution in law.

In this sphere, then, the Common Law has not been 'copious'. The Commonwealth as it now exists is a singularly lawless association. Certainly, the majesty of the Common Law of England is reflected with little diminution of its glory in the judicial institutions of each of the Dominions. But it shines in each separately; their relations with each other are shrouded in a mist of convention. The Commonwealth is even more lawless, though certainly less disorderly, than the comity of nations, for the nations have at least rules of international law which are copious though not observed. The Commonwealth has its habits and usages, which sometimes amount to 'conventional' rules, and it does on the whole observe them; but they are not rules of law.

This nebulous state of the general law of the Empire throws into relief the success of the Common Law within each particular dominion or dependency. Here it has been fruitful, copious, and strong. When, by reason of its unsociable character, it has come into conflict or rivalry with another system of law, it has usually had the better of the difference. In some parts of the Empire the whole of the

[1] 22 Geo. 5, c. 4.

[2] The reference is here to the central function of the League Covenant as a rudimentary international constitution for the prevention of war and the regulation of peace, not to its important subsidiary activities.

standing *corpus* of the law is English law; in others a foreign system exists alongside English law; in others the whole private law belongs to another legal tradition. But even in these last the English public law, the English manner of interpreting statutes, the English law of evidence, and the English system of precedent, intrude in some degree.[1]

But first it is necessary to pursue two aspects of the history of the extension of English law to the colonies: the extension of the English system as a whole, so far as applicable, to settled colonies, and the inevitable extension of a part of British public law to all territories under direct British sovereignty. These two topics will be followed only in the general law of the Empire as declared by British courts, not in their local development in the several colonies, however important; and the general constitutional development of the colonies, a subject which has been often enough expounded, will not be described.

The general law of the modern British Empire springs from and is continuous with the doctrine which the courts of England tardily, under pressure of fact, built up concerning the seventeenth-century 'plantations' in America and 'factories' in the Orient and Africa which Englishmen founded or conquered from other European Powers. To the legal theory of the medieval empire of the Kings of England (Normandy, the Channel Islands, Wales, Ireland, Gascony, Guienne, Calais, Berwick, &c.) the law of the new colonies owed no clear rules except the negative one that the conquest of a country does not necessarily destroy the legal system there existing and substitute that of the conqueror.[2] But the medieval law did offer theories of the absence of any territorial limitation to the Common Law[3] or to the authority of parliament[4] which became fundamental

[1] Only where, as in some protectorates and territories under 'indirect rule', native law is administered by native courts under native quasi-sovereignty, is there no element of the Common Law present. But even there the native courts are restrained by the suzerain from infringing 'natural justice', and natural justice as seen by a British Resident will often bear a close resemblance to the fundamental principles of the Common Law.

[2] For this rule see, e.g., Vaughan C.J.'s note on *Process into Wales*, in Vaugh. 395 (which was in fact an undelivered judgment in *Whitrong* v. *Blaney* (1674) 2 Mod. 10); and *Blankard* v. *Galdy* (1694) 2 Salk. 411.

[3] This appears, e.g., from Coke's two propositions that allegiance 'cannot be circumscribed within the predicament of *ubi*' and that '*ligeantia* [allegiance] *est quasi legis essentia*': *Calvin's Case* (1608) 7 Co. Rep. 1*a*, at 7*b*, and 4*b*. *Ergo*, there is nothing in the nature of the Common Law to limit it territorially.

[4] Schuyler, *Parliament and the British Empire*, pp. 36–7. James I sought to exclude parliament from colonial affairs: Keith, *Constitutional History of the First*

in the law of the new colonies. The medieval precedents on these points were less unambiguous than they were made to appear in the rationalizations of seventeenth-century Whig lawyers; but the Whig rationalizations prevailed, and were firmly established by the Revolution of 1689. To the legal theory of the personal union between England and Scotland, whose *locus classicus* is *Calvin's Case*,[1] the law of the colonies owed nothing. Observing the close similarity between the modern conventional-legal theory of the Commonwealth[2] and Coke's theory of the Union of the Crowns, one is tempted to speculate what the history of the Empire might have been if the courts had chosen Scotland instead of Ireland as the precedent for colonial status. But there was never any likelihood of such a choice, for the colonies were founded expressly in order to be the economic dominion of England.[3] One other ostensible source is suggested by the frequent references in the reports to *ius gentium* and the law of nature; but these are the merest apology.[4] No rule of international law really affected decisions; and unless eighteenth-century Whiggery be reckoned the law of nature, there is little natural law in the law of the colonies, though there is plenty of common sense.

Campbell v. *Hall*[5] was decided on the principles of the Glorious Revolution. In settling the fundamental principles of English nationality, feudal principles were followed.[6] Apart from these matters there is remarkably little that is doctrinaire in early colonial law. The law grew up around the plantations and factories; they were not planned and founded within an existing law. Always the law followed the facts at a respectful distance.

The two leading rules of the law of colonization furnish good examples of this empirical process. The first is the rule that a con-

British Empire, pp. 5 sqq. And the Barbados asserted their independence of Cromwell's authority: Schuyler, op. cit., pp. 110 sqq. But after the Restoration Parliament was left in full exercise of the power until the American Revolution.

[1] (1608) 7 Co. Rep. 1*a*.

[2] See, e.g., Schlosberg, *The King's Republics* (1927), which carried the view of the Commonwealth as a personal union farther than the law at the time warranted. See below, p. 526.

[3] For the relations of Scotland to the colonies during the Union of the Crowns, see below, p. 517.

[4] The Roman law of the acquisition of *res nullius* by occupation was occasionally cited to justify the exercise of sovereignty over plantations; and the law of nations was often invoked for the 'principle' that the lives of the conquered were in the hands of the conquerors.

[5] (1774) Lofft 655, 1 Cowp. 204, 20 St. Tr. 239. This *cause célèbre* decided that once the Crown has definitely granted representative institutions to a conquered colony its power to legislate for that colony by Order In Council ceases.

[6] *Calvin's Case* (1608) 7 Co. Rep. 1*a*; *Craw* v. *Ramsey* (1669) Vaugh. 274. See below, p. 520.

quered or ceded colony retains its previous law (with certain exceptions to be mentioned later)[1] except in so far as the Crown may alter it.[2] This rule is variously justified in the decisions, and has, as we have seen, some medieval authority,[3] but at all times its real ground has been the fact that conquered and ceded territories have been actually left in possession of their 'ancient laws'.

The other leading rule is that, when Englishmen found a colony in an uninhabited or savage[4] country, they carry with them the English law so far as it is applicable. This rule appears to have rested, not on the express provisions for the introduction of English law which were often, though not always, inserted in the charters,[5] nor upon the circumstance that the charters usually included a grant of the colonial land to be held of the English Crown 'as of our Manor of East Greenwich',[6] but on a vague attachment of English law to the persons of Englishmen, at least so long as they did not subject themselves to the law of another sovereign.[7] The process, therefore, by

[1] See below, pp. 518–20. Coke's exception, that the laws of infidels cease altogether, was qualified in *Blankard* v. *Galdy* (1694) 2 Salk. 411, 412, Comb. 225, and in the case of 1722 before the Privy Council referred to in 2 P. Will. 75. It was repudiated with undeserved vehemence by Lord Mansfield in *Campbell* v. *Hall* (1774) Lofft 655, 741. The case which it was intended to cover, that is to say, the acquisition of territories whose existing system of law is such that Englishmen cannot reasonably be expected to conform to it, is now in effect covered by the special rules as to Oriental 'factories', for which see below, p. 518.

[2] The leading dictum is that of Coke in *Calvin's Case* (1608) 7 Co. Rep. 1*a*, 17*b*. The Crown may alter the 'ancient law' by the terms of the capitulation: *Campbell* v. *Hall*, Lofft 655, 741; and the commander of the conquering forces has full power to arrange any terms of capitulation he pleases. After capitulation the Crown may legislate by order-in-council: *Forbes* v. *Cochrane* (1824) 2 B. & C. 448, by letters patent or charter: *Campbell* v. *Hall*, above; *Jephson* v. *Riera* (1835) 3 Knapp 130, 151, and possibly by order under the sign-manual or by a mere expression of the will of the Secretary of State: *Cameron* v. *Kyte* (1835) 3 Knapp 332; but the Governor alone cannot legislate: ibid.

[3] Above, p. 514.

[4] In theory, the distinction between settlement in savage territory and conquest from infidels (see above, n. 1) might not seem clear, but in practice, territory inhabited by American Indians was reckoned uninhabited, while settlements in Oriental countries were treated as 'factories'. See below, p. 518.

[5] Cf. Chalmers, *Political Annals of the United Colonies* (1780), p. 14, and Keith, *Constitutional History of the First British Empire*, p. 3.

[6] Some colonies were granted to their proprietors with the exceptional status of Counties Palatine.

[7] 'Then taking it as the Truth is, certain subjects of England, by Consent of their Prince, go and possess an uninhabited desert Country; the Common Law must be supposed their rule, as 'twas their Birthright, and as 'tis the best, and so to be presumed their Choice; and not only that, but even as Obligatory, 'tis so. When they went thither, they no more abandoned the English Laws, than they did their natural Allegiance; nay, they subjected themselves thereby no more to other Laws, than they did to another Allegiance, which they did not.' Argument of counsel before the House of Lords in *Dutton* v. *Howell* (1694) Show. Parl. Cas. 24, 32.

which the English law was extended to English settlements was primarily personal, not territorial, and it is always so treated in the authorities.[1] But as soon as the original settlers had reached the colony, their invisible and inescapable cargo of English law fell from their shoulders and attached itself to the soil on which they stood. Their personal law became the territorial law of the colony. Subsequent settlers did not, like the founders, bring with them the law of England as they left it, but entered into the colony as they would into any other country, becoming subject to the established territorial law.[2] Nor, as we have seen, did English law automatically follow Englishmen to colonies conquered from a civilized power.

It is remarkable that after the legislative union with Scotland in 1707, when England and Scotland merged into a single kingdom of Great Britain having two territorially limited systems of private law, equal in status, the law that followed citizens of the united realm to colonies subsequently founded was invariably the law of England.[3] There is nothing in the Acts of Union or elsewhere expressly prescribing this.[4] In fact, Scotland had just failed to establish a Scottish colony in Darien,[5] and her consent to the union with England amounted to a final adoption of the English colonies instead of an empire of her own as the domain of her future trade.[6] Scotsmen accordingly did not question the reflection of this policy in law, and were content to be Englishmen overseas.[7]

[1] In the exhaustive argument in *Dutton* v. *Howell*, already cited, counsel urged, *inter alia*, as a ground for the extension of English law to the colonies the rule (*semble*, of international law) that by occupying colonial land settlers acquired it for the Crown, and the fact that colonial land was held of the Crown. This is the only exception.

[2] Statutes subsequent to the settlement did, of course, apply to the colony if they could be construed as *intended* to apply. But prior statutes applied if their nature was such that they were *capable* of applying.

[3] Sir Maurice Amos observes that in capitulatory courts in Egypt, English law is treated as the national law of all British subjects.

[4] Unless, in view of the mercantilist view of colonies then prevailing, the provision in the Acts of Union that the laws of the United Kingdom as to trade should be those of England be thought to cover the point.

[5] Had it succeeded this colony would have been under Scottish sovereignty, as would Nova Scotia, for which a charter was given to Sir William Alexander by James I and VI under the Great Seal of Scotland. This colony also was abortive; Nova Scotia was subsequently acquired under English auspices.

[6] From 1603 to 1707 Scotsmen had the rights of Englishmen as well in the colonies as in England itself. Opinion of Sir John Hawles, S.-G., quoted in Chalmers, *Political Annals of the United Colonies*, p. 259. But Scottish ports did not enjoy the benefit of the Navigation Acts.

[7] Professor R. W. Lee points out as an interesting parallel that in the Dutch East Indian Colonies (including South Africa) the law of the Province of Holland prevailed over the law of any other of the seven provinces of the Netherlands. Cf. Lee, *Introduction to Roman-Dutch Law* (3rd ed.), p. 9, n. 4.

Three exceptions to the rule concerning conquered and ceded colonies are not very clear. One is the special position of Oriental factories.[1] Another is the rule, which seems to be established by *Lindsay* v. *Oriental Bank*,[2] that where it is not definitely shown that an alien system of law applies, the application of the Common Law will be presumed by the Privy Council.[3] Further, *Ruding* v. *Smith*[4] establishes some sort of exception to the dictum in *Campbell* v. *Hall*[5] that 'the law and legislation of every dominion equally effects all persons and property within the limits'.[6]

It remains to discuss the extent to which, during the formative period of the general colonial law, English sovereignty was held to introduce of necessity English public law to colonies which retained other legal systems. By reason of the absence from the British constitution of formally 'entrenched' principles of government, only a small proportion—one might almost say the bare minimum—of English law is so imposed.[7] This minimum has been eloquently defined by Lord Stowell:[8]

> 'No small portion of the ancient law is unavoidably superseded, by the revolution of government that has taken place. The allegiance of the subjects, and all the law that relates to it—the administration of the law in the Sovereign, and appellate jurisdictions—and all the laws connected with the exercise of the sovereign authority—must undergo alterations adapted to the change.'

In the Middle Ages the ambit of jurisdiction was the ambit of law, and the King's law ruled where the King's writs ran. The privileges and subordinations of his realms inferior to England varied with no clear common measure. But here, as elsewhere, it is unnecessary to go into the medieval law because what was authoritative for subse-

[1] *The Indian Chief* (1800) 3 Rob. Adm. 22, 28, 31; *Lautour* v. *Teesdale* (1816) 8 Taunt. 830; *Advocate-General of Bengal* v. *Ranee Surnomoyee Dossee* (1863) 2 Moo. P.C. (N.S.) 59; *Papayanni* v. *Russian Steamship Co.* (1863) 2 Moo. P.C. (N.S.) 161.

[2] (1860) 13 Moo. P.C. 401.

[3] This was a curious case, inadequately reported, where one would have expected the Roman-Dutch law to be presumed. It is doubtful if the presumption of the common law would now be applied rigidly.

[4] (1821) 2 Hagg. Cons. 371.

[5] (1774) Lofft 655, 741.

[6] The felicity of Lord Stowell's style in *Ruding* v. *Smith* is only equalled by the ambiguity of its *ratio decidendi*. Probably the case is best treated, as it was in *Armitage* v. *Armitage* (1866) L. R. 3 Eq. 343, as deciding simply that, where compliance with the full local formalities of marriage is impossible, compliance with the formalities of the *lex domicilii* will suffice. On this view, the case decides nothing pertinent to Imperial law as such.

[7] For a striking instance, see *in re Adam* (1887) 1 Moo. P.C. 460.

[8] In *Ruding* v. *Smith* (1821) 2 Hagg. Cons. 371, 382.

quent ages was not the medieval law itself, but what Coke and his seventeenth-century successors, ingenuously or disingenuously, said it had been. Coke distinguished between the writs of private remedies and writs which served to maintain the royal power.[1] The latter alone ran to the Dominions. They included what are now called the prerogative writs[2] and the cognate writ of error, which was in effect a restricted form of appeal.[3] From the first, writs of error were not used for appeals from the colonies, because the administrative jurisdiction of the Privy Council gave an opportunity for a wider and more satisfactory form of appeal. But they and the prerogative writs continued to be available, in strict law, until well into the nineteenth century.[4]

The 'Government and superintendency of the Crown', in the sense in which Vaughan, C.J., spoke of it,[5] came in fact to be maintained, not by the courts of common law through the awkward process of these writs, but by the King's Council itself. At first no distinction was drawn between its administrative and its judicial functions in the supervision of the colonies,[6] but by the end of the seventeenth century they were fairly well separated, though exercised by the same body of persons. Regular reports of cases before the Privy Council were first published in 1829.[7] Despite the transference of the judicial functions from the whole Council to the Judicial Committee constituted by the Acts of 1833 and 1844,[8] this remarkable court retains to the present-day forms of procedure which are appropriate to an administrative rather than to a judicial body. The general case law of the British Empire is almost entirely the creation of the Privy Council.

[1] *Calvin's Case* (1608) 7 Co. Rep. 1*a*, 9*b*. Vaughan, C.J., quoting Coke, expounds him thus: 'More intelligibly it may be said, That Writs in order to the Particular Rights and Properties of the Subject (which he called *Brevia mandatoria remedialia*) . . . issue not to the Dominions that are no part of England, but belonging to it: For surely, as they have their particular Laws, so consequently they must have their particular Mandates or Writs in order to them. . . . *Brevia mandatoria, et non remedialia*, are Writs that concern not the particular Rights or Properties of the subject, but the Government and Superintendency of the King, *ne quid res publica capiat detrimenti*': *Process into Wales* (1674) Vaugh., 395, 400.

[2] Habeas corpus, mandamus, prohibition, and certiorari; together with some other miscellaneous writs now mostly obsolete.

[3] See the dictum of Vaughan, C.J., in *Process into Wales* (1674) Vaugh. 395, 402, quoted below, p. 556.

[4] After the decision of the Queen's Bench in *in re Anderson* (1861) 30 L.R. (Q.B.) 129 that the Queen's Bench had jurisdiction to grant habeas corpus to a colonial court, the jurisdiction to grant this writ was abolished by 25 & 26 Vict. c. 20. See further Safford and Wheeler, *Privy Council Practice*, p. 713, n. (*k*).

[5] Above, n. 1.

[6] See, e.g., *Clayborne's Case* (1638), reported in Chalmers, *Political Annals of the United Colonies*, p. 233.

[7] Knapp's Reports.

[8] 3 & 4 Will. 4, c. 41; 7 & 8 Vict. c. 69.

For the theoretical reason of its close association with the person of the sovereign, and for the same practical reasons which Vaughan, C.J., cites[1] as a ground for the extension of the prerogative writs to the colonies, the jurisdiction of the Privy Council was held to extend to every territory of which the King was sovereign. The present position of this jurisdiction is discussed below.[2]

The sovereignty of the King, wherever it went, was held to carry with it a uniform law of allegiance. Although the actual importance of the law of nationality lies in the differentiation of the status of nationals and non-nationals for numerous purposes of public and private law, allegiance is in sentiment and in theory a direct and reciprocal relationship of king and subject, and is often spoken of as constituting the moral or philosophical basis of all municipal law.[3] At least, that was the view of seventeenth-century theory, which treated the King's protection as the correlative of the subject's obedience.[4] Accordingly, it was the law of the Crown of England—the common law or Imperial statute—which determined in all parts of the Empire alike whether a man was or was not a British subject.[5] But the rights and liabilities attached to that status were, and are, a matter of local law.[6] There is nothing to prevent the local law from conferring upon an alien or a class of aliens rights identical, within the territory, with those of British subjects. Naturalization in a subordinate dominion amounts, in effect, to this.[7]

The jurisdiction of the Privy Council and the law of allegiance do not only differ from the general common law in that they are introduced equally into all colonies by the mere fact of British sovereignty, but also in that they are immune from alteration by local legislative organs unless these are specifically empowered to that end by the Imperial parliament. They therefore constitute, from the colonial point of view, a sort of Imperial fundamental law, which will, amongst other things, be discussed in the next section.[8]

[1] Below, p. 556.
[2] Section 2 (ii).
[3] 'Ligeantia . . . est quasi essentia legis': *Calvin's Case* (1608) 7 Co. Rep. 1*a*, 4*b*.
[4] Ibid., at 5*a*; *Dutton* v. *Howell* (1694) Show. Parl. Cas. 24, 32.
[5] *Donegani* v. *Donegani* (1835) 3 Knapp 63; *in re Adam* (1857) 1 Moo. P.C. 460.
[6] *Donegani* v. *Donegani*; *in re Adam*.
[7] Local naturalization is no new thing. The rule was established in *Craw* v. *Ramsey* (1669) Vaugh. 274, a case which concerned naturalization in Ireland before the Union. Though the grounds of the decision might not now be accepted, the result is good law. That is to say, the general powers of self-government which a modern Dominion has do not include the power to grant a British nationality which will be valid all over the Empire. This can be done only under the British Nationality and Status of Aliens Act 1914. Cf. *Markwald* v. *Attorney-General*, [1920] 1 Ch. 348.
[8] Section 2 (iii) of this chapter.

II

Unity in Commonwealth Law

The heading of this section is no more than a vague rubric to cover some inquiries, selected arbitrarily for their interest rather than for exhaustiveness, into certain general phenomena in Commonwealth law. It will appear—as has already been foreshadowed in the foregoing section—that of recent years the law of the Commonwealth has been a by-product or epiphenomenon of its politics. For this reason, although the relation of various kinds of legal unity to the political cohesion of the Commonwealth will be discussed, they will not be approached primarily as 'bonds of Empire'. It is not assumed that it is either desirable or undesirable that the Empire should have bonds, or even that, given the desirability of bonds in general, legal bonds should or should not figure among them. It will rather appear from the ensuing discussion that the law is now incapable of supplying significant bonds, that in the present state of the Commonwealth the degree of its unity in law has no organic relation to its political unity. A succeeding section will consider the other régimes, the other principles of order in Commonwealth affairs, which present themselves as alternatives to strict law. All that will here be shown is that legal unity of any sort is not now a goal to be striven for by imperialists as such. The topics discussed in this section are so grouped merely by reason of their common historical derivation from the system which has been described in the last section.

Apology is perhaps due for the extent to which these discussions trespass upon philosophy on the one hand and politics on the other. But the general law of the Commonwealth is not ordinary law. It lies rather on the periphery of municipal law, where it marches with politics, with 'constitutional convention', and with international law. Questions on the margin of a subject necessarily stir more extraneous issues than do points which lie comfortably in the centre of established doctrine; in such frontier regions to require self-sufficiency of legal scholarship is to ensure not its chastity but its sterility.

One more prefatory warning or exculpation must be made. A simple pragmatic view of the nature of law is assumed throughout: that that only is law which is declared and enforced by the courts, or will be declared and applied by the courts if occasion arises; where it is not applied, it is not law. This is not the place to justify that definition; indeed, it is not for all purposes a satisfactory definition of law. But it has for the present purpose at least this merit, that it is the implicit traditional theory of English law, though possibly not of British speculation.

1. *Formal Unity.*

Every community has a multiplicity of authorities issuing rules and orders, general and particular, which have the force of law. For both practical and theoretical reasons it is of primary importance that these rules and orders should not contradict each other: that is to say, that the citizen should not be placed in the position of having to obey requirements of the law which are inconsistent with each other. Only to the extent that provision is made for resolving apparent conflicts of this nature does an agglomeration of laws become a *system* of law.[1]

The resolution of such conflicts is effected, and consistently with the nature of law can only be effected, by inquiring of each purported rule of law: by what authority does it speak? From what source is its legal character, its quality of being law, derived? The answer will always take the form of a more general proposition of law which, from the point of view of validity, is logically prior to the rule examined, and from which the validity of the rule can accordingly be deduced. Behind the prior rule a still more general rule will be discoverable, and so on. The relative validity of conflicting rules will be determined when a prior rule is reached from which both derive their validity. Analysis need then go no farther. But theory allows and practice may require the pursuit of the analysis to a point at which a proposition is found which is ultimate in law—behind which stands no prior legal proposition, but whose validity depends on non-legal considerations.[2] Such a rule is called by Kelsen a *Grundnorm.*[3]

[1] *Rechtsordnung* (Kelsen). The whole of the preliminary analysis upon which this discussion of formal unity rests is derived from Kelsen. But the adoption of Kelsen's calculus of formal validity and of his Kantian *a priori* derivation of it must not be taken to commit the writer to Kelsen's estimate of the actual importance of the purely rational or formal element in law. See Kelsen: *Allgemeine Staatslehre* (1925), pp. 248–51.

[2] The nature of the non-legal considerations which are called upon to justify obedience to law as such by the theorist, by the conscientious citizen seeking a reason for his obedience to the State, or by the judge examining the postulates of his office vary infinitely, and include considerations of ethics, religion, political principle, tradition, and mere blind reflex loyalty. They are preponderantly inexplicit in legal systems of long standing like that of Great Britain, and explicit by comparison where conflicts between systems have rendered the acceptance of judicial office, and even of the duties of citizenship, something like a choice between real alternatives.

[3] 'Ground-norm', or 'foundation-norm'. A norm in Kelsen's sense is a proposition of the form '*A* is, therefore *B* ought to be', where *A* and *B* are situations of fact (*Tatbestände*).

The *Grundnorm* is the ground of the validity of the system which depends on it, and its supremacy constitutes the assurance that there will be no conflict within that system. It may therefore be said to embody and express the formal unity of the system. From the point of view of their form, of their validity, all other rules in the system are particularizations of the *Grundnorm*.

It is usual in English constitutional writings, whose tacit jurisprudence is Austin's theory of law as command, to find the ultimate formal source of law in a dynamic authority, the 'sovereign', rather than in a static principle, the *Grundnorm*. A *Grundnorm* in the simple form *quod principi placuit legis habet vigorem*, that is to say, a *Grundnorm* prescribing simply that the sovereign is the sole source of authority, and identifying him, is *prima facie* conceivable, and may even have existed in some system of law. It would seem accordingly that Austinian sovereignty might be a legitimate special case under Kelsen's general theory of the *Grundnorm*.[1] But modern criticism makes it doubtful whether even the British constitution is exactly that special case. Where the purported sovereign is any one but a single actual person,[2] the designation of him must include the statement of rules for the ascertainment of his will,[3] and these rules, since their observance is a condition of the validity of his legislation, are rules of law logically prior to him.[4] Further, the mere assertion of the omnipotence of a sovereign leaves completely uncertain the fundamental question whether or not he can bind himself; but the addition of a ruling in either sense on this point makes the basic rule of the system something more than a mere designation of the sovereign. Thus even the theoretic possibility of sovereignty as a *Grundnorm* is questionable. But however that may be, and however happy the Austinian theory may be in its application to the British constitution, it manifestly breaks down when applied to a constitu-

[1] Professor C. A. W. Manning in his essay on Austin almost asserts this: *Modern Theories of Law* (Oxford University Press, 1933), pp. 192 sqq.

The word is cumbrous, but has no exact short equivalent in English; the nearest is 'basic rule'. Hereinafter the word *Grundnorm* will only be used where it is necessary to insist on the fact, expounded above, that the fundamental thing in a system of law is a *proposition*. Elsewhere it will be more seemly to speak of the 'root' of a system of law—an expression for which the writer is indebted to Meredith, J., in *Cahill* v. *Attorney-General*, quoted below, p. 536.

[2] Whether a body unincorporate, a corporation aggregate, or even a corporation sole. Where the succession to even the rankest despot is disputed, questions of fundamental law arise.

[3] Thus, the King, Lords, and Commons meeting in a single joint assembly, and voting by majority, or even unanimously, could not enact a statute.

[4] On this and the next point see *Attorney-General of New South Wales* v. *Trethowan*, [1932] A.C. 526; and Jennings, *The Law and the Constitution*, ch. iv.

tion where either a partition of powers between different authorities or fundamental guarantees are 'entrenched' behind a procedure of amendment more difficult than the process of ordinary legislation.[1] Here the *Grundnorm*, whether or not it coincides with the written constitution, is clearly prior and superior to the legislature and is daily so treated by the courts. The theory of the *Grundnorm*, then, provides a general scheme or calculus of the formal validity of law, a scheme, moreover, which follows inevitably from the nature of law itself. The theory of the sovereign, at best, provides neither. It is, however, approximately true for countries with unitary constitutions, and in general the language of the approximate theory is readily translatable into the language of the true theory. So in the next page or two the reader who boggles at exotic analysis will not err greatly if he understands identity and difference of *Grundnorm* as referring to identity and difference of sovereign.

That a system of law should have a *Grundnorm* is, as we have seen, implicit in the nature of law. But in practice this means merely that the existence of *some* single common *Grundnorm* is assumed whenever a body of law is treated as a coherent system, not that in order that any law shall be valid it must be shown that a *Grundnorm* has been explicitly formulated and that the law is derived from it. Where the constitution is written and law is codified, the *Grundnorm* may be explicit from the beginning. But in the English system of case-law fundamental principles are not stated, and the judicial process is not purely deductive. The data of the law are *rationes decidendi* of previously decided cases, which stand midway between the generality of the broader provisions of a code and the utter particularity of decisions 'on the facts'. Principles more general than existing *rationes decidendi* are ascertained, ostensibly by the process which logicians call induction, as and when they are required to explain existing decisions and to deal with situations not covered by existing authority. Once so ascertained, a principle becomes the *ratio decidendi* of the case in which it is ascertained and is established as an authority for future cases. Clearly in such a system there is no certainty that the most fundamental principle, the *Grundnorm*, will be reached and declared by the courts. It may be that no case will arise which necessitates resort to the ultimate rule. Yet at any time such a case may arise, for by definition the *Grundnorm* is a rule of law, and, also by

[1] Where there is only a partition of powers, the *Grundnorm* is complex, but still purely formal. Where there are constitutional guarantees, the *Grundnorm* is substantial as well as formal: it determines not only the validity but also some of the content of the rules of law below.

definition, since it is a rule of law, it must be capable of declaration and application by the courts.

In fact, such judicial induction is by no means pure;[1] indeed, it is naturally even more impure than judicial deduction is now universally conceded to be.[2] In both processes the general outlook of the judge is a powerful tacit major premise. This is particularly true in a field as little tilled by judicial decision as the ultimate constitutional theory of the Common Law. That this field is unexplored in England may be seen from the striking fact that Dicey was unable to cite a single decided case as authority for his classic exposition of the sovereignty of Parliament.[3] The courts entrusted with judicial review of legislation in the federal Dominions have to venture farther into the abstract and general, but still contrive to pitch their *rationes decidendi* fairly low.[4] Even so, the influence of their judges' general philosophies stands out more strongly in high constitutional decisions than in decisions on ordinary private law.[5] If this tendency is so marked at the penultimate degree, it is to be expected that decisions on the ultimate question, decisions defining the *Grundnorm*, will reflect still more strongly the basic beliefs of the judges themselves. It may then be said, and not in any cynical way, that the *Grundnorm* of a case-law system is simply the sum of those principles which command the ultimate allegiance of the courts. This loose definition opens up possibilities of indeterminacy of *Grundnorm* and of shifting of *Grundnorm* which will be illustrated in the next few pages.

Our purpose is to ascertain the extent to which there is formal unity in Commonwealth law. To this end it is fortunately not necessary to attempt to state the British or any other *Grundnorm*,[6] but only to discover whether all or any of the members of the Commonwealth share a common *Grundnorm*, whatever its terms may be. The

[1] If, indeed, any induction is pure, which logicians doubt.

[2] If their logic were pure, judges could not exercise their salutary function of creating case law.

[3] Dicey, *Law of the Constitution*, ch. i.

[4] *Trethowan's Case*, already cited, is an instance where the diffidence of the Privy Council amounted to timidity. The Board avoided a fundamental issue, squarely raised, by a decision 'on the words of the Statute'.

[5] The judgments of Isaacs and Higgins, JJ., on the Australian Constitution are a notable instance. Isaacs, J., was in the habit of stating with unusual fullness the considerations which influenced him.

[6] The limits within which the British *Grundnorm* must lie are, however, clear. It must assign supremacy in some sense to Parliament, and recognize, subject to that supremacy, the Common Laws of England and Scotland and the Prerogative. The only point outstanding is the extent to which Parliament may bind itself, as to which see above, p. 523, and Jennings, loc. cit.

fact that the *Grundnormen* we seek may be—and, as we shall discover, are—inexplicit hinders our task, but does not frustrate it. But first it is convenient to eliminate two possible sources of misunderstanding. In the first place, though the fact that the appellate jurisdiction of the Privy Council extends to a Dominion assists the maintenance of formal unity, it is not conclusive in its favour.[1] In the second place, the fact that the Imperial Parliament retains recognized legislative functions in relation to a Dominion, such as the amendment of the British North America Act,[2] may be consistent with a difference of *Grundnorm*. For already, in constitutional convention, the Imperial Parliament exercises these powers not on its own behalf, but as the mere agent of the Dominion. It is not at all impossible that the law of a Dominion should come to regard the Imperial Parliament's legislative power within the borders of the Dominion as now derivative—delegated by tolerance, if not expressly[3]—if only it can explain how its former supremacy was terminated.

Formal unity of law clearly exists between England, Scotland, and Northern Ireland, despite the partial bifurcation in legislative authority between Great Britain and Northern Ireland and the partial severance of Scots private law from that of the rest of the United Kingdom. The law of the dependent Empire of the United Kingdom, with the curious exception of the Indian States and certain other subordinate monarchies, clearly shares the same root. Newfoundland and New Zealand, Dominions which have never been strongly nationalist, have always looked to the United Kingdom for the formal source of their law.[4] Australia does likewise, not from lack of nationalism, but because Australian nationalism has always been interested rather in the substance than in the trappings and formal guarantees of independence.[5] If, however, Australia should at any time want to sever her law from the Imperial root, the nature of her federal system would create serious difficulties. Since the constitutions of the Com-

[1] For the relation of jurisdictional unity to formal unity, see below, pp. 543–5.

[2] And, *a fortiori*, the power of the Imperial Parliament to legislate for a Dominion with its request and consent, under s. 4 of the Statute of Westminster.

[3] This view was taken, prematurely perhaps, by Mr. Schlosberg in 1927: H. J. Schlosberg, *The King's Republics* (Stevens, 1927), pp. 21, 57, 68.

[4] Newfoundland was in 1933, at the request of her Government and Parliament, deprived of her self-governing constitution and put under a Commission, by Act of the Imperial Parliament: 24 & 25 Geo. V, c. 2. This is her present status.

[5] The reluctance with which an eminent Australian lawyer finds himself forced to realize that the Imperial *Grundnorm* is anywhere questioned as the root of Dominion law may be seen in Mr. Justice Dixon's address in 10 *Aust. Law Journ., Supp.* 96. See also the Commonwealth Attorney-General, ibid., p. 108.

monwealth and the States are not contained in a single instrument, but in so many separate Acts of the Imperial Parliament, there is no measure within Australia of the mutual status of the parties to Federation. Accordingly, if the Imperial Parliament ceased to be looked to as the original source of law, there would have to be a novation of the federal compact, a new fundamental agreement between Commonwealth and States.[1] But the situation is most unlikely to occur.

Despite the more meticulous temper of Canadian nationalism, it does not seek to deny history by repudiating the Imperial root of Canadian law.[2] Dissatisfaction with the legal status of Canada takes less high ground, and attacks the Privy Council appeal and the role of the Imperial Parliament in amending the Canadian constitution. As has been suggested above, these bonds, even while they continue, are not an insuperable obstacle to a breach of formal unity, but they are a serious discouragement. But if Canada does ever desire to establish a local root for her law, her federal system will offer no obstacles comparable to those in Australia, since the British North America Act is the constitution alike of the Dominion and of the Provinces.[3]

It is impossible to understand the constitutional policy of South Africa without reference to political conditions. South African nationalism is strong, developed, and legalistic, but not fanatical.[4] The peculiar objective of moderate South African nationalists has been the 'right of secession'. Like all legal or pseudo-legal terms which become the ammunition of political controversy, this phrase has been misused. It is in any case permissible to doubt whether the formula was ever a happy one to express the real desire of those

[1] The difficulties experienced in adapting the emancipatory provisions of the Statute of Westminster to Australia spring from the same source. The adaptation has been very imperfectly done, and will cause difficulties when the Statute is adopted by Australia. See W. A. Wynes, *Legislative and Executive Powers in Australia* (Law Book Co. of Australia, 1936), pp. 73–87.

[2] But for a suggestion by a Canadian scholar that in deciding *British Coal Corporation* v. *R.*, [1935] A.C. 500, the Judicial Committee of the Privy Council should have treated the Report of the Imperial Conference of 1926 as a first source of Canadian sovereign status in law, see Dean V. C. Macdonald in 13 Can. Bar Rev. 625. Compare this view with the South African developments discussed below.

[3] Dr. Maurice Ollivier, however, has suggested that Canada should assert her formal independence by enacting an amended Constitution in advance of imperial legislation approving thereof: *L'Avenir Constitutionnel du Canada* (Montreal, 1935), p. 150.

[4] 'The Afrikaner's forbears were Dutchmen, a people great in law and polemical theology, French Huguenots, of all men most logical, and West Germans, a highly schematic folk' (*Round Table*, vol. xviii, p. 651).

who used it. What the majority of them desired was rather freedom to secede if they should so wish—a purely political objective.

More precisely, the substance of their demand was for assurance that if the white South African nation should unequivocally declare its intention to secede from the Commonwealth, no compulsive or punitive action would in fact be taken by any other member of the Commonwealth, in the name of the law or otherwise, to frustrate the translation of that intention into fact. Without such freedom in fact, a legal right of secession would be useless. This freedom once assured, there was little that the establishment of the legal right could add. Yet there were two ways in which the legal right might buttress the political freedom. In the first place, it is conceivable, though not likely, that, if all other influences left the issue in the balance, Great Britain's decision whether to intervene actively might be determined by the British Government's view of the legality of secession.[1] In the second place—and this is a matter of importance among a people as law-abiding as most South African citizens are—it would hinder a movement for actual secession at all its stages, and might lead to some citizens withholding their loyalty from the Union after it was accomplished, if it could be said that secession was in the strict law of South Africa illegal.[2] If, on the other hand, secession were legal, the stigma of revolution would attach not to the secessionists but to those who refused to accept secession. Those nationalists who consciously intended in claiming the right of secession to claim something more than freedom to secede must be supposed to have had these considerations in mind.

Until their fusion in 1934 there was a line of cleavage between the two principal parties on 'the Imperial issue'. The Nationalist Party held, before 1926, that the right of secession did not exist, and ought to be established. After 1926, General Hertzog, its leader, held that the right of secession had been acquired at the Imperial Conference, while other members of the party thought that it was not yet secure. The South African Party, led by General Smuts, considered it not worth seeking, thinking that South Africa would best secure her substantial freedom by adhering firmly to the British Commonwealth. General Smuts differed from General Hertzog over the effect of the resolutions of the 1926 Imperial Conference, holding

[1] The point is of course unreal. At no time since the Great War has there been any possibility that Great Britain would actively oppose South African secession. But we are here seeking to find a meaning for the views of those who thought that there was such a possibility.

[2] It is probably no less true that the knowledge that secession is legal is likely to rob of its zest any movement for secession. But this does not affect the argument.

that they did not confer a right of secession in law. With the situation, so understood, his party was content. The enactment of the Statute of Westminster in 1931 made no difference in these alignments beyond increasing the confidence of the Nationalist Party in its view.

In 1933, however, the Nationalist and South African Parties made a coalition, which was followed in 1934 by fusion. The basis of the coalition, so far as constitutional policy was concerned, was an agreement that membership of the British Commonwealth should be accepted without reserve (which meant that actual secession would no longer be contemplated), but that South Africa should be shown unequivocally to have, within the Commonwealth, full freedom, formal as well as substantial (which implied, though they may not have admitted it in public, abandonment by South African party coalitionists of their opposition to the establishment of the formal right of secession). The Union Government was thus in effect commissioned to remove all vestiges of formal subordination of South Africa to the United Kingdom, subject to two overriding considerations: that the institutions to which Commonwealth sentiment properly attached (that is, in effect, the Crown) should not be attacked, and that good relations with the United Kingdom should not be even slightly disturbed.

The existing situation was not satisfactory by these standards. Apart altogether from minor provisions of the South Africa Act implying subordination, and the major question of the 'entrenched clauses',[1] the central issue of the right of secession was still outstanding. The Statute of Westminster, standing alone, was open to a construction which would make secession legal,[2] but it could not

[1] All these points have been 'cleaned up' by amendments of the South Africa Act by the Union Parliament. The 'entrenched clauses' have been removed from the fundamental law of the Union and converted into a solemn international obligation of good faith.

[2] There is, it is submitted with respect, no substance in Professor Keith's contention (*The King and the Imperial Crown* (Longmans, 1936), p. 449) that the preamble to the Statute of Westminster has the effect of rendering secession conventionally impossible. No preamble is an enactment of law. This exceptional preamble is a declaration of convention. There are no established canons of interpretation of declarations of constitutional convention. But since such a declaration derives any force it has from the *consensus* of the parties, it must be legitimate to look, in construing it, at the intention of the parties. It is notorious that two at least of the Dominions who in 1930 consented to the draft of this preamble did not regard it as establishing a convention prohibiting secession, and would not have consented to it in that sense. The South Africans actually declared that the right of secession was not to be taken to be prejudiced, and the declaration was noted by the Imperial Conference. In any case, would a law terminating the allegiance of a Dominion to the Throne be a law 'touching the Succession to the Throne'? In the first place, the Throne, in convention as in law, is a single throne. Its existence as a throne and the

be contended that it unequivocally did so. Yet a request for a further emancipatory Imperial statute so soon after the Statute of Westminster would not have been well received in the United Kingdom. But in any case there was this further difficulty, that established constitutional doctrine held that it was in strict law impossible for the Imperial Parliament to put it beyond its own power to repeal any of its own Acts.[1] Any measure of emancipation at the hands of the Imperial Parliament would therefore suffer from the vital flaw that it was revocable at the Imperial Parliament's pleasure. According to established theory, nothing that Westminster could do would remove this taint from its gifts. In other words, the revocability in strict law of Dominion emancipation seemed to be ineradicable so long as South African law adhered to its Imperial root. Accordingly, South African law had to be detached from its Imperial root without offending Great Britain. Escape from this dilemma demanded both courage and tact. Neither were wanting, and a delicate and radical stratagem was found, of whose success it is still too early to judge.

There has been in South Africa since 1926 a legal heresy which may be called the nationalist theory of status. This theory in the first place took a very wide view of the Balfour Report, regarding it as establishing or recognizing the complete independence of the Dominions within the Commonwealth—as was legitimate and, in the event, correct. The heresy consisted in treating the terms of the Report, thus construed, as themselves valid in constitutional law. It was clearly authoritative in constitutional convention, and it is arguable that it affected international law.[2] But convention, by definition, leaves the law intact; and British law, which on this point is also the law of the Dominions,[3] does not allow international law to intrude into municipal law unless expressly adopted.[4] Responsible scholars, including those of nationalist views in politics, did not adopt this obviously untenable view.[5] If such a fundamental change in the law of South Africa had occurred, it would hardly have passed unnoticed by either the legislature or the courts. A cognate but lesser

rules of succession to it are unaffected by the number of realms that owe it allegiance. In the second place, would even the abolition of all allegiance to the Throne be a change in the law relating to the succession to it?

[1] Dicey, *Law of the Constitution*, ch. i; for criticism see Jennings, *The Law and the Constitution*, ch. iv, and above, p. 525.

[2] On the effect of the Balfour Report upon the status of the Dominions in international law see P. J. Noel Baker, *The Juridical Status of the British Dominions in International Law*, ch. v, pp. 130 sqq.

[3] Except possibly the Irish Free State.

[4] *West Rand Central Gold Mining Co.* v. *R.*, [1905] 2 K.B. 391.

[5] e.g. Schlosberg, *The King's Republics*, ch. ix.

heresy is that the Statute of Westminster translated the constitutional declarations of 1926 *en masse* into law.

In 1934 the Union Parliament enacted the Status of the Union Act 1934,[1] the preamble whereof runs as follows in the English text:

> WHEREAS the delegates of His Majesty's Governments in the United Kingdom, the Dominion of Canada, the Commonwealth of Australia, the Dominion of New Zealand, the Union of South Africa, the Irish Free State and Newfoundland, at Imperial Conferences holden at Westminster in the years of our Lord 1926 and 1930, did concur in making the declarations and resolutions set forth in the Reports of the said Conferences, and more particularly in defining the group of self-governing communities composed of Great Britain and the Dominions as 'autonomous communities within the British Empire, equal in status, in no way subordinate one to another in any aspect of their domestic or external affairs, though united by a common allegiance to the Crown and freely associated as members of the British Commonwealth of Nations';
>
> And whereas the said resolutions and declarations in so far as they required legislative sanction on the part of the United Kingdom have been ratified, confirmed and established by the Parliament of the United Kingdom in an Act entitled the Statute of Westminster, 1931 (22 Geo. V, c. 4);
>
> And whereas it is expedient that the status of South Africa as a sovereign independent state as hereinbefore defined shall be adopted and declared by the Parliament of the Union and that the South Africa Act 1909 (9 Edw. VII, c. 9) be amended accordingly;
>
> And whereas it is expedient that the said Statute of Westminster, in so far as its provisions are applicable to the Union of South Africa, and an Afrikaans version thereof, shall be adopted as an Act of Parliament of the Union of South Africa;

Section 2 reads:

> The Parliament of the Union shall be the sovereign legislative power in and over the Union, and notwithstanding anything in any other law contained, no Act of the Parliament of the United Kingdom and Northern Ireland [*sic*] passed after the eleventh day of December, 1931, shall extend, or be deemed to extend, to the Union as part of the law of the Union, unless extended thereto by an Act of the Parliament of the Union.

Section 3 provides that the sections of the Statute of Westminster applying to the Union[2] (and its preamble) 'shall be deemed to be an

[1] No. 69 of 1934. Printed in Kennedy and Schlosberg, *The Law and Custom of the South African Constitution*, p. 614.

[2] Sections 1, 2, 3, 4, 5, 6, 11, and 12.

Act of the Parliament of the Union, and shall be construed accordingly'.[1]

In the preamble (whose force is, of course, only expository, not legal) there is one clear error of statement, the second recital. The Statute of Westminster did not ratify, confirm, and establish *all* the resolutions and declarations set forth in the reports of the 1926 and 1930 Conferences in so far as they required legislation by the Imperial Parliament, but only *certain* of them, as the preamble to the Statute itself accurately recites.[2] The recital in the Act follows the minor heresy mentioned above. Otherwise, the preamble is unexceptionable. Indeed, it is quite unusually unexceptionable, for it is equally consistent with the orthodox view of the law and with the major heresy. Even the striking declaration that South Africa is a 'sovereign independent state' has the disarming qualification 'as hereinbefore defined', a reference to the sentence quoted from the Balfour Memorandum.

It may even be doubted whether the first clause of section 2, which is generally regarded in orthodox circles as going beyond the Statute of Westminster,[3] necessarily does so. Of course, the establishment of a sovereign coequal with the Imperial Parliament is clearly neither achieved nor authorized by the Statute of Westminster. But the equation of sovereign independence with 1926 Dominion status in the preamble, coupled with the provision now to be found in section 1 of the South Africa Act[4] that 'the people of the Union humbly acknowledge the sovereignty of Almighty God', strongly suggest that in South Africa sovereignty is less a term of art than a complimentary expression.[5] The second part of the section, however, does go beyond the restriction of the power of the Imperial Parliament effected by section 4 of the Statute of Westminster[6] in requiring subsequent extension of an Imperial Act to the Union by the Union Parliament as well as prior request and consent by the Union Government.

[1] The remaining sections of the Act, though important, do not touch the issues here discussed.

[2] The preamble to the statute is printed in the Schedule to the Act. (This does not appear from Kennedy and Schlosberg's reprint.) Thus the Act contradicts itself upon its face.

[3] e.g. Professor A. B. Keith, in 16 *Journ. Comp. Leg.* 290.

[4] Inserted by the South Africa Act Amendment Act, No. 9 of 1925.

[5] Compare the dissenting judgment of Kennedy C.J. in *State* (*Ryan*) v. *Lennon*, [1935] I. R. 170, 204–5 (below, p. 538, n. 7) where legal effect is attributed to a similar acknowledgement.

[6] 'No Act of Parliament of the United Kingdom passed after the commencement of this Act shall extend, or be deemed to extend, to a Dominion as part of the law of that Dominion, unless it is expressly declared in that Act that that Dominion has requested, and consented to, the enactment thereof.'

To the extent to which the Act does go beyond the Statute, whether in its enactment of sovereign independence or in its restriction of the legislative authority of the Imperial Parliament, it is, of course, from the orthodox point of view, invalid. But from the orthodox point of view the remarkable feature of the Act is not that one or two of its provisions may be slightly *ultra vires*, but that some parts of it are utterly otiose, serving no conceivable purpose. Why does the preamble declare it 'expedient' that the status of South Africa, already (according to its own recital) established in law by the Statute of Westminster, should be 'adopted and declared' over again by the Union Parliament, and that the Statute should be re-enacted in the Union? What meaning can attach to section 3 of the Act? If the Statute is law in the Union, it is law, and no amount of repetition will make it more so.

But the legislature of a nation of jurists cannot have intended such elaborate futility. Consideration of the political background supplies a clue: construed by the canons, not of orthodoxy, but of either of the heresies above mentioned, the otiose provisions become significant. The Act must have been intended to be construed by these canons. Without offending against imperial theory, or offending as little as possible, it nevertheless proceeds on the assumption that not the imperial, but the nationalist theory is true. It only requires the re-enactment of the South Africa Act by the Union Parliament (odd imperial references have already been cleared out of its text),[1] and there will be no need to look beyond the Union statute-book for the whole of the written constitutional law of the Union.[2] The Status of the Union Act is an invitation to the South African courts to assert a local root for South African law and jurisdiction in place of the Imperial one.

Will the courts comply? No case since the Act has raised issues which compel a choice of *Grundnorm*, and until South African and British legislation clearly conflict on a practical point, the issue will not arise.[3] But if it should arise in the near future, it is difficult to

[1] By sections 5, 6, 7, 8, 9, 11 of the Status of the Union Act.

[2] Except the appeal by special leave to the Privy Council.

[3] Since this was written, His Majesty King Edward VIII's Declaration of Abdication Bill has been introduced into the Union parliament (January 1937). This bill assumes (and, for South Africa, authoritatively declares) a different view of the law concerning the abdication of a monarch than that taken by the Law Officers in the United Kingdom and implied in His Majesty's Declaration of Abdication Act, 1936, of the United Kingdom Parliament. But the South African Bill has indemnity clauses retrospectively validating acts done in the Union on either view of the law. It amounts, therefore, to another legislative assertion of the separateness of the South African from the Imperial legal system, but stops short of submitting the matter to the arbitrament of the courts.

predict what answer the courts will give. They are not the blind servants of the legislature; they are the servants of the law.[1] It is true that, as the authors of the leading text-book point out,[2] the South Africa Act does not 'vest' the judicial power in them, as the Australian Commonwealth Constitution does in its courts. But neither does the British North America Act in the Canadian courts, yet they exercise the power of judicial review.[3] The South African courts may well feel it their duty to maintain the Imperial *Grundnorm*, either by construing the Status of the Union Act narrowly or by holding some of it invalid. On the other hand, public opinion, the wish of the legislature, and local loyalty will tell in the opposite direction. The legislature might indirectly assist that tendency by requiring an oath of unequivocal local allegiance from newly appointed judges.[4]

The separate South African *Grundnorm*, if it comes to be established, may look to the Balfour Report or merely to the Status of the Union Act for the root of title of South African law. Or it may set up a fiction that the Statute of Westminster was a complete and irrevocable abdication of the power of the Imperial Parliament. In any case, it will do violence to law or to history, probably to both. But it may well be politically fortunate. There is much to be said for stealth and subtlety as methods of revolution,[5] if revolution there must be.

In Ireland we find for the first time an interest in the formal derivation of law for its own sake. The comparatively sophisticated utterances of intellectual revolutionaries[6] demand not merely freedom, but freedom springing from an Irish source, and the factious populace expresses the same thought when it paints on the walls of Dublin 'Damn your concessions, England!' The *Grundnorm* has

[1] Dr. van Themaat, in 53 *S.A.L.J.* 50, surely goes too far in assuming that the South African courts are 'subjected' (*onderworpe*) to the Union Parliament. For his general view see 15 *Journ. Comp. Leg.* 47.

[2] Kennedy and Schlosberg, *Law and Custom of the South African Constitution*, p. 87.

[3] For a suggestive discussion of the rivalry between the principle of parliamentary sovereignty and the principle of the supremacy of the law, see Mr. Justice Dixon in 51 *L.Q.R.* 590.

[4] The oath required of members of Parliament by s. 51 of the South Africa Act as amended by s. 7 of the Status of the Union Act is equivocal between imperial and local allegiance.

[5] Establishment of a separate *Grundnorm* in any of these senses would enable legislation for secession to be validly passed. There would remain the practical problem of securing the consent of the King as a member of the legislature. This problem is dealt with by s. 4 of the *Status of the Union Act* and by the *Royal Executive Functions and Seals Act* 1934 (No. 70 of 1934). See below, p. 590.

[6] e.g. T. MacSwiney, *Principles of Freedom* (Dublin, 1921), ch. xvii.

descended into the market-place. The abortive proclamation of Easter 1916 did not demand any alteration of British law. It repudiated it entirely, asserting in its stead native Irish right,[1] and it was on the basis of this proclamation that the rebels fought, off and on, until the truce of 1921.[2]

The treaty settlement of 1921–2 was a compromise which simultaneously satisfied the British Government that the twenty-six counties were receiving their freedom at the hands of the Imperial Parliament, and satisfied the majority of the rebels that they had won it for themselves. In the negotiations each side gave up something. The Irish representatives did not, as they would have liked, claim retrospective recognition in the new Constitution of the authority of the revolutionary Dáils, but contented themselves with making ratification by the existing Dáil under another name a condition precedent to the operation of the Constitution. The British delegates, satisfied on pure doctrinal grounds that the authority of the new Free State could have no derivation but from the Imperial Parliament, did not insist upon explicit recognition of this, and allowed the dangerous Article 2 to go into the Constitution.[3]

Controversy concerning the circumstances and meaning of the Treaty Settlement is endless and absorbing. Some account of it is given above.[4] From the lawyer's point of view, however, it is wholly inconclusive. We shall, therefore, in the best English and Irish tradition, confine this discussion to decided cases.

Until 1924 the judicial system operating in Southern Ireland under the Government of Ireland Act, 1920,[5] served, by virtue of Article 75 of the Constitution, as the judicial system of the Free State.[6] Upon the establishment of the Free State the judges of the existing courts

[1] 'We declare the right of the people of Ireland to the Ownership of Ireland, and to the unfettered control of Irish destinies, to be sovereign and indefeasible. The long usurpation of that right by a foreign power and government has not extinguished the right, nor can it ever be extinguished except by the destruction of the people.'

[2] See above, Chapter III, section iii.

[3] 'All powers of government and all authority legislative, executive, and judicial in Ireland, are derived from the people of Ireland and the same shall be exercised in the Irish Free State (Saorstát Éireann) through the organizations established by or under, and in accord with, this Constitution.'

[4] Chapter III, section iii. See Pakenham, *Peace by Ordeal*, and Mansergh, *The Irish Free State; its Government and Politics*. For an analytical jurist's view, Kohn, *The Constitution of the Irish Free State*, ch. vi.

[5] Except the Court of Appeal for All Ireland.

[6] The form of Art. 75 (like Art. 73, which continued the existing general law until amended) was not a saving of the existing situation so that it continued *suo proprio vigore*, but an adoption of the *de facto* situation existing at the time of coming into force of the Constitution, without reference to its origins: *R.* (*Armstrong*) v. *County Court Judge of Wicklow*, [1924] 2 I.R. 139.

were continued in office without reappointment, but judges of superior courts were given an opportunity of resigning. The majority did not resign. Accordingly for the first two years of the Free State the courts consisted preponderantly of men who had personally accepted the British allegiance during the Troubles. Naturally in the circumstances, these courts were chary of pronouncing authoritatively upon the fundamentals of the Free State Constitution; and in fact there was no case where the question of the ultimate formal source of Free State law came up clearly for decision. There are some equivocal *obiter dicta* of which the most that can be said is that they do not preclude the idea that the Treaty, the Constitution, and the Constituent Act, or some or one of them, may amount to a constitutional novation.[1] One point, however, was clearly decided: the acts of the first Dáil and its instrumentalities are, from the Free State point of view, not only void but illegal.[2] There is no constitutional continuity between the revolutionary Dáils and the Free State.[3]

The majority of the members of the permanent judicature constituted in 1924[4] were newly appointed.[5] A new confidence, and a willingness to pronounce upon ultimate questions even when they were not strictly in issue, were immediately apparent. Thus Meredith, J., in 1925 said that the 'Constitution must be recognized by the Courts as an original source of jurisdiction, and, as regards the whole code of law to be applied, it is the one and only root of title'.[6] A *dictum* of Kennedy, C.J., (with which, however, the rest of the Court did not associate itself) in *in re Reade*[7] suggests that in his view the Treaty rather than the Constitution is the beginning of the Free State; but it seems not to be intended to cover more than the question of valid state succession, which does not necessarily amount to constitutional

[1] *R.* (*Childers*) v. *Adjutant General*, [1923] 1 I.R. 5, 14 (on the Provisional Government of 1922); *R.* (*O'Connell*) v. *Military Governor*, [1924] 2 I.R. 104; *R.* (*Armstrong*) v. *County Court Judge of Wicklow*, [1924] 2 I.R. 139, 144, 146, 151, 153.

[2] *R.* (*Kelly*) v. *Maguire and O'Sheil*, [1923] 2 I.R. 58.

[3] The Dáil Courts and Instrumentalities Winding-Up Act, 1923, provided for the appointment of a Commissioner with a wide discretion to settle questions arising out of the jurisdiction of the former Dáil courts. The tendency of the Act was to save their judgements as far as possible. But though it treats them tenderly, it is clear that any force they may continue to have is *conferred*, not merely *recognized*, by the Act.

[4] Under the Courts of Justice Act, No. 10 of 1924. Mr. Justice Hanna writes of the new judicial system: 'It effectively secures the complete disruption of the system of British Courts in the Saorstát.' (*The Statutes of the Irish Free State, 1922 to 1928*, p. 18.) It is difficult to see what this can mean, beyond the mere fact that the existing Acts were repealed, for the new system is British in all respects except the method and extent of its decentralization.

[5] Two judges from the former courts were appointed to the new courts; there were seven new appointments.

[6] *Cahill* v. *Attorney-General*, [1925] 1 I.R. 70.

[7] [1927] I.R. 31, 49.

continuity.[1] Subsequent dicta of the Chief Justice confirm this view; thus, in *Lynam* v. *Butler* (*No. 2*)[2] he refers to 'the Constitution, the Bunreacht, or fundamental structure upon which the State was set by the Dáil sitting as a Constituent Assembly', a description which he repeats in his dissenting judgment in the great case of *State* (*Ryan*) v. *Lennon*.[3] In the latter case Fitzgibbon, J., one of the majority in the Supreme Court, quoted with assent counsel's proposition that 'the Constituent Assembly proclaimed the Constitution by virtue of its own supreme legislative authority'.[4]

A tendency to stress the element of popular sovereignty is exemplified by an *obiter dictum* of Hanna, J., in *Carolan* v. *Minister of Defence*,[5] that Article 2[6] 'established in law, not for the Saorstát alone, but for Ireland, and in no metaphorical sense, the sovereignty of the people of Ireland'.[7] In so far as this theory involves a presumption in favour of the rigidity of the Constitution, it is decisively rejected in *State* (*Ryan*) v. *Lennon*.[8] Meredith, J., in the High Court, is explicit on this point:

> 'The Constitution itself is the exclusive source from which this Court can derive any principle of law on the strength of which it has jurisdiction to declare any law to be invalid. Of course, to determine whether any law contravenes the Constitution the Court has to analyse what is contained in that law and what is contained in the Constitution, and then to determine whether the law is consistent with the Constitution; and this reasoning may, and indeed must, follow principles of construction. But these principles are not principles of law constituting part of the subject matter of the comparison involved in the question whether a law is consistent with the Constitution. So it is true to say that there are no principles of law in relation to which the validity of any law is to be tested except those enshrined in the Constitution. Our common law does not contain any principles of constitutional law, and Article 73

[1] In *Fogarty* v. *O'Donoghue*, [1926] I.R. 531 it was held by the Supreme Court that the Free State was equally entitled to the funds of the Republican Dáil whether by continuity of title or by mere *de facto* succession. It was accordingly unnecessary to decide by which right it held.

[2] [1933] I.R. 74, 94–5.

[3] [1935] I.R. 170, 203.

[4] [1935] I.R. 170, 225.

[5] [1927] I.R. 62, 70.

[6] 'Subject to this Constitution and to the extent to which they are not inconsistent therewith, the laws in force in the Irish Free State (Saorstát Éireann) at the date of the coming into operation of this Constitution shall continue to be of full force and effect until the same or any of them shall have been repealed or amended by enactment of the Oireachtas.'

[7] If this 'sovereignty of the people' is recognized as the ground of the validity of the power of the Third Dáil and therefore of the Constituent Act, it is relevant to the *Grundnorm*, and Article 2 is merely declaratory. If, on the other hand, it is merely enacted by Article 2 for the first time, it is irrelevant to the *Grundnorm*.

[8] [1935] I.R. 170.

of the Constitution[1] did not enact by reference any principles of constitutional law, in relation to which any law could be held by this Court to be valid or invalid.'[2]

This admirable exposition of the roots of Free State law is vitiated, from the point of view of the present study, by the fact that in the succeeding paragraph the learned judge makes it clear that his view is based, not on considerations of the source of Free State law, but on the limitations upon the Court's power of judicial review of legislation, which power he assumes to be conferred solely by Article 65.[3] In view of *Marbury* v. *Madison*[4] and the prevalence of judicial review throughout the British Empire, it seems preferable to regard Article 65 as in this respect merely declaratory. The other two judges of the High Court did not find it necessary to consider fundamental questions, and concurred in the result with Meredith, J., as did Fitzgibbon, J.[5], and Murnaghan, J., who formed the majority of the Supreme Court. Kennedy, C.J., in an interesting dissenting judgment, put forward the remarkable view that Acts of the Oireachtas[6] inconsistent with the Natural Law are void.[7]

Article 73[8] has been uniformly interpreted not as simply suffering the English law to continue, but as re-enacting as Free State law the *corpus* of United Kingdom law in force in the Free State area at the date of the Constitution.[9] On the other hand, it has not been ques-

[1] See below, n. 8.

[2] [1935] I.R. 170, 178–9.

[3] 'The judicial power of the High Court shall extend to the question of the validity of any law having regard to the provisions of the Constitution. In all cases in which such matters shall come into question, the High Court alone shall exercise original jurisdiction.'

[4] (1803) 1 Cranch 137. This decision of the Supreme Court of the United States established the right of that court to review legislation for conformity to the Constitution.

[5] A *dictum* in his judgment is cited above, p. 537.

[6] The Free State Legislature.

[7] From the acknowledgement in the preamble to the Constituent Act 'that all lawful authority comes from God to the people', coupled with Article 2 of the Constitution, he argued that 'if any legislation of the Oireachtas (including any purported amendment of the Constitution) were to offend against that acknowledged ultimate Source from which the legislative authority has come through the people to the Oireachtas, as, for instance, if it were repugnant to the Natural Law, such legislation would be unconstitutional and invalid': [1935] I.R. 170, 204–5. The Constitution (Amendment No. 17) Act, No. 37. of 1931, was, in the late Chief Justice's view, invalid on this ground.

[8] 'Subject to this Constitution and to the extent to which they are not inconsistent therewith, the laws in force in the Irish Free State (Saorstát Éireann) at the date of the coming into operation of this constitution shall continue to be of full force and effect until the same or any of them shall have been repealed or amended by enactment of the Oireachtas.' This Article is omitted from Keith's reprint, in *Speeches and Documents on the British Dominions, 1918–1931.*

[9] *O'Callaghan* v. *O'Sullivan*, [1925] 1 I.R. 90; *London Finance and Discount*

tioned that the 'law in force' referred to in that article is the British law, and not such law as the revolutionary Dáils had enacted.

In the few appeals that came to the Privy Council from the Free State before 1935, it was not necessary to consider what was the basis of Free State law. In *Moore* v. *Attorney-General for the Irish Free State*[1] the question arose squarely. Its treatment by the Board is unsatisfactory,[2] possibly owing to the fact that the Free State Government, which did not recognize the jurisdiction, was not represented by counsel, but the conclusion is simple and clear:

> 'Thus the Treaty received the force of law, both in the United Kingdom and in Ireland, by reason of the passing of an Act of the Imperial Parliament; and the Constitutional Act owed its validity to the same authority.'[3]

According to the principles laid down in the Canadian case of *British Coal Corporation* v. *R.*,[4] which was heard concurrently, it would seem that, in deciding *Moore's Case*, the Judicial Committee regarded itself as in effect an Irish court, deciding a question of Irish law, not as an imperial, still less a United Kingdom court.[5] The *dictum* quoted is therefore in direct and immediate conflict with all shades of doctrine in the Irish courts on the same point. But since the substantial decision in *Moore's Case* was that the appeal from the Free State to the Privy Council had been effectively abolished by Irish legislation, there will be no opportunity for a continuation of the conflict. And since the dictum quoted is that of a court which by its own decision had already ceased to be a court superior to the Irish courts, it would hardly be binding authority in the Irish courts, even if they were otherwise prepared to defer to Privy Council decisions, which is by no means likely.

We are left, then, with a mass of dicta of the Free State courts, not obviously consistent with one another, and all in some measure *obiter*, as the best available evidence of the root of Irish Free State law. He would be a bold man who would attempt, on these authorities, to define the Irish *Grundnorm*. Since the establishment of the

Company v. *Butler*, [1929] I.R. 90. The opinion of the Board in *Performing Right Society* v. *Bray*, [1930] A.C. 377, 399, [1930] I.R. 509, 528, tends in the opposite direction; but Privy Council decisions are no longer authoritative in the Free State.

[1] [1935] A.C. 484; [1935] I.R. 472.

[2] See an acute criticism by Dr. W. I. Jennings, 52 *L.Q.R.* 183 sqq.

[3] [1935] A.C. 484, 492; [1935] I.R. 472, 479.

[4] [1935] A.C. 500, 520–1.

[5] Contrast *Wakely* v. *Triumph Cycle Co.*, [1924] 1 K.B. 214, where the King's Bench Division had to construe the Free State Constitution as a matter of British law. In fact, the same point, arising in Irish law, was decided, on the same premises, in the opposite sense by the High Court of the Free State in *Gieves Ltd.* v. *O'Connor*, [1924] 2 I.R. 182.

permanent judicature, however, they all point unequivocally to its separateness from the United Kingdom *Grundnorm*. Despite the lack of a decision directly in point, no reader of the Irish Reports can be left in any doubt about the matter. Counsel in the Free State do not even argue the other view. For the Irish Free State, then, the breach with the formal unity of Imperial law has been consummated.

A change of *Grundnorm* is, by definition, an event outside and prior to the law. It constitutes a technical revolution, for the *Grundnorm* embodies the identity of the State. In the light of subsequent developments, the foundation of the Irish Free State proves to have been an instance not of extreme devolution by the Imperial Parliament, but of revolution coupled with reconciliation on a contractual basis.[1] Retrospectively, that is, from the orthodox British point of view; but the Irish view, though vague in detail, has been consistent throughout in this essential respect, and has been justified in the event. For this reason the separation of the Irish *Grundnorm* has not imposed the same strain on the intellectual integrity of those responsible for it as will the South African attempt, if it is successful. It is one thing to insist that an admittedly catastrophic change amounts to a juristic revolution; it is quite another to set up retrospectively by enacted fiction a catastrophe which never took place—to claim to have effected a revolution by due process of law.

The extreme fundamental vagueness which has rendered possible the shifting of the *Grundnorm* in South Africa and in Ireland is an anomalous quality of imperial law. For, just as the existence of a system of law as a system involves the postulation of a *Grundnorm*, so the working of the system normally involves the rendering of that *Grundnorm* explicit. In the British Commonwealth two peculiar factors have operated to postpone the latter process. One is the empirical character of the case-law method. The other is the circumstance that, by reason of the archaic inflexibility of the general constitutional law of the Empire, the forces of constitutional controversy which should have hammered out a new legal system have operated instead in the alternative field of constitutional convention.

2. *A Common Jurisdiction*

Among the important institutions of the former centralized Empire which have survived into the co-operative Commonwealth, a judicial

[1] The contractual quality of the Treaty was in effect recognized by the decision in *Moore's Case*, [1935] A.C. 484, 499.

institution, the jurisdiction of the Privy Council, is the most vigorous in its daily operation and at the same time the most archaic in form. The common legislature has in the Statute of Westminster to the best of its ability divested itself of its imperial character, and is lapsing into comparative desuetude. In function, though not in dignity, the common titular executive is being split asunder. But the Judicial Committee still sits in Whitehall, drawing its authority from the same prerogative which the Norman kings had, and observing in its proceedings a Standing Order of 1627. A succession of nineteenth-century statutes regulated its personnel, but without drastic change. In the general tactful *bouleversement* of ancient imperial institutions in the twentieth century, it suffered only three losses, if losses they can be called: in 1900 a newly created jurisdiction which it might have expected to acquire was denied it;[1] in 1933 it lost one jurisdiction which it had never been anxious to exercise,[2] and another, recently assigned to it, which it had never consolidated.[3] Meanwhile its territory was steadily and almost automatically extending with every new acquisition of a dependency by the Crown.[4]

The comparative vitality of this institution is no accident, because the maxim 'Self-government is better than good government', upon which the emancipation of the overseas dominions has proceeded, by its nature applies last of all and with the least force to the judicial arm. Judicial power as exercised by superior courts does not, or should not, belong to government at all except in a marginal sense. On any theory the faculty of judgment is at least more absolute and universal and less varying according to person, place, and circumstances than administration and legislation. There are some nationalists who, counting the objectivity of the courts a major part of freedom, think themselves never so free as when that objectivity is best secured. They are even prepared to regard an appeal to an external court as an addition to freedom if it increases that security. There are others who hold that the form, traditions, and personnel of a nation's judicial institutions are properly regarded as products of its national genius, and it does not lie well in the mouths of Englishmen —whose own history is the strongest argument for this view—to deny it categorically, still less to construe it as a claim for the corrup-

[1] Certain kinds of constitutional cases from Australia. See below, pp. 548–9.

[2] Criminal appeals from Canada by Canadian Act 23 and 24 Geo. V, c. 53. See below, pp. 549–50.

[3] Irish Free State appeals by the Constitution (Amendment No. 22) Act, No. 45 of 1933. See below, pp. 549–50.

[4] The latest extension is to the territories put under mandate to Great Britain and the Dominions.

tion of justice. In fact, a court of law needs to be both objective and *sympathique*. It is legitimate for, say, Calvinists to stress the one quality, and Celts the other. This very difference can be seen in the views of Irishmen and South Africans. Thus the first President of the Irish Free State wrote in 1923 to the members of the committee which was to draw up a new scheme of judicature for Ireland:[1]

> 'In the long struggle for the right to rule our own country there has been no sphere of the administration lately ended which impressed itself on the minds of our people as a standing monument of alien government more than the system, the machinery and the administration of law and justice, which supplanted in comparatively modern times[2] the laws and institutions till then a part of the living national organism. . . .
>
> 'Thus it comes that there is nothing more prized among our newly won liberties than the liberty to construct a system of judiciary and an administration of law and justice according to the dictates of our own needs and after a pattern of our own designing.'

And a judge of the High Court of the Free State writes:[3]

> 'One of the most effective institutions, forged more as a weapon against British administration than as a definite and perfect system, was the Dáil Judiciary.'

(The Dáil Courts[4] at one stage refused to hear British cases cited, and relied for inspiration on natural justice, Roman law, the *Code Civil*, and old Irish law.) Even when discounted as heavily as utterances of their type must be, these statements reveal a view, sincerely held, which is radically opposed to that of, say, Dr. Manfred Nathan, who writes[5] that:

> 'the continued existence of appeals to the Judicial Committee . . . does not affect the independent status of the Dominions, any more than the status of any international state is affected by the Permanent Court of International Justice at The Hague. The final appeal to the Judicial Committee is not a mark of the sovereignty of the Crown, but a matter of convenience in that there should be a final court of resort for members of the Commonwealth.'

A more nationalist South African jurist, attacking the Privy Council appeal, does so on the purely abstract ground that the Judicial Com-

[1] Letter of President W. T. Cosgrave, quoted in Hanna, *The Statute Law of the Irish Free State, 1922 to 1928* (Dublin, Thorn, 1929), p. 17.

[2] The supplanting was completed in the reign of James I (R.T.E.L.).

[3] Hanna, op. cit., p. 30.

[4] i.e. the courts set up by the authority of the revolutionary Dáil. See above, pp. 117–18.

[5] *Empire Government* (1928), p. 91.

mittee cannot recognize the 'sovereignty' of South Africa.[1] To the Irish nationalist, then, judgment by alien judges, however upright, is alien government; to the South African nationalist, it is not necessarily so. Neither view is to be preferred to the other, for nationalism is not a creed of objective reason.

Even in countries which take a thoroughly objective view of law, there are gradations in the objectivity of the courts. In practice the judicial function can nowhere be kept logically pure. Courts of first instance, especially petty courts, must and do temper the logic of the law with personal understanding, based on knowledge of the background of their cases. The superior courts, especially the appellate courts, which deal with considerable questions of private law, are more faithful to the canons of pure reason, but even in them the general outlook of the judge and his habit of thought play a large conscious and a larger unconscious part. And those tribunals which, under rigid constitutions, are charged with the exalted duty of interpreting and enunciating fundamental law must, if they are not to wreck the constitutional organism, pay more heed to 'public policy'[2] than do the courts of private law.

It is upon no more rigid assumptions than these that we shall discuss the only common jurisdiction of the countries comprising the British Empire or Commonwealth. We shall seek to discover the significance of this common jurisdiction in relation first to the formal unity of the Commonwealth discussed in the last section, then to the three political programmes of imperial unity, nationalism, and provincialism, and finally to the general quality of law and justice throughout the Empire.

The first question, which links up with the preceding section, can be answered upon grounds of general theory, apart from the peculiar character of the Privy Council jurisdiction. No court will assign different ultimate roots to different portions of its jurisdiction, or (which is perhaps the same thing) to different parts of the law which it applies, unless explicitly directed to do so. That is to say, there is a strong tendency, amounting to a presumption, that any court will apply the same ultimate criteria of validity to all the law that it administers. Can this presumption ever be displaced? Is it possible

[1] Professor H. ver Loren van Themaat, 53 *S. Afr. Law Journ.*, p. 49, quoted below, p. 544.

[2] 'Public policy' is a phrase used by judges to explain decisions for which they are unable to cite strictly legal grounds. Some principles first tentatively enunciated as 'public policy', such as those governing contracts in restraint of trade, have by repeated judicial adoption become in effect rules of common law.

for a court to have two quite unconnected sources of jurisdiction, to administer two systems of law which are, in the formal sense described in the last section, unrelated ? Dr. van Themaat thinks not. Having asserted the formal separateness of the South African system of law, he writes:[1]

> 'What will the position then be if the British Parliament passes an act conflicting with section 4 of the Statute of Westminster, or amending or repealing any section of the Statute ? The Privy Council, being the servant of the British Parliament, will fully acknowledge and apply the act; our own courts will not acknowledge and apply it, since they are subjected to the Union Parliament. . . . The retention of the Privy Council appeal is accordingly inconsistent with the legal position of the Union of South Africa, as laid down in the Status of the Union Act 1934.'

The assumption seems to be that a court can administer only that system of law to which the legislature constituting it belongs;[2] it must accept as its sole criteria of validity those of that system. But the present jurisdiction of the Appellate Division of the Supreme Court of South Africa itself demands a gloss upon this view, if indeed it does not refute it. The Appellate Division is constituted by South African law. Appeals lie to it also from the Supreme Court of Southern Rhodesia.[3] But Southern Rhodesia is unquestionably under the authority of the British Parliament, and belongs therefore to that British system of law from which Dr. van Themaat assumes that the South African system is separate. Therefore the Appellate Division derives its jurisdiction from two separate roots, and administers two formally independent systems of law.[4] The conclusion seems to

[1] 53 *S. Afr. Law Journ.* 49, 51. I am indebted to Sir de V. Graaff for assistance in the translation.

[2] The cruder and more obvious implication, that courts are always 'subjected' to legislatures, would preclude the possibility of judicial review, and so cannot be intended. For an exposition of Dr. van Themaat's view of the relation of courts to legislatures see his article, 15 *Journ. Comp. Leg.* 47.

[3] By Act No. 14 of 1931 of Southern Rhodesia, and Act No. 18 of 1931 of the Union.

[4] There is an interesting, though not complete, analogy in the position of Australian State courts which enjoy both federal and State jurisdictions. There is often great ambiguity whether a court is exercising federal or State jurisdiction, or both simultaneously. They are not in theory incommensurable, since the authority of both is derived from imperial legislation; but in fact they may prove to be so, since from State jurisdiction an optional appeal lies to the Privy Council, while the federal parliament has confined appeals from federal jurisdiction to the High Court, and the Privy Council and the High Court seem to take different views both of the validity of that federall egislation and of the distinction between State and federal jurisdiction. See Report of the Royal Commission on the Constitution of the Commonwealth (1929), pp. 108–10; J. G. Latham, *Australia and the British Commonwealth* (Macmillan, 1929), pp. 116–17.

be that if the laws of two systems concur in conferring jurisdictions in both systems upon a court (or if those laws reciprocally confer and permit the conferment of both jurisdictions), the court may exercise both jurisdictions. It may even, upon identical data which are significant in both systems, but in relation to which the provisions of their laws differ, reach different conclusions in its two jurisdictions. But if a conflict should arise through failure of the laws conferring jurisdiction to coincide, or through one system purporting to lay down criteria of validity for the other system different from the criteria which that other system itself accepts, the court will have to abandon one or other allegiance. In choosing, it will naturally adhere to the system by whose law it is actually constituted, upon which its very existence as a tribunal depends. If it is constituted equally by both, its choice will be free.

It appears, accordingly, that a common jurisdiction can be shared by formally separate systems of law without their merging, but only if the provisions setting up the common jurisdiction in each system are concurrent and clearly defined. If such definition is lacking, and the common jurisdiction is constantly exercised, the court will tend to apply the same criteria of validity over the whole range of its jurisdiction, which may destroy the separateness of the systems.[1] If, however, the jurisdiction is only rarely exercised in one or other system, it may not have that effect. It is only because the Judicial Committee is slow to entertain appeals from South Africa,[2] and that its jurisdiction for the Free State, while it lasted, was as far as possible boycotted and frustrated,[3] that the phenomena described in the last section have been possible.

Before the second and third questions can be answered, it is necessary to describe the constitution and jurisdiction of the Judicial Committee, to ascertain the extent and manner in which its jurisdiction may be controlled by the Dominions, and to compare the Judicial Committee in a general way with other courts of law.

Some account has been given in the first section of this chapter of

[1] A court which in different parts of its jurisdiction has to apply different kinds of law *in pari materia* (whether or not those kinds of law belong to formerly separate systems) is under a strong temptation to decide that both laws say the same thing, thus saving itself from having to draw the line between the jurisdictions. Cf. *Smith* v. *Davis*, [1878] Buch. (S. Afr.) 66 (for which reference the writer is indebted to Professor R. W. Lee) and the numerous Scotch appeals which the House of Lords has decided on English law without inquiring too carefully whether or not Scots law is identical on the point, e.g., *McAlister* (*or Donoghue*) v. *Stevenson*, [1932] A.C. 562.

[2] See below, p. 553.

[3] See Hughes, *Judicial Autonomy in the British Commonwealth of Nations.*

the origin and early history of the Privy Council jurisdiction.[1] The Judicial Committee Act, 1833, and its successors did no more than constitute a committee of the Privy Council to which all petitions to His Majesty in Council in the nature of judicial appeals must be referred. Where an ordinary court gives a judgment of its own authority, the Judicial Committee merely advises the King in Council to make an order, though that order is in fact always made. The source of the Privy Council's jurisdiction is accordingly still the royal prerogative. Signs of the administrative origin of the tribunal appear in these and other peculiar formalities, and in the rule that the opinion of the Board is embodied in a single judgment, from which no dissent is expressed. This practice is imposed by an Order in Council of 1627, which is still in force, prescribing that,

> 'In voting of any cause, the lowest councillor is to speak first, and so it is to be carried by most voices; because every councillor hath equal vote there: and when the business is carried according to most voices, no publication is afterwards to be made, by any man, how the particular voices and opinions went.'[2]

But the Judicial Committee is now as scrupulously and purely judicial as any court in the Empire.[3]

By the Act of 1833 and later Acts, the Judicial Committee consists of the President of the Council, the Lord Chancellor of England, ex-Lords President, ex-Lord Chancellors, and all Privy Councillors who are or have been Lords of Appeal in Ordinary, judges of the Supreme Courts of England or Northern Ireland, of the Court of Session in Scotland, of the Supreme Court of Canada, the High Court of Australia, the Supreme Court of South Africa, or the Supreme Court of Newfoundland, or the superior courts in New Zealand, the Canadian provinces, or the Australian states, or who are or have been Chief Justices or Judges of a High Court in India (but not more than two of this class at the same time) together with others specially appointed up to the number of four, of whom two must be specially qualified in Indian law. The laymen, if there are any (Lords President are usually laymen), do not sit. The quorum is three. Indian and colonial appeals, except a few of great importance, are heard by boards of three. The majority of Dominion appeals are now heard by boards of five.[4] The Lord Chancellor determines what members shall hear what appeals by issuing invitations to sit.

[1] Above, pp. 519–20.

[2] Printed in Safford and Wheeler, *Privy Council Practice*, p. 133.

[3] The contrary view dies hard in Canada. Cf. Ollivier, *Le Canada, pays souverain?* (Montreal, 1935), pp. 186–8.

[4] See Note I, below, p. 574.

The law lords (i.e. the Lord Chancellor, ex-Lord Chancellors, and the Lords of Appeal in Ordinary) form the backbone of the committee. The board of three for Indian appeals normally consists of a law lord, one of the specially appointed members for India (who may be Indian or Anglo-Indian), and one other from any category. Boards of five have three or four law lords. Ex-judges of English and Scottish courts are often brought in, especially when business is heavy. Scottish law lords do more than their proportionate share in the Privy Council: their presence is especially valuable in appeals from Roman Law countries such as Quebec, South Africa, and Ceylon, and their knowledge of comparative law fortifies the tribunal in dealing with other systems alien to the Common Law. Dominion chief justices and some Dominion puisne judges are usually sworn of the Privy Council and, when in England, are asked to sit; but this happens so rarely that they are a negligible element in its constitution.[1] No Irish Free State judge has sat.

There are usually two divisions sitting during term, but three divisions have, on occasion, sat simultaneously. Sittings are on four days a week only, in the Treasury building at the corner of Downing Street and Whitehall. Members of the Board do not wear robes, though counsel do. This practice, and the circumstance that there is no dais, lend the tribunal an air of comparative intimacy and informality. The right of audience is enjoyed by English barristers and Scottish advocates, and by members of the bar of any tribunal from which an appeal lies to the Privy Council.[2]

In addition to its appellate jurisdiction from the overseas Empire and under the Foreign Jurisdiction Act, the Judicial Committee has odd scraps of jurisdiction within the United Kingdom,[3] and hears appeals from the Channel Islands[4] and the Isle of Man. It has also jurisdiction to decide matters referred to it by Order in Council of the United Kingdom.[5] The most important matter which has hither-

[1] For statistics of the composition of recent boards see Notes III and IV, below, pp. 575–6.

[2] Safford and Wheeler, *Privy Council Practice*, p. 135, n. (*e*). Members of another overseas Bar than that from which the actual appeal comes have been heard by the board in recent years. So the writer is informed by Mr. W. A. Barton.

[3] It hears appeals from certain Admiralty courts, from all ecclesiastical courts, and from the Joint Exchequer Board of Great Britain and Northern Ireland. It determines on special reference constitutional questions affecting Northern Ireland, and exercises quasi-judicial powers in certain ecclesiastical matters, in hearing persons aggrieved under schemes for endowed schools, and in licensing republication of books after the death of the author.

[4] The jurisdiction of the Privy Council over the Channel Islands was the forerunner and prototype of its modern imperial jurisdiction: Holdsworth, *History of English Law*, vol. i, pp. 520, 599.

[5] 43 T.L.R. 289.

to been so referred is the Labrador Boundary Question between Canada and Newfoundland, in 1927.

Overseas appeals come to the Judicial Committee in two ways: as of right, and by special leave of the Judicial Committee itself. Appeals as of right exist only where a right of appeal in prescribed categories of cases has been specially created by statute, letters patent, Order in Council, or otherwise. The instrument creating the right of appeal usually entrusts to the court appealed from the duty of granting or refusing leave to appeal in accordance with its terms. If that court refuses leave to appeal as of right, the applicant may apply to the Judicial Committee itself for special leave to appeal. Where a colonial or Dominion legislature has power to regulate courts of justice, that power, apart from local constitutional provisions, probably includes the power to restrict or prohibit appeals as of right.[1] An enactment that the judgment of a local court shall be 'final and conclusive' is sufficient to prohibit such appeals.[2]

When leave to appeal to the King in Council is given not by another court under the terms of a grant, but by the Judicial Committee itself in its discretion, it is called special leave to appeal.[3] The right to apply for special leave to appeal is, as we have already shown,[4] in its nature a right coextensive with British sovereignty, extending equally to territories which themselves have common law systems and to those under other kinds of law. It has always been regarded as a right closely related to the imperial prerogative of the Crown and not a matter of local law, so that before the Statute of Westminster legislation of a dominion or colony prohibiting application to the Privy Council for special leave to appeal was invalid[5] in the absence of an express power to legislate to that end given by an Imperial Act. Such power was given to the parliament of South Africa,[6] and, in respect only of appeals from the High Court, to the parliament of the

[1] It was so assumed by all parties in *Nadan* v. *R.* [1926] A.C. 482. But the correctness of the assumption is questioned by Mr. Justice Dixon in 10 *Aust. Law Journ.*, *Supp.*, pp. 102–3.

[2] Appeals still lie as of right from the courts of Australian states, Canadian provinces, and New Zealand; but not from the Supreme Court of Canada, the High Court of Australia, or any South African Court. Appeals from the Colonies and India normally come as of right.

[3] Special leave to appeal may be sought not only where there is no appeal as of right from the court below, but also after the court below has refused leave to appeal as of right, and may be granted either on the ground that the refusal was wrong, or on the ground that the matter ought in any case to be determined by His Majesty in Council.

[4] Above, p. 520.

[5] *Cushing* v. *Dupuy* (1880) 5 App. Cas. 409; *Nadan* v. *R.*, [1926] A.C. 482.

[6] South Africa Act, 1909, s. 106.

Commonwealth of Australia,[1] subject in each case to 'reservation' of the abolishing Act for the royal assent. No legislation has been passed under either of these powers. But the Commonwealth Constitution itself forbids appeals from the High Court,

> 'upon any question, howsoever arising, as to the limits *inter se* of the Constitutional powers of the Commonwealth and those of any State or States, or as to the limits *inter se* of the Constitutional powers of any two or more States, unless the High Court shall certify that the question is one which ought to be determined by Her Majesty in Council.'[2]

The High Court has only once granted such a certificate, and will be slow to grant another.[3]

At the Imperial Conference of 1926 the law regarding the competence of the Dominions to bar appeals to the Privy Council suffered no change, since resolutions of a conference do not change law. But constitutional conventions were then declared which radically enlarge the actual powers of the Dominions in this respect. In the first place, the efficacy of the reservation of bills was destroyed by the establishment of the rule that, in consenting or refusing his consent to a reserved bill, the King acts on the advice of Dominion ministers. In the second place, it was declared that—

> 'it was no part of the policy of His Majesty's Government in Great Britain that questions affecting judicial appeals should be determined otherwise than in accordance with the wishes of the part of the Empire primarily affected.'

This admission sets up, in effect, a convention that the Imperial Parliament will, at the request of a Dominion, abolish or limit the jurisdiction of the Privy Council for the Dominion. In the federal Dominions (Canada and Australia) the views of the provinces and states would have to be taken into consideration, to the extent hereinafter explained.[4]

To this political emancipation a large measure of legal emancipation was added by the Statute of Westminster, 1931. In the leading cases of *Moore* v. *Attorney-General for the Irish Free State*[5] and *British*

[1] Constitution, s. 74. But appeals direct to the Privy Council from state courts in matters concerning the interpretation of the Constitution (whether '*inter se* questions' or not) have been in fact prevented by making the investment of the state courts with jurisdiction in such matters conditional upon there being no appeal save to the High Court: Judiciary Act 1903–7, ss. 39, 39B, 40, 40A. There is, however, some doubt of the effectiveness of this legislation, arising from the distinction between State and Federal jurisdiction. See above, p. 544, n. 4.

[2] Constitution, s. 74. [3] See below, pp. 565–7. [4] See below, pp. 550, 551.

[5] [1935] A.C. 484, [1934] I.R. 472, upholding the Constitution (Amendment No. 22) Act 1933 of the Free State.

Coal Corporation v. *R.*[1] the Judicial Committee, interpreting section 2 of the Statute broadly, held that, by acts passed in 1933 under the powers expressed by the Statute, the Oireachtas had validly abolished all appeals from the Free State, and the Canadian parliament all criminal appeals from Canada.[2]

We shall now consider for each Dominion in turn what is the present extent in law of the appeal to the Privy Council by special leave, and what are the steps, if any, which each Dominion now has the power in law or convention to take for its abolition or limitation. It must not be thought that within the limits to be stated the Privy Council will, like an ordinary appellate court, hear any and every reasonable appeal. As will be explained below,[3] the board restricts narrowly, and in different measure for different Dominions, the class of cases in which it will grant special leave to appeal. But these are restrictions of discretion, not restrictions of law, and the Dominions have no certain guarantee of their continuance.

In Canada appeals lie both from the Supreme Court of Canada and from the highest courts of the provinces. Criminal law being a subject assigned to the federal legislature,[4] that legislature has, as we have seen, validly abolished appeals in criminal matters from all courts in Canada.[5] Property and civil rights, and procedure in civil matters in provincial courts, are, however, provincial subjects.[6] In view of section 8 of the Statute of Westminster, it seems clear that the federal legislature alone could not eliminate the right of appeal in civil matters, but that with the concurrence of the provincial legislatures it might. How much the provincial legislatures alone could achieve in this direction is doubtful. An alternative and a surer method of abolishing or further limiting appeals would be a request to the United Kingdom Government to promote legislation in the imperial parliament. Under the 1926 Report, the government and parliament would be bound in convention to accede to such a request. But the request would, by reason of the conventions governing amendments of the British North America Act, require to be made by the provinces as well as the Dominion. It is to be noted that, since constitutional issues may arise in criminal cases, the Supreme Court

[1] [1935] A.C. 500, upholding Canadian Act 23 and 24 Geo. V, c. 53.

[2] See, for comment on these decisions, W. I. Jennings in 52 *L.Q.R.* 173, V. C. Macdonald in 13 *Can. Bar Rev.* 625, and Mr. Justice Dixon in 10 *Aust. Law Journ., Supp.* 96.

[3] Pp. 552–4.

[4] British North America Act, s. 91.

[5] Canadian Act 23–4 Geo. V, c. 53; *British Coal Corporation* v. *R.* [1935] A.C. 500.

[6] British North America Act, s. 92.

of Canada has now for the first time an opportunity to determine some constitutional matters finally, without the possibility of further appeal.[1]

In Australia, as we have seen, there is already in that preponderant number of constitutional cases which raise '*inter se* questions' no appeal to the Privy Council except by certificate of the High Court, which is now never granted.[2] In the residue of constitutional cases,[3] and in all other cases, an appeal by special leave lies from both Commonwealth and state courts.[4] The Statute of Westminster does not apply to Australia until adopted.[5] It might not appear at first sight that its adoption would confer any additional power to abolish or restrict the Privy Council appeal, since the Commonwealth parliament has already under the Constitution power to limit the appeal from the High Court and from state courts in matters of federal jurisdiction, and the Statute does not apply to, and cannot be adopted by, the States. It is probable, however, that, in view of the decision in *British Coal Corporation* v. *R.*[6] and the narrow terms of section 9 (1) of the Statute, it will give power to the Commonwealth parliament to abolish the appeals as of right and by special leave from state courts in matters of state jurisdiction.[7] In any case, those appeals can be abolished by constitutional amendment according to the prescribed procedure by referendum[8] or by imperial legislation requested by the Commonwealth and the states.

[1] The validity of legislation creating criminal offences can nevertheless still be considered by the Privy Council by way of appeal from an advisory opinion of the Supreme Court, as in *in re Section* 498A *of the Criminal Code, The Times,* 29 January, 1937, [1937] W.N. 56. But since the Supreme Court only gives advisory opinions on questions referred to it by Order in Council of the Dominion, the Dominion government could prevent such a question going to the Privy Council by raising it instead in the form of a test prosecution.

[2] Constitution, s. 74. See below, p. 567.

[3] i.e. cases concerning the interpretation of the Constitution, but not of those sections of it directly concerned with the distribution of powers among Commonwealth and states: e.g. *Shell Co. or Australia* v. *Federal Commission of Taxation,* [1931] A.C. 275 (whether vesting of judicial power in executive is permissible), and *James* v. *Commonwealth,* [1936] A.C. 578 (whether Commonwealth may infringe freedom of interstate trade). And, of course, cases concerning State constitutions, e.g. *McCawley* v. *R.* [1920] A.C. 691: *Attorney-General for New South Wales* v. *Trethowan,* [1932] A.C. 526. See below, pp. 566–7.

[4] Except in so far as appeals on constitutional questions from state courts direct to the Privy Council have been circumvented by the legislative device mentioned above, p. 549, n. 1.

[5] The Federal Attorney-General has announced the Commonwealth Government's intention of introducing legislation for the adoption of the Statute; 10 *Aust. Law Journ., Supp.* 108.

[6] [1935] A.C. 500.

[7] See Mr. Justice Dixon in 10 *Aust. Law Journ., Supp.,* at p. 101.

[8] Constitution, s. 128.

The South African Parliament, having already in effect full power under the South Africa Act[1] to abolish or limit Privy Council appeals, had nothing more to gain under the Statute of Westminster.[2]

The New Zealand Parliament cannot apart from the Statute of Westminster limit the appeal by special leave. If it adopted the Statute it would probably, despite section 8 of the Statute, have complete freedom in this respect.

There is now no appeal from the Irish Free State.[3]

It remains to consider the habitual limitations which the Judicial Committee has imposed upon itself by declaring the principles upon which it will grant special leave to appeal. In settling these limits, successive boards have frankly taken into consideration the advance of Dominion status and the different shades of opinion regarding the Privy Council appeal which prevail in different Dominions. In 1882, in *Prince* v. *Gagnon*,[4] the Board stated:

> 'Their Lordships are not prepared to advise Her Majesty to exercise her prerogative by admitting an appeal to Her Majesty in Council from the Supreme Court of a Dominion, save where the case is of gravity involving some matter of public interest or some important question of law, or affecting property of considerable amount, or where the case is otherwise of some public importance or of a very substantial character.'[5]

This rule was afterwards further strengthened by pronouncements that even cases coming within these limits would not be heard if the decision of the court below was clearly right in law,[6] and that where the appellant had already chosen to appeal to the Dominion Supreme Court rather than to the Privy Council, leave to appeal from the Supreme Court to the Privy Council should only be granted 'under special circumstances'.[7] Nor will the board entertain questions, of whatever public importance, which are not, or have ceased to be, practical issues.[8] Distinctions between one Dominion and another

[1] s. 106.

[2] See above, pp. 548–9.

[3] *Moore* v. *Attorney-General for the Irish Free State*, [1935] A.C. 484, [1934] I.R. 472.

[4] 8 App. Cas. 103, 105.

[5] The same rule was applied to Australian appeals in *Daily Telegraph* v. *McLaughlin*, [1904] A.C. 776.

[6] *Cité de Montreal* v. *Ecclésiastiques de St. Sulpice*, 14 App. Cas. 660. Followed in an Australian appeal: *Wilfley Ore Concentrator Syndicate Ltd.* v. *Guthridge*, [1906] A.C. 548.

[7] *Clergue* v. *Murray*, [1903] A.C. 521. Followed for Australia in *Victorian Railways Commissioners* v. *Brown*, [1906] A.C. 38.

[8] *Taylor* v. *Attorney-General for Queensland*, [1918] W.N. 85.

are first drawn in the post-war cases. In *Whittaker* v. *Durban Corporation*[1] Lord Haldane, for the Board, said:

> 'The effect of the Confederation was to say that South Africa shall dispose of its own appeals. . . . No doubt the prerogative is not wholly swept away, but it is obviously intended [by s. 106] that it should be exercised in a very restricted sense. . . . In the South Africa Act of 1909 there is express power given to Parliament to limit the prerogative. That shows an intention that the matter should be looked at from a South African point of view.'

As the case raised 'essentially a local question', special leave was not granted. Even for Canada, the limits were drawn tighter, appeals being restricted to 'far-reaching questions of law or questions of dominant public importance'.[2] In *Hull* v. *McKenna*, in 1923,[3] Lord Haldane explained the reluctance of the Judicial Committee to hear South African appeals as arising from the fact that South Africa, unlike Canada, was a unitary Dominion.[4] The same reluctance, he said, would be shown in entertaining appeals from the Irish Free State, another unitary Dominion. He acknowledged that 'the desire of the people' of the Dominion was a factor to be considered in deciding what appeals should be admitted.[5]

These dicta are vague and somewhat conflicting, and must be taken rather as indicating the general policy of the board than as destroying its discretion for the future. Too much importance has been attached to Lord Haldane's dicta in *Hull* v. *McKenna*,[6] which were clearly extempore and not intended to establish fixed principles of law. If they and similar dicta are taken as law, there is ground for the Irish complaint[7] that special leave should not have been given in *Lynam* v. *Butler* (*No. 1*)[8] and in *Moore* v. *Attorney-General of the Irish Free State*,[9] but not for the similar complaints that were made against the granting of special leave in the other Irish cases of *Wigg and Cochrane* v. *Attorney-General of the Irish Free State*[10] and *Performing Right*

[1] (1920) 90 L.J. (P.C.) 119; 36 T.L.R. 784.

[2] *Albright* v. *Hydro-Electric Power Company of Ontario*, [1923] A.C. 167.

[3] 67 Sol. J. 801; [1926] I.R. 402.

[4] This was a better explanation than that which he had given in *Whittaker* v. *Durban Corporation*, for the intention to restrict appeals is even more clearly shown in the Australian Constitution than in the South Africa Act. Yet Australia is treated in this matter like Canada, not like South Africa.

[5] [1926] I.R. 402, 405. This criterion, strictly applied, would have prevented the hearing of any appeals from the Irish Free State.

[6] Loc. cit.

[7] Made notably by Mr. Hector Hughes in *Judicial Autonomy in the British Commonwealth of Nations*, pp. 80 sqq.

[8] [1925] 2 I.R. 231.

[9] [1935] A.C. 484; [1934] 2 I.R. 472.

[10] [1927] A.C. 674; [1927] I.R. 285.

Society v. *Bray*[1] and in the South African case of *Pearl Assurance Co.* v. *Union Government*.[2]

Appeals in criminal cases are only entertained by the Judicial Committee where 'justice itself in its very foundations has been subverted'.[3]

Examination of the number of cases actually decided by the Judicial Committee in recent years shows that there is a considerable annual flow of appeals from Canada, and (considering the relative populations) a proportionate number from New Zealand, whose greater distance is compensated by the fact that appeals lie from its Supreme Court as of right. Australia, owing to its distance and to the restrictions on constitutional appeals, sends rather less than half as many in proportion. South African cases are very rare. There is a spate of appeals from India, which even the establishment of the new Federal Court may not suffice to check.[4]

There were times in the latter half of the nineteenth century when the reputation of the Judicial Committee was not high. The personnel of the Board was often senile and undistinguished; and it was said that the single-judgment rule had been providentially devised to enable all except the member who was going to write the judgment to sleep during the hearing.[5] In the twentieth century ground for these criticisms gradually disappeared, but until quite recently the complaint could still be heard that the law lords treated their duties on the Board as a holiday from their duties in the House, and that boards of three were set up to hear appeals from distinguished full benches of four, five, or six in the Dominions. But at the present time it is probably true to say that the Judicial Committee, which is formally the equal of the House of Lords, enjoys very nearly the same prestige in the opinion of the profession.[6] The single-judgment rule[7] tends to make a Privy Council decision more impersonal and a little cruder,[8] but considerably simpler and therefore more intel-

[1] [1930] A.C. 377; [1930] I.R. 509. [2] [1934] A.C. 571.

[3] Lord Shaw of Dunfermline in *Arnold* v. *King-Emperor*, [1914] A.C. 644, 650. See also *R.* v. *Bertrand* (1867) L.R. 1 P.C. 520, 529 sqq. and two recent cases, *Attygalle* v. *R.*, [1936] A.C. 338 and *Renouf* v. *Attorney-General for Jersey*, [1936] A.C. 445.

[4] For statistics of the origin of appeals, see Note II, below, p. 575.

[5] These faults did not go unnoticed in the Dominions. Cf., e.g., Senator Sir R. W. Scott in *Canadian Senate Debates*, 4th April 1894, p. 37.

[6] Its decisions, of course, are not imperatively binding on English and Scottish courts, nor are those of English and Scottish courts, including the House of Lords, on it.

[7] See above, p. 546.

[8] e.g. *King* v. *Victoria Insurance Company*, [1896] A.C. 250, and *Victorian Railway Commissioners* v. *Coultas* (1888) 3 App. Cas. 222.

ligible than the handful of three to five judgments which constitutes a decision of the House of Lords. Unlike the House, the Judicial Committee does not regard itself as imperatively bound by its own past decisions.[1] These peculiarities save it from becoming enmeshed in precedent's most complex nets,[2] and add to the authority of its decisions in appeals from primitive peoples on broad questions of justice and right. But the single-judgment rule makes its decisions on fine points in developed legal systems less copious, and therefore sometimes less instructive than those of the House of Lords.

It might be expected that the Judicial Committee would show less competence in alien laws than it does in the common law. But its reputation in Roman-Dutch law is high, both among scholars in that doctrine[3] and among those members of the profession who practise in it.[4] Between the private law of South Africa and the private law of England there is not, despite appearances, so great a gulf as that which divides public law under a rigid constitution from public law under full parliamentary sovereignty. Consideration of the competence of the Judicial Committee in this other exotic sphere will be postponed to a later stage of the argument.[5]

The Privy Council is often criticized for its expense. Its costs, by English standards, are not excessive. But litigation is notoriously expensive in England, more expensive than in any of the countries from which appeals to the Privy Council come.[6] Leave to appeal or defend *in forma pauperis* may be given by the Board, but only to parties who show that they are not worth £25 in the world, except their wearing apparel.[7] There is, of course, a large class of persons not paupers by this definition who cannot possibly face the costs of an appeal. The existence of the Privy Council appeal thus considerably increases the advantage of the rich over the poor litigant. Comparatively little hardship of this kind occurs, however, in constitutional cases. The protagonists in constitutional questions are usually public

[1] e.g. *Russell* v. *R.* (1882) 7 App. Cas. 829, and *Toronto Electric Commissioners* v. *Snider*, [1925] A.C. 396.

[2] An impasse such as that which arose in the reluctant attempt of the House of Lords in *Great Western Railway* v. *Mostyn*, [1928] A.C. 57, to discover a ratio decidendi in the conflicting judgments of *River Wear Commissioners* v. *Adamson* (1877) 2 App. Cas. 743, could not occur in the Privy Council.

[3] e.g. R. W. Lee in 51 *L.Q.R.* 274, 52 *S. Afr. Law Journ.* 318.

[4] But the Judicial Committee is criticized for applying to the Quebec Civil Code the rigid English canons of statutory interpretation, which are contrary to the traditions of French civil law: Mr. Justice Mignault in 1 *University of Toronto Law Journ.* 104.

[5] See below, pp. 560–3, 565–71.

[6] Except perhaps Canada.

[7] Such leave entitles the pauper to have solicitor and counsel assigned to him, and relieves him from all fees payable to the Privy Council office, but not from the expenses of preparing and printing the record.

bodies or other parties of substance, and where the nominal parties are men of straw, they are usually supported by adequately wealthy interests. In any event, it is so much in the public interest that constitutional decisions should be of the highest available quality that, if the Privy Council appeal contributes to that end, a good case can be made out for its continuance despite some hardship to individual litigants—if, indeed, such hardship is unavoidable. These considerations do not apply with equal force to appeals in private law.[1]

Because its jurisdiction cuts across the division of the Empire into those six autonomous units which are called the members of the Commonwealth, the Privy Council is necessarily praised and criticized not only by the standards which are applied to domestic courts, but in the light of the different views that are held of what the nature of the Commonwealth is, and of what it ought to be. It is not our present purpose to choose between imperialism, nationalism, and provincialism, but to discover how far the Privy Council jurisdiction can properly be said to further or to frustrate the cause of each.

Those whose chief concern is the unity of the Empire usually approve of the Privy Council jurisdiction. Three senses may be distinguished, in decreasing order of concreteness, in which the Privy Council is thought to promote Empire unity: it is regarded as a safeguard of unity, as a symbol of unity, and as an influence for solidarity of law.

The value of the Privy Council as a direct constitutional safeguard of imperial unity has been consistently overestimated in the United Kingdom since the earliest times. Vaughan, C.J., in 1674 assigned the following lucid reasons why English courts should supervise the courts of the colonies:[2]

> 'The reasons are, First for that without such writ, the Law appointed or permitted to such inferiour Dominion, might be insensibly changed within it self, without the assent of the Dominion Superiour. Secondly, Judgments might be then given to the disadvantage or lessening of the Superiority, which cannot be reasonable; or to make the Superiority to be only of the King, and not of the Crown of England (as King James once would have it in the case of Ireland, *ex relatione J. Selden mihi*, whom King James consulted in this Question).'

[1] Professor R. W. Lee informs the writer that the Privy Council has occasionally given special leave to appeal from the Supreme Court of Canada, where one of the parties was a wealthy corporation, only on the terms that the appellant pay the costs of both sides *in any event*.

[2] Vaugh. 395, 402.

This dictum referred to the jurisdiction of the common law courts of England to grant prerogative writs and writs of error running to the colonies, and as a statement of law it was already out of date when spoken, for this theoretical jurisdiction never really worked in relation to the 'plantations'.[1] As an expression of the reasons why imperialists support the Privy Council jurisdiction, it might have been uttered yesterday. But how effective has the Privy Council been to prevent these mischiefs? There could be no neater description of the developments in the Irish Free State and South Africa, discussed in the previous section, than that 'the Law appointed or permitted to the inferiour Dominion' has been 'insensibly changed within it self, without the assent of the Dominion Superiour'. What, again, are the decisions of the Board itself in *Moore* v. *Attorney-General of the Irish Free State*[2] and *British Coal Corporation* v. *R.*[3] but 'Judgments . . . given to the disadvantage or lessening of the Superiority'? And could there be clearer examples than the Irish Free State Constitution and the Status of the Union Act of measures 'to make the Superiority to be only of the King, and not of the Crown of England'? For the most part, it is true, the emancipation of the Dominions has been carried out by processes with which no court could interfere: by unequivocal legislation, which courts have to accept, and by the development of conventions, of which they can take only tardy notice, if indeed they can notice them at all. But where the law has been doubtful, the Board has usually preferred the view according the largest measure of autonomy, and it is arguable that in the two recent cases cited it even strained the law in favour of the plenitude of Dominion power.[4]

A symbol, like a metaphor, cannot be called true or untrue, but is judged by its felicity. And a symbol of unity, however felicitous it may be in the abstract, fails if it has not a universal appeal to those whom it purports to unite. The Privy Council jurisdiction is in the abstract a very felicitous symbol of imperial unity. The fiction that the appellant to the Judicial Committee is bringing his grievance to the very foot of the Throne has a particular charm not only for primitive peoples, but for that majority of the inhabitants of the Empire which has not read the iconoclastic judgment of the Board in *British Coal Corporation* v. *The King*.[5] But in the first place, the

[1] See above, p. 519. [2] [1935] A.C. 484. [3] [1935] A.C. 500.

[4] W. I. Jennings in 52 *L.Q.R.* 173; V. C. MacDonald in 13 *Can. Bar Rev.* 625; Mr. Justice Dixon in 10 *Aust. Law Journ., Supp.* 96.

[5] [1935] A.C. 500. In which several of the traditional doctrines concerning the Board were declared to be obsolete fictions even in the eyes of the law. Below, pp. 613–14.

suggestion of centralized power[1] was more appropriate to the old-style unity, which was imperialistic in the strict sense, than to the new unity-in-equality of the Commonwealth. Further, as we have seen, the principle of equality is not at all adequately represented in the composition of the Board. The Lord Chief Justice of England[2] and the Board in *British Coal Corporation* v. *R.*,[3] do it is true, by an effort of abstraction, see in the Judicial Committee not what is in effect a United Kingdom tribunal, but a true Commonwealth court. The average Dominion citizen, however, does not.[4] To Dominion nationalists, including many who are well disposed to imperial unity, the symbolism of the Privy Council jurisdiction seems definitely infelicitous.[5] The case for the Privy Council appeal as a symbol of unity in the Commonwealth accordingly fails. Its symbolic value for the dependent empire of the United Kingdom is, however, great.[6]

The Privy Council has a very real and important influence in maintaining uniformity in law and in standards of justice. But these benefits, though often stressed by imperialists, stand really upon their own feet, and could consistently be, although they seldom are, equally appreciated by those to whom imperial unity as a general objective makes no appeal. They will accordingly not be considered under the present head.

Over against imperialism—though not by any means necessarily in conflict with it—stands Dominion nationalism, certainly the most real and effective political force in British Commonwealth relations at the present time. The old formal nationalist argument against the

[1] Cf. above, p. 556 n.

[2] Lord Hewart, L.C.J., speaking extra-judicially at Johannesburg on 26 August 1936, said, 'No fallacy could be more complete or gratuitous than that which assumes or implies that appeal to the Privy Council is an appeal to England from some other part of the British Commonwealth of Nations.' Mentioning the fact that Dominion judges sit on the Board, he continues, 'The learning, experience and wisdom of the whole are brought to bear in the interests of any particular part' (*The Times*, 27 August 1936). If for 'England' we read 'English, Scottish, and Anglo-Indian judges' the 'fallacy' becomes substantially true. See Note III, below, p. 575.

[3] [1935] A.C. 500.

[4] For a summary by a French Canadian nationalist of expressions of hostility to the appeal, see Ollivier, *Le Canada, pays souverain ?'* ch. xvii, passim.

[5] For example, the juristic sub-committee of the unofficial Toronto Conference of 1933 (at which the Irish Free State was not represented), which went much farther than the Imperial Conference of 1930 in its desire to see established a permanent tribunal for inter-imperial disputes, rules out the Privy Council at the very beginning of its deliberations, for the reason stated in the text. See Toynbee, *British Commonwealth Relations*, pp. 85 sqq., 196 sqq.

[6] Note that India is, by comparison, well represented on the board which hears Indian appeals. Indeed, the board is often no less Indian in its composition than the court from which the appeal is brought. See above, loc. cit.

Privy Council jurisdiction—namely, that the mere existence of an uncontrollable external appellate tribunal is a limitation of Dominion autonomy—is, for what it is worth, unanswerable. The Board itself, in *British Coal Corporation* v. *R.*,[1] has admitted as much:

> 'Among the powers which go to constitute self-government there are necessarily included powers to constitute the Law Courts and to regulate their procedure. . . . A most essential part of the administration of justice consists of the system of appeals. . . . Such appeals seem to be essentially matters of Canadian concern, and the regulation and control of such appeals would thus seem to be a prime element in Canadian sovereignty as appertaining to matters of justice.'

As we have seen,[2] the extent to which such a theoretical limitation of self-government is also a practical one depends on the degree in which the prevalent ideal of law and justice departs from pure objectivity, and that in turn depends upon the temperament of the people. But the limitation has now ceased even in a formal sense to be an external limitation, since all the Dominions may now abolish the Privy Council appeal at least as easily as they can alter their constitutions in other respects.[3]

There remains, however, the substantial question, how far it is wise for a Dominion to let appeals from its courts to the Privy Council continue. Nationalism is, of course, only one factor, but so far as nationalism is concerned, the issue becomes: will the full and free development of the nation be hindered by the continuance of appeals? As we have already seen, a Dominion which is interested in the formal aspect of national independence may wish to establish its right of secession in strict law.[4] To establish this it will need to put itself outside the formal unity of Empire law; and this delicate process might be embarrassed by the Privy Council.[5] We have further seen that, apart from the matter of formal unity, the Judicial Committee is neither directly able to restrict the emancipation of the Dominions to any considerable extent, nor, to the extent that it is able, does it seem disposed to do so.[6] But the really important influence of the Privy Council is a more subtle one, lying outside the sphere of the law of the imperial constitution. In its jurisdiction over the domestic constitutional law and the private law of the Dominions, will the Judicial Committee take an 'anti-national' or an insufficiently 'national' line? This is the central question, by the answer to which the attitude of every Dominion to the Privy Council will,

[1] [1935] A.C. 500, 520–1.
[2] See above, pp. 541–3.
[3] See above, pp. 550–2.
[4] See above, pp. 527–8.
[5] See above, p. 545.
[6] See above, p. 557.

rightly or wrongly, in the long run be chiefly determined. Like most other questions concerning the Privy Council, it is governed by different considerations in the spheres of constitutional interpretation and of private law.

The relevance of nationalism to private law is at the present time universally exaggerated. Countries which have identical social and commercial systems require and achieve legal systems which are in fact closely similar, however nomenclature and adjective details may differ. Even on the continent of Europe, where general national traditions are strong and legal origins fairly diverse, the elements of *jurisprudence* that are genuinely national in their inspiration are very small, and amount in the last analysis to little more than local colour. The insistence that German law and German judgments should smack of 'blood and soil' make them not more German, but only worse judgments and worse law. Still less does a system like the Common Law, whose methodology is more peculiar and more resistant than that of the Civil Law systems of Europe, suffer upon transplantation sufficient modification of its spirit for it to be possible to speak of a rule of law as having a specifically Australian, or Canadian, or even American quality.

Nationalism is, however, highly relevant to public law, especially to the law of federal or other rigid systems. Dominion public law differs from the public law of the United Kingdom in omitting many ornamental institutions, and, in the case of the federal Dominions, adding a vast superstructure to support the federal system. In that part of the law which is common to both, namely, the rules determining the general character of legislature, executive, and judiciary and the general principles of administrative law, there is very little variation from the British model.[1] Even the Irish Free State, with the best will in the world to depart from British traditions wherever possible, has in fact followed British law and tradition closely for want of an available alternative.[2] But the superadded *corpus* of funda-

[1] Some departments of English public law which have been taken over by the Dominions have, however, reached a higher stage of development there. Note, for instance, the number of Australian decisions on the writ of prohibition. The law relating to injunctions in political cases needs, and will probably receive, clarification at the hands of Dominion courts. See Evatt, *The King and his Dominion Governors*, pp. 289, 290.

[2] e.g. *Leen* v. *President of the Executive Council*, [1926] I.R. 456 (the Free State has the same immunity from discovery as the Crown in England), *Carolan* v. *Minister of Defence*, [1927] I.R. 62 (the common law rule that superior servants of the Crown are not liable for the torts of inferior servants applies in the Free State), *Attorney-General* v. *O'Kelly*, [1928] I.R. 308 (Superior courts in the Free State have power to

mental constitutional law in the federal Dominions, is not only for the most part without parallel in British law so far as its actual rules are concerned, but differs in kind, in that there is no available legislature which can conveniently change those rules if, as interpreted by the courts, they are found to be unworkable. If interpretation of a British domestic statute by an English court renders the statute unworkable or frustrates the intention of its framers, it is possible, with a little trouble, to put an amendment through Parliament which will rectify the defect. The courts' traditional attitude of slight hostility to statute law, though awkward for administrators, is occasionally a safeguard of civil liberties, and always a useful discipline for draftsmen. The delay in carrying out the intention of the legislature is only temporary. But if the courts treat a rigid constitution in the same way—if they 'construe it as they would construe a Dog Act'—no such remedy is available. In Canada and Australia the difficulty of the process of constitutional amendment is such that in practice only non-contentious amendments can succeed. The courts are accordingly compelled in fact to adopt comparatively liberal rules of construction, whether or not they acknowledge them openly. The working of the constitution cannot be lightly wrecked because its framers occasionally expressed themselves unclearly, and did not foresee future circumstances. The difficulty of altering constitutional provisions means that, if they are literally construed, the constitution runs the risk of becoming out of harmony with contemporary conditions. In fact, the tendency of political opinion and economic forces in the two federal Dominions has been towards centralization. 'Progressive' interpretation of their constitutions will accordingly have a centralizing tendency. This tendency is readily identified, in public and professional opinion, with nationalism. In another age, nationalism and modernity may not coincide; for the moment, they do.

To the extent, then, that the Privy Council makes its interpretation of rigid constitutions march with the times, it will win the approval of nationalists. It must not be thought that such a demand is necessarily a demand for an illicit adulteration of law with politics. Statutes cannot be interpreted by their own light alone, and least of all can national constitutions. 'Where the text is explicit, the text is conclusive'—agreed. But where the text is inexplicit, one must

commit for contempt, whether or not that power is derived from the fiction of the presence of the King in Court), *State* (*Ryan*) v. *Lennon*, [1935] I.R. 170 (in the Free State Constitution, the principle of parliamentary sovereignty is more fundamental than the principle of fundamental rights).

look outside it. *Heydon's Case*[1] itself, the leading case of all our law of statutory interpretation, bids the court ascertain the mischief which the statute was designed to remedy, and adopt that construction of its terms which will best suppress the mischief and advance the remedy. The mischiefs against which the British North America Act, 1867, and the Commonwealth of Australia Constitution Act, 1900, were passed were the lack of political organisms corresponding to the geographical unities of the Canadian and Australian colonies. The remedy chosen in each case was to set up a national government for the common purposes. To assert, therefore, that the effective operation of the national system of government as a whole should be a postulate of constitutional construction is no violation even of the English tradition of statutory interpretation.

The problem for the nationalist is not to estimate the absolute degree in which the Judicial Committee complies with this requirement, but to compare it in this respect with the only available alternative courts of final appeal, namely the highest courts of the Dominions. There is no need to make this comparison in the abstract, for in the treatment of Canadian appeals by the Judicial Committee and of Australian appeals by the High Court of Australia we have an experience which is almost equivalent to a 'controlled' laboratory experiment. The ensuing account of how each tribunal has served its Dominion will also illustrate the merits of each tribunal from other points of view than that of nationalism.

Each had to find its bearings in strange seas, and each (except the High Court in its earliest years) chose to regard those seas as uncharted, though the rich experience of the United States was at hand.[2] It is therefore not surprising that neither has steered a course which can be described as straight. It is still too early to say whether their vagaries will ever be able to be regarded retrospectively as adroit tacking towards a definite goal, or whether they will appear to have been drifting at the mercy of wind and waves. Each tribunal has, alike for its inconsistencies and for its consistencies, been subjected to intense criticism from within and without the legal profession. Owing to the wide extent and highly litigious character of Australian industrial law, the High Court has come more often

[1] (1584) 3 Co. Rep. 7*a*, at 7*b*.

[2] The Privy Council, with considerable justification, never regarded United States authorities as applying at all closely to the Canadian constitution, a document of a very different type. On the other hand, the provisions of the Australian Constitution relating to the federal system as such follow the American constitution closely. The High Court followed American precedents in its early years, but abandoned them—in the opinion of the writer, without sufficient justification—in 1921.

into the arena of controversy. But so far as popular criticism at least is concerned, these attacks have usually spent their main force on the Arbitration Court, which has thus acted as a shock-absorber. In fact the Judicial Committee is probably more criticized, though, being remote from the scene and a body of shifting composition, it is less sensible of the fact. Neither court has ever incurred a tenth of the odium which is being heaped upon the Supreme Court of the United States at the present time.

The original bench of the High Court of Australia,[1] maturely wise without excess of cleverness, treated the constitution as a federal compact and saved as far as possible the integrity of both States and Commonwealth by applying the American doctrine of the immunity of federal and state instrumentalities, a sort of rule of mutual tolerance.[2] A brilliant minority, appointed to the bench in 1906, broke British judicial tradition by persisting in consistent dissent.[3] They repeatedly refused to recognize previous majority decisions *in pari materia* as binding in subsequent cases, and elaborated an heretical doctrine in exhaustive dissenting judgments.[4] As the older judges left the bench, and new appointments were made, this solid minority became the majority. The revolutionary *Engineers' Case*[5] in 1921 marks the point at which their heterodoxy became the new orthodoxy. The reasoning of this decision is open to all sorts of criticism. The case was decided on high constitutional ground, when a much simpler argument would have sufficed.[6] It cut off Australian constitutional law from American precedents, a copious source of thoroughly relevant learning, in favour of the crabbed English rules of statutory interpretation, which are one of the sorriest features of English law, and are, as we have seen, particularly unsuited to the interpretation of a rigid constitution. The majority judgment was, further, self-contradictory in two ways. It declared that the Constitution was

[1] Sir Samuel Griffith, Sir Edmund Barton, and Mr. Justice R. E. O'Connor.

[2] *D'Emden* v. *Pedder* (1904) 1 C.L.R. 91; *Deakin* v. *Webb* (1904) 1 C.L.R. 595; *Railway Servants' Case* (1906) 4 C.L.R. 488.

[3] Sir Isaac Isaacs and the late Mr. Justice H. B. Higgins.

[4] Such persistence in dissent is, however, usual in the Supreme Court of the United States.

[5] *Amalgamated Society of Engineers* v. *Adelaide S.S. Co.*, 28 C.L.R. 129. The actual decision was that the wages and conditions of labour laid down in an award of the Commonwealth Court of Conciliation and Arbitration set up by the Commonwealth Parliament under s. 51, pl. xxxv, of the Constitution bound the state of Western Australia as an employer in respect of its State saw-mills.

[6] It could have been decided on the ground that running saw-mills was a non-governmental activity involving no element of sovereignty, in respect of which the State stood in the same position as any other employer.

to be interpreted by its words alone; yet the court, in reaching that very proposition, took notice of responsible government, a matter far more extrinsic to strict law, and far less admissible by the English rules of statutory construction themselves, than the close verbal correspondence with the United States Constitution upon which the early High Court had relied[1] to bring American authorities in point. And this very judgment which abandoned American precedents would not have been possible if the majority had not followed the loose American rather than the strict English view of the binding authority of precedent.[2] The fundamental criticism of the decision is that its real ground is nowhere stated in the majority judgment. This real ground was the view held by the majority that the Constitution had been intended to create a nation, and that it had succeeded; that in the Great War the nation had in fact advanced in status while the states stood still, and (as was a patent fact) that the peace had not brought a relapse into the *status quo ante bellum*; that a merely contractual view of the Constitution was therefore out of date, and its persistence in the law was stultifying the Commonwealth industrial power, which they believed to be a real and vital power; and finally, that the words of the Constitution permitted the view of the federal relationship which the times demanded. A judgment on these lines would have made the *Engineers' Case* frankly a quasi-political decision, based on a far-sighted view of ultimate constitutional policy, of the type with which the Supreme Court of the United States in its greatest periods has made us familiar. It would have been no more political than several of Sir Isaac Isaac's most notable judgments, and, so far as judicial recognition of a constitutional *fait accompli* is concerned, there is good American precedent in *Texas* v. *White*.[3] The Judicial Committee has since shown itself almost as radical in *British Coal Corporation* v. *R.*[4] The majority judgment, however, still stands as it was given. There having been no more accessions of crusading judges, the High Court has returned to more or less orthodox principles of *stare decisis*,[5] and as a consequence the expressed *ratio decidendi* of that judgment remains as the leading authority in the law of the federal relationship. The actual power of the Commonwealth was notably advanced by *New South Wales* v. *Commonwealth*

[1] *D'Emden* v. *Pedder* (1904) 1 C.L.R. 91.

[2] See above, p. 563, n. 4.

[3] (1868) 7 Wall. 700.

[4] [1935] A.C. 500.

[5] For example, the court which threw over all existing precedents to decide the *Engineers' Case* would not have felt bound, as did the court in *James* v. *Commonwealth*, 52 C.L.R. 570, to follow its own decisions despite its disagreement with them, and ask the Privy Council to deliver it from chains of its own forging.

(*No.* 1),[1] a decision in the political crisis of 1932 upon the new section 105A of the Constitution which opens up the possibility that financial agreements under that section might be construed to authorize the Commonwealth to override almost any right of the States incidentally to the execution of the agreements. The recent *Aviation Case*,[2] which decides that the Commonwealth may under its power to legislate for external affairs legislate in execution of international conventions in excess of the domestic powers otherwise granted to it, marks yet another substantial access of power to the Commonwealth. In its construction of particular heads of Commonwealth legislative power, notably of the industrial arbitration power, the High Court has taken a generous line.[3] But the general principle that residuary power is in the States remains uninfringed, and applies even to matters which are utterly unsuited for local control, if they cannot be brought under any explicit head of Commonwealth power.[4]

On another major topic of the Constitution, namely, the provision in section 92 that 'trade, commerce, and intercourse between the States shall be absolutely free', the High Court in its middle period gave a number of mutually inconsistent decisions[5] which embarrassed it when it returned to the orthodox calculus of precedent. In *James* v. *Commonwealth*[6] it felt itself bound by its past decisions to give a decision which it thought wrong in principle, and at the same time expressed a hope that the Privy Council (whose aid in constitutional cases it had not been in the habit of welcoming)[7] would reverse it on appeal[8].

It is not fair to take the judgments of the Privy Council in Australian constitutional appeals as samples of its quality as an interpreter of fundamental law. The situation by which the decision of the central questions of the Constitution are assigned to a court which is in other respects of inferior rank, the superior court being only let in on peripheral issues, is unfortunate in every way. In

[1] 46 C.L.R. 155.

[2] *R.* v. *Burgess, ex p. Henry* (1936) 10 Aust. Law Journ. 335.

[3] In establishing that the nature of the power authorized by the Constitution to be conferred upon the Commonwealth Court of Conciliation and Arbitration is essentially legislative and not judicial, the High Court has made a notable advance on its early dicta, for which advance Sir Isaac Isaacs is chiefly to be thanked.

[4] *R.* v. *Burgess, ex p. Henry*, cited above.

[5] The *Wheat Case* (1915) 20 C.L.R. 54; *Foggitt Jones and Co.* v. *New South Wales* (1916) 21 C.L.R. 357; *Duncan* v. *Queensland* (1916) 22 C.L.R. 556, and *McArthur's Case* (1920) 28 C.L.R. 530 are some of them.

[6] (1935) 52 C.L.R. 570.

[7] *Flint* v. *Webb* (1907) 4 C.L.R. 1178.

[8] The Privy Council did: *James* v. *Commonwealth*, [1936] A.C. 578.

such circumstances it was inevitable that the judgments of the Privy Council should be desultory and lacking in profundity, as they have indeed been. This is in itself no proof that, had the Judicial Committee been entrusted with a general jurisdiction over the Australian Constitution, it would not have done much better. There is the further consolation that the quality of the decisions has steadily improved. The first was the worst. *Webb* v. *Outtrim*[1] contained one major blunder,[2] and showed complete incomprehension both of the reasoning which led the High Court to apply American authority to the Australian Constitution and of American constitutional doctrine itself, which is on any view a necessary background to the study of any rigid constitution under the common law. The latter errors were adequately exposed by the High Court in *Baxter* v. *Federal Commissioner of Taxation*,[3] and the decision was politely ignored thereafter.[4] Behind the greater sophistication of the *Sugar Case*[5] of 1915 there are concealed some fundamental errors springing from narrowness of outlook.[6] The decision of the Board in *Shell Co.* v. *Federal Commissioner of Taxation*[7] was neither better nor worse than that of the High Court[8] which it affirmed: the judgments in both courts were unanalytical and barren,[9] though right in the result. *Attorney-General for New South Wales* v. *Trethowan*[10] was rightly decided, but the opinion showed such excessive timidity that it hardly amounts to a statement of reasons for judgment at all.[11] *James* v. *Cowan*,[12] a sound decision on the freedom of interstate trade clause, failed to bring that illumination from above which alone

[1] [1907] A.C. 81.

[2] The view, expressed at p. 88, that the royal assent to a statute ousts judicial review. Lord Halsbury, L.C., during the argument said, in reply to counsel's contention that a law was *ultra vires*: 'That is a novelty to me. I thought an Act of Parliament was an Act of Parliament and you cannot go beyond it. . . . I do not know what an unconstitutional act means.' Quoted in Ollivier, *Le Canada, pays souverain ?*, p. 223.

[3] (1908) 4 C.L.R. 1087.

[4] The majority judgment in the *Engineers' Case*, 28 C.L.R. 129, although it upset the rule in *Baxter's Case*, adopted another ground, despite the courteous mention of *Webb* v. *Outtrim* at p. 150. It is regrettable that the Supreme Court of Canada should have based its decision in *Abbott* v. *City of St. John* (1908) 40 S.C.R. 597 on *Webb* v. *Outtrim*. See also *Attorney-General for Manitoba* v. *Worthington* (1934) 42 Manitoba Reports 540.

[5] *Attorney-General for the Commonwealth* v. *Colonial Sugar Refining Co.*, [1914] A.C. 237.

[6] See 9 *Aust. Law Journ.* 213, 248, and for a Canadian criticism of some dicta, Kennedy; *Essays in Constitutional Law*, pp. 36 sqq.

[7] [1931] A.C. 275.

[8] (1926) 38 C.L.R. 153.

[9] Cf. J. Finkelman, 1 *University of Toronto Law Journal*, pp. 339–40.

[10] [1932] A.C. 526. A case on a State constitution.

[11] Cf. above, p. 523.

[12] [1932] A.C. 542.

could have led the High Court out of its perplexities. The latest decision, *James* v. *Commonwealth*,[1] on another aspect of the same clause, is the best Australian constitutional decision of the Privy Council to date: it is nevertheless not a great decision.

The Judicial Committee has occasionally been criticized by Australian lawyers for greediness of jurisdiction. Its entertaining an appeal on an *inter se* question direct from a state court[2] was thought to be against the spirit of the Constitution at least, and the leak was stopped by an ingenious legislative device.[3] In the *Sugar Case*,[4] which is the only appeal which has gone to the Judicial Committee by certificate of the High Court under section 74 of the Constitution, the Judicial Committee went beyond its terms of reference in the High Court's certificate.[5] The decision that the question in *James* v. *Cowan*[6] was not an *inter se* question, and was therefore entertainable by the Judicial Committee, proceeded on narrow grounds, and was open to criticism in the then state of the law.

Objective comparison of the Supreme Court of Canada with the Judicial Committee and the High Court of Australia in respect of policy is almost impossible for the student, since the general appeal to the Privy Council has deprived the Supreme Court of the opportunity to form its own *jurisprudence*. Of the comparative merits of the Supreme Court and the Privy Council as tribunals there is deep division of professional opinion. Probably a majority would agree that for sheer competence in law the Judicial Committee is definitely superior; though some would say that the English tradition of competent lawyership, when applied without adjustment to the construction of constitutions, produces nothing more than dexterous but purblind manipulation of imperfectly analysed and over-literal concepts. These critics would go on to assert that the Supreme Court, if left to itself in constitutional matters, would develop a liberal tradition in constitutional interpretation whose value would outweigh any comparative deficiency it may have shown in the field of ordinary law.

The history of Privy Council interpretation of the Canadian consti-

[1] [1936] A.C. 578.

[2] *Webb* v. *Outtrim*, above.

[3] See above, p. 549, n. 1.

[4] *Attorney-General for the Commonwealth* v. *Colonial Sugar Refining Co.*, [1914] A.C. 237, 15 C.L.R. 182.

[5] The certificate is printed in 15 C.L.R. at p. 234. The criticism is suggested by J. G. Latham, *Australia and the British Commonwealth*, p. 115. But *quaere*, whether the High Court should have framed the certificate in such narrow terms. That, however, is a separate question.

[6] [1932] A.C. 542, 560.

tution falls into three periods, of which the third is just beginning. In 1935, Dean V. C. MacDonald was able to write as follows:[1]

'Up to the year 1925 the course of decision was marked by a definite increase of provincial jurisdiction, with a corresponding curtailment of Dominion jurisdiction; subsequent to that date the trend has been in the direction of expanding the jurisdiction of the Dominion with a corresponding contraction of provincial jurisdiction. The trend to 1925 was marked by three main processes:

(a) the declension of the general residuary power of the Dominion to the status of a reserve power to be used only in case of war, famine, pestilence, or other national emergency;

(b) the devitalization of the "trade and commerce" power to a point where its exercise was confined to supplementary Dominion powers elsewhere conferred;

(c) the enlargement of the provincial power over "property and civil rights" to the extent that "the real residuary power of legislation in normal times was held to be contained in the words 'property and civil rights'[2]."[3]

'The ebb-tide of Dominion power having reached its lowest mark with the *Snider Case* of 1925, that power has been borne along on a flowing tide of returning vitality which, if sustained, may yet give Canada the constitution which it was intended to have.... This pro-Dominion trend has manifested itself in judgments of the Privy Council which (a) enlarge the scope of the Dominion's residuary power, (b) affirm the Dominion's capacity to implement international engagements, (c) give great sweep to its "criminal law" power, and (d) *per dicta*, indicate (though without defining) that the "trade and commerce" power is not merely auxiliary but substantive.[4]

'Up until ten years ago the Privy Council approached the [British North America] Act as a statute to be treated "by the same methods of construction and exposition which they (courts of law) apply to other statutes".[5] Excluding extraneous evidence as to its purpose and meaning, they were compelled to seek for them in the text alone, aided only by the flickering illumination afforded by rules of textual construction evolved with respect to ordinary statutes. This literalistic approach held sway for over fifty years.... In 1930 the Privy Council broke away from its traditional approach and, *mirabile dictu*, promulgated the doc-

[1] In 1 *University of Toronto Law Journal* 260, at pp. 276–8.

[2] H. A. Smith, *The Residue of Power in Canada*, 4 *Can. Bar Rev.* 432 sqq.

[3] e.g., *In re Board of Commerce Act*, [1922] 1 A.C. 191; *Toronto Electric Commissioners* v. *Snider*, [1925] A.C. 396.

[4] This tendency has manifested itself in a dictum in *Edwards* v. *Attorney-General for Canada*, [1930] A.C. 124, 136–7, and in the decisions of *Proprietary Articles Trade Association* v. *Attorney-General for Canada*, [1931] A.C. 310; the *Aeronautics Case*, [1932] A.C. 54; the *Radio Case*, [1932] A.C. 304; and *British Coal Corporation* v. *R.*, [1935] A.C. 500.

[5] *Bank of Toronto* v. *Lambe* (1887) 2 App. Cas. 575, 579.

trine that the Act is a constitution as well as a statute. "The British North America Act", said Lord Sankey, L.C., "planted in Canada *a living tree* capable of growth and expansion within its natural limits.... Their Lordships do not conceive it to be the duty of this Board—it is certainly not their desire—to cut down the provisions of the Act by a narrow and technical construction, but rather to give it a large and liberal interpretation".[1]'

In January 1937, however, in its judgments in a group of appeals[2] concerning the validity of what has been called the 'New Deal' legislation of the former Conservative government in Canada, the 'flowing tide of returning vitality' began to ebb. Of the four progressive trends enumerated by Dean MacDonald, three received setbacks. The Dominion residuary power was cut down and the provincial power over 'property and civil rights' erected again into something like a general and superior residuary power.[3] It was decided that the fact that the Dominion is under a treaty obligation (otherwise than as part of the British Empire)[4] to legislate in a certain way does not authorize Dominion legislation implementing the treaty to invade the sphere of 'property and civil rights' thus widely construed.[5] Hopes that the trade and commerce power might be construed as a reality were dashed.[6] Whether the 'living tree' has merely been lopped, and will grow again, or whether it has been killed entirely it is impossible to tell. These decisions are a reversion to provincialism, but not an unequivocal reversion to literalism.[7] One general fact at least emerges: it cannot now be said that the judicial policy of the Privy Council is more stable than that of the High Court of Australia.[8] The range of the High Court's oscillations has

[1] *Edwards' Case*, [1930] A.C. 124, 136.

[2] Reported in *The Times*, 29 January 1937 and in [1937] W.N. 53–9. They will be reported in [1937] A.C.

[3] *in re Weekly Rest in Industrial Undertakings Act, &c.*, [1937] W.N. 53; *in re Employment and Social Insurance Act* [1937] W.N. 58; *in re Natural Products Marketing Act*, [1937] W.N. 57.

[4] Express power to implement British Empire treaties is given to the Dominion by s. 132 of the British North America Act.

[5] 'For the purposes of . . . the distribution of legislative powers between the Dominion and the Provinces, there is no such thing as treaty legislation as such. . . . As a treaty deals with a particular class of subjects, so will the legislative power of performing it be ascertained': *in re Weekly Rest in Industrial Undertakings Act*, [1937] [W.N.] 53.

[6] *In re Natural Products Marketing Act*, [1937] W.N. 57.

[7] It is worth noting that the Board justified its decision in the Labour Conventions case (*in re Weekly Rest Act*, [1937] W.N. 53) by reference to the inviolability of the 'separate jurisprudence' of the provinces, especially Quebec. This is a political consideration, inappropriate to a truly literalist decision.

[8] At the same time, its instability is less unedifying. It may be that a militant minority fights for its view within the Board, as Isaacs and Higgins, JJ., fought on the High Court bench; but the single judgment rule prevents the world from knowing.

been greater, but their period has hitherto been longer, and they are less recent.

In the decade preceding 1937, the Dominion nationalist was not able to urge against the Privy Council as a present complaint that it did not understand the full responsibilities of a court that is set rigidly in authority over the institutions of a nation. That complaint will now again be heard, and the case for it will be at least arguable. The abolition of constitutional appeals would not, however, necessarily provide a remedy, for Canadian courts have been brought up in the tradition of the Privy Council's first period, to which the bulk of authoritative cases on the British North America Act still belongs. They have, quite properly, not shown many signs of originality or restiveness. It may therefore be doubted whether their decisions, even if made unappealable, would satisfy the *desiderata* of the nationalist without an alteration in their personnel which might have an adverse effect on the mere quality, apart from the tendency, of their decisions.

Apart altogether from its judicial policy, there are reasons why, in certain circumstances, a Dominion nationalist can validly object to the Privy Council appeal. The carrying of domestic cases to an external tribunal is undoubtedly an infringement of the perfection of the formal sovereignty of his Dominion—a fact to which he may or may not attach importance. If he wishes to assert a local root for his system of law, he will be well advised to keep appeals within his borders. And only if a government controls judicial appointments can it resort, in crisis, to the *ultima ratio* of packing the Bench.[1]

The third political attitude to which the Privy Council jurisdiction is relevant is provincialism, that is to say, attachment to the rights of local units as against the federations of which they form part. In the present state of the world, for both political and economic reasons, true provincialism is not an advancing cause. The tendency is for devotion to the local unit either to become a unique loyalty, thereby rising to the status of nationalism, or to be swallowed up in the nationalism of the larger body. The true provincialist has no scruples about calling in the aid of imperial institutions against the common enemy, which is nationalism focused upon the federation. Probably the truest provincialisms in the British Commonwealth are those of the Australian States and of Natal. The status of Natal is

On the other hand, it is quite possible, in view of the inconstancy of the composition of the Board, that its contradictory decisions are all unanimously reached.

[1] As was done by President Lincoln in the Civil War, in order to upset a decision that the United States could not validly issue paper money. See *Hepburn* v. *Griswold* (1870) 8 Wall. 604 and the *Legal Tender Cases* (1871) 11 Wall. 682; 12 Wall. 528.

not guaranteed by fundamental law. No court, therefore, can protect it.[1] In Australia, those who hold the creed of 'States' rights' often favour the extension of the Privy Council appeal,[2] but there is little probability of this occurring.

Particularist sentiment in Quebec is a provincialism so strong that it verges upon nationalism. Quebec has felt in the past that an external court gives better than any Canadian court could the security which it most values—the security that there will always be a political organism corresponding to French-Canadian culture. In this they are right in principle, for in any federation there is a tendency for judges appointed to federal courts by central government to have a national rather than a local outlook; and in practice, apart from the short period between 1931 and 1937, they have been well served by the Judicial Committee. At the same time, the belief, common in Great Britain, that all French Canadians frequently refer with emotion to 'le droit sacré d'appel' is exaggerated. Among them the particularists *à outrance* are leaning at the moment to a common hostility to Dominion and Empire, while those who prefer to ally themselves with all-Canadian nationalism[3] can do so with less reserve than formerly, since the place of the French element in Canada's future is now in any event firmly assured.[4] The application of the Statute of Westminster to Canada, which necessarily added more to Dominion than to provincial power, was consented to by Quebec. It is therefore now quite possible that, if abolition or further limitation of the Privy Council jurisdiction for Canada is thought desirable on nationalist grounds, Quebec will not stand in the way.[5]

There remains the less obtrusive, but in solid fact by far the most important function of the Privy Council appeal—its function in maintaining the unity, and therefore the quality, of the private law of the common law countries of the Empire, and of that part of British public law which all the Empire shares. Few laymen realize that this function exists, and many lawyers underestimate its im-

[1] Nevertheless, Natal provincialists are attached to the Privy Council appeal.

[2] e.g. W. A. Holman, *The Australian Constitution* (Brisbane, 1928), p. 81; T. C. Brennan, *Interpreting the Constitution* (Sydney, 1935), ch. xxviii. Royal Commission on the Constitution, 1929, *Report*, p. 253.

[3] e.g. M. Maurice Ollivier, in *Le Canada, pays souverain?* (Montreal, 1935), ch. xvii.

[4] The proportion of French Canadians in the population of Canada (3,000,000 in 1936) is certainly not decreasing, and is probably increasing.

[5] It would be possible for Quebec to stand in the way not only if it turns out that provincial concurrence is necessary to the abolition of the appeal in civil matters (as to which see pp. 550–1 above) but by virtue of the strength of its representation in the Dominion parliament.

portance. It is known that the Judicial Committee occasionally corrects a rank miscarriage of justice which has occurred in some minor and remote jurisdiction. It is known, too, that in appeals from the more advanced of the dependencies and from the Dominions the daily work of the board is not so much the righting of plain injustice as the decision of refined points of law, and the significance of the jurisdiction for practising lawyers lies in the thin stream of decisions on such points, which enjoy high authority.

But it is wrong to regard the influence of an appellate court as merely corrective, or as operating only in the cases which actually come to it on appeal. The number of appeals it hears, and even the quality of its decisions, so long as it does not fall below a certain minimum level,[1] are more or less immaterial. The mere knowledge that there is a common appellate court above them whose decisions are not wholly capricious ensures that the courts below will adhere to certain standards of justice and of accuracy in law. In terms of the calculus of precedent, the potentiality of appeal to a common tribunal causes all courts below to accept its decisions as having binding authority, and each other's decisions as having stronger persuasive authority than decisions in an unconnected jurisdiction. The accident that the personnel of the Privy Council and the House of Lords are largely interchangeable[2] is in this respect most fortunate, for it creates an informal but effective link between the overseas jurisdictions which the Privy Council unites and the jurisdictions of the United Kingdom.[3]

A case-law system cannot flourish unless it has a continual stream of respectable reported decisions on all aspects of the law. In small isolated jurisdictions only the most litigated branches of the law remain living: the rest withers away. Because the appellate jurisdiction of the Privy Council renders the decisions of the courts of every (or nearly every) jurisdiction in the Empire available for the authoritative enlightenment of the other jurisdictions, it offers to the Dominions a disciplined wealth of precedent which enriches their local systems[4] to an extent otherwise impossible. In the United

[1] It is accordingly fallacious to imagine that advocacy of the Privy Council appeal in private law cases involves the imputation that the quality of Dominion justice is below that of the Privy Council. It may be even higher; the peculiar virtue of the Privy Council jurisdiction is not superlative quality, but its unifying effect.

[2] See Note IV, below, p. 576.

[3] The decisions of the Judicial Committee are not binding in Great Britain, nor are the decisions of the House of Lords overseas, but they are in each case of great persuasive authority. Decisions of British courts have high persuasive authority overseas, and the authority of Dominion judgments in England is growing.

[4] It is worth noting that no single overseas jurisdiction is comparable in size with

States there is an even greater—indeed, a quite embarrassing—wealth of case law. But owing to the lack of a single appellate court, the decisions of the courts of one State are under no obligation to agree with those of another, and each jurisdiction builds up for itself its own *jurisprudence*, differing in petty ways from that of the others. The Privy Council jurisdiction saves the Empire from this confusion.

Of course, this system imposes on the participant in it not only the merits of the common tradition of the common law, but its faults as well. Dominion courts, for example, are not free to develop for themselves a rational doctrine of statutory interpretation.[1] Defective rules of the common law can be, and regularly are, remedied by statutes. But those inarticulate defects which are inherent in the traditional approach of English courts to their work are not thus eradicable, and the existence of the Privy Council jurisdiction fastens them around the neck of every court in the Empire.[2]

But in general, in the opinion of the writer, so far as the private law of common law countries in the Empire is concerned, the advantages of the Privy Council appeal far outweigh its disadvantages, even when the hardship caused by expense is taken into account. For non-common law countries the same considerations do not apply.[3] Where there is a single alien system of law the only criterion by which the Privy Council appeal can be judged is the actual comparative competence of the Judicial Committee and of the court appealed from in the particular system of law concerned. This is a matter for the enlightened judgment of practitioners and scholars in that particular doctrine. Where, as in India, there is a multiplicity of communal laws, the Judicial Committee may well be in a better position than any local court of appeal to weld them by insensible steps into a coherent body of law.

We have shown above that unless a Dominion is seeking to break, but has not yet definitely broken, with the formal unity of Empire

England. Canada and Australia, the largest in population, are each split, for most purposes of private law and jurisdiction, into several units.

[1] Cf. above, pp. 563, 569–70.

[2] For example, the unfortunate decisions of the Privy Council enumerated above, p. 566, are constantly cited in the High Court of Australia, which cannot escape feeling itself to some extent bound by them. For the canons of interpretation which the Privy Council has forced upon the Civil Code of Quebec, see Mr. Justice Mignault in 1 *University of Toronto Law Journal*, p. 104.

[3] There is a pale parallel to the function of the Privy Council for the common law in the case of Roman-Dutch law, where the existence of the Privy Council jurisdiction makes South African decisions authoritative in Ceylon, and vice versa.

law, there is no necessary connexion—and at the present time not even a fortuitous connexion—between the interpretation of Dominion constitutions in a nationalist sense and the final determination of constitutional appeals within Dominion borders. We have also seen that, so far as simple competence is concerned, there is no clear superiority of the Judicial Committee over the only Dominion court which now finally disposes of constitutional cases. The argument, so strong in private law, that unity of jurisdiction broadens and enriches the law of the countries partaking in it, has no force for constitutional law, for between the constitutional doctrines of the different Dominions there is now little common ground. There is therefore no reason why the lawyer should oppose any disposition of constitutional appeals which the dominant political forces in his Dominion—whether they are nationalist, imperialist, or provincialist —may desire. But he can and should demand that, whatever court is chosen, it should hear all constitutional appeals from the Dominion without exception. The arbitrary division of the Australian field between the High Court and the Privy Council has been nothing but an embarrassment to both.[1] But the distinction between constitutional questions and private law is not hard to draw, and there is no reason why the political forces which will inevitably determine the disposal of constitutional appeals should touch the unifying influence of the Privy Council in private law, to which they are not relevant.

NOTES

Analytical Tables concerning the Business of the Judicial Committee from Michaelmas Term 1934 to Trinity Term 1936

These figures relate not to all cases heard during the period, but to cases in which judgments were delivered within the period. Consolidated appeals are treated as single cases.

I. *Size of Boards at Hearing*

Number of cases heard by Boards of:	*Five*	*Four*	*Three*	*Total*
Dominion Appeals	21	2	9	32
Channel Islands and Northern Ireland cases	2	..	1	3
Colonial Appeals	2	..	30	32
Indian Appeals	15	..	98	113
All cases	40	2	138	180

[1] The Royal Commission on the Constitution of the Commonwealth, 1929, recommended that all constitutional questions should be finally determined by the High Court: *Report*, p. 254.

II. *Provenance of Appeals*

Dominion Appeals:		
Canada (Federal courts 6, provincial courts 12)	18	
Australia (High Court 5, State Supreme Courts 3)	8	
New Zealand	5	
Irish Free State	1	
Total Dominion Appeals		32
Channel Island Appeals and Northern Ireland Constitutional References		3
Appeals from Colonies, Mandates, Protectorates, &c.:		
Mediterranean (Gibraltar, Malta, Palestine)	5	
Asiatic (Ceylon, Malaya, Hong Kong)	8	
African (East and West)	9	
American (West Indies and British Honduras)	8	
Pacific (Fiji)	2	
Total Colonial Appeals		32
Indian Appeals (including Burma)		113
TOTAL		180

The unit in the two succeeding tables is each occasion upon which each individual member takes his seat to hear a case.

III. *National Origins of Privy Councillors Sitting*

	Dominion Appeals (32)	*Chan. Is. and N.I. (3)*	*Colonial Appeals (32)*	*Indian Appeals (113)*	*All Cases (180)*
Members and ex-members of the English* judiciary (11)	81	8	73	87	249
Members and ex-members of the Scottish* judiciary (4)	34	3	16	84	137
Anglo-Indian ex-members of the Indian legal service (4)	12	2	10	123 }	213
Indian ex-members of the Indian legal service (1)	..	..	..	66 }	
Dominion judges (4)	4	..	..	1	5

* Lords of Appeal in Ordinary are appointed for the United Kingdom as a whole. They are here allocated to the countries of their professional careers.

IV. *Classes of Privy Councillors Sitting*

	Dominion Appeals (32)	*Chan. Is. and N.I. (3)*	*Colonial Appeals (32)*	*Indian Appeals (113)*	*All Cases (180)*
Lord Chancellor (1) . . .	6	2	3	..	11
Ex-Lord Chancellor (1) . .	2	..	..	..	2
Lords of Appeal in Ordinary and Master of the Rolls (9) . .	86	6	57	140	289
Ex-judges of English and Scottish courts (4) . . .	21	3	29	31	84
Members appointed for India (salaried) (5). . . .	12	2	10	189	213
Dominion judges (4) . .	4	..	..	1	5

3. *Fundamental Rules of the Commonwealth Association*

The first section of this chapter ended upon a distinction within the general law of the Empire between ordinary law and fundamental law. To speak of an imperial fundamental law may seem strange. For fundamental law in general jurisprudence means law which is not alterable by ordinary legislation, but only by some more difficult process, if at all; and it is a platitude that the British Parliament can change any law by ordinary legislation and cannot deprive itself of the freedom so to do. (It has been argued above,[1] it is true, that every system of law, even the British one, must have a *Grundnorm*, and a *Grundnorm* is by definition fundamental law; but the British *Grundnorm* is a very little one, and for most practical purposes the traditional doctrine is as nearly true as makes no difference.) To the extent that the technical legal supremacy of the Imperial Parliament is recognized—and, as we have seen, it is recognized everywhere in the Empire except in the Irish Free State and, possibly, South Africa—how can there be any talk of fundamental law in the Empire?

So long as legislation at Westminster is regarded as the *ordinary* process of legislation for all the Empire, the criticism is just. But since the very beginning of colonial constitutions, it has not been so regarded. For any colony which has local legislative institutions, the ordinary process of legislation is the local process. All law which cannot be changed by local legislation is therefore, from the colonial point of view, fundamental. The relation in which local legislation stands to such law is essentially the same relation as that in which

[1] Section II (1).

the statutes of the United States Congress stand to the Constitution of the United States.

In a colony or Dominion, though not in the United States, it is possible to distinguish two elements in the law which is called fundamental. Some (or all) of it is removed from colonial legislative control in order that the imperial supremacy over the colony may be maintained; there may also be (though there is not always) law which has fundamental status simply in order that the rigidity in certain respects of the colonial constitution may be ensured. The distinction is a purely political one, and in the case of a definitely subordinate colony it cannot be drawn with accuracy. Who can say, for example, how far the delimitation of the respective spheres of legislature and executive in Sierra Leone is directed merely to the efficient working of the domestic government of that colony, and how far to the maintenance of imperial control? But the distinction grows in political importance and in precision as the measure of colonial autonomy increases, and modern constitutional doctrine has for some time recognized a vital distinction between, for example, the provisions in the British North America Act which deal with the constitution and the powers of the Canadian provincial legislatures and the clauses in the Act of Settlement, 1701, laying down the succession to the Crown. Both affect Canada, and both have binding force there. Both are fundamental law there, that is to say, they are alterable only by Act of the Imperial Parliament. But a change in the former is recognized as concerning Canada alone, and the Imperial Parliament in amending the British North America Act in such respects now limits its discretion to ascertaining whether the wishes of Canada, both provinces and Dominion, concur in demanding the amendment; a change in the latter concerns the Empire as a whole, and Canada as a part of it. It is convenient to speak of the former as local fundamental law and the latter as imperial fundamental law.

Imperial fundamental law is, however, not the only or even the chief element in the rules which govern the Commonwealth association. The basis of the modern Commonwealth relationship is equality, but the intractable Austinianism of British legal theory makes it incapable of recognizing a relationship which is fundamentally equalitarian. Imperial fundamental law, in the sense defined above, is fundamental for the Dominions, but not for the United Kingdom, since the United Kingdom Parliament, the ordinary legislature of Great Britain, may in law repeal any part of it at pleasure. To redress this inequality that body of doctrine which is called Commonwealth convention has been called in. It operates in two ways: by hindering the United Kingdom from altering certain rules of law which are essential to the Commonwealth, and by facilitating the alteration at the instance of the Dominions of laws which, though not essential to the Commonwealth, have still fundamental status. A typical convention of the first type is the limitation of the supremacy of the Imperial Parliament by the recital in the Statute of Westminster that 'no law hereafter made by the Parliament of the United Kingdom shall extend to any of the . . . Dominions as part of the law of that Dominion otherwise than at the request and with the consent of that Dominion'. A typical convention of the second type is that which obliges the Imperial Parliament to make any amendment of the British North America Act which is requested by the Dominion of Canada and all the Provinces. There are, of course, other Commonwealth conventions which are not concerned with redressing inequalities of law.

It is easy to draw a distinction between ordinary and fundamental Commonwealth conventions analogous to that already drawn between ordinary and fundamental imperial law. Those conventions which are inalterable except by the common consent of members of the Commonwealth may properly be described as fundamental to the Commonwealth association. But it is hard to say precisely which among the many conventional obligations between members of the Commonwealth bear this character. The test of the fundamental quality of law is easy: legislation in breach of it is invalid, and will be so held by the courts. But convention consists, by definition, of rules not enforceable in courts of law, and so cannot invalidate law. Since, however, the Commonwealth is in convention a voluntary association,[1] it may be said that the sanction for breach of fundamental convention is exclusion from the Commonwealth association. But even this is not sufficiently precise, for the Commonwealth association is notoriously elastic, and things are now tolerated and approved in Dominions which not long ago would have been thought quite incompatible with imperial loyalty. There is, then, no sure test of the fundamental quality of a Commonwealth convention other than the behaviour of the Commonwealth as a whole when confronted with a breach of it, and that is not predictable with any accuracy. The only guide to its prediction is the prevalent opinion concerning the essentials of the Commonwealth, and it must be recognized that this opinion differs from Dominion to Dominion, and between

[1] Its members are 'freely associated': *Balfour Report*, Cmd. 2768, p. 14.

Great Britain and certain Dominions. There is, however, a sufficient consensus of opinion to establish certain conventions as fundamental.

The development of the Commonwealth into a voluntary association has changed the practical, though not the technical, significance of the imperial part of its fundamental law. It is still technically true that an act done in breach of fundamental law has no legal effect, for the sanction of all fundamental law is invalidity. Acts done *ultra vires* are, in the eye of the law, not done at all; and if the person doing them is anything but a natural person (i.e. an individual human being), it simply does not exist, in the eye of the law, to do anything but what it is authorized to do. When the political institutions of the colonies were first set up, these technical doctrines were in a certain sense parallel to the facts, for their constitutions were not intended to be the framework of a generally competent political organism, but only to exercise certain selected powers. But those institutions became in fact political frameworks for nations, the reality of whose nationhood transcended the institutions of its origin. The imperial acts which set up the constitutions of the various Dominions are rightly no longer regarded in the Dominions as the sole or even the principal ground of the existence in fact of their national identity and national institutions. The meaning of a legal institution cannot be assessed apart entirely from its practical social significance. In practice, observance of imperial fundamental law is not now for the Dominions a condition precedent to their national existence, but an obligation incident to their membership, as nations, of a voluntary association of nations, the British Commonwealth. This is true equally of the Dominions that have and of those that have not asserted local roots for their systems of law—indeed, the mere fact that such assertions have been possible is a testimony to the change.

Observance of imperial fundamental law being now for practical purposes an obligation upon nations incident to their membership of the Commonwealth, it is not easily distinguishable in function from fundamental Commonwealth convention, which bore that character from its beginning. There are only two differences, one of which gives law a higher efficacy than convention, the other a lower. In the Dominions which still form part of the formal imperial system of law, acts done in breach of imperial fundamental law are necessarily void in Dominion domestic law, whereas fundamental Commonwealth convention lacks this sanction of nullity. On the other hand, just because convention creates not literal obligations of law but vague obligations of a moral or political quality, its requirements may be less easily evaded by fulfilment of the letter and neglect of the spirit than the requirements of strict law.[1]

The tendency towards assimilation of imperial fundamental law to convention has had opposite incidental effects on local fundamental law in the Dominions which have preponderantly rigid and preponderantly flexible constitutions respectively. The two great federations have inevitably each a large *corpus* of domestic fundamental law, which they have had to preserve in full force in order that their federal character may not be destroyed. The frequent application of this law by the courts to invalidate statutes and executive acts has saved it from any sort of atrophy, and it has been expressly excepted from the operation of the Statute of Westminster for both Canada and Australia.[2]

In South Africa, on the other hand, where there was no element of rigidity in the domestic constitution except the relatively unimportant 'entrenched clauses' of the South Africa Act, the emancipatory effect of the Statute of Westminster has been allowed to extend to them as well.[3] The position in the Irish Free State is obscure. There are two possible sources of rigidity for Free State constitutional law: the Treaty and the Constitution. The Constitution is made fundamental law by its own Article 2, and the sanction of judicial review is provided by Article 65. Amendments may, by Article 50, only be made by the Oireachtas with the assent in a referendum of either the absolute majority of the registered voters or a two-thirds majority of those voting. But this article is made subject to a proviso that for the first eight years it may be amended by ordinary legislation. Under this proviso an amendment was passed in 1929[4] extending the duration of the operation of the proviso itself to sixteen years, and this amendment was held valid in *State* (*Ryan*) v. *Lennon*.[5] Accordingly the Constitution strictly so called of the Irish Free State is for the moment completely flexible, but it may be rendered rigid by amendment,[6] and in the absence

[1] See, e.g. the then Commonwealth Attorney-General in the Australian House of Representatives, 17th July 1931 (Keith, *Speeches and Documents on the British Dominions, 1918–1931*, pp. 264–5).

[2] In slightly different terms for each. See below, p. 589.

[3] Kennedy and Schlosberg, *Law and Custom of the South African Constitution*, pp. 100, 101.

[4] Constitution (Amendment No. 16) Act, No. 10 of 1929.

[5] 1935 I.R. 170.

[6] In this respect it is similar not to the British constitution but to the constitutions of those colonies and States which are governed by s. 5 of the Colonial Laws Validity Act 1865: *Attorney-General for New South Wales* v. *Trethowan*, [1932] A.C. 526.

of further amendment will automatically become rigid in 1938.[1] At the time of writing, an extensive recasting of the Constitution[2] is foreshadowed by the Free State Government.

The flexibility or otherwise of the Constitution strictly so called does not as such touch the Treaty, which was declared by section 2 of the Constituent Act[3] to have a force superior to any provision of the Constitution or amendment to the Constitution, and whose provisions were excepted from the power of amendment given by Article 50 of the Constitution. In 1933 an amendment of the Constitution repealing these limitations was passed,[4] and in 1935 a subsequent amendment of the Constitution[5] inconsistent with the Treaty was held valid in Irish Free State domestic law by the Privy Council.[6] But since the Privy Council has no longer jurisdiction in Irish appeals, its view is not binding on Free State Courts, and in fact there are dicta of the Free State Supreme Court in the earlier decision of *State (Ryan)* v. *Lennon*[7] tending to the opposite view. It may, however, be surmised that the Supreme Court will not regard the Treaty as fundamental if ever a square decision on the point is required of it.[8]

In short, the weakening of imperial fundamental law by the

[1] Lord Justice Greene suggests to the writer that on the view of the Statute of Westminster taken by the Judicial Committee in *Moore* v. *Attorney-General of the Irish Free State*, [1935] A.C. 484, the Constitution would remain amendable by ordinary legislative process after the expiry of the second eight-year period by virtue of the power which the Statute confers to amend imperial acts, the Constitution being part of an imperial act. This is a power quite separate from, and independent of, the amending power contained in Art. 50. But it is unlikely that the Irish courts will take the view that the Imperial Parliament is capable of conferring *ab extra* any such power on the Oireachtas.

[2] Beyond the Constitution (Amendment No. 27) Act, No. 57 of 1936, which was passed at the time of King Edward VIII's abdication. For its effect see below, p. 586, n. 2.

[3] Scheduled to 13 Geo. 5, c. 1.

[4] Constitution (Removal of Oath) Act, No. 6 of 1933.

[5] Constitution (Amendment No. 22) Act, No. 45 of 1933.

[6] *Moore* v. *Attorney-General of the Irish Free State*, [1935] A.C. 484; 1935 I.R. 472.

[7] [1935] I.R. 170. Fitzgibbon, J., at p. 227, states firmly that amendments inconsistent with the Treaty would be void; Murnaghan, J., the other member of the majority, countenances this view without expressly affirming it; the view of Kennedy, C.J., who dissented, is difficult to ascertain from his dicta at pp. 205–7, but seems to tend in the same direction. The effect of the Statute of Westminster, which was the sole ground of the Privy Council decision, is not adverted to in any of the judgments of the Supreme Court.

[8] If the Supreme Court were to declare the Treaty still fundamental, the Constitution (Amendment No. 27) Act, No. 57 of 1936, which removes the Governor-General from the Constitution, would almost certainly be invalid. All legislation passed since that Act would therefore be invalid, not having been signed by the Governor-General.

Statute of Westminster and by the assertion of local roots for Dominion systems of law has had the effect in unitary Dominions of weakening or eliminating rigid elements in the local constitutions. In the two federal Dominions, on the other hand, it has accentuated the difference between imperial and local fundamental law, the latter being preserved in full force.

It remains to state the fundamental rules of the Commonwealth association as it now is, and to estimate how far they are properly described as rules of convention, how far as rules of law. We have already suggested that fundamental Commonwealth convention must, from its subjective character, necessarily be vague. Some even question whether its provisions are sufficiently binding to be properly classed as rules at all. It is true that nearly all the standards which, politically speaking, imperialists consider essential have been infringed by the Irish Free State, and each infringement has been in greater or lesser degree condoned by the United Kingdom and the other members of the Commonwealth. Yet the principal unquestionable breaches of convention by the Free State[1] have been breaches not of general Commonwealth convention at all, but of the Anglo-Irish Treaty. This agreement certainly has, amongst other qualities, the quality of convention as between the parties to it; but it was concluded before the generalization of the conventions of Dominion status in 1926 first established the general character of the Commonwealth as a voluntary association of equals, and thereby first rendered conventions fundamental to the association possible. Breaches of the Treaty are accordingly merely breaches of a private bilateral 'contractual'[2] arrangement, not of the multilateral fundamental conventions establishing the status of a member of the Commonwealth as such.

That objection set aside, there seems no reason why the conventions stated in the Balfour Memorandum, with proper allowance for its slightly exalted language, should not be taken seriously as rules still regulating the conduct of Commonwealth affairs.

None of them are stated in so many words to be fundamental or to require common consent to their alteration. But in the crucial

[1] Exceptions are the introduction of the Bill for the Irish Nationality and Citizenship Act, 1935, without prior consultation, contrary to the Report of the 1930 Imperial Conference (Cmd. 3717, p. 22), and Mr. De Valera's ambiguous remarks in the Dáil on 11 December 1936. Mr. D. L. Keir rightly observes to the writer that even those breaches which break only a bilateral arrangement have nevertheless a deteriorating effect on the standing of Commonwealth convention generally.

[2] The Privy Council used this epithet in *Moore's Case*, [1935] A.C. 484, 499.

definition the members of the Commonwealth are said to be 'united by a common allegiance to the Crown'. It is hard to think that a member could remain a member if it utterly disavowed the common Crown. The 1930 Conference certainly interpreted one aspect of this requirement as fundamental when it laid down the corollary, afterwards recited for emphasis in the preamble to the Statute of Westminster, that

> 'it would be in accord with the established constitutional position of all the members of the Commonwealth in relation to one another that any alteration in the law touching the Succession to the Throne or the Royal Style and Titles shall hereafter require the assent as well of the Parliaments of all the Dominions as of the Parliament of the United Kingdom.'

On the only occasion which has hitherto arisen for its application, namely, the abdication of King Edward VIII and the institution of King George VI in 1936, this convention has worked, though not without creaking. The Australian Parliament was the only one to express its assent before His Majesty's Declaration of Abdication Act was passed at Westminster. The Dáil did not in so many words express its assent to the passing of the Act, but passed legislation making what amounts to an identical change in the succession, which came into effect on the following day. The other Dominion *parliaments* expressed their assent in various ways within the next few months. The change in the succession came into effect in all of them, except the Irish Free State, at the same time as in Great Britain; in Australia and New Zealand (which have not adopted the Statute) by virtue of the overriding force of imperial legislation under the Colonial Laws Validity Act, 1865; in Canada by virtue of the request and consent of the Canadian Government recited in the Act pursuant to section 4 of the Statute of Westminster; and in South Africa by virtue of section 3 of the South Africa Act, which defines the King in South Africa as the King for the time being under the laws of the United Kingdom.[1] The ancillary conventions governing the tendering of advice to the Crown in matters touching the succession are clearly not fundamental, for they were broken in 1936 by the governments of the United Kingdom and (possibly) the Irish Free State without impairing the Commonwealth association.[2]

[1] The text, which represents a view to which the writer still adheres, was written before His Majesty King Edward VIII's Abdication Bill was introduced into the Union Parliament. This Bill declares the abdication to have taken effect immediately upon the signing of the Instrument of Abdication, on 10 December. See below, p. 618.

[2] A more detailed account of the abdication in imperial constitutional law is given in the Appendix, below, pp. 616–30.

Concerning nationality, though there is, as we shall see, an indelible but impotent common status in fundamental law,[1] there is no fundamental convention, despite the reference in the Balfour Memorandum to a 'common allegiance' as the basis of Commonwealth unity. Grammatically, the allegiance there referred to is that of the 'communities' of the Commonwealth, not that of their citizens. But in any case, there was in 1926 no 'common allegiance', in the strict sense, of the citizens of all the member nations of the Commonwealth, because even at that time the incidents attached to allegiance in the Dominions were widely different, and the classes of persons regarded by the various Dominions as within that allegiance did not exactly coincide. There is no doubt, however, that the duty of maintaining the largest possible measure of effective common or mutual citizenship is one of the principal non-fundamental conventions of the Commonwealth.[2]

It is probable that there is another fundamental convention of the Commonwealth, not mentioned in the Balfour Memorandum: a rule that the admission of a new member of the Commonwealth requires the consent of all. This may seem startling, for the last member of the Commonwealth to be admitted—the Irish Free State, in 1921—was admitted by the sole authority of the United Kingdom, as all others had previously been. But the rule follows logically from the equal and consequently multilateral character of the Commonwealth relationship established in 1926.[3] Equality precludes the possibility that any one member of the Commonwealth should have the exclusive prerogative of admitting new members. Therefore, either new members can be admitted by any member acting alone, or they can only be admitted by common consent of all. Clearly, the admission of a foreign nation would require the consent of all. The admission of territories already within the Empire which have not previously been fully self-governing in every aspect of their internal and external affairs, whether they are dependencies of a member of the Commonwealth (e.g. India and Southern Rhodesia) or whether they form part of the domestic territory of a member of the Commonwealth (e.g. Western Australia, Quebec, Scotland) would raise difficult questions. Of course, complete self-governing status (in fact if not in form) is a pre-requisite for membership, and this can only be accorded by the member of the Commonwealth of which the candidate is a dependency

[1] Below, pp. 592–5.

[2] Report of Conference on the Operation of Dominion Legislation and Merchant Shipping, paras. 72–9, Cmd. 3479 of 1929, pp. 24–5; Report of 1930 Imperial Conference, section VI (b), Cmd. 3717, pp. 21–2.

[3] For the multilateral character of the modern Commonwealth, see below, pp. 597–8.

or a part. But when it has been accorded, does it *ipso facto* confer Commonwealth membership, without the consent of the other members? It is submitted that, in principle, their consent is necessary. This is so not because the present members of the Commonwealth have any sort of monopoly of status, but because the accession of a new member would render the general conventions of the Commonwealth automatically applicable between it and the existing members. This would amount to an extension of the conventional obligations of existing members, and as such it would require their consent.[1] But in practice this principle must, it would seem, be qualified by the consideration that in accepting—and indeed welcoming—the presence of Southern Rhodesian and Indian representatives at imperial conferences expressly in anticipation of their future full status in the Commonwealth, the present members of the Commonwealth must be taken to have consented in advance to their admission to the Commonwealth as soon as they shall have been granted full autonomy by the United Kingdom. The same argument would apply *a fortiori* to the restitution of Newfoundland to full Dominion status.[2]

These are the fundamental conventions of the Commonwealth association. There remain two other sorts of Commonwealth convention. There are those positive conventions of the Commonwealth association which are not fundamental, the chief of which are those concerning foreign affairs. These are of all conventions the most significant of the true nature of the Commonwealth relationship, but they do not touch the present topic. There are also those negative and supplementary conventions of Dominion status which fill up the remaining inequalities in law between the United Kingdom and the Dominions to an effective practical equality of status. It was once the main task of the constitutional student of the Empire to enunciate these conventions separately, and estimate how far each had gone in the direction of complete emancipation. But it is now not only easier but more accurate simply to state that the Dominions have in convention complete equality of status according to the definition in the Balfour Memorandum. All conventions necessary to implement that status are implied. The extent of the conventions so implied corresponds exactly with the extent of the remaining in-

[1] It is true that the Report of the Committee of Both Houses on the Receivability of the Petition of Western Australia for Secession (Parl. Pap. 1935, H.C. 88) asserted only that the consent of the Commonwealth of Australia would be necessary to legislation erecting the State of Western Australia into a separate Dominion. But the question of the consent of the other Dominions was not raised, and the absence in fact of the consent of the Australian government was sufficient to dispose of the matter.

[2] See above, p. 526, n. 4.

equality in strict law. Some of the conventions of this class will of necessity be mentioned in the ensuing account of imperial fundamental law.

In stating the imperial fundamental law of the present day it is necessary to consider not only the extent of its provisions, but also the derivation of, and the security for, its fundamental character. In both these respects it has been debilitated by modern developments: in its extent by legislation, principally the Statute of Westminster, and in its fundamental character by the assertion of local roots for Dominion systems of law.

The effective assertion of a local root for the law of a Dominion has two quite separate effects on the application of imperial fundamental law to that Dominion. In the first place, it removes from the law of that Dominion the theoretical possibility that any or all of the laws of the Dominion might at any time be overborne by imperial legislation. In the second place, it definitely separates imperial fundamental law from local fundamental law. Thus there is translated into legal theory the political distinction which we have drawn between imperial and local fundamental law, and also the change in the function of imperial fundamental law which we have mentioned above, whereby from being the ground of the national existence of the Dominion it has become merely the embodiment of some of the terms of the Dominion's membership of a voluntary association, the Commonwealth. It may retain fundamental status in the Dominion, so that ordinary legislation repugnant to it is void; but if it does, it enjoys that status no longer in virtue of logical priority to (or at least parity with) the local fundamental law, but in virtue of its adoption by the latter, in the same manner as international treaties are by the United States Constitution[1] adopted into American law.

The institution of the Crown and the law of succession to it as enacted by the Parliament of the United Kingdom are still fundamental law in each of the Dominions, except the Irish Free State.[2] This exception, however, does not disprove the rule, because of the

[1] Art. 6. 2.

[2] Art. 51 of the Free State Constitution, as amended by the Constitution (Amendment No. 27) Act, No. 57 of 1936, provides only that any 'organ' used as a constitutional organ for the appointment of diplomatic and consular agents and the conclusion of international agreements by any of the nations of the Commonwealth may be availed of by the Free State Executive Council for those purposes 'to the extent and subject to any conditions which may be determined by law' (i.e. by ordinary legislation). Pursuant to this provision, the King recognized by the Commonwealth nations 'as the symbol of their co-operation' is by the Executive Authority (External

anomalous nature of the Free State's membership of the Commonwealth. Imperial fundamental law requires that the monarch remain, in name at least, head of the executive throughout the Empire. Are any inalienable powers coupled with this headship, or is it wholly nominal? Apart from the Statute of Westminster, the Crown retains in law all those prerogatives in relation to the Dominions which are not vested in the Governors-General and Governors by the Dominion constitutions or delegated to them by royal instructions; and, apart from power expressly given in the constitutions, Dominion parliaments cannot derogate from these retained powers. The exact limits of these powers has long been a matter of dispute, and their determination has been rendered unnecessary in practice by the establishment of conventions that, whatever their extent may be, they are exercisable only on the advice of Dominion ministers, so that in fact Dominion cabinets exercise all executive power in relation to their Dominions, whether it is legally vested in the Governor-General or in the monarch in person. The question how far the King's prerogative is incapable of being taken from him by Dominion statute therefore loses much, though not all, of its importance. Not all, because circumstances are conceivable in which a monarch might disregard his conventional duty to a Dominion in which he was not resident, particularly if the performance of that duty should be inconsistent with his conventional duty to another member of the Commonwealth, as it would be if the advice of their cabinets on a common matter were to conflict.

The common matters, in which the King cannot act differently for different parts of the Empire, but must do a single act for all, include on the one hand matters concerning his life as an individual, such as his marriage and his bodily locomotion (for he cannot be corporally partitioned among the members of the Commonwealth),[1] and on the other hand matters in which his function is deemed to be indivisible by imperial fundamental law. Issues of peace and war have usually been regarded as belonging to the latter category. Actually, the states of belligerency and neutrality, though by a compendious metaphor they are spoken of as attributes or conditions of states or heads of states, are significant principally in their application to nationals of those states. The real juristic difficulty in regarding the

Relations) Act, No. 58 of 1936, authorized to act for the Free State in such matters when advised by the Executive Council. There is now no other mention of the King in the Constitution. The King is accordingly eliminated from the internal affairs of the Free State.

[1] See the Appendix (below, p. 616) for a discussion of some of the conventions, fundamental and otherwise, touching the monarch's personal life.

Commonwealth as divisible in matters of peace and war lies not in any supposed indivisibility of the Crown in this respect—for the Crown, like any other fictitious entity, exists only to have arbitrary meanings given to it—but in the extreme difficulty of distinguishing in such matters between the nationals of one member of the Commonwealth and those of another, so long as and to the extent that the status of British subject is for these purposes the common nationality of the citizens of all members of the Commonwealth.

The only provisions of the Statute of Westminster which affect the power of the Dominions to deprive the Crown of its prerogatives, namely sections 2 and 3, appear at first sight to many orthdox lawyers to do no more than free Dominion legislation which is otherwise *intra vires* from two general restrictions which had hitherto been imposed on it apart from the limits contained in the original grant of power: the restriction (whatever it may be) on extra-territorial effect, and invalidity for repugnancy to imperial Acts expressly or by necessary implication extending to the Dominions. The abolition of an external limitation on a granted power does not enlarge the grant itself. On this view, these sections would not enable the Dominion Parliaments to affect matters, such as royal prerogatives of an imperial, not a local character, which the law had hitherto simply deemed not to be included in the original grants of legislative power to the Dominions.[1] But a less literal view of the effect of those sections prevailed in *British Coal Corporation* v. *R.*[2] and *Moore* v. *Attorney-General for the Irish Free State.*[3] These cases establish that sections 2 and 3 are to be construed as an independent grant of power. It is impossible now to say what are the legal limits to the powers of those Dominion Parliaments which take the full benefit of these sections of the Statute. It seems unlikely that any measure circumscribing the powers of the Crown in such Dominions, however radically, would now be held invalid. There is, then, probably nothing in imperial fundamental law to prevent those Dominions (i.e. the Union of South Africa and the Irish Free State) from legislating to deprive the monarch of every power and dignity except his bare status as monarch and perhaps his established royal style and titles.[4]

The precise extent of the additional powers which the Statute has

[1] See Dean V. C. MacDonald in 13 *Can. Bar. Rev.* 625, and Mr. Justice Dixon in 10 *Aust. Law Journ.*, *Supp.* 96.

[2] [1935] A.C. 500.

[3] [1935] A.C. 484.

[4] Instances of Dominion legislation regulating the Crown's prerogatives in a radical way are the Status of the Union Act, No. 69 of 1934 (South Africa) and the Constitution (Amendment No. 27) Act, No. 57 of 1936 (Irish Free State) with which must be read the Royal Executive Functions and Seals Act, No. 70 of 1934 (South

conferred upon the Canadian and will, if fully adopted, confer on the New Zealand and Australian Commonwealth legislatures, is uncertain. The section[1] saving the Constitutions of Australia and New Zealand probably prohibits only legislation which alters those instruments textually or declares rules for their construction, and imposes no obstacle to legislation by the Dominion parliaments outside the powers conferred on them by the Constitutions, under the new powers conferred by sections 2 and 3 as now broadly construed.[2] The section saving the British North America Act, however, provides further that the additional powers conferred on Dominion and provincial legislatures shall not extend beyond the subject-matters at present allotted to the competence of each.[3] The benefit of the Statute extends to the legislatures of the Canadian provinces, but not to the Parliaments of the Australian States. It seems probable, then, that the New Zealand parliament and, in relation to federal matters, the Australian Commonwealth parliament would have, on adopting the Statute, as full power to minimize the royal office as the Irish and South African legislatures have, but that the State Parliaments in Australia have gained no new freedom in this respect.[4] The decision in *British Coal Corporation* v. *R.*[5] suggests that the powers of both federal and provincial legislatures in Canada to limit the royal prerogative have been considerably increased by the Statute. It cannot therefore be said with certainty that in the remaining Dominions the royal powers are any better protected from the inroads of Dominion legislation than they are in South Africa and the Irish Free State.

Canada, Australia, and New Zealand have in fact taken no steps derogating from the powers or dignity of the imperial Crown, unless Canada's abolition of the Privy Council appeal in criminal cases can be so regarded. Indeed, the change in the position of the Governor-General which was effected at the 1926 Conference, whereby he became in theory the direct personal representative of the Crown, and not at all of the British government (this does not yet apply in New Zealand) increased, nominally at least, the intimacy of the connexion between the Crown and the Dominions, though in fact the right which Dominion governments acquired at the same time to be

Africa) and the Executive Authority (External Relations) Act, No. 58 of 1936 (Irish Free State) respectively.

[1] s. 8. [2] Cf. Dixon, op. cit., p. 99. [3] s. 7.

[4] The Commonwealth Parliament's power would probably include even the regulation of matters now regulated by Imperial act which are of purely State concern, provided only that they are not 'within the authority of a State'. Dixon, op. cit., p. 101. [5] [1935] A.C. 500.

the exclusive advisers of the Crown in the appointment of Governors-General has as often as not been exercised with more regard to the closeness of the appointee's connexion with the Dominion than to his personal acquaintance with the monarch. The Irish Free State first minimized the dignity of the Crown in the Free State by appointing as its representative a nonentity who merely signed documents, and then, in 1936, eliminated it entirely from the internal constitution of the Free State, though retaining it for Commonwealth affairs.[1] South Africa has, on the other hand, done nothing to detract from the dignity of the Crown, but has effectively nullified the personal power of the King by statutorily empowering the Governor-General to act on his behalf in practically all circumstances.[2]

Imperial fundamental law is, then, no effective safeguard for common monarchical institutions in the Commonwealth. Convention is a somewhat better safeguard; but the real assurance of the continuance of the monarchy lies in two political facts: the strength of the monarchical tradition and the difficulty which would be experienced in adjusting the form of the Commonwealth association to any other kind of régime.

From the consideration of the Privy Council appeal above[3] it appears that the appeal now figures very little, if at all, in imperial fundamental law.

The most important matter in imperial fundamental law is the legislative supremacy of the Imperial Parliament. In the last analysis, this supremacy is absolute for Dominions belonging to the imperial system of law, since for them the imperial parliament may validly repeal even the Statute of Westminster, and non-existent for Dominions which treat their law as having local roots, since in their view any legislative functions which the imperial parliament exercises for them it exercises merely by the authority or at the sufferance of the local Constitution or legislature.[4] Since, however, the repeal of the Statute is not a practical possibility to be reckoned with, it is desirable to estimate what powers to pass legislation for the Dominions unrepealable by Dominion parliaments the imperial parliament has while the Statute stands. There is a general power under s. 4

[1] Constitution (Amendment No. 27) Act, No. 57 of 1936, and the Executive Authority (External Relations) Act, No. 58 of 1936. See above, p. 586, n. 2. The precise effect of these enactments will take some time to become apparent. They were drafted and passed in a hurry, and will probably need further amendment.

[2] By the Royal Executive Functions and Seals Act, No. 70 of 1934.

[3] Pp. 550–2.

[4] Cf. the position with regard to amendment of the Irish Free State Constitution, see above, p. 581, n. 1.

of the Statute to legislate for the Dominions with the request and consent of the Dominion governments. Except for Australia, where the request and consent required are the request and consent of the Commonwealth parliament,[1] a Dominion government could under this section secure the enactment of an imperial statute over the head of its parliament—a power which might be useful to it in case of a conflict with an upper house. Such legislation would necessarily have the character of local rather than imperial fundamental law, because its repeal could be secured in the same manner as its enactment. It might, however, be rendered fundamental in convention if it were requested and consented to by all the Dominions, and a convention against unilateral repeal were set up analogous to the convention concerning the succession in the preamble to the Statute of Westminster. The present power of the imperial parliament to amend the British North America Act is fully preserved. It is in fact exercised according to strict conventions: no amendment affecting the provinces is passed without the consent of the provinces affected. The imperial parliament is, however, the judge whether or not an amendment requested by the Dominion alone does affect the provinces. The greater part of the local fundamental law in Australia is contained in the Commonwealth Constitution, which is amendable by a local process; but it is usually assumed that the 'covering clauses' (i.e. the first eight sections of the Commonwealth of Australia Constitution Act, 1900, of which the Constitution is section 9) are not amendable by that process.[2] Amendments of the terms of those clauses—and, possibly, amendments of the Constitution proper repugnant to those clauses[3]—must accordingly be made by imperial Act, and by section 8 of the Statute of Westminster the law and conventions touching such measures are preserved. There is little doubt that the same conventions which govern Canadian constitutional amendments govern such Australian amendments equally.[4]

The remaining topic of imperial fundamental law is nationality.

[1] s. 9 (3).

[2] So the Joint Committee on the Receivability of the Western Australia Secession Petition held (Parl. Pap. 1935, H.C. 88, Report, para. 6). But compare the opinion of Mr. Owen Dixon, K.C. (now Mr. Justice Dixon), printed as Appendix F to the Report of the Royal Commission on the Constitution, 1929, in which he holds that the federal nature of the Constitution could be validly destroyed by an amendment under s. 128, despite the reference in Covering Clause 3 to the Commonwealth as a 'Federal Commonwealth'. The ground for this view is presumably that the inability of the Commonwealth Parliament to amend the words of the covering clauses does not necessarily entail the invalidity of amendments which do not purport to amend those clauses but are in fact inconsistent with them. Cf. above, p. 589.

[3] On which see Mr. Justice Dixon, in *10 Aust. Law Journ., Supp.* 99.

[4] Parl. Pap. 1935, H.C. 88, Report, para. 9.

There is in the modern Commonwealth a welter of nationalities, citizenships, and unnamed personal statuses which exist for a multitude of purposes. The various categories of 'citizenship' and 'nationality' created by dominion legislation can obviously be regulated in any way by dominion legislation, and so have no fundamental quality. Older than any of them is the status of British subject. The common law, and now the general provisions of the British Nationality and Status of Aliens Acts, 1914–22, which have been substituted for it, confer this status upon all persons born within the King's dominions[1] and a few born out of them, and provide that persons who have fulfilled certain requirements may acquire it by certificate of the Home Secretary of the United Kingdom or of a minister of a Dominion which has 'adopted' the Act.[2] The status so obtained is valid, for what it is worth, throughout the Empire, and must be distinguished from the status which a foreigner may acquire under Dominion Acts,[3] which can only be valid within the Dominion conferring it, and (since the Statute of Westminster at any rate) in relation to Dominion diplomatic and consular representatives abroad.

There is a common law rule of long standing that within its general legislative competence the legislature of every self-governing colony can regulate the *incidents or consequences* of the imperially valid status of British subject, but not the *status* itself.[4] This is still law. Prima facie, therefore, the *desiderata* for acquisition and loss of the imperially valid status of British subject, whether by birth, marriage, naturalization, or otherwise, are inalterable by Dominion legislation, and therefore constitute imperial fundamental law. But the legal significance of any status consists solely in its consequences in law. The imperially valid status of British subject is capable of having, and has in fact, consequences in law for its possessor in three spheres: in his own municipal[5] law, in the municipal laws of other parts of the Commonwealth, and in international law. We must therefore inquire to what extent its consequences in each of these spheres are guaranteed by imperial fundamental law.

The Canadian, the Australian, or the New Zealander enjoys his political rights and most other domestic rights of citizenship in his

[1] The King's dominions (which it is convenient to distinguish from the self-governing Dominions by the use of a small 'd') are all places which are under the Crown for the purposes of constitutional (not international) law. They do not include Protectorates or Mandated Territories.

[2] i.e. has adopted Part II of the British Nationality and Status of Aliens Act, 1914, pursuant to s. 9 thereof.

[3] For an account of this and other local statuses see *The British Empire*, chapter xx.

[4] See above, p. 520.

[5] See below, p. 595, n. 1.

Dominion in virtue of his status as a British subject. The Irishman or the South African, on the other hand, now enjoys these rights in his Dominion in virtue of his Irish citizenship or his South African nationality.[1] There is no doubt of the validity of the legislation which has created this state of affairs, and the other three Dominions could pass similar legislation if they wished.

Except in the Irish Free State,[2] the title by which some or all of the rights and duties of local citizenship are enjoyed by persons from other parts of the Commonwealth is their status as British subjects. But, clearly, a self-governing nation will extend privileges within its borders only to persons and categories of persons which it approves; nor, if it has decided by its law to accord or deny such privileges to a given person or category of persons, will it be restrained by anything in the law of the country of origin of these persons.[3] The legislatures of the Dominions and Great Britain are therefore free, if they wish, to substitute other qualifications instead of the status of British subject as the title to such privileges, as the Irish Free State has already done.[2] No incidents of this kind, then, are attached to the status of British subject by imperial fundamental law.

The determination of the categories of persons to whom a diplomatic or consular representative of Great Britain or a Dominion will accord protection is as much a function of the municipal law of the member of the Commonwealth which he serves as the determination of privileged categories in internal affairs.[4] Any doubt of the Domi-

[1] For accounts of Irish citizenship and South African nationality, see *The British Empire*, loc. cit. Not all British subjects are Irish citizens or South African nationals.

[2] In the Free State, most of the rights of citizenship are by the Aliens Order, 1935, extended not to British subjects as such, but to 'nationals or citizens' of Australia, Canada, Great Britain, South Africa, and New Zealand.

[3] Thus s. 33 of the Irish Nationality and Citizenship Act, No. 13 of 1935, provides that:

'(1) The British Nationality and Status of Aliens Act, 1914, and the British Nationality and Status of Aliens Act, 1918, if and so far as they respectively are or ever were in force in Saorstát Éireann, are hereby repealed.

(2) The common law relating to British nationality, if, and so far as it is, or ever was, either wholly or in part, in force in Saorstát Éireann, shall cease to have effect.

(3) The facts or events by reason of which a person is at any time a natural-born citizen of Saorstát Éireann shall not of themselves operate to confer on such person any other citizenship or nationality.'

But this enactment does not affect the law of the rest of the Commonwealth whereby Irishmen are British subjects, and are treated as such.

[4] The Irish Free State, however, by the Constitution (Amendment No. 27) Act, No. 57 of 1936 and the Executive Authority (External Relations) Act, No. 58 of 1936, empowers the Executive Council in future to advise the King in the appointment of diplomatic and consular representatives. A representative appointed by the King for the United Kingdom with the advice or concurrence of the Free State Executive Council would thus be deemed in Irish law at least to protect Irish

nion's competence in this respect springing from the alleged territorial limitation of Dominion legislative power has been removed by section 3 of the Statute of Westminster.

It is indeed difficult to think of any incident or consequence in municipal law of the status of British subject[1] which is since the Statute of Westminster preserved from the control of the legislatures of the Dominions by imperial fundamental law.[2]

The question who may regulate the possession of the status of British subject in international law is quite another matter, and one of extreme obscurity. The suggestion may, however, be hazarded that if the Dominions which have erected categories of nationality of their own (i.e. Canada, South Africa, and the Irish Free State) were so to define these categories as to make them serviceable categories for the purposes of international law,[3] then, by reason of the undoubted international personality of these Dominions, a foreign nation would be justified in treating Dominion nationality as a true nationality for international purposes, and consequently applying the law of the Dominion, rather than any alleged imperial fundamental law conflicting with it, in determining whether or not a national of the Dominion had also the additional status of a British subject.[4] If this suggestion is correct, then the consequences in international law also of the status of British subject are controllable by Dominion legislatures.

It therefore seems likely that in law the consequences of that status of British subject whose acquisition is purported to be governed by imperial fundamental law are entirely malleable. So far as it confers rights and duties under the municipal laws of Commonwealth countries, those rights and duties are controlled by the relevant

citizens as such and by Irish authority. But if the Irish government or legislature should give him instructions incompatible with those given by the United Kingdom, he would doubtless follow the instructions of the government that paid him. No representative has yet been appointed in the manner contemplated. British representatives therefore continue to protect Irish citizens who are British subjects, by reason of their being British subjects, and Irish citizens who are not British subjects, by courtesy alone.

[1] The right of appeal to the Privy Council is not, as is often erroneously thought, a right attaching to British subjects as such, but extends to any party competent to bring or defend an action in a court from which the appeal lies.

[2] Some consequences may be prescribed by rigid constitutions, and thus be removed from the control of the legislature by *local* fundamental law; e.g., s. 23 of the British North America Act, 1867, requires Canadian senators to be British subjects.

[3] Dr. Baty, in 18 *Journ. Comp. Leg.* 195, 199 suggests that Canadian nationality is not yet serviceable in this respect. Irish Free State nationality, on the other hand, since the Irish Nationality and Citizenship Act, No. 13 of 1935, undoubtedly is.

[4] It is only in such circumstances that s. 33 (3) of the Irish Nationality and Citizenship Act, No. 13 of 1935 (quoted above, p. 593, n. 3) could have practical significance.

vant legislatures; so far as it confers a status in international law, the terms upon which that status may be acquired are controllable by the legislature of the member of the Commonwealth to which the relevant foreign power regards the person as primarily belonging. There is no certainty about it, but it is probably safer to deny than to assert that any rights or duties are firmly secured by imperial fundamental law to those upon whom it confers the name of British subject.

III

The Nature and Future of Commonwealth Obligation

A number of conventions, understandings, political practices and obligations, both general and particular, have come into existence to perform for the Commonwealth the function which is performed for centralized empires, for the most part, by constitutional law, and for the comity of nations, so far as it is performed at all, by international law—that is, to regulate the mutual relations of its members so far as they are capable of and require regulation by established and explicit rules. Neither municipal[1] law (of which constitutional law is an integral part) nor international law is merely a convenient descriptive classification of a number of essentially unrelated rules; both form more or less coherent systems—municipal law more, international law less. The question therefore arises whether the conventions, understandings, and obligations of the Commonwealth form likewise in any degree a coherent system, or are merely a congeries of rules connected only by a certain similarity of subject-matter. If they should be found to constitute a coherent system, the further question will arise, what is the relation of that system to municipal law on the one hand and international law on the other; and the possibility must not be excluded that Commonwealth conventions may prove to be or to have become indistinguishable from rules of municipal or of international law. These questions constitute at the moment a vital legal problem of the Commonwealth. It is a problem rich in theoretical interest and weighty with practical consequence, for upon the solution of it depends the possibility of establishing an effective tribunal which can guarantee the rule of some intelligible principle of order in Commonwealth affairs. The present essay does not assume or argue that Commonwealth affairs must be intelligibly ordered: there is virtue also in judicious disarray. It seeks only to

[1] By 'municipal law' international lawyers mean the system of law of each state, as distinct from international law. The word is used here in that sense.

examine what possible forms the rules of the Commonwealth might assume, if the Commonwealth is to be regulated by rules at all.

Where rules, whatever their origin, are administered in the same tribunal, and that tribunal operates fairly continuously, it will inevitably so interpret the rules as to make them cohere. In doing this, it treats them as belonging to a single system of law: and, as we have seen, courts in the English tradition are capable in practice of administering a system although its limits remain undefined and its *Grundnorm* shrouded in mystery. But there is no tribunal which has a general jurisdiction in Commonwealth convention, still less one in regular operation. The timid recommendation of the 1930 Imperial Conference in favour of *ad hoc* tribunals for Commonwealth disputes[1] has not once been applied, and in the only dispute in connexion with which its application was discussed, namely the Land Annuities dispute of 1932, the parties were unable to agree upon the composition of such a tribunal.[2] None of the tribunals which have actually taken cognizance of questions of Commonwealth convention has had any pretence to a general jurisdiction in that sphere. The Judicial Committee of the Privy Council considered and adjudged questions of convention in *British Coal Corporation* v. *R.*,[3] but only incidentally to its proper task, which lay in the sphere of strict law. The Joint Committee of the House of Lords and the House of Commons on the receivability of the Western Australian petition for secession from the Australian Commonwealth construed its task as extending to the ascertainment of the matters relevant to that issue and to that only, law being treated as ancillary and political merits neglected. Its report[4] is a valuable document in the authoritative literature of convention. But it was an *ad hoc* body, and acted solely under the authority and on behalf of the Parliament at Westminster.[5] Certain controversies between the India Office and the War Office concerning the liability of Indian revenues for the training of British troops for Indian service have indeed been dignified by the British Government with the appearance of a dispute between members of the Commonwealth, and an eminent Australian lawyer was called in to preside over the Tribunal which was set up in 1932 to advise on

[1] Cmd. 3717, pp. 23–5. [2] Below, p. 607. [3] [1935] A.C. 500. Below, pp. 613–14.

[4] *Parliamentary Papers*, 1935, H.L. 75, H.C. 88.

[5] Its members were Viscount Goschen (formerly Governor of Madras and for a short time Viceroy of India; with Australian experience); the Marquis of Lothian (formerly active in South African politics under Lord Milner; Secretary to the Rhodes Trust; imperial publicist), Lord Wright (Master of the Rolls, a law lord); Mr. L. C. M. S. Amery, M.P. (formerly Colonial and Dominions Secretary), Mr. Isaac Foot, M.P. (Solicitor), Mr. William Lunn, M.P. (formerly Parliamentary Under-Secretary for the Colonies and Dominions). Lord Goschen presided

the question. Its other members were two British and two Indian judges.[1] But India, not being self-governing, is a member of the Commonwealth only in an honorific and anticipatory sense,[2] and in any case the issue was not one of convention but of 'fair, just and equitable adjustment'.[3] There does not at present exist any jurisdiction which could conceivably of itself reduce Commonwealth convention to order and coherence. If it is a coherent system, or has a tendency towards coherence, that must spring from other causes and will be discernible from other considerations.

The distinction has already been drawn[4] between the conventions of status, which are rules inhibiting the operation of imperial institutions that are not in strict law equalitarian, and the conventions of co-operation, which have equality of status not as their end but as their basis. The former are mainly customary in origin. They operate on particular institutions such as the Crown, the United Kingdom cabinet, and the imperial parliament, imposing upon them in favour of Dominion freedom duties of abstention, and sometimes of action, over and above their duties in strict law. To a convention of this class there are normally only two parties: the Dominion interested and the imperial institution whose freedom is restricted. Conventions of co-operation may be customary, but are now more often contractual. The parties to them are the separate members of the Commonwealth regarded as political units, and they may be multilateral, like the general resolutions of imperial conferences, or bilateral, like the Ottawa agreements.

The early conventions of the self-governing colonies which were to become the Commonwealth were mostly, though not entirely, of the former, the inhibitory kind.[5] They developed from departmental and political practices which arose to meet particular needs. They bore no relation to each other beyond the resemblance of the circumstances in which they were conceived and the fact that many of them were administered by a single body, the Colonial Office. Formally, the degree of emancipation of each colony was a matter between it and the Colonial Office; there was no general status in convention which colonies, or colonies of a particular class, enjoyed as such. We can now see that the meeting of representatives of the colonies at

[1] The members were Sir Robert Garran (chairman), Lord Dunedin, Lord Tomlin (both law lords), Sir Shadi Lal and Sir Muhammad Sulaiman (Indian Chief Justices).

[2] For India's inchoate Commonwealth status, see p. 169, above.

[3] Report, Cmd. 4473, p. 12.

[4] Above, pp. 585–6.

[5] For an exhaustive examination of the early Commonwealth conventions, see a forthcoming book by K. C. Wheare on *Usage and Convention in the British Commonwealth*, which the writer has had the privilege of consulting in manuscript.

colonial (later called imperial) conferences had to lead to an ultimate standardization of colonial self-governing status. As soon as it was recognized that questions of status were proper to be discussed there, it was inevitable that the status of the self-governing Dominions would come to be not merely accidentally, but essentially similar, despite their unequal political development. In the War of 1914–18, a common equal status of the Dominions was a patent fact. In 1921 the Irish Treaty expressly prescribed that the new Irish Free State should have the same constitutional status as the Dominions,[1] and in 1922 its constitution provided that it should be 'a co-equal member of the Community of Nations forming the British Commonwealth of Nations'.[2] The Balfour Report of 1926 assumed throughout that each member of the Commonwealth was bound to each other member by ties that were essentially the same. Thus from being a number of isolated alleviations of the strict law, the conventions of status became a body of general doctrine. Most of the conventions of status now existing might indeed be summed up in a single rule: where laws create inequality of status, they are to be so administered by all parties as to give substantial equality in fact.

The general conventions of co-operation were under no comparable compulsion from circumstances to cohere, and they have been diversely interpreted and are not seldom disobeyed. But the coherence which they lack in execution they possess in intention. Unlike the conventions of status, they have been for the most part planned. Reports of imperial conferences repeatedly enunciate comprehensive rules for the conduct of treaty negotiations and other matters of foreign policy, and shorter sets of rules for such matters as legislation touching the succession to the Crown. All these rules are expressed in similar terms, and refer constantly to one another and to the conventions of status. Whether particular co-operative agreements are made within the context of the general conventions of co-operation or as isolated bargains is a matter which may affect the force and precision of those agreements themselves,[3] but does not affect the coherence of the general conventions.

Concerning the intimacy of the relationship between the conventions of status and the conventions of co-operation there is a differ-

[1] Treaty, Art. 1.

[2] Constitution, Art. 1.

[3] No contract can by its express terms cover all contingencies which may arise under it. The experience of private law shows the necessity of a background of general doctrine concerning contracts which is either incorporated into particular contracts by reference or governs them *suo proprio vigore*. International law has a similar though less well-developed doctrine concerning treaties. Commonwealth agreements are not exempt from these necessities.

ence of view between the United Kingdom and the more radical Dominions which is none the less marked because it is seldom clearly expressed. The radical Dominions naturally exalt the conventions of status, which are their title-deeds to nationhood; the United Kingdom clings to the conventions of co-operation, which are the surviving formal embodiment of imperial unity. If the government of the United Kingdom can succeed in linking the co-operative conventions intimately with the conventions of status, the Dominions may accord to the former something of the inviolability which, they insist, attaches to the latter. Documents of United Kingdom origin are thus apt to stress the mutual coherence, almost the interdependence, of conventions of status and conventions of co-operation. The classical example is the leading section of the Balfour Report[1]—a document bearing all the marks of United Kingdom authorship[2]—in which each paragraph, each sentence, almost each word imputing emancipation is balanced immediately by an assertion of association. An observer unacquainted with other terrestrial institutions might well assume, upon reading the Report, that national status and the Commonwealth association were in some sense inevitable correlatives. The radical Dominions on the other hand, who have come, perhaps a little unhistorically, to assert that they enjoy national status as of natural right, regard the conventions establishing it as tardy recognitions of eternal facts, and do not think of their emancipation as in any way qualified, still less conditioned, by the vague co-operative undertakings which of their grace they have given to their fellow-nations in the Commonwealth.

Thus the conventions of the Commonwealth are not a congeries of unrelated imperatives lacking entirely a common measure or a common design. Each of the two great classes of them shows a tendency towards that formal coherence which is one of the marks of a system of law.[3] Whether there is real coherence between the two classes themselves is more doubtful. But further speculation on this point must be postponed until after the consideration of the relation of the conventions of each class to the flanking and overshadowing systems of municipal and international law.

The present strict separation of international law from municipal systems of law dates only from the Renaissance and the Reformation,

[1] Cmd. 2768, pp. 14–15.

[2] It is not suggested that the United Kingdom imposed anything in the substance of the report upon the Dominions. But it is generally accepted that the drafting of the crucial parts owes more to Lord Balfour's hand than to any other.

[3] Above, p. 522.

when the sovereign state was first exalted above all other human collectivities. There is nothing in the nature of the world or of men which demands that the particular human grouping called the nation-state should be preferred above all others as it has been by the conventional morality and the law of the last three centuries. The nation did not claim primary loyalty in the Middle Ages, and the absolute claims of the Roman Empire rested not on its character as a nation among other nations, but on the false assumption that it was coterminous with civilization as a whole coupled with the truth that it was coterminous with a particular civilization and with a particular economic system. There is therefore no reason for assuming that the nation-state will for all future time be the most formally potent grouping of men. While now in some quarters nationalism is being further inflated, so that from being the prevailing it shall become the only loyalty of citizens, there are other quarters where it is losing its power. If the supremacy of the nation-state should break down in fact, its breakdown in law will doubtless follow at the usual respectful interval.

But for the present, in every civilized jurisdiction in the world municipal law prevails over all other kinds of law. Any duties the state as such may owe can only be owed to other states, and the law of states between themselves forms no part of their respective municipal laws, nor has it access to the sanctions of municipal law. Municipal law, the only law which touches and effectively governs the actions of men, is not allowed to look beyond the state and its acts except by its special grace, and, conversely, the law which alone purports to have world order as its goal may not touch a citizen of the world except by grace of his government, even though that government itself is the principal transgressor against the peace.[1] So municipal law may compel a citizen to commit an international crime, and the observance of international law or even the acknowledgment of an international loyalty may be an offence in municipal law. In a world where international contacts are by no means limited to meetings of sovereigns on fields of cloth of gold, this unnatural barrier between the instruments of international and national order is a major symptom of our present ills, and in so far as those ills are attributable to defects in institutions as distinct from policies, it is a major cause of them.[2]

[1] Above, p. 511. The existence of an international obligation binding Canada to legislate in a certain way does not even enlarge the power of the Dominion parliament to enable it to implement the obligation: *in re Weekly Rest in Industrial Undertakings Act &c.*, [1937] W.N. 53. But otherwise in Australia: *R.* v. *Burgess, ex. p. Henry* (1936) 10 Aust. Law Journ. 335.

[2] See, for an analysis of the fallacies which surround the idea of state sovereignty

The analogous barrier in British Commonwealth law and convention between domestic rules and the rules of the Commonwealth association is not nearly so absolute and impenetrable. This is not due to exceptional wisdom in Commonwealth as compared with international statesmen, but follows inevitably from the long uncertainty whether the true nation, the proper object of unique allegiance, was each separate member of the Commonwealth or the British Empire as a whole, and the persistence, after the matter had been settled substantially in favour of the former, of extensive formal and sentimental vestiges in the contrary sense.[1] But some of the consequences of the present anomalous transitional situation are none the less fortunate for being in this sense fortuitous. In particular, it avoids one of the most barbarous of the logical consequences of the hypertrophy of the sovereign state: the ticketing of all mankind with five or six dozen sorts of labels called nationalities, each sort imposing upon its wearers the moral and social absurdity of a unique allegiance. The common status of British subject, though not securely anchored in imperial fundamental law,[2] remains potent in existing municipal law, and secures, at least to those of its possessors whose skins are white, a large measure of equal treatment over a quarter of the surface of the earth. Although for various purposes local statuses have been created, they are not yet, even in the intention of their authors (except in the Irish Free State),[3] mutually exclusive. This and similar humane rules in the purely political sphere have suggested to many of the liberal philosophers of the Empire the hope that the Commonwealth relationship may be a precursor and model for a new and saner system of international order.

The counterpart of this hope in the juristic sphere would be the hope that Commonwealth convention should succeed in integrating the domestic laws of the nations of the Commonwealth with the rules of their mutual relations into a single articulated system, in which the loyalties claimed from the citizen by local, regional, and oecumenical institutions should be better proportioned in their strength and extent to the necessary and proper functions of those institutions

in international law, J. L. Brierly in *British Year Book of International Law*, 1924, pp. 12 sqq.

[1] The chief of these, the *inter se* doctrine, described below, pp. 602–7, is a good deal more than a vestige.

[2] Above, pp. 594–5.

[3] Though the Irish Nationality and Citizenship Act, 1935, purports to make Irish nationality exclusive of other national statuses, the other parts of the Commonwealth still treat the vast majority of Irish nationals as British subjects, and the citizens of other parts of the Commonwealth in the Free State are exempted from many of the consequences of alienage by executive order. Cf. above, p. 593.

than are the national and international allegiances now imposed upon the citizen. Though this would be a most admirable achievement, there is little to indicate that Commonwealth law and convention can attain it. Key concepts of the older systems, such as sovereignty and nationality, have filtered through to popular consciousness, and, albeit in a distorted form, command the loyalties and thereby influence the actions of men. Commonwealth law and convention have produced no concept which has comparable power over men's minds.[1]

This optimism is, perhaps a little paradoxically, one of the supports of what is called the *inter se* doctrine in the Commonwealth—a doctrine whose essence is that relations between members of the Commonwealth are *sui generis* and more intimate than relations between other nations, and that for the preservation of this uniqueness and intimacy they should be separated from international relations. Since, in the liberal optimist view, Commonwealth relations are superior in quality to international relations, and are destined to supersede them, they must be kept uncontaminated by contact with international affairs while the latter remain unregenerate. This feeling, which might be called the Liberal root of the *inter se* doctrine, overlaps and insensibly merges into its stronger Tory root, which is the sentiment that British institutions are in the nature of things superior to foreign institutions, and therefore not to be mixed with them. The *inter se* doctrine, however arrived at, may take one or other of two opposite forms. It may demand that advantage be taken of the good will between Commonwealth nations to clarify and elaborate rules to cover every contingency in the Commonwealth which is capable of regulation by law, and the institution of a Commonwealth tribunal to interpret and apply those rules; or it may hold that rules are not necessary where good will exists, and look forward to Commonwealth relations becoming like those of a family, or of the Communist classless state when law has withered away. The *inter se* doctrine in one or other of these senses, or in an intermediate form, is dominant in the United Kingdom, Australia and New Zealand, and strong in Canada. On the other hand 'radicals' in Ireland, South Africa and Canada feel that their national independence against the encroachments of Great Britain or a co-operative Commonwealth conspiracy[2] must not lack whatever prestige or protection the recognition of their full and perfect sovereignty in international law can bring. Of these two benefits, prestige must be uppermost in their minds, else the quest would be pointless at a

[1] Imperial symbols (Crown, flag, &c.) are not essentially *Commonwealth* ideas.

[2] Those Dominion nationalists who hold the theory of the 'Liberal Conspiracy' think advocacy of co-operation merely camouflages British 'imperialism'.

time like the present, when the security given by international law is almost negligible.

The *inter se* doctrine manifests itself in every department of Commonwealth affairs, cultural, political, legal, and conventional. It resorts to expedients of various types: where Commonwealth and international institutions differ in substance, the difference is stressed; where they do not differ in substance, they are made to differ in form; and where they do not differ even in form they are made to differ in name. Its manifestations include trivial matters of precedence and nomenclature, such as the practice whereby the mutual envoys of members are called not Ambassadors but High Commissioners, matters of some importance, such as the refusal to allow foreigners to participate in the settlement of Commonwealth disputes, and matters of supreme importance, such as the symbolism attached to the Crown and the fact of common citizenship. It is indeed the *differentia* of the Commonwealth among international associations.[1]

The *inter se* doctrine is perverted in many ways, notably by those who meet arguments for international co-operation either with the plea that imperial co-operation on the same lines must come first,[2] or with the plea that, since institutions or obligations of the kind proposed are not found necessary within the Empire, they are not necessary outside it.[3] Even in British official and orthodox imperialist pronouncements it often serves—in effect, if not in intention—no other purpose than that of endowing statements which are in fact controversial with a spuriously axiomatic appearance and a gratuitous emotive force. The classical expression of the application of the doctrine to the question of the international character of intra-Commonwealth relations, which is our present concern, is an example of this perversion. Sir Cecil Hurst states it thus:[4]

> 'If I may put the matter in one short sentence, I would say that the common allegiance to the Crown prevents the relations between the different communities being international relations.'

The word 'allegiance', though heavy with emotional content, has

[1] The Little Entente, for example, is knit closer by geography and by strategic common interest, and the mutual obligations of its members go in many respects beyond those of the Commonwealth; but the lack of an *inter se* doctrine places it in a different and looser class.

[2] This is the perversion suggested by the phrase 'Empire Free Trade'.

[3] This perversion is commonly used by apologists for the reluctance of Great Britain to enter into definite obligations to play her part in restraining breaches of the peace in Europe.

[4] In Lowell and Hall (ed.), *The British Commonwealth of Nations* (1927), pp. 54–5.

no meaning in law except in the particular consequences which the law ascribes to the status which it creates. Those consequences had even in 1927, when Sir Cecil Hurst wrote, not prevented the Dominions from entering into direct relations with foreign powers which were inconsistent in the sense that as a result thereof contradictory duties might be laid upon the citizens of different Dominions. If the Dominions have international personality for those purposes, it seems difficult to assert that they are *incapable* of having it for the purpose of contracting with one another. Sir Cecil Hurst's statement, then, by attributing the non-international character of Commonwealth relations to common allegiance does not explain it; it merely attaches to it the emotional reaction which is evoked by that word.[1]

In the inconclusive and intermittent controversy on this question which has gone on since the Peace, successive British governments have wavered between the view that Commonwealth relations are incapable of the character of international relations and the view that they are capable of that character, but it is undesirable that they should have it. At the other extreme, Irish governments have asserted the completely and exclusively international character of the Free State's relations with other members of the Commonwealth; with this *nuance*, that the Cumann na nGaedheal Government was at pains to assert the validity of the Treaty of 1922 in international law, while the Fianna Fáil Government has taken the line that it is either invalid upon the ground of duress or so unconscionable that its binding force is thereby impaired. South African governments, at least since General Hertzog took office in 1924, have consistently held that South Africa's relations with other Commonwealth nations are potentially international, but that South Africa applies the *inter se* doctrine of her own free will. Liberal, but not Conservative, governments in Canada have taken a similar line.

The basic question whether the Covenant of the League of Nations could be invoked by a member of the Commonwealth in a dispute with another member has never been decided.[2] But it is the separate membership of the Dominions in the League of Nations that has been the chief ground of most subsequent assertions of the separate international personality of the Dominions both in substance and in law.

[1] See, for another criticism of this dictum, P. J. Noel Baker, *The Present Juridical Status of the British Dominions in International Law* (1929), pp. 298 sqq. Sir Stafford Cripps expressed the same verbalistic outlook when he said of the Irish Treaty: 'It is an agreement. It is impossible in law for one sovereign to enter into a treaty with himself.' (259 *H. C. Deb.*, 5*s*., 695, 17th June 1932.)

[2] For an exhaustive and able discussion of this question, see P. J. Noel Baker, op. cit., pp. 305–18.

The first formal dispute was that concerning the registration of the Anglo-Irish Treaty of 1921 with the Secretariat of the League under Article 18 of the Covenant.[1] In 1924 the Free State Government presented the Treaty for registration, and the Secretary-General of the League, whose functions under the Article are automatic, registered it. The British Government wrote to the Secretary-General that:

> 'Since the Covenant of the League of Nations came into force, His Majesty's Government have consistently taken the view that neither it, nor any conventions concluded under the auspices of the League, are intended to govern the relations *inter se* of the various parts of the British Commonwealth. His Majesty's Government consider, therefore, that the terms of Article 18 of the Covenant are not applicable to the Articles of Agreement of 6th December, 1921.'[2]

The Free State Government replied:

> 'The obligations contained in Article 18 are, in their opinion, imposed in the most specific terms on every member of the League and they are unable to accept the contention that the clear and unequivocal language of that Article is susceptible of any interpretation compatible with the limitation which the British Government now seek to read into it.'[3]

The controversy went no farther.

In 1926 the Imperial Conference made the following declaration:[4]

> 'The making of [a] treaty in the name of the King as the symbol of the special relationship between the different parts of the Empire will render superfluous the inclusion of any provision that its terms must not be regarded as regulating *inter se* the rights and obligations of the various territories on behalf of which it has been signed by the King. In this connexion it must be borne in mind that the question was discussed at the Arms Traffic Conference in 1925, and that the Legal Committee of that Conference laid it down that the principle to which the foregoing sentence gives expression underlies all international conventions.
>
> 'In the case of some international agreements the Governments of different parts of the Empire may be willing to apply between themselves some of the provisions as an administrative measure. In this case they should state the extent to which and the terms on which such provisions are to apply. Where international agreements are to be

[1] Article 18 reads: 'Every treaty or international engagement entered into hereafter by any member of the League shall be forthwith registered with the Secretariat and shall as soon as possible be published by it. No such treaty or international engagement shall be binding until so registered.'

[2] League of Nations, *Treaty Series*, xxvii. Printed in the *Survey of International Affairs for 1924*, p. 474. See pp. 150, 321, above.

[3] Loc. cit.

[4] Cmd. 2768, p. 23.

applied between different parts of the Empire, the form of a treaty between Heads of States should be avoided.'

These words form part of a set of rules, which are perhaps hardly more than recommendations,[1] for the making of treaties by the members of the Commonwealth, and touch our problem only obliquely. They were undoubtedly drawn up with the Irish Treaty question in mind. Being an agreed text, they cannot even be construed as amounting to an abandonment by Great Britain of the view that international treaties are *incapable* of applying to members of the Commonwealth *inter se*, though upon a strict construction this might be inferred from the admission that either an express contrary provision or signature in the name of the King is required to prevent a treaty from so applying. It is suggested rather than laid down that it is not desirable that future treaties should be made to apply *suo proprio vigore*, by virtue of international law, between members of the Commonwealth. Nothing is said of the Irish Treaty, or of the eligibility of intra-Commonwealth agreements in general for registration under Article 18 of the Covenant.[2] The question whether imperial relations shall be international relations is left open, with a suggestion that they should not normally be given an international character. It now becomes clear, however, that the issue will be determined by practice and, possibly, agreement, not by dogma.

The attitude of the governments of the Commonwealth to the submission of Commonwealth disputes to the Permanent Court of International Justice exhibits with unusual clarity the way in which the *inter se* doctrine is regarded in the various Dominions.[3] In 1929 Great Britain and all the Dominions adhered for the first time to the 'Optional Clause' of the Statute of the Court. States so adhering recognize the jurisdiction of the Court as 'compulsory, *ipso facto* and without special agreement' in relation to all other States adhering to the Clause in practically all disputes of a legal character. The Court is not an arbitral body or tribunal in equity, but a tribunal of strict international law. To admit the competence of the Court in a dispute is, therefore, to admit that the dispute is one of international law.

[1] The part quoted cannot be taken as laying down hard-and-fast rules, for its principal recommendation, namely, that treaties should be made in the names of Heads of States, requires the concurrence of the foreign parties.

[2] The view taken by Mr. Noel Baker in his extended treatment of the matter (op. cit., pp. 289–301), that the Conference resolution amounts to a defeat for the Irish view, seems therefore to go too far.

[3] See, for a fuller account of the adhesions of 1929, Sir John Fischer Williams in *British Year Book of International Law*, 1930, p. 63.

The United Kingdom made its adherence subject to the reservation of—

> 'Disputes with the Government of any other member of the League which is a member of the British Commonwealth of Nations, all of which disputes shall be settled in such manner as the parties have agreed or shall agree.'[1]

Mr. Henderson, the Foreign Secretary, explained the reservation by the official theory that—

> 'the Members of the Commonwealth, though international units individually in the fullest sense of the term, are united by their common allegiance to the Crown. Disputes between them should therefore be dealt with by some other mode of settlement.'[2]

Canada, Australia, South Africa, New Zealand, and India made the same reservation. The Canadian and South African delegates made supplementary declarations to the effect that they withheld jurisdiction in Commonwealth disputes not because they considered them incapable of submission to the Permanent Court, but as a matter of policy. The Irish Free State adhered without any reservation at all.

In 1930 the Imperial Conference drew up a scheme for voluntary *ad hoc* tribunals in justiciable inter-Imperial disputes.[3] Nothing was said of the law to be applied by these bodies, but the *inter se* principle appeared in the shape of a provision that the personnel of tribunals should be drawn entirely from within the Commonwealth. There is, of course, nothing to prevent Commonwealth judges applying international law. In the controversy between the Irish Free State and the United Kingdom over the Land Annuities in 1932, the Free State government refused to accept the restriction of the membership of a proposed arbitral body to the Commonwealth. This demand, conversely, does not strictly amount to an assertion that Commonwealth relations are governed by international law. There is, however, no doubt that Mr. de Valera's government holds even more emphatically than did its predecessor that they are.

While no progress has been made towards the ultimate decision whether or not the rules of the Commonwealth will come within the fold of general international law or remain a separate system, Commonwealth law and convention have undergone several changes

[1] Cmd. 3452, p. 5; *Documents on International Affairs*, 1929, p. 39.
[2] Cmd. 3452, p. 6; ibid., p. 42. Cf. Hurst, above, p. 603.
[3] Cmd. 3717, pp. 22–4.

which bring them nearer in character to international law, and farther from municipal law. Most of these have already been referred to in other connexions. The assertion of local roots for the law of certain Dominions[1] endows them with formally separate systems of municipal law, and therefore separate individualities in ultimate constitutional theory, parallel to the separate personalities which all the Dominions have for some time enjoyed in international law. For the Dominions which have not asserted local roots for their laws, the growth of the distinction between imperial and local fundamental law[2] has performed a similar service in a milder way, accentuating the distinctness of their constitutional individualities without severing them entirely from the United Kingdom and each other in their ultimate constitutional theory. More important than either of these developments in strict law is the tendency towards clearer demarcation between the conventions of status, which supplement municipal law, and the conventions of co-operation, whose function is in all respects analogous to that of international law.[3]

A small but significant phenomenon is the endowment of the members of the Commonwealth as such with rudimentary corporate personalities (which must be distinguished from the constitutional individualities above referred to)[4] in strict imperial constitutional law. It has long been a convention of Commonwealth relations, as of international affairs, that a nation expresses its will only through its executive government. Suggestions that leaders of Oppositions as well as Prime Ministers might attend Imperial Conferences have been repeatedly rejected on this ground. But not until very recently have 'Canada', 'Australia'—or even 'the United Kingdom'—appeared as dramatis personae as distinct from mere properties on the stage of strict law. These names have long been used in statutes in adjectival phrases descriptive of institutions corporate and incorporate, and alone as geographical substantives, but never by themselves to designate national entities deemed to have single corporate wills of their own. 'Great Britain' and 'Ireland', persons hitherto unknown to the law, appeared as the parties to the 'Articles of Agreement for a Treaty' which were scheduled to the Irish Free State (Agreement) Act 1922. These mysterious and commanding figures presided, like premature Magi, over the birth of the Free

[1] Above, Section II (1). [2] Above, pp. 577, 582. [3] Above, pp. 597–9.

[4] Personality in the strict legal sense means the quality of being the subject of legal rights and duties. It is possessed by natural persons (human beings) and by 'bodies corporate', but not by 'unincorporated' collectivities or organisms. The law is said to 'incorporate' an entity when it makes it capable of rights and duties. 'Individuality' is here used descriptively, without any technical meaning.

State, and have not appeared again. Heads still ache all over the Commonwealth, and skulls are still cracked in Ireland, over the question of their identity and the significance of their brief act. (But these matters are less urgent now, for the spells they wove have almost ceased to bind.) Section 2 of the Statute of Westminster provides that no future statute of the Imperial Parliament shall apply to a Dominion as part of the law of that Dominion unless the request and consent *of that Dominion* are declared in the preamble. Who is this person, the Dominion, who has a tongue to request and a mind to consent? When the Statute was drafted the Australian representatives, affecting a proper judicial ignorance, complained of the imprecision of the reference. But the other Dominions were not to be cheated of the scintilla of personal status which the section implied, and in a supplementary section[1] the phrase was defined for Australia, but for no other Dominion, as meaning the request and consent of the Parliament of the Dominion. In His Majesty's Declaration of Abdication Act, 1936, the 'request and consent' recited was that of 'Canada' *simpliciter*, and the 'assents' recited were likewise those of 'Australia', 'South Africa', and 'New Zealand'. In fact, the expressions of approval of the Act to which the recital referred all emanated from the governments concerned and not from the parliaments, with the single exception, again, of Australia.[2] Thus the new legal persons performed their first act in law. We may expect that in future imperial statutes applying to the Dominions—if there are any—the veil will be drawn more thickly over the internal organization of the Dominions, and the single will of the Dominion government will wherever possible be left to speak alone, in the name of the Dominion as a legal person, to the outside world, equally within or without the Commonwealth. The assimilation to international practice is clear.

In sum, it appears that the law and convention of the Commonwealth is likely to disappoint those who hoped it would bring a positive contribution to the framing of a new and better rule of international order. As its doctrine becomes more definite its shape follows more and more exactly the familiar outlines of international law, despite its remaining for the present, in the view of most members of the Commonwealth, a formally separate system. This

[1] s. 9 (1).

[2] The resolution of the Australian Parliament on 11th December 1936 was not designed to satisfy s. 9 (1), for the Statute of Westminster does not yet apply to Australia, and the Abdication Act came into effect there *suo proprio vigore*. It was designed to satisfy the convention concerning laws regarding the succession agreed upon in 1929 and 1930 and recited in the preamble to the Statute.

does not mean that certain of its negative aspects may not fulfil a modest but not negligible fraction of liberal hopes. Its greatest achievement in this direction has been in the matter of common citizenship. Experience has shown that within an association such as the Commonwealth, in which the contingency of war between the members need not be provided for, the fullest measure of national self-government under the traditional form of the sovereign state does not necessitate the confining of civic and political rights in the several nations to persons belonging to mutually exclusive national categories.[1] National sovereignty is compatible with common or reciprocal citizenship within any group of nations which does not contemplate internecine war. The demonstration of the possibility of such a common citizenship arrangement is a real contribution to the technique of a world order.

It remains to consider the relation of Commonwealth conventions to municipal law. The very definition of constitutional convention is a negative one: it consists of those usages of public men and public bodies which are thought of as obligatory for some other reason than that they are cognizable in a court of law. A convention may be thought obligatory for that reason as well, that is to say, a law may coincide with it; but in such cases the convention is normally superfluous because of the superior authority and efficacy of law. Only where the force of law is for some reason attenuated is it worth while inquiring whether a rule of convention exists parallel to the rule of law.

A convention may be derived from custom or from agreement. In domestic affairs agreement rarely, if ever, creates constitutional convention, because the usual parties—namely ministers, members of Parliament, the Houses of Parliament, and the King—have not moral authority to bind their successors by mere agreement apart from precedent. But in Commonwealth relations it has long been recognized that the agreement of the executive government of a member binds its successors, because it would be derogatory to its autonomy if other members, in order to ascertain their rights and obligations in relation to it, were compelled to examine its internal affairs. Agreed conventions are accordingly common in Common-

[1] The Irish Free State, which is the only member of the Commonwealth which seeks to make its citizenship exclusive of other Commonwealth citizenships—and even that with such palliatives as to make the British or Dominion visitor in effect much more nearly a citizen than an alien—is the exception which proves the rule, for it is the only Dominion where there is not an overwhelming conviction that war with another member of the Commonwealth is unthinkable.

wealth affairs, the chief of them being the conventions agreed upon at Imperial Conferences. A certain difficulty arises over those conventions of status to which the parties are a Dominion or Dominions on the one side and some organ in the United Kingdom constitution other than the executive government, such as the Imperial Parliament, on the other. It is very doubtful whether Parliament would be prepared to assent to the proposition that the United Kingdom government of the day has general authority to commit even the existing parliament, let alone its successors, to whatever conventional obligations ministers may concert with Dominion governments.[1] At least, one can easily imagine circumstances in which a succeeding, or even the same parliament, might revolt against such obligations.[2] So far as the current parliament at least is concerned, the recital of such conventions in a preamble to a statute may be thought to mend matters somewhat, by expressing Parliament's consent.[3] The difficulty is less where the convention is negative, binding Parliament *not* to act, than where it imposes a positive obligation to legislate to a certain effect: Parliament is less likely to jib at being told not to legislate[4] than at being told that it

[1] Professor J. L. Brierly has drawn the attention of the writer to the circumstances in which the Empire Marketing Board was established. Mr. Baldwin at the Imperial Conference of 1923 promised the Dominions certain preferential duties. He was put out of office before he could implement this promise, and regained office in the next year on a pledge not to impose a tariff. He and his majority, however, felt so far bound by the pledge that a sum equivalent to the amount of the intended remission of duties to the Dominions was voted for the establishment of the Empire Marketing Board. Any obligation there may have been in this case was, of course, not a general convention of status, but an isolated co-operative convention. In such matters it is probable that Commonwealth arrangements will be treated in the same way as international agreements, for whose coming into force Great Britain does not, but the Dominions generally do, insist on parliamentary ratification.

[2] Some hold the view (with which the writer does not agree) that the second recital in the Statute of Westminster requires the *prior* assent of all the parliaments of the Commonwealth before legislation touching the succession can be properly passed by the imperial parliament. On this view, the enactment of His Majesty's Declaration of Abdication Act, 1936, before the *Parliaments* of Canada, South Africa, New Zealand, and the Irish Free State had assented to it was a breach of convention, and furnishes an admirable instance of the difficulty of binding Parliament even by a negative contractual convention.

[3] It is difficult to assign any other force than this to such recitals, and therefore difficult to regard recital in a preamble as a third mode of creating convention, in addition to precedent and agreement, as Dr. Jennings does (*The Law and the Constitution*, p. 86). Conventions so recited would have no force unless they had been agreed upon beforehand by the governments of the Commonwealth, at an imperial conference or otherwise; and once so agreed upon, they bind the governments without recital in a statute.

[4] Since a government nowadays can always prevent legislation, it is really sufficient, to secure the observance by Parliament of negative conventions, that the government is bound by them.

has to pass automatically without amendment some text from overseas.

There is some difficulty in distinguishing between law and convention in Commonwealth affairs, because many major topics in the Commonwealth are so seldom adjudicated upon by the courts that it is a matter of speculation what rules the courts would recognize and what they would not. The task of distinguishing has not been rendered easier by the ambiguities and the conflicts of view concerning the formal derivation of Dominion law, or by the developments described in the preceding section of this chapter. In that section we have seen how, in certain respects and for certain Dominions, rules of imperial unity which formerly rested on law have come to be regarded as having the force of convention merely,[1] so that they are not distinguishable in effect from the conventions of co-operation.

But if Commonwealth co-operation is becoming increasingly a sphere of convention, and decreasingly of law, the equal status of the members of the Commonwealth, which was established almost entirely by the development of conventions, is steadily acquiring the quality of law. By one means and another, the conventions of status are being translated into law. A parallel transformation is taking place in the domestic sphere: the Parliament Act, 1911, and the Irish Free State Constitution[2] are instances of the substitution of law for domestic constitutional convention;[3] but there the pace is slow. In the Commonwealth there have been only a few statutes of this type, but the gap between law and fact has been so wide, and the consequent pressure for its reduction so great that these few statutes have been the vehicle of a change out of proportion to the modesty of their wording, at least as that wording is read by the lawyer accustomed to the ungenerous English tradition of statutory interpretation.[4]

[1] Above, p. 582.

[2] e.g. Art. 24 (Oireachtas to fix the beginning and end of its sessions); Art. 24 as amended in 1936 (Chairman of Dáil to summon and dissolve Dáil on advice of Executive Council); Art. 28 (Dáil not to be dissolved except on such advice); Art. 35 (definition of money bills); Art. 41 as amended in 1936 (duty of Chairman to sign bills presented to him); Art. 51 until 1936 (see above, p. 586); Art. 51 (Executive Council to be responsible to Dáil Éireann); Art. 53 (Dáil to choose President of the Executive Council; President to choose members of Executive Council; Dáil not to be dissolved by Executive Council without a majority in Dáil); Art. 54 (collective responsibility of Executive Council).

[3] Mr. Justice Evatt's recent book, *The King and his Dominion Governors*, is a plea for the conversion of the conventions governing the relation between King (or Governor) and Parliament into law.

[4] e.g. *British Coal Corporation* v. *R.*, [1935] A.C. 500. See above, p. 557.

The first notable instance of the translation of Commonwealth convention into law is to be seen in the Irish Treaty, which provided[1] that

> 'Subject to the provisions hereinafter set out the position of the Irish Free State in relation to the Imperial Parliament and Government and otherwise shall be that of the Dominion of Canada, and the law, practice and constitutional usage governing the relationship of the Crown or of the Representative of the Crown and of the Imperial Parliament to the Dominion of Canada shall govern their relationship to the Irish Free State.'

By the Constitution of the Irish Free State (Saorstát Éireann) Act[2] and the Irish Free State Constitution Act, 1922,[3] this provision was 'given the force of law'. Thus the 'practice and constitutional usage' referred to was not merely applied in its original character to the new Dominion but given the character of law there.[4] This situation was remarkable in that the existence of the conventions which were to become law was left to be determined by the courts which might have occasion to apply the law.[5]

Other statutes have enacted as law rules which cover ground which was previously covered by convention. The chief of these are the Statute of Westminster, 1931,[6] the Status of the Union Act, 1934,[7] and Royal Executive Functions and Seals Act, 1934,[8] of South Africa, and the Constitution (Amendment No. 27) Act, 1936,[9] and Executive Authority (External Relations) Act, 1936,[10] of the Irish Free State. The effect of these statutes cannot be summarized here, but they have converted a considerable proportion of the conventions of status, in their application to Canada, South Africa, and the Irish Free State, into law.

It has been suggested that the opinion read by Lord Sankey for the Judicial Committee in *British Coal Corporation* v. *R.*[11] opens up the prospect that the Courts may take it upon themselves to recog-

[1] Art. 2. [2] No. 1 of 1922 of the Constituent Assembly, s. 2.

[3] 13 Geo. 5, c. 1, s. 1.

[4] S. 2 of the Constituent Act has been repealed by the Constitution (Removal of Oath) Act, No. 6 of 1933. Whether this repeal undoes the incorporation of convention into law referred to in the text is doubtful.

[5] But in fact, by reason of the reluctance of bench, bar, and litigants to emphasize the Dominion status as against the national status of the Free State, this section and the corresponding provision of s. 51 until its amendment in 1926 have seldom been invoked in Free State courts. It was cited in vain before the Judicial Committee in *Performing Right Society* v. *Bray U.D.C.*, [1930] A.C. 377, 383.

[6] 22 Geo. 5, c. 4. [7] No. 69 of 1934. Above, pp. 531. Below, p. 617.

[8] No. 70 of 1934. Above, p. 590. [9] No. 57 of 1936. Above, p. 586, n. 2.

[10] No. 58 of 1936. Above, p. 586, n. 2. [11] [1935] A.C. 500.

nize judicially certain well-established conventions, thereby giving them the force of law. In the view of Dr. Jennings,[1] the Board in this case confessedly took into account two conventions in arriving at the conclusion that, apart from external fetters, the power of the Canadian parliament under the British North America Act, 1867, includes the power to abolish the jurisdiction of the Judicial Committee in criminal appeals from Canada—the convention that the Judicial Committee, though legally part of an executive body, is a court of law, and the convention that, though in law it belongs to the executive of the United Kingdom, it is really a Canadian, or at least not merely a United Kingdom court. The words of the opinion certainly lend colour to this view; but it would take more than a single decision of the Judicial Committee to establish such a radical innovation in the law. It is perhaps best to treat the case as an extreme instance of the liberal or 'living tree' interpretation of the Canadian Constitution, and one which is by no means certain to be followed in later cases. Such confusion, from the lawyer's point of view, would result from a breakdown of the barrier between law and convention that it can hardly be anticipated that the courts will allow it to occur. But the case does serve to show how thin that barrier has become.

It seems accordingly to be the destiny of the conventions of Commonwealth status to be gradually incorporated into strict municipal law, possibly with the aid of judicial decision but principally by the instrumentality of imperial and Dominion statutes. This means that the *corpus* of Commonwealth convention will come to consist preponderantly, if not entirely, of the conventions of co-operation. They, and not the decreasing residue of conventions of status, will determine the general character of Commonwealth convention. Except on one point, generalizations concerning their future can be no more than speculation. But it seems certain that, whatever the formal relation of Commonwealth convention to the system of international law may come to be, the substance of its rules and concepts is likely, for want of intrinsic fertility or an alternative model, to approximate more and more closely to the analogy of international law. Any superiority which its rules may have over those of international law will be a negative one, arising from the refusal of the members of the Commonwealth to apply in their mutual relations the more extreme perversities of excessive nationalism. Now, as in the seventeenth century, the rules of the British Empire, whether

[1] 52 *L.Q.R.* 177–9.

they are called law or convention, will follow the facts. It has never been the British habit that they should do otherwise. All that can fairly be demanded of them is that, in a time when the very essence of the institutions to which they are attached is rapidly changing, they too should accelerate their rate of change, so as not to lag too far behind.

If Commonwealth convention joins the system of international law, it will cease to have a separate doctrinal history. If it stays separate, the alternatives of greater precision and vague equity, whose ideals are the 'Commonwealth tribunal' and the 'happy family' respectively, will remain. Prediction is difficult, but at present it seems probable that precision will prevail. There can be no real precision in any body of rules without a permanent tribunal having a general jurisdiction to interpret and apply them in a strictly judicial manner. The *ad hoc* tribunals of the 1930 Conference would be nearly useless for this purpose, even if the necessity for preliminary agreement on their personnel and terms of reference did not render them unattainable in a dispute of any acerbity. But before an effective tribunal having jurisdiction in Commonwealth convention can be set up, the relation of Commonwealth convention to international and municipal law must be settled by agreement. To many it is a matter of surprise and regret that the members of the Commonwealth, who were ready in 1929 to accord a large measure of compulsory jurisdiction to a predominantly foreign court in disputes with foreign nations, have not been able to reach a similarly reasonable arrangement among themselves. But in committing these disputes to the Hague Court, to be judged by international law, they had some idea of what they were committing themselves to. If at the present moment the members of the Commonwealth were to set up a court with the same power which the Hague Court in effect enjoys to 'find its own law', there is no knowing what its judges, set to find their way through the maze of Commonwealth rules by the light of reason alone, might not decide.

APPENDIX

THE ABDICATION OF KING EDWARD VIII IN COMMONWEALTH LAW AND CONVENTION

THE RELEVANT RULES OF LAW

I. The abdication of a monarch and the installation of a successor, whether or not the successor installed is the next in natural succession to the Throne, cannot take effect in the law of the United Kingdom or of any of the Dominions by act of the monarch, or otherwise except by statute.

This seems the best view. There is no true precedent of a voluntary abdication.[1] But the rule as stated seems to follow inevitably from the fact that the title to the Throne is parliamentary. The law officers in the United Kingdom and in all the Dominions except South Africa concurred in this view. The writer, with respect, agrees.

The view of the advisers of the South African government, which was accepted by that government,[2] is that a monarch may abdicate by his own act,[3] but, *semble*, that such abdication does not of itself disinherit his unborn issue, if any.[4]

II. (*a*) In United Kingdom law,[5] a statute of the United Kingdom parliament for the removal of a monarch and the installation of a successor validly effects that change for the United Kingdom, Australia, New Zealand, Newfoundland, and their dependencies independently of any recitals in its preamble.

(*b*) In United Kingdom law, *semble*, such a statute likewise effects that change for the Union of South Africa and its dependencies.

(*c*) *Quaere*, whether in United Kingdom law such a statute takes effect for Canada or the Irish Free State unless the request and consent of Canada or the Irish Free State, as the case may be, is recited in its preamble.

[1] For a clear exposition of the precedents, see the speech of Mr. Menzies in the Australian House of Representatives, 12th December 1936.

[2] The terms of the proclamation of the accession of King George VI in the Union on 12th December are the first evidence of the adoption of this view. On 11th December General Hertzog addressed a telegram to his predecessor as King, although on this view of the law he had ceased to be King on 10th December. General Hertzog later explained in the House of Assembly on 25th January 1937 that this style was used for reasons of courtesy.

[3] Mr. R. B. Bennett appeared to give his adherence to this view in the Canadian House of Commons on 18th January.

[4] This factor, Mr. Pirow explained in the House of Assembly on 27th January, was what necessitated legislation by the South African Parliament. His view is reflected in the wording of His Majesty King Edward VIII's Abdication Bill, 1937, cl. 2.

[5] i.e. in the law applied by the courts of the United Kingdom of Great Britain and Northern Ireland and its dependencies.

(*d*) *Et quaere*, whether in United Kingdom law, in the absence of a United Kingdom statute containing such a recital, a statute of the Oireachtas or of the Canadian parliament, as the case may be, can validly effect the change for its Dominion.

(*a*) Since the Statute of Westminster does not apply to Australia, New Zealand, and Newfoundland, the United Kingdom statute applies there of its own force as an imperial statute extending thereto by 'express words or necessary intendment' within the meaning of the Colonial Laws Validity Act, 1865, s. 1.

(*b*) The Statute of Westminster does apply to the Union of South Africa, but its operation in this particular matter is, in the opinion of the writer, circumvented by ss. 2 (as amended by s. 5 of the Status of the Union Act, 1934) and 3 of the South Africa Act, 1909. These sections, taken together, have provided since 1934 that the King for the purposes of the South Africa Act shall include 'His Majesty's heirs in the sovereignty of the United Kingdom of Great Britain and Ireland[1] as determined by the laws relating to the succession of the Crown of the United Kingdom of Great Britain and Ireland'. There is no doubt that the amendment in this sense of the South Africa Act by the Status of the Union Act is valid, whatever may be thought of the validity of other sections of the Status of the Union Act.[2] Nor is there, in the opinion of the writer, any doubt that, by reason of its greater particularity, s. 5 of the Status of the Union Act prevails over the provision of s. 2 of the same Act that no statute of the United Kingdom parliament shall apply to the Union unless adopted by the Union Parliament,[3] whatever the validity of that provision may be.[2] But it may be doubted whether the laws of the United Kingdom thus adopted include statutes passed after the date of the Status of the Union Act itself, such as His Majesty's Declaration of Abdication Act, 1936. In view of the provision of the latter Act for a demise of the Crown, there is little doubt that in this particular instance King George VI took the Throne as 'heir'. The South African government, however, did not regard the Act as applying to the Union.[4]

(*c*) Section 4 of the Statute of Westminster provides that 'No Act of Parliament of the United Kingdom passed after the commencement of this Act shall extend, or be deemed to extend, to a Dominion as part of the law of that Dominion, unless it is expressly declared in that Act that that Dominion has requested, and consented to, the enactment thereof.' The predominant view among United Kingdom jurists is that the inalienable sovereignty of the United Kingdom parliament enables it validly to pass an Act disregarding the limitation which this section purports to impose. On this view the section has no effect in law beyond raising a presumption, in cases of ambiguity whether or not an Act is intended to apply to the Dominions, that it does not apply if the requirements of the

[1] *Sic.* The Status of the Union Act throughout erroneously refers to 'the United Kingdom of Great Britain and Ireland' instead of 'the United Kingdom of Great Britain and Northern Ireland'.

[2] See above, pp. 532–4.

[3] But Mr. John Foster is not certain on this point. See *The Nineteenth Century*, February 1937, p. 234.

[4] General Hertzog in the House of Assembly, 25th January.

section have not been complied with. Others hold that the section is valid until repealed expressly or by implication by an Act which itself recites the request and consent of the Dominions in respect of which it is desired to repeal the section. The section applies without qualification to Canada and the Irish Free State.

(*d*) The British North America Act and the various constituent documents of the Irish Free State do not, in the view of United Kingdom law, themselves grant to their respective parliaments power to pass legislation affecting the succession to the Throne. It is a matter of doubt whether, in United Kingdom law, the additional power conferred by s. 2 of the Statute of Westminster extends to authorize such legislation.[1]

III. The laws of Canada, Australia, New Zealand, and Newfoundland concur with the law of the United Kingdom in the above rules.

The legal systems of Canada, Australia, New Zealand, and Newfoundland belong to the imperial system of law, and therefore cannot conflict with the law of the United Kingdom.[2]

IV. (*a*) *Semble*, in the law of South Africa, Rule I will no longer hold good, and a monarch may abdicate on his own behalf, but not on behalf of his unborn issue (*quaere*, as to existing issue), by his own act, both for South Africa and for the other parts of the Commonwealth.

(*b*) *Semble*, the law of South Africa concurs with the law of the United Kingdom in Rule II (*b*).

(*c*) In all other respects, the law of South Africa concurs with the law of the United Kingdom.

(*a*) See comments on Rule I. His Majesty King Edward VIII's Declaration of Abdication Bill, 1937,[3] of the Union expressly purports to establish in South African law the view taken by the government, and will probably be effective in doing so.[4]

(*b*) The government of the Union dissents from Rule II (*b*), and therefore from the rule here stated. The Bill does not touch the question. The writer, with respect, prefers the view here stated.[5]

V. Probably, in the law of the Irish Free State, an Act of the United Kingdom parliament to the above effect, whatever its recitals, true or false, does not effect the change for the Free State, and has effect in the other parts of the British Commonwealth according to their respective laws.

If this is so, an Act of the Oireachtas is competent, in the view of the law of the Irish Free State, to effect the change for the Irish Free State.

The position is complicated and obscure. In Free State law, the United Kingdom enjoys no inherent right to legislate, by any procedure, for the

[1] See above, pp. 588–9. [2] See above, pp. 526–7.

[3] This Bill had not been passed at the time of going to press. The writer has assumed that it would be passed in its then form.

[4] See above, pp. 532–4.

[5] For the reasons stated in the comment to Rule II (*b*), above.

Free State. Any right it has so to legislate must be conferred by the Treaty. *Quaere*, whether the Treaty does purport to confer any such right. In the view of the present government of the Free State, and probably, but not certainly, in the view of the Free State courts (from which no appeal now lies to the Privy Council), the Constitution of the Free State is no longer subject to the Treaty. But *quaere* whether, if the Treaty has been effectively removed from the fundamental law of the Free State by the Constitution (Removal of Oath) Act, 1933, the provisions of the Treaty, if any, identifying the Irish with the English law of succession were not still, at the time of the passing of the United Kingdom Abdication Act, valid ordinary law of the Free State.

If in Free State law the Constitution is not now subject to the Treaty, there is no doubt of the power of the Oireachtas to pass legislation affecting the succession for the Free State. If it is so subject, it is very questionable whether, apart from the Statute of Westminster, the Oireachtas has such power. The view of the present government that the Statute cannot confer any additional power rests on its view that the Constitution is not subject to the Treaty: so *quaere* whether, if the Constitution is subject to the Treaty, the Statute may not operate to confer the necessary power.

The Relevant Conventions

I. It is the constitutional duty of any parliament in the Commonwealth (or at least of the United Kingdom parliament) not to enact any alteration of the law touching the succession to the Throne or the royal style and titles unless the other parliaments of the Commonwealth have first assented thereto; but where such legislation is urgently necessary and the prior consultation of all the parliaments is impracticable within the time available, subsequent assent by the parliaments is sufficient, if before the enactment the initiating government has obtained from the other governments their assent, their promise that they will seek the assent of their parliaments, and their assurance that there is a reasonable certainty that that assent will not be withheld.

This rule results from the convention agreed upon at the Imperial Conference of 1930[1] which appears as the second recital of the Statute of Westminster, that

> 'inasmuch as the Crown is the symbol of the free association of the members of the British Commonwealth of Nations, and as they are united by a common allegiance to the Crown, it would be in accord with the established constitutional position of all the members of the Commonwealth in relation to one another that any alteration in the law touching the Succession to the Throne or the Royal Style and Titles shall hereafter require the assent as well of the Parliaments of all the Dominions as of the Parliament of the United Kingdom.'

The provision in an abdication statute for an artificial demise of the Crown is perhaps not technically an alteration in the law touching the succession; but the inevitable clause disinheriting the issue of the abdicating monarch is.

[1] Cmd. 3717, p. 21.

The gloss for cases of urgency is a practical necessity. Its introduction is justified by the rule, which governs the interpretation of all convention, that conventions are made to work.

II. It is the constitutional duty of any minister or government in the Commonwealth not to do anything from which a situation necessitating legislation of the above categories may result, without first consulting the other governments of the Commonwealth.

This is a corollary of Rule I, on the assumption that constitutional conventions are concerned rather with the substance than with the form of Commonwealth relations. On this view, the creation without consultation of a situation where legislation of the specified kind is inevitable is no less obnoxious to the convention than the enactment of it without consultation.

III. Independently of the two preceding rules, it is the constitutional duty of any minister or government in the Commonwealth not to tender to the monarch constitutionally significant advice in a matter of common concern, without first consulting the other governments of the Commonwealth.

IV. For the purpose of Rule III, advice is constitutionally significant whether it is tendered formally or informally, finally or tentatively, subject or not subject to reservation, if it is of such a character that in all the circumstances it is reasonably to be contemplated that the monarch may, rightly or wrongly, feel a constitutional obligation to comply with it.

V. For the purposes of Rule III, a matter is of common concern to the extent that it directly affects more than one member of the Commonwealth if in relation to that matter the monarch cannot, whether for reasons of nature, of law, or of convention, take separate action on behalf of each member concerned.

VI. For the purposes of these rules, the obligation to consult another government is satisfied if that government is accurately informed of the proposed action, and is given an opportunity to express its views to the initiating party before action is taken and, if the contemplated action is advice to the Crown, to tender advice of its own at the same time as advice is tendered by the initiating party.

VII. It is the constitutional duty of the monarch to see to the best of his ability that the conventions of Commonwealth consultation are complied with in respect of advice tendered to him, and therefore probably to disregard advice tendered in breach of them.

These rules, especially Rules III to V, are difficult to formulate, and some will disagree with the above formulation of them, especially with Rule IV. There is not space to justify them in detail here, but in the opinion of the writer they follow from three established principles: (*a*) that the members of the Commonwealth have equal status in their mutual relations in all substantial respects; (*b*) that the Crown is a common Crown, belonging to all equally; (*c*) that Commonwealth constitutional convention, in the absence of express provision to the contrary, is a matter of good sense and good faith, looking not to formalities, but to the substance of transactions.[1]

The Course of Events

1936. 20th January.

King Edward VIII acceded to the Throne. For some time before his accession he had associated consistently with Mrs. Ernest Simpson, a lady of American birth possessing British nationality by virtue of her marriage to her second husband. Her first, an American citizen, had been divorced by her in the United States, and was at all relevant times still living.

The association continued after the King's accession. He sought neither concealment nor publicity for it.

August, September, and October.

Reports of the matter, compounded in varying degrees of fact and fiction, appeared in the American and foreign press. During this period these reports came to exceed by far the proportions of ordinary speculative gossip on such subjects both in volume and in credibility.

Practically the whole of the press of the British Empire, whether by unanimous coincidence of individual decisions (as some newspapers afterwards asserted) or by concerted action, and whether freely or with knowledge of the wide and uncertain scope of the law of seditious libel, made no open allusion to the matter and suppressed most of the reports and photographs which were evidence of it. Except in Canada, where American newspapers are imported and read in large quantities, the great bulk of public opinion in the Empire was accordingly unaware of the matter.

The Prime Minister of Canada was in the United Kingdom on a private visit from 16th October to 31st October. During this visit he saw the Prime Minister of the United Kingdom. It would be remarkable if the two prime ministers did not discuss the King's association with Mrs. Simpson. There was no other opportunity for personal discussion between Mr. Baldwin and Dominion ministers. Subsequent statements by the various prime ministers give the impression that there was no communication on the subject until 27th November.

Early in October Mrs. Simpson lodged a petition for divorce, which was set down for trial at Ipswich Assizes.

18th October.

The Prime Minister of the United Kingdom asked the King for an interview under conditions of secrecy, naming the subject-matter, and stating that it was urgent.[2]

[1] Contrast the view of Mr. John Foster in *The Nineteenth Century*, February 1937, p. 234.

[2] Speech of Mr. Baldwin in the House of Commons on 10th December 1936, 318 *House of Commons Debates*, *5s.*, 2186–96 (hereinafter cited as 'Speech'), col. 2188.

He informed neither his colleagues in the United Kingdom cabinet nor the Dominions of this step.

20th October.

The interview[1] took place at Fort Belvedere. It appears from Mr. Baldwin's account of it to the House that it took the form of a courteous admonition to the King. His advice was subject to every reserve in a formal sense: that is, he did not profess to be speaking on behalf of his cabinet, or of the Dominions, but only for himself. He spoke, nevertheless, in the character of prime minister, as well as in the character of a friend:[2] no prime minister, whatever his independent personal friendship with a monarch may be, can do otherwise. He did not press for an answer.[3] He spoke without reserve.[4]

He expressed the view that the British monarchy was an immense power for good; that it was by no means invulnerable; that reports of the kind then current were likely, if they continued, to do it damage; and that such damage might be irreparable. He expressed his 'anxiety and desire that such criticism might not have cause to go on'.[5] He referred to the pending divorce proceedings, and to the 'danger' of the 'period of suspense' that might result from the granting of a decree *nisi*.[6]

The King, it seems, said: 'You and I must settle this matter together; I will not have any one interfering.'[7] He also expressed a desire to 'take this action quickly'.[8]

Mr. Baldwin reported his interview to a few of his senior colleagues, but not to the whole Cabinet. Neither he nor the King reported it to the Dominions.

27th October.

At Ipswich Assizes a decree *nisi* was made by Mr. Justice Hawke in the case of *Simpson* v. *Simpson*, which was undefended, after evidence of the usual type.

16th November.

The King sent for Mr. Baldwin (who had already formed the intention of seeking an interview with him) and the second interview took place at

[1] Reported in speech, cols. 2188–90.

[2] 'I felt that in the circumstances there was only one man who could speak to him and talk the matter over with him, and that man was the Prime Minister. I felt doubly bound to do it by my duty, as I conceived it, to the country and my duty to him not only as a counsellor but as a friend.' Speech, col. 2188. 'I told him I had come—naturally, I was his Prime Minister—but I wanted to talk it over with him as a friend to see if I could help him in this matter.' Speech, col. 2189.

[3] Speech, col. 2188.

[4] 'There is nothing I have not told His Majesty of which I thought he ought to be aware—nothing.' Speech, col. 2188.

[5] Speech, col. 2189.

[6] Speech, col. 2190.

[7] Speech, col. 2190. Mr. Baldwin narrates these as the King's words.

[8] Speech, col. 2190. The words are Mr. Baldwin's. The context does not show what action is referred to.

Buckingham Palace.[1] Mr. Baldwin spoke first. His advice was again subject to formal reserves, but its substance appears to have been imperative.

Mr. Baldwin spoke first, for fifteen to twenty minutes. The gist of his argument appears from his own account of it to have been: the King must obey the voice of the people in public matters; the identity of the Queen is a public matter; therefore, the King must obey the voice of the people in choosing a Queen. The people would not give its approbation to Mrs. Simpson's being Queen; therefore, the King must not marry her.[2] The King replied, 'I am going to marry Mrs. Simpson and I am prepared to go.' Mr. Baldwin expressed concern, and made no further comment.[3]

25th November.

The King sent for Mr. Baldwin. At the interview he inquired what possibility there was of legislation authorizing a morganatic marriage.[4] Mr. Baldwin refused to give a formal answer, but replied to a further inquiry from the King that his informal reaction was that the United Kingdom parliament would never pass such a bill. He told the King that he could not give a formal answer without first consulting the whole cabinet and the Dominion prime ministers. The King asked that a formal examination of the question on those lines should be made.[5]

27th November.

Mr. Baldwin informed the Dominion prime ministers of the interview of 25th November and presented to them an enumeration of the three possibilities of normal marriage, morganatic marriage, and abdication, with his views thereon. He requested the *personal* opinions of the Prime Ministers, and their assessments of the views of their peoples, on the alternatives.[6] It appears that the request was expressed to be made informally and confidentially.

[1] Speech, col. 2190. [2] Speech, cols. 2190–1.

[3] Speech, col. 2191. Mr. Baldwin on 27th November telegraphed an account of this and the preceding interview to dominion prime ministers. Their accounts to their parliaments of the contents of this telegram are second-hand accounts of the interviews. Mr. Lyons, in the Australian House of Representatives on 11th December, reported the telegram as stating 'that His Majesty had stated his intention of marrying Mrs. Simpson, but that at the same time His Majesty had said that he appreciated that the idea of her becoming Queen and her children successors to the Throne was out of the question, and that consequently he contemplated abdicating and leaving the Duke of York to ascend the Throne' (*Sydney Morning Herald*, 12th December). General Hertzog, in the South African House of Assembly on 25th January, said that the telegram informed him 'of a discussion between the King and himself [Mr. Baldwin] on 16th November at which the King informed him of his fixed intention to marry a certain lady, and that he contemplated abdicating in favour of the Duke of York' (*Cape Times*, 26th January).

[4] i.e. a marriage which, while making the lady the King's wife, would not make her Queen. [5] Speech, cols. 2191–2.

[6] The request was so described by General Hertzog to the House of Assembly on 25th January. Presumably it was made to the other Dominions in the same form.

On the same day the United Kingdom cabinet met and decided against a morganatic marriage.

28th November–1st December.

Mr. Lyons replied to Mr. Baldwin's message of 27th November that in his view 'the proposed marriage, if it led to Mrs. Simpson becoming Queen, must incur widespread condemnation, and that the alternative proposal, or something in the nature of a specially sanctioned morganatic marriage, would run counter to the best popular conceptions of the Royal Family.'[1]

General Hertzog replied on 30th November that the King should be dissuaded from the marriage; of the alternative evils, abdication was the less. 'The one would be a great shock, but the other would prove a permanent wound.'[2]

Mr. Mackenzie King, on a date not stated, 'advised Premier Baldwin the people of Canada would not approve of marriage to Mrs. Simpson, whether she was to become Queen or not.'[3]

None of these three prime ministers had consulted their cabinets.

The remaining prime ministers, with one lukewarm exception, took a similar line. Whether their cabinets were consulted does not appear.

2nd December.

The King called Mr. Baldwin to a fourth interview and asked for an answer to his question. Mr. Baldwin replied that the inquiries he had thought proper to make were not complete,[4] but that they 'had gone far enough to show that neither the Dominions nor [in the United Kingdom] would there be any prospect of such legislation being accepted'.

Mr. Baldwin, in his narration, goes on to state that the King thereafter regarded the morganatic question as closed, and that thereafter only two alternatives were considered: complete abandonment of the project of marriage, and abdication.[5]

Two English provincial newspapers, taking as their cue or as their pretext a remark by the Bishop of Bradford on the preceding day which had no obvious connexion with the matter, published the news of the King's desire to marry Mrs. Simpson.

3rd December.

The morning press of the whole United Kingdom and all the newspapers of the Empire followed.

[1] Mr. Lyons's speech in the House of Representatives, 11th December (*Sydney Morning Herald*, 12th December).

[2] General Hertzog's speech in the House of Assembly, 25th January (*Cape Times*, 26th January).

[3] In the House of Commons, on 18th January (*Montreal Gazette*, 19th January).

[4] This, presumably, was a reference to the fact that Mr. Baldwin had not yet complied with the King's request that the Dominion prime ministers should be asked to examine the morganatic question *formally*.

[5] Speech, col. 2192.

4th–9th December.

There was public discussion throughout the Empire. The Australian Commonwealth Parliament and the Dáil were summoned; the United Kingdom parliament was already in session. The Canadian, South African, and New Zealand parliaments remained in recess.

On or about 5th December, Mr. Baldwin suggested that Dominion *governments* might like formally to advise the King direct. On 5th December the Australian cabinet,[1] on 6th December the South African cabinet,[2] on 8th December the Canadian cabinet,[3] and on 9th December the United Kingdom cabinet,[4] gave formal advice. This advice in each case asked the King to remain on the Throne, and assumed or stated that he could not remain on the Throne if he should marry Mrs. Simpson. Each of the four governments preferred abdication to marriage of any kind. What advice, if any, the New Zealand government tendered has not been disclosed. The Irish Free State government did not tender any formal advice.[5] Both of these governments, however, at least let it be understood that they had no objection to the actions which were in fact taken by the British government.

10th December.

The King executed an 'instrument of abdication' in the following terms:

> 'I, Edward VIII, of Great Britain, Ireland, and the British Dominions beyond the Seas, King, Emperor of India, do hereby declare My irrevocable determination to renounce the Throne for Myself and for My descendants, and My desire that effect should be given to this Instrument of Abdication immediately.'

This document was not addressed to any particular person.

In a message to the House of Commons the King announced his decision, reciting the instrument of abdication, and expressed his anxiety 'that there should be no delay of any kind in giving effect to this instrument'.[6] Similar messages were sent to the Dominion parliaments.

Upon the motion that the Message be considered, Mr. Baldwin made the speech from which the foregoing account of events has been principally drawn.

At 6.40 p.m. His Majesty's Declaration of Abdication Bill was brought in to the House of Commons and given a first reading.

On the same day the Canadian Privy Council passed an Order in Council expressing the request and consent of Canada to the Bill.

[1] Mr. Lyons in the House of Representatives, 11th December.
[2] General Hertzog in the House of Assembly, 25th January.
[3] Mr. Mackenzie King in the House of Commons, 18th January.
[4] Speech, col. 2195.
[5] Mr. De Valera in Dáil Éireann, 11th December.
[6] 318 *H. C. Deb., 5s.*, 2185–6.

11th December.

Each House of the Australian Commonwealth parliament passed during the day a resolution expressing its assent to the enactment of His Majesty's Declaration of Abdication Act, 1936, by the United Kingdom parliament. Since Canberra time is ten hours in advance of Greenwich time, the resolutions were passed before the House of Commons met.

The House of Commons and the House of Lords passed the Bill through all remaining stages, and it received the Royal assent by Royal Commission in the House of Lords at 1.52 p.m. By its terms it came into force immediately.

The Act[1] recites that—

> 'the Dominion of Canada pursuant to the provisions of section four of the Statute of Westminster, 1931, has requested and consented to the enactment of this Act, and the Commonwealth of Australia, the Dominion of New Zealand, and the Union of South Africa have assented thereto.'

Section I (1) enacts that the instrument of abdication shall have effect, that Edward VIII shall cease to be King, that there shall be a demise of the Crown, and that 'the member of the Royal Family then next in succession to the Throne shall succeed thereto'. Section I (2) deprives Edward VIII and his descendants of any title to the Throne. Section I (3) frees him and his descendants from the operation of the Royal Marriages Act.

On the same day, Dáil Éireann passed the Constitution (Amendment No. 27) Act, 1937.[2] It eliminates all reference to the King and the Governor-General from the Constitution of the Free State, but authorizes the Executive Council 'to the extent and subject to any conditions which may be determined by law' to avail itself, for the purpose of diplomatic appointments and international agreements, of any organ used for the purposes by the other nations of the British Commonwealth.[3]

12th December.

King George VI was proclaimed in London, Ottawa, Canberra, Pretoria, St. John's, and in many other places throughout the Empire.[4]

Dáil Éireann passed the Executive Authority (External Relations) Act, 1937,[5] and it was signed by the Chairman of the Dáil. It provided, first, that:[6]

> 'It is hereby declared and enacted that, so long as Saorstát Éireann is associated with the following nations, that is to say, Australia, Canada, Great Britain, New Zealand, and South Africa, and so long as the king [*sic*] recognized by those nations as the symbol of their co-operation continues to act on behalf of each of these nations (on the

[1] 1 Edw. 8, c. 3. [2] No. 57 of 1936. [3] s. 51, as amended.

[4] The Proclamation appeared in the *New Zealand Gazette* on the same day, but was not read in the Dominion until 14th December.

[5] No. 58 of 1936. [6] s. 3 (1).

advice of the several Governments thereof) for the purposes of the appointment of diplomatic and consular representatives and the conclusion of international agreements, the king so recognized may, and is hereby authorized to, act on behalf of Saorstát Éireann for the like purposes as and when advised by the Executive Council so to do.'

Secondly, it enacted[1] that upon the passing of the Act the Instrument of Abdication should have effect according to its tenor, and that the King should be the person who would, if King Edward had died on 10th December, be his successor under Free State law.

Events in the Dominions during January 1937 (at the end of which month this note went to press) are mentioned in the ensuing comments upon the situation in each Dominion. For most of these events the writer has had to rely on newspaper reports.

Legal and Constitutional Position

King Edward VIII

King Edward behaved throughout in accordance with law. An absolute renunciation of the throne might conceivably be regarded as a dereliction of statutory duty; but the Instrument of Abdication was merely a request that he should be relieved of his statutory duties.

His statement to Mr. Baldwin that 'you and I must settle this matter together; I will not have any one interfering', indicates a misapprehension of the constitutional rights of his Dominion advisers, and must therefore be regarded as constitutionally unfortunate.

If, in forming his decision to abdicate, he allowed himself to be influenced by anything the Prime Minister of the United Kingdom said, he acted, in the opinion of the writer, unconstitutionally in not first allowing his Dominion advisers an equal opportunity to influence his decision.[2] If, however, he came to his decision independently of anything he was told by Mr. Baldwin, he broke no convention.

The reflection may be ventured that the present conventional situation places too great a responsibility on the shoulders of an inexperienced monarch, so long as he has, comparatively speaking, no opportunity of intimacy with Dominion advisers.

The United Kingdom

The abdication of King Edward VIII and the succession of King George VI were, so far as the United Kingdom was concerned, in every way regular from the point of view of strict law.

In the opinion of the writer, the convention requiring the assent of Dominion parliaments was sufficiently complied with by the assents subsequently given. The absence from the preamble of His Majesty's Declaration of Abdication Act, 1936, of a recital of the assent of the Irish

[1] s. 3 (2). [2] The view here stated does not command universal assent.

Free State government is immaterial, since no such recital is required by law or convention.

If, when he advised the King informally against marriage with Mrs. Simpson on 16th November, Mr. Baldwin believed that his advice would, or might, affect the decision of the King, either with regard to the marriage or with regard to abdication, he committed, in the opinion of the writer, a breach of convention in so acting without having consulted the Dominion prime ministers beforehand.[1] For such a breach of convention the United Kingdom government was vicariously responsible. If, on the other hand, the King's mind was believed by Mr. Baldwin to be, and was in fact, irrevocably made up on both these issues, so that the advice neither had nor was expected to have any effect, it constituted no breach of convention.

Canada

Section 4 of the Statute of Westminster having been complied with by virtue of the Canadian Order in Council of 10th December and the consequent recital of Canada's request and consent, His Majesty's Declaration of Abdication Act, 1936, validly effected the change of monarch for Canada simultaneously with the United Kingdom.

Upon its meeting in January the Canadian parliament regularized the conventional position by passing an Act expressing its assent to the United Kingdom Act.

Mr. Bennett's criticism,[2] if valid, does not detract from the validity of the succession, but merely places it twenty-four hours earlier. The view of Mr. Woodsworth, leader of the C.C.F. Party,[3] that convention required the assent of the Dominion parliament to precede the enactment of a change in the law of the succession by the United Kingdom, is, in the opinion of the writer, erroneous. Mr. Woodsworth further accused Mr. Mackenzie King of conspiring to force King Edward off the Throne,[4] alleging that Mr. Baldwin put the King in a position which left him no alternative.[5] Mr. King's vindication of Mr. Baldwin, as reported,[6] does not tally with Mr. Baldwin's own account. But as against Mr. King the accusation is merely political; whatever view is taken of Mr. Baldwin's action, Mr. King broke no convention in assenting to it subsequently or in accepting its results.

Canadian action was therefore regular in both law and convention.

[1] This view is not accepted by some authorities. See, e.g., Mr. John Foster in *The Nineteenth Century*, loc. cit.

[2] Above, pp. 616, n. 3.

[3] House of Commons, 14th and 15th January (*Montreal Gazette*, 15th and 16th January).

[4] House of Commons, 19th January (*Montreal Gazette*, 20th January).

[5] House of Commons, 15th January (*Winnipeg Free Press*, 16th January).

[6] 'King Edward had first consulted Mr. Baldwin about his proposed marriage, and Mr. Baldwin had given his opinion. He had not placed the King in any position': Mr. King in the House of Commons, 15th January (*Winnipeg Free Press*, 16th January).

Australia

The means by which the succession was effected in Australia are legally and constitutionally impeccable from every point of view.

His Majesty's Declaration of Abdication Act, 1936, applied to Australia *suo proprio vigore*, independently of the Statute of Westminster. The recital therein of Australia's assent was a mere courtesy. The Commonwealth parliament alone of Dominion parliaments complied fully and literally with convention by assenting to the Act before it was passed.

New Zealand

The Act applied to New Zealand *suo proprio vigore*.

At the time of going to press Parliament had not met, but there was no doubt that it would express its assent either by Act, as in Canada, or by resolution, as in Australia.

South Africa

The writer is unable to accept the view of the South African government on the effect of s. 5 of the Status of the Union Act, and its view that unilateral abdication is possible and on this occasion took place. But it is not suggested that these views can by any means be dismissed as perverse. Competent authorities outside South Africa can be found who agree with both of them.

The government's view on abdication is declared by His Majesty King Edward VIII's Declaration of Abdication Bill, and will on that account probably be accepted in South African courts; but the Bill is so drafted that it is unlikely that the question will fall to be decided in litigation.

In the official South African view, the abdication of King Edward and the accession of King George took effect for the whole Empire upon the execution of the Instrument of Abdication on 10th December. The disinheritance of King Edward's possible issue and descendants, however, does not, in this view, take effect for South Africa until the passing of His Majesty King Edward VIII's Abdication Bill.[1]

On the alternative views that the United Kingdom Act effected for South Africa either the whole change or the disinheritance of the possible issue and dependants, the South African Bill will adequately serve the purpose of expressing the assent of the South African parliament within the convention.

On any view, therefore, the succession in South Africa will be legally and conventionally regular.

Irish Free State

It is not appropriate to discuss here the change in the relation of the Crown to the Free State which was brought about by the Irish legislation summarized above. Nor is there room to consider the arguments for the

[1] There seemed at the time of going to press no doubt that the Bill would be passed in its then form, and this is here assumed.

various views which are held concerning the dates of the abdication and accession respectively.

The principal possible views are: that the abdication and the accession occurred simultaneously on the passing of the United Kingdom Act on 11th December; that they occurred simultaneously on the passing of the Executive Authority (External Relations) Act on 12th December; that they occurred simultaneously on the execution of the Instrument of Abdication on 10th December; that King Edward abdicated on 10th December, and King George acceded simultaneously, but was removed on 11th December and reinstated on 12th December; that King Edward was removed on 11th December and King George adopted on 12th December. It is also theoretically arguable that King Edward was not at any time validly removed from the throne for the Free State.

The writer does not presume to express a preference among these views. It is, however, likely that, if the Free State Courts had to express a view, they would hold that King Edward was removed by the constitutional amendment of 11th December, and King George adopted by the Act of 12th December.

The Acts of 11th and 12th December, even if they had not purported to create a kingless interregnum of one day, would have been, and are, breaches both of the Irish Treaty and, in the opinion of the writer, of that fundamental convention of the Commonwealth which declares that the members of the Commonwealth are united by a common allegiance to the Crown. It should be added that the present government of the Free State does not regard the Treaty or the conventions of the Commonwealth as binding.

The conventions specifically relating to the law of succession were not, however, infringed. Mr. De Valera, in the Dáil on 11th December, declared that his government was under no obligation to consult other Commonwealth governments before initiating legislation touching the succession to the throne.[1] This was a repudiation of an undoubted convention. But since the effect of the legislation introduced without consultation was, so far as it touched the succession, merely to bring Free State law into line with the alteration proposed by the initiating government, which was the United Kingdom government, consultation could have made no difference. Convention, being a matter of common sense, does not demand otiose acts. No convention, therefore, seems to have been broken.

[1] *Irish Times*, 12th December.

LIST OF CASES CITED

INDEX

PRINTED IN
GREAT BRITAIN
AT THE
UNIVERSITY PRESS
OXFORD
BY
JOHN JOHNSON
PRINTER
TO THE
UNIVERSITY